Community Planning
Integrating social and physical environments

Phil Heywood

Queensland University of Technology
Department of Urban and Regional Planning
Brisbane
Australia

WILEY-BLACKWELL

A John Wiley & Sons, Ltd., Publication

This edition first published 2011 © 2011 Phil Heywood

Blackwell Publishing was acquired by John Wiley & Sons in February 2007. Blackwell's publishing program has been merged with Wiley's global Scientific, Technical and Medical business to form Wiley-Blackwell.

Registered office: John Wiley & Sons Ltd, The Atrium, Southern Gate, Chichester, West Sussex, PO19 8SQ, UK

Editorial offices: 9600 Garsington Road, Oxford, OX4 2DQ, UK
                       The Atrium, Southern Gate, Chichester, West Sussex, PO19 8SQ, UK
                       2121 State Avenue, Ames, Iowa 50014-8300, USA

For details of our global editorial offices, for customer services and for information about how to apply for permission to reuse the copyright material in this book please see our website at www.wiley.com/wiley-blackwell.

The right of the author to be identified as the author of this work has been asserted in accordance with the UK Copyright, Designs and Patents Act 1988.

Library of Congress Cataloging-in-Publication Data
Heywood, Philip.
    Community planning : integrating social and physical environments / Phil Heywood.
        p. cm.
    Includes bibliographical references and index.
    ISBN 978-1-4051-9887-5 (pbk. : alk. paper)   1. Community life.   2. Communities–Planning.   3. Community organization.   4. Community development–Planning.   5. Urban ecology (Sociology)   I. Title.
    HM761.H49 2011
    307.1′2–dc22
                            2010042182

A catalogue record for this book is available from the British Library.

Set in 9 on 11 pt Palatino by Toppan Best-set Premedia Limited
Printed and bound in Malaysia by Vivar Printing Sdn Bhd

1   2011

Cover illustration: *Earth's Creation* © Emily Kame Kngwarreye/Licensed by Viscopy, 2010.

Alex O'Reilly writes of Emily's *Earth's Creation*: 'This painting to me has a strong energy with elements of centres, traces of space and passages of movement ... at a deep level, it implies that community and community planning have many different perspectives, ultimately with changing shapes that unite in art both collectives and individuals.'

Contents

The book's companion website at **www.wiley.com/go/heywood** offers invaluable resources for practitioners, lecturers, students and community activists with generously illustrated sets of PowerPoint slides to accompany each chapter. Links to the websites of useful bodies are also provided.

Preface

This book is intended for the many practitioners, planners and students whose dedicated work is already shaping community life throughout the world, in fields as varied as the built environment, community and cultural development, local economic policy, education, health, transport, recreation and social services. All play essential roles in creating community life. Such people, caught up in the daily demands of collaborating with disciplines quite different from their own, often find themselves having to create and manage new relationships in order to make their own work effective. In the course of this book, a simple and widely applicable vocabulary of needs, wants, activities and choices is developed that can assist the necessary collaboration. In order to relate the increasing number of levels of community resulting from today's communications revolution, a transparent planning method is derived, which is equally relevant to localities and regions. Methods are developed and examples provided to suggest paths of collaboration that can lead to lively, healthy and holistic communities for living, learning, working and playing. Participatory place-making and governance are related to the regular practices of community planning.

The first five chapters review the general issues of spirit and purpose of contemporary community life and planning. Chapter 1 examines the causes and consequences of the cascades of change that are currently affecting community life and evaluates the capacities of the competing paradigms of order, productivity, control and cooperation to respond to them effectively. Chapter 2 widens this review to consider how communication, consultation, participation and negotiation can contribute to purposive planning. In particular, the expanding impact of instantaneous modern communications on the three related fields of community action, development and organisation are considered. Chapters 3 and 4 explore the many different scales, or levels, of communities of both contact and interest, spanning from the local and urban, through the regional and national to the supranational and global. The psychological importance of 'mixed scanning', which repeatedly refocuses between immediate and distant places and times, is considered as a way to manage simultaneous membership of the many communities of which people may increasingly find themselves part. Competing values and goals and their significance for community life and planning are considered in Chapter 5, focusing on the four major themes of prosperity, liberty, justice and sustainability, and how they can support each other in developing productive, free, just and sustainable communities.

Chapters 6 to 9 develop and apply general methods and techniques to the planning of shelter, work, learning and health. Common methods of community planning are developed in Chapter 6, combining the creativity and intuition of art, the hypothesis-testing of science and the regularity and groundedness of craft. Simple modelling techniques are explored in Chapter 7, to promote understanding of the specific activities which we need to enhance and integrate with each other. Chapters 8 and 9 apply these methods and techniques to the crucial fields of homes, communities, work, learning and health.

The last three chapters draw together the threads to illustrate how integrated and attractive places can be made, how people can participate in achieving good governance and how community planning can help manage the insistent challenges of changing community life. Chapter 10 relates holistic practices of community design to the natural physical unity of places. Chapter 11 considers the crucial relations between community participation and representative governance, and differentiates between roles of regulation and service, and agency and participation. In conclusion, Chapter 12 shows how the challenges of rapidly intensifying impacts of communication, interaction and scale can be managed by employing the more stable but nonetheless evolving patterns of values, methods and participatory practices to help shape essential future roles of social integration. Community planning in localities, cities and regions should be well equipped to help both long-established and newly arriving individuals and groups to get the best out of themselves and each other in times when the costs of misunderstanding and conflict are too great to be lightly risked.

Philip Heywood

Acknowledgements

Of all stages of producing a book, writing the acknowledgements is among the most satisfying. Recording the contributions of friends, associates and helpful sources, whose ideas and assistance have enlivened the content and form of the work, is a major psychological satisfaction. Equally gratifying are the reminders of many moments of illumination, intellectual companionship, good advice and thoughtful encouragement that have been shared in the course of its compilation.

First, thanks are due to the friends and colleagues whose ideas and insights over many years to my understanding of community life have made major contributions. John Taylor and Jon Allison have been organisers and companions on numerous explorations through towns, countryside and the world of ideas. I am deeply grateful for their enquiring minds and reflective, creative spirits. To the late Ian Crowther, talented practitioner and administrator of regional planning, I am equally grateful for a lifetime of friendship and example of practical goodwill and idealism, which started on the first day of my first job in regional planning, when he strode down the corridor, hand extended well in front of his tall frame, exclaiming 'You must be the new chap!'. Ian is sorely missed by both friends and family. Chris Buckley, founding partner of one of Queensland's most innovative and enlightened planning consultancies, and a good companion on planning delegations to Timor Loro S'ae and urban rambles around Brisbane, has provided a heartening reminder of how a clear mind can combine with a good heart to make a better world, step by step. I am also grateful to Fiona Caniglia, whose insight and community development skills have provided much needed examples of the roles that dedicated community activists can play in steering regions of rapidly growing wealth and population, such as South East Queensland, away from descents into self congratulation and materialism. I also owe incalculable thanks to generations of students and community activists in Nigeria, England and Australia whose energy and imagination has enriched my teaching career and community life, and provided much of the material in this book.

Reading early drafts of other people's writing is a demanding task, but it shouldn't be a thankless one. The overall intentions, logic and writing style of this book have all benefitted from the comments of a number of friends, colleagues and family members, who have commented on different chapters and sections. The advice of Peter Roberts, Director of the United Kingdom's Homes and Communities Academy which combined empathy and insight, proved invaluable in clarifying the intentions and structure of the book. Doug Baker, Anna Hassett, Anne and Brian Hudson, Laurel Johnson, Mark Limb, Alex O'Reilly and Greg Vann have provided valuable commentary on different chapters. Between them, my wife Sheila and daughters Lucy and Eileen have read every word of this long text (some sections many times) and have applied their knowledge of the fields of community health, appreciative inquiry and social development to improve its relevance. Thanks also go to my son-in-law Dean Saffron for his photographic skills.

Different people have made particular contributions of knowledge and research. David Cant, CEO of Brisbane Housing Company has not only assisted with commentary, information and photographs for the chapter on Homes and Communities, but has also provided an inspiring example through his energetic leadership of that organisation. Jon Mongard's trail blazing work on place making throughout Australia has helped inform much of the content and many of the illustrations of the chapter on Place, Space and Community Design. Justine Lacey, Mark Conlan, Sherry She and Jessica Chatwin have undertaken invaluable work on research, analysis and presentation of information, transforming sketchy ideas and information into clear diagrams and figures. I'm also grateful for Jessica's invaluable technical and interpretative skills in the compilation of the final text.

The author and publishers are grateful to the following for permission to reproduce copyright material: Viscopy for reproduction Emily Kame Kngwarreye's *Earth's Creation*, both as the cover of this book and as Plate 6.2; to Steve Oliver for photo reproduction rights for Plate 5.1, David Hockney's *Road Across the Wolds,* and Plate 6.2, *The Diver;* to John Mongard Landscape Architects for Plate 10.3 and Figures 10.16, 10.17, 10.18 and 10.19; to the Brisbane Housing Company for Plates 8.1, 8.2 and 8.3 and for Figs 8.3, 8.4, 8.5, 8.6, 8.7, and 8.8 of their housing developments in Brisbane; to the Vancouver City Council for Figs 8.1 and 8.2 of the South East False Creek Redevelopment Site Plan and Scheme; the International Council on Monuments and Sites for Fig 10.4; John Hill and Creative Commons for Fig 10.5; and to Catherine Oakley for Figs 10.9 and 10.10.

Finally, my heartfelt thanks go to Madeleine Metcalfe, Senior Commissioning Editor, and the other editorial and production staff at Wiley-Blackwell, whose insight and guidance have bestowed on the writing of this book much of the experience of an enjoyable long distance conversation rather than the familiar back-breaking labour in the vineyards of theorising!

Phil Heywood

1 The Nature and Planning of Community Life

This chapter examines the ways in which recent rapid social and economic changes have increased the need for effective community planning. Part One considers the impacts of:

- information and communication innovation;
- economic fluctuations;
- expanding transport technologies and nodes;
- radical administrative reorganisation;
- major political changes;
- destabilised international relations;
- increasing intellectual relativism and loss of confidence.

Part Two relates these challenges to contemporary community life and planning responses. Part Three examines and evaluates the capacity of the competing paradigms of order, productivity, control and cooperation to respond to these challenges of change. Part Four reviews how people and organisations can cooperate in planning their communities, and leads on to the concluding section of the chapter, which relate these roles to current trends towards collaborative planning.

Part One: Social and Economic Changes

The current cascade of change

The justification for planning is no longer simply the age-old desire to create a better world; it is also to improve prospects for securing survival in the face of increasingly volatile social, economic and environmental conditions. Though many of the causes can be readily identified, solutions require new agreements on values, practices and distribution of costs and benefits. Coordinated responses are needed to match and manage the impacts resulting from increased personal and social mobility, economic uncertainty, environmental instability and technological change, all of which are causing community life throughout the world to become less secure and more problematic.

Such rapid and accelerating changes may fragment relations among parallel social programmes. Coherent and inclusive planning is needed to ensure that the success of one programme is not achieved at the cost of failure in others.[i] This will mean bringing together not only different specialists, but also community members, business groups and political leaders, because sustainable solutions must ultimately be built upon consent, communication and collaboration. This is equally true in the ethnically riven communities of England's West Midlands and north Lancashire and in the flood-prone villages of the Sunderbans of the Ganges delta (Ghosh, 2004).

COMPONENTS OF CHANGE

At the global scale, current impacts, such as climate change are exerting far-reaching effects on human health, freshwater resources, ecosystems, crop production, coastal systems in low-lying areas, industry and settlements (Intergovernmental Panel on Climate Change, 2007). The period since 1990 could be viewed as a time of accelerated change, or 'punctuated equilibrium', during which a number of very rapid transformations have coincided and interacted to create revolutionary transitions in a number of systems.[ii] In the physical environment, the early effects of global warming are producing climatic instability and threatening sea levels rises (Stern, 2007). Economically, cumulative over-consumption and production have triggered the global financial crisis. In politics, international stability has collapsed at the end of the Cold War. These converging crises in our physical, economic and social environments pose challenging questions for contemporary humanity. Just as fears recede of border wars between power blocs and international groupings escalating towards the notorious 'mutual assured destruction' (MAD) of nuclear conflict and reprisals, local riots and killings and the rise of international terrorism have increased fears of a 'clash of civilisations' (Huntington, 1996). As a result, in times of unprecedented physical mastery and invention, humanity is stalked by threats of failures of coexistence, locally, nationally and globally.

Solutions will often require major innovations and painful adjustments. Widespread personal anger and social resentments may flare among people facing disruptions to accustomed patterns of life and policymakers may need to manage and assuage these reactions. People will require help and tools to adjust their lifestyles to accommodate the 'shock of the new'. Sensitive and sustainable community planning will be needed to assist individuals and communities to manage changes which may arrive without warning or fully understood causes. In each of a number of arenas, discussed below, the forces of entropy, pulling things apart, will have to be matched by integration to hold them together.[iii] In this situation, communities will need to develop capacities to scan changing conditions, rapidly in order to develop cooperative responses to and to evaluate options for, unintended consequences: in short, they will need to plan.

INFORMATION AND COMMUNICATION INNOVATION

Extraordinary recent advances in information and communications technologies have made the contemporary world a place of instant and universal communication and greatly expanded the potential scale of communities of association. 'Glocal' awareness, transcending communities of place, is stimulating loosely linked initiatives, such as the carbon reduction schemes embraced by many local communities throughout developed countries (see, for example, Oxfordshire Climate Exchange, 2010; Transition Towns, 2010). Networks of environmental and social activists are making use of instantaneous Internet and e-mail links to assemble powerful coalitions of public, political and media opinion-formers to champion or oppose action on global issues. One such campaign prevented the proposed introductions by the World Trade Organization of extensions of the global economy into fields such as local land ownership.[iv] Where contact is daily and direct, communities may retain intensive local links. Where they are widespread and open-edged to draw in newcomers, they frequently become more influential, and may well help to bolster the vitality of community life in quite remote local societies (Environmental Change Institute, 2009).

ECONOMIC FLUCTUATIONS

Economics has become one of the most contested fields of knowledge and interpretation in the lives of local communities. The prevailing wisdom of the mid-twentieth century of managed economies balancing demand and supply to produce full employment without inflation (Galbraith, 1972) rapidly gave way in its closing decades to the militant ideas of supply side economics working through foreign direct investment (FDI) to maximise economic growth in the belief, criticised by Friedmann and Weaver (1979), 'that a rising tide will float all boats'. This orthodoxy is now itself challenged by the current concern to stimulate economic demand to forestall a prolonged world economic recession and massive local unemployment. As government funds and credibility are used to bolster private sector financial institutions, community life is being dramatically impacted by these radical swings in economic policy. These changes may also present well-organised communities with opportunities to play larger roles in shaping their own destinies, with support from central government funding. All members of the G20 group of the world's most economically developed nations, for instance, committed themselves to this programme at the 2009 London Summit (London Summit, 2009). In particular Clause 26 obliges the twenty nations to:

> Support those affected by the crisis by creating employment opportunities and through income support measures [to] build a fair and family-friendly labour market for both women and men. We will support employment by stimulating growth, investing in education and training, and through active labour market policies, focusing on the most vulnerable.

Clauses 27 and 28 go on to commit governments to intervene to promote clean, resilient and green economies, and to combat climate change. These changes in economic orthodoxy present major opportunities for proactive community planning.

EXPANDING TRANSPORT TECHNOLOGIES AND NODES

All scales of transport and trade are also experiencing great changes. The container revolution of the last thirty years has both advanced the international division of labour (by promoting routine long-distance exchange of manufactured products) and revolutionised the spatial patterns of port cities throughout the world. From Baltimore and San Francisco to London and Rotterdam, dock locations have been moved downstream to new deepwater locations, freeing large swathes of old docklands for commercial and residential development in central areas (London Dockland Redevelopment Agency, 2008). International airports have gone through a similarly explosive phase of development, rationalised by concepts such as the Aviopolis and the Aerotropolis (Kasarda, 2009). These developments have seen very large and often privatised new airports in cities throughout the world as diverse as Tokyo, Bangkok, Los Angeles, Amsterdam and London becoming not only major elements of the regional settlement pattern but also increasingly significant centres of employment. They may also compete as regional shopping centres with established metropolitan cores, resulting in recurrent major traffic congestion and disruption to established regional transport systems. At the same time, their noise and traffic impacts are causing often bitter conflicts over proposals for new runways, flight paths and night-time curfews.

International trade and transport are not only binding global networks together ever more securely and stamping out giant footprints in key locations within metropolitan regions. They are implanting new economic pacemakers near the hearts of long-established urban and rural communities. Community planning is required to negotiate sustainable outcomes that balance the needs and concerns of existing local and regional communities with the insistent demands for ever more space and investment of supersonic technology and global economics.

RADICAL ADMINISTRATIVE REORGANISATION

Community administration too has experienced great changes. While new technologies of production and communication have increased the scale of private business, tax revolts and business domination of mass media have publicised the attractions of 'small government' (Osborne and Gaebler, 1992), though this has been brought into question by the failure of such small governments to match and oversee the activities of big business. Nevertheless, the retreat from central control, coinciding with the growing scale of settlements, has also led to a revival of interest in regions and regionalism. In the European Community, this has taken the form of the infusion of new life into existing communities by injecting funds from above (Balchin, Sykora & Bull, 1999). Elsewhere, in British Columbia and Oregon, top-down and bottom-up approaches have been drawn together to create regional governments with strong planning and implementation powers (Heywood, 1997). Meanwhile, in the United States and the United Kingdom, looser, more voluntary associations of the 'new regionalism' are creating regional coalitions to negotiate continuous problem-solving, often without the formality of publicly adopted 'plans' (Wheeler, 2002). The snowballing failures and collapses of the economy of risk of the first decade of this century has led to a more cautious and negotiative attitude of the private sector towards social organisation and to the recognition of a renewed role for government in public administration. Alliances between communities and government, already being promoted by the United Kingdom's new Homes and Communities Agency (2009), for instance, could become far more significant in the next few years.

MAJOR POLITICAL CHANGE

In politics, too, established orders have splintered. Politically regulated command economies have failed and largely disappeared, which is due as much to internal inefficiencies as to external competition. In market economies, attempts to replace political decisions by economic choice have produced mixed results and often created severe disparities and social injustice (Monbiot, 2003), making the regulatory merits and efficiency of market mechanisms look increasingly questionable. Sectionalism, fragmentation and individualism have disrupted the old established order of a fraternal left in constructive dialogue with a freedom-seeking right. The cause of representative democracy has ebbed and flowed, advancing in Europe and Latin America, scarcely holding its own in Asia and North America, and collapsing in parts of Central Africa. Meanwhile, in the new 'millionaire' cities which now accommodate a third of the world's population (United Nations, 2009), local and regional systems of governance have struggled to manage the demands and impacts of rapid urbanisation and to produce effective systems of urban management.

International relations have also exerted powerful impacts on the lives of local communities. Mounting instability, beyond the capacities of national governments or international organisations to control or resolve, has sent waves of refugees across borders and oceans, compounding the challenges facing community planning in host regions throughout the world. After the collapse of the Soviet Union ended the icy stability of the Cold Car between communism and capitalism, a brief 'new world order' of economic and military dominance by the United States was scarcely proclaimed before it was violently challenged by international insurgency and terrorism. Their huge productive power has also projected China and India onto the world stage as major players. Europe has similarly stepped out from the shadows of American leadership. Meanwhile, in Africa the shocking conflicts of the early 1990s between Hutus and Tutsis in Rwanda, Burundi and the Democratic Republic of Congo unleashed waves of ethnic violence which continued to ravage community life across the entire region for almost two decades.

Such outbreaks of bitter communal violence have occurred in all parts of the world, between Serbs and Bosnians in Europe, Han Chinese and Tibetans in Tibet, left- and right-wing groups in Latin America, militarists and minorities in Burma, Christians and Muslims in Sulawesi, Timor-Leste and northern Nigeria, and Chechens and Russians in the Caucasus region. Meanwhile, in this fracturing and conflict-ridden situation of an unstable and multilateral world, the United Nations struggles to maintain its global roles of reconciliation, negotiation and leadership. Failures of local community life may escalate into national and international conflicts, which are in turn carried by refugees and economic migrants to impact on other localities throughout the world. The implication that we are inescapably 'members one of another' presents both challenges and opportunities for community planning at all scales.

Philosophical thought both reflects the ideas and activities of its own age and in turn helps to influence new conceptual and physical development.[v] The well-differentiated philosophical arguments of the last two and half thousand years between the great traditions of empiricism, idealism and rationalism have been radically challenged by a welter of new ideas, which can be conveniently mustered into a performing arena under the title of 'post structuralism'. 'Deconstruction' has become a favourite discursive technique and 'meta narratives' a potent put-down.[vi] Nevertheless, as the air clears, it becomes apparent that the Aristotelian tradition of empiricism (of knowledge through experience) is alive and well in the arguments of the American Pragmatists (Rorty, 1996), who continue to assert that 'mental knives are what won't cut real bread' (James, quoted in Passmore, 1980), while the contribution of ideas, however reshuffled and neon-lit, continues in the neo-idealism of writers like Derrida and Foucault, who employ paradox and contradiction to question conventional interpretations (Foucault, 1963, 1980, 1981) and 'deconstruct' received truth (Derrida, 1976, 1993, 1995).

Another field of socially engaged critical philosophers also divides into temperamentally contrasted streams. On the one hand, the Critical Rationalists provide a powerful and persuasive explanation of science and justification for technological optimism of the mid-twentieth century in the form of the upward spiral of conjecture and refutation (Popper, 1972; Magee, 1973). On the other hand, the more idealist Frankfurt School of Critical Method recognises the importance not only of individual interests and hypotheses but also of the crucial roles of discussion and exchange between equally privileged participants around a notional 'policy table', whereby both knowledge and action can be resolved in open exchange between interested parties in a process which they term 'communicative action' (Habermas, 1972, 1987, 1990).

These ideas can be related to concepts, programmes and actions in everyday life and community planning. American Pragmatism can be seen as the rationalisation of material mastery and physical evidence in asserting that 'handsome is as handsome does', and incidentally justifying mass production and consumption. One variant of this view can develop into the questionable justification of the material self-serving of walled estates, patrolled shopping centres and military campaigns of 'shock and awe' (on the basis that they support material progress and diversity). It is nevertheless important to recognise the contributions that pragmatism can make to the testing of ideas against evidence. Three distinct contributions can be identified:

1. Recognising the importance of material outcomes.
2. Developing and justifying evidence-based policy.
3. The need to maintain democratic support of voting majorities.

Critical Rationalism, by contrast, emphasises progressive problem-solving, social engineering and scientific improvements which aim to keep pace with the inevitable effects of social and physical changes and challenges. These result in suitably cyclical open-edged and open-ended methods to allow communities to plan their own evolution to meet constantly emerging challenges of current times. There are undoubted contributions to community planning:

1. Problem-solving methods which can drive a cyclical and purposive approach to social change.
2. The virtues of conjecture and refutation in ensuring that people listen to each other.
3. The rights of minority groups in pluralist societies to be part of continuing social debates.

Communicative Action places ideas of individual problem-solving within a social context and seems to respond particularly well to a number of contemporary situations. Its negotiative and cumulative capacities match many of the dominant characteristics of the current times, particularly those of universal and instantaneous communications, the worldwide spread of education and knowledge, insistent demands of previously excluded groups to have their interests taken into account in allocating opportunities and resources, and the increasingly deadly capacity of excluded and dissident groups to be able to wreak havoc on those whom they see as oppressors or opponents. Communicative Action is therefore particularly relevant to contemporary community planning, and has a number of important contributions to make, providing:

● a coherent framework for community engagement;
● a powerful and fertile source of objectives through discussion;
● incorporation of community experience in information collection and review;
● inclusion of communities of practitioners and their specialised knowledge in policy development;
● insights into key aspects, such as the importance and role of public space in maintaining social dialogue.

The rapid splintering of philosophical thought into contending and often unrelated views of meaning, method and purpose is thus not altogether negative for community planning. Insight can be gained into the very wide range of views and beliefs prevalent in increasingly diverse contemporary communities, and situations can be matched with their underlying values and concepts to seek acceptable and appropriate solutions. Pragmatic achievement can be incorporated into the development of evidence-based policy. Innovative problem-solving can be encouraged by the active involvement of energetic individuals. The innate human capacity for communication can be harnessed in festivals, discussion groups, speakers' corners and the potentially democratic conversations of the Internet. Modern philosophy can be heard as a symphony of different themes and instruments as well as a confusing and solipsistic babble of personal insights.[vii]

Part Two: Community Life and Change

Contemporary challenges to community life

Communities consist of groups of people who experience and acknowledge significant links, expectations and responsibilities towards each other. They do not need to be neighbours, but they do need to share neighbourly feelings, which may be based on shared spaces, interests or realms of interaction. Nevertheless, 'community' may mean different things at different scales and to different people. 'Friendly association' is the most all-embracing of its many meanings, encompassing such alternatives as ' all the people in a particular district', 'a group of people living together as a smaller social unit within a larger one' and 'ownership and participation in common' (Guralnik, 1974). Friendly association both promotes, and is in turn promoted by, community life. Through the self-expression that links people and groups, personal energies can be combined to form the community synergy to create cities and their infrastructure of roads, aqueducts and ultimately global communications systems. Settlements that benefit from friendly association gain the strength and capacity to transform their environments into places of lasting achievement and beauty through cooperation in production, art, science and technology. Though cities may well have originated through enforced association within containing walls (Mumford, 1961) as well as mutual aid (Kropotkin, 1939), their rapid growth to accommodate half of all humanity has depended on networks of association, exchange and collaboration, which are most sustainable where they are voluntary, mutually advantageous and pleasurable. Depictions of the life of the earliest cities by their artists are full of scenes of people singing and dancing together (Desroches-Noblecourt, 1976) just as paintings of medieval cities like Lorenzetti's

Figure 1.1   Lorenzetti's *Allegory of Good Government*.

Allegory of Good Government and *Allegory of Bad Government* in thirteenth-century Siena show repeated acts of quiet neighbourliness and mutual appreciation (Figure 1.1).

Nevertheless, successful cities inevitably bring people into enforced and sometimes unwanted contact with those who do not share their culture, interests, religion or even language. City life also creates situations where fear, hostility and exploitation can create conflict or the subjugation of whole groups as servants, serfs or slaves. Settlements where friendly association has been lost may become dangerous places where vulnerable individuals and groups suffer random assault or systematic exploitation. As a result, the fostering of community life to support and sustain healthy societies requires careful planning and management, which will involve choices and decisions about which values and interests will be pursued – whether, for instance, to adopt the elaborate caste systems of traditional Hindu society (Naipaul, 1979) or to develop more voluntary networks like those of the craftsmen and artisans of medieval and renaissance Tuscany (Heywood, 1904; Hibbert, 1979; Putnam, 1993).

The first decades of the twenty-first century present particularly acute challenges to the roles of communities as places where change can be assimilated and the shock of the new absorbed into a continually readjusted balance. The increased personal mobility and power of the modern era has accentuated to dangerous extents the effects of interpersonal conflicts of belief and interest. These influences have, in turn, been amplified by the global reach of mass media, publicising the attractions of the world's most prosperous regions to the most remote corners of all continents, and encouraging flights from famine which may involve many tens of thousands of people. There is also the added possibility of mass migrations resulting from sea level rises fuelled by global warming. We are facing a future where the capacity of communities to integrate newcomers will become even more essential to both successful local life and global harmony.

CURRENT TRENDS

Opportunities to do this have been much assisted by developments of mass education and technological reach throughout the twentieth century, climaxing in the digital revolution of the cell phone, which is increasingly being used in all parts of the world to access the global Internet. Most societies now aim to provide some sort of primary education for their children and the universal reach of global communications has also brought the informal education of satellite 'infotainment' to every village, however poor or remote. Individuals in all parts of the world now have the confidence and the capacity to communicate their ideas and needs and aims with each other and with power holders. Even though we are approaching a resources crisis, we are experiencing the potential for education and learning to become major focus points for community life at all scales (Table 1.1).

The role of communication in community building is by no means limited to education; it plays key roles in governance, culture and social life. Many of the worst failures of community life in recent times have occurred where there have been breakdowns in communications.

Table 1.1 Community forming role of education at different scales

Physical scale	Educational facility	Nature of community	Frequency of intensive interaction
Family	Radio, TV, cell phone	Extended family	Continual
Locality	Child care centre, primary school	Neighbourhood	Daily
District	Secondary school, library, video store	Suburb	Daily/weekly
Town	Vocational college internet cafe	Work catchment	Daily/weekly
City or rural province	Regional university, voluntary organisations, regional newspaper, radio stations, agricultural college	City or rural region	Weekly
Metropolis	Metropolitan university, creative culture precincts; TV stations, major libraries and museums, research facilities	Metropolitan community	Monthly
Country	International universities, national education hub, access to national educational and employment opportunities	National community	Annual/life phase.
Global	Global knowledge networks of cell phones, satellites and internet UNESCO.	Human community	Physical: once or twice a lifetime; Virtual: daily/continuous

FAILING COMMUNITIES

There are many vivid and well publicised failures to manage cultural diversity peacefully and positively. Cases like the Khmer Rouge and Serbian extermination camps, Rwandan and Chechen massacres, and riots in Los Angeles in 1992, Mumbai in 1993 and 2008 and Sydney in 2007 have become recurrent themes of contemporary life (Robertson, 1999). Nevertheless, these are far outweighed by more significant but less dramatic achievements of cooperation and mutual aid. Examples such as Bangladesh's Grameen Bank (Box 1.1), the Mondragon workers cooperatives (Boxes 1.2 and 1.3) and the international community development schemes of organisations like Oxfam and World Vision have brought personal autonomy and essential physical and social resources such as clean water and education to countless small communities throughout Africa, Asia and Latin America (Oxfam Australia, 2006). It is significant that despite the dramatic destructiveness of explosions of violence, the long-term imperatives of cooperation and voluntary exchange have always re-asserted themselves, because community life is a necessity for civilised and prosperous societies, which depend upon harnessing human skill, ingenuity and creative talent in networks of exchange and development. The prosperity and individual fulfilment of their members relies on the support of networks of trust, which in their turn rest upon the friendly associations of community life.

The psychological basis of community living has been explored by Jane Jacobs, the celebrated planning theorist, in her 1992 book *Systems of Survival*, in which she argues that humans have evolved as 'dealers' far more capable of developing robust systems of mutual advantage than the 'guardians' who see it as their prerogative to lay down rules to regulate the behaviour of their fellow citizens. These ideas have great significance for community planning, and for the promotion of person-to-person methods of developing policies and plans as against the top-down ones, which guardians in the spirit of Plato, More, Marx and Skinner would advocate. In his seminal book *The Open Society and its Enemies*, Karl Popper (1998) relates the repressive failings of closed communities to their inability to acknowledge and integrate the experience of their members into the evolution of those communities' future directions. They thus become caught in a vicious cycle of resentment, repression, resistance and rejection. If, on the other hand, people are obliged to negotiate with each other, policies will become better informed, more detailed and more widely and securely based.

Jacobs' ideas therefore powerfully support the methods of 'collaborative planning' (Healey, 2006, 2007) which are currently emerging to replace the 'systems thinking' of the mid-twentieth century (Chadwick, 1969; McLoughlin, 1971). Such systems planners, in creating descriptive systems often of great subtlety, scope and explanatory power, frequently slid

Box 1.1 Micro credit in Bangladesh

At the end of its bloody war of independence in 1972, when Bangladesh emerged as one of the world's poorest nations, Mohamed Yunus returned from the United States, where he had been teaching as a professor of economics. Depressed by the inability of academic theories to explain or redress the cycle of poverty in which chronic debt trapped most of the country's population of more than one hundred million people, he experimented, by making 42 small loans totalling $27 in a nearby village (Bornstein, 1996). Based on the success of this initiative in enabling the recipients to work and trade their way out of debt and poverty, he developed a general approach to micro credit, in which the traditional financial collateral demanded by banks, which the poor do not have, was replaced by social collateral, which their daily lives and mutual knowledge provide in abundance (Yunus, 1998). Over a period of four years, he and his colleagues organised the Grameen, or 'Seed', Bank of small local groups linked to form centres of about thirty members, in turn joined to district branches each serving sixty centres. The bank's success depends upon hard work, small sums of money, accountability and respect for human dignity

Because it lends to 'the poorest of the poor' who are used to tight budgeting, and relies on weekly meetings to decide on loans and collect repayments, the bank has always enjoyed an excellent repayment rate, which is currently running at 98%. Its workers must spend two-thirds of their time travelling to villages and participating in weekly branch meetings of local members. Its lending has grown in 30 years to over $7.59 billion to over seven million members (over 97% of them formerly impoverished women) organised in 1.2 million groups (Grameen Bank, 2009a, b). By the end of the century, the movement had spread to include partner organisations in twenty different countries in all six settled continents and is still growing (Grameen Dialogue, October, 1999; Grameen Bank, 2009b).

The achievements of the Grameen Bank are widely celebrated. Mohamed Yunus has been awarded the Nobel Peace Prize, the Bank has gained an international architecture award for its contribution to improved rural housing and construction of over 600000 homes has also been financed (Grameen Bank, 2009a). Grameen Phone, Grameen Knitwear (a weaver's cooperative) and Grameen Health Care Services have been formed to use the excess funds contributed by members after they have finished repaying their loans. Grameen Phone has transformed the former rural isolation of the country by having one or more 'telephone ladies' with a mobile phone able to reach any resident in any of the 83000 villages where there are groups.

By the turn of the century, the Grameen Bank started to look worldwide, aiming to reach a hundred million of the world's poorest families, especially women, providing credit for self-employment, and other financial and business services, in pursuit of the basic aims of:

- reaching the poorest;
- reaching women;
- building financially self-sufficient institutions;
- ensuring impact on the lives of clients and their families.

The bank continues to expand in many directions: upwards to influence the policies of the World Bank to support micro credit; downwards to make its members more self-sufficient, in enterprises like Grameen Knitwear and Healthcare Service; and sideways to establish over 150 branches in all six settled continents (Grameen Trust, 2000).

into the error of seeing themselves as appointed experts with responsibilities to project current needs into the future and make provisions for such decisive innovations as land use transportation systems designed around massive urban freeways capable of accommodating all the forecast increased traffic flows, irrespective of community concerns about demolition, pollution and distributional effects (Heywood, 1974).

CONTRIBUTIONS OF COLLABORATIVE PLANNING

There are many practical examples of the contributions which these community-building collaborations can

Box 1.2   Worker and community self-management in Spain

The Mondragon Workers Cooperative (now the Mondragon Corporation Cooperative) is a notable example of the power of creative ideas and cooperation to transform unsatisfactory and unjust economic and physical conditions. In the early 1940s, Father José Arizmendi, emerging from one of Franco's prisons, founded a democratically managed polytechnic school and began to explore cooperative ideas as an option to avoid each of a number of unattractive alternatives, including the repressive excesses of the dictatorship then ruling Spain, the rigid and unproductive standardisation of Stalin's Soviet Union and the social inequities of contemporary capitalism, which had produced the mass unemployment of the 1930s. In 1956, five unemployed graduates of the polytechnic pooled their savings and joined with him to establish the basis for a workers cooperative. ULGOR became the first of the network of cooperatives, producing white goods and domestic appliances, which happened to be the items with which they had industrial experience (Whyte & Whyte, 1989).

ULGOR was an immediate success and by the early Sixties had grown to a network of enterprises comprising over 3000 worker partners. All members have a financial stake in their work places, which is bought out if they leave, so that only the workers can own the enterprise. Control of the factories and appointments of senior management is by means of works councils with all workers as voting members, appointing and sharing power with plant managers. By 2008, the original network had grown to include over 23000 member owners, and became Spain's largest producer of white goods, with the highest worker productivity of any Spanish enterprise. The wider international network now includes more than 100000 members (Mondragon Corporation Cooperative, 2008).

The Contract of Association stipulates that not less than 10% of the profits must go to community and social services of schools, colleges, health insurance, clinics and research institutes. These 'second degree' cooperatives are governed by representatives of the factory co-ops. No factory may expand beyond 500 workers, in order to maintain the reality of workers' control and good human communications. Wage differentials, originally fixed at a ratio of 1:3, have since been expanded to 1:6 in order to ensure that the co-op network retains its pool of highly talented and energetic young managers and technical experts, to keep it competitive in times of very rapid technological and economic change, as Spain adjusts to membership of the mainstream European Community.

Because membership confers the automatic right to a job, the global restructuring of employment owing to the automation of the 1980s and 1990s posed particularly sharp challenges to the co-ops. Employment growth slowed, and remuneration fell for the first time to about the average elsewhere in Spain's industrial sector. Employment levels, however, remained at 100%. This achievement of consensual decision-taking in the workers councils involved creative innovation by management and rational choices by members to accept reduced wages to stay competitive.

The co-op begins new enterprises with a group of people who are friends, and sees the natural bonds of friendship as a building block for successful ventures, echoing the definition of community as 'friendly association' with which we started this section. Its successful application of radical social and economic ideas is assisting a traditional community to thrive in its home setting and to maintain a deeply valued heritage of language, culture and economic autonomy, which has elsewhere in the Basque region been expressed in acts of social dissent and terrorism.

make to flourishing human cities and regions, including, for example, micro credit to assist economically struggling communities, worker participation and management and the more pervasive but smaller-scale ones of local community development. One, deceptively modest example can be found in the City Farm movement, by which environmental activists in cities across the world are reintroducing the restorative effects of contact with nature to underprivileged inner-city communities. Box 1.1 illustrates how community trust can offer the social collateral to provide micro credit to relieve the exclusion of the 'poorest of the poor' in Bangladesh, one of the world's most impoverished countries. Boxes 1.2 and 1.3 describe how the collaborative management of the Mondragon workers cooperative has assisted a previously marginalised

> **Box 1.3**   Social enterprises in Santander
>
> The entrepreneurial ideas of the Social Enterprise Movement can also be grafted on to the communitarian and cooperative stock of workers cooperatives. In 2008, a former Director of Mondragon's Innovation and Knowledge Institute, Fernandez Isoird, left to establish Business Innovation Brokers (BIB), in the Basque capital of Santander, maintaining cooperative principles while seeking international capital to build a new industrial park to employ a thousand formerly unemployed people in innovative small-scale enterprises. His aim is to offer 'self-sufficiency, a safety net and a solidarity network that reduces dependency on the State' (Benjamin, 2009). BIB also wants to explore the black economy: 'We want to see how we can help (social security) claimants turn what they are doing into a legitimate social business. That way they come off welfare and pay taxes' (Benjamin 2009).
>
> Alison Benjamin reports Isoird as hopeful that out of the ashes of the present economic collapse will come more equitable ways of operating: 'First we have to democratize companies, and then we have to build the organization on principles and values, so they become part of the community and part of the solution in tackling social problems.'
>
> The ideas of such social entrepreneurs are immersed in the 'deal-doing' philosophy of Jane Jacobs discussed in the preceding section; their community planning approaches can be traced as far back as the model settlements of Robert Owen in New Lanark and New Harmony at the beginning of the nineteenth century (Taylor, 1989).

minority community to achieve and maintain prosperity since its establishment in 1956. Box 1.4 presents one such example in the heart of London, one of the world's most intensively developed cities.

Part Three: Competing Interpretations of Community Structure and Change

In both developed and developing countries, current challenges of rapid change and conflict are testing to breaking point long-established processes of community life (Diamond, 2005; Ridley, 1996; Pilger, 1992). Increasingly bitter communal clashes over conflicting beliefs and interests raise insistent questions about social policy. More inclusive and better informed community planning is a valid response that is being energetically pursued in the United Kingdom, the Netherlands, South Africa and elsewhere (Hamdi & Goethert, 1997; Department of Communities and Local Government, 2007, 2008viii; Healey, 2007; Homes and Communities Agency, 2009; Homes and Communities Agency Academy, 2009a, b). Such practical activities need a sound theoretical basis to help understand the character, development and workings of the communities in question. An accurate and shared understanding of their nature and that of the forces which are acting upon them is required if we are to be fully effective in promoting their success. Are they, for instance, primarily means of establishing order and avoiding

violence, or promoting productivity and exchange; or maintaining class control; or a framework for communication and mutual learning? To what extent are they, in short, driven by order, production, class interests or collaboration?

This section therefore explores four competing accounts of the nature of communities, based on the following different main aims:

- order: genetically driven dominance;
- productivity and exchange: through market competition;
- control through transcendence of conflict: equality through struggle;
- collaboration: through negotiation, adjustment and mutual aid.

Order: genetically driven dominance

In exploring the nature of human communities, one prime consideration must be the human nature of their members. No ideas have influenced thinking on this matter more than those of Charles Darwin (2008), who argued that humanity, like all other species, has been competitively shaped by the natural selection of the survival of the fittest, as amplified by randomly produced new mutations.[ix] A school of 'Social Darwinists' developed who applied these competitive principles to social organisation, suggesting that communities would advance best by promot-

Box 1.4 Surrey docks city farm

The aim of city farms like Surrey Docks, in the heart of inner London, is to involve local people and environmental activists in land care, food production and animal husbandry. City farms are areas of repose, centres of conservation of natural life and places for reconnecting with nature to balance the intensity of modern city life. They depend upon support from their local communities, often providing out-of-curriculum activities for local schools and youth clubs, and in turn relying upon the services of local volunteers. There are no fewer than 15 of them in London, all members of the Federation of City Farms and Community Gardens, a national scale network (Federation of City Farms and Community Gardens, 2010).

Surrey Docks City Farm is one of the smallest and most central, occupying two acres of an old docks site at the northern tip of the Rotherhithe peninsula, immediately across the Thames from the towering bulk of the 75-storey Canary Wharf and the spreading mass of London's new international office precinct of Docklands. The farm was originally founded in 1975 by Hilary Peters, who recalls that

> The dreadful alienation of people in the abandoned docks wasn't just the result of unemployment. They were alienated from themselves, each other and their surroundings. When I started to dig the silt and graze my goats and poultry in Surrey Docks, I was surprised by the urgency with which everyone wanted to join in… People who had never related to anyone or anything started to relate to animals. The farm grew due to people who recognized that it met some buried need in them. (Peters, 2009)

Now the farm is run by Surrey Docks Farm Provident Association, involving schools, businesses, youth organisations, volunteers of all ages including a blacksmith/artist, who work on site every day, providing farm equipment, art objects and continuing interest. It is

> a focus for local community life, the site of recurrent fairs and festivals, its café a regular stopping off point for walkers and cyclists travelling along the Thameside Path. The small site is densely used and includes in the words of Hilary Peters: *fields for grazing, a vegetable patch along the river, a herb garden, a compost area, a duck pond, a wild life patch, at least one yurt (which also go out to schools), a willow walk housing the bee hives … an orchard full of geese and sculpture. The blacksmith does extremely inventive work with local children collecting the grot off the river beach and making recycled portraits of the farm's animals.* (Peters, 2009)

Although frequently small and very local in their organization and links, these city farms contribute significantly to making inner cities physically attractive, interesting, socially inclusive and open-hearted. Many readers will immediately associate this story with similar community organisations and spaces in their own or nearby cities. Such places and groups express well how community life and organisations can help people to take possession of their own living areas and lives in ways which welcome all others who also want, in whatever ways, to contribute.

ing the 'survival of the fittest'. Darwin's friend Thomas Carlyle, for instance, propounded a 'great man' view in which history is shaped by dominant leaders. He condemned the democratic Chartist movement of the 1830s and 1840s for seeking egalitarian rights including universal suffrage as 'this bitter discontent grown fierce and mad' and argued instead for the Machiavellian motivation of natural leaders to maximise the worth of their possessions, and therefore of the communities which constituted them. (Desmond & Moore, 1991).

Twentieth-century experience has cast dark shadows across the capacity of such unconstrained leadership to achieve lasting social progress. The German cultural tradition stalled under Hitler; Spain and Portugal suffered socially and stagnated economically under Franco and Salazar, and Mussolini's regime proved disastrous for Italy, climaxing in his being torn limb from limb by a vengeful crowd in Milan in 1944. Currently, the Burmese military regime has perpetrated social injustice, political autocracy, economic penury and multiple ethnic conflicts. As a result of these many failures, Social Darwinism has lost appeal as a basis for community life (Ridley, 1996). Sociologists and ethnologists have tended to turn more to the mutual aid theories of thinkers like Peter Kropotkin, who argued that 'admitting that swiftness, strength, cunning and endurance contribute to survival under certain conditions … sociability is always the greatest advantage in the struggle for life' (1939).

Nevertheless, lasting subconscious effects of Social Darwinism have influenced many of the explanatory ideas of twentieth-century urban sociology and economics. In the first three decades of the twentieth century, for instance, Robert Park, Ernest Burgess and Roderick McKenzie (1925) and their colleagues in the Chicago School of Urban Sociology developed ideas of urban processes resulting from endless struggles for space and resources. The new urban communities were seen as being continually reshaped by the dynamic of externally driven economic investment and technological change, giving rise to waves of renewal rippling outwards through concentric zones of uniform development. As the city grew, the high-intensity commercial core expanded to redevelop the surrounding environmentally blighted zone in transition, sending further ripples of redevelopment through the successive rings of inner-residential suburbs, zones of working men's housing and outer fringes of low-cost accommodation. The language adopted to describe this process, 'invasion and succession', reflected Darwinian ideas of competitive evolution: one group was invading the territory of another and succeeding to its ownership. Later, Martin Anderson (1964) and Jane Jacobs (1961) described how these forces were able to annex the powers of city and federal governments, using instruments of 'eminent domain' to acquire land compulsorily and speed the process of economic appropriation. The dominant elites of the 'property machine' (Ambrose & Colenutt, 1975) and the 'growth machine' (Logan & Molotch, 1987) claimed to be acting in the best interests of the whole urban community. It is not surprising that opposing schools of Marxist urbanists, discussed later, developed the counter-interpretation of class conflict.

Twentieth-century developments in genetics both reinforced and modified these ideas of the sociobiology of communities (Wilson, 1992). Richard Dawkins argued that human evolution was driven by the struggle of the 'selfish gene' to dominate over the competing genes of others of its own species (Dawkins, 1976, 1988, 2009). Although he discounted the ability of human beings to rationally control these drives in the interests of cooperative success and survival, he argued that in the drive to promote our own genes we will support siblings and others within our own communities having some common genetic material. These interpretations may seem to explain some of the collapses of community life and 'ethnic cleansing' of the end of the twentieth century, where groups of individuals of shared ancestry seem to have combined to attack and exterminate neighbours alongside whom they had been living more or less peacefully for decades in Bosnia, Rwanda and northern Nigeria. However, closer examination often identifies other economic and environmental factors, which more satisfactorily explain the patterns of violence and social disintegration. Diamond (2005) argues that the economic scarcity had stretched these communities' capacities for cooperation to breaking point, so that in Rwanda, a survivor explained 'the people whose children had to walk barefoot to school killed the people who could buy shoes for theirs' irrespective of whether they were Hutu or Tutsi (Diamond, 2005).

However, it is not only in such marginalised and stressed communities that evolutionary biology has offered explanations or influenced social organisation. The cult of the outstanding business leader, and the unique gladiatorial sportsperson (both rewarded with annual salaries of many tens of millions of dollars a year), reached its climax in the first decade of this century, only to falter in the face of the global financial crisis of 2008 and the failure of the 'world leader' and 'shock and awe' policies in the Middle East and Africa.

Community planning doctrines of order imposed through dominant power have changed the face of many metropolitan regions, introducing segregated and walled residential and tourist communities, recreational and shopping centres and theme parks, often patrolled by private security staff, and closed to local access or use. In Los Angeles County and elsewhere in the United States 'cities by contract' (Miller, 1981) have incorporated as local governments where the wealthy gather to isolate themselves, making no contribution to the upkeep of the social needs of the wider metropolis. Such communities suffer from being both provocative and vulnerable to attack from the excluded workers on whom they depend and Miller, for instance, accurately forecast Los Angeles' 1992 urban riots a decade before they occurred.[x]

This view of communities, based on unconstrained rights of control and exclusion may well become self-defeating. Such places are prone to become vulnerable to violence instigated by the equally 'selfish genes' of those who see themselves as excluded and exploited, as is already happening in urban riots and atrocities around the world. The evolutionary biology underlying these ideas is intellectually insecure because it relies on extrapolating observations of other species onto our own, leaving scope for the double error of subjective misinterpretation and uncritical application of animal to human life. Even more crippling is the naturalistic fallacy that 'is implies ought', that observations of competitive tendencies in evolution should guide us in shaping the life of communities, which are created by intention and maintained by consent, and drawn towards the achievement of better living.

Nevertheless, there are some positive and important contributions that genetic science can make to community planning. By establishing the role of the deeply inscribed structures of genomes and individual DNA in deciding individuals' innate characteristics and competences, genetic science reinforces the arguments of thinkers as diverse as Karl Popper and Noam Chomsky that human beings have their own innate characteristics and are not infinitely malleable (Popper, 1972; Chomsky, 1972, 1992; Lyons, 1970, 1991). Their deep-seated competences and values should be respected as valid guides to objectives in planning for communities and settlements, rather than being subjected to attempts at moulding by behavioural conditioning. It is not the science but the selective interpretation of genetic determinism that is faulty.

Productivity and exchange: through market competition

A different model of individualism more appropriate to a productive society than the social dominance of a caste 'born to rule' emerged from the combination of the humanism of the Enlightenment and the physical transformations of the Industrial Revolution. More open meritocracies replaced closed aristocracies. Thinkers as different as John Locke, Adam Smith and John Stuart Mill sought to expand the scope of individual freedom, and the rapidly growing manufacturing communities proved a fertile soil for these ideas where people of talent could work and trade their way into success or even pre-eminence, and therefore, it was argued, confer advantages on the whole community.[xi] Competition was seen as the road to progress and choice.

In many pioneer industrial nations, the liberalism of the market and the social and physical mobility of the twentieth century combined to form communities afflicted by alienation, insecurity and great disparities of wealth and living conditions (Williams, 1973). There were few constraints on technological innovation, which introduced potent new developments promot-

ing the interests of the affluent. Urban motorways rapidly replaced long-established systems of public transport of trams and trains, often obliterating existing inner-city communities by broad swathes of new roads and associated clover leaf connectors. Mass-produced high-rise public housing, fuelled by corrupt contracts, ignored needs for human contact, convenience and family life (Jephcott, 1971; Heywood, 1974; Booker, 1980). In the United States, the 'federal bulldozer' flattened inner-city ghettos without opening up the new suburbs to people of Afro-American or Hispanic descent (Davidoff, Davidoff & Gold, 1970). The assumption that, given choice, people would create the communities that they wanted through market preference foundered on grossly unequal incomes and the reality of self-maintaining class systems and institutionalised racism.

By the second half of the twentieth century, the cumulative and often unregulated impacts of neo-liberal permissive planning were afflicting community life in cities throughout the Western world, generating massive pollution, destroying settled neighbourhoods and their green spaces and often failing to distribute equitably the social benefits from newfound material affluence. Then, in the opening years of the new century, environmental, economic and political effects began to encounter internal contradictions and global limits in the form of the triple disasters of climate change, financial collapse and urban terrorism.

Another of the potent impacts of neo-liberal doctrines for community planning has been the extrapolation of its inherent materialism to justify the belief that human behaviour is largely shaped by material conditions, and that values can very rapidly be moulded by physical stimuli.[xii] This view has major community planning implications, including standardised and mechanistic living environments, shopping centres arranged to suspend people's critical faculties and manipulative abuse of public consultation. In their pursuit of perfect competition, productivity-driven policies have created places for consumption without community and residential communities afflicted by almost intolerable sameness. It is a strange paradox that a view of society originally grounded in the desire to maximise liberty should reach a stage where its proponents are using mass-conditioning techniques to replace genuine human choice.

Another result has been pervasive privatisation. The view of Margaret Thatcher, prime minister of the United Kingdom from 1979 to 1991, that 'There is no such thing as society; there are only individuals and their families' briefly became a self-fulfilling prophecy. The results in Britain were repetitious, badly serviced and poorly coordinated suburbs in southern growth areas and devastated and alienated ones of contraction in declining parts of the north of the country, like South Yorkshire, Clydeside and Durham. The individualist competition of neo-liberalism seems unable to provide the inclusion, direction and lively social dialogue that are needed to create healthy community life.

Control through transcendence of conflict: equality through struggle

The opposing way of interpreting the nature and evolution of human society developed by Karl Marx and Friedrich Engels (1998) elevated the liberal competition of the marketplace to the clash of classes in the struggle for control of the means of production as part of an inexorable dialectic of class conflict. Progressing from primitive accumulation, through its antithesis of feudal power to the further opposite of capitalist urban competition, Marx advocated a final synthesis of socialist cooperation under the control of the representatives of the proletariat. In this view, Carlyle's 'great leaders' and the systems planners of the mid-twentieth century were alike reduced to mere temporary expressions of underlying class struggles for control of the land, capital and labour which will decide who commands the means of production, who pays and who benefits.

Community problems and controversies are likewise seen as local expressions of national and international scale contradictions resulting from the exploitation of labour by capital, through the instruments of rentier landlordism. As late as the mid-1980s David Harvey (1996) was arguing that resort to the idea of community was a veil to disguise the potent and naked economic exploitation of labour by capital, and that 'urban-regional planners' were the bailiffs and apologists of this process of adaptation and co-option. Harvey illustrates his interpretation by an example of a situation where housing stress is occurring in an impoverished community:

> If labour lacks organization and power in the community, but is well organized and powerful in the workplace, a rising rate of appropriation may result in the pursuit of higher wages in the workplace, which, if granted may lower the rate of profit and accumulation. A rational response of the capitalist class under these conditions is to seek an alliance with labour to curb excessive rental appropriations, to free land for new construction and to see to it that cheap (perhaps even subsidised) housing is built for the labouring classes.

> We can see this sort of coalition in action when large corporate interest in suburban locations join with civil rights groups in trying to break suburban zoning restrictions that exclude low wage populations from the suburbs. (Harvey, 1996)

This Olympian standpoint allows Harvey to reinterpret a victory for decent housing opportunities and social justice as the outcome of a 'coalition' among civil rights groups and corporate interests that neither would recognise. It is highly possible that Harvey is making a direct reference (the circumstances are certainly very similar) to the celebrated and influential community action work of Paul and Linda Davidoff and their associate Newton Gold in the previous decades in establishing Suburban Action Inc in 1969 to fight, often successfully, against discrimination in housing throughout the more desirable outer suburbs of the United States. As both lawyers and planners, they arraigned zoning restrictions which effectively kept people of Afro-American and Hispanic descent out of these jurisdictions at the edges of the spreading new metropolitan areas, enjoying good job prospects and community facilities, as breaches of the second amendment to the United States' constitution, which guarantees equality of opportunity (Davidoff, Davidoff & Gold, 1970).

While the Davidoffs and Gold's struggles in the communities and courts and Harvey's in the fields of theory-building are equally valid, the evidence is that the activist commitment to pluralist evolution has proved more effective and relevant. American society has integrated quite rapidly since the 1970s, and neighbourhoods are continuing to desegregate their housing; dozens of cities have Black and Latino mayors and senior officers, and in 2008, the country elected an African American President, who had come into politics by way of community development work in Chicago, one of the United States' most stressed cities (Obama, 2004). Meanwhile, in Russia and a number of East European countries, overtly Marxist-Leninist regimes that discounted community organisation and life in favour of wider class conflict and solidarity have been overthrown by their own people, to widespread relief (Bater, 1984; Ascherson, 1996).[xiii]

Of course, deeply humanitarian theorists like David Harvey would be the first to criticise and oppose such cruel and repressive regimes, but they could not point to other examples where dialectical materialism or conflict models of social development have produced better results. Even the Community Development Project running in England from 1970 to 1976 produced negligible or negative results where they were based on neo-Marxist interpretations, while those pursuing social familiarisation, seeking to transform the relations between local communities and local governments (Topping & Smith, 1977) were far more successful and contributed to the development of the many community development and community organisation movements which are now working to combat the devastating local effects of global economics. If we follow Popper's argument (1989), that every theory only deserves credence until it is falsified in practice, when it should be abandoned or modified, there is a clear conclusion. The criticism that community planning is, in reality, a veil worn by social apologists for continuing class exploitation is based on inadequate evidence and over-generalised interpretation which makes them, in Popper's terms, 'non-sense', neither true nor certainly false, but merely personal speculations, though they to now seem to be falsified by the accumulating evidence becoming available.

One distinguished example of this re-evaluation is the early work of Manuel Castells (1977, 1983). Examining the actual evolution of urban and community life in Madrid in the closing years of Franco's fascist regime in Spain up to 1975, Castells observed the important role of community groups in shaping regime change from below (rather than by seizing the central organs of power from above as had been advocated by Lenin). Castells was involved in the Madrid Citizen's Movement (summarised in Box 1.5), and it is this direct experience which allowed him to transform the abstract Marxist model into a practical understanding of how different groups negotiate with each other and evolve to match external changes and improve living conditions. What emerges is not so much a class conflict model of community life and social change as a group interaction version. Although Stuart Lowe (1986) has looked at the significance of Castells ideas for community action and housing campaigns in Britain in the 1980s, the importance of urban social movements deserve more attention than has been paid to them, partly because Castells himself has chosen to turn his attention instead to the social and political implications of modern communications technology (Castells, 1989).

In considering conflict models we must look therefore at their practical applications in their own terms. They have proved far from libertarian; many have resulted in authoritarian, top-down and generally repressive urban and community regulation, failing to acknowledge the human determinants of community life. Under the general justification that it is 'necessary to break many eggs to make a good omelette', the pursuit of order and uniformity has devastated the natural creativity of community life. In Stalin's Russia, acquisition of the basic necessities of life became a daily challenge and community life was driven underground and into the deprived outposts of the so-called gulag archipelago of prison camps (Solzhenitsyn, 1974) before being overthrown by internal rejection; Chairman Mao's Cultural Revolution is now universally excoriated by its survivors; and the devastating effects of the imposed emptying of Cambodia's towns into the 'killing fields' of the Khmer Rouge has caused lasting social damage (Bater, 1980; Ridley, 1996, Solzhenitsyn, 1968, 1974; Pilger, 1992). Physically, the resulting communities have been ugly, inefficient and marked by standardised repetition; socially, they have created deprivation and alienation.

By denying the cooperative capacities of community life, the conflict theorists have justified regimes based on the crudest use of naked coercion, and justified this by selective historical analysis. Dialectical materialists have found themselves caught in an iron cage of regressive causality of action and reaction of their own making, from which most of them cannot escape. If, for Margaret Thatcher, 'There is no such thing as society; there are only individuals and their families', for the conflict theorists there is no such thing as community: only classes fighting to control the State. Well-argued alternatives are available in the form of the roles played within the life of communities by cooperation (Kropotkin, 1939, 1974), by insightful deal doing (Jacobs, 1969, 1992) and by celebration, play and trust (Putnam, 1993; Landry, 2000). These are discussed in the next section.

Collaboration: through negotiation, adjustment and mutual aid

Conflict theorists tend to dismiss communicative approaches as social therapy and diversionary tactics, while communicative activists point to the wasteful character of social conflicts and the tendency for them to polarise complex situations into hostile camps that accentuate the worst aspects of both sides.[xiv] Although the adversarial structure of legal systems based on English law make use of challenge and response, elsewhere little common ground can be found between conflict and communication. Even there, pure conflict is constrained by principles of natural justice, rights of defendants and access to advocacy, so that elements of cooperation are involved. Recent developments in alternative dispute resolution combine communication and cooperation. Once people find themselves talking with someone, there is always the tendency for

Box 1.5   Urban social movements in Madrid

Throughout the second half of the twentieth century, urban social movements transformed the capacities of communities to share in shaping their local and urban environments, as new political systems and mass communications created opportunities for local democratic politics. Ways in which these processes of local and urban change could be linked to improve access to political power, identified by Castells (1983) in his native Madrid in the 1970s, suggest that grassroots associations can combine to create effective urban social coalitions to achieve change.

In Madrid, the poor maintenance of public housing estates, badly planned and located private housing without urban services and middle-class residential suburbs needing better facilities were active causes of discontent. Originally separate campaigns to build local democracy, provide basic urban services, redevelop shanty towns and rehouse slum dwellers converged to form an effective coalition for change, the Federation of Citizens Movements. Meanwhile, in central Madrid, a number of active pressure groups campaigned for physical and social conservation, rather than the massive redevelopment favoured by the Phalange Party and its business backers. Within four years, schools were built, slums demolished, a preservation agency created for central Madrid and processes of public participation in planning established that survive up to the present, though the community coalition has dissolved. Writing in the aftermath of this period, Castells saw urban social movements as potentially the most powerful force for change in contemporary society, with three necessary conditions for success:

1. Widespread concern for items of collective consumption (such as work, housing or health).
2. The significant cultural affiliations of groups with historic or ethnic origins.
3. The capacity for autonomy or decentralisation in service delivery.

To these hindsights can be added the cultural capacity for different groups to communicate and cooperate. Given these conditions, urban movements can be effective agents in the struggle for a free city. While established political processes tend to represent dominant class interests, citizen movements represent 'civil society' with the ability to balance and ultimately overcome the capacity of the 'growth machine' to destroy diversity and homogenise urban environments in the interests of investment. In this process, metropolitan governments can be captured, sensitised and adjusted towards fairer and more sustainable distributions of social provisions and economic and political power between groups. Where democratic politics, universal education and miniaturised, decentralised technology are combined, they can produce better informed and more assertive electorates. Regular elections should alert governments to community priorities, and global electronic networks can spread knowledge more evenly across and between regions.

Since the 1980s, such urban movements have stopped urban motorways in their tracks in Toronto and San Francisco, prevented their construction in Brisbane and Vancouver, generated urban conservation of whole suburbs in Adelaide's Hackney, Sydney's Woolloomooloo and Melbourne's Kensington, and protected valued urban open space in the forms of creeks, corridors and wetlands throughout the Western world (Gutstein, 1983; Lemon, 1985; Harris, 1986; Stretton, 1989; Heywood, 1997). Though yet to fulfil the more ambitious agenda of shifting political power from established elites to organised communities, they have created a climate of debate over urban development, where the voices of social activists and community groups have become an accepted and essential part of the context of contemporary urban governance and planning.

them to be drawn into a dialogue that may modify and diminish the sharp clarity of pure conflict. There are thus very strong links between communication and collaboration (Margerum, 1999, 2002): mutual understanding provides both the motive and the capacity to work together.

The case for linking communication and collaboration within a single model of community planning is therefore practical as much as theoretical: they are interdependent. Communication involves not only speakers but also active listeners to whose psychology and needs the speakers must pay attention. Most communication has an element of persuasion, and the development of a statement into a discussion implies the expectation of a positive outcome, paving the way for subsequent cooperation. Equally, it is simply impossible to collaborate without prior or simultaneous communication: people can't work together until they have discussed and agreed purposes, activities, roles and rewards. Though closely related, it is clear that the two modes are not identical: communication is about meaning and collaboration about action. It is worthwhile examining the role of each before combining them to consider collaborative communicative planning as an integrated process.

COMMUNICATION AND COMMUNITY

The communicative turn in planning theory (Healey, 1996, 2006) was anticipated by such earlier collaborations as those involved in actual and ideal communities like Plato's Academy, Anglo-Saxon folk moots and More's *Utopia* (Mumford, 1961; More, 1965).[xv] As the major theorist of communicative action, Jurgen Habermas (1990) points out, discussion plays an essential role in reaching valid interpretations and good policies, which emerge not so much from isolated individual thinkers but from the vigorous debate and winnowing of arguments that is favoured by free and critical discussion in open societies.[xvi]

The basic role of communication in the evolution of settled societies is supported by findings from archaeology, biology, linguistics and ethnology. The archaeologist and ethnologist Richard Leakey argues that whereas hunting and food gathering might not have necessitated the use of vocal language, social organisation and food sharing certainly did. His conclusion is significant for community organisation and planning:

> In a small hunter gatherer community social rules, elaborated through language, produce a cohesion that would be impossible to produce in any other way. (Leakey, 1981)

Developing communication was thus basic to the evolution of the first human communities around half a million years ago. The earliest yet found, at Terra Amata on the slopes of Mount Boron overlooking the Mediterranean above Nice, and the Choukoutien caves, an hour's drive south-west of Beijing, both offer evidence of highly organised community life, which must have depended on the transmission of experience and skills and their application in cooperative social activities (Leakey, 1981). On the Terra Amata site, footings have been unearthed of a series of eleven large wicker work huts, each twelve by six metres, constructed in successive years. Inside, there are the remains of domestic fires, animal prey and pigments for body painting. Excavations of the large cave site in Choukoutien have likewise unearthed many years of ceremonial burials signifying highly organised and stable societies. Both these societies must have possessed communication skills to support patterned and productive community life. Fossil remains of skulls from these sites support this conclusion, containing much enlarged brain spaces for Broca's area, which controls and coordinates the muscles of the tongue, mouth and lips and Wernicke's area, which is responsible for the structure and sense of language, than those of earlier sites (Leakey, 1981). This correlation suggests an upward spiral of improved language skills helping the development of elaborated social organisation. Leakey comments:

> Communicating with others, not just about practical affairs, but about feelings and fears … and the elaboration of a shared mythology produces a shared consciousness on the scale of the community. Language is without doubt an enormously powerful force holding together the intense social network that characterizes human existence (Leakey, 1981).

In making the link between communication, collaboration and social organisation so explicit, Leakey is leading us very far from abstract conflict and selfish-gene theories. Marshal McLuhan (1964) also interpreted improvements in communications technology as the mainspring of social development, coining his celebrated dictum that 'the medium is the message'. If speech created the conditions for an evolving human culture, he argues, writing promoted the growth of the great valley empires of five thousand years ago; printing generated the rise of the nation state; and the telegraph, telephone and radio promoted the development of the global economy. To this may be added the universalising impacts of the Internet and the growth of information and communications technology, which are promoting the spread of a universal commercial culture. It appears that communication creates the conditions for the collaborative success of communities which may then subsequently modified by competition.[xvii]

An equally significant role of the communication of ideas is to alert society to impending threats. This provides the theme of Jared Diamond's (2005) closely argued book *Collapse: How societies choose to fail or survive.* Diamond reviews a wide range of failed and successful societies in all six settled continents, spanning a period from several thousand years ago to the present. Many of his societies, like those of Easter Island and Norse Greenland, collapsed because they could not modify destructive practices or adapt to threatening environmental conditions. They were unscientific and conservative and generally either excessively pious or narrow-minded. They were not thinking enough about their changing situations, and if they were, they were not discussing their ideas enough. Others, like Tokugawa Japan of the seventeenth century, though socially conservative, were energetically reviewing their situations and promoting policies to correct threatening problems like deforestation and overpopulation.

Diamond specifically asks what lessons his many case studies have for modern societies. His conclusions focus around three principles:

1. Investigate conditions and face the facts.
2. Recognise and review unintended consequences of current actions.
3. Collaborate in social problem solving.

Insofar as Diamond discusses competition, he regrets the role it played in amplifying unwise behaviour, like the erection of ever-larger statues on Easter Island, the aim to rear more cattle in the declining climatic conditions of thirteenth-century Greenland or the killing frenzies of Rwanda. He notes how the feudal organisation of Tokugawa Japan succeeded in preventing the continuation of the competitive excesses which had destroyed so much of the country's vital forests in the preceding century.

His conclusions are that awareness, investigation and open communication are the keys to survival in times of external or internal threats or rapid change. These views on avoiding disasters are paralleled by those of Richard Florida on achieving economic success, when he argues (2005) that the 'creative class', on whose inventions and skills modern society increasingly depend, can only develop and thrive in mixed, diverse and experimental communities like those of inner-city San Francisco, Greenwich Village in New York, inner-Austin, central Amsterdam, Hong Kong and Melbourne. These models, where communicative action supports cooperation, have great significance for community planning.

COMMUNICATIVE ACTION AND COMMUNITY PLANNING

Progress towards valid social policy as well as philosophical truth, according to Habermas (1990), should emerge from open and purposeful discussion, with people speaking out about the experience of their daily lives. These discussions can occur across a wide variety of scales and types of community. He argues for such face-to-face debates and against the distanced and abstracted virtual discourses of the 'system world' of generalised administration or theoretical economics. Everyone, including both policymakers and local residents, has an equal right to be heard at the policy table, and thus to public participation in community planning. He deprecates the traditional self-allocated role of the philosopher as flunkey (discussed in more detail in the section dealing with intersubjectivity in Chapter 2 of this volume) as both servile and arrogant, preferring the more explicit and open advocacy of individuals' own ideas. Though he accepts that action is the most important basis for knowledge, he strongly asserts the importance of 'speech acts' which can power and coordinate so much physical action, again supporting citizen participation and suggesting how it might be organised. Habermas particularly emphasises the importance of abundant, lively and accessible public open spaces to promote the easy contact between people on which good social communication depends.

APPLICATIONS OF COMMUNICATION IN COMMUNITY PLANNING

There are a number of more specific planning implications of this commitment to communication:

1. Community festivals, art and cultural events in public spaces to initiate, promote and communicate different community values, needs and strengths, which can help to share, shape and accept ideas and aims through events such as public art, radio and online discussion groups, talkback radio, community forums, peer group discussions and appreciative workshops (Hammond & Royal, 1998).
2. Neighbourhood committees and councils that can take responsibility for neighbourhood communication and such communal functions, as public parks, street closure, neighbourhood watch, young people's vacation activities and comment on development proposals (Ward, 1973; Heywood, 1997).
3. Focus and mixed interest groups: groups of volunteers and invitees with particular interest in specific topics who work together to produce aims, problems and solutions, in specific topics or for a particular planning area.

4. Advisory and reference groups, selected, elected or self-nominated to provide ongoing advice on matters referred to them, based either on specific topics (such as the needs of young people or conservation historic buildings) or on physical areas; these bodies can become 'learning groups', provided with resources to gain further information on their topics so that evidence based policies can emerge from a combination of values and facts.
5. Consultation kits summarising accessible and interestingly presented information can be provided to large numbers of local organisations to promote discussions and responses that can make useful contributions to policy development.
6. Community visioning: to promote reflection and speculation among a group about values, goals, fears and hopes to drive future strategic plans.
7. Design workshops and charettes: occasions at which local residents and other participants work together with planners, designers and others to produce a draft schemes to fulfil their shared or negotiated aims.
8. Public meetings: publicised occasions open to all, featuring specified speakers addressing identified topics, with opportunities provided for open questioning.
9. Attitude surveys, community preference lists and semi-structured surveys: statistically valid questionnaires sample to identify people's attitudes to specific issues that can provide reliable guides to perceived problems and preferences.
10. Collaborative planning: involving local people and stakeholders with investors and implementation agents (responsible for land use, social, transport and economic planning) in cycles of proposal, review and negotiation to produce schemes which can integrate the necessary mix of activities (Healey, 2006).

One interesting aspect of the communicative turn in planning is the shift in consultation techniques from problem-solving to more positive approaches that involve individuals and groups thinking about successful experiences and their hopeful visions for the future. Whereas Critical Rationalists tend to extract objectives from the frustrated wants of felt problems, the emphasis of 'appreciative inquiry' is on searching for recognition of good experiences and positive values in people's previous experiences (Hammond & Royal, 1998). This not only helps to build participants' self-esteem and enlist their energies in the process of shaping beneficial change; it also identifies successful models and mechanisms which can be developed to help implement plans. Good cases can be made out for both approaches. While problem-solving is more radical and potentially comprehensive, appreciative inquiry can be more engaging, less threatening and is well suited to form part of ongoing community development and capacity building.

Part Four: The Roles of Cooperation

The history of human cooperation is closely linked to the evolution of communication discussed earlier. Each has assisted the other. At the dawn of the species, more than three million years ago, one of the earliest of archaeological findings shows the steps of a young hominin child, recorded in the volcanic ash at Laetoli south of the Olduvai Gorge in Tanzania, skipping her way around the heavier and more purposive path of her parents, implying both cooperative family life and some level of communication required to maintain guidance and confidence (Leakey, 1981). Much later, when the first cities were established around 4000 years ago, the tablets of Hammurabi and the epic of Gilgamesh depict worlds where the strands of cooperation, conflict and order were closely woven together to create societies capable of sustaining themselves over many generations and centuries (Sandars, 2006). Peter Kropotkin (1939) extends his belief in the basic role of cooperation in the evolution of all species to apply particularly to human societies. Greatest progress, he believes, is made in phases where cooperation predominates, as in the development of the self-governing communes of the central Italian city states which according to subsequent historical research, grew to number more than 80 by 1300 (Toynbee, quoted in Mumford, 1938). Kropotkin's view that the guild and civic arrangements in twelfth-century Italy promoted the evolution of modern city life provides valuable explanation and support for Robert Putnam's (1993) influential book on social capital, *Making Democracy Work*. Putnam shows how the thriving continuation of this tradition of medieval and renaissance cooperation, mediated into celebrations and festivities like the Palio of Siena and the Gioco del Ponte in Pisa (Heywood, 1904). These later created the basis for the associational economics of 'Third Italy' with its networks and clusters of small mutually supportive enterprises.[xviii]

Central and northern Italy are interesting cases of community cooperation. Through all of the vicissitudes of recent Italian politics, the cooperative regional economies have continued to create significant innovation and wealth and to sustain a community life that is one of the most celebrated models of contemporary social organisation. This example of the resilience of systems combining social cooperation and personal prosperity is particularly significant for ideas of collaborative planning (Healey, 2006), which have to operate in the times of fractured control, prolonged disorder and occasional foreign domination of the post-modern world.[xix]

The paradox of splintering centres and coherent localities, poses the persistent question 'What are the social forces (the "social capital") holding these communities together?' Putnam (1993) argues that the most convincing answer is the capacity to cooperate, which both generates and is generated by the singing, dancing and other performances which characterise the many festivals and social activities of Tuscany, Umbria and Emilia Romagna. Cooperation, drawing its energy from mutual understanding, reliance and exchange, is then expressed in art, play and performance and reinforced in cooperative production and enjoyment. The way that this millennium-old model combines cooperation and competition to produce a stable and evolving order has been explored and termed 'associational economics' (Cooke & Morgan, 1998). It is a social invention that in turn shapes social, economic and physical environments.

This kind of guild and civic life also developed in northern Europe, particularly in the Baltic states, Germany, Britain and the Low Countries, and played a significant role in the development of the 'polder model' of sixteenth- and seventeenth-century Holland. Communal work established and maintained the canals and dykes, and established the basis of trust that supported the development of the highly dynamic form of capitalism that continues to make Amsterdam and Rotterdam major centres of today's global economy. In England, similar cooperative management of village commons and the 'three fields' fallowing system, which persisted until the Enclosure Acts of the eighteenth and nineteen centuries, helped build the democratic awareness that re-emerged in such British political reform movements as Chartism, the Cooperative Movement and universal suffrage (Hamilton, 1946; Hammond & Hammond, 1978; Thompson, 1980). Elsewhere, in the monsoon lands of South-East Asia, communal water and land management in Bali (Ridley, 1996; Suarja & Thyssen, 2003) and New Guinea (Diamond, 2005) built strong cooperative institutions which survive to the present. Many such collaborative ideas underlying worker, housing and urban farm cooperatives can be traced back to similar roots in medieval notions of cooperation.[xx]

Cooperation in practice

In order to explore the practical capacities of cooperation to achieve successful outcomes in contemporary times, this section examines examples drawn from shelter, natural environment, place and production.

SHELTER

Housing, which is one of the most basic prerequisites of life in settled communities, combines the three critical elements of:

- firm grounding in the basic human values of shelter, nurture, procreation, play and learning;
- strong interconnectivity with many other social activities;
- expense far beyond the immediate and unaided scope of average individuals.

As both a basic human need and a social product, shelter is therefore a good candidate for cooperative planning and provision. There is anecdotal evidence that a number of early agricultural societies did indeed practise cooperative house-building and planning with sites being approved by village elders for young newlyweds, and construction being assisted by working parties of friends and relations, rewarded by the staging of a subsequent feast.[xxi] Although the industrialisation of the eighteenth and nineteenth centuries produced a dominant market in low-cost mass housing, cooperative responses rapidly re-emerged. In the 1770s in Britain's industrialising regions of the West Midlands and West Yorkshire, groups of working men collaborated to form 'terminating building societies', whereby each agreed to contribute a fixed sum every month so that houses could be built, one by one, until all members had been accommodated in homes of their own (Garrett-Holden, 1970). When all land and houses had been paid for, the society terminated, but out of this successful social invention grew the 'permanent building society', which has done so much to extend the 'trust principle' to bring home ownership within the reach of large proportions of the total population of many such advanced nations as the United Kingdom, the United States, Australia and Canada, either owning or buying their own homes. This process has done much to transform 'classic capitalism' into the 'welfare capitalism' that has managed to evolve and survive for over two centuries. A particular interest of this example is the illustration it provides of the ways in which cooperation in producing desired goods can coexist with market mechanisms in deciding their allocation and distribution.

Nonetheless, at the time of writing, this long-standing and productive social invention is showing signs of severe strain owing to erosion of its trust base. The cooperative machinery linking sincere borrowers to willing lenders broke down following the competitive excesses of hedge funds and remote subprime portfolio operators. Only the subventions of thousands of billions of dollars, extending to unprecedented programmes of planned economic stimulus from governments as distant from the original problem as those in Beijing and Delhi, saved the international economy from a prolonged period of recession and mass unemployment. Re-establishment of trust, confidence and cooperative capacity to recreate sustainable conditions for an exchange economy is proving challenging and protracted. Reviewing the causes of the crisis, it appears that, although the banks had physical collateral in the form of the dwellings themselves, they lacked a collaborative basis. The subprime lenders and hedgefund operators had little knowledge and even less interest in the lives and living conditions of their borrowers. This resulted in ill-judged and unreflective lending policies leading to a downward spiral of repayment failure, foreclosure, dispossession and competitive disinvestment. Much that should have been learnt from the 'social collateral' model of the micro credit movement had been ignored. Many of the commercial bankers, and initially staff of the World Bank, had refused to support and even mocked micro credit when it was proposed to them as a means of providing grassroots security to the commercial banking system (Yunus, 1998).

NATURAL ENVIRONMENT

Collaborative interest groups have become very important environmental actors. In Britain, foresters and commoners associations have historically enjoyed rights to the benefits, control and upkeep of the common land and forests which once constituted much of the total land area. This spirit of local and personal stewardship has spread through organisations like the Ramblers (formerly the Ramblers Association), with over 100 000 members, the Council for the Preservation of Rural England and the Yorkshire Wildlife Preservation Trust to influence not only ideas and access but also land tenure and management, and influenced the designation, as early as 1949, of the country's comprehensive system of national parks, areas of outstanding natural beauty, public rights of way, long-distance footpaths and nature conservation areas (Cullingworth, 1976). Elsewhere, similar bodies work individually and together to promote habitat awareness and conservation, including Australia's National Parks Associations and Landcare and Watercare groups, the United States' Audubon Society and local and regional ecological preservation societies, and worldwide countless environmental action groups. They often combine community and academic concerns, to contest habitat loss and promote reforestation and wetland protection, in areas as widely separated as Russia's Lake Baikal and Malaysia's Penang Island (Anenkhonov & Pronin, 2010; University Sains Malaysia, 2010). Increasing numbers of local organisations, loosely organised into regional and international coalitions, are also taking action on matters such as carbon reduction to safeguard global environmental health (see, for instance, Oxfordshire Climate Exchange, 2010). Making excellent use of modern information and communications technology, these organisations aim to combine local action and advocacy to produce consciousness change at the wider scale.

On an international scale, this has spread to encompass the activities of groups such as Greenpeace, asserting wider environmental interests against national and sectional ones in activities including forest clearance for plantation agriculture in Indonesia and Brazil and Japanese whale harpooning in international waters. Others, such as the World Wildlife Fund and the United Nations' Intergovernmental Panel on Climate Change (IPCC; 2007), are equally effective across a broader range of issues. Nowhere is the injunction 'Think Global, Act Local!' more effective than in the sphere of the physical environment. There is widespread sensing that the excesses of competitive capitalism and command communism have produced equally unsustainable results in the natural environment that need to be redressed by conscious action, normally involving community organisation and cooperation, academic research and commitment to the principles of symbiosis and mutual aid (Suzuki & McConnell, 2008). Peter Kropotkin (1939) would approve.

PLACE MANAGEMENT

Cooperation is particularly appropriate to the holistic management of living places. This recognition inspired Ebenezer Howard's 'invention' of the Garden City (Howard, 1898, 1965; Moss Eckhardt, 1973). Subtitling his book *A Peaceful Path to Real Reform*, Howard (1898) insisted that the cooperative principle should be infused into every aspect of life and government of his new garden cities. These were planned to be the largest cooperatives ever developed up to that time, with memberships including all 32000 people of their proposed populations. Both Letchworth and Welwyn were run by Garden City Companies, and it was Howard's original intention that the members of the cooperative companies would own the land in perpetuity, pay modest rents for their houses and spend the profits from the inevitable increases in land values on job creation and environmental conservation. Peter Hall (2002) quoting from an unpublished writing of Howard's (*The Vanishing Point of Landlord's Rent*) explained that land values would flow back to the community, in order to:

> found pensions with liberty for our aged poor, now imprisoned in work houses, to banish despair and awaken hope in the breasts of those that have fallen; to silence the harsh voice of anger; and waken the soft notes of brotherhood and goodwill. (Hall, 2002)

Later, Howard came to propose that houses could be built by a variety of means, including people building their own homes with funds provided through building, friendly societies or cooperative societies or trade unions. The garden city idea in its various expressions of new towns, garden suburbs and regional cluster cities has spread throughout the world and remains a powerful force to help humanity manage urban development in an era of unprecedented population growth and technological change.

Other cooperative approaches to place-making have followed apace. In the United States, Kevin Lynch's (1984) wide-ranging *Good City Form*, Randolph Hester's *Community Design* (2002) and the *New Urbanism* of Peter Calthorpe and associates (Calthorpe, 1993; Calthorpe & Fulton, 2001) have developed a plethora of paths to good place-making through community consultation and participation. In Britain, the highly influential *Responsive Environments* of Bentley *et al.* (1985) base their design methods entirely on how people do and may respond to present and future features. In the face of recent commercial pressures for privatised and socially segregated layouts, such ideas have supported a place-making movement which aims to create interacting, sociable and cooperative communities. Their methods, too, are based on inclusion and cooperative social inquiry like 'enquiry by design' and community charettes. Later, in Chapter 10, one such method is explored in which John Mongard makes use of the outcomes of a series of community engagement 'set-up shops' to build a strategy of place-making for a set of four country towns on Queensland's Atherton Tableland.

TRANSPORT

Freedom of movement can be seen as an inherently individual value, allowing serfs to walk off their feudal master's demesne, factory workers to move to a new town in search of better jobs or qualifications and contemporary international economic refugees to seek new lives in more promising places. Personal as these freedoms are, none of them may be possible without arrangements and provisions of a wider scale of social organisation. Rights of way need to be communally identified, agreed and maintained. Large-scale movements of goods and people require shared paths and international travel calls into play the most complex sets of cooperative arrangements. At the most local level, small networks of parents throughout the world are combining to organise 'walking buses' to get children to and from school safely, healthily and in sociable groups. Community buses and car pooling arrangements are being organised by local communities and urban coalitions are campaigning for better public transport based on cooperative principles (Cervero, 1998, 2009; 1000 Friends of Oregon, 2009). Public subventions to maintain a public transport system that can sustain public life are being levied and accepted in great cities throughout the world, with notable examples in London, Toronto, Vancouver, Curitiba, Bogotá, Portland (Oregon), Kolkata and Singapore (Heywood, 1997; Cervero 1998, 2009). These examples form part of a pattern that is becoming a model of worldwide best practice rather than the exception.

PRODUCTION, EXCHANGE AND ECONOMY

Contending views dispute the conditions necessary for the creation of surplus production. Karl Marx saw wealth production as dependent on class control. Adam Smith discerned the hidden hand of the laws of supply and demand, making possible the division of labour and specialisation of function. Galbraith (1972), Kropotkin, Marshall and Keynes interpreted economics rather differently, as the study of ways to achieve and maintain effective communal activity. In all these models, practical cooperation is crucial to production and prosperity, though there is no agreement on the best ways to achieve that cooperation, whether by the discipline of competition, the imperative of control or the inducements of collaboration. Earlier in this chapter, we discussed the successful cooperative approach developed by the Mondragon Corporation Cooperative (2008). While highly significant, this remains a challenging exception in a world controlled by competitive venture capitalism particularly dominant in four of the world's most populous countries: China, India, the United States and Russia, with the other, Indonesia, moving rapidly in the same direction. The intention of the Mondragon workers cooperatives and the ideas of its original designer, Father Arizmendi, that workers cooperatives grow up inside capitalism and supersede it, are singularly compatible with the synthesising philosophy and iterative approaches of community planning and development, unlike the competitive conflict and imposed order models of social change (Whyte & Whyte, 1989).

In such cooperative models, ownership, investment and credit arrangements will all require transitional arrangements. Despite the recent contraction of the international economy and the failure of investment banks and finance corporations to manage their own models, the view that they could be replaced overnight by alternative systems is unrealistic. Indeed, part of their excesses can be explained by the oversimplifications and inaccuracies of the opposing doctrine of exclusive State investment and control, whose collapse in the last decades of the twentieth century encouraged merchant bankers' illusions of invincibility which seem to have suspended their capacities for self-criticism and critical judgement. On the other hand, cooperative investment, incorporating the micro credit principles of social collateral and personal responsibility of the Grameen Bank, offers an approach that is well suited to stimulate grassroots development of the sort which venture capitalism so signally failed to foster. Now that governments have acquired a substantial degree of control over banks, the moves towards cooperative credit unions and societies of the 1990s and 2000s may well be further assisted, and become important levers to increase activities and tools available to community planning.

These can build on existing initiatives as diverse as Spain's Mondragon Corporation Cooperative, Britain's large and successful Cooperative Wholesale Society (150 years old in 2008); the John Lewis Partnership (the worker-owned British retail chain); the range of cooperatives established in the United States by the Office of Economic Opportunity under Lyndon Johnson's Great Society programme in the 1960s; and the rapid growth of farmers' markets and local bulk-buying co-ops which are springing up in communities throughout the world. There is every reason to promote the alliance between government and communities in achieving productive local investment and employment. Commercial banks will have to pay more regard to public interest and community support now that governments are such significant stakeholders and, indeed, shareholders in many of their enterprises.

Conclusions

ATTRIBUTES AND DEFINITIONS

Both 'community' and 'planning' are words loaded with significance and high expectations in these opening decades of the twenty-first century. The concept of community has graduated from being seen as too nebulous for serious use to being recognised as a convenient summary for many of the most important attributes of social life, in the same way that 'home' is increasingly used to capture the human reality of dwelling and residence. Community includes the links that people acknowledge with each other, involving expectations both of themselves and of others. It implies the reciprocity that constitutes a major factor in sustaining social life. The alternatives are less convincing than ever before. Law and order are not enough because they can no longer be sustained without consent. By itself, competition can cause a race to the bottom as often as an ascent to new pinnacles: poisoned environments, self-voted bonus payments for firms only surviving on government handouts after collapses caused by bad business decisions and ritual crowd violence at sporting occasions are among the more obvious examples. Naked coercion and military control attract universal condemnation in free societies, and heroic opposition from inside regimented ones. The collaborative basis of community life is thus supported both by its own arguments of shared objectives and activities and also by the painful failures of alternative, single-minded rationales for community life and organisation.

'Planning' is also a term which has recently emerged from the shadows of bureaucratic regimentation into the more spacious fields of human choice and intention. Remarkable new capacities to shape physical environments and unlock new resource wealth may also exert devastating impacts over distant places and people. They pose the inescapable need to accept responsibility for the effects of our actions. Rapid changes in the external environments of climate, water supply and circulation, species habitats and fossil fuel reserves have further focused attention on the need to think carefully about unintended consequences, and our abilities to anticipate and manage changed material situations.

Planning, once an activity poised uneasily between the rigours of emergency rationing, the narrow logic of project implementation and the self-assertion of architectural formalism, has become a widely accepted and welcome means to involve whole communities in thinking about their futures. In so doing, they can develop and mould feasible means to achieve desirable ends. Planning courses in universities are oversubscribed with talented young people seeking the tools to shape future societies to reflect their own values and those of their fellow community members. Government departments compete to recruit planners to develop purposive policies, implement community consultation and collaborate with others in community building and governance. The voluntary sector also plays leading roles in developing collaborative community plans for whole sectors and communities. No less important, community groups and activists are insisting on making their voices heard, both to oppose schemes which threaten their values and to propose often comprehensive alternative approaches. Planning, in short, has emerged from the wings to take centre stage, where the leading players must collaborate with each other or face losing control of events altogether.

CASCADES OF CHANGE AND CHOICE

The capacity to achieve effective shared action is essential if we are to navigate successfully the currants of physical, economic, social and political change which are flowing increasingly rapidly through our daily lives. In the face of such pervasive changes, it is clear that we must face and take choices about the future, which must take account of each other's needs and hopes, if we are to avoid self-destructive conflicts. Actions varying from suicide bomb attacks of politically motivated terrorists to voter revolts and mass demonstrations against medical reforms that would involve people in contributing to the health maintenance of other members of society provide illustrations of the disastrous effects of perceived exclusion. In the words of Gordon Campbell (1993), addressing the Greater Vancouver District Council of Councils, 'You can have anything you want, but you can't have everything, and you can't have it right now – you must take choices.' It is that spirit of honest realism and mutual acceptance of responsibility which makes cooperation possible, and which can in turn make it such an effective tool in creating sustainable communities.

COLLABORATIVE PLANNING IN PRACTICE

In practice, collaborative planning can promote effective change management within and among such essential activities as shelter, work, play, movement, communication culture and governance, to sustain and enrich the lives of both individuals and groups. At the same time, planning can also help communities embrace the inescapable challenges of integrating new members and adapting to changed external conditions. In identifying and achieving good overall outcomes, communication, consultation, participation and negotiation can play invaluable roles. They form the main themes of the next chapter.

Endnotes

  i Examples of this are such familiar cases as a new sewage outlet being located upstream of an important marine habitat or a neighbourhood engagement programme requiring its participants to sign an undertaking of confidentiality.
 ii Although these changes may be the most acute experienced by humanity since the ending of the ice ages of about 10 000 years ago, they are by no means unprecedented in the longer geological history. Geologists have long recognised that their record of the rocks points not to steady deposition of sediments in generally constant or slowly evolving conditions but to the separation of a series of relatively stable epochs by horizons of very rapid and sometimes cataclysmic change. These may result from a number of external causes, including volcanic activity, meteor impacts, changes in the Earth's axis and orbit and solar activity (Gould, 1988). Gould speculates that this 'punctuated equilibrium' may also explain the successive epochs of human history better than the prevalent assumption of steady evolution to increased knowledge, wisdom and power, which still retains a strong hold as the conventional wisdom of contemporary intellectual life. Such an interpretation invites the speculation that human society may have passed through a number of similar transformations. These may have been triggered by external events, such as the ice ages (which may have stimulated the growth of agriculture by concentrating population in the relatively limited areas of well-watered valleys). Alternatively, they may have resulted from social and technological revolutions such as the positive inventions of writing and the wheel, or the negative ones of organised warfare and slavery.
iii Karl Popper in a memorable phrase (1974) described life itself as 'negative entropy' – keeping things together by the progressive problem-solving which he believes underlies all life.

iv The World Trade Organization produced in the early years of this century proposals for a Multilateral Agreement on Investment (MAI) which would have made legislation by national governments to protect local land ownership illegal (Monbiot, 2003). This proposal, which would have opened the way to dispossession of the only economic resource of billions of rural dwellers in economically disadvantaged nations, had to be abandoned owing to the campaigning and lobbying of coalitions making use of global information networks.

v The enquiring spirit of the Renaissance, for instance, was both influenced by such inventions of the age as printing, compasses, horse stirrups and gunpowder, and also became a stimulus to their further use and development in the improved education, great city building and colonial enterprises of their own times. In a similar way, the current rapid change and contending welter of philosophical thought has diverted previously well-defined streams of ideas into fast-flowing and often conflicting eddies, reflecting the growing mix of interests in a turbulent and unstable world.

vi This spirit was prophetically caught by the Irish poet W. B. Yeats at its outset of the twentieth century, when he wrote:

> Things fall apart, the centre cannot hold…
> The falcon cannot hear the falconer
> The best lack all conviction and the worst
> Are full of a passionate intensity.

vii The novel *Babel Tower* (1996) by A. S. Byatt explores this theme brilliantly, relating it to the difficulty of establishing ideal communities among groups who have not had the opportunity to understand each others' ideas and values.

viii Now Homes and Communities Agency.

ix In his *On the Origin of Species* (1859) and *Descent of Man* (1871), Darwin never precisely defined the mechanisms of natural selection, though the full title of the first edition of the former is instructive: *On the Origin of Species by Natural Selection or the Preservation of Favoured Races in the Struggle for Life*. His colleague and disciple, Thomas Huxley, equated this struggle as being like 'nothing as much as a giant gladiatorial contest' and spoke of 'Nature red in tooth and claw' (Kropotkin, 1939). A parallel powerful school of 'Social Darwinists' including theorists like Darwin's friend Thomas Carlyle, and satirised by Charles Dickens in the character of 'Gradgrind' in *Hard Times* (1861) developed these views to depict human communities as depending on dominant leaders such as Julius Caesar, Genghis Khan and the new Captains of Industry. This interpretation has them emerging by force of character and determination and creating, out of spasms of conflict, the stable conditions in which great civilisations could flourish, and local communities could shelter under their paternal mantles.

x Exploring the same theme, David Williamson's play *Sanctuary* traces a two-and-a-half-hour dialogue between a wealthy playwright resident in one such walled sanctuary and the angry young political activist who has come intending to kill the older man (Williamson, 2000). The play explores the self-defeating nature of the dialectic of dominance and conflict which is driving the young man's deadly idealism.

xi Mill (1983) was advocating as early as 1861 that democratically elected governments maintain standards in such other-affecting activities as public health, environmental quality and educational provisions which were so badly needed in the rapidly densifying new settlements. Despite Mill's recognition of the crucial roles of governments in creating healthy and accountable communities, others who subsequently developed the liberal tradition chose to emphasise more individual rights than social responsibilities. By the mid-twentieth century, Friedrich Hayek (1944) was railing against the 'The Road to Serfdom', resulting from government intervention in community life.

xii The American behavioural psychologist B. F. Skinner accurately conveys the intentions of behaviourism in the title of his book *Beyond Freedom and Dignity* (1974), in which he advocates a totally conditioned community life, rather like that uneasily anticipated by Aldous Huxley in *Brave New World* (1955).

xiii Forty years earlier, Karl Popper had vigorously demonstrated how these absolutist theories were directly linked to the terrible results of intergroup conflict and extermination of the mid-twentieth century in Nazi Germany and Soviet Russia. In his *Open Society and its Enemies* (1998), he laid the basis for the pluralism which justified the community activism of Paul and Linda Davidoff, who argued that every interest should have its own watchdog (Davidoff, 1965). This gave a community application to the upward spiral of social problem-solving that Popper (1972) termed 'social engineering' and saw as a more continuous, connected and less destructive path to social evolution than either the dialectical materialism of Marx and the Neo-Marxists or the rigid social order of Plato's *Republic* (1980) or Machiavelli's princely dictatorship (1961).

xiv As in Shakespeare's *Romeo and Juliet* where the Montagus and the Capulets license their mutually murderous behaviour by pointing to each other's sins.

xv This long period of latency reflects the age old dialectic between rationalists like Buddha, Descartes, Spinoza, Kant and Popper, developing and testing new ideas against principles of consistency, utility and logic; and more practical activists such as Moses, Ignatius Loyola, Voltaire, Mill and Habermas seeking to involve whole communities in their social prescriptions.

xvi Critical Rationalists like Karl Popper (1972) might respond that without the critical thinking and idea-forming of reflective individuals there would be no contributions to exchange. The two positions are more compatible, and even mutually supportive than their protagonists sometimes imply.

xvii However, McLuhan's argument veers dangerously close to technological determinism (Heywood, 1970). The medium is not always the message. Values also drive outcomes. The Lindisfarne Gospels, for instance, were produced at a time when England lived under the constant threat of Viking invasion, only for their Christian message of stable community life to later reassert itself (Brown, 2008). Contemporaries of McLuhan, like Melvin Webber (1964, 1969), thought that modern communications technology spelt the end of local community life, which would be absorbed into a 'non-place urban realm' ignoring the fact that, however globally linked elites may be by Skype, eBay, Amazon and international blogs, they still depend for their daily satisfactions on family life and community contact (Heywood, 1970).

xviii These have lent the regional economy a life-saving resilience throughout the remarkable political vicissitudes of the twentieth century, including the fiercely imposed order of Mussolini's fascism, the corrupt and unstable disorder of the mid-century Christian Democrat regimes and the more recent media-sponsored politicking of Berlusconi's Forza Italia.

xix The successful intellectual, scientific, social and economic history of Tuscany, Emilia Romagna and Umbria has been shaped to a quite remarkable extent over the past eight centuries by the accumulated social capital of these city communities. Since the late twelfth century, when St Francis first sent his messages of universal cooperation throughout Western Europe from the small Umbrian hilltop town of Assisi, this spirit of mutual aid has contrasted with and overcome the bleak warring political and military history of those city regions (Heywood, 1904).

xx The fourteenth- and fifteenth-century British Lollards and Bohemian Hussites, for instance, advocated replacing lordly and priestly control by independent and self-regulating congregations (Cole & Postgate, 1976). Later, Thomas Paine and William Godwin advocated a society built on this cooperative basis, as did Fourier with his proposals for phalansteries, or cooperative workshops, in nineteenth-century France. Robert Owen, though ambiguous about adopting cooperative principles in his own New Lanark model industrial settlement (1800–1821), did provide a clear and effective explanation of them in his 'Report to the County of Lanark' of 1817 (Hamilton, 1946; Mumford, 1961).

xxi This was the pattern which still applied in Igbo land in Nigeria in the early 1960s, and was still recalled by old-timers in the Forest of Dean in 1980, when I conducted a community preference survey there with students of the Gloucestershire College of Art and Design.

References

1000 Friends of Oregon (2009) *Transportation for Oregon's Future*, http://www.friends.org/issues/transportation, accessed 2 June 2009.

Ambrose, P., Colenutt, J. (1975) *The Property Machine*. Harmondsworth, Penguin.

Anderson, M. (1964) *The Federal Bulldozer: A critical review of urban renewal 1949–1963*. Cambridge, MA, MIT Press.

Anenkhonov, O., Pronin, N. (2010) *Lake Baikal's Selenga River Delta: Biodiversity, conservation and sustainable development*. Institute of General and Experimental Biology, Siberian Branch, Russian Academy of Sciences, http://deltas.usgs.gov/presentations/Anenkhonov_Pronin.pdf, accessed 20 March 2010.

Ascherson, N. (1996) *Black Sea*. London, Vintage.

Balchin, P., Sykora, L., Bull, G. (1999) *Regional Policy and Planning in Europe*. London, Routledge.

Bater, J. (1984) *The Soviet City: Ideal and reality*. London, Arnold.

Benjamin, A. (2009) 'The new revolution starts here', *Guardian Weekly*, 16 January 2009.

Bentley, I., Alcock, A., Murrain, P. *et al.* (1985) *Responsive Environments: A manual for designers*. London, The Architectural Press.

Booker, C. (1980) *The Seventies: Portrait of a decade*. Harmondsworth, Penguin.

Bornstein, D. (1996) *The Price of a Dream: The story of the Grameen Bank*. Dhaka, Bangladesh, Grameen Press.

Brown, M. (2008) *The Lindisfarne Gospels: Society, spirituality and the scribe*. Toronto, University of Toronto Press.

Calthorpe, P. (1993) *The Next American Metropolis: Ecology, community, and the American dream*. New York, Princeton Architectural Press.

Calthorpe, P., Fulton. W. (2001) *The Regional City: Planning for the end of sprawl*. Washington, Island Press.

Campbell, G. (1993) *Chairman's Keynote Address to Council of Councils*. Greater Vancouver Regional District, Vancouver.

Castells, M. (1977) *The Urban Question*. London, Edward Arnold.

Castells, M. (1983) *The City and the Grassroots*. London, Edward Arnold.

Castells, M. (1989) *The Informational City: Information technology, economic restructuring, and the urban-regional process*. Oxford, Blackwell Publishing Ltd.

Cervero, R. (1998) *The Transit Metropolis: A global inquiry*. Washington, Island Press.

Cervero, R. (2009) TOD and car sharing: A natural marriage. *Access, Transport Research at the University of California* **35**(Fall).

Chadwick, G. (1969) *A Systems View of Planning*. Oxford, Pergamon.

Chomsky, N. (1972) *Language and Mind*. New York, Harcourt Brace Jovanovich.

Chomsky, N. (1992) *Deterring Democracy*. London, Vintage.

Cole, G., Postgate, R. (1976) *The Common People 1746–1946*. London, Methuen.

Cooke P., Morgan, K. (1998) *The Associational Economy: Firms, regions and innovation*. Oxford, Oxford University Press.

Cullingworth, J. (1976) *Town and Country Planning in Britain*, revised 6th edn. London, Allen & Unwin.

Darwin, C. (2008) *On the Origin of Species*. Oxford, Oxford University Press.

Davidoff, D. (1965) Advocacy and pluralism in planning. *Journal of American Institute of Planners* **31**(November).

Davidoff, P. L., Davidoff, D., Gold, N. (1970) Suburban action: Advocate planning for an open society. *Journal of American Institute of Planners* **36**(1).

Dawkins, R. (1976) *The Selfish Gene*. Oxford, Oxford University Press.

Dawkins, R. (1998) *The Blind Watchmaker*. London, Penguin.

Dawkins, R. (2009) *The Greatest Show on Earth: The evidence for evolution*. London, Bantam.

Department of Communities and Local Government (2007) *Third Sector Strategy for Communities & Local Government*, http://www.communities.gov.uk/publications/communities/thirdsectorstrategy, accessed 12 October 2010.

Department of Communities and Local Government (2008) *Communities in Control: Real People, Real Power*, http://www.communities.gov.uk/publications/communities/communitiesincontrol, accessed 12 October 2010.

Derrida, J. (1976) *Of Grammatolgy*, (trans. G. Spivak). Baltimore, Johns Hopkins University Press.

Derrida, J. (1993) *Circumfession*. Chicago, University of Chicago Press, (published jointly with Geoffrey Bennington's *Derridabase* as *Jacques Derrida*).

Derrida, J. (1995) *On the Name*. Stanford, CA, Stanford University Press.

Desmond, A., Moore, J. (1991) *Darwin*. London, Penguin.

Desroches-Noblecourt, C. (1976) *Tutankhamen*. Boston, New York Graphic Society.

Diamond, J. (2005) *Collapse: How societies choose to fail or succeed*. New York, Viking Adult.

Environmental Change Institute (2009) *New strategies to cope with global environmental change on food systems and security and advancing networked science in Amazonia*, http://www.eci.ox.ac.uk/, accessed 31 May 2009.

Federation of City Farms and Community Gardens (2010) *Places to visit*, http://www.farmgarden.org.uk/component/places/?task=list, accessed 17 October 2010.

Florida, R. (2005) *Cities and the Creative Class*. New York, Routledge.

Foucault, M. (1963) *The Birth of the Clinic*. New York, Vintage, (first published in English in 1975).

Foucault, M. (1980) *Power/Knowledge*. New York, Pantheon.

Foucault, M. (1981) *Discipline and Punish*. Harmondsworth, Penguin.

Friedmann, J., Weaver, C. (1979) *Territory and Function*. London, Arnold.

Galbraith, J. (1972) *The New Industrial State*. Harmondsworth, Penguin.

Garrett-Holden, C. (1970) Building society. In: *Chambers Encyclopaedia*. London, International Learning Systems.

Ghosh, A. (2004) *The Hungry Tide*. London, HarperCollins.

Gould, S. (1988) *Time's Cycle, Time's Arrow: Myth and metaphor in the discovery of geological time*. London, Penguin.

Grameen Bank (2009a) *Historical Data*, http://www.grameen-info.org/index.php?option=com_content&task=view&id=177&Itemid=144, accessed 15 January 2009.

Grameen Bank (2009b) *Monthly Update: December 2008*, http://www.grameen-info.org/index.php?option=com_content&task=view&id=453&Itemid=527, accessed 15 January 2009.

Grameen Trust (2000) *Grameen Dialogue 39*. Chittagong, Bangladesh, Grameen Trust.

Guralnik, D. (ed.) (1974) *Webster's New World Dictionary: Concise edition*. Nashville, TN, The Southwestern Company.

Gutstein, D. (1983) Vancouver. In: W. Magnusson, A. Sancton (eds), *City Politics in Canada*. Toronto, University of Toronto Press.

Habermas, J. (1972) *Knowledge and Human Interests*, (trans. J. Shapiro). London, Heinemann.

Habermas, J. (1987) *The Theory of Communicative Action*. Cambridge, Polity Press.

Habermas, J. (1990) *Moral Consciousness and Communicative Action*. London, Heinemann.

Hall, P. (2002) *Cities of Tomorrow*, 3rd edn. Oxford, Blackwell Publishing Ltd.

Hamdi, N., Goethert, R. (1997) *Action Planning for Cities: A guide for community practice*. New York, John Wiley & Sons.

Hamilton, H. (1946) *History of the Homeland*. London, Allen & Unwin.

Hammond, J., Hammond, B. (1978) *The Town Labourer*. London, Longman.

Hammond, S., Royal, C. (1998) *Lessons from the Field: Applying appreciative inquiry*. Plano, TX, Thin Book Publishing Co.

Harris, S. (1986) Economic, social and heritage goals in metropolitan planning: Achievement in three inner Sydney suburbs. *Queensland Planner* **38**(3–4).

Harvey, D. (1996) On planning the ideology of planning. In: S. Campbell, S. Fainstein (eds), *The Urbanization of Capital*. Baltimore, Johns Hopkins University Press.

Hayek, F. von (1944) *The Road to Serfdom*. London, Routledge & Kegan Paul.

Healey, P. (1996) Planning through debate: The communicative turn in planning theory. In S. Campbell, S. Fainstein (eds), *Readings in Planning Theory*. Maldon, MA, Blackwell Publishing Ltd.

Healey, P. (2006) *Collaborative Planning: Shaping places in fragmented societies*, 2nd edn. Basingstoke, Palgrave.

Healey, P. (2007) *Urban Complexity and Spatial Strategies*. London, Routledge.

Hester, R. (2002) Community design. In: S. Swaffield (ed.), *Theory in Landscape Architecture: A reader*. Philadelphia, University of Philadelphia Press.

Heywood, P. (1970) Plangloss: A critique of permissive planning. *Town Planning Review* **43**(3).

Heywood, P. (1974) *Planning and Human Need*. Newton Abbott, David & Charles.

Heywood, P. (1997) The emerging social metropolis. In: *Progress in Planning*. Oxford, Pergamon/Elsevier.

Heywood, W. (1904) *Palio and Ponte: An account of the sports of central Italy from the age of Dante to the XXth century*. London, Methuen.

Hibbert, C. (1979) *The Rise and Fall of the House of Medici*. Harmondsworth, Penguin.

Homes and Communities Agency (2009) *The National Housing and Regeneration Agency*, http://www.homesandcommunities.co.uk/, accessed 1 June 2009.

Homes and Communities Agency Academy (2009a) *Transformation of Northmoor, Manchester*, http://showcase.hcaacademy.co.uk/case-study/transformation-of-northmoor-manchester.html, accessed 1 June 2009.

Homes and Communities Agency Academy (2009b) *Sustainable Communities*, http://www.hcaacademy.co.uk/sustainable-communities, accessed 2 June 2009.

Howard, E. (1898) *Tomorrow: A peaceful path to real reform.* London, Swann Sonnershein.

Howard, E. (1965) *Garden Cities of Tomorrow.* London, Faber & Faber.

Huntington, S. (1996) *The Clash of Civilizations and the Remaking of World Order.* New York, Simon & Schuster.

Huxley, A. (1955) *Brave New World: A novel.* Harmondsworth, Penguin/Chatto & Windus.

Intergovernmental Panel on Climate Change (IPCC) (2007) Summary for policymakers. In: M. L. Parry, O. F. Canziani, J. P. Palutikof *et al.* (eds), *Climate Change 2007: Impacts, adaptation and vulnerability: Contribution of Working Group II to the Fourth Assessment Report of the Intergovernmental Panel on Climate Change*, http://www.ipcc.ch/ipccreports/assessments-reports.htm, accessed 31 May 2009.

Jacobs, J. (1961) *The Death and Life of Great American Cities.* Harmondsworth, Penguin.

Jacobs, J. (1969) *The Economy of Cities.* Harmondsworth, Penguin.

Jacobs, J. (1992) *Systems of Survival.* London, Hodder & Stoughton.

Jephcott, P. (1971) *Homes in High Flats.* Edinburgh, Oliver & Boyd.

Kasarda, J. (2009) *Aerotropolis*, http://www.aerotropolis.com/aerotropolis.html, accessed 30 May 2009.

Kropotkin, P. (1939) *Mutual Aid.* London, Penguin.

Kropotkin, P. (1974) *Fields, Farms and Workshops of Tomorrow.* London, Allen & Unwin, (first published 1899).

Landry, C. (2000) *The Creative City: A toolkit for urban innovators.* London, Earthscan.

Leakey, R. (1981) *The Making of Mankind.* London, Abacus.

Lemon, J. (1985) *Toronto since 1918.* Toronto, Lorimer.

Logan, J., Molotch, H. (1987) *Urban Fortunes: The political economy of place.* Berkeley, CA, University of California Press.

London Dockland Redevelopment Agency (2008) *Vision for London Riverside and Prospects for Prosperity.* London, Author.

London Summit (2009) *Global plan for recovery and reform*, http://www.londonsummit.gov.uk/resources/en/news/15766232/communique-020409, accessed 31 May 2009.

Lowe, S. (1986) *Urban Social Movements: The city after Castells.* Basingstoke, Macmillan.

Lynch, K. (1984) *Good City Form.* Cambridge, MA. MIT Press.

Lyons, J. (ed.) (1970) *New Horizons in Linguistics.* Harmondsworth, Penguin.

Lyons, J. (1991) *Chomsky.* London, Fontana.

Machiavelli, N. (1961) *The Prince*, (trans. G. Bull). Harmondsworth, Penguin.

McLoughlin, J. (1971) *Urban and Regional Planning: A system's approach.* London, Faber & Faber.

McLuhan, M. (1964) *Understanding Media: The extensions of man.* New York, McGraw-Hill.

Magee, B. (1973) *Popper.* Glasgow, Fontana.

Margerum, R. (1999) Getting past yes: From capital creation to action. *Journal of the American Planning Association* **65**(2): 181–92.

Margerum, R. (2002) Evaluating collaborative planning. *Journal of the American Planning Association* **68**(2): 171–92.

Marx, K., Engels, F. (1998) *The Communist Manifesto.* New York, Signet Classics.

Mill, J. S. (1983) *Utilitarianism: On liberty and considerations on representative government.* London, Dent, (first published 1861).

Miller, G. (1981) *Cities by Contract.* Cambridge, MA, MIT Press.

Monbiot, G. (2003) *The Age of Consent*, http://www.monbiot.com/archives/2003/10/13/the-age-of-consent-a-manifesto-for-a-new-world-order/, accessed 13 October 2010.

Mondragon, Corporation Cooperative (2008) *Mondragon Corporacion Cooperativa, Spain*, http://www.iisd.org/50comm/commdb/desc/d13.htm, accessed 15 January 2008.

More, T. (1965) *Utopia.* Harmondsworth, Penguin, (first published 1516).

Moss Eckhardt, J. (1973) *Ebenezer Howard 1850–1928.* Aylesbury, Shire Publications.

Mumford, L. (1938) *The Culture of Cities.* London, Secker and Warburg.

Mumford, L. (1961) *The City in History.* New York, Harcourt Brace and World.

Naipaul, V. (1979) *India: A wounded civilization.* Harmondsworth, Penguin.

Obama, B. (2004) (2nd edition) *Dreams From My Father.* Melbourne, Text Publishing.

Osborne, D., Gaebler, T. (1992) *Reinventing Government.* New York, Penguin.

Oxfam Australia (2006) Oxfam *Horizons* and Oxfam *News* Quarterlies containing accounts of community action in Africa and Asia.

Oxfordshire Climate Exchange (2010) *Wolvercote: A low carbon village*, http://climatex.org/articles/news/climatex_update_57/, accessed 19 March 2010; http://climatex.org.articles/lo-carb-communities/wolvervcote-low-carbon-village/, accessed 30 July 2008.

Passmore, J. (1980) *A Hundred Years of Philosophy.* Harmondsworth, Penguin.

Peters, H. (2009) *Surrey Docks Farm: Agri-culture in the city*, http://www.sovereignty.org.uk/features/footnmouth/cfarm.html, accessed 1 June 2009.

Pilger, J. (1992) *Distant Voices.* London, Vintage.

Plato (1980) *The Republic*, (trans. H. Lee). Harmondsworth, Penguin.

Popper, K. (1972) *Conjectures and Refutations*. Oxford, Oxford University Press.

Popper, K. (1989) *Objective Knowledge*: *An evolutionary approach*. Oxford, Clarendon.

Popper, K. (1998) *The Open Society and Its Enemies: Vol. 2: Marx and Hegel*, 2nd edn. London, Routledge & Kegan Paul, (first published 1945).

Putnam, R. (1993) *Making Democracy Work: Civic traditions in modern Italy*. Princeton, Princeton University Press, (with Leonardi, R., Nanetti, R.).

Ridley, M. (1996) *The Origins of Virtue*. London, Penguin.

Robertson, G. (1999) *Crimes against Humanity*. London, Penguin.

Rorty, R. (1996) The challenge of relativism. In: J. Niznik, J. T. Sanders (eds), *Debating the State of Philosophy*: *Habermas, Rorty and Kolakowski*. Westport, CT, Praeger.

Sandars, N. (2006) *The Epic of Gilgamesh*, (trans. N. K. Sandars). London, Penguin.

Skinner, B. (1974) *Beyond Freedom and Dignity*. London, Penguin.

Solzhenitsyn, A. (1968) *Cancer Ward*, (trans. N. Bethell, D. Burg). London, Bodley Head.

Solzhenitsyn, A. (1974) *The Gulag Archipelago 1918–1956: An experiment in literary investigation: I–II*, (trans. T. P. Whitney). New York, Harper & Row.

Stern, N. (2007) *The Economics of Climate Change*. London, HMSO.

Stretton, H. (1989) *Ideas for Australian Cities*. Melbourne, Transit.

Suarja, I., Thyssen, R. (2003) Traditional water management in Bali. *Liesa Magazine* **September**, http://www.fao.org/prods/gap/database/gap/files/597_WATER_MGMT_BALI.PDF, accessed 17 October 2010.

Suzuki, D., McConnell, A. (2008) *The Sacred Balance: Rediscovering our place in nature*, 2nd edn. St Leonards, Australia, Allen & Unwin.

Taylor, A. (1989) *Vision of Harmony*. Oxford, Oxford University Press.

Thompson, E. (1980) *The Making of the English Working Class*. Harmondsworth, Penguin.

Topping, P., Smith, G. (1977) *Government against Poverty?* Liverpool Community Development Project 1970–1975. Oxford, Social Evaluation Unit, Oxford University.

Transition Towns (2010) *Transition Towns Network/ Transition Communities*, http://transitiontowns.org/TransitionNetwork/TransitionCommunities, accessed 2 March 2010.

United Nations (2009) *World Urbanization Prospects: The 2009 Revision*, http://esa.un.org/unpd/wup/index.htm, accessed 10 October 2010.

University Sains Malaysia (2010) *Regional Centers of Excellence: Penang*, http://www.ias.unu.edu/resource_centre/RCE%20Penang.pdf, accessed 20 March 2010.

Ward, C. (1973), *Anarchy in Action*, London, Freedom Press.

Webber M. (1964) The urban place and the non-place urban realm. In M. Webber (ed.), *Explorations into Urban Structure*. Philadelphia, Pennsylvania University Press.

Webber, M. (1969) Planning in an environment of change: Part 11: Permissive planning. *Town Planning Review* **39**(4).

Wheeler, S. (2002) The New Regionalism. *Journal of the American Planning Association* **68**(3): 267–78.

Whyte, W., Whyte K. (1989) *Making Mondragon: The growth and dynamics of a workers co-operative complex*. Ithaca, NY, ILR Press.

Williams, R. (1973) *The Country and the City*. London, Chatto & Windus.

Williamson, D. (2000) *The Great Man/Sanctuary: Two plays*. Strawberry Hills, Australia, Currency Press.

Wilson, E. O. (1992) *The Diversity of Life* Cambridge Mass., Belknap Press of Harvard University Press, 1992.

Yunus, M. (1998) *Socially Conscious Capitalism towards a Poverty Free World*. Public Lecture Transcript. Brisbane, Queensland University of Technology.

2 The Spirit and Characteristics of Community Planning

Chapter 1 showed how active community life can help societies adjust to the rapid pace of current social and environmental change. Part One of this chapter examines the following four major ways in which planning can both shape and respond to these changes:

- communication;
- consultation;
- participation;
- negotiation.

The second part provides specific examples showing how these capacities can best be applied in effective community planning. The chapter concludes with an examination of the relations among community planning, action, development and organisation, and the contributions which they can together make to a fulfilling and successful community life.

Creative and sustainable community planning requires a combination of all four factors of communication, consultation, participation and negotiation. Good communication is needed to both shape and implement plans. Consultation is necessary to achieve relevance and engagement. Without willing and widespread participation, plans will remain paper or electronic inventions, less influential than journalism and more imaginary than fiction. Negotiation will be needed to achieve support, traction and the stimulus to solve emerging problems.

Part One: Themes

Communication

The 'communicative turn' in contemporary thought of the last third of the twentieth century, drawing on developments in science, technology and philosophy, also provided a powerful stimulus to improved planning methods (McLuhan, 1964; Habermas, 1987;

Healey, 1995; Heywood, 1997). More respect started to be paid to the speech acts which form the basic building blocks of communication and less to trend projections of statistics. Innovations such as focus and search groups, community visioning, 'enquiry by design', 'charettes' and collaborative planning within policy communities enriched the previously rather brittle reliance on the quantitative techniques of statistical analysis, opinion polling and market research.

Parallel trends in economics and information and communication technology have provided powerful support for this communicative shift. Global markets, driven by instant and universal transmissions of data on demand and consumption, pulse hourly indicators and trends around the world to audiences in every nation and city. Wiki groups transcend the constraints of time and space to build new knowledge out of the views and experiences of people who might otherwise never meet, and chat rooms dissolve the boundaries between audiences and actors in exchanges which span local and global spaces. The growth and character of many different kinds and scales of communities are influenced by the various forms of communication on which they are based: local meetings, regional associations, national cultural debates and global cyber exchanges. Communication has become a value in itself, but one strongly influenced by the nature and reach of its media, the ideas and experiences of its

Community Planning, First Edition. Phil Heywood.
© 2011 Phil Heywood.
Published 2011 by Blackwell Publishing Ltd.

participants and people's capacities for communicative action, each of which are briefly discussed in the following sections.

THE RANGE AND REACH OF MEDIA

Improvements in communications have created communities of interest at much wider scales than ever before.[i] For some time now, the extraordinary capacities of electronic and satellite communications have made possible a 'non-place urban realm' (Webber, 1964), consisting of communities of cultural and financial interests, scholars, activists and enthusiasts for such causes as environmental conservation and social justice. Within these global and national realms, regional communities have developed in response to the growing scale and impact of modern settlements. This has not, however, diminished the importance to individuals and families of local community life. Shared daily experiences of local spaces and the opportunities and threats posed by the wider environment have resulted in local community life gaining rather than losing personal significance. As people respond to daily streams of information about comparative global conditions, they turn their attention back towards local action or improvement (Oxfordshire Climate Exchange, 2008). Ease of communication is enriching community life at all scales. In the course of one day, a typical urban resident may experience the reassurance of neighbourly contact and care; the stimulus to regional awareness and participation of traffic and environmental pollution; involvement in a national community, through drawing benefits, paying tax or membership of a trade union or political party; and participation in global life, through belonging to an international organisation such as Oxfam, World Vision or Green Peace or through work in an office or processing industry deeply embedded in the global economy.[ii] Because communities span scales from the neighbourhood to the global, they require at each level some means of accountability to the people whose future is being planned. The communications revolution which has created this need also offers techniques of involvement like e-mail and Wiki networks, and capacities for universal education and electronic transmission of information about facts and values to support inclusive planning at each scale.

EXPERIENCE

People's own experiences and priorities also provide powerful direction for community planning. The directly felt truth of experience within the 'lifeworld'

shapes the 'subconscious landscapes of the heart' (in the memorable words of Randy Hester), which can in turn provide the energy to prompt action (Hester, 1985; Habermas, 1987; Lefebvre, 1991). The smell of newly cut grass in a suburban park, of charcoal and bitter leaf soup in an African neighbourhood, the sight of a throng of children playing in a clean urban waterfront, or pollution gathering around the high-rise buildings of a great metropolitan centre, may each send a powerful message, which can help build consensus over community policies and planning. A sensational film like Danny Boyle's 2009 *Slumdog Millionaire* may do more to build experiential empathy and motivation to action than a more cerebral and intellectual one, such as Richard Attenborough's *Ghandi* of 1982. Poetry, fiction and drama as well as cinema often capture the immediacy and impact of these common human experiences. They have the capacity to reach across differences of class, ethnicity, age and gender to make the links essential to thriving community life and planning.

IDEAS AND IDEALS

Though communication is often triggered by something we have seen or sensed, such experiences are reflected onto our deep-seated ideas and beliefs to create meanings. The observation that people who would not argue over the price of a meal will die for an idea is reinforced in Bertrand Russell's (1971) celebrated aphorism that 'the world is divided into hard headed idealists and crackpot realists'. In the world of community planning, ideals such as community focus, social justice and environmental conservation are demonstrably very important and have proved more durable than the destructive but short-lived trends triggered by such technological changes as high-rise public housing and massive urban motorway construction of the mid-twentieth century. Shared commitment to ideas such as garden cities and new towns, greenbelts and greenheart metropolises (Hall, 2002) make possible the celebrated Dutch 'polder model' of community consensus and the conflict resolution and problem-solving processes of the 'policy communities' which shape outcomes and inform collaborative planning (Faludi & Valk, 1996; Faludi, 2005; Healey, 2007).

COMMUNICATIVE ACTION

Since the 1980s, theories of communicative action developed by Jurgen Habermas (1987) have emphasised the importance of the exchange of speech acts to establish truth and build collaboration. Links with community planning have been sketched in the work of planning theorists including Forester (1999, 2009) and Healey (2006, 2007). Out of the galaxy of ideas that Jurgen Habermas (1987) draws together in his *Theory of Communicative Action*, four are particularly important for participatory community planning: intersubjectivity, open dialogue round policy tables, the distinction between the 'lifeworld' and the 'systemworld', and the major role of public open space in providing physical arenas where human contact and communication can occur naturally and continuously.

Intersubjectivity approaches the age-old arguments between idealists and empiricists by accepting that while ideas are mental formulations, based upon interpretation of sensory evidence, they may well be prone to error, which is best identified and eliminated in the free and open exchange of ideas between communicating equals. From this basis, Habermas develops the idea of the 'policy table', where all have a right to a seat and to be heard and a duty to participate. He criticises the tradition of philosophers abstaining from debate about the issues of the day as being both arrogant and servile – 'Do not hover round the table like a flunkey', he seems to command, 'showing each of the participants to their allotted places, but instead take your own seat and have your say!' This balance is also well illuminated by his distinction between the lifeworld, of direct human experience and action, and the systemworld, of statistics, forms, indicators, criteria, performance measures and mass regulation. No argument about participation could be more relevant for the practice of community planning, which has constantly to weigh between the impulses of objective social indicators and those of lived experience. Habermas's arguments do not discount the value of quantitative measures in a world of mass organisation, but they do suggest that the abstract indicators of the systemworld cannot substitute for the genuine and personally validated judgements of people's own lives. Finally, his championing of the rights of communities to accessible, usable and attractive public open space where people can meet and talk about the issues of the day and familiarise themselves with the appearance, style, interests and needs of new and old neighbours is itself an indication of the daily significance and value of the lifeworld.[iii]

COMMUNICATION AS A VALUE AND THE VALUES OF COMMUNICATION

Communication also serves to promote other important values. For more than thirty years now, Habermas has been developing a powerful argument that communication is an innate human skill which has very significant implications for individual and species evolution and survival (Habermas, 1987, 1990). Without the guidance of truth, he argues, individuals and societies will be prone to blunder into life-threatening and socially destructive situations.[iv] Truth, in turn, can only be established by open challenge and criticism because the mix and flux of external conditions demand repeated testing against new observations and other ideas (a view also powerfully argued by Popper, 1972). These open challenges require the guarantee of a free society, because people who fear for their lives or material advancement are unlikely to subject authoritarian orthodoxy to the necessary rigorous scrutiny. Lack of this criticism or 'prudent' self-censorship may have disastrous consequences, such as the collapse of agriculture and science under Soviet Behaviourism during the sway of Pavlov and Lysenko (Koestler, 1971; Ridley, 1997). Truth therefore requires liberty, including the unrestricted expression of personal views and beliefs. Public policy and planning depend upon valid information and interpretation and should be based on open, unconstrained and energetic debate.

The fullest contributions of communication therefore depend on the parallel promotion of other values of personal freedom, free expression, equal participation and social equality. If any of these values are consistently ignored or infringed, communication may be falsified and fail. If they are genuinely sought and achieved, communication should ultimately succeed. Community planning, which depends so much on good communication, must therefore also become a participatory and negotiative activity, not a morally neutral one, merely seeking to adjust groups of people to static or changing circumstances. This logic of the basic and instrumental roles of communication in achieving survival and sustainability has powerful implications for the style and conduct of community planning, which are summarised in Table 2.1.

PRACTICAL COMMUNICATION FOR COMMUNITY PLANNING

These values and activities clearly suggest a number of planning techniques, but the compilation of any list can be at best tentative, because highly fecund communications technology is constantly creating new techniques and approaches. Nevertheless, readers may find the summary of a number of the more prominent, effective and widely used ones, provided in Box 2.1, helpful in prompting their own ideas.

The value of these techniques is neatly summarised in the phrase with which one of the most distinguished

Table 2.1 Roles of basic and instrumental values of communication in community planning

Degree of durability	Value	Activity	Planning implication
Basic values – genetically inscribed	Survival	Recognition of truth (objective or intersubjective)	Exploratory discussion protected by law or custom
Instrumental values – culturally entrenched	Knowledge	Challenge and response; conjecture and refutation in open debate	Critical and tolerant culture
Active values – socially encouraged	Debate public	Free speech and personal equality of rights	Practice, protection and funding of opposition and critiques
Demonstrable outcomes – constitutionally defined	Equality	Equality before the law; constitutional rights and responsibilities	Individual rights constrained only by equal rights of others

---

Box 2.1 Communication-based techniques in community planning

- Qualitative consultation (including focus and mixed-interest groups).
- Sample, snowballing and universal surveys.
- Learning and problem-solving groups (including 'enquiry by design' and charettes).
- Community engagement (including visioning and advisory groups, round tables).
- Community stimulus and leadership (including community recognition, awards and competitions to encourage activism, participation and self-confidence).
- Cultural activities (including festivals and celebrations).
- Community art and cultural mapping (including photography, news and art walls).
- Media methods (including Internet, radio, television and print).
- Liaison with interest and advocacy groups.
- Consultation with schools and other organised youth groups.
- Public place workshops and performances.

---

of twentieth-century English writers prefaced many of his novels: 'Only connect' (Forster, 1941, 1978, 2005). Such communication can provide the crucial missing link between understanding and changing the world, leading individuals from personal understanding to communal action and opening the way for wide and innovative participation and open-minded negotiation.

Consultation

Countless examples of the political and administrative rewards of involvement and the penalties of social exclusion have given rise to flourishing consultation and facilitation activities throughout contemporary mass societies. Where the effects of time and distance inevitably exclude many people from direct involvement in decisions crucially affecting their daily lives, the opportunity to contribute and have publicly recorded information on values, preferences and facts can itself become a useful form of engagement. If the purpose and the use of outcomes are made clear and

incorporated transparently into decision-making processes, consultation can become a useful tool of governance and planning.

ADVANTAGES OF THOROUGH CONSULTATION

There is a strong theoretical case for engaging stakeholders and future users in developing ideas for future conservation and development in line with such contractarian ideas as those of John Rawls (1971), which are discussed in more detail in a later section of this chapter, on participation. It is the ideal of shaping and reshaping society and settlements to meet their citizens' needs, by encouraging public contribution to defining those needs. There are also powerful practical reasons for incorporating thorough consultation in decision-taking: local and outside knowledge can improve the relevance of proposals; the process of public debate should improve ultimate design detail and quality; and open discussion will increase public understanding and support for the ultimate proposals and reduce the dangers of delay and rejection.

The most basic technical role for early and energetic consultation is to improve the quality of outcomes.

Local residents and future users will simply know more about the site and their own needs than experts coming in to the area from elsewhere, particularly if the latter are nationally or internationally based. However, consultation should not be confined to future users. Suppliers and stakeholders, too, will have invaluable knowledge to share; early involvement in discussions and objective setting will lead to better subsequent acceptance of their roles in implementation and monitoring. Next, there is the crucial advantage of debate in improving understanding and testing and adapting proposals. Christopher Alexander (1979) points out the importance of 'eliminating misfit' between innovations and their existing context, and the difficulty of doing this in societies as technologically dynamic as ours, where there is seldom time for testing by experience. In these circumstances, public consultation and debate can be invaluable means of advance testing options and proposals. One example is provided by an ambitious scheme produced in 2007 (at the climax of the 'merchant adventurer' phase of the first decade of the century) by the Queensland State Government in conjunction with a large commercial developer. This scheme would have narrowed the Brisbane River by 70 metres and constructed a number of very high office blocks and tourist features on reclaimed riverfront land on the north bank of the river, linked to the city centre by access routes built over an existing elevated freeway. In response to immediate and very critical reaction from residents, architects, environmentalists and economists, the government commendably instituted an open 'enquiry by design' process, which confirmed the environmental and traffic costs of flooding, construction and traffic impacts and added further doubts about the cost implications and risk-avoidance requirements of building over the freeway (Queensland Government, Department of Infrastructure & Planning, 2008). This resulted in the 2008 abandonment of the entire scheme, just before the Global Financial Crisis plunged the intending developer into a major insolvency crisis. Though late, the open consultation, when it came, was highly effective in highlighting and avoiding potentially disastrous problems of cost, unintended environmental consequences and public rejection.

A final advantage of consultation is that it can build up a constituency for change and forestall the chances of ultimate failure through funding fatigue or simple political apathy. The one-year programme conducted in 1991 and 1992 by the strategic planners of the Greater Vancouver Regional District (now Metro Vancouver) to determine the values and priorities of the metropolitan community for the future develop-ment of their city region produced top rankings for environmental quality and community life, ahead of economic opportunity. Maintaining their community dialogue throughout the decade, the strategic planners succeeded in introducing strong regional planning, restricting the use of the private motor car for the journey to work, increasing densities in central areas and improving environmental quality through quite stringent controls (Greater Vancouver Regional District, 1993; Heywood, 1997; Punter, 2003). Such early and inclusive consultation can avoid unnecessary conflict, delay and rejection.

DISADVANTAGES OF EXCLUSION

There is a realistic case for consulting the future users of planned developments, since insensitive and pre-conceived plans suffer from two major disadvantages. First, they have a greater chance of delay or actual prevention by public opposition. A significant example, also drawn from Brisbane, which has significantly affected the life and appearance of the city centre, was the ultimate rejection in 1990 of the 'River City 2000' proposals, to redevelop the site of the successful 1988 World Expo for high-rise privatised commercial development, despite being originally supported by the state government (Heywood, 1995). Lack of consultation and the 'extreme development' style of the proposals including islands in the Brisbane River, an exclusive city canal housing estate and a quarter of a million square metres of new offices, increasing by a half the total available office space in the central area, resulted in widespread public reaction involving professionals, academics and politicians, including the city's lord mayor. Mass meetings and newspaper polls and campaigns contributed to the proposals being overturned and new tenders were called, resulting in the current Southbank Gardens, which play major and widely celebrated roles in the social, cultural, economic and aesthetic life of the city.

There is also a greater likelihood of subsequent failure if insufficiently examined schemes do go ahead. Well-known examples in the United Kingdom and the United States in the 1960s and 1970s involve residential mega structures which had to be radically redesigned or demolished like Thamesmead in London and Pruitt–Igoe in St Louis (Newman, 1973; Heywood, 1974). One of Australia's most notable planning failures, the aborted Victorian Housing Commission flats programme in Melbourne in the Seventies, also resulted from a determined professional resolve to ignore public opinion (Sandercock, 1975). The tarnished picture of planners and developers as know-alls needs to be remodelled into an image of more enquiring humanism.

DISCUSSION OF OBJECTIONS TO CONSULTATION

Nevertheless, strong and entrenched objections to consultation, often voiced by planners, politicians and developers, need to be acknowledged and resolved before launching into thorough-going public programmes for long-term strategies and plans. The most important of these objections are considered below.

1. Lack of knowledge of complex matters by ordinary people

The question is: 'Do ordinary people know enough about the complexities of modern society and the requirements of planning processes to make valid judgements?' In considering this concern, it is important to identify the kinds of knowledge required to contribute to consultation on desired directions. People remain the greatest experts on their own life situations, problems and objectives, which should be the most important concerns in planning consultation, even though they may know little, for instance, about construction techniques, methods of coordination or social impact analysis. Social and political history indicates that others cannot be relied upon to identify these matters for us. It is also relevant that democracy, which has survived for over two centuries of the modern era, depends upon the idea that individuals are capable of making informed decisions about community interests in the present (Arrow, 1973). When we come to planning for a common future, there are no less cogent reasons to maintain democratic principles.

2. Consultation may result in bad choices

The questions are: 'Will people want what is not good for them? Are they driven by self-destructive and compulsive desires and conditioned by false consciousnesses instilled, for instance, by mass media, controlled by self-serving magnates?'[v] If people sometimes want what is not good for them (such as another drink or another packet of cigarettes, or the power to punish cruelly those they do not like) it is often for one of two reasons. First, they may have been conditioned by cynical advertising or sensationalist journalism. While it is true that many of these attitudes are reinforced by money-driven mass media, the better answer is to create alternative information sources, like council, community and planning newsletters and open-access websites, rather than to compound commercial brainwashing by further excluding the public from information, influence and the experience of choice. Another aspect which deserves respect is the distinction between compulsive behaviour, which we all exhibit at some stage, and the capacity for clear thought in conditions of reflective equilibrium. Unwise personal behaviour does not mean that we cannot at other times think straight about social priorities.

3. Lack of experience in making choices and decision-taking

The question needs to be considered whether many people have had sufficient experience in the skills of making choices from their childhood up to be able to practise them with confidence as adults. Daily survival does demand the exercise of this sort of judgement. Asking people what they think is right for their neighbourhood or city will get them thinking about wider issues and improve their capacity for exercising their judgement, while excluding them will further stunt their decision-making, self-esteem and sense of social responsibility. The choice is between optimistic realism and pessimistic repression.

4. Different people may want different things

The question is whether the many objectives of thousands of people will conflict so hopelessly that it becomes unwise to raise public expectations of overall solutions. It is true that objectives will conflict (not just between households, but also within them, and even within the psyches of individual people). Any relevant strategy will have to resolve these conflicts through creative problem-solving and a thorough understanding of group preferences. As Alexander (1979) shows, the more information that planners, policymakers and community members have on conflicting objectives, the better able they will be to identify and resolve conflicts to produce effective and coherent plans, whereas ignoring conflicts will prevent their being recognised, let alone resolved. Multiple criteria decision making is a well understood process, discussed in more detail in Chapter 6.

5. Raising unrealistic expectations

The question whether it is unwise to raise expectations that cannot be fulfilled was well posed by a very honest and distinguished English city planning officer when he asked, 'Why ask people what they want, when they are going to have to like what they get?' This question is, nevertheless, based on the assumption of the 'niggardliness of nature', which is not altogether true: capacities for the creation of wealth are powered by human ingenuity for the compatible transformation of matter. Our weakness is in the distribution, management and recycling of resources, all of which are amenable to good planning. Without the search for better satisfaction of people's wants and needs, there would be no challenge to achieve social progress. Lacking incentives, society would tend to be forced back on naked coercion, instead of being drawn forward by hope. Far from stirring up unnecessary trouble, social enquiry is an indispensable path towards social progress.

Participation and exclusion

Participation and exclusion are the opposite sides of the common coin of citizen rights, itself one of the most contested currencies of contemporary life. This is an age of both dissent and consent. It is an age of dissent in that individuals, groups and whole societies are refusing to accept the policies that others are attempting to impose on them on the basis of economic power, trading imperatives or rights of investors. The so-called clash of civilisations between a prosperous and activist Christian West and a resurgent and sometimes theocratic Islamic East is one example of the resulting conflicts (Huntington, 1996). There are others: the urbanisation of rural areas, for example, which brings local residents face to face with investors, government planning departments and an influx of new people from neighbouring towns and cities, with all of their urban expectations and experiences.

However, this is also an age of consent where national and local regimes have to justify policies to critical electorates, by some form of validation (Habermas, 1976). These conflicts and conciliations arise when the expanding reach of communications technology, promoting ever-larger organisations, collides with the increased personal power and independence of individuals. Organisations in countries as far apart as North America, eastern, southern and western Asia and Europe, whose prosperity depends upon the participation of consumers spread throughout the world, are constantly striving to draw decisions to their centres in the interests of their top executives and investors, while local communities and individuals may be struggling to regain control of decisions, drawing them closer to the action points where their environments and daily lives are most affected. In such situations, there is a tendency for

action and reaction to be equal and opposite. In one sense, the argument is not about participation, but the extent to which it is willing or enforced.[vi]

Where this balance entirely breaks down and there is mutual rejection, as in such troubled states as Somalia or in forest clearance disputes in Amazonia, acrid conflict occurs and provides such vivid images of contemporary market failures as swarming Somali pirates boarding Western oil tankers and local Amerindian protesters being shot by Brazilian farm settlers and police. Other even more dramatic examples are provided by the daily bombings and killings in Iraq and Afghanistan. By contrast, multilateral intervention by a United Nations peacekeeping force to create local participation in the organisation and government of the tiny island state of Timor-Leste in 2001 has, though far from perfect, established democracy, the rule of law, reconciliation between old enemies, and the ability to retain a major proportion of its own oil revenues.[vii]

Similar issues affect rural regions throughout the developed and developing worlds. Nobel Prize winner Arundhati Roy (1999) describes movingly the struggle of the tribal people of the Narmada Valley to maintain their land and livelihoods against the construction of a huge dam to feed Mumbai's thirst for water and electric power. Similar issues affect the several hundred thousand villagers displaced to make way for China's Three Gorges dam. Even in the politically activist democracy of the Australian state of Queensland, the rural community of Traveston Crossing has been faced with construction of a dam to supply water for metropolitan Brisbane that would have obliterated the community with no prior consultation. Subsequent protests and Commonwealth Government environmental impact assessment has caused the whole proposal to be shelved (Meredith, 2008; Lacey & Heywood, 2009). Exclusion can create its own costs.

Urban localities experience no less frequent crises of consent and participation, which feature in the daily output of the news media. The mass clearance of African housing in the old Orlando and Sophiatown settlements of Johannesburg and their relocation in the regimented Soweto by the previous regime in the face of fierce local protests and the resulting repression and police killings remain among the most notorious events in the history of South African apartheid.

Less deadly, but scarcely less dramatic, were the clearances of old inner-city areas in Liverpool, London, Glasgow, Leeds, Sheffield and Newcastle to make way for unloved and unlovely marshalled ranks of tower blocks, assembled from mass-produced component panels (Davies, 1972; Heywood, 1974; Booker, 1980). Lack of consultation and participation resulted in designs of unprecedented ugliness and dreadful living conditions (Jephcott & Robinson, 1971). Happier outcomes were achieved where stronger local organisations and more responsive local governments ultimately negotiated in the redevelopment of both Covent Garden in central London and Coin Street on its South Bank; and in inner Sydney's Woolloomooloo, following 'Green Bans' resulting from the alliance between local residents and the Building Labourers Federation (Harris, 1986). The successful outcome of the conservation of the Annex in inner Toronto in the Seventies also involved a coalition of local community groups including Jane Jacobs and Jim Lemon working with a sympathetic city mayor to convince an initially hostile metropolitan government (Lemon, 1985).

The significance of participatory theories

Community planning often involves the contentious reallocation of powers and opportunities from well-established private and public bodies to empower community organisations. Theories of participation become important justifications, and may be hotly contested. Where such rights to profits and opportunities for benefits are involved, recourse is therefore frequently made to ideas of justice and social purpose. These have two main skeins:

1. Concepts of natural justice and a notional social contract between citizens and State.
2. Theories of cooperation and mutual aid.

A most appropriate starting point for social contract theories is presented by Socrates' *Apologia* of 399 BC, explaining his choice of death before retraction and justifying his dissent from the policies of the city government of Athens (Kitto, 1967; Fox, 2005). He argued that it was the duty of the good citizen not only to participate in government but also to question public decisions and prompt others to do likewise, even if that meant being condemned to death for sedition. Similar responsibilities of individuals to their communities were enshrined in the later teachings of St Francis of Assisi and the practices of participatory brotherhood and sisterhood of the Franciscan friars and the Little Sisters of St Clare. Rights of personal faith and interpretation were added to community responsibilities in the active participation proclaimed in the religious revivals of the fourteenth century by John Wycliffe and Jan Huss. Both rights and responsibilities were explored by Sir Thomas More (1965) in his *Utopia* of 1516. He developed ideas for the fictional island of Amaurote, where there would be enforced but recipro-

cal participation in all aspects of community life, from street kitchens and communal dinners to common and equal hours of each day devoted to sleep, work and recreation, and where the entire island would be governed by a conclave of mayors. Such a conformist but consensual community might, in practice, have evolved to embrace freer and more spontaneous community life.

Later in the seventeenth century, such speculations were developed into the formal social contract theories of Thomas Hobbes and John Locke. In his *Two Treatises on Government* of 1690, Locke (1993) enunciates the four rights that government should guarantee to citizens in return for obedience and payment of taxes:

- freedom of expression;
- the right to elect representative governments;
- rights to religious toleration;
- freedom from taxation without representation.

These principles were to reappear in the American Declaration of Independence nearly ninety years later. Social contract theories have continued to be dominant in the social philosophy of the United States, underwriting Jeffersonian localism and being powerfully restated in John Rawls' *Theory of Justice* (1971). Rawls evolves and tests his theory by constructing a notional discussion among a group of equally advantaged individuals about how society should be organised. The two principles that he argues they would adopt, on which he bases a very comprehensive view of constitutional justice, are:

1. A utilitarian commitment to maximum personal liberty compatible with a like freedom for others.
2. An arrangement of the inevitable inequalities which will arise from that freedom so as to confer greatest benefit upon the least advantaged – a dictum which has been severally described as 'giving most to those who have least' and 'advancing the back marker' (Hare, 1978; Heywood, 1990).

Rawls powerfully justifies this position by pointing out that those who are still better off should have no complaint about assistance for those who are still worse off. This skein of participatory theory has great significance for contemporary society and communities. First, communities are seen as social organisms whose totals are more than the sum of their parts, and whose overall health depends upon the health and welfare of each other member. Second, Rawls' long book offers throughout examples of the careful weighing of ideas and interests that is essential to effective and sustainable community planning. His view is very different from that of Margaret Thatcher when she pronounced 'There is no such thing as society; there are only individuals and their families' (Ridley, 1997). Rawls offers not only a concept of cohesive societies but also guidelines for their regulation based on careful and transparent logic, which can be reworked as evolving conditions and consequences may require.

Theories of mutual aid are also important to ideas of participation. Peter Kropotkin (1939) traces them far back to the advantages enjoyed by sociable species in the struggle for existence, and goes on to identify their resurfacing in the earliest days of revived urban life of the dawn of the Renaissance in twelfth-century century Italy, where cooperative guilds played a major role in the organisation of city life and government (Heywood, 1910; Kropotkin, 1939; Hall, 2002). Similar ideas underlay the philosophy of Indian ashrams and through them the agrarian village cooperatives advocated by Mahatma Gandhi. Ideal communities and model towns like those of Robert Owen and his son Robert Dale Owen in New Lanark in Scotland and New Harmony in Indiana were based on similar ideas, which were well developed into coherent social proposals in Owen's *Report to the County of Lanark* of 1819 (Hamilton, 1946). Owen himself was a conflicted character and something of a pied piper who sometimes abandoned those who had trusted him (Taylor, 1989), but nevertheless he put his ideas into practice, at least in New Lanark, and later in the foundation of the Rochdale Pioneers Cooperative society, with great success, demonstrating that cooperation was an even more effective basis for successful social organisation than the unconstrained capitalist competition which dominated his age.

The communitarian skein in participation theory has been carried forward into the twenty-first century in Britain by the well-known syndicalist writer Colin Ward (1973, 1974), who was for many years a project officer with the British Town and Country Planning Association. In books like *Tenants Take Over*, *Anarchy in Action*, *Streetwork* and his 1974 edition of Kropotkin's classic *Fields, Farms and Workshops of Tomorrow*, Ward keeps alive the theory of participation as not only a right but also a powerful means to successful social organisation. In the United States, Amitai Etzioni and colleagues (Etzioni, 2004; Etzioni, Volmert & Rothschild, 2004) have produced a powerful stream of books and articles advocating and describing communitarian social arrangements, which would draw both roles and powers away from national and state governments. Such alterations to free-market methods of social organisation have gained further credibility, following the worldwide collapse of the speculative housing mortgage market in the period from 2008 to 2010.

PRACTICAL APPLICATIONS OF PARTICIPATION IN COMMUNITY LIFE AND PLANNING

Some examples of participation have already been discussed in Chapter 1: worker's self management in the Mondragon workers cooperatives, the micro credit transformation wrought by the Grameen Bank of Bangladesh, the environmental activism of urban and city farms, and carbon-reduction groups are all eloquent testimonies to the power of motivated groups to transform their communities.

Another form of participation is offered by the local community boards and neighbourhood councils which have been integrated into the administrative and planning systems in Portland, Oregon and New Zealand. In Portland there are now more than one hundred neighbourhood councils registered with the City's Office of Neighbourhood Involvement (ONI), who receive modest funding to maintain their organisation and communications and to undertake local initiatives, in return for meeting minimum standards of accountability and open election of office holders.[viii] They have rights of comment on issues affecting their areas and act as grassroots feeders of information and concerns for the city council with its population of 545 000 (City of Portland, 2009). The New Zealand model of community boards, of which there are 143 throughout the country, in both urban and rural areas, is rather more formal, being resourced by local governments, who oversee methods of selection to ensure that they are openly constituted and representative. Community boards have official rights of consultation and perform advisory roles, which are particularly significant in cases of development assessment and control, providing local communities with a routine and regular way to voice opinions on development proposals before decisions are made. They are also able to undertake some initiatives of their own by precepting on the local rates. They thus perform both consultative and participatory roles (Heywood, 1997; Local Government, New Zealand, 2009).

Loosely representative bodies of this sort have long been common within metropolitan organisation and planning in the United Kingdom. They played major roles in the community engagement of Liverpool, London and other cities in the early Seventies (Heywood, 1974). Later, the national Community Development Project with its twelve local projects throughout the country also employed this approach to achieve local involvement and responsiveness. Now the Homes and Communities Agency (HCA) and the HCA Academy are fostering community participation as a major plank of their policy of urban regeneration, encouraging both organisations like faith-based housing associations and local residents associations to apply for government support and grants to help transform declining and often crime-ridden inner areas like Longsight in inner-Manchester (Homes and Communities Agency 2009). This area's housing stock was modernised by building new homes, refurbishing existing ones and converting two-up, two-down terraces into spacious four-bedroom town houses. The introduction of a new community centre and community gardens has fostered a strong new community spirit in Northmoor. Interventions are based on the concept plan developed at the start of the project in partnership with local residents. In 2002, the schemes originator, Manchester Methodist Housing Association (now Great Places), had no waiting list for Northmoor and gave vouchers to encourage residents to move there. By 2007, after the implementation of the collaborative improvement scheme, the waiting time for a two-bedroom house in the area stretched to four years. Rental property vacancies had more than halved to three weeks.

The successful transformation of Northmoor has been recognised by a number of awards, including the Housing Corporation Awards for Excellence and the then Deputy Prime Minister's Awards for Sustainable Communities. What is most significant about this story is the recognition by central government of the key role that local involvement can play in implementing national improvement policies in the localities where change is needed. The evolution of the names of the responsible government department is, itself, significant: from 'Housing and Local Government' through 'Department of Environment' and 'Department of Communities and Local Government' to 'Homes and Communities Agency'. In the same way, the consistent showcasing of best practice by the HCA Academy and its Awards recognises the importance of nurturing community participation (HCA Academy, 2009).

On the opposite side of the world, in Australia, the same pattern is evident. Since 1998, the Queensland Community Renewal Program has made use of advisory committees and community reference groups to enhance the knowledge and authenticity of the 24 local schemes which have been run in disadvantaged communities throughout the state, nineteen of which are still active (Queensland Government Department of Housing, 2009). Other examples include environmental management by local creek catchments coordinat-

ing committees in Brisbane (Brisbane City Council, 2009), and land, coast and river care groups and committees throughout the Australian Outback (Landcare Australia, 2009). As the scale and impersonality of modern mass societies and cities increase, local extensions of representative democracy of this sort can play an increasingly important role in maintaining healthy connections between local communities and governments, especially if recent moves are continued towards governments divesting themselves of community service roles onto the shoulders of those communities themselves.[ix] Genuine empowering of such local and regional groups could give new meanings to the phrases 'small government' and 'big society'.

Leadership has also important roles to play in promoting community participation. In England the Academy of Sustainable Communities (now the Homes and Communities Agency Academy), is making significant contributions to effective participation by developing and running numerous courses to help develop leadership within local communities. Foundation degree courses are offered in sustainable communities, providing a pathway for local leaders to develop their own skills and become more effective agents of change and engagement. The Academy also offers a wide range of shorter courses in general leadership and team-building, including skills development in combating crime and anticipating and managing the future. Annual awards recognise community performance in a very wide range of activities, including innovation, place-making, rural housing, stronger communities and sustainable futures. These awards both provide leadership in themselves and recognise and award it in local communities (Homes and Communities Academy, 2010). One of the key roles of such local leadership, to imbue in others the confidence to participate in effective negotiations, is the topic of the following section.

Negotiation

Cyclical processes of consensus building and alternative dispute resolution (ADR) create new paths to reach acceptable outcomes in community negotiations (Susskind & Cruikshank, 1987). Irrespective of planning, community life goes on. People participate. They cross the threshold of the community centre, the city hall or the school entrance, or they join a local group dedicated to song, dance, religious activities or even cooking, walking or adult education. As they communicate within this group and then with other groups, they learn of each others' needs, contributions and difficulties. A degree of solidarity is created, and a sense of understanding and sympathy may evolve, but inevitably differences will occur within and between groups. There will be competition for attention, time, space, resources and opportunities. Principles for resolving allocations will assist and goodwill will be needed.[x]

Communication can assist in clarifying core concerns, winnowing out social attitudes from actual needs and enriching understanding of the situations and attitudes of others. Such informal negotiations tend to occur in situations where people are able to learn a great deal about the aims, beliefs and priorities of each other. Elsewhere, in the daily flux of business life, constant and unrehearsed contact with unknown others is regulated more by market relations. Conflicts of interest may arise among groups not sharing a high level of prior contact or sympathy, and more formal processes will be needed to develop mutual understanding.

Widespread attention is being focused on the potentialities of negotiation to resolve disputes because of the multiple conflicts, collapses and splintering of community life and the increasing individualism of contemporary societies. Theories of group dynamics and processes of ADR have been developed to assist in these situations. As early as 1933, Kurt Lewin, arriving in the United States from Nazi Germany, applied systems theory to work out patterns of interpersonal relations, concluding that one of the key factors was for participants to commit to building and maintaining networks and relationships with each other (Lewin, 1997).[xi] He combined his academic and practical interests to develop 'action research' techniques that acknowledged participants' perceptions of their situation, to help to ensure that outcomes would be relevant. His work in developing group dynamics (discussed later in this section) was intended to provide analytical and problem-solving tools to make negotiation more purposeful and effective. The ability of problem-solving methods to actually throw up new solutions, objectively better than those originally advocated by any of the participants, was supported by subsequent work by design theorists such as Christopher Alexander (1979), who used set theory to develop multiple criteria planning solutions, as described in Chapter 6.

Applying ADR, and consensus-building, Laurence Susskind and Andrew Cruikshank (1987) illustrate how it is possible to break the impasse by draining negotiations of their emotional charge and assisting protagonists to differentiate their key interests from rhetorical commitments and marginal preferences.

Other approaches avoid the conflicts addressed by ADR and instead build on positive elements in people's relationships and expectations of each other to construct model links and outcomes in the privileged space of the workshop or focus group, which can then be transferred to transform participants' original views of the situation and each other (Cooperrider, 2008; Hammond & Royal, 1997). This process, termed 'appreciative inquiry', builds on the natural bonds of mutual acceptance that exist in even the most dysfunctional of communities, to resolve strained relations and produce good outcomes in situations which may at first have seemed unpromising. Donald Schon (1983) has analysed how reflective practice can assist those in negotiations to review their own actions and values and improve their skills to find ways forward for themselves and others. Others have investigated how participants can achieve *Getting to YES* (Fisher & Ury, 1981) and *Getting beyond yes* (Margerum, 1999) in more programmatic ways. John Forester (1989, 1999, 2009) illustrates ways in which positive listening, imaginative empathy and informed use of associational logic can generate positive outcomes.

COMMUNITY PLANNING AND NEGOTIATION

Community planning provides a practical field for the processes of social negotiation, offering a framework that can take participants beyond their present discontents and problems into a future, where everyone has equal rights to be heard and to have their interests considered in the distribution of potentially amplified resources.[xii] Such a world offers an ideal space for building consensus, directing attention away from past resentments and current conflicting interests into notional discussions of better futures.

MODELS OF NEGOTIATION

The negotiative principles of mutual respect, honest and open communication, active listening, reflective evaluation and purposive proposition are all well understood and widely advocated (Susskind & Cruikshank, 1987; Forester, 2009). Planners also need practical models which can be confidently applied in their regular activities. Four which offer useful approaches are those deriving from group dynamics, ADR, action planning and advocacy planning.

Group dynamics is a young field of study, stemming from the original work of Kurt Lewin (1997) on ways to resolve social conflicts in the Thirties and Forties of the last century. Using his 'force field' theory, Lewin's basic equation $B = F (p, e)$ states that human behaviour is a product of both environment and personality, and does not result solely from either. He thus avoids the excesses of both environmental determinists like Lysenko and Skinner (Ridley, 1997) and the genetic determinists like Carlyle (Desmond & Moore, 1991), Galton (Magnussen, 1990) and Dawkins (1976, 2009). Lewin recognised that in order to resolve conflicts involving change it was necessary to increase the incentives relative to the constraining factors acting on participants, which may include all the influences shaping their 'life spaces': their values, goals, needs, motivations and anxieties. He applied this approach in practical work to improve relations in situations of potential conflict between industrial workers and managers in factories and between Jewish minorities and the gentile majority in the state of Connecticut in the United States. By these means, Lewin developed some key principles that remain the basic building blocks of group dynamics:

- Negotiative planning and action research should be based on direct face-to-face involvement.
- Democratic leadership and organisation are best fitted to achieve sustainable outcomes.[xiii]
- Continuity and commitment are necessary to achieve consensual conclusions, unlike judicial approaches, which produce decisions that can be recorded and left to others to implement.

Group dynamics relies on enhancing participants' self-awareness and building social networks to expand understanding and relationships. There are two clear implications for community planning. First, communities need to be well informed about changing external conditions and the potential impacts on their own lives, in ways similar to those being promoted by the United Kingdom's Homes and Communities Agency Academy, discussed earlier. Second, consensual change will require clear advantages for local communities, with the number and intensity of perceived benefits outstripping perceived disadvantages. This implies the possibility of sum-plus situations, based on creative problem-solving and new proposals. A similar recognition of the rights of everyone to seek their own best interests and futures is central to the work of ADR, with similar commitment to the search for win–win situations to provide better alternatives to entrenched and recurrent conflicts. Later in the chapter, we shall examine instances where some of these conflict resolution principles and techniques have been applied.

CONSENSUS BUILDING AND ALTERNATIVE DISPUTE RESOLUTION

Consensus building is a wider and more proactive approach than dispute resolution, but both owe much to Lewin's pioneering work on resolving social conflicts and force field analysis. Consensus can be built around solutions developed to resolve earlier rejections of proposals perceived as threatening communities' interests. One vivid example is provided by Toronto's Stop Spadina/Save Our City Coordinating Committee (SSSOCCC) of the Seventies, which flowered into support for community development in the adjacent suburb of the Annex and public transport improvements throughout Metro Toronto (Lemon, 1985). Even more dramatic developments occurred in Madrid with the urban social movements of the Seventies flowering into a transformation of local government and planning in the city (Castells, 1983). The rapid three-year development of Brisbane's 1990 Campaign Against Route Twenty (CART) into Citizens Advocating Responsible Transport (still CART!) (Engwicht, 1993) played a significant role in the successful introduction in the period from 1995 to 2000 of world-class busways, which have reversed the decline in public transport patronage and continue to be expanded as a major part of the city's movement system. The many examples of this upward spiral of proposition, criticism and conflict resolution leading to coherent new community plans create a clear pattern and model for beneficial social change.

Another element which ADR derives from its social psychology origins is the logic of the best alternative to negotiated agreements (BATNA), which determines whether it is worthwhile for interest groups to engage in negotiations (Susskind & Cruikshank, 1987). If they are able to achieve a better outcome by lobbying, recourse to legal systems or responding to existing incentives, then there is no point in their entering into negotiations which may prove long, difficult or unrewarding. Viewed in this light, community planning processes need to offer community groups and individuals genuine prospects of substantial success. Susskind and Cruikshank (1987) provide an interesting notional example, based on an actual case where a local community, supported by university experts, oppose the establishment of a dioxin treatment plant in a redundant federal navy yard on the grounds of the likelihood of neighbouring contamination. At one point in the ADR process, the leading academic expert for the objectors states the conditions on which the community would be justified in accepting the opening of the plant: legally binding guarantees for transparent and regular monitoring, automatic closure if emissions exceeded the permitted level and joint acceptance of all liability for any necessary compensation by the city council and the contracting company involved. The city's Department of Sanitation immediately accepted these conditions, and this established the basis for ultimate successful resolution of the dispute.

Such alternative dispute resolution processes can be adopted either by the groups involved or by making use of expert intermediaries. It is significant that five US states – Hawaii, New Jersey, Massachusetts, Minnesota and Wisconsin – have established offices to mediate distributional disputes (Susskind & Cruikshank, 1987). Both Wisconsin and Rhode Island have adopted hazardous-waste disposal laws that require mediation to precede formal siting decisions. Similar approaches could be adopted elsewhere and across a wider range of functions to ensure that community planning systems include negotiative and consensual practices in developing their plans. Numerous examples of such approaches already exist, but they need to be more systematically adopted and implemented as extensions of democratic involvement. Oregon's State Planning Goal Number One: Citizen Involvement, for instance, requires the formation, funding and incorporation of 'citizen involvement committees' wherever community plans are being produced, and this has proved a valuable basis for community organisations like the 1000 Friends of Oregon to campaign for public transport and habitat conservation throughout the state, and particularly in the major metropolis of Portland (Knaap & Nelson; 1992, Ozawa, 2003). Elsewhere, in the Netherlands, Canada, Australia and the United Kingdom, there are provisions of varying effectiveness for citizens to oppose proposals that they distrust, and in some situations to contribute to objectives for planning 'at the formative stages' (Skeffington, 1969). In order to cross the threshold from tokenism to achieve genuine participation and creative problem-solving, these provisions need to be greatly expanded.

ACTION PLANNING

Action planning involves people making plans for the future development of their own communities and spaces in face-to-face discussions in the actual places where changes are proposed (Hamdi & Goethert, 1997). This down-to-earth, humanistic approach to planned social change aims to deconstruct the very technical and often complex modernist methods of top-down and centralised strategic planning into more local, spontaneous and responsive projects which can initiate small-scale local changes. These can later flow together to create overall strategic outcomes. This approach draws both on Castells' ideas of *The City and the Grassroots* (1983) and on the 'small state' views of the 1980s of 'not rowing but steering' and of preferring catalytic support roles to ones of centralised state provision (Osborne & Gaebler, 1992). This method works in concentrated three- and four-day workshops with a mixture of local activists, residents, government and non-government stakeholders, providers and policy-makers. Short cycles are devoted to identifying objectives, recognising constraints and opportunities, developing options and preparing programmes. There is a heavy emphasis on informality, authenticity and local implementation. The process is designed to produce consensus that can be rapidly actioned. Unearthing potential conflicts that may need to be negotiated is neither proposed nor encouraged. There is thus a strong element of 'appreciative inquiry'.

These processes are well designed to melt such deep-frozen landscapes of centralised planning as those of the Nineties World Bank and Soviet ministries of the Seventies and Eighties, but they would benefit from development to incorporate the logic and problem-solving thoroughness of the ADR systems developed by the social psychologists discussed in the preceding section. The reality of conflicting interests, which are always involved in community planning, is glossed over or sidestepped. The resultant hastily developed plans may well be forestalled by the opposition or abstention of powerful forces that have not been represented in the workshops. (In the Schweitzer-Renate workshop in the north-western province of South Africa, for instance, the powerful white community residents of the local establishment were not involved, though their privileged access to water supplies was a major factor in the community development problems faced by the majority black community) (Hamdi & Goethert, 1997). More comprehensive community planning would have given time and energy to starting the conversations that could have led to improved understanding between the different communities who shared the area. Though annual repetition of the workshops is recommended in a general way, continuity is neither emphasised nor specified.

Similar problems had affected the Springfield (Belfast) workshop of 1986, which brought participants from three different continents and five different countries to face the huge problems of social and political reconciliation, housing provision and improvement and economic regeneration in Northern Ireland's troubled capital of Belfast (Hamdi & Goethert, 1997). Within a week of the workshop's conclusion, violence had broken out again, but no provisions had been made for the ongoing review that could have adjusted proposals to the renewed difficulties of this quite predictable occurrence, which could have helped to develop much needed realistic, viable long-term community plans.

The valuable lessons to be learnt from these action planning examples is that although such vivid and engaging systems for producing proposals on site and with the local people have great contributions to make ~~ns~~ of engagement and option development, their short timeframe and narrow focus needs to be expanded to enable the negotiations needed to produce deeply-founded solutions that can meet the tests of lasting social change and tackle ingrained opposition. To do this, they would have to be part of continuing community dialogue, not a substitute for it. The fact that they allow hard-pressed planners to 'Get in, get started and get out' is not really the advantage that it may seem. Valuable as they are, communication and participation alone are not enough: opportunities for negotiation are also necessary if lasting beneficial change is to be achieved.

ADVOCACY PLANNING, NEGOTIATION AND COMMUNITY ACTION

Negotiation therefore plays an integral role in the resolution of many community planning campaigns and controversies to achieve positive change. A general sequence can be discerned, including the following four broad stages (Figure 2.1):

This four-stage sequence can be demonstrated in a number of instances, illustrated in the accompanying boxes describing Saul Alinsky's landmark work in Chicago's Back o' the Yards inner-city area and industrial councils throughout the United States (1939–1960), the evolution of Brisbane's Norman Creek Waterway Park and Common (1986–1992) and the establishment of Southbank Gardens (1987–1994). Recognition of this pattern, with its prospect of light at the end of the tunnel, can be empowering to local communities, who find themselves caught in complex requirements placed by governments on objectors and participants. Willingness to engage and persevere in opposing unwanted proposals and developing the community's own agenda should, in consensual democracies, eventually evoke offers of negotiation.

There are logical reasons why this pattern affecting community involvement in major planning proposals is so prevalent. Initial agenda setting and publicity are necessary to establish the facts of the existing situation and the proposed development, providing opportunities for different stakeholders to identify unintended consequences and to propose alternatives. Opposition and conflict can then test the validity of competing proposals and bring a wide range of different participants to the negotiating table. Resulting discussions may produce several potential options, which may need some time to be considered and further developed. Finally, negotiated outcomes will need to be inscribed in binding agreements with secure funding and adoption by legitimating agencies. This sequence may often take a number of years, and it is reassuring for participant groups engaged in this arduous process to know that it is a well-trodden route with good prospects for ultimate success.

It may be objected that these instances all demonstrate only the reactive capacity of concerned communities to oppose unwanted development schemes and to refine them through local knowledge and enlistment of alternative experts. However, looked at from a greater distance, these processes of negotiation can be seen as an inherent and necessary component of beneficial physical change in pluralist and consensual democracies (Davidoff, 1973).

Viewed in this light, community action may be seen as a constructive and integral phase in the processes of evolving acceptable and beneficial local policies within a democratic mixed economy society. In such societies, organisations and business concerns are free to propose any scheme they wish to achieve profits through meeting commercial aims, often being actively encouraged to do so by governments in the interest of full employment and social prosperity. Such proposals

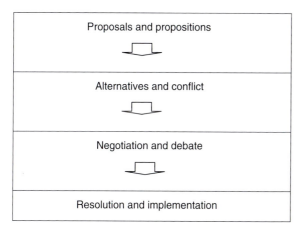

Figure 2.1   Phases in community action.

may well have a negative impact on the perceived interests of existing residents and users of the area. If these interests are to be fairly addressed, alternative proposals will need to be developed and considered (Davidoff, 1973). Time will be required for competing campaigns to allow their relative merits to be recognised and evaluated. Limits to the powers and political clout of each will emerge and compromise solutions will have to be considered. Negotiation will again be needed to build consensus around composite solutions, to assemble funds and approve enacting powers. It is a heartening fact that in each of the three cases (Boxes 2.2, 2.3 and 2.4) such a process did ultimately succeed. The evidence is that more proactive and inclusive systems of community planning should prove less controversial and accident prone. Community planning will benefit from incorporating, rather than avoiding or repressing, this well-established sequence of proposition and proposal, leading to review and contestation, followed by negotiation and debate, resulting in resolution and implementation of acceptable change.

Part Two: Applications

All four themes – communication, consultation, participation and negotiation – contribute to the range of methods and techniques available to assist community planning and can be readily discerned in the methods and techniques outlined in this section. Communication is the basis of many of these techniques. Consultation is involved in almost every activity of good planning. Negotiation provides the litmus test of the willingness of controlling bodies to share their power. Participation is the most complex of the four factors because of the wide range of meanings and activities to which it is attached, well illustrated by Sherry Arnstein's celebrated 'Ladder of Participation' (1969), which ascends from a bottom rung of therapy through tokenism, consultation, placation, shared control and delegated powers to a top rung of full citizen control. Techniques will vary according to the position which has been reached on this ladder. Therapy may well involve the formation of groups of local worthies who meet from time to time to advise decision-takers on emergent issues. Tokenism will invoke more structured approaches including allocating a formal advisory role to such groups. Consultation, increasingly widely practised throughout organised societies, will require mechanisms to establish representativeness and transparency. Considerable attention is paid to it in the fol-

lowing section because of its major role in improving the quality of planning proposals, as well as in developing community awareness and involvement. Placation will involve actions to meet aspects of perceived public preferences. Shared programmes may include a measure of community development. Delegated powers move towards community organisation. Finally, citizen control involves the sponsorship and support of political evolution. Inevitably, the higher rungs of this ladder take practitioners into fields of politics, economics and social organisation. We have seen that local groups can run their own urban farms, micro credit organisations and take responsibility for the upkeep of creek catchment management and protection. All of these very specific implementation techniques will involve a need for accurate information concerning facts and values that will depend upon open and transparent methods of consultation. These are discussed in the following section.

Necessary conditions for effective community consultation

It is important to define the preconditions which should be achieved before any collaborative method can be effective. Even the simplest processes of consultation demand very careful shaping to reflect their purpose and context if they are to achieve valid and effective contributions. Attention needs to be given to the following conditions:

- The purpose of the consultation and questions should be clearly identified at the outset.
- Topics should be within people's personal experience.
- Respondents should know what use is to be made of their responses, and what degree of anonymity will be preserved for them.
- Questions should focus on what ought to be done for the good of the community in question, not the individual's personal preference, so that responses will be about the same things (community priorities and not thousands of different personal preference lists) and can therefore logically be combined (Arrow, 1973).
- Participants should be encouraged to trade off with each other, and to indulge in creative problem-solving.
- People should be discouraged from expressing objectives trespassing on someone else's human rights (e.g. "No more this or that group here").

Box 2.2   Contested rights in inner-city Chicago

Saul Alinsky's work in inner Chicago from the 1930s to the 1960s aimed to help the poor and discounted, including the families of people in prison, fight for their rights as citizens, by creating 'people's organizations' that could wield community power. Starting as a Chicago criminology research student in the late 1930s, he organised the Back o' the Yards People's Congress to identify and tackle the community's many problems. The Congress first met in 1939 in a stressed inner-city area, where there were high concentrations of the families of prisoners and ex-prisoners (Alinsky, 1971). It was the community itself which identified the wide range of problems of powerlessness from which it suffered: social isolation, proneness to violence, environmental decay and lack of independence or opportunities for home ownership.

Under the slogan of 'We, the People, will work out our own destiny', the Back o' the Yards People's Congress soon came to exercise many of the functions of local government that had gone by default in the area for many years. For more than twenty years, the Congress met annually to elect officers and formulate the programme for the following year. Each of the key problems of environmental and housing decay, bad landlordism, mortgage blacklisting and city council neglect was in turn targeted in effective campaigns. Between 1953 and 1956 alone, for instance, 5000 dwellings were rehabilitated in the area without any residents being relocated (Jacobs, 1961).

Incorporating these lessons, Alinsky also organised the nation-wide Industrial Areas Foundation, which sought to mobilise communities to solve their own problems throughout the country. He developed the influential doctrine of 'community power', encouraging disadvantaged communities to learn from their actions and take responsibility for their own lives and those of their neighbourhoods. Alinsky summarises his view of the relations between action and learning in the following way:

> Through action, reflection, study, testing and synthesis, I have learned to distil experience from living, integrating the actions and events of life so that they assemble themselves into a meaningful universal pattern. (Alinsky, 1971)

Alinsky was reacting against the intolerable injustices that riddled American society. For him 'the real action is the reaction'. He was a populist, who worked regardless of accepted social and moral theories, believing in the purifying effects of open process, advocating:

> Get them to move in the right direction first. They'll explain to themselves later why they moved in that direction and that explanation will be better learning than anything else we can do. (Alinsky, 1971)

Alinsky only worked for causes for which he had sympathy and then participated fully in shaping an appropriate course of action. He returned to the Back o' the Yards in the 1950s to help organise in opposition to the leaders he had worked with fifteen years earlier who were now opposing the entry into the neighbourhood of African Americans, arriving from the Deep South in search of work in Chicago's factories. He was a committed activist, self-confident and neither superior nor deferential. Reflecting many years later, Alinsky muses:

> It seems as though a good part of our knowledge ... and philosophy and attitudes are not things that we carefully and laboriously think through but are the rationalizations or self justifications for acts we have already committed. (Alinsky, 1979)

His work, too, falls into the same pattern of Agendas > Conflict > Negotiation > Implementation. His example and achievements remain excellent examples of the importance of 'the propaganda of the deed'. He would rejoice at the national and, indeed, global success of his distinguished successor as a Chicago inner-city community organiser, Barack Obama.

Box 2.3   Norman Creek Flood Mitigation and Waterway Common

Norman Creek is a short, flood-prone stream which flows through Brisbane's inner, eastern suburbs to join the Brisbane River estuary a few kilometres downstream from the city centre, for which competing plans were being developed in the mid-1980s. The local Norman Creek Flood Action Group (NCFAG) aimed to link flood mitigation to open space and habitat conservation, improved residential amenity, and regulation of industrial development and traffic. It aimed to preserve the area as a mixed status creek-side inner-city suburb. Simultaneously, a Sydney finance company, Turbo Investments, bought a large disused industrial site on the southern slopes of the valley and proposed a scheme which would solve the flooding problem at no cost to the city council by straightening and culverting the creek and creating a large area of approximately twenty hectares of flat land for industrial development with direct access to major road and rail routes to the city centre and south-east.

Different sections of Brisbane's city council and the state government were lobbied by both sides, with responses varying between occasions and departments. Support for the Turbo proposals came from the city works, parks and industrial promotion sections, impressed by cost savings to the public purse. The city planners adopted studied neutrality, unimpressed by the demanding style of the NCFAG, and the implications of a 'planning led' approach to local development. The state government's departments of transport and education were interested because of issues of major road construction, and potential impacts on several school sites, and kept careful watching briefs.

The NCFAG worked with planning staff and students of the Queensland Institute of Technology (now Queensland University of Technology) to produce an alternative scheme that would preserve the existing valley and meanders for open space and habitat conservation. By creating a medium-level floodway across the meanders, excess water would be quickly removed from the valley in times of flooding, preventing the accumulation of water that had previously caused flooding and transforming the creek from a barrier to a focus for recreation, conservation and transportation. This plan was enthusiastically adopted by the local community who resolutely maintained their commitment through the succeeding four years of conflict and negotiation. The lord mayor formed a liaison committee, which received promises of state and federal funding for flood mitigation, but passive resistance by council officers, who disliked the implied 'local area management' approach, resulted in two years of abortive discussions and the eventual collapse of the committee.

Following this period of deadlock, and under the shadow of a council election, the lord mayor, Alderman Sallyanne Atkinson, instructed the manager of her Inner Suburbs Action programme to resolve the issue. Consultants were appointed to produce a scheme under the guidance of a community consultative committee with equal numbers of NCFAG, schools and industry members. Council officers were to be co-opted, as necessary without voting rights, though ultimate decisions remained with the city council. The resulting scheme, adopted by the council in 1990 and gaining a 1991 Planning Institute award for strategic planning, largely incorporated the 1986 QIT scheme for balanced conservation, mitigation, integrated industrial and educational sites and residential improvement. In November 1990, the Norman Creek Community Common was opened, where the first of several community festivals was held the following year. By 1994, the council was referring to the area as 'Norman Creek Waterway Park'. For nearly twenty years the creek corridor has provided a network of bike and walking paths and inner-city natural habitats which link the service hub of Stones Corner to the residential areas of Coorparoo and Norman Park to the shores of the Brisbane River estuary. Community participation has continued to thrive. In 1994, a proposal for a massive flyover spanning the creek was successfully opposed, and the city council is now in partnership with the local *N4C* (Norman Creek Catchment Coordinating Committee) to maintain and extend areas of public access and nature conservation along the creek's meandering course (Figures 2.2, 2.3 and 2.4).

Box 2.4   Brisbane's Expo site redevelopment and Southbank Gardens

The Bicentennial 1988 Brisbane Expo occupied a riverside site of 37.5 hectares immediately opposite the city centre, which had been compulsorily acquired under a special Act of Parliament. The original redevelopment guidelines encouraged maximum commercial, hotel and luxury residential uses, and the winning tender, submitted by a group headed by a former treasurer of the ruling National Party, proposed nearly half a million square metres of new development. Two high-rise hotels, a casino and convention centre would have dominated the site, increasing by a half the city centre's commercial floor space. Luxury canal housing and a river island would have transformed the city centre. Office towers would have dwarfed and shadowed the city's Cultural Centre Complex, creating a canyon effect over the river, and excluding public riverside access by commercial ownership. Relocation of heritage buildings would have removed important historic landmarks.

Forceful opposition from professional and community groups and academics, supported by politicians and reflected in the media, resulted in large public demonstrations. A newspaper survey showed that most people thought the site should be a 'people place', include significant areas of riverside parkland and maintain public access to the waterfront. Competing agendas were evident. Later in 1988, a new premier responded by designating a new Southbank Development Corporation with equal representation from city and state governments to balance financial viability and public interest and called for new tenders. The successful new scheme devoted the entire waterfront to public access and parks, including three hectares of artificial lakes with extensive bathing beaches and a middle section of restaurants and entertainment areas and hotels, with luxury housing and offices behind, terraced well back from the river. General responses were overwhelmingly favourable, singling out public access, bikeways and parkland and entertainment facilities for approval.

Comments from organised community and professional groups included a number of criticisms that proved crucial in improving the quality and feasibility of the scheme. Proposals to expand almost tenfold the area under the planning control of the Development Authority – to 'reap a profit from the enlarged area' with sweeping powers over one of the city's most sensitive concentrations of rental housing – were criticised. The proposed freehold tenure would have pre-empted coordinated management of a complex site with half of its area in public parkland and swimming areas. The corporation accepted the recommendation of the consultant reporting on the consultation outcome, to adopt a new form of government leasehold, giving overall responsibility for the site to the corporation and leaving the surrounding area within the control of the city council. Extension of the corporation's planning powers beyond the old Expo site was quietly dropped. The Cabinet accepted this submission.

The Southbank Gardens, which were opened to the public in June 1992, benefited from public objections to the earlier proposals. Public access has replaced private and commercial exclusion throughout the site. Riverside and parkland access runs from the neighbouring residential suburb of West End through the parkland down to the waterfront, which is devoted to public parks, pools and entertainment. Housing and hotels occupy the middle of the site. There are now countless opportunities for local people and international and interstate visitors to rub shoulders, share a public environment and meet informally, and Southbank's first year coincided with a dramatic increase of over 50% in the number of tourists visiting Brisbane to over a million in 1992–3. The development certainly adds a distinctive feature to a 'gateway' city that formerly lacked a characteristic attraction of its own.

Had the original scheme gone ahead, Brisbane would not have gained the rewards of continuous riverside parks with their views and opportunities to enjoy the constantly varying reflections of buildings, bridges and night-time lights. The city may instead have been left with a mass of very tall and unlettable office space, seriously damaging its urban economy. Southbank has released the potential of this central riverside location to capture and express the subtropical, open-air and convivial character of Brisbane. In so doing, it provides the meeting place that every great city needs for its residents and tourists (Plate 2.1).

Figure 2.2 Norman Creek Greenway: Athletics track, cycle path and creek corridor bush regeneration in inner Brisbane.

Figure 2.3 Saturday morning at the creek-side skatepark.

Figure 2.4 Team training in Greenway playing field with playground and creek-side re-vegetation behind.

● As far as possible, discussions should be held in situations of 'reflective equilibrium': calm, convenient and comfortable situations. Thought needs to be given as to the most comfortable and suitable location for consultation. Indigenous people, for instance, often do not like formal meetings with agendas and intrusive recording procedures, but prefer discussions held on 'country', linked to storytelling by the elders, so that people can 'walk the talk' and communicate in an informal way. Similarly, elderly people can be consulted in day centres or at recreation clubs. Young people in care can be approached informally, by peer researchers, or in 'hang out' locations. Each group will have its own favourite locations.

The role and themes of consultation

Many of these conditions demand careful reflection and early decisions about the intended purposes of consultation. Although light can be shed on important matters of fact, these can, to some extent, be established by good observation, well-informed research and recourse to existing reports. The values and objectives which should drive plans, by contrast, can only be ascertained by asking people directly and perceptively about what they believe is right for their communities and areas. Observation may only record existing power relations, injustices and ingenious adaptations to unwanted situations. However, if the planners are already committed to methods not based on social values or human objectives – such as policy analysis, trend projection or 'big picture' professional goals – it may be best not to conduct community consultation, which may simply lead to subsequent disillusionment, bitterness and the familiar phenomenon of 'consultation fatigue'. In many of these cases, it is not that people are tired of being consulted but that they are frustrated at not being told how their contributions will be used, or how they will influence the development of proposals, and therefore at seeing no result from their contributions. These questions of the significance of choice of methods to the role, reputation and relevance of planning are discussed in more detail in Chapter 6.

COMMUNITIES OF METHOD

In seeking to define objectives, the general point also needs to be made that people are often more familiar with their daily problems than with 'technical' objectives. We notice misfit more than congruence. If one naked person, for instance, is walking down a street where all the others are fully clad, it is highly likely that it is the naked person who would attract our attention (and the reverse would also be true). Thus, asking people to identify their problems can be a useful first step to identifying what they think should be done. It all depends upon the group you are working with, and the style of thought with which they are familiar.

Methods of consultation

Every worthwhile new consultation programme creates and adopts some original means to suit its unique needs. The following well-established and successful methods can all be adapted and applied to specific situations:

- **Focus groups** of people with particular relevant knowledge and interests; such groups contain a considerable pool of knowledge and insight and can produce well-informed background understanding and sectional objectives in their own areas of concern.
- **Mixed-interest groups** can be composed in the opposite way so that they contain a full cross-section of interests in the study area, making them ideal consensus-building and conflict-resolution groups.
- **Service providers** whose 'coalface' experience brings them into contact with community problems and needs. Such people can often produce detailed lists of relevant problems and objectives. Examples are community development officers, social workers, human service providers, parks officers, public transport managers, housing providers and association members, and religious leaders. Their contributions can be tapped by helping them to reflect on the significance of their daily actions, and their early involvement will assist subsequent informed collaboration in implementation and monitoring.
- **Promotional and pressure groups** can be interviewed, organised into focus groups and approached by means of a standard loose-leaf 'consultation kit', with prepared information and response sheets allowing the group to consult its own members and to debate attitudes before reaching decisions on priorities and proposals.
- **Public attitude surveys** can be administered at the point of activities such as shopping, recreation or work, or, more validly, on the basis of representative samples, conducted by interview questionnaire in people's own homes, or by phone or post. (Point of activity surveys should generally take less than five minutes, phone interviews may go up to 8–10 minutes and home interview surveys may be designed for up to 25–30 minutes.) These surveys can also give information on activities and behaviour patterns.
- **Self surveys** can also be conducted by local people within their own neighbourhoods, either independently or working in conjunction with a local university or school. They can be very influential, forestalling the accusation that the silent majority has been ignored, particularly if such neutral personalities as academics, teachers or clerics are involved in their design or conduct.
- **Schools** will often agree to integrate 'alternative futures' projects into appropriate classes, such as geography, social studies, home economics or citizenship. They may even invite speakers to address morning assembly, and have survey forms completed in class time. This is particularly useful because today's school children will be the generation most affected by strategic planning.
- **Various media** – talkback radio, post-in newspaper coupons, TV link-ups of Future Visioning meetings and use of the Internet – can all help balance the normal diet of often trivialised and frequently biased news. Local government, community and planning participation newspapers are widely used and can be most successful in generating and maintaining a dialogue with the community.
- **Representation on steering committees and reference groups** can be an invaluable way of maintaining a voice at the decision table, particularly when linked to careful arrangements for reporting back to constituent groups. The dangers of co-option can be limited by good arrangements for regular renewal of mandate and support for maintaining contact between members.
- **Neighbourhood, progress or ward associations** with elected locality and interest group representatives performing such regular roles as responding to council initiatives, preparing locality profiles and distributing information and collecting community preferences.
- **Consultative and advisory committees** run the dangers of co-option and unrepresentativeness, but they have the merits of continuity, the capacity to act as 'learning groups' and often a high level of expertise and a strong sense of public service. They are a useful addition to any public consultation programme, but they are not a substitute for more representative approaches.

Consultation techniques

Each of these forms of consultation will require appropriate techniques. There is much to be said for composing or inventing these as one goes along in response to the particular needs of the situation and community. A few of the more popular ones are outlined below.

BRAINSTORMING

Small groups, ideally of not more than seven people, work with a facilitator and a scribe to undertake a specific task or explore a particular question, with no rules except that no criticism is allowed of anyone else's contribution. Originality is encouraged. Members are asked to convert negative comments into positive responses, which are recorded by a scribe. This is an appropriate technique for developing a wide range of objectives, which can then be evaluated and ranked, possibly by voting.

NOMINAL GROUP WORK

This approach can be used for larger groups where it is thought there may be people whose voices may not be heard without some structure to the session. All members are initially asked to ponder the same question and write down their conclusions. Each person's top priority is then declared round the group and recorded by the facilitator, and the process is repeated until all of the top three or four have been recorded. Subsequently, more wide-ranging and free-flowing discussion may be encouraged. Again, ranking can be done by voting. This highly structured approach may be rather restrictive, but it can be very effective with task-orientated groups having to accomplish a lot of work in a short space of time.

PIN BOARDING

This is another structured form of brainstorming. Quite large numbers of people attending a meeting can be organised to work in small groups of 6–7 people with each person writing down objectives on pieces of paper and pinning or sticking them up on walls, where they can be grouped into categories and then voted on, to produce ranked lists. Members can be asked to rearrange the objectives to form related sets, and this process often produces very interesting patterns of association and clusters of concern.

ROLE PLAY

This useful simulation technique can involve up to a dozen individuals, pairs or teams. Different participants are asked to research and advocate the attitudes and needs of the widest possible range of relevant groups or stakeholders, in a simulated situation, such as a committee meeting, with objectives being recorded in the form of meeting outcomes. A period of one or two weeks between the selection of roles and the performance of the role play will allow time for necessary research, although this is not essential. Of course, the validity of this approach to generating objectives is limited because people are not speaking for themselves, but it does have the considerable educational advantage of putting participants into the situations of those for whom they are planning.

LEARNING GROUPS

Groups may be specially formed to interact with decision-makers and information analysts. After each meeting, members are supplied with information relevant to the preferences they have stated. They are asked to develop their original ideas in more detail, or to change them in response to what they have learnt. In many ways, all continuing consultation creates learning groups, capable of developing steadily improving skills of interpretation and judgement.

Conclusion: relations among community planning, community action, community development and community organisation

Many of these methods and techniques can also be applied to a number of other activities intended to improve the quality of life within local and wider communities, including those directed towards action, development and organisation. Some definitions may help to clarify these distinctions and the relations with and between community action, community development and community organisation. These are all linked to community planning and to each other in a strong framework of mutual support, which is discussed in the following section, and illustrated in Figure 2.5. Because the whole book is directed to explore the scope and practice of community planning, a summary of the field is not offered at this stage, but can instead be found in Chapter 12, where it is linked to the discussions of scale, values, methods, systems, facets, design and governance of Chapters 3–11.

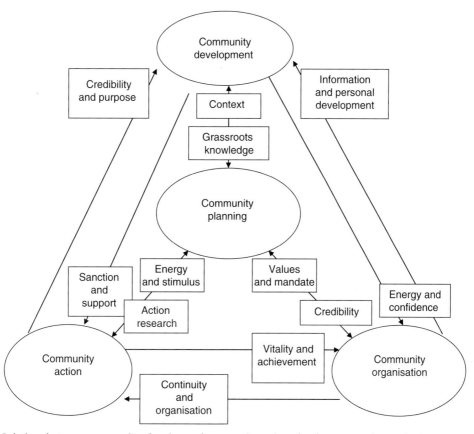

Figure 2.5 Relations between community planning and community action, development and organisation.

A. COMMUNITY ACTION

Joint action by groups of people to solve problems or achieve aims in matters of shared special concern, such as provision or loss of housing, traffic safety or public open space.

Contemporary community action often starts in campaigns against bad conditions or threats of worsening ones. Later, it may develop into positive movements to achieve better futures, which can make major contributions to community planning, as indicated in the earlier section on the roles of advocacy and negotiation. Activities of blocking streets, physical obstruction of bulldozers assembled for forest clearance or non-cooperation campaigns to impede village removal to make way for new plantation agriculture or dams are all familiar forms of community action. There are more positive versions: collective action is a pervasive and long-established aspect of most social life, extending from communal construction of buildings in traditional societies of West Africa and New Guinea to the

organisation of bulk food buying and urban farming in modern metropolitan milieu. Another example is the 'reverse strike', first practised by Danilo Dolci in Partinico in 1958, when he and his supporters insisted, in the face of local government prohibition, on repairing a public road to improve local conditions for a community suffering from severe problems of isolation (Dolci, 1959a). Dolci was to persevere with this approach for forty years. The rehabilitation of the Back o' the Yards neighbourhood in Chicago, discussed in Box 2.2 similarly demonstrated the power that communities can muster, as well as the close and supportive relations between community development, community action and community organisation.

Protest movements worldwide engage in community action on the basis of 'Where there's a will there's a wont!' Bridges have been halted in mid-construction. Schemes of massive urban clearance have been cancelled after initial government approval: the success of the Stop Spadina Freeway/Save our Cities

Coordinating Committee in Toronto in the 1970s led to preservation of the Annex as a vibrant mixed-use, inner-city suburb (Lemon, 1985); the defeat of the Covent Garden commercial redevelopment proposals in London a little earlier resulted in the present productive and agreeable mix of craft, art, cultural and tourist activities (Heywood, 1974); and the urban conservation of Woolloomooloo in Sydney in the 1970s resulted from collaboration between the Australian Builders Labourers Federation and local protest groups to defeat proposals for massive commercial redevelopment of the area (Harris, 1986). Community action continues to provide a potent source of energy in fields as diverse as forest conservation in Amazonia, opposition to dam construction in India and Australia (Roy, 1999; Meredith, 2008), habitat conservation in Rwanda and species protection worldwide (Greenpeace, 2010).

Although Alinsky (1971) recognised that community action often started as a reaction to threatening proposals, he saw this as the first step in a positive process of logical steps towards establishing durable organisational structures. Examples can be found in his own work in helping to found the Back o' the Yards Congress and the Industrial Areas Foundation. Other much longer-established examples can be found in the Indonesian island of Bali, where the community-based committees, or subaks, discussed in Chapter 3, work collaboratively to maintain and regulate the island's supplies of water for irrigation (Lansing, 1996). Elsewhere, the neighbourhood organisations and federations of Portland, Oregon channel the spirit of community action into more than a hundred local organisations recognised and supported by the city council (City of Portland, 2009).

Future directions for community action will be largely shaped by the inherent capacities of people and communities to take their own initiatives, which neither can nor should be ordained from outside or above. Future agendas and directions are therefore likely to be influenced by the style and pace of urban and rural change. The dynamic systems of capital investment prevalent in mixed economies are likely to produce a variety of proposals, which may have considerable merits in terms of profitable innovation but may contain the seeds of other unwelcome consequences, including threats to existing communities and environments and the loss of irreplaceable features of urban life, involving, for instance, the demolition of existing inner-city suburbs to make way for high-rise luxury residential and commercial extensions of the city centre, habitat destruction, dam building, airport expansion, stadium construction and many other such proposals, with unintended consequences that need to be examined to help decide if schemes should be enacted, modified or rejected. Community action offers invaluable feedback loops to scrutinise such proposals for both error and impact. Regular ways therefore need to be developed to acknowledge and incorporate its role into the regular processes of community planning.

B. COMMUNITY DEVELOPMENT

The creation of lasting beneficial change within a community by developing the energy and skills of local people to achieve their own psychological, social and material well-being and progress.

Community development combines ameliorative social work and proactive social policy, to improve the psychological, social, economic and political skills of individuals and groups so that they can exert more power over their own futures. It has become a respected and influential profession, providing higher education which draws upon contributions in practice and theory from fields as diverse as architecture, education, health, politics, public administration, planning and sociology (Freire, 1976; Osborne & Gaebler, 1992; Wates, 1996; Lewin, 1997; Ife, 2001; Wilkinson & Pickett, 2009). Many of its most celebrated examples demonstrate a transformational quality. Danilo Dolci, moving from action to development with the establishment of the Centre of Research and Initiatives for Full Employment, aimed to provide leadership and ideas for community renewal in Sicily (Dolci, 1959b).[xiv] Mohamed Yunus, whose work is described in Box 1.1 in Chapter 1, successfully established the Grameen Bank to provide seed money to assist 'the poorest of the poor' to work their own way out of penury and dependence. The bank's structure of groups, centres and branches was based on community development principles of mutual support and collaboration at each scale (Bornstein, 1998). Father Trevor Huddleston battled against apartheid and helped to develop ideals and leaders for the Anti-Apartheit movement in a sequence of roles as missionary in Sophiatown; teacher in St Peter's College in the Republic of South Africa; and leader as Bishop of Masasi in Tanganyika and Archbishop of the Indian Ocean in Mauritius (Huddleston, 1956; Brockman, 1994).

The less dramatic daily instances of dedicated community building which are being carried on by community development staff in urban and regional communities throughout the world are no less significant. One such example with which the author is personally familiar is the work of the New Farm

Neighborhood Center in inner Brisbane, one of a score of such community centres in the city. New Farm is a picturesque inner-city suburb, a metropolitan cul de sac, enclosed within a curve of the Brisbane River undergoing rapid social and economic change, including gentrification, city centre encroachment, massive urban redevelopment, road and bridge construction and demolition of old housing stock including nearly thirty boarding houses with a total capacity of three hundred bed spaces. In the face of these pressures, successive Neighborhood Center coordinators have mounted sustained campaigns of community development to maintain resilience and hold the balance between local needs and metropolitan opportunities. These activities have had numerous strands:[xv]

- affordable housing support and research, including brokerage, advocacy, research, programme planning and development of alliances;
- boarding house involvement, monitoring and support;
- community awards for local participation, personal contribution and community achievement;
- community organisation and advocacy, including a neighbourhood action group (NAG), incorporating people from marginalised groups, which developed into a more broadly based community action network (CAN);
- food collection and distribution programmes, including breakfast and coffee cart provision;
- personal development programmes involving learning skills, leadership, recreation, fitness, literacy, negotiation, reconciliation and planning;
- Politics in the Pub, promoting community communication and debate;
- review and participation in the preparation of the city council's urban renewal and development control plans for the neighbourhood;
- community support schemes, including:
  - Alcoholics Anonymous
  - breakfast and coffee carts
  - day care for the elderly
  - drug dependency support
  - housing referral
  - Meals on Wheels
  - mental health
  - youth support.

Many of the activities generate or draw upon community action initiatives in which the centre and its staff are also involved, such as Boarding House Vigils, conducted in 2003, when a group of thirty local community activists and people in housing stress conducted a walking tour of twelve recently closed boarding houses in the neighbourhood, pausing for a sung tribute and silent vigil at each site, before moving on to the next. A more recent initiative, conducted in March 2010, involved the launch of a programme of housing provision for homeless people in the adjacent central city area of Fortitude Valley. Entitled Under 1 Roof, the consortium of agencies draws together business groups, housing advocacy bodies, housing and social service providers, youth services, Mission Australia, New Farm Neighborhood Center and State government tenant advisory services with people in housing stress, to improve planning, provision and brokerage services and to promote a coordinated community response to the needs for shelter of the people of this stressed inner city suburb.

Current activities of community development are thus geared to meeting and ameliorating present pressing problems, by bringing together those in need and those with potentially relevant skills and available resources of funds, services and powers. Future directions are likely to build on this collaborative approach to expand balanced and bridging roles between communities and governments. All parties will need to share ownership of community development, in order to preserve the ethical and activist independence of its practitioners.

C. COMMUNITY ORGANISATION

An approach to community governance that aims to create institutions that can wield community power to achieve lasting goals of social justice and material advancement for particular areas and communities.

This is a radical political approach which can be used by organisers of both the left and the right to alter the balance of power within jurisdictions, in pursuit of such explicit objectives as citizen empowerment, economic justice, 'home rule' agendas or community involvement in decision-taking. While radical reformers like Saul Alinsky and Manuel Castells have helped to create people's and workers' organisations to promote inclusion, affluent US communities have sometimes organised community development corporations (CDCs) to exclude poor and minority groups, for opposite purposes (Miller, 1981). In New Zealand, the Netherlands, the United Kingdom and Portland, Oregon moderate reformers have also created structures to link community organisations to the political process, as described earlier in this chapter in the sections discussing participation.

Community organisation contributes the continuity and regularity that can promote positive roles for community action, and provide cumulative long-term direction for the changes sought by community development. Lack of it may have contributed to the stalling and diminution of the early promise of the work of both Danilo Dolci in Sicily and Robert Owen in the Clyde Valley in Scotland and Indiana in the United States. Both were inspired initiators of action and development, but may have lacked the conceptual or psychological capacity to pass on their contributions to self-regulating or autonomous organisations (Dolci, 1959a, b; Taylor, 1989). Other successful examples abound. Alinsky's own community organisation activities with Back o' the Yards Congress and the Industrial Area Foundation are examples. An even more significant example is the encouragement given by the Indian government over the past twenty years to develop thousands of village *panchayati* into responsible bodies able to advocate the interests of their village and urban communities and to undertake significant local initiatives (Mitra, 2001). This policy, enshrined in the 1993 Local Government Act, could help to build grassroots participation to sustain Indian democracy to face the challenges of internal opposition from Maoist insurgents and external competition from a geopolitically conscious China and its uneasy subcontinental neighbour, Pakistan.

A similar and even more radical experiment in local democracy is currently being pursued in Venezuela, where 19 000 'community councils', rapidly established in the wake of the 2006 Law of Community Councils, now dispense the equivalent of more than a billion US dollars annually.[xvi] Steve Ellner, a distinguished Venezuelan academic and political commentator, is cautiously optimistic about these community organisations, which appear to be genuinely popular and effective, and to be developing the kind of transparent organisational structure necessary to safeguard the rights of individuals and ensure opportunities for the criticism that is essential to maintain political health (Ellner, 2009).

More local examples of community organisation may be no less significant. Neighbourhood Watch committees of local people working together to ensure community surveillance of activities and to control crime in their neighbourhoods are common in most Western countries, and similar informal networks exist in all non-totalitarian societies. Another instance of community organisation at the local scale which has already been discussed (Box 2.3) is the successful role played by the appointment of a carefully constituted public corporation to run the Southbank Gardens site in Brisbane. This may offer useful lessons for other cities wishing to safeguard public interests in the redevelopment of increasingly common festival sites. Brisbane offers further examples in the work of the city's '4C' bodies (creek catchment coordinating committees), which consist of volunteers who take responsibility for maintaining the quality and upkeep of the city's crucial creek corridors.

Such organisations enjoy the advantages of spontaneity and responsiveness, but also face the associated dangers of manipulation and abuse of power.[xvii] The Chinese Cultural Revolution, with its years of licensed atrocities by the Red Guards (Chang, 1991) and the more recent repression and thuggery of President Mugabe's Veterans Militia in Zimbabwe are both examples of organic democracy and 'people's organisations' that have deteriorated into instruments of the worst kind of lawless and self-interested repression. Clearly, strong checks on authenticity and accountability are needed. The most recent impartial accounts of the workings of such systems in India and Venezuela give cause for qualified optimism (Ellner, 2009). In India, the reservations relate to the variable effectiveness of village *panchayati*, and in Venezuela to the government's tendency to arrest and arraign the most vocal opponents.

Community organisation and planning have much to gain from each other. Planning can offer directions and purpose to maintain the energy and activism of community organisations, and it is significant that the generally favourable view of commentators on Venezuelan community councils stems from their capacity to implement effective, beneficial and honest programmes of health, education and environmental improvements. Planning itself, however, can confer neither authenticity nor accountability. Those characteristics must be sought in the fields of politics, public administration and institutional theory and practice. People's organisations can only be securely defined as belonging to their members and communities if they contain transparent mechanisms of accountability and opportunities for criticism, as provided by the New Zealand community boards at regular local government elections, and by the provisions of the Portland neighbourhood organisations for regular and open nominations and elections of office holders.

The future direction of community organisations appears to lie in creating opportunities and support for local groups to be formed, gain official support, be integrated into governance structures as recognised partners and in return adopt transparent measures of accountability and representativeness. Such organisations can then constitute invaluable agencies and arenas for community planning at levels ranging from the local neighbourhood to the global network.

WHOLE COMMUNITIES

Each of these four fields of community activity is holistic in its own way – community action in participation, community development in seeking to work with the whole person, community organisation in involving, over time, whole communities and community planning in seeking to span the wide range of human activities, and all levels of governance. Their shared aim is to deal with whole communities composed of whole people, by coordinating activities at all levels of government: local, city, regional, state, national and global. We shall review these themes in the next two chapters, which consider the local scale of direct contact (Chapter 3) and the wider scales of communities of interest and interaction (Chapter 4), before returning, in Chapters 11 and 12, to devote more specific attention to community governance and its future directions.

Endnotes

i For several millennia, communities have been increasingly less bounded by interpersonal contact. The introduction of writing into the early civilisations of five thousand years ago extended the reach of communities of governance over whole regions and empires (Childe, 1976). The invention of printing later reinforced common community life throughout nation states and religious networks. Religious communities have also transcended international boundaries (for well over two thousand years in the case of Buddhism and for more than one thousand years in the cases of Christianity and Islam). Orders of friars, monks and nuns provide clear examples of international scale community planning.

ii George Monbiot (2003) argues that, since our daily lives are all incontestably shaped by global economic forces, the spirit of government by consent demands the progressive development of some form of worldwide accountability, linked to a system of democratic global governance. This would bring with it the prospect of new forms of coherent planning for the human community more just and sustainable than those currently imposed by global economics with their trends towards negative environmental impacts, global warming, economic polarisation, international division of labour and the triggering of military interventions as a result of direct foreign investment. These matters are discussed in more detail in Chapter 11.

iii The long history of participation dates back to ancient Greece and the institutions for Athenian democracy

where decisions were taken by the open vote of all free citizens and everyone was expected to participate in the military, judicial and cultural offices of the city (Kitto, 1967; Popper, 1998; Fox, 2005). Roman republicanism also involved forms of participation with balances of rights and responsibilities for each of the different classes of citizens, highlighted by short-lived attempts to extend these to more thorough-going democratic practices by reformers such as the Gracchae brothers and Spartacus. The speeches of Pericles, the *strategoi* of Athens in the fifth century BC and the writings of Cicero in the Rome of the first century BC make out powerful cases for the need for willing citizen participation to ensure a healthy society (Fox, 2005).

Later, as Europe's middle ages evolved into the Renaissance, the Lollards and Hussites both insisted that congregations should be able to participate in religious and civil life by understanding and reading for themselves the bible and the civil statutes (Tawney, 1961). The egalitarian skein of participation was well caught in the provocative question posed by Jack Cade: 'When Adam delved and Eve span, who was then the gentleman?' However it was not until the 16th century that the first signs of modern participatory theory surfaced in the assumptions of the otherwise gloomy ideas of Thomas Hobbes who developed the concept of a 'social contract' in which citizens sacrificed their 'natural rights' to the Leviathan of state power in return for protection of their rights to preservation of life, civil order and property (Russell, 1972). John Locke, writing 55 years later expanded this doctrine to a much wider definition of human rights including freedom of expression, right to elect representative governments, rights to religious toleration, and freedom from taxation without representation, principles that were to reappear not surprisingly in the American Declaration of Independence nearly ninety years later. At the same time Voltaire's Candide and Cunegonde travelled the world in search of transcendent truth only to return, battered and disabused of their former idealistic convictions to practice the simple joys of controlling their own activities as they tended their garden and participated in the regulation of their own lives and environment (Voltaire, 2006).

iv Well-known examples are the early enthusiasts who believed that by equipping themselves with mechanical wings they could fly from mountain tops, or zealots who proclaimed themselves members of master races, both of which illusions led to defeat, disaster and death, and thus prevented individual and regime survival.

v One of the earliest-recorded cases of this corruption of public opinion by wealthy demagogues happy to spend money in order to extend their personal influence and power is that of Cleon, the Athenian butcher and leader of the populist faction in late fourth century BC Athens, who spoke powerfully against Socrates in order to remove a political rival and thereby buttress his own position as a leader of the extreme democrats (Popper, 1998).

vi In democratic societies the idea of participation has become synonymous with willing involvement; though, of course, dictatorial and authoritarian regimes often attempt to achieve participation by coercion. For example in the Soviet Union of the mid-twentieth century (Solzhenitsyn, 1974; Bater, 1984), and in South Africa during the same period (Paton, 1959; Gordimer, 1981) workers were required to register as residents in a particular locality where they were employed. If they were found in areas for which they did not have a valid permit, under the hated Pass Laws, they were liable to be deported to overcrowded tribal homelands or, in the Soviet Union, sent to enforced labour camps in Siberia. In practice, such enforced participation resulted in conflict, abstention and finally civil unrest leading to ultimate regime change, as happened in both those countries. The aphorism describing relations between Polish workers and the Communist Party of the late seventies whereby workers say to the party 'You pretend to pay us and we pretend to work', neatly summarises this downward spiral. There is thus ample justification for now applying the term, 'participation' to mean willing and positive engagement.

vii See for instance the accounts of legal proceedings in the Timor-Leste courts, as recorded by the Judicial System Monitoring Programme (East Timor JSMP, 2010). Through the provision of independent legal analysis, court monitoring and community outreach activities JSMP aims to contribute to and evaluate the ongoing process of building a strong and sustainable justice system in Timor-Leste.

viii ONI coordinates the City of Portland's public participation activities through seven district coalitions, 95 neighbourhood associations, and 40 business district associations. In partnership with the Neighbourhood Resource Center, these community-based organisations engage thousands of dedicated volunteers participating in neighbourhood activities and governmental affairs. Working together, these organisations address land use and transportation issues, organise neighbourhood clean-ups and community celebrations, tackle crime prevention, business district marketing and a wide range of neighbourhood liveability issues. ONI coordinates its programmes through six centres funded through a combination of city general funds and intergovernmental agreements with other city, county, state and federal agencies to provide a wide range of information, referral and liveability services in their own neighbourhoods (City of Portland, 2009).

ix In Queensland, however, centralising tendencies, have led to radical mergers of local governments in preference to the preservation or development of new local grassroots organisations. This outcome may have been prompted by by increases in the scale of technology and the search for economies of scale as well as dislike of administrative complexity.

x Negotiation is required to mediate change within and between communities undergoing constant reshaping as founding members age or leave and are replaced by newcomers. As individuals constantly navigate their ways from past experiences towards future actions, they must also scan carefully the links between their own places and the many surrounding ones, which exert significant impacts upon them. Adjustments have to be made to meet economic, social and physical pressures from external environments, often themselves experiencing radical change. In these situations, the word 'negotiate' may mean both finding one's own way and seeking an acceptable outcome to differences with others. In established communities, this may often build on relationships from earlier phases of participation and communication that have established people's roles, and by inferences their reciprocal rights.

xi Social philosophers have produced theoretical models like John Rawls' 'initial position' in which people come to negotiations agreeing to draw a 'veil of ignorance' over their personal advantages on the basis that since no one can be sure what will happen to them in the future, they will prefer to protect the rights of the least advantaged. This, he argued, would lead them to accept a 'maximin' outcome of maximum possible benefit from minimum necessary risk (ranking alternatives upwards from their worst possible consequences) rather than to chance a 'minimax' one (seeking minimum inescapable risk from maximum possible benefit) (Rawls, 1971). Earlier liberal theorists suggested that by differentiating between 'self-regarding' and 'other-regarding' issues, it is possible to logically establish whose voice should be given greatest attention in each situation; and which situations require the impartial intervention of elected governments and which should be left to the discretion of individuals (Mill, 1983).

xii These classical processes of 'proposition and response', very similar to Karl Popper's 'conjecture and refutation', encourage the development of new solutions, which may generate the consent of former opponents by giving them a shared interest in the proposed outcome.

xiii Dolci's entry in Wikipedia (http://en.wikipedia.org/wiki/Danilo_Dolci) is full of interest for its current indication of the continuing significance of his practice and teaching:

'Dolci became convinced that the key to progress was through education. With the money he received for the Lenin Peace Prize in 1958, he founded the Centro Studie Iniziative per la Piena Occupazione (Center of Research and Initiatives for Full Employment) in Partenico, the village in the Palermo hinterland that became his home.

The centre was one of the most important examples of community development in Italy and especially in the south since the war. It became both a form of self-organisation of local communities and a training school for a generation of socially and politically committed young people, who found their cohesion as a group and attempted to construct a process of social aggregation through the methods and instruments of active non-violence ... His pedagogical methods, with their emphasis on social awareness and cultural interaction, won him a worldwide reputation, and a small but ardent following at home that took his ideas, over the years, across Sicily and into mainland Italy.'

xiv Many of these programmes were initiated by Fiona Caniglia, Neighbourhood Centre coordinator for a number of years in the 1990s, who still lives in New Farm and continues to contribute knowledge and energy to programmes to combat the area's mounting problems of homelessness.

xv The Law of Community Councils, enacted in April 2006, offers funding to neighbourhoods, once they are organised democratically and submit feasible projects to state agencies. Each council represents between 200 and 400 families who approve of priority projects in neighbourhood assemblies. As of March 2007, 19 500 councils have been registered. By planning, administering and financing public works and housing construction in their barrios, the community councils represent not only the government's most recent success in jump-starting popular participation but also a radical break with the past, when these activities were undertaken by the city, state, or national government (Ellner, 2009). Ellner comments that the communal councils have been wildly popular. Eight months after the law was passed, over 16 000 councils had already formed throughout the country. Twelve thousand of them had received funding for community projects – $1 billion total, out of a national budget of $53 billion. The councils have established nearly 300 communal banks, which have received $70 million for micro loans. In January 2007, the government announced a transfer of the equivalent of US$5 billion available for the use by communal councils. Thanks to such funds, the councils have implemented thousands of community projects, such as street pavings, sports fields, medical centers, and sewage and water systems.

xvi These dangers were memorably explored by George Orwell in his 1945 novel *Animal Farm*, with its animal organisations formed and led by the pigs who changed their ritual chant of 'Two legs bad – four legs good!' to 'Four legs bad – two legs good!' once they had taught themselves to walk on their hind legs, like their overthrown former rulers.

References

Alexander, C. (1979) *Notes on the Synthesis of Form*. Cambridge, MA, Harvard University Press.

Alinsky, S. (1971) *Reveille for Radicals*. New York, Bantam.

Alinsky, S. (1979) *Rules for Radicals*. New York, Bantam.

Arnstein, S. (1969) The Ladder of Participation. *Journal of the Association of American Planners* **July**.

Arrow, K. (1973) Values and collective decision making. In: E. S. Phelps (ed.), *Economic Justice*. Harmondsworth, Penguin Modern Economic Readings.

Bater, J. (1984) *The Soviet City: Ideal and reality*. London, Arnold.

Booker, C. (1980) *The Seventies: Portrait of a decade*. Harmondsworth, Penguin.

Bornstein, D. (1998) *The Price of a Dream: The story of the Grameen Bank*, Sydney, Grameen Books.

Brisbane City Council (2009) *Brisbane's Catchment Network: A regional voice for Brisbane's waterways*, http://www.brisbanecatchments.net.au/default.asp, accessed 30 May 2009.

Brockman, N. (1994) Trevor Huddleston. In: N. Brockman (ed.) *An African Biographical Dictionary*. New York, Grey House.

Castells, M. (1983) *The City and the Grassroots*. London, Arnold.

Chang, J. (1991) *Wild Swans: Three daughters of China*. London, Simon & Schuster.

Childe, G. (1976) *What Happened in History*. Harmondsworth, Penguin.

City of Portland (2009) *What is the Office of Neighborhood Involvement (ONI) and Neighborhood Involvement Directory?* http://www.portlandonline.com/oni/index, accessed 30 May 2009.

Cooperrider, D. (2008) *The Appreciative Inquiry Handbook*, San Francisco, Berrett-Koehler Publishers, [electronic resource].

Davidoff, P. (1973) Advocacy and pluralism in planning. In: A Faludi (ed.), *A Reader in Planning Theory*. Oxford, Pergamon.

Davies, J. (1972) *The Evangelistic Bureaucrat: Study of a planning exercise in Newcastle upon Tyne*. London, Tavistock.

Dawkins, R. (1976) *The Selfish Gene*. Oxford, Oxford University Press.

Dawkins, R. (2009) *The Ancestor's Tale*. Oxford, Oxford University Press.

Desmond, A., Moore, J. (1991) *Darwin*. London, Penguin.

Dolci, D. (1959a) *Report from Palermo*. New York, Orion Press, Inc.

Dolci, D. (1959b) *To Feed the Hungry*. London, McGibbon & Kee.

East Timor JSMP (2010) *Dili District Court acquits defendants in case of attack in Fatu-Ahi*, http://www.jsmp.minihub.org/, accessed 23 October 2010.

Ellner, S. (2009) *A new model with rough edges: Venezuela's community councils*, http://venezuelanalysis.com/analysis/4512, accessed 27 March 2010.

Engwicht, D. (1993) *EcoCity*. Sydney, Envirobooks.

Etzioni, A. (2004) *The Common Good*. Cambridge, Polity Press.

Etzioni, A., Volmert, A., Rothschild, E. (eds) (2004) *The Communitarian Reader: Beyond the essentials*. Lanham, MD, Rowman & Littlefield.

Faludi, A. (2005) The Netherlands: A culture with a soft spot for planning. In: B. Sanyal (ed.), *Comparative Planning Cultures*. New York, Routledge.

Faludi, A., Valk, A. van der (1996) Planners come out for the green heart. *Journal of Economic and Social Geography* **97**(5).

Fisher R., Ury, W. (1981) *Getting to YES: Negotiating agreement without giving in.* Boston, Houghton Mifflin.

Forester, J. (1989) *Planning in the Face of Power.* Berkeley, CA, University of California Press.

Forester, J. (1999) *The Deliberative Practitioner.* Cambridge, MA, MIT Press.

Forester, J. (2009) *Dealing with Differences: Dramas of mediating public disputes.* Oxford, Oxford University Press.

Forster, E. (1941) *Howard's End.* Harmondsworth, Penguin.

Forster, E. (1978) *A Room with a View.* Harmondsworth, Penguin.

Forster, E. (2005) *A Passage to India.* London, Penguin.

Fox, R. (2005) *The Classical World.* London, Penguin.

Freire, P. (1976) *Education: The practice of freedom.* London, Writers and Readers Publishing Cooperative.

Gordimer, N. (1981) *Burger's Daughter.* London, Penguin.

Greater Vancouver Regional District (1993) *Creating Our Future.* Vancouver, Author.

Greenpeace (2010) *Green actions speak louder than words,* http://www.greenpeace.org.uk/taxonomy/term/524, accessed 28 March 2010.

Habermas, J. (1976) *The Legitimation Crisis.* London, Heinemann.

Habermas, J. (1987) *The Theory of Communicative Action.* Cambridge, Polity Press.

Habermas, J. (1990) *Moral Consciousness and Communicative Action.* London, Heinemann.

Hall, P. (2002) *Cities of Tomorrow: An intellectual history of urban planning & design in the twentieth century.* Oxford, Blackwell Publishing Ltd.

Hamdi, N., Goethert, R. (1997) *Action Planning for Cities: A guide for community practice.* New York, John Wiley & Sons.

Hamilton, H. (1946) *History of the Homeland.* London, Allen & Unwin.

Hammond, S., Royal, C. (1997) *Lessons from the Field: Applying appreciative inquiry.* Plano, TX, Thin Book Publishing.

Hare, R. (1978) Coloured balloons and moral judgement. *Listener,* 16 March.

Harris, S. (1986) Social conservation in inner Sydney. *Queensland Planner* **26**: 3–4.

Healey, P. (1995) Planning through debate: The communicative turn in planning theory. In: S. Campbell, S. Fainstein (eds), *Readings in Planning Theory.* Maldon, MA, Blackwell Publishing Ltd.

Healey, P. (2006) *Collaborative Planning: Shaping places in fragmented societies.* New York, Palgrave Macmillan.

Healey, P. (2007) *Urban Complexity and Spatial Strategies: Towards a relational planning for our times.* London, RTPI/Routledge.

Hester, R. (1985) Subconscious landscapes of the heart. *Places* **2**(3).

Heywood, P. (1974) *Planning and Human Need.* Newton Abbott, David & Charles.

Heywood, P. (1990) Social justice and planning for the public interest. *Urban Policy and Research* **8**(2).

Heywood, P. (1995) The social context of tourism. *Landscape Australia,* 1995/3, http://www.aila.org.au/landscapeaustralia/index.htm.

Heywood, P. (1997) The emerging social metropolis. In: *Progress in Planning.* Oxford, Pergamon/Elsevier.

Heywood, W. (1910) *History of Perugia.* London, Methuen.

Homes and Communities Agency (2009) *Northmoor, Longsight, Manchester,* http://www.englishpartnerships.co.uk/northmoor, accessed 30 May 2009.

Homes and Communities Agency Academy (2009) *Showcase,* http://showcase.hcaacademy.co.uk/index.html, accessed 30 May 2009.

Homes and Communities Agency Academy (2010) *Homes & Communities Awards 2010,* http://skills.homesandcommunities.co.uk/awards, accessed 25 March 2010.

Huddleston, T. (1956) *Naught for Your Comfort.* London, Collins.

Huntington, S. (1996) *The Clash of Civilizations and the Remaking of World Order.* New York, Simon & Schuster.

Ife, J. (2001) *Community Development: Community-based alternatives in an age of globalisation.* Frenchs Forest, New South Wales, Pearson Education.

Jacobs, J. (1961) *The Death and Life of Great American Cities.* Harmondsworth, Penguin.

Jephcott, P., Robinson, H. (1971) *Homes in High Flats: Some of the human problems involved in multi-storey housing.* Edinburgh, Oliver & Boyd.

Kitto, H. (1967) *The Greeks.* Harmondsworth, Penguin.

Knaap G., Nelson A. (1992) *The Regulated Landscape: Lessons on state land use planning from Oregon.* Cambridge, MA, Lincoln Institute of Land Policy.

Koestler, A. (1971) *The Case of the Midwife Toad.* New York, Random House.

Kropotkin, P. (1939) *Mutual Aid.* London, Penguin, (first published 1899).

Kropotkin, P. (1974) *Fields, Farms and Workshops of Tomorrow.* London, Allen & Unwin, (first published 1899).

Lacey, J., Heywood, P. (2009) The ethics of regional water planning: Planning and management of water resources in a growth region. In: T. Yigitcanlar (ed.), *Sustainable Urban and Regional Infrastructure: Technology, planning and management.* New York, IGI Global.

Landcare Australia (2009) *Landcare Partners,* http://www.landcareonline.com.au/, accessed 30 May 2009.

Lansing, J. (1996) *Priests and Programmers: Technology of power in the engineered landscape of Bali.* New York, Princeton University Press.

Lefebvre, H. (1991) *The Production of Space.* Oxford, Blackwell Publishing Ltd.

Lemon, J. (1985) *Toronto since 1918.* Toronto, Lorimer.

Lewin, K. (1997) *Resolving Social Conflicts and Field Theory in Social Science.* Washington, American Psychological Association.

Local Government New Zealand (2009) *Community Boards,* http://www.lgnz.co.nz/lg-sector/community-boards/index.html, accessed 30 May 2009.

Locke, J. (1993) *Two Treatises on Government.* London, Cambridge University Press.

McLuhan, M. (1964) *Understanding Media: The extensions of man.* New York, McGraw-Hill.

Magnussen, M. (ed.) (1990) *Chambers Biographical Dictionary.* Edinburgh, Chambers.

Margerum, R. (1999) Getting past yes: From capital creation to action. *Journal of the American Planning Association* **65**(2): 181–92.

Meredith, P. (2008) To paradise and beyond. *Griffith Review* **20**: 62–84.

Mill, J. (1983) *Utilitarianism: On liberty and considerations on representative government.* London, Dent, (first published 1861).

Miller, G. (1981) *Cities by Contract.* Cambridge, MA, MIT Press.

Mitra, S. (2001) Making local government work: Local elites, panchayati raj and governance in India. In: A. Kohli (ed.), *The Success of India's Democracy.* Cambridge, Cambridge University Press.

Monbiot, G. (2003) *The Age of Consent*, http://www. monbiot.com/archives/2003/10/13/the-age-of-consent-a-manifesto-for-a-new-world-order/, accessed 13 October 2010.

More, T. (1965) *Utopia.* Harmondsworth, Penguin, (first published 1516).

Newman, O. (1973) *Defensible Space: People and design in the violent city.* London, Architectural Press.

Orwell, G. (1945) *Animal Farm.* Harmondsworth, Penguin.

Osborne, D., Gaebler, T. (1992) *Reinventing Government.* New York, Penguin.

Oxfordshire Climate Exchange (2008) *Wolvercote: A low carbon village*, http://climatex.org.articles/lo-carb-communities/ wolvervcote-low-carbon-village/, accessed 30 July 2008.

Ozawa, C. (ed.) (2003) *The Portland Edge.* Washington, Island Press.

Paton, A. (1959) *Cry the Beloved Country.* London, Jonathon Cape.

Popper, K. (1972) *Conjectures and Refutations.* Oxford, Oxford University Press.

Popper, K. (1998) *The Open Society and Its Enemies: Vol 2: Marx and Hegel*, 2nd edn. London, Routledge & Kegan Paul, (first published 1947).

Punter, J. (2003) *The Vancouver Achievement: Urban planning and design.* Vancouver, UBC Press.

Queensland Government Department of Housing (2009) *About Community Renewal*, http://www.communityrenewal. qld.gov.au/aboutus/, accessed 30 May 2009.

Queensland Government, Department of Infrastructure & Planning (2008) *North Bank*, http://www.dip.qld.gov.au/ projects/residential-and-accommodation/north-bank, accessed 30 May 2009.

Rawls, J. (1971) *A Theory of Justice.* Oxford, Oxford University Press.

Ridley, M. (1997) *The Origins of Virtue.* London, Penguin.

Roy, A. (1999) *The Cost of Living.* London, Flamingo.

Russell, B. (1971) *The Problems of Philosophy.* London, Oxford University Press.

Russell, B. (1972) *A History of Western Philosophy.* New York, Simon & Schuster, (first published 1945).

Sandercock, L. (1975) *Cities for Sale: Property, politics and urban planning in Australia.* London, Heinemann.

Schon, D. (1983) *The Reflective Practitioner: How professionals think in action.* New York, Basic Books.

Skeffington, A. (1969) *Report of the Committee on Public Participation in Planning.* London, Ministry of Housing & Local Government/HMSO.

Solzhenitsyn, A. (1974) *The Gulag Archipelago 1918–1956: An experiment in literary investigation: I–II*, (trans. T. P. Whitney). New York, Harper & Row.

Susskind, L., Cruikshank, AJ. (1987) *Breaking the Impasse: Consensual approaches to resolving public disputes.* New York, HarperCollins.

Tawney, R. (1961) *Religion and the Rise of Capitalism.* London, Penguin, (first published 1926).

Taylor, A. (1989) *Vision of Harmony.* Oxford, Oxford University Press.

Voltaire (2006) *Candide and other stories*, (trans. R. Pearson). Oxford, Oxford University Press.

Ward, C. (1973) *Anarchy in Action.* London, Allen & Unwin.

Ward, C. (1974) *Tenants Take Over.* London, Architectural Press.

Wates, N. (1996) *Action Planning: How to use planning weekends and urban design action teams to improve your environment.* London, The Prince of Wales's Institute of Architecture.

Webber, M. (1964) The urban place and the non-place urban realm. In: M. Webber (ed.), *Explorations into Urban Structure.* Philadelphia, Pennsylvania University Press.

Wilkinson, R., Pickett, K. (2009) *The Spirit Level: Why more equal societies almost always do better.* London, Penguin.

3 Local Communities of Place and Contact

Communities may be defined as groups of people who experience and acknowledge significant links, expectations and responsibilities towards each other. They do not need to be neighbours, but they do need to share neighbourly feelings, which may be based on shared spaces, realms of interaction or interests. Six scales of communities of these sorts can be identified in the contemporary world, ranging from the local to the global. This chapter focuses on local communities of place and contact, which are the most numerous of all the six types. Assuming the average upper population size of three thousand, which is adopted in Table 3.1, there may be as many as two million identifiable local communities throughout the world, making them a most significant element of human life. The characteristics and significance of the remaining five types of communities (based more on shared interests and levels of interaction and less on regular physical contact) are discussed in Chapter 4. In order to explore the social, physical, ethical, planning and political aspects of the local communities on which it is focused, this chapter is organised into the following five sections:

- social and organisational characteristics of local communities;
- the physical forms of communities;
- spatial justice;
- planning places;
- community participation and governance.

The chapter concludes with a consideration at the durability of local communities of place and contact.

The success of local communities depends largely upon how far their regular personal contact develops into cooperation, and coexistence evolves into sustainable community organisation. This chapter proceeds from a review of these characteristics through consideration of different measures that may promote their success to develop general principles for effective and integrated local community planning.

Social and organisational characteristics of local communities

CONTACT AND COOPERATION

The capacity to cooperate has survival value with roots deep in the history of human evolution. Evidence of

Community Planning, First Edition. Phil Heywood.
© 2011 Phil Heywood.
Published 2011 by Blackwell Publishing Ltd.

such cooperation has been traced as far back as Neolithic farming villages by Lewis Mumford (1961) and to medieval market towns, out of which the modern European city evolved, by Peter Kropotkin (1939).[i] In India, Mahatma Ghandi and his followers identified village cooperation as the constructive core of Hindu culture and proposed on this basis a model of village democracy, which is still proving very influential.

This spirit of cooperation is also well expressed in recent developments of economic and social theory which started to attract increasing attention at the end of the twentieth century. 'Associational economics', discussed by Cooke and Morgan (1998), draws on analysis of the successful network economies of Emilia Romagna in northern Italy, Baden-Württemberg in western Germany and the Basque region of northern Spain to show how shared support of funding and training facilities for numerous small enterprises has assisted flexibility and productive dynamism in times when volatility in the global market threatened local

Table 3.1 Bases, scope and scales of communities

Scale	Population size and range	Nature of links, expectations and responsibilities
Local	100–3000	Opportunities for regular personal contact within shared physical spaces
City/District	10 000–1 million	Exchange of goods and services
Region/Metropolis	0.5 million–10 million	Shared social, economic and environmental spaces
National	1 million–1000 million	Common culture, interests and laws
Supranational	100 million–2000 million	Capacity for mutually beneficial joint action
Global	1000–10 billion people (by 2050)	Common interests

economies elsewhere. The theme of cooperating locally in order to compete globally is particularly relevant as national economies struggle to emerge from the current global financial crisis with its associations with the competitive excesses of profit-seeking by remote financial operators. Cooke and Morgan (1998) also draw attention to the collaborative achievements of the Mondragon Cooperative Corporation (MCC), which they describe as Spain's most successful economic performer since the 1980s. (These aspects are discussed in more detail in Chapter 9.)

Economic cooperation is a widespread but sometimes elusive theme of contemporary community life, with links to social and human capital. City farms, bulk-buying and workers' cooperatives like the MCC are prominent examples. The continuing importance of community societies and clubs dedicated to the human skills of singing, dancing, play and performance has been identified by Putnam (2000) as crucial to the continuing success of the societies of Tuscany, Veneto and Emilia Romagna, and as essential for any future recovery of community life in the United States. Nevertheless, other interpretations extol the economic virtues of competition, so that the roles of cooperation are strongly contested issues in both developed and developing countries.

The International Monetary Fund and the World Bank, for instance, advocate competition rather than cooperation, and support direct foreign investment rather than communal land ownership (Friere & Yuen, 2004; Heywood, 2006). World Bank support for the privatisation of water provision has favoured development of the situation where over 300 million customers in 100 countries now depend upon private international companies such as Veolia from France, RWE-AG from Germany and Thames Water from England, who made global profits of over 12 billion in 2002, leaving local communities powerless to influence prices or distribution systems (Barlow & Clarke, 2004).[ii] By contrast, the ancient system of Balinese water management, discussed later in this chapter, continues to operate well, both maintaining in local hands the complex pattern of irrigation canals and water distribution and reinforcing the bonds of social solidarity which underlie Balinese community life (Lansing, 1996; Suarja & Thyssen, 2003).

Other examples are more geared to transformation than management. For instance, the Grameen Bank, the micro credit network described in Box 1.1 in Chapter 1, has built a multi-layered, multi-billion-dollar organisation with over four million members in a period of thirty years (Bornstein, 1997). Mohamed Yunus, the Grameen founder, explains that the system was designed to replace 'financial collateral' of traditional banking by 'social collateral' of established community life in order to promote collaboration amongst 'the poorest of the poor' (particularly landless peasant women) in Bangladesh, which is one of the world's poorest, most heavily populated and environmentally threatened countries (Yunus, 1998). While these individual successes do not mean that collaboration is poised to succeed competition in the conduct of global community life, they do suggest that cooperation can make, and is increasingly making increasingly significant contributions to balance competition in local economic life and promote distributional justice and efficiency.

ORGANISATION

Many of these examples of social and economic cooperation have flowered into cases of successful community organisation. The collaborative spirit of Howard's garden city associations has re-emerged in initiatives such as the UK's eco towns and those community development corporations (CDCs) of the United States which are dedicated to affordable housing and job creation (Community Wealth Org, 2010). By 2006, there were 4600 of these CDCs, promoting community life and prosperity, especially among disadvantaged black communities. Since they first emerged in the late 1960s as part of President Johnson's

Great Society programme, they have produced nearly a quarter of a million private sector jobs and over half a million units of affordable housing. They are currently developing 86 000 units of affordable housing and nearly nine million square feet of commercial and industrial space a year.

Amitai Etzioni (2006), who is often seen as a spokesperson for the Communitarian Movement in the United States, widens the ambit of community activism to include organised religion. He interprets the performance of an increasing range of service roles by community organisations as a means to balance the centralising tendencies of nationalism in contemporary life. He cites 'charitable choice', introduced under the 1996 Welfare Reform Act, as a significant example of how religious and other organisations can expand their social activities to create new centres of local power to balance the role of the State (Etzioni, 2006). Charitable choice encourages states to provide funds for the provision of social services by religious and other charitable groups rather than delivering those services themselves.

Across the Atlantic, Britain's experiment with 'third way' politics has encouraged the development of social and not-for-profit enterprises to take over some of the State's traditional service roles. It was inspired by a similar philosophy of 'not rowing but steering'. Advocated by activists like the Reverend Andrew Mawson (2008) and academics like Anthony Giddens (1994), these ideas were enthusiastically taken up by New Labour's policymakers, and seem to have entered the mainstream of shared political doctrine. Andrew Mawson is a United Reformed minister who took over the derelict East End parish of Bromley-by-Bow in London in the late 1980s and set about a process of community development involving social entrepreneurship, assisting communities and individuals to help themselves to renew their own lives and those of their communities. He founded the United Kingdom Community Action Network to promote the concept and support new initiatives around the country (Australian Broadcasting Commission, 2000).

This approach builds on earlier Fabian and Syndicalist ideas already being applied in the many thousands of housing associations providing over a million dwellings under the umbrella of the National Housing Corporation (now the Housing and Communities Agency). Chapter 2 discussed one recent award-winning example of the community organisational aspects of this in the inner Manchester locality Northmoor, where the Manchester Methodist Housing Association (now part of the Great Places Housing Association working across the entire north-western region of the United Kingdom) provided 35 new homes in an area previously rejected as a place for families to live (English Partnerships, 2009). Such approaches involve collaboration between government, voluntary and private sectors at a number of levels of community scale, both regional and local. The intention of the Homes and Communities Agency and the HCA Academy is to encourage maximum local ownership and participation in such schemes.

English Partnerships is working with a number of key partners and has made £2.4 million of funding available to support the acquisition strategy and the refurbishment and development programme.

Community organisation is also a major issue in developing nations. In India the *panchayati raj* system, long advocated by the Gandhian movement, has been formally integrated into Indian National legislation under the 1992 seventy-third amendment to its constitution, giving constitutional and institutionalised status to a three-tiered system with *panchayati* at the village, block and district levels. The amendment also stipulated that all panchayat members be selected for five-year terms in elections supervised by state election commissions (Mitra, 2001). These democratically elected *panchayati*, or village councils, have appropriate planning and implementation powers. In Bali, the comprehensive framework of subaks has been developed over a thousand years to manage water supply and irrigation. Over 1500 local groups, each with an average of 200 members, administer areas of a little under one square kilometre each. In all 1500 subaks are responsible for 90 000 hectares of irrigated land. Suarja and Thyssen (2003) report that all members of the local water-consuming communities are members of the 'general assembly', which appoints a board to decide distribution of water rights and responsibilities as well as taking on other roles in local agricultural administration. It is significant that although this system grew out of the traditional Hindu culture of the island, membership is open to all water users, whichever religion they practise or whenever they acquired their water rights. As open-edged communities, the subaks provide a highly relevant model for the contemporary world where community membership is often subject to rapid change.

The physical forms of communities

Such patterns of cooperation and organisation do much to shape the physical form of communities where people live, meet and make the contacts that mould their daily lives. Despite varying in scale and size, they have recognisably similar social and physical structures, normally including a central focus, containing shared activities and uses such as a market, wayside stalls or shops, some form of school, a religious centre or shrine and often access to public or community transport. Centres are connected to surrounding dwellings by networks of paths or streets. This centre, in turn, is normally traversed by one or more roads leading to other similar centres of neighbouring communities on the same, or a greater, scale. Such forms have evolved to promote ease of movement, convenient focus and mix of uses. The way that such communities actually work is also influenced by characteristics such as density, structure, grain, permeability, mix and meeting points. These both reflect the way people live and influence the future form and quality of their lives. Being matters that can be affected by conscious choice, they can become very significant levers in planning to improve community life.

If we assume an average community size of around 3000 people, rather more than two million communities will make up the human family of the twenty-first century world with its population approaching seven billion people.[iii] In the urban communities, the population densities may vary from as much as 1000 per hectare in the crowded inner-cities of developing nations, such as Kolkata, Mumbai, Wuhan, Hong Kong and São Paulo, to as little as twenty to the hectare in the low-density affluent suburbs of cities such as Houston, Perth and Los Angeles of the more developed nations. In the rural village communities, densities will also tend to be quite high, as much as 100 people to the hectare as populations cluster to conserve productive land and resources and promote security.

DENSITY

Density is an issue that often concerns local communities and individual residents and families. Collective and individual interests may clash. Established authorities and governments may favour increased densities to promote commercial prosperity and the convenient provision of common services. Individual households and families, on the other hand, often express their consumer preference by favouring more generous provision of personal and family space, privacy and amenity. Actual densities vary widely between and within different cultures. In the one- and two-storey residential areas of the souks, kasbahs and bustees of northern Africa and southern Asia, intensively developed networks of courtyard dwellings result in densi-

ties of around 100 dwellings to the hectare, while in the quarter-acre blocks of New World suburbs, urban sprawl and large private gardens produce much lower densities of ten dwellings to the hectare (Newman & Kenworthy, 1989). Population densities vary accordingly. For instance, Dhaka, the capital of Bangladesh, accommodates its population of approximately twelve million on roughly 1400 sq km, at an average density of 8500 people to the square kilometre or 85 people to the hectare, whereas Brisbane, a typical low-density New World city, accommodates a population of just over one million people on a similar area of approximately 1200 sq km at an average density of approximately ten people to the hectare, or less than one-eighth of the population density of Dhaka.

However, this is not purely a distinction between more and less developed communities. In Manhattan, with its densely packed and often high-rise development, average population per hectare rises to as much as 261, three times the Dhaka average and 26 times the Brisbane one. In New York City, overall, the average density of 26 429 people per square mile is 103 people per hectare, which it is interesting to note is about 20% higher than Dhaka.[iv] For comparison, the density in San Francisco, the next most densely developed city in the USA, is about 65 people per hectare (Ginsburg, 2003). This is clearly an issue where policy, land values and technology can exert major influences. There are basic needs involved, including access to private and public open space for young children to exercise, day lighting standards for dwellings and adequate scale of communities to promote ease of access to primary schools, local shops and public transport. Communities' attitudes towards high-rise development, solar access, traffic generation and choice of form of transport, whether active, private or public will also be significant. Choices are available (Adams, 2009). Work recently published for Melbourne (discussed further in Chapter 10) suggests that remarkably high densities can be achieved by selectively concentrating medium-rise development, of 6–8 storeys, along radial corridors with good access to public transport, in similar ways to that which has evolved in many European cities over the twentieth century, such as Milan, Berlin and Paris.

In considering residential densities, account also needs to be taken of emerging population patterns. For several decades, throughout the developed world, communities will continue to age as baby boomer generations are succeeded by ones with smaller families. In Australia, for instance, more than half of all households already consist of two or fewer people, and this proportion is steadily increasing. As a result, there is scope in new schemes to increase the proportion of small dwellings, including attached and medium-rise apartments. Even so, this may not result in dramatic increases in overall population densities, because of reduced average household sizes.

SETTLEMENT STRUCTURE

The physical structure of local communities directly affects many aspects of our daily lives: how much contact we have with neighbours, whether we walk, cycle, drive or bus to work, play or school, and whether we drive to a large supermarket chain or shop locally. Structure, in turn, includes the factors of grain, mix, permeability and meeting places. 'Grain' is the descriptive term that has come to be used for the scale of the basic building blocks which go to make up settlements. Fine grain consists of short streets with many intersections, many small local parks and play areas, and a tendency for many buildings to be at the human scale. Pedestrian movements are then spread fairly evenly throughout whole districts, encouraging a mix of small shops and other uses. Coarse grain, on the other hand, results from large-scale elements, such as big apartments blocks, whether in terms of height, bulk or basic floor plan. Jane Jacobs (1961) memorably castigated coarse-grained open space plans in many major America cities, contrasting the sociable virtues of small local open spaces with the array of large public spaces, proudly created in many great American cities, which generated 'border vacuums' and provided such extensive areas away from the protective scrutiny of 'eyes on the street' that she catalogued them as 'Rapists Parks, Perverts Parks, Mugging Parks, and Misdemeanour Open Spaces'.

Mixed uses can thrive where there is a fine grain of physical form because access and custom are both encouraged. However, rigid and doctrinaire segregation of activities separating residential, commercial, home office and small-scale craft production can discourage the development of a lively street life and frustrate the natural evolution of new activities within communities. Members of the 'creative class' identified by Richard Florida (2005) both like and need the variety and opportunity which mixed uses and positive attitudes towards new development can provide. These characteristics enable them to meet easily and casually and exchange the ideas that can help develop new approaches and products.

'Permeability' is another convenient word that captures the movement characteristics of fine-grained communities, where people experience a sense of easy flow along a choice of routes, to reach a variety of interesting destinations. Lanes and arcades can provide this, while walled and gated communities destroy informal contact. It is not difficult to frame planning regulations that will enhance permeability in new developments and prevent the development of coarse-grained new suburbs, which would result in physical exclusion. For instance, a rule that no new development may receive planning permission if any residence is more than 50 metres from a public right of way would effectively prevent the establishment of disruptive walled estates and encourage permeability.

Where permeability provides the paths, meeting places offer the destinations. There are many ways to develop the focus points round which communities can build a strong sense of the image and ownership of their localities. Small portions of streets may be closed to traffic or pavements widened to create little squares, pocket parks or play areas. New public spaces can occupy, for instance, one corner of a significant road intersection. Landmarks need not be large or dominating features. Often their cultural significance rather than their bulk creates a sense of place for residents and regular users, as with the celebrated small statue of the little mermaid which sits on a rock in Copenhagen's harbour, or the small bronzes statues of deer and other native animals that are placed at intervals along the pavements of the main street linking Portland's city centre to the state university campus. Together, grain, permeability, mix of uses and meeting points can give localities the spatial qualities that endear them to their residents. However, the other side to these tactical concerns of local character involves strategic issues of distributional justice. These extend to the spatial justice and equality, which are discussed in the next section.

Spatial justice

At the global scale, landless peasants and others whose property has been rendered worthless by desiccation are increasingly setting out on perilous journeys across deserts and oceans to seek employment in cities such as Los Angeles, San Diego, Frankfurt, Hamburg, Paris, London and Melbourne. Those who reach their destinations frequently experience poor living conditions and quality of life relative to longer established residents in their countries of arrival, with the most acute problems including isolation and alienation as well as standards of physical shelter and services.

Host communities in the pioneer Western industrial societies may themselves experience major problems of historic concentrations of densely packed, inadequately serviced and economically decaying inner areas, into which the special difficulties and needs of immigrants may now be additionally injected. Notable examples occur in London's Brixton and Tower Hamlets, Glasgow's Easterhouse, Manchester's Droylsden and Cheetham Hill and Liverpool's inner ring of relative deprivation in suburbs such as Toxteth and Walton (Yates, 2009). Such communities may, of course, possess resources of social capital and community spirit producing, for instance, the irrepressible music of the silver and brass bands and choirs of the old Yorkshire and Lancashire mining and mill towns of the United Kingdom, and of Detroit's Motown bands and performers. Nevertheless, the life chances there are often shadowed by poor opportunities in education, health and work, compounded by the stigma of social segregation. In the 'rustbelt' communities of the north-east of the United States, for instance, places such as Detroit and Cleveland severely affected by the collapse of the automobile industry are now experiencing high rates of unemployment and increased competition for jobs.

Planned communities may face different problems. Many of these localities resulted from the confluence of two unhealthy streams of mid-twentieth century administration: the assumption of some administrators that disadvantaged individuals and families should be conveniently concentrated in areas where they would not offend the sensibilities of more successful neighbours; and the authoritarian design principles of modernist architects, which favoured construction of corridors and clumps of high-rise dwelling blocks. These sprouted in places like Tower Hamlets in East London, Manchester's notorious Oldham and Rochdale Roads, Liverpool's Scotland Road and the infamous Pruitt–Igoe development of St Louis (Newman, 1973; Heywood, 1974; Gray, 1976). There are countless others.

Other variants, reflecting the more traditional values of the garden city, resulted in well-intentioned and carefully shaped swathes of public housing, such as Manchester's Wythenshawe, Liverpool's Kirby and numerous council estates scattered throughout London County Council's and Birmingham City's middle suburbs. Although decent and carefully designed, these places were socially segregated, sterile and lacking in social mix and activation. They gave rise to feelings of alienation and despondency, often summarised in the generalised phrase 'new town blues'. These reactions were cogently expressed in the social realism and stinging rhetoric of the 'angry young men' of Britain's plays, novels and films of the 1950 and 1960s, including John Osborne's *Look back in Anger* (1956) Alan Sillitoe's *Saturday Night and Sunday Morning* (1958) and Stan Barstow's *A Kind of Loving* (1960), protesting against drab environments and utilitarian community life.

In extreme cases, these places of planned segregation deteriorated to form 'sink estates'. In places such as Pruitt–Igoe and Easterhouse, groups of people such as single-parent families, immigrants, long-term unemployed and ex-prisoners, who were unwanted as neighbours by economically and socially more successful groups, were concentrated in such socially isolating high-rise public housing estates, whose fate was sealed when they were subjected to sensationalised labelling and given unsavoury reputations by the mass media.

SPATIAL INEQUALITY AS THE PHYSICAL EXPRESSION OF THE FREE MARKET

It is, however, unfair to blame physical inequality solely on designers and administrators. The free market system itself has implications for the social and physical organisation of cities that were well understood and explored a century ago by the theorists of the Chicago School of Urban Sociology. They recognised that as the city's population and economy grew and central business districts expanded, the original occupants of the inner suburbs, who mainly consisted of families of workers employed in the manufacturing activities of the inner city and living in rented housing, would be forced to seek cheap new accommodation on the urban fringe and commute back into their work places. This sequence would give rise to a rippling process of 'invasion and succession' driven by a continuing but irregular escalation in the values of land and dwellings (Burgess, 1925). This process of property acquisition, demolition and reconstruction would create a constantly changing and unstable 'zone in transition', where short-term rental housing would be mixed with derelict building and land assembly to prepare the ground for the next phase of expansion of the central business district. Later, further waves of displaced working families and new migrants would be drawn to new rings of low-cost housing on the expanding fringes of the city.

These outer suburbs were often dominated by public housing, created with the best of intentions. Rents were low and tenure was relatively secure, but the new estates tended to suffer from poor accessibility, standardised design and lack of physical variety. They supplied most of what was necessary for survival, but little that was sufficient to the development of lively and productive community life. Thus free market economics and rather perfunctory administration of public bureaucracies combined to produce two forms of spatial inequality. On the one hand, there were decaying inner areas like the 'Back o' the Yards' described by Alinsky (1971) in the inner Chicago of the 1930s, with investors and the area's bankers waiting for the next wave of redevelopment opportunities to complete the process of 'invasion and succession'. On the other, there were the soulless and stigmatised reception areas of social exclusion typified by Anthony Burgess in his celebrated novel *Clockwork Orange*, the film of which was set in the Greater London council housing estate of Thamesmead.

THE STRATEGIES OF SOCIAL JUSTICE

Global influences on local conditions are especially strong in matters of social justice. The international division of labour continues to assemble new urban communities of workers to manufacture industrial components to power the global economy. In cities like Shenzhen, Mumbai, São Paulo and Mexico City, conditions may vary from the sterile to the squalid. The global division of labour may seem a large issue to be tackled by such localised means as community planning. Nevertheless, the dedicated action of voluntary bodies such as Oxfam, World Vision, Care and other global social justice organisations are tackling these manifest injustices through campaigns such as Fair Trade, water provision projects and squatter upgrading schemes. Other organisations like the Asian Development Bank and the Japan International Cooperation Agency are also playing their part with support for large infrastructure investment programmes to improve living conditions in rapidly expanding cities.

Technology transfer is another widely advocated strategy, encouraging the establishment of Western-owned enterprises in the hope that the development of skills will stimulate local economic development to support such outcomes. This has clearly achieved some success with the 'young tiger' economies of eastern and southern Asia, such as Thailand, Taiwan and South Korea, and is now being adopted in parts of Vietnam and Indonesia. The World Bank actively encourages direct foreign investment. Nevertheless, there are well-justified concerns that the long-term effects of such policies may generate economic dependency, political influence and even military interventions (Heywood, 2006). Worldwide, more collaborative arrangements based on national government agencies and local enterprises cooperating through contracts with international partners are becoming more common and appear to offer a more secure and productive long-term approach. In China, Malaysia, Taiwan and Korea, government agencies and private enterprises are increasingly forming their own international trading partnerships.

The spatial injustices of the international division of labour are also entrenched by the mechanisms of world debt regulated by the International Monetary Fund and the World Trade Organization (Monbiot, 2003). The increasing support for debt redemption (on the basis that the debtor nations have already many times paid off their original loans) could cause a significant improvement in spatial justice within the global community. Debt redemption could offer a level playing field; Fair Trade would provide even-handed rules; and local ownership and control of enterprises would ensure the presence of local players in the home team.

BIDONVILLES AND SHANTY TOWNS

For those driven to international migration to escape from such life-threatening conflicts such as those affecting Sudan, Somalia, Congo, Iraq or Afghanistan, or in search of a more secure livelihood, the immediate prospects may be ones of acute spatial inequality in their adopted countries of adoption. Bidonvilles[v], shanty towns, sink estates and crowded rental accommodation in physically decaying terrace housing are their most likely reception areas. Examples are the older areas of declining industrial towns like Oldham, Burnley and Bradford in the United Kingdom, parts of Lille, Marseilles and the old Moselle Valley industrial towns in France and shanty towns on the fringes of Madrid and Milan (Lucassen, 2005; Reuters, 2009a, b). The threat of clearance and forcible removal constantly hangs over their heads, and in the present the communities suffer from social and physical exclusion, and very poor housing and environment. Despite polices of dispersion in the United Kingdom, immigrant communities have become concentrated in such old northern industrial towns, where feelings of alienation have given rise to outbreaks of violence. In 2001, race riots involved Pakistani and other Muslim communities in repeated battles with police riot squads for nearly a week.

Part of the difficulty faced by newcomers in securing suitable housing and integrating into new communities results from the sense of exclusion and disadvantage already felt by long-standing members of the host community, who themselves lack satisfactory and socially desirable housing. Throughout Western

Europe, many migrants are drawn to such declining industrial communities, already afflicted by strained services and insufficient jobs. Massive clearance and re-housing programmes tried as solutions to the problems of older initial areas have been found wanting (Heywood, 1974; Hall, 2002). They are not only economically infeasible, socially insensitive and culturally destructive. They are also environmentally wasteful, in an age rightly concerned with sustainability. However, the polar opposite of leaving the solution to the areas' problems to market forces would do nothing to help current residents or future seekers of affordable accommodation: it would merely continue the cycle of invasion and succession to produce constant social conflict and family stress.

In the Netherlands, public housing provision to help integrate immigrants from Surinam and Sumatra from the 1960s and 1970s onwards has been, on balance, more purposive and successful, based on the traditionally active role of Dutch local government in providing affordable housing and the country's long-standing tradition of welcoming newcomers and refugees. Responsibility for providing public housing for legal migrants was accepted by housing authorities such as the city of Amsterdam, where many were accommodated in the large planned suburb of Bijlmermeer. Largely composed of 11-storey blocks served by aerial corridors, this new south-eastern suburb was very similar in form to the demolished slab blocks of Pruitt–Igoe, though having a much larger population, which originally approached 50 000 residents. However, the housing was not attractive to local people and came to be largely occupied by recently arrived immigrants (Freiling, 2004). Soon, familiar problems akin to those of Britain's sink estates started to emerge, with instances of crime and drug-taking, leading to labelling and stigma. This developed to the extent that by the mid-1980s, the city council was considering mass demolition, along the lines of the St Louis housing authorities of Pruitt–Igoe.

However, Amsterdam's system of active local community councils in each of its major divisions meant that local views were clearly formulated and expressed. They favoured physically and socially reshaping the district rather than mass clearance. Surveys indicated that about one-quarter of residents wanted to preserve the estates in their original modernist design, a further quarter wanted to leave the district altogether and the remaining half supported progressive remodelling to a more mixed form and tenure (Bijlmermeer Renovation Planning Office, 2008). This policy of selective redevelopment, originally adopted in 1992, involves selective demolition of about a quarter of the original slab blocks, quadrupling the amount of single-family housing to constitute over a third of the total housing stock and sale of a fifth of all dwellings to private buyers (Bijlmermeer Renovation Planning Office, 2008). While the Netherlands as a nation still has major problems of mutual distrust between Muslim and Christian communities, the combination of physical and social aspects of community planning in Bijlmermeer must be counted an overall success. Many people in both communities want to join hands across the barriers of race and religion, and the renovated Bijlmermeer is a good example of this healthy community spirit.

Many English local government authorities are also trying their best to meet fairly migrant needs for housing on the basis of combined need and time on waiting lists (Rutter & Latorre, 2009). However, this is made more difficult by much reduced total social housing stocks, following twenty years of continual enforced sales of dwellings to current occupiers. The figure of 2% of all council housing being occupied by recently arrived immigrants suggests a cautious but fair-minded approach, but the widespread resentment of other local residents against any provision of this sort highlights the difficulties involved in inclusive community building. Community-run social enterprises can go some way to overcome these objections. One successful example is the Mitali Housing Association, founded in Bethnal Green by a Bangladeshi migrant activist to assist people in Tower Hamlets Borough to acquire decent housing. Mitali enjoys excellent relations with both the borough and the Greater London councils and is able to access support funds, along with other housing associations, from the Homes and Communities Agency. After 25 years of operation, Mitali now provides over 400 homes to people in housing need, across several London boroughs, irrespective of their ethnic group (Social Enterprise, 2010).

SINK ESTATES AND TRANSIT ZONES

The spatial disadvantages of the high-density, and often high-rise, inner-city public housing estates – associated with Pruitt–Igoe, Thamesmead, Easterhouse, Tower Hamlets, inner Philadelphia, Melbourne's Housing Commission tower blocks in Kensington and the original Bijlmermeer development – often seem to invite dramatic and revolutionary solutions, such as mass demolition. Nevertheless, this is seldom necessary or justified. The mixed and collaborative solutions applied in Bijlmermeer constitute a more sensible community planning response. The combination of two approaches is required to solve the problems of poverty and disadvantage, which bedevil such areas. The first is to stop creating new single-class, single-minded designs that treat people as units of space consumption. Social housing needs to be a policy, not a construction programme. Affordable social housing can be integrated with in the normal processes of mixed-economy physical development, by subsidised and regulated market providers as well as by social enterprise providers such as housing associations and publicly sponsored housing companies (as will be discussed later in Chapter 8).

Second, the often well-intentioned mistakes of the mid-twentieth century can often be reclaimed, by selective conversion of some public housing blocks to individual ownership. Suitable buyers include one- and two-person households, of young people, empty nesters, student housing associations and childless couples. The communities that evolve from these less centralised and more inclusive policies can then be endowed with the realities of responsibility and ownership, through clear legal and financial control.

It is clear that such problems require the kind of 'joined up' cumulative and inclusive approaches of sensitive community planning. This will involve community consultation and engagement, as in Manchester's Northmoor; coherent mixing of social and physical activation, as in Bijlmermeer; implementation involving cooperation between public private and social enterprises, as in the Lea valley redevelopment in East London; and physical plans that involve sharing of spaces, facilities, transport corridors and human capital, as in Metro Portland's 2040 Growth Concept (discussed in Chapter 6). Despite many shortcomings, such processes are being developed and applied in many communities in both more and less developed countries (Bijlmermeer Renovation Planning Office, 2008; Thames Gateway Development Authority, 2008a, b; Great Places, 2009; Metro Portland, 2010).

The planning of places

Planning places, like home-making, requires collaboration, active listening and confident participation. In communities, as in families, roles need to be identified and organised, personal spaces shaped and equipped, communal access planned and provided, and methods of participation and negotiation agreed.

THE ORGANISATION OF ACTIVITIES

Social inclusion to provide full scope for individuals and families to express their personalities as active social beings is one of the most important roles of community planning. This will demand not only equal access to existing systems of shelter, work, play, learning, health and transport, but also to newly organised activities such as communal childcare and retirement living. Essential inks among these are often easy to identify but difficult to organise. Issues of scale and access will influence how activities can best be co-located or integrated. For instance, primary schools need to be small enough for all their students to live within walking or cycling distance but large enough to justify necessary facilities such as a library, playing fields and varied learning spaces. Similar principles will apply in different ways to clinics and health centres, shops and parks, causing the task of place-making to involve challenging sequences of progressive problem-solving (Alexander, 1964).

'Central place' theories have also been developed over the last 150 years to guide decisions about how activities can be distributed in space and between population levels, to promote convenient and accessible co-location of such activities as shopping, education, health and transport (Hall, 1985). Ideas of hierarchies of centres have evolved to include interconnected nets of activity centres, whose scale and characteristics are discussed later in Chapter 8. For now, it is enough to note that such theories offer a suitably flexible frame for patterns of service distribution from central points to those who need them throughout definable hinterlands. The scale of such fields of activity will vary from the global distribution of electronic information to local organisation of children's play and collection of solid refuse. Within these local communities, good interagency communication and collaboration will improve capacities to cooperate in making life in the communities secure, convenient and sociable. Schools, clinics, play spaces, local government offices, and shops and active and community transport systems can all be planned and operated to promote each others' success.

THE SHAPING OF SPACE

Local communities often indicate particular concern over issues of urban design (Menzies, Rogan, Heywood & Smith, 1997). Community planning presents invaluable opportunities to shape the scale, density and appearance of a development to reflect their preferences. A firmly based starting point for this local design can be derived from the human scale of people's average height of about 1.75 metres, and eye level of about 10 centimetres less. On this basis, Kevin Lynch (1961, 1983) has developed a most useful vocabulary based on people's perceptions of urban space (which is discussed in more detail in Chapter 10). Consulting different samples of city dwellers, Lynch identified the elements of districts, nodes, landmarks, paths and edges, to which may be added the seams linking neighbouring communities. Christopher Alexander (1979; Alexander, Ishikawa & Siverstein, 1977) took this approach a stage further to develop a pattern language of 253 models of ideal features of settlements, which can provide a well-stocked palette from which communities can choose materials to meet their own local needs.

Such vocabularies and patterns can provide valuable resources to match and empower people's perceptions and experiences. More recently, Alexander (2002) has developed this thinking to distil fifteen principles of good design, including such matters as 'levels of scale', 'roughness' and 'repeated alternation'. Deficiencies and strengths of existing environments can be discovered, mapped and used to determine the appropriate contributions that can be drawn from universal models and patterns. In these ways, design schemes can be developed that combine user objectives across a wide array of activities, with the most imaginative possible new solutions.

As well as providing a persuasive vision, this process can also produce actual designs and implementation programmes to ensure that development on the ground is coherent and well connected. For instance, rationales for the quantity, scale and style of housing, based on local community participation, can be combined in multi-criteria design schemes to produce local plans that also integrate health, education and work thresholds and facilities. The local primary school, for instance, can play an invaluable role in establishing, maintaining and supporting community life and acting as an early-warning system for social malaise, as well as providing a convenient location for after-hours and weekend community activities.

PLACE-MAKING

Places for meeting and mutual support can provide communities with focus and opportunities for empowerment. People can meet in shared spaces or buildings to which they have guaranteed access rights, such as the local park or school, or a space over local shops or behind a coffee or milk bar. Existing communities will tend to have developed such places, which need to be protected from redevelopment; new communities will benefit from their being provided from the outset. Designing for casual and informal meeting, and 'loose fit', can also support community life. Established communities have often evolved incidental open spaces, which may be linked to cultural characteristics. New Zealand 'marae', for instance, protected from development by the New Zealand Planning Act, provide ideal meeting places as well as spaces for traditional ceremonies (New Zealand Government, 1991). Similar spaces can be designed into new communities and linked to community associations or sporting clubs. In such ways, play and culture can help to maintain and enhance community life.

ACCESS

Place-based communities enjoy daily access to children's play, weekly spaces for adolescent sport and opportunities for adult recreation, self-expression and performance. Such access, linking centres of provision to their fields of service, maintains choice in an epoch of mounting specialisation. Lacking access, people become mere spectators of life enacted on distant stages. Four different forms of access are available to local communities to bridge these gaps:

- **active movement** of walking and cycling;
- **community transport** of communal provision;
- **public transport** of mass transit, by bus, train or ferry;
- **private transport**, normally involving the use of individual motor vehicles.

Active movement of walking, cycling and running is deeply enshrined within our genes. It has great survival value in terms of health, awareness and personal security, and still predominates at the local scale in most communities, bringing many advantages to individuals and groups (Solnit, 2000). A well-walked neighbourhood is far safer than one mainly traversed at 30 mph, while driving a private car and half listening to the radio. Permeability plans can be carefully linked to the natural topography and drainage of localities. Foot and cycle paths can lead past schools and shops and link to creek corridors, which can in turn run down to suburban and city centres and up to nature reserves and forest parks. These open space networks can extend onwards to wilderness areas in the regional hinterland, forming part of a connected system that can encourage individuals and families to combine essential daily movements with health-giving exercise and promote invaluable community awareness and oversight.

Community transport is a field of considerable undeveloped potential. Car pooling for the journey to work is already widely practised in many parts of the United States, and Cervero (2009) shows that it frequently correlates positively with the transit-orientated development (discussed below). People car pool into a rail or bus station, and they are encouraged to get rid of their car or not to acquire one at all if there is good public transport. Their ridesharing and car pooling than becomes a financial contribution to the costs of the other members of the group who retain their vehicles. Other forms of community transport could involve different forms of sharing. These days, a typical outer suburban community may be separately served by a school bus, hospital and day care collection vehicles and shopping buses provided by partnerships between local government and shopping centres and yet still remain full of isolated individuals and households. A system of community transport convened by local government and operated by a local community transport group could combine many of these functions, using a council-purchased and -maintained vehicle, managed and driven by suitably qualified people drawn from the local community. Local councils may also fund 'council cab' schemes, which allow otherwise housebound elderly people to take taxis to shops and community services for a nominal charge for each visit, thus ameliorating the worst effects of the isolation of the elderly and the disabled.

At the younger end of the age scale, 'walking buses' can make use of a roster of parents to take groups of schoolchildren to school together, combining healthy exercise, social contact and the development of children's capacities for observation and conversation. Such community induction into active transport can establish good habits to help reduce the carbon footprint of individuals.

Provision of good **public transport** is often the tipping point between a vital and confident community and an isolated and alienated one, enabling people to join in community life, instead of staying at home watching moving shadows on a screen. The profit and loss account of public transport should therefore not be calculated solely in terms of ticket sales: equally important are its contributions to other attributes. Community safety can encourage people to move around the streets at many times of the day and night. Social contact can help people to visit friends and establish informal relationships with other regular travellers. Commercial prosperity can result in shops and employers enjoying an expanded clientele and labour pool. The personal autonomy of young and old people and those disqualified from driving on health

grounds can be assisted to become equal participants in an active society. Local rail and bus stations can be located as the knots in a net of local cycle and footpaths and designed as the bustling entrances to the district centre with its shops, clinics, council services and close access to the primary school.

Private transport cannot, and should not, be overlooked. For over five thousand years, ever since the invention of the wheel and the introduction of horse drawn transport, there has been a succession of private vehicles extending from the chariots of the ruling classes of the early city states to contemporary motor cars and SUVs, which have been enthusiastically adopted as emblems of personal independence and status. The car has come to be the symbol of a libertarian society where people can move freely to choose from among a wide range of jobs, schools, play spaces, entertainment opportunities and living locations. Its strengths are choice and flexibility; its weaknesses include consumption of space and resources and creation of pollution and conflict. The use of the private motor car is therefore an apt reflection of J. S. Mill's dictum that 'the boundary of one person's freedom is that of another' (Mill, 1983). Private transport thus requires careful community planning, with evaluation of options, weighing of unintended consequences and consideration of alternative provisions. Whether we are London commuters, Californian residents of outer suburbs or newly affluent Beijing knowledge workers, we cannot all drive 10 cubic metres of steel or extruded plastic at an average vehicle occupancy of 1.3 people to the same places at the same time along the same congested roads, emitting an average of more than a kilogram of carbon dioxide every 100 kilometres of our journey.

However, there are very many positive aspects of car ownership and use. Cars and their drivers and passengers bring life and vitality to local shopping centres, and parking provisions need to be made nearby. Many mountain and beach resorts are most easily accessed by car, and the social advantages of a private vehicle for maintaining family contact at weekends and during holiday times are enormous. However, unregulated journeys to work in city centres are simply unsustainable for reasons of space, pollution and resource consumption. They need to be managed by planning policies and parking controls. In London and Singapore, success has been achieved with congestion charges. In Vienna, Rome and Padua, central areas have been closed to daytime traffic and parking – as nature has also ordained for a thousand years in Venice. Worldwide, parking controls are being applied with increasing effect. Private vehicles have become an integral part of human life, but that does not mean that they should be given free reign at all times of the day and in all places, irrespective of their effects upon others.[vi]

Looking at the life of a local community in a Western metropolitan suburb over the span of a day from dawn to late night, an interesting pattern of movement emerges. Early in the day, active transport predominates as people jog and walk to greet the new day, maintain personal fitness and exercise their pet dogs. Soon commuters emerge from their homes to walk or cycle to local railways station or bus stops. Later again, almost-empty cars begin to filter through the streets on their way towards their daily battles with city centre congestion. Mothers and carers gather children together to escort them to school. By mid-morning, there is a low intensity of activity with cars taking housewives and carers to shops, gyms and part-time jobs. In the evening, the pattern is reversed. By the time dinner is finished, and homework is starting, there is only an intermittent flow of socialising people walking to bus stops and driving through the quiet streets.

The inherent manageability of this pattern of access has given rise to the ideas of 'transit-orientated development', often known simply as 'TOD', which seeks to integrate transport and land use planning around public transport nodes, linked to hinterlands of about 5 to 10 minutes' walking distance, or a radius of approximately 500 to 1000 metres. Within this area, intensive development is concentrated, with commercial buildings and residential apartment blocks rising to as much as 6–8 storeys (or 16 to 24 metres) in height. TODs of this sort can achieve densities of 200–300 people per hectare, producing populations as high as 50 000 people in their compact core within 500–1000 metres of the central station. Such development is capable of supporting a good array of commercial, health, educational and recreational and cultural facilities. Metropolitan areas such as Toronto, Vancouver and Portland provide good examples of this approach, where they have often resulted from the innovations in community engagement and governance, which are discussed in the next section.

Community participation and governance

Community governance involves far more than the representation of local wards by elected councillors. Equally important are individual and group participation, functional management of activities and the tireless work of voluntary organisations, summarised in Table 3.2. In the most successful and self-sustaining communities, many of these activities are being performed in parallel and support each other (Putnam 1993, 2000; Etzioni, 2006).

INDIVIDUAL PARTICIPATION

The basis of participation is the rights of individuals over their own bodies, energies and actions. This extends from the most local levels of the 'walking buses' and street gardens of community activists to the internationally significant social and urban movements of the last quarter of the twentieth century, which generated the energy for the reform of city life and government in countries throughout the world. This extended to include societies such as Spain (Castells, 1983), East Germany and Poland (Dobbs, Karol & Trevisan, 1981). This pooling of individual energies powered the transformation of the Gdansk shipyards and later the entire Polish system of government by 'Solidarity' in the 1980s, and was again evident in the tides of individual energy which resulted in the destruction of the Berlin Wall in 1989 and the later collapse of the Soviet regime in Russia.

GROUPS AND VOLUNTARY ORGANISATIONS

Less adversarily, groups such as Bali's water subaks have for centuries worked together to manage open space, common areas and shared resource systems. Such bodies often grow to become as highly significant as the Grameen Bank and Mondragon Cooperative Corporation, taking over important roles in the governance of education, housing and community life as well as finance and production. Such self-expression also generates the community choirs, theatres, dance groups, ramblers associations, cultural organisations and book clubs that create the social capital which sustains community life through collaboration rather than coercion. In so doing they have also helped to shape events, such as the local emergence of gay and lesbian communities into the mainstreams of life in Western democracies since the 1990s, symbolised by occasions such as Sydney's annual Gay and Lesbian Mardi Gras.

Voluntary organisations of this sort may follow a lifecycle from birth, through maturity to decline, but in reality their influence is indestructible. It reappears in new forms and organisations that create, for instance, the street gardens and international environmental networks which aim to transform community life in developed countries and support the rights of communities as far afield as South Pacific and Indian

Table 3.2 Forms of local community governance

Source	Personal participation	Voluntary organisations	Functional management	Official representation
Individual	People's ownership of personal energies and rights to apply them in free association: street gardens city farms and low-carbon networks	Membership of councils of social service and environmental action, conservation and resource management groups; participation in mass movements	Community space and conservation management	Membership of political parties and support groups
Groups	Management and maintenance of local systems of open space and natural habitats	Churches and charities, community care and outreach, particularly involving welfare and health services	Schools, community housing, child care centres	Elected school boards (United States and Canada)
Voluntary organisations	Workers cooperatives, housing co-ops	Housing, sport, play and sheltered workshop activities run by charitable groups	Management boards of public and community enterprises	Elected membership of management boards
Events	Street parties, vacation camps and holiday schemes	Play groups, sporting associations, bulk-buying and recycling networks	Community festivals, social support activities: home visiting and 'meals on wheels'	Elected community boards, neighbourhood associations with open election of office holders
Community life	Sharing and self-expression of choirs, dance clubs, community theatres etc.	Resource conservation, urban agriculture and active transport initiatives of bodies like Transition Towns	Community stakeholder in local plan preparation and administration	Community councils representing local activist, functional and voluntary groups

Ocean island states threatened by sea level rises resulting from global warming (Oxfordshire Climate Exchange, 2008). They therefore play significant roles in both local and global governance. George Monbiot (2003) refers to them variously as 'the movement' and 'the social justice movement'.

Churches and charities, both inside and outside this movement, are involved. In the United States, Charitable Choice (Etzioni, 2006) recognises their roles by devolving major responsibilities in the administration of welfare to such organisations. Devolution of powers and funds to voluntary agencies is also a major theme in 'third way' politics. As they develop and take on formal structures, they often evolve into social enterprises, such as housing associations and companies, and become managers of major social assets in education, income and health such as the Salvation Army, the Saint Vincent de Paul Society and the United Way. Such organisations are involved in daily events at scales ranging from the provision of morning breakfasts to boarding house residents to regular local and national clean-up days and systematic recycling programmes.

Such networks may grow very quickly. Transition Towns, for instance, spreading from its origin in the small English seaside town of Totnes in 2005, has grown in less than five years to be involved in Transition Hubs in nearly 300 cities and towns in 16 countries in five continents, all aiming to create initiatives to help communities make the transition from fossil-fuel dependency and mass consumption to living within logical limits (Transition Towns, 2010). After the collapse of the 2009 Copenhagen Climate Change Conference, as governments turned their attention away from global environmental management, such voluntary organisations redoubled their efforts to change global ecological governance by voluntary action (Avaaz Organisation, 2010).

FUNCTIONAL MANAGEMENT

Much of the governance that most directly affects our daily lives is controlled by indirectly elected or nominated bodies, such as transport and water boards, catchment committees, national parks and broadcasting corporations. They often do a very good job, as for instance do the Toronto Transit Commission (TTC), Transport for London, the Dutch *Rijkdienst voor der Ijsselmeerpolders* and the British and Australian Broadcasting Corporations. Labelling them as qangos (quasi-autonomous national governmental organisations) has sometimes served to give them a bad name, but, in fact, the combination of very high levels of professional expertise, constant public scrutiny and transparency and an evident public service ethic of responsibility has tended to produce consistent levels of good public service at times when more systematically and explicitly accountable representative democratic governments have been experiencing recurrent crises of confidence in countries such as the United Kingdom, France, the United States, Zimbabwe and Thailand.

OFFICIAL REPRESENTATION

There is a widening gap between small scale local communities which continue to be grounded in relatively intimate daily personal contact (Table 3.1) and local electoral units, which are generally being enlarged in response to the expanding extent of the city region. In Toronto, for instance, in 1996 electoral reform increased the most local level of city government to a scale to 2.3 million people, since grown to 2.7 million; the city's 44 wards thus now have an average population of over 60 000 people each. In Brisbane, a population of just above one million is similarly divided into 26 wards forming the most local level of representation of around 40 000 people each (Demographia, 1997; Brisbane City Council, 2010; City of Toronto, 2010). This rapid escalation of scale, which is removing people further and further from direct contact with their elected representatives, is increasing the importance of participation by individuals and voluntary organisations in self-identified roles of local governance. In the United States and Canada, elected school boards provide a special case of representative governance bodies, often credited with providing a fertile training ground for larger and wider forms of government.

Despite problems of distance, motivation and commercial co-option, representative democracy remains the most successful and sustainable system of government of the modern era. As Winston Churchill is credited with commenting, 'The only thing that can be said in its favour is that all alternatives are worse.' This should not prevent us from seeking to rectify its evident current failures of venality, populist pandering to electorates' baser instincts, short-sightedness and avoidance of major long-term issues. Measures to

tackle some of these problems are discussed in Chapter 10. These should certainly include attempts to mitigate the intrusive power of majorities, which were of such concern to Mill (1983) 150 years ago, when he wrote *On Liberty*. Electorates should be small enough to allow genuine communication and representation. Safeguards are needed to forestall collusive arrangements between media owners and political party establishments. Blatant factional interests must be prevented from taking priority over more widely felt and important public concerns.

There are some simple ways to improve communication and representativeness:

- Ward community boards may be elected at the same time as local government councillors, as has been mandated in New Zealand since 1993. This could do much to bring life back to the grassroots of local democracy, which elsewhere are often withering for want of cultivation.
- Systematic support for neighbourhood associations along the model successfully adopted since the 1980s in Portland, Oregon (discussed in Chapter 11) has equal potential to transform the relations between local governments and local communities, by accurately reflecting and balancing the different and complementary roles of participatory and representative democracy.
- Community governance and planning can benefit immeasurably from recognising the potentialities of informal and participatory arrangements and devolution of powers, roles and funds to local groups. The field of governance is much wider and more fertile than simply electing a preferred government at intervals of three to five years.

Conclusion: the durability of local communities of place and contact

Despite the universal impact of electronic communications and the Internet, the importance of local community life has never been greater. The local community remains the place where children acquire their values and attitudes, learn how to socialise, develop skills of living and thinking, negotiate conflicts and establish positive or negative attitudes towards personal responsibility and social life. New roles are also emerging. The local community is where people must now learn to manage the 'shock of the new' in times of unprecedented rates of change; to deal with newcomers or adjust to host communities; and to evaluate whether new possibilities should be welcomed, modified or rejected. In an increasingly systematised world, the local community provides both the nursery for healthy development and the stage where physical, playful and personal aspects of life can and should be enacted.

Endnotes

i Kropotkin went on to develop the theme into an advocacy of collaborative local governance in his *Fields, Farms and Worships of Tomorrow* (1974). In Renaissance Europe, Sir Thomas More (1965) had advocated a society in which local groups cooperated in work and recreation, with collaborative involvement in such enjoyable communal activities as cooking, eating and discussion. Robert Owen's large model industrial community of New Lanark (1799–1821), involving 1600 workers organised on cooperative principles, was taken to further levels of mutual aid in Fourier's proposals for phalansteries, or collaborative communities of shared production, advocated in his 1829 *New Industrial and Societal World*. Ebenezer Howard's garden cities (Hall, 2002) were deeply imbued with these cooperative principles in their organisational basis of community associations that owned in common the entire array of community land and dwellings. They also made social provision for all citizens of whatever condition including the blind, the deaf, the orphaned, the inebriate and the impoverished (Fishman, 1982).

ii Barlow and Clarke (2004) of the Polaris Institute describe the situation: 'There are ten major corporate players now delivering fresh water services for profit. Between them, the three biggest – Suez and Vivendi [recently renamed Veolia Environment] of France and RWE-AG of Germany – deliver water and wastewater services to almost 300 million customers in over 100 countries, and are in a race, along with the others such as Bouygues SAUR, Thames Water (owned by RWE) and Bechtel-United Utilities, to expand to every corner of the globe. Their growth is exponential; a decade ago, they serviced around 51 million people in just 12 countries. And, although less than 10 percent of the world's water systems are currently under private control, at the rate they are expanding, the top three alone will control over 70 percent of the water systems in Europe and North America in a decade … The World Bank serves the interests of water companies both through its regular loan programs to governments, which often come with conditions that explicitly require the privatisation of water provision, and through its private sector arm, the International Finance Corporation, which invests in privatisation projects and makes loans to companies carrying them out. Lending about $20 billion to water supply projects over the last decade, the World Bank has been the principal financer of privatisation. A year-long study by the International Consortium of Investigative Journalists, a project of the Washington-based Center for Public Integrity, released in February, 2003, found that the majority of World Bank loans for water in the last five years have required the conversion of public systems to private as a condition for the transaction. The performance of these companies in Europe and the developing world has been well documented: huge profits, higher prices for water, cut-offs to customers who cannot pay, little transparency in their dealings, reduced water quality, bribery, and corruption.'

iii In the compact communities of the developing world, five minutes' walk will take everyone the 150–200 metres to the centre of the community, while five minutes' driving time will be needed for the 1–2 kilometres to reach the local centre of the spread-out, auto-dependent communities of the metropolitan suburbs of Australasia and North America. The figure of 3000 in each urban community is constituted by the number of people living within sufficiently close distance to be in easy contact with each other in a period of 5–10 minutes.

iv However, this rises to as much as 66 940 people per square mile in Manhattan or 26 148 people per square kilometre or approximately 261.5 people per hectare.

v *Webster's* definition of 'bidonville' is 'a shantytown on the outskirts of a city, characterised by squalor and extreme poverty, as in France and formerly Algeria or Tunisia' (Guralnik, 1974).

vi A celebrated *Mr Magoo* cartoon of the Sixties depicts the bumbling everyman character of Mr Magoo, emerging from his front door as an amiable and smiling Mr Walker, patting his dog on the head, greeting passing neighbourhood children and walking to his car, where he is transformed into a snarling, fierce and fanged Mr Wheeler who drives out of his garage and spreads death, destruction and dangerous fumes throughout the city.

References

Adams, R. (2009) *Transforming Australian Cities*. Melbourne, City of Melbourne.

Alexander, C. (1964) *Notes on the Synthesis of Form*. Cambridge, MA, Harvard University Press, (reprinted 1979).

Alexander, C., Ishikawa, S., Siverstein, M. (1977) *A Pattern Language*. New York, Oxford University Press.

Alexander, C. (1979) *A Timeless Way of Building*. New York, Oxford University Press.

Alexander, C. (2002) *The Nature of Order*. Berkeley, CA, Center for Environmental Structure.

Alinsky, S. (1971) *Reveille for Radicals*. New York, Bantam.

Australian Broadcasting Commission (2000) *Welfare, Competition and the Third Way*, http://www.abc.net.au/rn/talks/8.30/relrpt/stories/s117972.htm (broadcast on 12 April 2010), accessed 21 February 2010.

Avaaz Organization (2010) *New Year Poll: Setting the agenda for 2010*, https://www.surveymonkey.com/s/98GWM55, accessed 7 March 2010.

Barlow, M., Clarke, T. (2004) *Water Privatization: The WB's Latest Market Fantasy*, http://www.cadtm.org/Water-Privatization-The-WB-s, accessed 26 October 2010.

Barstow, S. (1960) A Kind of Loving, London, Michael Joseph.

Bijlmermeer Renovation Planning Office (2008) *The Bijlmermeer Renovation: Facts and figures*, http://www.vernieuwdebijlmer.nl/bijlmer/component/option,com…/gid,86/, accessed 27 February 2010.

Bornstein, D. (1997) *The Price of a Dream: The story of the Grameen Bank*. Dhaka, Bangladesh, Grameen Press.

Brisbane City Council (2010) *Brisbane Catchment Networks*, http://www.brisbanecatchments.net.au/, accessed 11 March 2010.

Burgess, E. (1925) The growth of the city. In: R. Park, R. D. McKenzie, E. Burgess (eds), *The City: Suggestions for the study of human nature in the urban environment*. Chicago, University of Chicago Press.

Castells, M. (1983) *The City and the Grassroots*. London, Arnold.

Cervero, R. (2009) TOD and car sharing: A natural marriage. *Access, Transport Research at the University of California* 35(Fall).

City of Toronto (2010) *Ward Profiles*, (http://app.toronto.ca/wards/jsp/wards.jsp), accessed 2 March 2010.

Community Wealth Org (2010) *Community Development Corporations*, http://www.community-wealth.org/strategies/panel/cdcs/index, accessed 21 February 2010.

Cooke, P., Morgan, K. (1998) *The Associational Economy: Firms, regions and innovation*. Oxford, Oxford University Press.

Demographia (1997) *Local Government Reorganization in the Greater Toronto Area: A review of alternatives*, http://www.publicpurpose.com/tor-demo.htm, accessed 7 March 2010.

Dobbs, M., Karol, K., Trevisan, D. (1981) *Poland, Solidarity, Walesa*. Oxford, Pergamon.

English Partnerships (2009) *Northmoor, Longsight, South Manchester, 2010*, http://www.englishpartnerships.co.uk/northmoor.htm, accessed, 30 March 2010.

Etzioni, A. (2006) *The Common Good*. Cambridge, Polity Press.

Fishman, R. (1982) *Urban Utopias of the Twentieth Century*. Cambridge, MA, MIT Press.

Florida, R. (2005) *Cities and the Creative Class*. New York, Routledge.

Freiling, D. (2004) *Bijlmermeer: Compressed urbanism*, http://www.deltametropool.nl/v1/pages/english/Bijlmermeer,%20compressed%20urbanism.php, accessed 27 February 2010.

Friere, M., Yuen, B. (eds) (2004) *Enhancing Urban Management in East Asia*. Aldershot, Ashgate.

Giddens, A. (1994) *Beyond Left and Right: The future of radical politics*. Cambridge, Polity Press.

Ginsburg, M. (2003) *New York City: A case study in density after 9/11*, http://www.architects.org/emplibrary/C6_b.pdf, accessed 25 February 2010.

Gray, F. (1976) Selection and allocation in council housing. *Transaction of the Institute of British Geographers* **1**: 34–46.

Great Places (2009) *Northmoor receives Government Award*, hhtp://www.housingexcellence.co.uk/news/northmoor-receives-government-award-239932, accessed 31 March 2010.

Guralnik, D. B. (1974) *Webster's New World Dictionary*. Cleveland, OH, Collins.

Hall, P. (1985) *Urban & Regional Planning*. London, Allen & Unwin.

Hall, P. (2002) *Cities of Tomorrow: An intellectual history of urban planning & design in the twentieth century*. Oxford, Blackwell Publishing Ltd.

Heywood, P. (1974) *Planning and Human Need*. Newton Abbott, David & Charles.

Heywood, P. (2006) Universal rights and global wrongs. *Commonwealth Association of Planners Newsletter* **15**: 19–25.

Jacobs, J. (1961) *The Death and Life of Great American Cities*. Harmondsworth, Penguin.

Kropotkin, P. (1974) *Fields, Farms & Workshops of Tomorrow*. London, Allen & Unwin, (first published 1899).

Kropotkin, P. (1939) *Mutual Aid*, Penguin, London first published 1899).

Lansing, J. (1996) *Priests and Programmers: Technology of power in the engineered landscape of Bali*. New York, Princeton University Press.

London Thames Gateway Development Corporation (2008a) *Vision for London Riverside: Regeneration for East London*. London, Author.

London Thames Gateway Development Corporation (2008b) *Vision for London Riverside: Regeneration for the Lower Lea Valley*. London, Author.

Lucassen, L. (2005) *The Immigrant Threat: The integration of old and new residents*. Chicago, University of Illinois Press.

Lynch, K. (1961) *The Image of the City*. Cambridge, MA. MIT Press.

Lynch, K. (1983) *A Theory of Good City Form*. Cambridge, MA, MIT Press.

Mawson, A. (2008) *The Social Entrepreneur: Making communities work*. London, Atlantic Books.

Menzies, C., Rogan, B., Heywood, P. (1997) *Social Planning Guidelines*, Brisbane, Local Government Association of Queensland.

Metro Portland (2010) *Metro Portland 2040 Growth Concept*, http://www.metro-region.org/index.cfm/go/by.web/id=25104, accessed 30 March 2010.

Mill, J. S. (1983) *Utilitarianism: On liberty and considerations on representative government*. London, Dent.

Mitra, S. (2001) Making local government work: Local elites, panchayati raj and governance in India. In: Atul Kohli (ed.), *The Success of India's Democracy*. Cambridge, Cambridge University Press.

Monbiot, G. (2003) *The Age of Consent: A manifesto for a new world*. London, Flamingo.

More, T. (1965) *Utopia*. Harmondsworth, Penguin, (first published 1516).

Mumford, L. (1961) *The City in History: Its origins, its transformations, and its prospects*. New York, Harcourt World & Brace.

Newman, O. (1973) *Defensible Space: People and design in the violent city*. London, Architectural Press.

Newman, P., Kenworthy, J. (1989) *Cities and Automobile Dependence: A sourcebook*. Aldershot, Gower.

New Zealand Government (1991) *Resource Management Act*, Wellington, Author.

Oregon Land Conservation & Development Commission, (1996).

Osborne, J. (1956) *Look Back in Anger*. New York, Penguin.

Oxfordshire Climate Exchange (2008) *Wolvercote: A low carbon village*, http://climatex.org.articles/lo-carb-communities/ wolvervcote-low-carbon-village/, accessed 30 July 2008.

Putnam, R. (1993) *Making Democracy Work: Civic traditions in modern Italy*. Princeton, Princeton University Press, (with Leonardi, R., Nanetti, R.).

Putnam, R. (2000) *Bowling Alone: The collapse and revival of American community*. New York, Simon & Schuster.

Reuters (2009a) *Madrid calls time on shameful shanty town*, http://www.reuters.com/article/idUSTRE56R0P020090728, accessed 27 February 2010.

Reuters (2009b) *Gypsy slum a world away from Milan's fortunes*, http://www.reuters.com/article/idUSL098416920070116, accessed 27 February 2010.

Rutter, J., Latorre, S. (2009) *Social Housing Allocation and Immigrant Communities*. London, Equality and Human Rights Commission.

Sillitoe, A. (1958) *Saturday Night and Sunday Morning*. New York, Plume.

Social Enterprise (2010) *Housing association founded by Bangladeshi immigrants celebrates 25th anniversary*, http://www.socialenterpriselive.com/your-news/housing-association-founded-bangladeshi-immigrants-celebrates-25th-anniversary, accessed 27 February 2010.

Solnit, R. (2000) *Wanderlust: A history of walking*. Harmondsworth, Penguin.

Suarja, I., Thyssen R. (2003) Traditional water management in Bali, *Liesa Magazine* **September**, http://www.fao.org/prods/gap/database/gap/files/597_WATER_MGMT_BALI.PDF, accessed 17 October 2010.

Transition Towns (2010) *Transition Towns Network/Transition Communities*, http://transitiontowns.org/TransitionNetwork/TransitionCommunities, accessed 2 March 2010.

Yates, R. (2009) Inside broken Britain. *The Guardian*, 22 November 2009, http://www.guardian.co.uk/lifeandstyle/2009/nov/22/liverpool-deprivation-broken-britain, accessed 24 January 2010.

Yunus, M. (1998) *Socially Conscious Capitalism towards a Poverty Free World*. Public Lecture Transcript, Brisbane, Queensland University of Technology.

4 Communities of Interest and Interaction

Chapter 3 focused on local communities, where many of the daily activities of life take place. This chapter widens the spectrum of review to include the larger scales of community life which are becoming increasingly significant in the contemporary world. In ascending scale, five such types of communities can be identified, associated with cities, regions, nations and supranational and global affiliation. They all interact and influence each other, but are identifiably distinct, as indicated in Table 4.1.

The growing significance of the global community is clearly demonstrated by the increasing numbers of international agreements that are being adopted, affecting environmental conservation, human rights, international trade, reduction of carbon emissions and many other aspects of contemporary life. Once ratified, these then become binding on national governments. Supranational bodies such as the European Union (EU), the Association of South East Asian Nations (ASEAN) and the North American Free Trade Area (NAFTA) are similarly exerting increasingly strong influences on the lives of the peoples in their regions. These two levels of global and international communities provide the context within which nation states operate. Figure 4.1 indicates that these nation state communities are themselves composed of regional and local ones, frequently represented by their own tiers of government. However, the grassroots of all levels are to be found in the truly local communities discussed in Chapter 3, which are enlivened by daily interpersonal contact, and reinforced by their many and vigorous associations and organisations. Figure 4.1 also indicates the very wide range of activities that go to make up all levels of community life, including not only living, working and moving but also learning, maintaining health and participating in social life and community governance, which are therefore also essential building blocks of community planning.

A separate section of this chapter is accordingly devoted to each of these levels:

- city communities;
- regional communities;
- national communities;
- supranational communities;
- global communities;
- the many levels of community planning.

Two concluding sections then draw together the common themes of the contributions of 'mixed scanning' and the psychology of managing spatial dissonance.

City communities

Cities are now the world's most significant form of settlement, accommodating more than half of all population (United Nations, 2007). They are also the places where shelter, work, play and social life most regularly overlap with administration and regulation. People

Community Planning, First Edition. Phil Heywood.
© 2011 Phil Heywood.
Published 2011 by Blackwell Publishing Ltd.

associate very strongly with the combination of contact, place, culture and history offered by cities. Most now have some form of responsible governance, reflecting the needs for coordination of their high levels of daily and weekly interaction. Because they have accommodated much of the explosive population growth of population of the last century, they have become the greatest consumers of natural resources, and their dynamism gives rise to inherent problems of sustainable planning. Writing in 1958, in the midst of this period of explosive growth, the American sociologist Don Martindale commented:

Table 4.1 Types and characteristics of communities in the contemporary world

Type	Basis of community	Characteristics	Typical problems	Approximate indicative population range
Cities	Exchange and administration goods and services	Economic and social interdependence	Conflicts of interests between communal and class groups	10 000–1 million
Metropolitan and provincial regions	Complementary economic interests and common environmental contexts	Intensifying impacts of physical and communication networks	Environmental degradation and social and spatial polarisation	500 000–10 million
Nations	Legal, linguistic and cultural affiliations	Organisational, policing and military powers	Liability to internal and external conflicts	1 million–1 billion
Supra national associations	Trade, culture and peacekeeping	Geopolitical interests in economic promotion and conflict resolution	Problems of rapid growth in size, membership, roles and influence	100 million–2 billion
Global associations	Shared human values, and economic and environmental interests	Global environmental, communication and economic systems	Conflicts arising from entrenched national economic, military and class interests	Increasing to 10 billion global citizens by 2050

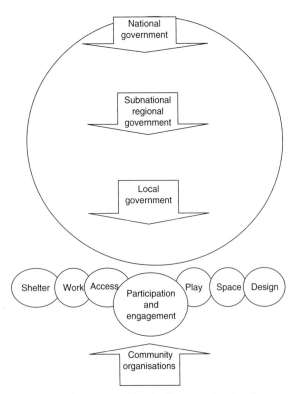

Figure 4.1 The scope and levels of community planning.

Every city … is an argument in millions of kilowatt hours, millions of short tons of coal, iron, steel, concrete and brick. It is a metric assertion in linear miles of steel rails. It is a rebuttal in cubic feet of air space … It is a protest expressed in terms of percentages of criminality, juvenile delinquency, prostitution, recidivism, mental illness and senility. It is a suave assurance in volumes of transactions, in gross sales, in amounts of credit, in retail and wholesale vales, in the size of payrolls, in cash services and balances.

It is not, however, lacking in institutions of service and governance. He goes on to ask:

What is a city without political parties, bosses, machines, chambers of commerce, credit associations, labour unions, factories, newspapers, churches, schools, welfare agencies philanthropic societies, humane societies, museums, art galleries, lodges, zoos, auditoriums, parks, playgrounds, slums, red light districts … jungles, sanitation plants and taxi cab companies?

Martindale's synoptic view suggests that a wide and sensitive application of community planning responses is required if the vitality of the city is to be managed without destroying its energy. Jane Jacobs, in a series of milestone books over a period of more than forty years, investigated the ideas which enliven such city communities and economies (Jacobs, 1961, 1969, 1985, 1992). Recognising the needs for both cooperation and competition, she views the city as a zone of confrontation where ideas and goods can be created and displayed in a stream of comparison and exchange. Deals are done and honoured because people trust each other to the extent that they can recognise mutual advantage from relations with trading partners who stand to gain long-term benefits from further trust-based associations and transactions. This approach led Jacobs to devote much time and energy to promoting micro credit, which, as we have seen in Chapter 1, makes use of collaborative 'social collateral' to replace conventional financial collateral and support the successful participation of formerly poor people and communities in local and wider markets. In rather similar ways, the participants in Cooke and Morgan's (1998) 'associational economies', discussed in Chapter 3, rely on each other to enable the whole productive community to adjust rapidly and effectively to new market preferences.

Jacobs celebrates cities as markets and centres of exchange. She also draws attention to the disastrous effects of the 'self-destruction of diversity', which she observed in the centres of great American cities where trading successes had attracted tidal waves of what she terms 'cataclysmic money' bent on concentrating new development in 'best and highest uses' to achieve short-term profits. These then swamped and replaced the original mixed uses and set in train processes of over concentration, which resulted in economic and physical blight. In order to forestall these market failures, Jacobs was prepared to advocate a measure of cautious community planning, supporting diversity and constraining market monopolies.

An equally important role of the city, which is naturally supported by local democracy, is to act as a centre for the provision of common services. Whereas local communities focus around human and physical contact, cities and districts tend to be the units of administrative organisation, where services can be planned, managed and coordinated. This requires ways to link the location and operations of such closely related systems as economy, health, education, housing and transport, in which cities have long-standing histories of broadly successful provision. The city is the ideal place to integrate these activities. General principles of urban structure and shape, discussed in Chapter 10, can be applied to link related activities, promote personal contact and support spontaneous meeting. Planning methods, described in Chapter 6, can be designed to guide this coordination without retreating to rigid or sterile 'cookie cutter' formulae which would tend to stamp out rigid and repetitious patterns on the ground, irrespective of people's preferences or local situations or histories.

Cities have always been the basic generators of economic wealth. Similar forces have made them the centres for other activities. They provide the focus for journeys to work and public transport systems, whether publicly owned or privately provided. The planning, building and management of public housing has also been a function of government in societies such as the Netherlands and Britain. The management of public parks and gardens and other open spaces is likewise a major and much-valued role of city governments. Cultural activities are frequently most vigorously developed at the urban scale, which is large enough to generate a community of interest but small enough for shared interests, activities and performances. Health is a common concern, and many countries have local health officers based in their city halls to oversee standards of health and prevent overcrowding and unsanitary practices which might lead to the spread of disease. Though schools are more often provided at the scale of neighbourhoods and localities, coordination with public transport and open-space facilities demands city-scale planning. The social and physical services of libraries, solid waste collection and community planning and development are also most usually provided at this level. The interaction of many of these major activities is summarised in Table 4.2.

THREE GENERAL PRINCIPLES FOR CITY PLANNING

In addition to the advantages of collaboration identified in Table 4.2, three general principles, concerned with administration, space and form, can be applied to the community planning of cities:

- administrative subsidiarity;
- integrated spatial design;
- physical urban containment.

Subsidiarity has been mentioned earlier. It is the principle of devolving responsibilities and roles to the lowest level at which they can be well performed, in the interests of sensitive decision-making, prompt feedback and opportunities for community involvement. These practices can be applied to new and existing local hubs, clustering facilities such as schools, clinics and libraries around public transport nodes.

Integrated spatial design has become all the more important because of the likely effects of climate

Table 4.2 Interaction among urban activities and arenas

Activities	Housing	Economy	Transport	Environment, recreation and parks	Culture
Housing		Avoidance of pollution; promotion of mixed uses	Integrated local transport in new and existing localities	Public open space provision and systems	Issues of design, density, heritage and grain
Economy			Mass transit by bus and rail	Buffers to noxious industry	Inventories of community skills
Transport				Active movement networks	Access to community facilities
Environment, recreation and parks					Informal organised sport and festivals
Culture					
Education					
Health					
Social and physical services					
Land use planning					

change producing more volatile and extreme flooding events. Collaboration between environmental, land use, transport, health, educational and economic planners can concentrate housing, employment and human services away from river valleys, creek corridors and coastal wetlands, which can instead be dedicated to open space networks. These can form continuous open space systems that shape and serve the local settlement patterns at the same time as providing active transport routes and spaces for recreation and habitat conservation. Public transport routes joining neighbourhoods and district centres to the central

activities core of the city centre will help to maintain the circulating life blood of the city. Applied through the cyclical activities of community planning, these principles can progressively steer evolving urban communities and settlements towards more sustainable and attractive forms.

Urban containment aims to prevent urban sprawl from re-creating inconvenient and unmanageable megacities, where congestion, conflict and pollution reduce amenity in inner parts of old industrial cities to the level of solidly built and heavily trafficked barracks. In modern times, containment has often taken

Education	Health	Social and physical services	Land use planning	Governance
Accessible primary and secondary schools; shared facilities for play, meeting and libraries	Location of antenatal clinics and day care centres for the elderly	Integrated local service hubs	Planned land allocation and release to meet needs	Community and tenant participation and consultation
Numeracy, literacy and vocational skills	Pollution and emission controls	Disability employment. Service Clubs and community involvement	Strategic planning to balance job need and creation	Micro credit support and workers co-ops
School and tertiary service systems of active and public transport	Active movement promotion	Active, community and public transport access community hubs	Integrated land use transport planning	Integrated management and community participation in public transport systems
Shared use of open spaces	Exercise trails and health maintenance	Keep-fit activities and planning	Open-space system planning	Collaborative space management: creek conservation committees and land care and water care
Values formation and cultural awareness	Community health programmes	Community development and inclusion	Cultural mapping and planning	Involvement of community, cultural, ethnic and indigenous groups
	Education about healthy lifestyles, drug and substance abuse	Planned links between schools and child welfare activities	Integrated planning of neighbourhoods and hubs	School parents and citizens committees: possibilities of school boards on US model
		Wellness and healthy lifestyle promotion	Integrated community wellness planning	Community health boards overseeing hospitals and local practice
			Collocation of facilities in local centres	Local Community Boards and Neighbourhood Associations
				Community involvement in plan preparation and assessment of development proposals

the form of greenbelts around cities, such as London and Manchester (Hall *et al.*, 1973). Cities such as Vancouver, Portland, Brisbane and Melbourne have also introduced urban growth boundaries, green zones and urban footprints, beyond which land is to be maintained in open space to preserve rural amenity and natural resources and act as reservoirs for habitat conservation and recreation. These approaches are evolving to produce proposals for regional networks of cities linked by fast public transport and set in attractive open space, thus meeting many widely held community objectives concerning scale, amenity and rural conservation.

Regional interest communities

Championing of regional communities rests on long-standing traditions dating back to the *urbs in rure* (cities in the countryside), which is well caught in Lorenzetti's fourteenth-century painting *Allegory of Good Government* where the peasants and farm workers can be seen filing in at sunset from the rural areas to enjoy the security, social life and economic activity of the city. Such regions developed a harmonious relationship between urban demands and rural supplies of air, water, food and natural resources. The evolution of European governance since the 1970s has built on these foundations to strengthen the bonds within such regions where actions taken in one part increasingly exert widespread and powerful repercussions elsewhere. On the one hand, job creation and new educational opportunities, and on the other pollution and resource depletion impact throughout regions. Significant administrative devolution has resulted in Spain, France, Austria and Italy (Balchin & Sykora, 1999).

Such regional communities, where cities and nets of rural settlements have for centuries developed a shared regional consciousness, are attracting increasing attention. In mainland Europe, regions such as Tuscany, Provence, Catalonia and Scania are all focusing on regional economic development. England's South-East region and Scotland's Strathclyde have become the focus of study and investment (Roberts, 1999a, b, 2000). In India, the states of Kerala, West Bengal and Rajasthan, among others, plan development on a regional scale. Such regions often express the cultural self-consciousness of historic cultures and patterns of association. This is now converging with the desire to decentralise governance and management within nation states. The European Union is particularly active in promoting this kind of regionalism, building on long-established feelings of affiliation to promote economic equality by distributing assistance under inter-regional programmes such as the EU's Structural Adjustment and Objective Three Funds (Balchin & Sykora, 1999). The European Spatial Development Perspective also promotes regional planning (Faludi & Waterhout, 2002). Designation of annual 'Cities of European Culture' in such regional centres as Athens, Glasgow, Lisbon and Liverpool have further stimulated awareness of regional communities (Gold & Gold, 2002).

Another form of regional planning is based on natural resource conservation of ecological communities and has deep roots in the natural sciences.[i] Rachel Carson in her The *Silent Spring* (1961) demonstrated the need to recognise the interconnectedness of life forms, combining to make up the unique character of localities and ecosystems. Practical theorists such as Benton MacKaye (1928), Lewis Mumford (1938, 1961) and Marion Clawson and colleagues (1960) created a synthesis of natural resource conservation, social progress and physical planning that continues to

inspire succeeding generations of regional planners and provide firm theoretical grounding for the conservation and regional planning movements of the new century. Their ideas can be recognised in the trailblazing regional planning schemes, introduced in many parts of the world during the second half of the last century (Friedmann & Weaver, 1979). The Tennessee Valley Authority (TVA) adopted resource management principles to tackle social and physical problems through a very large area, including all or part of six states, thereby demonstrating the relevance of the concept of the 'valley region' (Lilienthall, 1944; Hartshorne, 1960; Selznick, 1984; Gray & Johnson, 2005). Playing a centrepiece role in President Roosevelt's New Deal programme, the TVA tackled the three challenges of water on the ground, water in the channel and the transformational role of regional planning. Dams and roads were built that stimulated agriculture and brought cheap power to formerly backward communities. Eroded slopes were re-forested and the TVA became the world's greatest producer of softwood for paper pulp. Isolation was reduced as new lakes and old construction camps became the focus of thriving new tourist industries. Farming practices were improved and local economies benefited.

After sixty years, the region is still one of the less prosperous parts of the country but it has rejoined the mainstream of national life and avoided some of the more toxic outbreaks of racial violence and bigotry that characterised other less impoverished areas, which lacked a powerful public employer practising strict 'equal quota' employment policies. An early chair of the management board, David Lilienthall was led by these achievements to describe its record as 'democracy on the march'. This was not a centralist planning approach. Almost all of the 40 000 new jobs created were located in the region and only ten were in Washington (Lilienthall, 1944).

Integrated catchment management is now being attempted by regional authorities, national governments and international commissions worldwide in locations as widely separated as the Mekong Valley, the Murray Darling Basin, the Punjab development programme and the Rhine River Commission. It has been widened to take in the claims of entire 'bio regions' in areas such as the North American Rockies and Cascadia, the Siberian taiga, Australia's mulga woodlands and Brazil's El Chaco. Such valley regions are developing their own regional consciousness and administrative arrangements.

Australia's large Murray Darling Basin is one such example, facing major problems of desiccation and erosion. Environmental degradation and maldistribution of water flow has occurred between its upper reaches in Queensland, its middle ones in New South Wales, Victoria and its lower ones in South Australia, where for several years prior to 2010 hardly any water was reaching the sea at Lakes Entrance. These widespread geographic areas are not natural 'community of interest' regions, and experience a far lesser sense of cultural affinity than the city regions discussed above. Nevertheless, they do have shared environmental resources and natural impacts. Increasingly, they are being seen as necessary entities for subnational planning, often well suited to governance by designated bodies, whose members may indirectly elected by nomination from constituent jurisdictions (Papas, 2007; Council of Australian Governments, 2008).

A third, very different and even more dynamic, type of regional community which has experienced explosive growth over the last century is the metropolitan region.

Metropolises such as London, Tokyo, Toronto, Mexico City, Mumbai and Shanghai may have populations approaching or exceeding ten million and include as many forty or fifty local governments originally designated in response to movement patterns dictated by the horse and cart or rickshaw. Such metropolitan communities are now the most rapidly growing demographic units in the contemporary world. They currently accommodate more than one in five of the world's population of nearly seven billion in concentrations of one million or more people. This proportion is forecast to rise to more than one in three by 2025, which is an extraordinary level of spatial concentration for any species (United Nations, 2001, 2007). They form approximately four hundred such conurbations of very dense, populous and interdependent settlements, each composed of aggregations of hundreds of much more local, spatially based, communities. The most recent UN study has discerned the growth of forty even more populous mega-regions, often developing in heavily urbanised areas like Hong Kong–Shenzhen–Guangzhou, which is already home to 120 million people. Other mega-regions have formed in Brazil and Japan and are developing in India and West Africa, where they spread across national borders to include cities in Nigeria, Togo, Benin and Ghana (United Nations, 2010). The age of the international urban community has arrived.

Despite increases in population and falling densities, the world's forty largest mega-regions cover only a tiny fraction of the earth's habitable surface, but now accommodate almost one in five of its population (Vidal, 2010). The concentrated populations of these metropolitan regions favours ready communication. Negotiation of values, attitudes and options is assisted. Such regional communities thus have both the capacity as well as the absolute need to plan. The requirements will be to balance the consumption and conservation of resources: to match demands and supply for housing; to provide infrastructure to meet needs within available resources; and to reconcile urban needs with rural sustainability. These metropolitan regions are apt units for planning. They tend to have developed common systems of employment, education, health, communications and physical resources. They normally enjoy good access to national demographic data and the scientific information systems associated with of metropolitan universities.

Community governance and planning are required to manage these emerging metropolitan regions, and there are increasing numbers of experiments to review (Heywood, 1997). By contrast with traditional cities, such new metropolitan communities tend not yet to have acquired acknowledged administrative roles. In the United States, only Portland, Oregon has a directly elected level of metropolitan governance, while Miami, Atlanta and Minneapolis–St Paul have looser indirectly constituted metropolitan planning organisations. Most, like Kansas, with its admirable but under-funded Mid-America Regional Council (MARC; www.marc.org), rely on well-intentioned coordinating agencies. In Canada, too, the tendency is for indirectly elected bodies, such as Metro Vancouver and the Greater Toronto Service District, to be nominated from members of their constituent cities. Such bodies offer very convenient and suitably accountable public authorities to provide such services as water supply, public transport, regional park management and environmental monitoring throughout entire regional areas sharing common air sheds, watersheds and commuter sheds. Elsewhere, as in London and Bangkok, elected mayors and supporting metropolitan authorities take responsibility for strategic land use and transport planning, while many other functions continue to be divided up between local and national governments. Whether it is such power-sharing arrangements, or devolution of powers as in the rejuvenated regional provinces of France and Scotland, or fully elective regional bodies on the Italian, Spanish, German, Oregon and New Zealand models, the dramatically expanding metropolitan regions that are increasingly accommodating a large proportion of the world's population will require effective, innovative and imaginative community planning and governance.

National communities

The nation state is almost as old as the city itself: Upper and Lower Egypt were unified by Menes as long as five thousand years ago (Gibb, 1970). A thousand years later, Gilgamesh lauded the marriage of city and mountain that created the ancient kingdoms of Mesopotamia (Sandars, 2006). Persian and Roman empires spread far beyond the edges of their continents of origin and Chinese dynasties extended Han culture over areas approaching a million square miles. It is a commonplace that the spread of the use of gunpowder and printing from East Asia in the fourteen and fifteenth centuries expanded the power of the nation state to become universal within the space of five centuries (McLuhan, 1964). In the contemporary era, national regimes have come to correlate well with language, culture, economy, communication and governance. Few people living today fail to associate themselves with some nation or other. Even the United Nations is based on the gathering of over two hundred separate countries, and is dominated by often unstable coalitions of nation states. Nations are centres of power, prestige and privilege, which rest on the sanctions of military strength. They also generate their own self-sustaining cultures and national community life.

Their strengths include cultural, social and economic aspects. Culturally, they normally possess a common language, even where minority groups have maintained their own original ones. This supports common literary, oral and artistic heritages which may provide the basis for shared social values. Religion, too, tends to become a unifying factor and often reinforces other common bonds. The contribution of national cultures to human heritage is demonstrated in the way that people often refer to 'Indian dance and music', 'English drama and poetry', 'Greek philosophy' and 'Roman law'. Economically, the rise of the nation state has also been the era of most remarkable increases in human productivity. Allowing concentrations of military power to create long periods of relatively peaceful conditions. The Pax Britannica of the nineteenth century, for instance, promoted maximum specialisation of function and ideal conditions for the 'hidden hand' of the laws of supply and demand to develop trade within and between nations, in line with the doctrines of Adam Smith's *Wealth of Nations* (1950). Equally significant, the institution of progressive taxation has made possible the material support of community life in the forms of public education, health, welfare, transport and communication systems.

Socially, nations have been successful in creating bonds of mutual responsibility that can support the needy and create systems of social sharing to ensure that societies are more able to survive in difficult times and prosper in good ones. Social and human capital is often nurtured within the protective perimeter of the nation state. Nations have also come increasingly to recognise the collective nature of wealth creation and the need for its progressive redistribution to forestall destructive social conflicts. At a time when there is increasing acceptance of the fundamental importance of communication in community life and planning (Habermas, 1987; Healey, 1995; Forester, 1999, 2009) the capacity of national communities to communicate in common languages, using established channels and calling upon shared symbols and images is of the utmost significance.

However, there are also many negative aspects to nationalism, which have caused, for instance, Amitai Etzioni (2006) to look for communitarian alternatives to national community life. John Stiglitz (2002) is also scathing about the self-interest of wealthy Western nations in maintaining the conditions for permanent debt dependency of 'third world' nations struggling to develop, but constantly obliged to reduce necessary services to their own people to repay outstanding debt on loans which have already, in total, been repaid many times over. Such injustices have led George Monbiot (2003) to search for means to establish a global body that could supersede nation states.

Tribal exclusiveness frequently flowed freely in the outbreaks of intercommunal bloodletting which damaged the life of many nations throughout the twentieth century and has continued in many places into the present century. The atrocities of Germany's Third Reich against Jews and other ethnic minorities were later replicated in the rump of the old Yugoslavia under Slobodan Milosevic and Radovan Karadžić against Bosnian Muslims, and in the Hutu slaughter of Tutsi neighbours in Rwanda (Robertson, 1999). In a less dramatic but nonetheless similar pattern, there is a tendency for national communities to sustain their joint allegiance by denigrating other groups and practising social exclusion against newcomers, even though they may, like the Huguenots and Jews of past times in Europe and the economic migrants of the current world, have much to contribute to the economic vitality of their host communities. Another negative aspect of nationalism, expressed in recent history, is the strong motivation it provides for the economic and military colonialism, which may have contributed to the social collapse of such colonised societies as those of the

Congo region of central Africa, to the current conflicts in Tibet, and to repression of minorities on the borders of Burma.

Despite these dangers of destructive dominance, national communities are amongst the most powerful sources of positive human energy in the contemporary world. Long-established political systems of representation provide a widely understood forum for democratic control. Whether one is considering land use, transport, cultural development, environmental care, resource conservation or climate change, community planning at the national scale is often the key to effective action. Examples are not hard to find. The New Towns programme of Britain's mid-twentieth century, creating more than twenty new communities that now accommodate over a million people is one well-known example (Osborn & Whittock, 1963). The refashioning of social, physical and economic life throughout the six-state extent of the Tennessee Valley Authority in the United States, still continuing after sixty years of unwavering Federal support, is another instance. The Netherlands' reclamation of the IJsselmeerpolders and the integration of the reclaimed lands into a new province with a population of over half a million is a third. Canada's determination to confront many decades of abuse and exploitation of its indigenous communities is a further instance. In the field of health, the controversies over the proposed introduction of health insurance by the Obama administration in the United States was a clear case where community planning had to look to the national scale to unlock a stalled situation. Community planners cannot afford to disregard the powers of nation states to shape community life for good or ill.

It is not surprising that much of the most effective community planning is instigated from national commitment and discussions. Healey (2007) and Faludi (2005) both point to the way that policy communities at that level can provide the funds, energy and, above all, mandate for community planning policies that have profound effects on local life throughout the nation. Good examples of the influence of national policy communities include the provision of high-quality public housing and open space in the Netherlands and Britain's greenbelt policies and commitment to urban containment. The national tier is an indispensable arena for community planning. Where it becomes the 'dog which does not bark' as in Conan Doyle's celebrated detective novel *The Hound of the Baskervilles*, the silence frequently provides the clue to what is going wrong. When, by contrast, community planning draws strength from grassroots' commitment and organisation as occurred in the United States in

2008, this may then used to sustain national initiatives, and the results of such connectivity may be to transform national life and attitudes at all levels.

Supranational political communities

The recent development of supranational political and economic alliances such as the European Community (EU), the North American Free Trade Area (NAFTA) and the Association of South East Asian Nations (ASEAN) provides convincing examples of the importance of this newest form of community. At the time of writing, new regional organisations that reflect newly emerging interests are still coming into being. A Latin American regional body, not including the United States and Canada, is being formed to represent the interests of 32 Latin American and Caribbean countries, following a 'unity summit' held in Cancún in February 2010. Influenced by their increased political independence and the collapse of the IMF's credit cartel, which removed the most important source of Washington's influence in the region, member nations have been emboldened by the recognition that they increasingly have other sources of investment capital and political leadership (Weisbrot, 2010). Meanwhile, the South East Asian Treaty Organisation is considering expanding its sphere of operations to include a customs union, and the Organisation of African Unity continues to provide a forum for continental cooperation, despite the many difficulties being experienced throughout the continent.

The first of such continental alliances in the modern era, the European Union (EU), developed out of the post-World War Two Common Market ,which comprised a customs union of the six nations of France, Germany, Italy, Belgium, the Netherlands and Luxembourg. Since its foundation in 1947, it has grown at a remarkable rate to its current scale of 27 member nations with a combined population of almost half a billion. After a history of over two thousand years of mutual devastation, terror and atrocity, the European nations have come together to create one of the most effective international collaborative organisations ever known, bringing increases in prosperity and stability to all member nations, and extending their influence far beyond the boundaries of their continent of origin to include associate members in Africa, Asia and the Caribbean. The EU now has its own parliament and president, selected not for reasons of personal charisma but to reflect consensual values of compromise.

The EU is much involved in community planning at both the continental and regional levels, with equalisation incentives to rectify long-standing competitive disadvantages of rural regions such as the Mezzogiorno, Sardinia, Brittany, Andalusia, the Greek Peloponnese and parts of southern Poland. As a supranational organisation, the EU has shown remarkable self-confidence in admitting a series of new members from Central and Eastern Europe, including Poland, Rumania and Bulgaria, which are suffering from many decades of impoverishment under the sway of autocratic and often corrupt totalitarian regimes. Now the Union is considering applications for membership from Turkey, Croatia, Macedonia and Iceland. The Turkish application is particularly significant, because of the large population of over sixty million and the great diversity of the country. In addition, its accession would expand the boundaries of the union into Asia to include a Muslim country. Such a link could become a very significant first step towards transcending old religious divisions and enmities, and establishing freedom of movement across ancient political and religious boundaries.

The EU has also played significant roles in intervening in Bosnia and Kosovo to prevent continued genocide of minority populations. At the time of writing, the European Court of International Justice is currently trying Radovan Karadžić for war crimes committed when he was the Bosnian Serb political leader and military commander. He now faces eleven counts, ranging from the mass murders at Srebrenica to the 43-month siege of Sarajevo carried out by forces under his command (Associated Press, 2010). It is significant that it is the European Convention on Human Rights that provides the framework for this case to be brought, rather than the United Nation's International Declaration of Human Rights, which does not contain provisions for bringing violations and their perpetrators to justice.

Community planning at this supranational scale is destined to become increasingly significant as the major world regions recognise the advantages of economic trade, political stability and social progress that can be achieved by regional bodies developed through negotiation and treaties. Long-ignored traditions of cultural commonality, benefits of enlarged markets of labour and consumption, the development of common currencies and the enjoyment of personal freedom of movement combine to provide fertile fields for economic, social and spatial planning that transcend national borders.

Global communities

As international events and influences impact on local communities more directly than ever before, global networks are spreading rapidly in response. Their forerunners in the religious communities of Buddhism, Christianity and Islam spread throughout the known world, as much by example as conscious conversion or conquest. They introduced early instances of universalism into the everyday lives of people wherever they were practiced. Now information and communication technologies have transformed global communities to a new level of significance in both their range and scope.[ii] Relatively new global communities established to regulate economics and trade, such as the International Monetary Fund and the World Trade Organization, have become increasingly significant (Stiglitz, 2002), and charitable organisations such as Amnesty International, Greenpeace, Oxfam, World Vision and the World Wildlife Fund are spreading their own networks to match and influence their more official cousins. Such community networks prepare their plans on public or community interest bases, rather than commercial ones, because their aims are mutual benefit and shared values rather than financial profit. The influence of such global interest groups is giving rise to the concept of the 'glocal' – the local community expressing and pursuing global values and causes, and global communities having local outcomes as their ultimate aim, whether concerned with increasing production or enhancing such qualities of local life as social justice and environmental conservation. George Monbiot (2003) discerns a loose coalition of activists in a 'world democracy movement' or a 'social justice movement' associated with the World Social Forum, whose principles are dedicated to promoting global social justice and combating poverty (World Social Forum, 2001).

These trends fit well with the ideas of new place-less communities developed by theorists like Melvin Webber (1964, 1969). His 'non-place urban realm' relies on extensive use of modern communications and information technology to transcend local contexts and to create communities of interest with a global span. Nevertheless, it is important o recognise that such global networks exist to generate, coordinate or prevent actions in local space, not to supersede them. These are therefore not 'virtual communities' but associative ones that draw strength from powerful technologies of communication to enliven local actions. These global communities are of four main sorts. They may be value-based, like World Vision, Oxfam or Greenpeace; religious, like the Jesuits or the

Muslim Brotherhood; economic, like the World Trade Organisation or the International Monetary Fund; or governance based, like the United Nations, World Health Organization or Food and Agriculture Organization. They are assisted by the rapid expansion in information and communications technology of recent times, but their concerns remain the local occurrences and outcomes that happen to actual people in real places.

There are strong arguments for world government to control the rapidly expanding power and reach of the global economy, which is subjecting billions of poor people throughout the world to unfair terms of trade and causing cycles of indebtedness and devastation of irreplaceable natural resources (Stiglitz, 2002; Monbiot, 2003). Monbiot discounts the capacity of the United Nations to evolve into this broader role because of the entrenched and veto-based position of the Security Council that ensures that the organisation serves the interests of the original founding powers, including the United States, the United Kingdom, France and China. He therefore argues for the establishment of a new and parallel organisation based on electorates of approximately ten million people together providing a parliament of around 600 representatives, bound to no existing national power structures. He envisages funding the world government from adoption of the 1945 proposal by John Maynard Keynes to establish an International Reserve Bank (which would replace the IMF and the World Bank) and deploy its funds to promote international development and finance the pay for the policing operations of the world government.

The mechanism envisaged to achieve this transition is multilateral action on the part of the world's poorer and less economically powerful nations to refuse all future loan and debt repayments, thereby forcing the currently dominant powers to consider more fair and sustainable arrangements to promote global trade and governance. It is possible that Monbiot's scepticism about the capacity of the UN to evolve towards the role of world government is too pessimistic: for much of its period of involvement in international affairs, the United States, for instance, has been a dedicated supporter of the causes of equality and justice, and may well resume those attitudes under its current leadership. The mounting threats of environmental, economic and social chaos may also cause leaders and electorates to consider necessary reforms to meet mounting challenges.

In the meantime, the vitality of global communities of different sorts is demonstrably strong, and destined to become more so. Five webs of values, economy,

religion, governance and communications are identified and summarised in Table 4.3.

Such global communities combine local actions and connections with the worldwide sharing of values and information. They do not supersede local communities but support them with better awareness and understanding of themselves and each other. As constellations of people experiencing and practising self-expression, global and local communities are closely linked by widely based flows of moral, legal and financial support. They share information on the wider contexts within which plans will have to operate. They benefit from a wide range of shared examples of successes and failures. Most importantly, they draw strength from global alliances, enlivened through activism and the exchange of information.

What are the implications for community planning? Global communities are increasingly significant planning organisations, both individually like the World Bank, Habitat and Greenpeace and in networks like the World Social Forum and the World Trade Organization. The same principles of inclusion and communication which apply within smaller, more face-to-face organisations become even more important because of the potentially distorting effects of scale and distance. Accountability, two-way communication of facts and values and frequent reviews of outcome are all essential. Basic planning processes, like those developed in Chapter 6, retain their value. It is still important, for instance, to retain a clear planning cycle which links appraisal and goals, to information and analysis, and through options and evaluation, to plans and implementation. Collaboration at each of these stages becomes even more essential, but these extra complexities are more than balanced by the richness of information and support which is available from the shared values and diverse experiences available from the global reach of these communities

The many levels of community planning

An example based on the actual case of Brisbane's Norman Creek (introduced earlier in Box 2.3 in Chapter 2) can help to illustrate this simultaneous involvement of many different scales of community life and planning in a single, superficially quite local, issue. Norman Creek's community action and planning grew out of local concerns to tackle repeated flooding of neighbouring housing, and a general concern about the lack of environmental maintenance and management that

Table 4.3 Types of global communities

Basis	Sphere of activity	Examples	Directions
Values	Social justice	World Vision Amnesty International World Social Forum	Sharing information, funds and resources and involvement in direct action
	Global health	World Health Organisation Médecins Sans Frontières	Global conventions and agreements
	Environmental conservation	World Wildlife Fund Greenpeace	Concerted action and engagement
	Combating climate change	Intergovernmental Panel on Climate Change Transition Towns	Science, research and publicity Direct action on the ground Global networking and local action
Economy	Investment	International Monetary Fund and World Bank	Global division of labour Technology transfer
	Trade	World Trade Organization	Direct foreign investment
	Productivity	World Economic Forum	Increased production and consumption Multilateral agreement on investment
Religion	Social and spiritual welfare	Christian churches and Islamic movements	Increasing participation in social action and support
	Conversion	Buddhist associations	'Clash of civilisations'
	Piety and social conformity	Religious revival groups	Possibilities of expanded religious extremism
Governance	Prudential rules International justice Agreements and concerted action Peacekeeping	United Nations International Court of Justice International Labour Organization UN support for regional peacekeeping initiatives (e.g. Bosnia, Kosovo, Timor-Leste, Sudan)	Increasing levels of participation and accountability Growth on international public service Development of international peacekeeping capacity
Communication	Knowledge	Social networking	Rapid and universal spread of information and knowledge
	Choice	Organisations such as Facebook, MySpace, Twitter	Struggles over creative and intellectual property rights
	Information dissemination	Open access networks	Growth of open edged 'Wiki' and similar networks and media counterattacks

was causing a potential local asset to run downhill to a state where it was starting to attract unwanted uses, such as fly-tipping and industrial encroachment. The Norman Creek Flood Action Group (NCFAG) was formed on a stormy summer's afternoon in a local school, where speakers had to shout to make themselves heard above the pounding of a tropical rain storm on the tin roof of the old school building. Links were made with local universities, who collected systematic information on population, employment, environment, flood characteristics, traffic flows, open space patterns and governance issues in the area and around the creek catchment. Extensive research was conducted at the city level on the separate policies of the parks, engineers and planning departments and the city's Office of Economic Development. In particular, the Lord Mayor's Office was involved because of the membership of one of the associated academics on her Citizen's Advisory Committee.

It soon transpired that the creek corridor which contained open space of three adjacent schools was a significant concern of the state Education Department. Equally, the Commonwealth government was the body responsible for providing flood mitigation funding, and the local MP was approached and confirmed that funds would be available for a scheme produced by the collaborative work of the local universities and the local NCFAG. Metropolitan access needs were also involved because it emerged in the course of investigations that the State Department of Main Roads was planning to take advantage of the tacitly acknowledged likelihood of massive consolidation and tipping of the valley to create a new industrial estate, to construct a new 160-metre flyover running diagonally across the valley to carry a major radial road over both the creek and a suburban commuter railway line. This proposal had both traffic generation and aesthetic implications which caused a great deal of local concern.

Within a couple of years of a local community meeting the issue had grown to involve two universities, five sections of local government, three state government departments and two commonwealth government agencies, as well as a major national scale property developer and voluntary groups concerned with environmental conservation. Not surprisingly, there was no consensus and the situation became deadlocked. The city government would not accept the local community's flood mitigation scheme, even though it was guaranteed funding by the Commonwealth Government. No one else, apart from the property developers, accepted the City Engineer's Department's preference for a culverting and tipping scheme. Different sections of the state government held opposing positions, Main Roads favouring the flyover, and Education sympathetic to retaining an open space corridor. The resolution, which took another three years to set in train, resulted from the active participation of the Lord Mayor, Alderman Sallyanne Atkinson, in global community networks which took her on international visits to locations in North America and Europe afflicted by advanced urban blight and the city rot of the Eighties. She reacted by creating a new city council section, which she named Inner Suburbs Action, dedicated to community participation, development of mixed uses and environmental improvement to forestall disasters she had seen develop elsewhere.

Despite the strong reservations of many of her own Liberal Party about such an interventionist agenda, the prospect of a forthcoming election meant that the Norman Creek imbroglio had to be resolved and resolved in a manner consistent with the objectives of the high profile and highly publicised Inner Suburbs Action – which in turn meant reverting to the original collaborative community and university plan for an open space creek corridor to combine flood mitigation with habitat conservation, residential improvement, limited extension of the existing industrial estate, emphasis on active transport rather than urban freeways and a viaduct, and integration of public and private open space including school grounds and

flood plain into A council-promoted Norman Creek Waterway Park running for six kilometres from an inner-city suburban node to the estuary of the Brisbane River (Brisbane City Council, 1992). The Norman Creek Catchment Coordinating Committee, which included a number of people who had been involved with the local action group, has become the model for the city's most successful initiative in citizen participation in open space management: a comprehensive set of Creek Catchment Coordinating Committees (Brisbane City Council, 2010). One of the most significant aspects of this story is that it is not unusual. Most cities could produce several similar ones, illustrating how the different scales of community coexist and intersect, involving each other in a dense web of mutual support.

Conclusion: mixed scanning for integrated community planning

LONG- AND SHORT-TERM CONSIDERATIONS

For these reasons of overlapping spheres of influence, the practice of 'mixed scanning' is of the greatest importance, applying across both time and space (Etzioni, 1973). To move confidently into the future, but avoid striding resolutely up dry gullies, we need to identify long-term directions as well short-term actions. Equally, in considering physical scale, we need not only to be very well informed about local conditions but also to be well briefed on the wider contexts which influence them and in turn will be affected by our own plans. By these means, we are better positioned to gain the benefits of collaborative and sustainable progress.[iii] These issues of balancing short-term needs to 'muddle through', with longer perspectives to achieve purposive beneficial change give rise to methods of 'cumulative innovation', which are developed in Chapter 6. Essentially, they consist of adopting a cyclical approach to planning, with regular reviews of long-term directions provided by goals and objectives, being informed and adjusted in the light of evidence of successes and failures of recent actions and current policies, to give rise to new sets of proposals for action. Starting in the present, these can propose careful and signposted paths towards better futures.

LOCAL AND WIDER ISSUES

Mixed scanning also offers useful methods to relate the different levels of planning (including the six identified in this chapter) to each other. An obvious cases are the needs for local transport planning to take account of citywide policies and journey-to-work problems, and for city transport planning to be based in a sensitive understanding of local conditions. Global warming impacts will also, of course, be highly relevant, as will national policies on reducing carbon emissions. By contrast, the narrow incremental planning approaches of the Land Use Transport Plans of the 1960s and 1970s, have left a damaging inheritance for many metropolitan communities, and begin to look like predictable and avoidable mistakes (Heywood, 1974).

Etzioni (1973) provides an example of the need for mixed scanning to take account of different scales of operation. He illustrates, by reference to an earlier study (Wilson, 1960), the futility of trying to take a decision about building a new hospital in a black area of racially segregated Chicago of those times, without taking account of the ferment of city, state and, national policies that were involved. Incrementalism would have oiled the squeaky wheel of immediate needs by constructing a segregated hospital in the middle of the South Side Afro-American area though this would have perpetuated the separate and unequal health provision which had become a hallmark of American society, and ignored growing national commitments to social justice. A wider range of concern might have produced a very different policy of guaranteeing equal access to a differently located new hospital. This would have been more difficult but well worth doing. It would have constituted a case of community planning contributing to a better future instead of continuing inherited divisions and injustices.

This need for community planning to take account of the different scales of contemporary community life is reflected closely in matters of governance (discussed in Chapter 11). Mixed scanning, which allows us to switch focus to different timescales and spaces at different times, can help to integrate common methods and values with the activities of different levels of government. In these ways, community planners can help different tiers to move their political and administrative styles towards more appreciative collaboration and away from the current destructive tendency towards mutual criticism and ascription of blame and failure. In purely operational terms, there is great advantage for different levels of community planning to be well informed about each others' concerns, motivations and initiatives which increasingly impinge decisively on their own actions and communities.

THE PSYCHOLOGY OF MANAGING SPATIAL DISSONANCE

Psychologically, mixed scanning also has considerable contributions to make to contemporary life where rapid developments in transport, communications and information technologies have brought individuals into contact with a far wider range of mental and emotional stimuli than ever before. By focusing on one scale at one time, and consciously suspending our immersion in the others, we can regain a sense of clarity, agency and mastery over our lives as individual and community members. Later, we can switch the focus of our attention, and scan at a more general level the major forces acting upon us, again experiencing a sense of satisfaction at personal control over the ideas which act as levers of engagement with events in the outside world. Later again, we can refocus on a different scale, applying awareness of the broad categories of concern and expectation that we have gained from our broader scan.

In such ways, individuals can come to terms with and benefit from the dramatic increases in stimuli and impacts of contemporary life. Feelings of individual satisfaction and agency can be increased rather than diminished by selectively taking control of the ways we use and respond to these enlarged capacities to know and act. Such potential benefits apply equally to the cultural, emotional, and cognitive worlds, by constantly expanding opportunities for people to understand better themselves and their own cultures by looking through the prism of the eyes of others, as expressed in novels, plays, poetry, dance, song and music. These benefits extend to our appreciation of the physical world. On the one hand, its diversity and detail are constantly expanding sources of wonder. On the other, by momentarily discarding thoughts of the polluted city and the warming world, we are able to enter fully into such moments of physical elation as when we burst into total commitment movement, or sense the perfect coincidence of the warmth of the early-morning sun on our skin and its harmony with the temperatures of our own bodies. Later, we can return refreshed to the different satisfactions of planning better futures, with opportunities for more such moments of self-actualisation for ourselves and our communities. In such moments, we are enough for ourselves.

We are all simultaneously members of many communities. Daily life takes place in a local community of familiar neighbours and accustomed places. The city is where we work and vote for the local government which provides many of our services.

The region provides our resources of refreshing air, drinkable water and available space on which we depend for life support and where we frequently go for recreation. The nation enacts the laws which guide our lives, and maintains our borders. International communities are increasingly widening our perspectives of trade, contact and culture towards a continental scale. The global community reduces contact time between all parts of the connected world to a matter of seconds, creating communities of scholars, traders, activists and investors. Integrated community planning will typically involve an awareness of all these global, national, regional, metropolitan and local levels. It is not helpful to select and champion the claims of one scale to take precedence over others. The 'non-place urban realm' (Webber, 1964) has certainly not superseded cities as centres of community life and organisation. Instead, they have doubled their total populations and increased their influence since the non-place urban realm was first mooted (United Nations, 2010). Nation states have also stubbornly failed to dwindle in the face of globalisation. Simultaneous participation in many of these communities contributes to both the strains and the satisfactions of being alive and active in the twenty-first century.

Endnotes

i Linnaeus in the eighteenth century provided the taxonomy to describe the distribution and relations of species, and Gilbert White recorded their daily and yearly interactions. Later, Aldo Leopold in his *Sand County Almanac* (1947) and a *Land Ethic* (2004) and geographers including Herbertson in England and Passarge in Germany attempted to classify the world into natural resource types based on combinations of such influential factors as climate, soil types and topography (Hartshorne, 1960). In France, Buache recognised the way that valley regions bring together many elements of topography, geology, microclimate, settlement and movement patterns to form clearly defined regions for the purposes of classification, study and management (Hartshorne, 1960). Starting in Russia, Peter Kropotkin (1939) applied his observations of symbiotic responses to changing natural conditions to develop a theory of mutual aid within and between species that is still highly significant for all forms of community planning.

ii Buddhist teachings travelled from northern India to China, Japan, Sri Lanka and Thailand; Christianity from its Mediterranean origins to Northern Europe, Scandinavia, Southern Africa, the Americas and Australasia and Islam from Arabia to northern Africa, south-eastern Europe and central and southern Asia. Each now forms a family of communities, based on shared values and beliefs, reinforced through daily local religious observances. Strong emphases on attendance at church, madrasahs and regular communal prayers support powerful feelings of local affiliation. Administrative and mutual aid networks also predate modern electronic communications, such as the Knights Templar, Masons and Free Foresters.

iii Etzioni (1973) acknowledges that the classic rationalist planning approach of concentrating on long-term goals may make people insensitive to immediate conditions, and their capacities for beneficial change, and they may even blind practitioners to the potential contribution of the evidence of unintended consequences to forestall unwise policies. On the other hand, he demonstrates the potentially deadly consequences of the conservative assumptions of incrementalism, which are biased to respond to immediate pressures, thus serving currently dominant interests and placating those who hold positions of economic, political or military power. In so doing incremental planning frequently fails to identify crucial long-term issues, even in times of clearly radical change. Preoccupied with maintaining the status quo and preserving the current allocation of roles and rights, such planning often fails to recognise emerging and deadly dangers. Diamond (2005) describes these vividly in the cases of the Easter Islanders and Anasazi Indians, deforesting their fragile environments; Greenland Vikings, persevering with increasingly inappropriate land use and animal husbandry in the face of deteriorating climatic conditions; and vanished Mayan civilisations, practicing too intensive cultivation in vulnerable environments. Mixed scanning, refocusing between different scales of time and places, could have enabled each of these once thriving civilizations to compare their practices with other possibilities and to evaluate their short term activities within the context of long term goals, needs, trends and consequences.

References

Associated Press (2010) *War crimes court rejects Karadzic trial delay bid*, http://www.google.com/hostednews/ap/article/, accessed 2 April 2010.

Balchin B., Sykora, L. (1999) *Regional Policy and Planning in Europe*. London, Routledge.

Brisbane City Council (1992) *Norman Creek Waterway Park*. Brisbane, Author.

Brisbane City Council (2010) *Brisbane catchment networks*, http://www.brisbanecatchments.net.au/, accessed 11 March 2010.

Carson, R. (1961) *The Silent Spring*. London, Penguin.

Clawson, M., Burnell, H., Stoddard. C. (1960) *Land for the Future*. Baltimore, Johns Hopkins Press.

Cooke, P., Morgan, K. (1998) *The Associational Economy: Firms, regions and innovation.* Oxford, Oxford University Press.

Council of Australian Governments (2008) *Agreement on Murray Darling Basin Reform,* http://www.coag.gov.au/intergov_agreements/docs/murray_darling_basin_referral.pdf, accessed 2 April 2010.

Diamond, J. (2005) *Collapse: How Societies Choose to Fail or Survive.* London, Allen Lane.

Etzioni, A. (1973) *Mixed scanning: A third approach.* In: Faludi A. (ed.), *A Reader in Planning Theory.*

Etzioni, A. (2006) *The Common Good.* Cambridge, Polity Press.

Faludi, A. (2005) The Netherlands: A culture with a soft spot for planning. In: B. Sanyal (ed.), *Comparative Planning Cultures.* New York, Routledge.

Faludi, A., Waterhout, B. (2002) *The Making of the European Spatial Development Perspective: No masterplan.* London, Routledge.

Forester, J. (1999) *The Deliberative Practitioner.* Cambridge, MA, MIT Press.

Forester, J. (2009) *Dealing with Differences: Dramas of mediating public disputes.* Oxford, Oxford University Press.

Friedmann, J., Weaver, C. (1979) *Territory and Function: The evolution of regional planning.* London, Arnold.

Gibb, H. (1970) Egyptian history. *Encyclopaedia Britannica: Vol. 5.* London, International Learning Systems.

Gold, J., Gold, M. (2002) *Cities of Culture.* London, Ashgate.

Gray, A., Johnson, D. (2005) *The TVA Regional Planning and Development Program.* Aldershot, Ashgate.

Habermas J. (1987) *The Theory of Communicative Action,* Cambridge, Polity Press.

Hall, P., Thomas, R., Gracey, H., Drewett, R. (1973) *The Containment of Urban England.* London, George Allen & Unwin.

Hartshorne, R. (1960) *Perspective on the Nature of Geography.* London, John Murray.

Healey, P. (1995) Planning through debate: The communicative turn in planning theory. In: S. Campbell, S. Fainstein (eds), *Readings in Planning Theory.* Maldon, MA, Blackwell Publishing Ltd.

Healey, P. (2007) *Urban Complexity and Spatial Strategies.* London, Routledge.

Heywood, P. (1974) *Planning and Human Need.* Newton Abbott, David & Charles.

Heywood, P. (1997) The emerging social metropolis. In: *Progress in Planning.* Oxford, Pergamon/Elsevier.

Jacobs, J. (1961) *The Death and Life of Great American Cities.* Harmondsworth, Penguin.

Jacobs, J. (1969) *The Economy of Cities.* Harmondsworth, Penguin.

Jacobs, J. (1985) *Cities and the Wealth of Nations.* Harmondsworth, Viking.

Jacobs, J. (1992) *Systems of Survival.* London, Hodder & Stoughton.

Kropotkin, P. (1939) *Mutual Aid.* London, Penguin.

Leopold, A. (1947) *A Sand County Almanac.* New York, Oxford University Press.

Leopold, A. (2004) A land ethic. In: S. M. Wheeler, T. Beatley (eds), *The Sustainable Urban Development Reader.* New York, Routledge.

Lilienthall, D. (1944) *The TVA Democracy on the March.* New York, Harper.

MacKaye, B. (1928) *The New Exploration: A philosophy of regional planning.* New York, Harcourt Brace.

McLuhan, M. (1964) *Understanding Media: The extensions of man.* New York, McGraw-Hill.

Martindale, D. (1958) Prefatory remarks: The theory of the city. In: M. Weber, *The City.* New York, Free Press.

Monbiot, G. (2003) *The Age of Consent: A manifesto for a new world.* London, Flamingo.

Mumford, L. (1938) *The Culture of Cities.* New York, Harcourt Brace.

Mumford, L. (1961) *The City in History.* New York, Harcourt Brace.

Osborn, F., Whittock, A. (1963) *The New Towns: The answer to megalopolis.* London, Hill & Leonard.

Papas, M. (2007) Proposed governance framework for the Murray-Darling Basin. *Macquarie Journal of International and Comparative Environmental Law* **4**: 77–90.

Roberts, P. (1999a) The New Regional Agenda in the UK: Changing Roles, Structures & Functions of Regional Development Agencies. Dublin, Regional Science Association 39th European Congress.

Roberts, P. (1999b) A new agenda for regional planning and development in Europe: Taking stock and looking forward. *Regional Contact* **13**(14).

Roberts, P. (2000) *The New Territorial Governance: Planning, developing and managing the United Kingdom in an era of devolution.* London, Town & Country Planning Association.

Robertson, G. (1999) *Crimes against Humanity.* London, Penguin.

Sandars, N. (2006) *The Epic of Gilgamesh,* (trans. N. K. Sandars). London, Penguin.

Selznick, P. (1984) *TVA and the Grass Roots: A study of politics and organization.* Berkeley, CA, University of California Press.

Smith, A. (1950) *An Inquiry into the Nature and Causes of the Wealth of Nations.* London, Methuen.

Stiglitz, J. (2002) *Globalization and its Discontents.* London, Penguin.

United Nations (2001) *World Urbanization Prospects: The 1999 Revision,* http://www.un.org/esa/population/publications/wup1999/WUP99, accessed 17 October 2007.

United Nations (2007) *State of the World Cities Report, 2006/7: United Nations Chronicle,* http://www.un.org/Pubs/chronicle/2006/issue2/0206p24.htm, accessed 30 March 2010.

United Nations (2010) *State of the World's Cities 2010–2011,* http://www.unhabitat.org/pmss/listItemDetails.aspx?publicationID=2917, accessed 2 April 2010.

Vidal, J. (2010) UN surveys a world of 'endless cities'. *Guardian Weekly,* 25 March 2010.

Webber, M. (1964) The urban place and the non-place urban realm. In: M. Webber (ed.), *Explorations into Urban Structure*. Philadelphia, University of Pennsylvania Press.

Webber, M. (1969) Planning in an environment of change: Part 11: Permissive planning. *Town Planning Review* **39**(4).

Weisbrot, M. (2010) Changing balance of freedom. *Guardian Weekly*, 5–11 March 2010.

Wilson, J. (1960) *Negro Politics*. New York, Free Press.

World Social Forum (2001) *Charter of principles*, http://en.wikisource.org/wiki/Charter_of_Principles_(World_Social_Forum), accessed 12 February 2010.

5 Human Values and Community Goals

Values should drive planning. As David Hume observed, 'Reason is, and ought only to be, the slave of the passions' (Norton, 1999). Although the original stimulus to plan may often spring from instinctive responses to pressing needs, unless these problems are traced back to their underlying human wants and the values which generated them, there is a danger that the resulting plans will be shallow and poorly considered.[i] However, it is not only for reasons of logic that it is necessary to look behind everyday land uses and activities to discern their underlying values. There are also two cogent practical and ethical reasons why this is necessary:

i   There may be better and more effective ways of fulfilling these values than by promoting existing activities.
ii Existing patterns of behaviour may be poor guides to true needs, because people do not do things solely because they want to but also because they may be coerced into that pattern of behaviour by poor existing conditions or repressive power relationships. Their objectives and values may be frustrated but can, nonetheless, be discovered through questioning and reflection and satisfied through planning.

Values are therefore of the first importance in planning. In order to explore their place and contributions, the chapter is organised into six sections. Following a brief review of the processes of value formation, successive sections explore the planning implications of four major human values which are shown to be of particular importance for community life and organisation. The following section examines relations among these values, and the chapter concludes with a discussion of how they may be combined to solve problems and shape creative and humanly fulfilling plans. The specific sections are:

● value formation;
● the value of prosperity;
● the value of liberty;
● the value of social justice;
● values for sustainable communities;
● relations among the four community values.

The chapter concludes with a consideration of how values can combine to help solve problems and shape creative plans.

Value formation

Basic needs like health and sustenance give rise to values, which are essential to our survival. People who ignore them diminish their survival chances, and over time their genes will be lost to the species. As a result, values based on survival needs have become essential parts of our genetic endowment. There are, however, very significant other values, like choice, knowledge and beauty, that are products of our self-consciousness and have come to be scarcely less important to us than the primary survival values. Endless debate is possible as to which values derive from biological drives, and which are products of self-consciousness, because self-consciousness values such as knowledge and social justice may acquire survival value and over the many millennia of humanity's evolution may also become incorporated by natural selection within our genetic structure. Nevertheless, the distinction is a useful one, because we share our primary drives with all forms of primate life, and ignoring them will rapidly lead to extinction or degradation. Values of self-consciousness are distinctively human, and are necessary to the pursuit of our highest ideals and self-fulfilment and community life. They may often assist us in interpreting the best way to channel the expression of

Community Planning, First Edition. Phil Heywood.
© 2011 Phil Heywood.
Published 2011 by Blackwell Publishing Ltd.

Table 5.1 Examples of survival needs and values of self-consciousness

Primary survival needs		Values of self-consciousness	
Shelter	Security	Choice	Fraternity
Sustenance	Nurture	Knowledge	Justice
Health	Procreation	Glamour	Wealth
Liberty	Recreation	Beauty	Progress
Rest		Diversity	Self-expression

Figure 5.1 Value sets in community planning.

more basic primary drives. The classification in Table 5.1 is based on this distinction between these survival drives, based on biological needs and values of self-consciousness, which have derived from the development of intellect and culture.

Such primary survival needs as health, sustenance and shelter provide a firm basis for planning, but the ways they are interpreted may be influenced by the priority that is accorded to such values of self-consciousness as choice, knowledge, diversity, fraternity, justice, progress and sustainability. Figure 5.1 illustrates how one grouping of these values relate to each other and their significance for community planning.

Four values of prosperity, liberty, justice and sustainability emerge as being central to clusters of related values; it is they which are explored in this chapter. As will be seen from Figure 5.1, they overlap and synthesise many of the other most important human needs and community values and in so doing

make basic contributions to human life and community planning. Prosperity creates the physical conditions to maintain life and nurture children, and is reflected in our daily search for sustenance, from the first need for mother's milk to the creation of complex systems of production and transport. Individual liberty is no less necessary to survival, allowing us to escape from danger, find favourable living conditions and develop our own inventive capacities. Social justice, the other side of liberty, is essential for a gregarious species who must share space, activities and resources. Perception of its loss can provoke resentments which endanger continued community life, as is demonstrated in national and global threats of civil war and terrorism. Finally, sustaining physical and human resources is a categorical imperative for societies' survival. Time's arrow, which drives all planning, necessitates prudent conservation to sustain successful community life. Proposals can and should be scanned to discover and forestall unintended consequences affecting resources needed to achieve successful futures. Community planning can therefore be expected, as a mimimum, to contribute the achievement of these four values.

The value of prosperity

Floating at the back of most people's minds is a latent vision of abundance, replete with freely flowing sources of sun, air, water, food and space, offering endless opportunities for play and pleasure, free of any trace of conflict or strain. However great our daily pressures of work or health may be, this image of plenty is always available to filter back into our minds, ready to prompt us to continue the search for a better future. Such a vision is well caught in David Hockney's painting of England's north country in his *Road across the Wolds* (Plate 5.1), painted in 1997, depicting the abundant prosperity of the unfolding landscape of his native Yorkshire, first glimpsed in his youth and still intact. Community life promotes such prosperity in a number of ways:

- Communities foster the creation and transmission of productive skills, by creating conditions for profitable exchange of specialist products.
- They make possible the combination of individual energies and skills required in large-scale projects and production.
- They support the growth and mix of population that promotes the collaboration necessary to produce innovation to build new enterprises.

- They act as incubators for the technical innovation and collective investment necessary for the mass production of such items of beneficial collective consumption as carbon-coated optical fibres, cell phones and communications satellites.

CREATION AND TRANSMISSION OF PRODUCTIVE SKILLS

The regular contact of community life fosters new productive skills through collaboration between different specialists. As these skills develop, so too do the communication methods to ensure their transmission. This pattern of contact, collaboration and exchange within stable but open communities encourages creativity and further invention of new goods and ideas. The pattern is not new.[ii] In similar ways, the pace and reach of today's innovation in fields including information technology, space exploration and genetic engineering often come from the transmission of skills promoted by the free exchange of ideas at the meeting points of previously separate fields of knowledge. Jane Jacobs argues in both *The Economy of Cities* (1969) and *Systems of Survival* (1992) that the contact, communication and exchanges of ideas, goods and money of city life create not only prosperity but also social justice and cohesion, as people who are trading skills, knowledge and goods with each other develop self-sustaining relationships of mutual advantage.

COMBINATION OF ENERGIES AND SKILLS

Larger communities may produce economies of scale which result in further economies of transfer, labour, localisation and urbanisation (Isard, 1956, 1975; Richardson, 1973, 1978). Transfer economies occur when the outputs of one activity are the inputs of another and give rise to industrial complexes like the petroleum and chemical industries in major port areas such as Europort, Los Angeles and the Baton Rouge and Corpus Christi complexes on the Gulf of Mexico. Labour economies relate to the capacity of locations to provide adequate pools of skilled labour to encourage industries to take up opportunities for expansion and new developments.

Urban communities also provide the urbanisation economies that are essential to high productivity, including local markets, commercial banking, financial and information technology facilities, transport terminals such as container depots, attractive social and cultural amenities, public service economies and technical, vocational and higher education. Localisation economies favour the development of whole industries and include pools of skilled labour, proximity to auxiliary industries (such as specialist electrical engineering for automotive and aerospace industries) and subcontracting facilities, such as information technology and access to research and development, which are often linked to higher education. In these ways, the goals of exchange, innovation and communication flow from and support the basic survival values of prosperity.

COMMUNITIES AS SEEDBEDS OF INNOVATION

Urban communities are also seedbeds of innovation, providing industrial nurseries for new activities in cheap premises, which have long since paid off their acquisition and development costs. These offer opportunities for convenient links between local enterprises, which can spin off related specialist activities to provide components and services in a process which is described as 'horizontal integration' (Richardson, 1975). It is significant that the twentieth-century phase of massive vertical integration (diverting much employment away from long-established city centres to large greenfield sites for production-line assembly plants extending over many hectares like those of Ford in Detroit and the Austin group in Longbridge, Birmingham) is now receding in the face of major threats of mass unemployment. Large concentrations of highly specialised labour in expanding 'rustbelt' regions of the old 'Fordist' production-line society in cities like Detroit, Cleveland and Coventry are experiencing great difficulty in finding alternative employment. Economic dynamism and success are instead coming from knowledge-based activities (including the celebrated FIRE quartet of finance, insurance, research and education), which are clustering where innovative and problem-solving practitioners want to live in open-textured and supportive communities. Florida (2005) shows that it is such inclusive communities which are attracting the 'creative class', who are making the inventions that are maintaining jobs and rebuilding full employment, despite rapid losses in the manufacturing sector. Florida (2005) identifies the three 'Ts' of technology, talent and tolerance as the vital ingredients of the creative capital which is driving these successes and explicitly relates them to the fluid community life identified and advocated by Jane Jacobs (1969). The values of prosperity and productivity, clearly apparent at the dawn of civilisation in the dense networks of specialist workshops in Mohenjo-daro and in the bustling life of the medieval European city, are still apparent in contemporary metropolitan cores like those of the City of London, New York's Greenwich Village, the Galleria of Milan and the crowded streets of inner-city Amsterdam, San Francisco and Boston.

As a result, the values of prosperity remain a driving force in community life. The former roles of medieval monarchs in providing peace and patronage have been replaced by those of modern governments ensuring public investment in human services of education, culture and the common goods of community access, exchange, play and communication. These favour the production and exchange of ideas and products in 'associational economies' (Cooke & Morgan, 1998). They may find their homes either in long-established regional communities like those of Tuscany, Catalonia, Kerala and Kalkutta benefiting from well-based social capital. Or they may develop in the fertile soil and creative capital of rapidly evolving knowledge industry districts like downtown San Francisco, Silicon Valley, Austin (Texas) and Cambridge (Massachusetts) (Florida, 2005; Heywood, 2008). In such seedbeds of innovation, community life is daily making possible new links between people who had formerly been strangers. In so doing, new human capital is continually being generated.

The value of liberty

These characteristics are strongly supported by values of liberty, since freedom of movement, speech, exchange and association are all crucial to the success and resilience of communities. Humanity has evolved to seek and practise personal liberty, often moderated by the 'emotional intelligence' to avoid destructive conflicts and permit cooperation. Humanity has evolved to seek and practise personal liberty, often moderated by the 'emotional intelligence' to avoid destructive conflicts and permit cooperation. These skills remain as important today in the boardroom, the council chamber and the football field as they once were on the prehistoric tribal hunt (Leakey, 1982). Such values are also well demonstrated in the ancient and classical worlds.[iii] Their enduring relevance for community planning is well captured in the words of Pericles' funeral oration, in which he commends the people of Athens, because they defend their city as free citizens, whereas those of Sparta must fight for their city as little better than slaves:

Our administration favours the many instead of the few: this is why it is called a democracy. The laws afford equal justice to all alike in their private disputes, but we do not ignore the claims of excellence. When a citizen distinguishes himself then he will be called to serve the state, in preference to others, not as a matter of privilege, but as a reward of merit; and poverty is no bar … The freedom we enjoy extends also to ordinary life; we are not suspicious of one another, and do not nag our neighbour if he chooses to go his own way. But this freedom does not make us lawless. We are taught to respect the magistrates and the laws, and never to forget that we must protect the injured. (Popper, 1974)

With all their flaws of sexism and slavery, such liberal values of Athens have lasting significance for the human community. They survived the widespread destruction of the settled community life of the 'dark ages' to help inspire the medieval dawn of the European Renaissance.[iv] This spirit of free association and mutual aid is well captured in the early–fourteenth-century painting of Ambrogio Lorenzetti's *Allegory of Good Government* (see Chapter 1, Figure 1.1) which celebrates the abundance of the rich productive civic life of Siena, where it was painted and remains on the walls of the Palazzo Pubblico as a reminder of the rich civic traditions of cooperation of this and the other emerging city states of the early Renaissance. More than four centuries later, in North America, the claim of the *Declaration of Independence* (1776) that the self-evident truth that human beings are born with equal rights to life, liberty and the pursuit of happiness, is still working its way through community life, having influenced the abandonment of the institution of slavery (never achieved in ancient Athens) and the adoption of strong national social justice and environmental protection laws (Cullingworth, 1993).

PERSONAL LIBERTY AND SELF-EXPRESSION

However, elsewhere and in other fields, liberty has proved to be the human value that the twentieth century most badly failed to respect, although great energy was expended and significant successes were sometimes achieved. The newly founded 'Parliament of Peoples', the United Nations, has struggled to uphold the liberal ideals proclaimed by Mill and developed by such political visionary leaders as Franklin D. Roosevelt, Clement Atlee, Mahatma

Gandhi, Pandit Nehru, Salvador Allende, Willy Brandt, John F. Kennedy, Nelson Mandela and the founding fathers of the European Union like Guy Mollet (Robertson, 1999, 2009). The *Declaration of Human Rights*, a monument to the conviction and energy of Franklin Roosevelt's widow, Eleanor, is an enduring benchmark and shield for individual liberty, proclaiming 'the advent of a world in which human beings shall enjoy freedom of speech and belief and freedom from fear … as the highest aspiration of the common people' (United Nations General Assembly, 2008).

It is, however, a set of criteria which has more often served to condemn failure than to measure success.

Liberty attracts literary and cultural expressions and many idealist and existentialist philosophers and writers have been drawn to its purest forms. Writing in 1871, Fyodor Dostoevsky (1977) proclaimed the angry assertiveness of the extreme individualist in his *Notes from the Underground*, speaking in the words of a despairing minor public servant contemplating suicide:

> Your advantages are wealth, freedom, and peace and so on, and so on … but you know this is what is surprising: why does it happen that all these sages, statisticians and lovers of humanity, when they reckon up human advantages invariably leave one out? That is that Man everywhere and at all times, whoever he may be, has preferred to act as he chose and not in the least as his reason and advantage dictated … one's own free unfettered choice, one's own caprice, however wild it may be, one's own fancy worked up, at times to frenzy, is that very most advantageous advantage which we have overlooked, which comes under no classification, and against which all systems and all theories are continually being shattered to atoms.[v]

CHARTERS OF RIGHTS AND LIBERTIES

Political defence of these rights of the individual take on more practical forms in the development of bills and charters of rights and liberties, which have set the benchmarks for the evolution of contemporary consensual community life.[vi] A significant milestone on the path of human progress was reached in the 1948 United Nations *Universal Declaration of Human Rights* (United Nations General Assembly, 2008), which has become a benchmark of liberty for all members of the global community. Applied in the *International Covenant on Civil and Political Rights* and the *International*

Covenant on Economic, Social and Cultural Rights (both adopted in 1976), these charters have influenced many different bills of rights worldwide and set standards for guarantees of liberty which states should provide to their citizens (Hellenic Resources Network, 1995). The *Universal Declaration of Human Rights* has also inspired other highly significant initiatives, including the *European Convention on Human Rights* of 1950, guaranteeing life, liberty, freedom of expression, assembly, personal security rights to private property, privacy and family life, and freedom from discrimination and, significantly, torture. The Council of Europe, having produced the convention, went the crucial stage further of establishing two administering bodies, the European Commission of Human Rights and the European Court of Human Rights, which continue to safeguard the rights of individuals and minorities throughout all member countries of the European Union and to bring to justice the perpetrators of war crimes in places such as Bosnia and Croatia (Robertson, 1999).

Britain followed suit in 1998 with the Human Rights Act, incorporating most of the provisions of the European Convention and establishing a Parliamentary Joint Committee on Human Rights to scrutinise all new bills and to report on their compatibility with the Act. In the first ten years of its operation, the courts granted 26 declarations of incompatibility, leading to amendments of legislation to protect the rights of homeless children and mothers, mental health patients, children of artificial insemination procedures, detainees held without trial and homosexuals (Robertson, 2009). Robertson quotes the view of the country's former Lord Chancellor, Lord Gardiner, that the effects of the Human Rights Act had been 'hugely beneficial' with 'very many of the beneficial effects coming from the fact that the state, whether it be central government departments or local authorities, now have to consider legislation in the context of "Does what I do affect people to the minimum in terms of infringing their human rights?"'

Robertson analyses outcomes under the Act to conclude that groups and individuals are being encouraged to use human rights law, often independent of lawyers, because its language and ideas have inspired and empowered them to challenge poor treatment and to negotiate improvements to their public services. Numerous examples of reform of practices without cases having to be taken to court include recognising the rights of disabled housing clients, hospital patients, people threatened with domestic violence involving inaction by public authorities and racial minority prisoners.

Welcome as these results may be, some may question whether benefits to such numerically small minority groups are really significant in the wider scale of overall community wellbeing. There are three reasons why such recognition of the rights of minorities is very important indeed. First is the inherent interdependence of community life, meaning that what goes around comes around, and injustices to anyone threatens injustice to all. Second, a majority of people are members of minorities of one sort or another in some aspect of their lives (including the writer and readers of these lines) and self-interest should ensure that we want protection of our own minority rights in such matters. Third, perceived infringements of the social conventions of harmonious and tolerant community life often result in those at the receiving end rejecting the legitimacy not only of those laws but also of the wider community which is enforcing them. Such disadvantaged groups may then react with dire, destructive and all too familiar consequences of terrorism and sabotage. Community life is based on reciprocal recognition and acceptance of the rights of others, and perceptions of casual or premeditated disregard of one's own rights within the community may trigger rejection of the whole set of laws when they seem not to take account of our own rights.

There are also more universal aspects to human rights. In his *Statute of Liberty* (2009) prepared as a contribution to Australia's National Human Rights Consultation process which was then reviewing the absence of any human rights bill, act or charter in Australia, Geoffrey Robertson proposes the inclusion of universal rights to work, well-being, education, democracy, justice and pristine and healthy environments among citizens' legal entitlements, along with freedoms from slavery, torture and arbitrary arrest, and rights to freedom of thought, religion, expression, movement, privacy and fair trial. These are all incontestably necessary aspects of a full and satisfactory life. It is a satisfying paradox of social life that individual liberty can only be fully experienced and safeguarded within healthy and prosperous communities.

The values of social justice

Social justice often competes with freedom in the setting of goals for community planning. The logic of liberty, that too much for one person may result in too little for another, is highlighted by the utilitarian argument that individual rights should not be allowed to

stand in the way of the 'greatest happiness for the greatest number' (Mill, 1983). The dangers posed for overall social justice by excessive freedoms for particular individuals were vividly demonstrated in the unconstrained impacts of the dramatically increased technical power of the Industrial Revolution, which is still exerting significant effects on the distribution of wealth and power in contemporary society.[vii] Rationalisations of necessity were based on the need to submit to instructions of the hidden hand of the laws of supply and demand. They were combined with interpretations of human nature, such as Carlyle's and Nietzsche's commitment to the unfettered role and rights of leadership of the 'Superman', to justify distributing liberty in dangerously uneven ways, with vast power for the few and very little freedom for the many.[viii]

BALANCING THE RIGHTS OF INDIVIDUALS AND COMMUNITIES

Contemporary political theory is still strongly influenced by these debates. Tom Paine's proclamation of *Rights of Man* (1792) and Godwin's *Enquiry Concerning Political Justice* (1793) both resoundingly proclaimed individual human rights,[ix] while John Stuart Mill looked more carefully into their unintended consequences and human implications for the whole range of citizens, male and female, white and black, rich and poor, and urban and rural alike, in an inquiry that was to prove even more influential, and more in keeping with the practical spirit of both his and our own ages. In his seminal essay *On Liberty* (1983), he argues that many human activities such as those of belief, lifestyle, freedom of speech and writing and choice of association are primarily 'self-regarding' matters which should be left to the free choice of each individual and included in a national bill of rights or constitutional establishment. Others, however, are clearly 'other regarding' and should be decided by the representatives of the whole adult population, based on people's choices expressed through use of their rights to vote in regular democratic elections with universal suffrage, working at both national and local levels. Mill regarded local government as particularly important because of the opportunities provided to increase individual and local participation in decisions affecting social justice and its role as a training ground for politicians who could later rise to perform well-grounded roles in national politics. The matters requiring democratic control and planning include:

- public health and safety;
- working conditions in places of employment;

- minimum rates of pay;
- housing quality and affordability;
- environmental health;
- public access to urban and rural open space;
- forms and levels of taxation;
- educational provision and participation (see more detailed discussion below).

By refining the logical and deductive formula of 'the greatest happiness for the greatest number' of the Utilitarians with the more radical libertarianism of such theorists and poets as Godwin and Shelley, a sustainable basis was laid for the representative democracy and inclusive community activities which sustain political life in contemporary mass societies. At their best, such systems aim to balance values of liberty and social justice.[x]

Mill also recognised the need to give special attention to activities where the self and other regarding arguments were more evenly balanced. He chose education, both as a good example of how such issues should be analysed and addressed and because the development and transmission of knowledge is so crucially important to the evolution of healthy and just societies. On the one hand, education involves people's nurture and rearing of their own children and is therefore close to the hearts of all parents, wanting both to pass on their own deeply held values and to provide the best possible preparation for their children's future lives. On the other hand, society has the right and need to ensure the younger generation develop knowledge and skills to maintain social prosperity and progress, even where parents may be negligent. Just rights and responsibilities are therefore allocated to each. While the State should provide opportunities for free and compulsory education for all, parents should be able, if they so wish, to select and shape the value systems that inform their children's education, and be free to develop religious and secular academies of their own devoted to different educational philosophies (as was later done by Rudolf Steiner, Maria Montessori and A. S. Neill) or to educate their children at home, in each case provided that they meet certain basic regularly inspected public and published standards. Broadly speaking, this system has, often after various vicissitudes, been adopted by the contemporary democratic world. Where conflicts of attitude have surfaced, this kind of careful analytical approach to determining the rights of each party has normally succeeded in defusing potential conflict and is a good model of 'inspired hair splitting' for those involved in developing broadly acceptable and just social policies.[xi]

This approach can be readily applied to other activities. In physical planning and urban design, for instance, there is a clear need for some form of physical and aesthetic control over developments capable of exerting vivid and continuing impacts on immediate neighbours and the general public. On the other hand, people should be free to exercise routine rights to shape their own home spaces to reflect their own needs and values. The outcome developed to balance these two sets of rights in the original *British General Development Order of 1946* (Cullingworth, 1979) is a good example of applied social problem-solving: people are free to develop and adapt their own dwellings as they wish up to extensions of 50% of total existing floor area, as long as they are in keeping with the building laws and do not obtrude into the public domain or unreasonably impact on their neighbour's views and privacy).[xii] Where the proposal goes beyond these limits, they must seek and obtain planning permission before undertaking the development.

Apart from its logic, this approach has the added advantage of appealing to a natural sense of justice. Most people would agree that personal convictions and revelations should not be encouraged to encroach on the freedoms of others, endangering amicable and sustainable community life.[xiii] Resolution of conflict between perceived public, private and sectional interests therefore demands constant attention. It would be glib to assume that a liberal division between the rights of the individual and the State resolves once and for all problems of the public interest. Problems remain where bad relations between the individual, groups and the State prevent one participant from recognising the legitimacy of the other. There is also the problem of how public policies should be shaped and validated once they are addressed by elected decision-takers. It is very well and good that elected representative should frame laws and actions to achieve the public good in other affecting matters, but the question remains: 'What principles should they adopt when implementing the public interest?'

GIVING MOST TO THOSE WHO HAVE LEAST

The previous section discussing liberty presented the idea of community life as the product of a bargain or contract between the individual and the State (Robertson, 1999, 2009). This contractarian tradition, developed over nearly four centuries of experimentation, application and criticism has been drawn together by John Rawls in his masterly work *A Theory of Justice* (Rawls, 1971), referred to in Chapter 2. Accepting the idea of a social contract as the basis for an organised society, Rawls asks: 'What principles would people themselves choose to regulate that society?' He develops an 'initial position' in which people would adopt the 'maximin' principle of maximum possible benefit from minimum acceptable risk (a version of the so-called precautionary principle) rather than the chancier 'minimax' principle of minimum inescapable risk from maximum possible benefit. They would, in short, prefer security to gambling on windfall benefits – a basis which looks even more rational in the twenty-first century than forty years ago when Rawls proposed it. This position would influence participants not to base decisions on their own current bargaining advantages (which may have changed by the time the principles and decisions came to be applied) but on the circumstances of a typical least advantaged member. Applying this approach, Rawls develops two basic principles that people in this 'initial position' would adopt:

1. The greatest possible freedom and benefit for each person compatible with a like freedom and benefit for others (adopting Mill's position in *On Liberty*).
2. Distribution of economic irregularities (differences in levels of benefit) to bring most benefit to the least advantaged (giving most to those who have least).

This second, so-called differences principle has attracted and survived a great deal of attention and review. Marxist criticism that the State should tolerate *no* irregularities has collapsed in the face of almost universal condemnation of the gross disparities of power which developed in regimes of this type in the former Soviet Union, Eastern Europe and Southeast Asia, where assumption of totalitarian powers to prevent economic irregularities resulted in the greatest imaginable disparities of actual power between the party and its officials on the one hand and the rest of society on the other, corroborating Lord Acton's (Creighton, 1904) celebrated dictum that 'Power tends to corrupt and absolute power corrupts absolutely'. Clearly, people should have sufficient control over their lives to make their own trade-offs between one activity and another, to decide for instance whether they want to take glamorous holidays and live in a basic dwelling, or to forego all holidays and devote their savings to more luxurious shelter. These are self-regarding choices.

Opposite criticisms come from economic rationalists and conservatives, who urge that government in mixed economy societies should limit interventions to promoting overall social benefit, so that there is no logical reason to give most to those who have least. Such criticisms, however, must still answer Rawls'

argument that those who still have more have no ethical grievance against redistribution of *public* wealth in favour of those who have less, because overall they remain well in advance. Rawls' view that society is a column, where it is dangerous to allow large gaps to develop between the pace makers, the middle rankers and the back markers, intuitively speaks to us in an age whose practical interdependence is becoming daily more apparent. He goes on to examine the implications of these views for the conduct of social life, justifying bills of rights (as open and acceptable bases for social organisation), civil disobedience (as a useful contribution to social dialogue), tolerance for the intolerant (on the grounds of the self-inflicted damage that descent into intolerance would do those who were initially tolerant), public consultation (as a practical application of his 'initial position') and regular and open debates on social directions. By updating and integrating the contractarian and liberal traditions of Locke, Jefferson, Lincoln, Mill and Russell, Rawls presents a spacious and comprehensive framework for the political economy of contemporary communities and demonstrates how the values of social justice can be applied in practice.

The meticulous philosophical rationality of these arguments and their attention to the rights, responsibilities, expectations and consequences of all parties may not always be achievable. In the 'lifeworld' of daily experiences and demands, careful logical deductive processes may tend to be dismissed as products of an intellectual 'systemworld'. In situations of unavoidable stress, when widely accepted methods of problem-solving are most needed, people may be drawn to more compulsive and visceral approaches, and tend to form their views of what to do next on the basis of their personal experiences of reciprocity, or its absence, constrained only by their acceptance of common laws. This compliance will be based partly on acceptance of the police powers of the State, but in the many situations where the enforcing power is no longer present, compliant behaviour will have to be based largely on willing assent. In a free society, consent thus becomes the decisive factor in acceptance of the rule of law.

Psychologically, it can be argued that this consent to the rule of law starts when we first recognise in childhood that others are experiencing the same feelings and emotions, and by extension should enjoy the same rights, as we ourselves do. We are then able to accept common rules, and ultimately to develop shared cultures and loyalties. The rule of law is based more on this recognition that our own rights are the mirror image of those of other members of our community than on statutes or stun guns. When people feel that reciprocal respect for their own rights is grossly infringed by other members of their communities of place, work or interest, there is a strong tendency for their acceptance of the bonds of law to be loosened or abandoned. Examples of such situations occur when people feel themselves to be treated unjustly or contemptuously, because their religion or value systems are ridiculed, culture or practices rejected, persons discounted on the basis of skin colour or appearance, resources seized, or the countries of their families or places of origin occupied. In such situations, there is an immediate need for ways to re-establish mutual understanding that can reshape daily events, rectify perceived injustices and avoid corrosive dissension.

In these circumstances, the communicative ideas of Jurgen Habermas (1987), discussed in Chapter 2, offer ways forward. The idea that truth can best be established by the exchange and adjustment of views and interpretations between the different people who constitute a situation, provides a structure to develop socially just policies and actions. It can also generate actual methods for deciding consensual directions. Such methods are 'intersubjective' because they come not from appeal to the authority of revelation or elevating individual experience into universal truth but from constructive debate between equals expected to justify their arguments around a policy table where each has an equal right and responsibility to participate. Their 'speech acts' can pool a multiplicity of experiences and ideas and winnow one against many others. By these means, arguments can be moved forwards rather than fall back to previously adopted positions. This approach displaces the more abstract, objective and positivist definition of the truths of the 'systemworld'. These often incorporate influential but hidden assumptions, which may subconsciously influence those who benefit from them, in their roles in charge of traditional bureaucratic decision-taking processes. Instead, communicative and intersubjective methods, including not only consultation but also cooperative action and encouragement to individual and group initiative, can constantly refresh values of social justice and contribute significantly to creating socially sustainable communities.

Values for sustainable communities

People's intuitive recognition of the importance of conserving the wholeness of communities and places is demonstrated across many different cultures and in many different times.[xiv] Such conservation of resources continues to form the basis for the sustainability which is increasingly imperative for all social and environmental policy. This must similarly aim to conserve resources to maintain the capacity to achieve desired future outcomes. Community life, as much as the physical environment, depends upon the sustainable use of resources of all types. Whole civilisations like those of Easter Island, Viking Greenland and the Anasazi Indians have been extinguished through overconsumption of the resources on which they relied. Today, climate change and resource depletion pose global threats. At the regional level, community life is menaced by deforestation, soil exhaustion and radioactive contamination as well as by climate change. At the local level, contamination of land, air and water, subsidence, flooding, dereliction, traffic gridlock, civil unrest and riots can all prevent the success and continuity of communities. Nevertheless, the great advocates of conservation are overwhelmingly positive in their worldviews; they want to celebrate wholeness and interdependence rather than to decry entropy and destruction.[xv]

This constructive interdependence can extend to the relations between town and country, as depicted in Lorenzetti's vivid *Allegory of Good Government* reproduced earlier, and still expressed in the associational economies of Tuscany and Baden-Württemberg, supporting the exchange of specialist skills among many differentiated producers (Cooke & Morgan, 1998). At the national level, policies of reuse, recycling and reclamation can foster balanced relations between communities, countryside and natural resources. At the global level, 'harmony' implies conservation of habitats and climates, symbiosis within and between species and preservation of stable relationships between the many different forms of life associated with the 'Gaia hypothesis' (Lovelock, 1988). Fostering this harmony can produce rich rewards for humanity by sustaining support systems that maintain life and enhance social justice. Grassroots community associations and organisations, matched and encouraged by energetic government action, can help develop the educational, cultural, health and environmental services to foster the development of social and cultural capital (see, for example, ClimateX, 2007).

RECIPROCITY AS A FACTOR IN SUSTAINABILITY

Socially sustainable systems rest on a broad basis of reciprocity, which is recognised by many religions and ethical systems. Christ's Sermon on the Mount with its instruction to 'Do unto others as you would be done by' is one of its most telling and compelling expressions and Immanuel Kant's 'categorical imperative' of 'Never to act otherwise than so that I could also will that my maxim should become a universal law' is another (Kant, 1934). Reciprocity is also a value which lies at the root of many aspects of animal as well as human society. Grooming rituals are recorded as a powerful bonding activity among many forms of primates. In human communities, indications of mutual aid are extensively noted by Peter Kropotkin (1939) from the Neolithic villages of ten thousand years ago up to the nineteenth century, enabling communal systems of agriculture, water supply and irrigation to be practised in Bali, Morocco and India. Practices recorded by the anthropologist C. Daryll Forde, in the first half of the twentieth century in the Trobriand Island group of Melanesia, describe the ceremonial interchange of gifts between individuals making adventurous expeditions between different islands in a process known as Kula. Gifts of red shell necklaces, which circulate in opposite directions to ones of armlets of white shell, accompanying presents of food and other products, constitute an invaluable framework for trade in an otherwise very warlike culture (Forde, 1957).[xvi] Richard Titmuss (1973) explores the roles of such 'gift relationships' in promoting the continuance of social organisation in advanced societies, using as an example voluntary donations of human blood to medical 'blood banks'. Contemporary micro credit, discussed earlier, also explicitly relies on mutual aid between people having very little else to offer each other except their trustworthiness (Bornstein, 1997; Yunus, 1998). Such behaviours may not offer direct benefits to participating individuals but nonetheless make significant long-term contributions to group welfare, and therefore have great survival value. The support which reciprocity offers to diversity can also help to sustain social systems, by favouring the survival of a wider range of individual characteristics and genes than would result from unalloyed competition, thereby expanding the gene pool to adapt more readily to changes in external conditions (Ridley, 1996).

Suzuki widens the scope of functional reciprocity even further by arguing that the inextricable links between all forms of life give rise to a universal reciprocity. Suzuki and McConnell quote Shapley's calculations about the common particle of argon, which we breathe in and out every second, leading to the conclusion that 'Your next breath will contain 400000 of the Argon atoms that Ghandi breathed in his long life' (Shapley quoted in Suzuki & McConnell, 1998). Suzuki and McConnell therefore see as a role and duty for humanity, as a sentient species, the promotion of well-being of all forms of life, as a sort of global expansion of Kant's categorical imperative of two hundred years earlier.

CONTINUITY AND TRANSFORMATIONS

Two celebrated philosophical aphorisms neatly summarise important common principles of social and physical sustainability. The first, that of Heraclitus in the fifth century BC, 'I step, yet do not step, in the same river twice', demonstrates the futility of attempts at total preservation because all life and matter is undergoing constant change (Graham, 1999). The second, from the eighteenth-century French scientist Lavoisier summarising the philosophy of Anaxagoras of two thousand years earlier, is hauntingly similar: 'Nothing is lost; nothing created: everything is transformed' (Direct Essays, 2010). The community planning significance of both statements is the need for good stewardship to involve caring and conservative use rather than the passive appreciation of the watchdog, because nothing can be maintained in exactly its present form. Sustainability is therefore more a matter of devising cyclical or reversible transformations, rather than, for instance, reducing all issues to demands for ever-tighter levels of population control in particular localities. Conservation and progress are thus compatible, but at the cost of careful, considerable and consistent forethought about desired outcomes and unintended consequences. Sustainability and planning indissolubly need each other.[xvii]

The need to conserve natural resources is strongly implied in the celebrated definition of sustainability by the World Commission on Environment and Development (1987) as 'development meeting the needs of the present generation without compromising the ability of future generations to meet their own needs'. This also supports the view of the physical world as 'natural capital' proposed by Paul Hawken and Amory and Hunter Lovins (1999), who suggest that each generation should confine its consumption to renewable material (the 'interest') without diminishing the total scale or variety of the natural endowment of the globe and biosphere, which constitutes the world's 'natural capital'. Because of the web of connections linking all life, this applies equally at local, regional and global levels. Local action is required to stem global warming; regional action is necessary to prevent the poisoning of watersheds, which percolate into every tract of local environments; and global agreements are needed to provide funds to protect threatened local environments in places like Amazonia and the South Pacific. Sustainability is

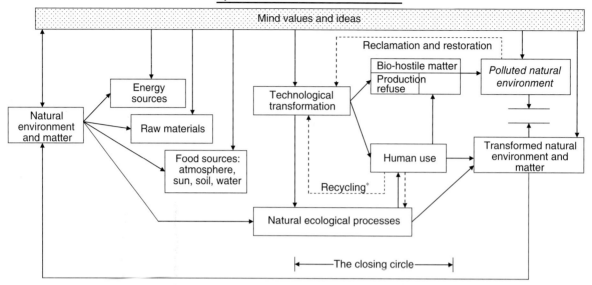

Figure 5.2 showing:

Cycle of human use of natural resources

* Recycling: water, metals, paper, glass, sewerage, animal waste
+ Reclamation: mining spoil, chemicals, plastics, concrete, bricks, domestic refuse, derelict land

Figure 5.2 Cycle of human use of natural resources.

equally important for social and economic systems as it is for physical ones: slavery and war, for instance, ultimately destabilised Bronze Age societies and those of the world of classical antiquity (Childe, 1976) and continue to menace modern life on every continent. In terms of physical conservation, however, we are fortunate that there are numerous methods to promote sustainability. These methods are briefly outlined below.

THE SEVEN *R*'S OF RESOURCE CONSERVATION

Sustainability can be an elusive, as well as a highly important, concept and needs to be approached along a variety of paths. One valuable first step is to apply the term in its original role as an adjective describing specific resources such as water supplies, atmospheric management and sources of building materials, settlement form and extent, traffic generation and community governance, with immediate benefits of clarity about what is and may be involved. In this way, the discussion is moved towards achievable objectives that can be defined and sought within a political process, making them at once more democratic and implementable and moving them away from visionary, cloudy and often dogmatic personal convictions. Another useful approach is to engage simultaneously in reflective review, observing ourselves in action, and

considering the impacts that we are having on people, species, spaces and systems around us. Figure 5.2 is an example of this kind of 'Reflection-in-Action' (Schon, 1995). This model suggests some of the techniques which can help sustain the human and biospheric systems on which we depend and which we influence, including the seven *r*'s of reuse, recycling, reclamation, rehabilitation, reservation, rationing and regulation, which are briefly outlined below.

Reuse involves reconditioning and recirculating such items of repeatable use as batteries, cartridges, clothing and containers. In its most extensive form on the outskirts of productive and dynamic cities like Kolkata and Lagos, it can provide a lucrative income for energetic people seeking to establish themselves in the city, at the same time as saving enormous areas from destruction by landfill. In Western societies, stores and enterprises to promote reuse are springing up throughout the suburbs of great cities

Recycling, the conversion and concentration of important resources such as construction material, paper and water, can drastically reduce the need for such environmentally damaging activities as new dam building, quarrying and deforestation. One well-known and important example is the reverse osmosis treatment of domestic and industrial water and its return to reservoirs for further use.

Reclamation, increasingly important in today's times of rapid technological change, can bring back spaces and resources to healthy use from formerly ruinous activities involving the redevelopment of old 'brownfield' sites such as docks for office spaces and urban farms, as well as the reinstatement of polluted areas such as Sydney's Homebush district of massive chemical contamination for the 2000 Olympic Games and London's Lea Valley for housing, modern industry, sports facilities and ancillary public open space associated with the 2012 Olympic Games.

Rehabilitation involves restoring damage and blight resulting from superseded uses, often associated with extractive industries, which can be converted to habitat conservation, sport, recreation and open space buffers to constitute one of the most satisfying and inspiring activities of community planning, with examples including the redevelopment of old spoil tips for ski slopes and the use of water bodies caused by subsidence for bathing and boating.

Reservation is being recognised as an increasingly important technique to safeguard areas to sustain, preserve and recuperate habitats and species. One celebrated example is Australia's Great Barrier Reef Marine Park, occupying an area of more than 200 000 square kilometres and presided over by a statutory authority with strong zoning and planning powers. Most of the world's many National Parks are such reserves, and more are needed, nowhere more urgently than in the fish-breeding grounds of the North Sea, Atlantic and western Pacific Ocean. Locally, small reserves are needed to safeguard threatened habitats, protect places of cultural significance (as with New Zealand's Marae) and provide sites for play and refuge.

Rationing, the control of access to an area or item of limited supply, can be based on democratic decision, market choice or a combination of both. 'Resident only' parking permits are one example, congestion charges another and emissions trading schemes a third, indicating the very wide range of levels at which this important control may be operated.

Regulation has come to be associated very closely with planning in mixed economy democracies, which tend to rely on controls over private development to achieve their land use intentions. It remains one of the most effective ways of achieving sustainable land use, a notable example being the Urban Growth Boundaries and Urban Footprints that are increasingly being adopted to limit the urban sprawl of great metropolitan regions and preserve precious habitats and environments of rural areas in North America, Europe, East Asia, Africa and Australia.

Relations among the four community values

The strength and resilience of communities is greatly influenced by the ways their shaping and sustaining values support and reinforce each other or sow the seeds for future dissension. Although the four values of prosperity, liberty, justice and sustainability emerge well from this compatibility analysis, each provides a limiting case for the others, like a corner tent peg holding in place the overall canvas of community life, a pattern of relationship which is summarised in Table 5.2.

THE IMPACTS OF PROSPERITY

The contributions of prosperity to liberty

Prosperity not only makes powerful direct contributions to community life but also promotes companion values of liberty, social justice and sustainability. Freeing people from the tyranny of necessity, by creating and storing food surpluses and providing comfortable shelter and financial security, helps to develop the independence and freedom of thought for sound personal reflection, judgement and decision (Rawls, 1971).[xviii] Economic strength can also advance political power. The emancipation of women of the last fifty years, for instance, has been greatly assisted by growth of their economic power as dexterity and organisational skills of office work in the knowledge economy has displaced the dominance of strength-based manufacture. In similar ways, the global development of consumer society has supported the rise of representative democracy. The increasing adoption of community consultation and participation has owed as much to the growth of the economic as to the political power of workers, consumers and voters.

In both India and China, current economic developments are encouraging an upward spiral of increased personal freedom, which is replacing the old vicious cycle of penury and repression. 'Dalits' (previously termed 'Untouchables'), who have never dared to claim the most basic political rights in India, are now, encouraged by economic advancement, stepping bravely into the highest levels of Indian political life. At a more local level, micro credit in Bangladesh and elsewhere is helping to emancipate people, many of them landless peasant women, who were previously 'the poorest of the poor' not only from their destitution but also from their powerlessness (Bornstein, 1997). The productive activities of exchange, contact and free

Table 5.2   Relationships among four community planning values

	Contributions to achievement of other values			
	Prosperity	Liberty	Social justice	Sustainability
Prosperity		Supports personal independence, self-expression and educational attainment, but may be used to justify inequality	Supports personal and mutual esteem and interdependence, but may threaten fair shares for all	Supports reflective equilibrium and sound judgement, but may consume natural capital
Liberty	Stimulus to individual creativity, inventiveness and exchange		Promotes free criticism, participation and protection for fair shares, but may intrude on equal rights	Favours personal responsibility and reflexivity, but can devour common goods and rights
Social justice	Promotes productive social capital and capacity to contribute	Safeguards human rights and personal initiative, but may develop excessive regulations		Protects common goods from destruction for short-term individual profit
Sustainability	Maintains resource base, environmental capital and long-term investment	Protects living environment but can be misapplied in authoritarian shortcuts	Safeguards natural resources and rights of future generations, but should observe distributional justice	

movement also contribute to the growth of liberty, and trade has promoted both individual enterprise and the spread of knowledge (Jacobs, 1969). It is not necessary to be an economic determinist to appreciate how much human independence benefits from a basic level of personal prosperity, allowing individuals to enjoy a secure home, income and personal access to health and education.

Productive societies also need and create mass literacy, which encourages individuals to aspire to be 'as good as their masters'. The grammar and maths schools and universities of the Renaissance, originally intended to produce administrators to serve the interests of the captains of State and commerce, rapidly expanded their role to nurture scientists such as Copernicus, Galileo and Newton, who revolutionised the worldviews and material mastery of their times, and philosophers such as Peter Abelard, John Wycliffe, Immanuel Kant and John Stuart Mill, who constantly raised the questions which have shaped the development of liberty in community life.

The impacts of prosperity on social justice

Social justice is concerned with the distribution of wealth and power: who will have what freedoms and how collective wealth will be distributed. Aggregate levels of prosperity in the form of indicators like the gross domestic product or average income levels may

tell us very little about social justice. While some prosperous mixed economy societies like Sweden enjoy egalitarian distributions of wealth and power, other equally affluent ones such as the United States and Australia experience much lower equity (Wilkinson & Pickett, 2009). Elsewhere, relatively poor societies such as Cuba and Vietnam may have quite egalitarian distributions of wealth. Widely differing levels of economic justice may operate in different parts of a single society, as in mid-twentieth-century Spain, where the rapidly expanding numbers of members of the Mondragon Workers Cooperative (rising to over 90 000 by 2008) maintained an absolute differential of six times the pay of its lowest paid operative for its highest paid managers, compared with ones many times that in the rest of the country (Whyte & Whyte, 1988). By comparison, in contemporary Australia, the ratio for chief executive officers is approaching sixty times the nation's minimum wage. Programmes aimed solely to increase gross national product may do nothing to improve social justice.

Appetites for prosperity can also lead successful individuals and groups to seek to devour the opportunities of their fellow citizens. Pay differentials of 60:1 between captains of business and investment bankers and, for instance, the essential workers of water supply and refuse collection not only offend people's sense of justice and thereby threaten the stability and sustainability of community life, they also endanger the prosperity which was their original justification, as senior executive officers in search of performance bonuses pursue short-term profits and ignore reinvestment in the infrastructure for tomorrow's production in favour of insecure investment in hedge funds derivatives and 'subprime' housing markets at high rates of interest. At the global scale, there is also evidence that the international division of labour and direct foreign investment can result in economic exploitation and even armed enforcement and military invasion (Monbiot, 2003; Heywood, 2006). Community planners can make invaluable contributions to human flourishing by balancing the dynamism of prosperity with the concerns of social justice.

Relations between prosperity and sustainability

In the short term, prosperity has often been won at the cost of the conservation of resources and, therefore, of sustainability. Statesmen and economists tend not to be notably interested in the long-term future with which sustainability is most concerned. 'In the long run', as John Maynard Keynes (1964) observed in his *General Theory of Employment, Interest and Money* of 1936, 'we are all dead.'[xix] Nevertheless, if societies are to succeed and contribute to building social and environmental capital to maintain an upward spiral of social evolution, we should plan to forestall social disasters. Greek landscapes were stripped of trees to smelt bronze and iron and build trading ships, until the peninsula was no longer capable of supporting its own population without emigration to new colonies. Greenland colonists from Iceland and Norway committed similar mistakes, resulting in their isolation in a marginal and cooling environment until they were condemned to a slow extinction through starvation and hypothermia, their skeletons becoming smaller and more diseased in their increasingly frozen and shallow graves (Diamond, 2005). The pursuit of prosperity is often conceived in such short time spans of enjoyment of abundance from immediate consumption of resources that conflicts with environmental sustainability become inevitable.

Of course, it is true that consideration for long-term prosperity can also lead communities towards sustainable practices, like the forest preservation and reforestation of Tokugawa Japan and democratic Scandinavia and the irrigation practices of Bali and Sri Lanka (Diamond, 2005). It is also often argued that only prosperity can produce sufficient wealth to avoid the necessity which drives people to destroy the very resources on which their future should depend. Such surplus wealth, it is argued, can fund the extra costs of environmentally compatible production, recycling of resources, rehabilitation and reforestation of damaged landscapes and conservative reuse of resources. The reintroduction of adequate fuel supplies to Timor-Leste in 2001, for instance, ended the tragic necessity to strip trees of their branches, day by day, branch by branch, to provide the wood for essential cooking. Local people returning to the Dili waterfront from their flight from the marauding militia in 2000 would circle sadly round well-loved local trees, with their machetes, trying to select a branch whose loss would not prove fatal to the whole tree. As soon as fuel supplies were reinstated, careful conservation of local timber was resumed, to prevent erosion and to nurture local insect life and fauna.

A similar process of tree preservation is also desperately needed on the unstable steep slopes of western and central Nepal. Viewed properly, prosperity may thus offer powerful support for sustainable practices. It need not be, as it often is, reduced to use as a wedge to provide short-term wealth for entrepreneurs by prising long-term resources away from their source locations. Sustainability, like social justice, can produce highly significant benefits for long-term prosperity by ensuring, in the famous phrase of the World Commission on Environment and Development (1987), that humanity 'makes development sustainable to ensure that it meets the needs of the present without compromising the ability of future generations to meet their own needs'.

THE IMPACTS OF LIBERTY

The independent judgement required to build the knowledge on which prosperity is based depends on freedom of speech and publication. Without freedom to contest conventional truth, there can be, in the words of John Stuart Mill, 'no force to keep truth vital' (1983). It was, for instance, the enquiring atmosphere of the free societies of Renaissance England, the Netherlands and the Italian city states which did most to create the scientific revolution on which the Industrial Revolution and the prosperity of the modern epoch has rested. Equally, the creative genius of inventors from Leonardo da Vinci to the innovators of the Silicon Valley required talented, tolerant and open-textured societies to attract lateral thinkers and promote the exchange of ideas and skills (Florida, 2005).

The close relations between liberty and justice are demonstrated in the bills, charters and declarations of rights which have provided the milestones of social progress since the signing of Magna Carta in 1215.

Reading the United Nations' *Universal Declaration of Human Rights* of 1948, one is struck by how many of its 30 articles concern equality of rights among all people. Article 2, for instance, opens:

> Everyone is entitled to all the rights and freedoms set forth in this Declaration, without distinction of any kind, such as race, colour, sex, language, religion, political of other opinion, national or social origin, property, birth or other status. (United Nations General Assembly, 2008)

No fewer than 23 of the 30 articles commence with the words 'everyone' or 'all'. The strong reciprocal links between liberty and justice focus on the bonds of reciprocity, which hold communities together, frequently balancing or overcoming the strains of competition, misunderstanding, suspicion and free-floating anger to which they have also been prone.

The relations between liberty and sustainability are more complex. When balanced with social justice, there is a positive three-way equilibrium between equal liberties, sustainable resources and just distributions, in which one person's liberty to consume is constrained by the prudent use and conservation of resources to ensure a like liberty for others. Worldwide legislation against pollution of water courses, for instance, is widely regarded as compatible with human rights. Nevertheless, extreme libertarians and individualists proclaiming their rights to do as they wish run the risk of promoting a 'race to the bottom', in which neither society nor its natural environment can be long sustained. Once again, the need is clear for synergy between values in community planning.

THE IMPACTS OF SOCIAL JUSTICE

Social justice supports the charters, bills of rights and legislative safeguards which safeguard equal liberties and provide protection from the excessive liberty of one person causing the loss of liberty of others. Mill's criterion of whether a matter is primarily self-regarding or other regarding, or which aspects of it are in one category or another, provides the practical means to separate personal liberty from public licence. Social justice is also being increasingly recognised as a key component in the long-term creation of wealth (Hutcheson, 2004; Putnam, 2004). For instance, the importance of singing and dancing in the economic vitality of the 'third Italy' of Tuscany, Emilia Romagna, Umbria and Veneto, and promoting the 'associational economics' that flexibly combines existing skills to generate new products in times of changing economic demands like our own has been highlighted (Putnam 1993; Cooke & Morgan, 1998). This is all welcome evidence that 'the society that plays together, stays together' and learns to prosper through cooperation.

Sustainability is also favoured by this social justice. Communities of plants, species and people are all maintained within an ecological framework that is robust in its balance until excessive dominance of one element takes the whole system to a tipping point and massive dislocation results. Social justice concerns reinforce the sustainability needs of society to maintain environmental and social systems for the benefit of all in this and future generations.

SUSTAINABILITY IMPACTS

Sustainability provides the long-term underpinning for prosperity, securing the future resources of natural and environmental capital, prompting conservative use of natural products, such as bamboo, hemp and timber, and encouraging development of such renewable energy sources as tidal, solar, wind geothermal and wave power. The important strategy of demand management, reducing individual consumption of water, energy, road space and building land, originated in people's recognition of the need to conserve scarce resources. Jared Diamond reminds us that sustainability is not 'a once and for all' set of principles, but demands constant scanning of the changing physical, economic and social environments to respond to new threats and unintended consequences.

The contributions of sustainability to social justice are often subtle but nonetheless important. To be sustainable, communities will also have to integrate the economic benefits of social, human and creative capital into the community life of both their local and regional networks. Recognising and conserving common resources, rights and shared culture will require collaborative planning, now and in the future, to conserve natural resources of air, water, soil, species and habitats for the prudent use of the whole society. Principles of caution and recuperation link the two values of sustainability and social justice.

Like landscapes, communities evolve over time and develop strengths through building relationships and capacities for mutual aid. Like landscapes, they depend on sustainable systems, services and networks to maintain their resources and governance. Their conservation requires negotiation and personal self-control and involves not being greedy. Common caring, communication and reciprocity are the common ground of sustainable communities.

Conclusions: how values can combine to help solve problems and shape creative plans

Needs and values are the core from which community planning grows. They provide the motivation and direction for each of its phases of comparison, debate, development of ideas, evaluation and political commitment. While such basic human needs as food, water, shelter and exercise provide universals that shape the process, direction is drawn from productive debate between the competing priorities proposed by such distinctive human values as liberty, justice, knowledge and choice. The value of universality itself has particular contributions to offer, harmonising different attributes in ways which mirror the ecological symbiosis within and between species (Kropotkin, 1939; Sheldrake, 1990; Ridley, 1996; Suzuki & McConnell, 1998). Many different elements combine to hold each other in balance, and meet each others' needs to maintain the functioning of the human ecosystem. Too much freedom for one may destroy justice and eventually threaten the survival of another. When one element becomes too strong and consumes the space and resources needed by others, the consequences will be damaging to the whole system and may eventually prove fatal. For instance, too single minded a concentration on meeting the total demands of sustaining a particular privileged space or perceived resource may impact so badly on social justice or human prosperity in others that there may be disastrous outcomes. One notorious example is the extremism of the Khmer Rouge's emptying the towns of Cambodia, and instituting a process of recidivist extermination of people viewed as supporters of Western materialism or bourgeois progress, under the justification of a future-orientated vision of environmental and political purity (Pilger, 1992). Instead, many values must be identified, acknowledged and unfolded, so that their implications can be understood and compared and their eventual collaboration be negotiated through egalitarian debate. This is why Habermas (1987) proposes 'communicative action' as a daily means of human conduct and social decision.

The four values discussed in this chapter are intended to evoke and support many others, as in indicated in Figure 5.1. Their mutual compatibility offers a model for relating different values more widely. Apparent conflicts can give rise to constructive resolutions that in turn generate feasible solutions and policies. For instance, tensions between prosperity and sustainability should prompt proposals and inventions of methods of production designed to meet the finite limitations of renewable resources, and therefore to incorporate many of the seven r's of reuse, recycling, reclaiming, rehabilitation, rationing, reservation and regulation. Similarly, the competing claims of personal liberty and social justice can combine to create policies of mutual aid and cooperation that apply the powers of human agency at the expanded scale of whole communities, cities, regions and beyond. Extraordinary collaborative achievements may result, such as global systems of satellite communication, tsunami warnings and post-disaster international aid in such situations as the global responses to the 2010 Haitian and Chilean earthquakes, and the regular operations of the World Health Organization in conquering cholera, combating malaria and managing the scourge of global epidemics.

Debate over values is well constituted to produce constructive outcomes. Multiple criteria objectives, evaluation and policy development thrive on the challenge of interrelated problem-solving. This often results in the well-known pattern where the most highly constrained situations with the most difficult problems may give rise to the most original design solutions. One celebrated example is the design and construction of the Sydney Opera House, successfully aiming to combine values of environment, aesthetics, metropolitan focus, national and international culture, performance requirements and entertainment quality. In a similar way, but at a much greater scale (earlier examined in Box 1.1 in Chapter 1), the values of liberty, justice and sustainability have been combined in pursuit of prosperity for impoverished rural women and their families in contemporary Bangladesh in the highly creative policy of micro credit, which was stimulated in response to a formidable array of entrenched and intractable problems of ingrained privilege, traditionally licensed exploitation, self-serving gender discrimination, economic isolation and marginalisation, an established culture of poverty, poor communications, extreme exposure to environmental catastrophe and perceived political impotence. The resulting policy of decentralised and small-scale financial stimulus owed much of its extraordinary and exemplary success to its roots in its lively awareness of all these problems, which spanned not only the four major values of prosperity, liberty, justice and sustainability but also other related ones of choice, communication, contact, leadership, nurture self-expression and shelter (Yunus, 1998). A wide range of values, even where they may appear to compete, are far from being impediments to successful community planning. Constructively approached, they may be brought together to build the mainspring for its most important innovations. Such methods of planning call upon contributions from all our ways of thinking and knowing to invent better solutions to satisfy our values, in line with Hume's aphorism with this chapter opened, that 'Reason is, and should only be, the slave of the passions'. These reasoned methods will include those of art, science and craft, which are discussed in the next chapter.

Endnotes

i Land uses develop and structures are built to accommodate activities such as residence, work, play, movement and administration, and can therefore be interpreted as responses to basic needs and wants. These may be described as 'values' because they are what people are drawn to value in their lives. Work, for example, may be performed in pursuit of a number of values, including providing sustenance to maintain life for ourselves and our families, as well as to express our natural creativity or to achieve prosperity, power, status or self-esteem. Play similarly expresses not only its own values but also those of skills development and therefore, indirectly, sustenance. Similarly, movement may be sought for reasons of choice, recreation, productivity or autonomy. The implications of these considerations are explored in more detail in Chapter 6.

ii The rapid transmission of such technical skills as pottery, metallurgy and wheel use (for irrigation, transport and pottery iteslf) of the fifth and sixth millennia BC coincided with the development of settled societies with stable community organisation (Childe, 1976). In Mohenjo-daro in the Indus Valley in particular, excavations indicate the existence of specific quarters of potters, armourers, wheelwrights and dyers, supporting the storing and transmission of specialised skills and knowledge, which would have been far more difficult in nomadic or widely scattered societies. In *Man Makes Himself*, Childe (2003) describes the evidence for the existence in the Bronze Age of specialist copper workers and even potters, who travelled from settlement to settlement providing scarce skills in ways which anticipated the wandering artists of the medieval era in Europe, whose journeys from community to community can be traced by the murals and carvings that they executed on the early churches and friaries of the time.

iii They must also have assisted the species in responding to the dramatic changes of climate associated with the coming and passing of the ice ages. There is likewise an impressive array of signs of choice and freedom in the evidence of productivity and nurturing of the Neolithic villages of ten thousand years ago collected by Peter Kropotkin for his monumental work *Mutual Aid* (1939). The epoch's characteristic activities of weaving, spinning, pottery, crop breeding, harvesting and making

flint tools must have relied on skills of individual and cooperative effort rather than mass regulation. This interpretation is supported by Childe (1976), who comments that it is impossible 'to detect any indications of chieftainship in a [typical] Danubian Village' of this Neolithic period. The extensive trading patterns, which distributed products across and between continents, also indicate notable individual enterprise to undertake the many perilous journeys involved in these often hazardous sequences of exchange.

Individual freedom to travel and trade is also evident in the epoch of the great valley civilisations of five thousand years ago. Though much reshaped by the new dominance of military and religious elites, the spirit of liberty still shines through the earliest written records of four thousand years ago. The Mesopotamian *Epic of Gilgamesh* records the transitions between hunting, farming and urban life, from the standpoint of an heroic individual ruler of Uruk, who makes dangerous journeys to the mountain forests to secure cedar timber for his temples and befriends Enkidu, the wild hunter, who proclaims: 'I am the strongest here, I have come to change the old order, I am he who was born in the hills, I am he who is strongest of all' (Sandars, 1972). Later, and further to the east in India around 500 BC, Gautama Buddha offered enlightened individuals a very different and sevenfold path to true personal liberty leading through moral virtues, respect for all living creatures and truthfulness to an escape from the thraldom of material conditions and desires. Later, in the reign of Asoka (273–231 BC), these ideas were applied to influence the practical world of government in the edicts of the Emperor, inscribed on the many stellae erected around his dominions, declaring universal rights of thought and expression (Childe, 1976).

More assertive impulses towards initiative and self-expression are demonstrated in the Greek and Phoenician establishment of colonies around the shores of the Mediterranean, with independent and aggressive values vividly illustrated in the epic sagas of the Trojan War, with the brittle heroics of Achilles and the wily durability of Odysseus' exploits in Homer's *Iliad* and *Odyssey*. This creative self-confidence is also expressed in the grandeur of the Parthenon and surrounding temples of Athens' Acropolis and the carvings, statues and ornamental pottery of the city's classical and Hellenistic periods. Distilled into the social philosophy of Plato's *Symposium* and his *Apology*, they still inspire contemporary social theorists with the questioning spirit of liberty that proclaims the god-given right to question the policies and practices of the State and of one's fellow citizens.

iv When city life re-emerged in the ninth and tenth centuries AD, serfs who were absent for a year from their feudal demesnes became free citizens and the idea that 'it is city air which makes men free' became a commonplace. Throughout the tenth to twelfth centuries, as Kropotkin notes (1939):

Thousands of fortified centres were built by the energies of the village communities, and once they had built their walls, once a common interest had been created in this new sanctuary – the town walls – they now understood that they could resist the encroachment of their internal enemies, the lords, as well as invasions of foreigners. A new life of freedom began to develop within the fortified enclosures. The medieval city was born.

For Kropotkin, it was liberty which shaped modern community life and these links between community life and liberty were strengthened through their productive invention of craft guilds, frequently combining to form city governments in a staged movement towards local democracy.

Citizens' rights were also to shape the continued social evolution of the great trading cities of the Renaissance – the North European Hanseatic League and the international trading centres of Amsterdam, Haarlem, Antwerp, London, Hamburg and Venice, recorded in the individualistic elegance and opulence of such painters as Rembrandt, Vermeer, Veronese and Canaletto. Support for personal liberty in this life and salvation in the next was provided by the Protestant doctrines of Luther and Calvin, adding a religious basis to justify belief in personal responsibility.

Similar Renaissance values of individualism and originality were expressed in the experiments of artists and engineers such as Leonardo da Vinci, with his inventions of flying machines, submarines and siege machines and the haunting psychological interpretations of canvas and mural painting like the *Mona Lisa* and *The Last Supper* proclaiming the triumphs and tribulations of personal freedom and unfettered mental inquiry (Rizzati, 1968). The scientists, including Galileo and Isaac Newton, who transformed human understanding of the world also made good use of their liberty to question and reinterpret both received truths and the evidence of their own senses. Newton benefited from the relative freedom of life in seventeenth-century Cambridge and Galileo successfully stepped a perilous path between religious observance and independent thought to help lay the foundations for modern science.

Shakespeare's intuitive empathy with such dilemmas is still recalled every day in the contemporary world. Thirty years before Galileo was given the choice between torture and recantation by Pope Urban in Rome, the playwright's character of Hamlet captures the heroic agony of such personal responsibility and choice when he asks himself in his celebrated soliloquy:

To be or not to be: That is the question;
Whether tis nobler in the mind to suffer
The slings and arrows of outrageous fortune
Or to take arms against a sea of troubles
And by opposing end them.

The challenge to reconcile these conflicting goals of liberty and responsibility were readily accepted by the humanistic social philosophers of the time. In 1644, Hobbes proffered a 'social contract' according to which people gained rights to preservation of life and property in return for submission to the laws and taxes of the State. Within fifty years, John Locke was arguing that these rights of the individual should be extended to representative government and freedom of belief and that political power should exist and be exercised only for the public good (Locke, 1978).

v Dostoevsky's novels *Crime and Punishment*, *The Brothers Karamazov*, *The Gambler*, *The Idiot* and many others contain such wonderful insights into human nature and motivation that they should be prescribed reading for any course or programme of conflict resolution.

vi Starting with England's *Magna Carta* in 1215, declaring rights of justice and equality before the law, trial by jury and freedom from arbitrary imprisonment, the scope of human rights has been continually advanced. The 1628 *Declaration of Rights* extended the rights of the feudal lords of Magna Carta to include elected parliaments (Robertson, 1999). The 1689 *Bill of Rights*, guaranteeing freedom of speech and writing, prompted the publication in the following year of John Locke's long-contemplated *Two Treatises of Government* and *Letters concerning Toleration* (1978), creating the effective foundations for the contractarian doctrine, which now provides a bridge between the values of human liberty and social justice.

vii The command of the entrepreneurs and investors of the Industrial Revolution spread rapidly from its origins in mid-eighteenth-century Britain throughout Europe and North America. Within a century it came to dominate global life. Large workforces were required to live in cramped, unsanitary and often polluted environments and to work long hours in noisy factories and dangerous mines (Engels, 1987).

viii Nietzsche himself, a powerful protagonist of such 'Man and Superman' theories, nicely raises questions about the relevance of the ideas of self-proclaimed leaders for those subjected to their control, when he exclaimed, 'What? A great man – I see only the actor of his own ideal!' A contemporary philosophical commentator, Dave Robinson (1999), writes:

It is, however, not clear whether [Nietzsche's] Overman is an ideal, a recommended attitude of mind, a realistic future philosophy or a Darwinian inevitability. As a philosophical idea, its influence has been huge in both literature and life. The frequent misinterpretations and political applications of the doctrine have not always been benign.

ix These ideas were reflected in the libertarian views of Godwin's son in law, the visionary poet, Percy Bysshe Shelley.

x Mill was the godfather and guide of Bertrand Russell, who was to become one of the strongest voices proclaiming the rational rights of liberty (Russell, 1988a, 1988b, 1988c).

xi Australia's religious education controversy of the 1950s, resolved by the Commonwealth Government's funding support for minority groups' own education systems, is an illustration of the application of liberal and Fabian principles of encouraging individual and group participation in providing nationally guaranteed services. After a long, bitter and divisive dispute in the Australian Labor Party between two polarised wings composed of a large minority of Roman Catholic members and others suspected of Marxist sympathies, the party accepted the then Liberal government's funding model for education which allocated generous support for Roman Catholic schools to provide their own generally academically high-quality education, including religious education of their own choice and devising. This has worked well in academic terms with bipartisan support for nearly half a century and religious education is no longer a significant issue in Australian politics. The nation performs well in terms of literacy, numeracy and scientific and technological innovation.

xii The most recent revision, the Town and Country Planning (General Permitted Development Order of 2008 (Secretary of State for Communities and Local Government, 2008), maintains the spirit of requiring permission for development which obtrudes into the public realm or would impact directly on neighbours, before work can be undertaken. Specific requirements are that new building should be: behind the front building line, less than four metres in height, less than three or four metres from the neighbouring buildings on either side (depending upon whether they are one or two storeys high) and project no more than four metres to the rear.

xiii If the individual liberties of powerful or influential people are allowed free rein, they may result, for instance in 'the free rights of Englishmen to make life a hell on earth for themselves and for their neighbours', in the telling phrase of the historian of England's nineteenth century, David Thompson (1978). The turbulent course of the twentieth century also provides countless unwelcome examples of a tendency for painstakingly created social progress, unless adequately protected by cultural sanctions or legal force, to be devastated by explosions or episodes of unconstrained competition, ethnic antagonism or demonic energy.

xiv Reverence for unity with nature and respect for its conservation can be found within a number of religious and philosophical doctrines: in the ideas of Gautama Buddha on the sacredness of life, the teachings of the Chinese mystic Lao Tze, on the self-rewarding virtues of harmony, the words and actions of the Christian Saint Francis of Assisi on the joyous responsibilities of universal nurture, the message ascribed to the American Indian Chief Seattle on the imperishability of nature, the arguments of the contemporary ecologist David Suzuki on the inter-relatedness of all matter, and those of the

scientific theorists, Lynn Margolis and James Lovelock on the importance of the spirit of Gaia, adjusting, if not over-burdened by change, the different elements of life to each other (Lovelock, 1988; Suzuki & McConnell, 1998).

xv It is interesting here to note Karl Popper's (1989) definition of 'life' as 'negative entropy'. Entropy is what makes things fly apart. Harmony is what makes them hold together.

xvi The gifts were passed in opposite directions from individual to individual in the many villages of the Trobriand Islands, the Amphletts and the neighbouring mainland of New Guinea, uniting communities which are now separated under different national regimes of New Guinea and Solomon Islands, and riven with civil wars related to complex competing claims to control the copper mines of Pangui. C. D. Forde (1957), the eminent anthropologist, describes a practice which was contributing to peaceful community life throughout the first half of the twentieth century as follows:

> The red shell necklaces always move clockwise and the armlets anticlockwise, so that an individual participating in the exchange receives a necklace from one side and repays it with an armlet received from the other. The objects themselves are valuable ornaments only shown at festivals. To ensure friendly relations and to obtain moral lien on the best articles that come into the hands of his nearer colleagues, a member of the Kula 'ring' makes gifts of other objects to his fellow traders. Each journey of a Kula trader is also the occasion for extensive transactions of a more commercial character of food products and utensils. But even here the barter has the nature of an exchange of presents … The bigger journeys are events prepared long in advance and enjoyed by the whole community. The Kula maintains friendly intercourse between distant areas and gives a stability to economic relations which is lacking in most parts of Melanesia.

xvii There are many good reasons for working hard to achieve sustainability. One is the brittleness of recourse to the belief that 'After me, the deluge!': the floodwaters may not be so long delayed. Then there is the natural love that binds one generation to the next and that makes us want to bequeath a liveable world to our children (Rawls, 1971). Most people prefer the prospect of progress and productivity to that of dissolution and disaster. Finally, one of the most compelling justifications for living is the promotion of life itself, the whole project of species survival and evolution, first of our own kind and then of the entire biosphere. Whether one subscribes to Dawkins' selfish gene, Kropotkin's sociable species or Singer's moral being, there is no lasting satisfaction in creating devastation.

xviii Plato's *Symposium* vividly depicts a society where leisured aristocrats of the blood, like Alcibiades, and aristocrats of the mind, like Socrates, could formulate ideas of freedom that they could later enact, choosing to support or defy the conventional wisdom of their day. Even without slaves to bring the wine and food, which were such constant supports to their free speculations, their judicious balance of simple needs and ample resources laid the basis for the freedom which was the safeguard of Athenian democracy.

xix This quote comes from Keynes' *General Theory of Money*. During the Great Depression, the prevailing economic orthodoxy was the classic view that markets would adjust to disequilibrium without government intervention. Therefore, when the Great Depression occurred in 1930, the classic response was to do nothing – because in the long run the markets would solve the problem (real wages would fall, people would return to work and the economy would return to full employment).

However, Keynes regarded this as folly, in the depth of a recession, why not try to rectify the situation, rather than leave the solution to market forces? Although in the long run, the recession may end, the long run could be ten years away. Keynes wanted to try to solve the depression now rather than wait for however long the 'long run' may prove to be (Economic Essays, 2010).

References

Bornstein, D. (1997) *The Price of a Dream: The story of the Grameen Bank*. Dhaka, Bangladesh, Grameen Press.

Childe, V. (1976) *What Happened in History*. London, Penguin.

Childe, V. (2003) *Man Makes Himself*. Nottingham, Spokesman Books.

ClimateX (2007) *Wolvercote: A low carbon village?* http://climatex.org/articles/lo-carb-communities/wolvercote-low-carbon-village/, accessed 1 November 2010.

Cooke, P., Morgan, K. (1998) *The Associational Economy: Firms, regions, and innovation*. Oxford, Oxford University Press.

Creighton, L. (1904) *Life and Letters of Mandell Creighten: Vol. 1*. London, Longmans, Green & Co.

Cullingworth, J. (1979) *Town and Country Planning in Britain*. London, Allen & Unwin.

Cullingworth, J. (1993) *The Political Culture of Planning: American land use planning in comparative perspective*. New York, Routledge.

Diamond, J. (2005) *Collapse: How societies choose to fail or survive*. London, Allen Lane.

Direct Essays (2010) *Antoine Lavoisier*, http://www.directessays.com/viewpaper/41663.html, accessed 4 April 2010.

Dostoevsky, F. (1977) Notes from the underground. In: D. Magarshack (ed.), *The Best Short Stories of Dostoevsky*. New York, Modern Library.

Economic Essays (2010) *In the Long Run, We Are All Dead: J. M. Keynes*, http://econ.economicshelp.org/2008/10/in-long-run-we-are-all-dead-jm-keynes.html, accessed 4 April 2010.

Engels, F. (1987) *The Condition of the Working Class in England*. London, Penguin, (first published 1844).

Florida, R. (2005) *Cities and the Creative Class*. New York, Routledge.

Forde, C. D. (1957) *Habitat, Economy and Society*. London, Methuen.

Graham, D. (1999) Heraclitus. In: R. Audi (ed.), *Cambridge Dictionary of Philosophy*. New York, Cambridge University Press.

Habermas, J. (1987) *The Theory of Communicative Action*. Cambridge, Polity Press.

Hawken, P., Lovins, A., Lovins, H. (1999) *Natural Capitalism: Creating the next Industrial Revolution*. Boston, Little, Brown & Co.

Hellenic Resources Network (1995) *The European Convention on Human rights*, http://www.hri.org/docs/ECHR50.html, accessed 6 August 2009.

Heywood, P. (2006) Universal rights and global wrongs. *Commonwealth Association of Planners Newsletter*.

Heywood, P. (2008) The place of knowledge-based development in the metropolitan region. In: T. Yigitcanlar (ed.), *Knowledge-based Urban Development: Planning and applications in the information era*. Hershey, PA., Idea Group.

Hutcheson, J. (2004) Social capital. *Journal of American Planning Association* **70**(2).

Isard, W. (1956) *Location and Space Economy*. Cambridge, MA, MIT Press.

Isard, W. (1975) *Introduction to Regional Science*. Englewood Cliffs, NJ, Prentice Hall.

Jacobs, J. (1969) *The Economy of Cities*. Harmondsworth, Penguin.

Jacobs, J. (1992) *Systems of Survival*. London, Hodder & Stoughton.

Kant, I. (1934) *Fundamental principles of the metaphysics of ethics*, (trans. T. Kingsmill Abbott). New York, Longmans, Green & Co.

Keynes, J. (1964) *The General Theory of Employment, Interest, and Money*. New York, Harcourt Brace & World, (first published 1936).

Kropotkin, P. (1939) *Mutual Aid*. London, Penguin.

Leakey, R. (1982) *The Making of Mankind*. London, Abacus.

Locke, J. (1978) *Two Treatises on Government*. Guildford, Evesryman, (first published 1690).

Lovelock, J. (1988) *The Ages of Gaia: A biography of our living earth*. Oxford, Oxford University Press.

Mill, J. S. (1983) *Utilitarianism: On liberty and considerations on representative government*. London, Dent, (first published 1861).

Monbiot, G. (2003) *The Age of Consent*. London, HarperCollins.

Norton, D. (1999) David Hume. In: R. Audi (ed.), *The Cambridge Dictionary of Philosophy* (2nd edn). Cambridge, Cambridge University Press.

Pilger, J. (1992) *Distant Voices*. London, Vintage.

Popper, K. (1974) *The Open Society and Its Enemies: Vol. 1: Plato: Vol. 2: Marx and Hegel*, (5th edn). London, Routledge, Kegan Paul.

Popper, K. (1989) *Objective Knowledge: An evolutionary approach*, (revised edition, 5th printing). Oxford, Clarendon.

Putnam, R. (1993) *Making Democracy Work: Civic traditions in modern Italy*. Princeton, Princeton University Press, (with Leonardi, R., Nanetti, R.).

Putnam, R. (ed.) (2004) Social capital. *Journal of American Planning Association* **70**(2).

Rawls, J. (1971) *A Theory of Justice*. Oxford, Oxford University Press.

Richardson, H. (1973) *Elements of Regional Economics*. Harmondsworth, Penguin.

Richardson, H. (1975) *Regional & Urban Economics*. Harmondsworth, Penguin.

Richardson, H. (1978) *Regional & Urban Economics*. Harmondsworth, Penguin.

Ridley, M. (1996) *The Origins of Virtue*. London, Viking.

Rizzati, M. (1968) *The Life and Times of Michelangelo*, (trans. C. J. Richards), Feltham, Hamlyn.

Robertson, G. (1999) *Crimes against Humanity*. London, Hamlyn.

Robertson, G. (2009) *The Statute of Liberty*. Sydney, Vintage.

Robinson, D. (1999) *Nietzsche and Postmodernism*. New York, Totem.

Russell, B. (1988a) *In Praise of Idleness*. London, Unwin, (first published 1935).

Russell, B. (1988b) *Power*. London, Unwin, (first published 1940).

Russell, B. (1988c) *Unpopular Essays*. London, Unwin, (first published 1950).

Sandars, N. (1972) *The Epic of Gilgamesh*. Harmondsworth, Penguin.

Schon, D. (1995) *The Reflective Practitioner: How professionals think in action*. Aldershot, Arena.

Secretary of State for Communities & Local Government (2008) *Town and Country Planning General Permitted Development Order: Amendment number 2 (England) Order, 2008*. London, HMSO.

Sheldrake, R. (1990) *The Rebirth of Nature, The Greening of Science & Nature*. London, Century.

Suzuki, D., McConnell, A. (1998) *The Sacred Balance: Rediscovering our place in nature*. Vancouver, Greystone Books.

Thompson, D. (1978) *England in the Nineteenth Century 1815–1914*. Harmondsworth, Penguin.

Titmuss, R. (1973) *The Gift Relationship: From human blood to social policy*. Harmondsworth, Penguin.

United Nations General Assembly (2008) *International Declaration of Human Rights*, Allen & Unwin, (first published 1948).

Whyte, W., Whyte, K. (1988) *Making Mondragon: The growth and dynamics of a workers co-operative complex*. Ithaca, NY, ILR Press.

Wilkinson, R., Pickett, K. (2009), *The Spirit Level: Why more equal societies almost always do better*. London, Allen Lane.

World Commission on Environment and Development (1987) *Our Common Future*. Oxford, Oxford University Press.

Yunus, M. (1998) *Socially Conscious Capitalism towards a Poverty Free World*. Public Lecture Transcript, Brisbane, Queensland University of Technology.

6 Communities of Method

To succeed in linking the many scales and activities of contemporary life, community planning requires methods which are equally comprehensive and able to embrace the variety of ways in which people live, work, move and associate. This will involve combining techniques drawn from the creativity of art, the precision of science and the productivity of craft to help shape communities which will need all those characteristics if they are to succeed in pursuit of values of prosperity, liberty, justice and sustainability in times of rapid change. Planning is artistic when it creatively draws together ideas and materials to shape new events and places. It is scientific when it tests ideas against evidence, even though it cannot claim to develop universal laws or predictions. As an acquired skill, communicated through actions, words and drawings that can be repeatedly applied to new situations, it is also a craft. Finally, as a public activity it must be under political control and informed by community participation. Accordingly, the chapter is organised into the following four sections:

- art and creativity in planning;
- science and knowledge in planning method;
- planning as a craft;
- political control and community participation.

The concluding section indicates the ways in which values-based methods provide the common ground where those engaged in planning very different activities for different levels of community can collaborate in the confidence of compatible methods based on communicable aims.

Art and creativity in planning

To think about the future at all requires imagination, and to think about improving the quality of human living conditions, as community planning is committed to do, involves practical social idealism. Planning is therefore concerned with what *should* be, rather than purely describing what *is*. Like art, it involves sensing, interpreting and re-creating the observed world in forms, sounds and writing. Creative planning interprets information to understand and improve activities, by searching out causes and effects, in similar ways to those by which art combines feelings and ideas to create its own outcomes.

Community Planning, First Edition. Phil Heywood.
© 2011 Phil Heywood.
Published 2011 by Blackwell Publishing Ltd.

EVIDENCE OF CAVE PAINTINGS AND ROCK ART OF EARLY COMMUNITY PLANNING

Evidence that such creative impulses are deeply embedded in the human psyche is provided throughout the archaeological record. Amongst the earliest works of art are the astounding cave paintings of the Cro-Magnon peoples who inhabited Europe from 28 000 to 12 000 years ago. The most dramatic examples of these are from the Lascaux caves. They depict the huge bison, mammoths, deer and horses which the Cro-Magnons hunted. Expert interpretation suggests that their creators were seeking to capture the essence or spirits of the animals (Campbell, 1985). It is doubtful if their intentions were purely decorative because the most spectacular examples of Cro-Magnon art are confined to caves, in deep underground fissures with long galleries and passages that were quite unsuitable for habitation or everyday use. Their large size and careful preservation suggest that they were highly significant for the whole hunting group, who must have supported the artists' work, implying pantheistic religious significance. Campbell concludes that 'the prodigious [artistic] output of Cro-Magnons is closely associated with their spiritual life', and was a vehicle for sympathetic hunting magic. The artists were not only imitating life but also making magic. In this way, these Palaeolithic cave paintings could be read as an early, and highly effective, form of planning to promote the future activities and productive success of their communities.[i]

ART IN AUSTRALIAN ABORIGINAL CULTURE

A similar spiritual significance pervades the work of Australian Aboriginal artists going back as far as 30 000 years ago. Strongly stylised rock drawings depict the pantheistic Rainbow Serpent, the creation spirit of the world, and the numerous other animal ancestor spirits who were believed to have given rise to the land and people who inhabit them to this day. In the oldest paintings, hand stencils literally put people's mark on the rocks, and abstract networks of criss-cross lines proclaimed the tribe's possession of the land. In the middle period, stick figures seem to celebrate human existence, and the activities of hunting, fishing and dancing. Later so-called X-ray pictures are both creative and analytical, searching for the inner essence of the creatures they depict – in some ways anticipating Picasso's combination of full face and profile figures. They certainly create a synthesis of elements that transcends mere observation and aspires to capture the spirit of the life and land it celebrates.

Aboriginal art is thriving and evolving into new combinations of traditional elements and abstract relations. One example is Emily Kngwarreye, who died in 1996 in her mid-eighties after an extraordinary flowering of creativity in the last eight years of her life (Neale, 1998). She painted many hundreds of canvases in a remarkable range of styles, using dots, nodes, stripes derived from body painting and startlingly beautiful Monet-like areas of rich primary colours, mainly blues, green, reds and ochres, as illustrated in Plate 6.1, *Earth's Creation* of 1994, which also provides the image for the cover of this book. Many of the later works were so large that a small machine had to be constructed to wind the canvases forward as her work went on at a rapid but steady pace. When asked to explain what her paintings depicted, she replied:

> My dreaming, pencil yam, mountain devil lizard, grass seed, Dreamtime pup, emu, emu food plant, green bean and yam seed. That's what I paint: whole lot. (Neale, 1998)

Put simply, Emily was creating a comprehensive vision. By re-conceiving, depicting the whole landscape, she was maintaining the tradition by which its essence could be understood and protected. The community planner aiming to create a fruitful and useful community appraisal is embarking on similar roles of understanding, interpretation, translation and communication.

THE GIFT OF FORM

Planning, like art, thus translates its ideas, values and proposals into tangible forms of one sort or another. This inventive capacity may generate remarkable transformations in the hands of architects and civil engineers. Bold schemes can evoke whole trains of personal association and affiliation in the minds of viewers, which greatly increase their impacts on emotions and commitment. The other side of this power of the image is its capacity to suspend critical faculties, which has strong implications for the adoption of the 'precautionary principle' to ensure advance evaluation of unintended consequences of proposed actions.[ii] These are discussed later in the chapter, in reviewing the roles of evaluation to produce well-tested rather than spectacular but possibly damaging proposals. Nevertheless, because nothing comes out of nothing, the creative impulse of invention remains a mainspring of all planning as well as an integral part of the processes of evaluation.[iii]

The universality of the creative impulse, integrating art, design and science in the activities of a single person and a common method is well demonstrated in the life and work of Leonardo da Vinci (1452–1519). His artistic works, including *The Last Supper* and the *Mona Lisa* are masterpieces of interpretation. In science, his designs for mechanics, anatomy, hydraulics, flight and flying machines, submarines and engineering anticipated technological developments by as much as five hundred years; and in physical planning, his schemes for fortified towns and ducal palaces combined elegance and efficiency (Mannering, 1981). In his case, the creative drive was so dominant that many of his artistic works were never finished. Extracts from his sketchbooks, vividly displayed in the Museo della Scienza in Milan, show him starting with a basic idea, working it through a series of detailed tests for feasibility of individual parts and making amendments until he is satisfied that it could work. His sketches for paintings show the same exploratory sequence.

The reason that the resulting works such as the *Mona Lisa*, the *Annunciation* and the *Last Supper* possess a marvellous coherence is that they flow from a unified original idea. Awareness is giving rise to understanding and interpretation, which are in turn shaping design. This also constitutes an effective model for planning method. Throughout the work of Leonardo's contemporary, Michelangelo, too, there is evident the same drive to free this intuition or idea of the artist from latent form into solid reality.[iv] Although it may seem presumptuous for others without this level of cosmic genius to aspire to such transformational creativity, in many ways the tasks being undertaken in shaping or reshaping whole communities to reflect the interests and hopes of their many thousands of members is no less challenging, and will demand similarly universal intentions.

Even as depictive an art form as landscape painting depends on the ideas of the artist. The French eighteenth-century classical painter Poussin, for instance, aimed to tame the 'disorder of natural scenery' by applying the logical form and harmonious balance of the 'golden section' to the vertical and horizontal elements of his paintings (Clark, 1956). Rather than merely recording observations, Poussin and later landscape painters such as Claude de Lorraine and Constable came to influence the ideas of landscape designers like Capability Brown and Humphrey Repton, who then created landscapes in the image of the idealised paintings. Ideas were shaping reality as much as observations of reality were shaping ideas. In planning method, as in art, ideas play a driving role.

THE CREATIVE IMPULSE IN COMMUNITY PLANNING

Evidence of this spirit of invention in the physical planning of communities abounds in historical records. In much the same way that nests of birds can tell us much about nature and conditions of life of their occupants, remains of civilisations throughout the last 5000 years display settlement patterns and public spaces that express their dominant ideas and values. Mohenjo-daro and Harappa, the Indus Valley cities of about 2000 BC, for instance, show strongly geometric development with rectilinear street patterns, centrally placed large public baths (as shown in Plate 10.1 in Chapter 10), and segregation of residential, industrial, religious and administrative quarters, which imply the imposition of ideas of order to transform the natural landscape into a city (Mumford, 1961; Whitehouse, 1977). Another celebrated example of early planning is Maru-Aten, the Pharaoh Akhenaten's planned new town of approximately 1400 BC (Desroches-Noblecourt, 1976). The influence of Hippodamus' strongly idealist plans, satirised by Aristophanes in Athens in the fourth century BC, can still be traced in the unvarying geometry with which the street system of Athens' new port of Piraeus, developed at that time, sits over the hilly topography of its steep peninsula. Aristotle, in his Politics, records the logic which underlies Hippodamus' plan. The city was composed of 10 000 citizens, and divided into three parts, one each for artisans, farmers and warriors. The three triads met at the central city square, or *agora*, the focus of the gridiron street pattern. Likewise, the surrounding land was to be divided into three parts, one sacred and dedicated to the worship of the gods, one public and in the keeping of the warriors and the third private and for use by the farmers (Mumford, 1961).

Later, the Romans were to spread the ideal urban form of the grid across Europe in the innumerable colonial *castrae*, or fortified towns, which they established wherever the empire extended. The same form was borrowed to reflect the different set of values which inspired the contemplative cloister of the early medieval abbeys and cathedrals, and was passed on to form the model for the town squares, piazzas and places of the Renaissance city. The intellectual vigour and artistic energy of the European Renaissance inevitably modified and developed the public square as a focus for activities and buildings, reflecting the dominant values and activities of the age of order, elegance and display.[v] Their widely influential designs helped to create a heritage of places of timeless beauty and order that has survived war and industrialisation, to create physical models still suited to the human scale of community life.

THE CONTRIBUTIONS OF ART IN SOCIAL AND CULTURAL DEVELOPMENT

The creative visions of the arts have helped shape the development of community planning and remain a driving force. Painting, sculpture, music, dance and writing each express and help develop the spirit of communities and places. By recording, interpreting and celebrating the features and forces of life, the arts foster social and cultural capital and create messages that help to maintain communication and cooperation. Music, song and dance allow people simultaneously to express themselves and understand and appreciate each other. Whether it is Beethoven's *Pastoral* and *Choral* symphonies, the ragas of Indian music or contemporary soul and rap, music evokes values which help unify its audiences. The surging life force of Mozart's fortieth symphony and Bjork's ballads energise and raise the spirits of those who hear them. In a similar way, Philip Glass's *Heroes* and *Light* symphonies capture the challenges to human values and perception of the rapidly expanding boundaries of the Space Age. The singing of choirs can express the common humanity of both individuals and groups of otherwise very different people, and the act of choral creation can become a powerful symbol as well as a source of community cohesion.[vi] It is significant that choral societies are prominent among the cooperative social institutions that Putnam (1993) identifies as the source of the social capital that has played a major role in the economic and cultural success of the Emilia–Romagna, Tuscany and Umbria regions in the 'Third Italy'.

In Africa, it is often dance that allows people to express their joy in living and relationships. Amongst Australian Aboriginal communities, too, dance may express very basic truths and interpretations. For instance, native title and land rights have been recognised by West Australian courts based on evidence of continued association of tribal groups with land from which they had been forcibly removed, on the evidence of the dances that had been memorised and were still performed to express the spirit of that land.

The capacities of painting to capture and portray the spirit of humanity and community have already been discussed. Painters have often supplied the emblems and symbols to communicate the rich variety of human experience and community life far more directly than words can, whether it is the vision of cooperative and harmonious communities of farmers and craftsmen sharing the common religious faith of Lorenzetti's *Allegory of Good and Bad Government* of Sienna in 1337–39, or the wonderful vitality of David Hockney's *The Diver*, painted in California in 1978 (Plate 6.2).

The written word also demonstrates the uniquely powerful capacity of art to transform life into meaning. Writing and records are both cornerstones of civilisation, enabling knowledge to be developed and stored and ideas and goods to be exchanged between people and over time. As well as being essential tools of method, they are also incomparably effective ways to develop and evaluate ideas of what constitutes a good society. Plato's *Republic*, More's *Utopia*, the celebrated prayer of St Francis's of Assisi, and J. S. Mill's *On Liberty* (1983), for instance, have all contributed basic ideas which have helped to shape community planning. Contemporary writers such as Margaret Attwood, A. S. Byatt, J. M. Coetzee, Doris Lessing, Nadine Gordimer and Arundhati Roy all present ideas which shape the goals and drive the processes of community planning as much as did earlier religious and secular writers.[vii] While many writers warn of dysto-

pias, others, including advocates of conservation such as Commoner (1972) and Suzuki (2009), are more positive in their world views, aiming to solve problems and celebrate wholeness and interdependence as well as to warn of entropy and destruction. The English poet William Wordsworth (1946) caught this spirit well in 1802, at the turn of the eighteenth and nineteenth centuries when he exclaimed over the beauty of Thames-side London in the early morning and produced a vision of harmonious relations between humanity and nature that survived the excesses of the Industrial Revolution:

> This city now doth like a garment wear
> The beauty of the morning, silent, bare;
> Ships, towers, domes, theatres, and temples lie
> Open unto the fields and to the sky,
> All bright and glittering in the smokeless air.
> Never did sun more beautifully steep
> In his first splendour, valley, rock or hill;
> Ne'er saw I, never felt, a calm so deep!
> The river glideth at his own sweet will;
> Dear God! The very houses seem asleep;
> And all that mighty heart is lying still.

The sense of harmony expressed in these lines vividly celebrates the community life of the great metropolis, balancing and integrating the many hundreds of places and thousands of human energy sources which interact to form and sustain the life of the city. Viewed in this way, the forces of community life appear as basic as those of nature, where gravity and mutual attraction hold together the physical forces of the universe.

CREATING WHOLENESS WITHIN NEW AND EXISTING COMMUNITIES

Community planning needs to design ways to bring together the many activities performed by thousands of people in new and self-sustaining relationships. New spatial forms will often be required. Ebenezer Howard's ideas of garden cities interacting within the regional network of the 'social city' are an example of this. He aimed to merge the values of rural space, peace and resources with those of urban intensity and productive capacity to create bounded and energetic communities that would avoid both rural isolation and inner city over-intensity. Current regional plans which often aim to focus metropolitan growth in linked clusters of activity centres are similar problem-solving inventions (Metro Portland, 2003; Queensland Government Office of Urban Management, 2005). They aim to combine innovative proposals for:

- integrated transport plans to replace reactive road building of urban motorways;
- regional economic development schemes to provide information technology, educational support and environmental quality to lead innovation rather than responding to market trends;
- regional open space systems to conserve valuable spaces and habitats and shape and complement intensive networks of regional settlement;
- cultural and local engagement that supports and involves local communities in planning and organising local and metropolitan life.

Over the last fifty years, the architect, mathematician and planner Christopher Alexander has been exploring and promoting such synthesising or 'multiple criteria' processes to conserve and recreate wholeness in existing and new settlements. Each one of a series of books, (often written jointly with colleagues in the Berkeley, California, Center for Environmental Studies), has unfolded further the ideas of its predecessor, starting with *Notes on the Synthesis of Form* (1979a), first published in 1964, continuing through the *Oregon Experiment* of 1975, *A Pattern Language* of 1977, *A Timeless Way of Building* (1979b), and *A New Theory of Urban Design* of 1987 to the definitive set of four volumes making up *The Nature of Order* (2002–2004), published by the *Center for Environmental Studies* over a three-year period.

Alexander, who also has qualifications in mathematics, has combined systems and set theory, scientific observations of pattern repetition at different levels of scale, and architectural theories of the elimination of misfit between form and context to create a general field theory of building and place-making. The intention of these new approaches is to more aptly accommodate activities and express values, than do current practices, often based on trend planning, technological determinism or architectural fashion.

His starting point is the observation that much traditional design of towns and countryside demonstrates an almost perfect fit between new forms and existing contexts. Examples that spring to mind include the countryside villages and small country towns of the English Cotswolds, Yorkshire Dales and Italian regions such as Tuscany and Umbria, perfectly settling into the contours, field patterns and woodlands of their surrounding landscape, so that the honey-coloured or grey-stone structures of the settlements appear as natural intensifications and knotting together the roads, walls and scattered farmhouses of their surroundings, rather than as separate elements. By contrast, much elaborate and systematically designed modern urban development is jarring, repressive and widely disliked by many of its thousands and millions of daily users. Such developments, he observes, result from ignorance or lack of respect for the preferences and needs of the people who will use them – and express a kind of contempt for the whole complex evolved pattern of the existing world into which these new developments should fit (1979a).

Alexander's explanation of this contrast in quality is that in traditional societies, where both technologies and social organisation are stable, design is able to evolve through cycles of trial and error over long periods in subsets of related activities which can be well differentiated from each other. Adaptations can therefore interact with a limited number of other factors to rapidly achieve a new balance. 'Failure and correction go side by side. There is no deliberation between the recognition of a failure and the reaction to it' (Alexander, 1979a). Inappropriate elements are continually replaced while appropriate ones are protected by taboos or custom. Repercussions throughout the system are minimised.

People who are familiar with the rural landscapes and country towns of Britain, France, Italy or Greece will often exclaim over the perfect relationships which exist between form and function and between the various elements of buildings, farmsteads and local settlements. Alexander's argument is that this resulted from stable social conditions in times of static technology and materials. A builder would erect a structure whose failings would soon become apparent and he would correct that mistake, and continue in a process of progressive error elimination until he had improved the quality of his design, in much the same way that evolution is thought to improve the capacity for survival of species by natural selection. Even if he didn't achieve complete success, the chances were that his son would continue in the family craft and would soon solve the old man's errors, as has been the delight of young people throughout the ages. In the same way, whole settlements would be developed to reflect the lives and needs of their residents.

Early in his career, in 1962, Alexander applied these ideas of synthesis through systematic and cumulative problem-solving while working as a consultant on village planning to the government of Gujerat in north-west India. This exemplary Indian village study is reported in detail in Appendix 1 to his *Notes on the Synthesis of Form* (1979a). Taking as axiomatic that the role of planning is to fulfil wants and aspirations, he identified an array of 141 objectives. These were drawn from three sources:

- values and needs expressed by villagers themselves during a period of six months of continuous contact with village life;
- goals and objectives of the national and regional economy and social purpose;
- preservation of values, which he observed were satisfied implicitly in existing village life and form.

Using set theory and mathematical modelling of the relationships between these objectives, he identified the following twelve major issues requiring attention:

- A. Cattle
  - cattle grazing
  - cattle care, stalling
  - cattle security, access;
- B. Land
  - cash cropping
  - agricultural organisation
  - operational efficiency
  - landownership, conservation and development;
- C. Social life
  - commercial life and organisation
  - social and community development;
- D. Family life
  - 1. domestic organisation
  - 2. family life
  - 3. traditional and religious customs.

Alexander's method focuses on producing solutions, one by one, to each of these twelve sets of objectives, before proceeding in cycles of progressive adjustment to tackle conflicts and embrace synergies between them. For example, the land ownership and conservation proposals, including soil and forest conservation of slopes lying above the village's cultivated fields, interact with the needs for agricultural organisation to include family ownership of land and rights to water for irrigation. Relating and reconciling these two concerns produces proposals for water collection in reafforested and orchard production areas separated from the arable fields below by a bund of raised land, along which runs the spinal road of the village land. Wells for water extraction are placed immediately below the bund and linked by distribution canals to the land holdings of each family, laid out in ridge and furrow form to assist the process of water distribution, with meters to record consumption. By such means of cumulative problem-solving and adjustment, Alexander creates a unified plan which integrates physical, social, economic and cultural concerns to meet all of the plan's 141 objectives, at the same time as respecting the existing values, traditions and forms

of the settlement. Five themes can be discerned in the resulting village plan:

1. Respect for traditional materials and settlement forms, and their use in new development;
2. Reliance on local vernacular design based on established cultural values;
3. Integrated design through careful adjustment and combination of related elements;
4. Use of traditional values and forms to identify appropriate activities and guide the invention of new forms;
5. Local design that reflects universal principles of spatial organisation, which he develops further in his later *A Pattern Language* (1977).

In an interesting example of parallel creativity, similar methods for evaluating designs have been produced for squatter and spontaneous settlements in north-western India and Delhi by the Indian architect-planner Neha Goel. In a paper entitled *Squatter Settlements: The urban vernacular*, delivered to the 2010 Conference of the International Planning History Society in Istanbul, she develops a methodology to understand the human, functional and spatial needs of squatter and self-help settlements in the adjacent region of the Kutch. Although not previously familiar with the work of Alexander, Goel adopted a similar method of deriving design criteria for the squatter village of Biodada in the Kutch and the self-help settlement of Khichripur in Delhi from the cultural, social and physical values of the people of those settlements and their people. Her functional and physical analyses of the settlements were based on the observed and recorded needs and existing success stories of the area's residents and traditional building styles and materials. Specific attention is given to each of the necessary residential functions of sleeping, cooking, washing, eating, procurement of water, family and social interaction and conducive conditions for the performance of chores. She notes that the arrangement of public space reflects natural patterns of centrality and assembly in small square and triangular areas where pathways meet. The interest of Goel's analysis and Alexander's proposals lies not only in their empathetic and consultative methods, but also in the brilliantly inventive solutions that Alexander produces, meeting objectives of care for cattle, land conservation, economic development, community vitality and domestic life. His approaches both empower existing communities and allow them to continue to develop where their members have grown up and acquired attachments to each other and to their common places. Neha Goel's ideas also reflect many of the principles of good design discussed in Chapter 10 of this book. They resonate with the case study (Box 10.1) which is recounted there of the upgrading of the Kolkata inner-city bustees by cooperation between the Calcutta Metropolitan Development Authority and the local communities in the period 1974–1986. This achieved spectacularly successful improvement of living conditions at costs of land, labour and capital that were much more affordable than those originally proposed by more conventional proposals that would have cleared and replaced these extensive areas, which accommodate almost two million of Kolkata's population (Heywood, 1987). These later approaches to partnership in settlement upgrading could provide the basis for similarly successful results for Delhi and other rapidly expanding Asian cities.

Moreover, these methods of successive problem-solving are also applicable elsewhere in dynamic contemporary societies, wherever the multiple changes of the scientific, industrial and information revolutions have replaced the stable conditions that fostered progressive elimination of misfit by repeated tides of change. In city centres and transportation hubs, for instance, design challenges constantly change; materials supersede each other before their inherent characteristics and limitations can be explored. The multiple-criteria design processes employed by Alexander and Goel offer highly appropriate methods to eliminate misfit between different elements and to establish harmony with their wider contexts. They simulate in design models the winnowing effects exerted by the passage of time in more static situations. By such means, we may avoid creating more of what Peter Hall (1980) calls 'great planning disasters' such as freeways carving up living cities and tower blocks separating young mothers from their children's play spaces. Alexander is at pains to point out in *The Process of Creating Life* (Volume Two of *The Nature of Order*) that this search to recognise, maintain and create wholeness is an inherently artistic and craftsman-like activity, leading him to demonstrate its workings by illustrations of Impressionist painting and classical Persian and Turkish carpets, in which each diverse feature is related harmoniously to the overall design. He is not seeking to displace creativity by the use of advanced mathematical analysis but rather to maximise its effect by successively concentrating attention on each of a comprehensive array of quite specific problems. Later stages then apply similar techniques to resolve conflicts between proposed solutions in an ascending process of cumulative invention which provides an effective method to achieve multiple-criteria design. This is the approach advocated for the synthesis stage of the planning process described later in this chapter.

Science, knowledge and planning method

SCIENCE AND ART

Like many of the best explanatory approaches, Alexander's methods often seem to combine the techniques of science and art, reflecting the findings of the thinker and theorist of scientific method, Karl Popper, who lived from 1902 to 1998. Popper (1959, 1972, 1989) argues that art, science and evolution are unified by their dependence on common creative problem-solving methods and patterns. The objection may be posed, however that science is different from art and design, being the realm of objective observation, classification, logical deduction and precise measurement.

SCIENCE AS MEASUREMENT

For three hundred years, the popularly held view of scientific method, as defined by Francis Bacon in his *Novum Organum* of 1620, was just this. He laid out a comprehensive model which commenced with careful classification of phenomena and proceeded to an exhaustive collection of facts and attributes in each category (Popper, 1989). After these were subjected to a number of universal tests, to determine their correct classification, experiments could be conducted to produce results on which explanatory and predictive theories could be based, as shown in Figure 6.1.

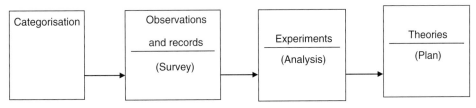

Figure 6.1 Traditional (Baconian) view of the scientific method (1616–1932).

This process begs numerous questions. How will the categories be decided if not on the basis of some pre-existing theories? How will experiments be devised to explore the nature of the phenomena? In short, how will theories be invented?

David Hume, writing in the eighteenth century, raised further doubts in his 'Enquiry concerning human understanding' (1990), which questioned the logical basis of prediction. A century later, in order to protect the empirical approach based on systematic observations, J. S. Mill tried to make sense of Bacon's model by accepting the idea of induction, drawing inferences from valid experiences (Passmore, 1980). This would allow the human mind to deduce universal patterns from a limited amount of evidence, rather like someone connecting points in a dot-to-dot puzzle to make up a pattern or a picture. Despite the apparent common sense of this idea, the stubborn problem remains that though phenomena or events may have been associated with each other in particular ways in the past this does not *prove* that there will be similar links in the future. Not all swans are white: Australian ones are black. Not all bread nourishes: bad wheat germ leads to ergotism and madness. In other words, causality is, in the words of Karl Popper, a probability hypothesis rather than a 'scientific' certainty (1989). Scientific theories themselves become hypotheses which have been imagined, tested and not yet disproved rather than truths which have been discovered and verified. Nevertheless, the fiction of inductive logic was so convenient, with its encouragement of the 'good habits' of systematic recording and careful observation, that it remained largely unchallenged for nearly ninety years, and remains a scarcely questioned view of many science teachers.

THE LOGIC OF SCIENTIFIC DISCOVERY

Thinking on scientific method was revolutionised with the 1935 publication in Vienna of Karl Popper's *Logic of Scientific Discovery*, redirecting attention to the question of how scientists actually develop new ideas and theories. Popper (1959, 1972) argued that science could not rely on inductive logic, since facts do not speak for themselves but can only be interpreted in the light of the ideas of their users. This is well summarised by Magee, explaining Popper's and Einstein's views. Magee (1973) writes:

There is no such thing as a logical method of having new ideas … every discovery contains an irrational element or 'a creative intuition' … In a similar way Einstein speaks of the 'search for

these highly universal laws … from which a picture of the world can be obtained by pure deduction'. 'There is no logical path,' he says, 'leading to these … laws. They can only be reached by intuition, based upon something like intellectual love of the objects of experience.'

Popper's views are optimistic. He argues that imaginative conjectures produce new hypotheses which can be refuted if they fail to explain observed facts or generate accurate predictions. Those that succeed become the best *available* truth given existing limitations of ideas and information. He envisages an upward spiralling evolution of knowledge, but rejects the possibility of finite human intelligences ever discovering *total* truth, which, being infinite, would require infinite intelligence and infinite information to comprehend. As a result:

All organisms are constantly, day and night, engaged in problem solving, and so are all evolutionary sequences of organisms. (Popper, 1989)

Natural selection is interpreted as a form of error elimination, through the failure to survive of an organism which has not made a necessary change and the success of one which has developed controls to rectify inappropriate changes (Popper, 1989). Reliance on this evolved capacity for problem-solving allows critical rationalists to welcome a continuous flow of initiatives, which can be tested against objective conditions of the real world:

Life is problem solving and discovery – the discovery of new facts, new possibilities – by way of trying out possibilities conceived in our imagination [is] trying to get nearer to the truth, to a fuller, a more complete, a more interesting, logically stronger and more relevant truth – to a truth relevant to our problems. (Popper, 1989)

This all-embracing view of the role of problem-solving in the evolution of life provides a model for the thought experiments which Popper advocates to speed up the evolution of knowledge:

While animal and pre-scientific knowledge grow mainly through the elimination of those holding the unfit hypotheses, scientific criticism often makes our theories perish in our stead, eliminating our mistaken beliefs before such beliefs lead to our own elimination. (Popper, 1989)

The relevance of this to planning is very clear: it becomes a prime means to recognise and solve problems posed by existing conditions, to produce new arrangements better able to match the nature and meet the needs of individuals and communities. Popper's tests, which have come to replace Baconian experiments, involve rigorous attempts to refute each new hypothesis, which may result in its being falsified and discarded or reformulated as a new theory, thus adding to the store of our objective knowledge.[viii]

In order to clarify this process of developing valid ideas, Popper refers to 'three worlds' of knowledge, each of equal validity and each supporting the others. World 1 is the observed world of external matter, existing more or less as recorded by the senses, and corroborated by a high level of successful use in everyday life and scientific predictions. World 2 consists of intelligent consciousness, typified in Descartes' celebrated aphorism 'I think, therefore I am'. It is the world each of us knows best and with which we are continuously familiar. World 3 consist of objective knowledge, and takes the form of scientific theories and recorded truths. Though produced by the interaction of consciousness and matter, it has its own independent existence, in books, on films and disks. If these were to be despatched into space, and the world destroyed by a calamity, some non-terrestrial intelligence could re-create an understanding of the nature of our world through interpreting these objects, indicating the independent existence of the objective knowledge of World 3 (Popper, 1989). Plans, as well as theories and works of art, are special cases of entities which exist in this 'third world' of ideas.

MISTAKES, PROBLEM-SOLVING AND HUMAN AND
SOCIAL PROGRESS

Together with other critical rationalists like Lakatos, and scientists like Medawar and Eccles, Popper has widened discussion about the evolution of knowledge to include social philosophy, politics and biological and mental evolution. He argues (1989; Popper & Eccles, 1984) that the evolution of the brain derives from the innate drives of organisms to solve problems which may diminish their chances of success or threaten their survival. Genes producing neurones which can store relevant information and help to create and test expectations of success in the light of experience are favoured by natural selection. Knowledge thus develops through mental processing of information about the observable world by the five senses, confirming or refuting expectations based on stored experience. Recognition of mistakes refines expectations and produces new and better ideas. Given the infinity of knowledge and relationships, first attempts at explanations are likely to be at least partly wrong.

Mistakes therefore are the starting point for the process of conjecture, refutation and improved conjecture which has taken humankind from superstition to science.

While Baconian empiricism abhors and tries to avoid mistakes, Popper's critical rationalism embraces them, shifting the focus of good method from justifying answers to exploring questions. The brain is no longer expected to collect and sift all available information impartially to produce explanatory theories, as Bacon believed, but to winnow out the information which is relevant to our interests and intentions. Thus, basic human problem-solving and idea-forming, not observation and accumulation of facts, become the basis of scientific knowledge, artistic endeavour and other purposive human activities, including planning. In the contemporary world of increasing scientific and technological specialisation, this is an empowering perspective, encouraging us to develop wide-ranging and radical new ideas, insisting that individuals have the problem-solving skills to continually renew the changing world, and freeing everyone, particularly planners and other decision-makers, from the impossible but self-imposed burden of know-alls, pretending that we have all the answers.

CRITICAL RATIONALIST APPROACH TO PLANNING

The basic beliefs of critical rationalists can be summarised as:

- Intellectual progress depends upon conjecture, attempted refutation and reformulation of ideas.
- Criticism is potentially constructive and provides the best path to valid knowledge.
- The value and truth content of statements increases with their audacity or unlikeliness because a trite or obvious truth adds little or nothing to human knowledge.

One of the interests of Popper's ideas for people involved in planning communities and settlements is that they span an even-wider range of interests than those of any one activity, even one as wide-ranging as community planning, extending far enough to embrace explanations of biological and human evolution. Not surprisingly, his theories are often open-textured, and do not precisely explain all phenomena in their field, but by so doing they leave space for new explorations, conjectures and refutations. As a result, such critical rationalism offers a coherent and encouraging context to understand and interpret existing conditions and to develop better options. It develops a perspective of planning and policy-making as successive open-minded conjectures which can welcome and incorporate new thinking rather than being driven to reject or suppress criticism. These views make planning and design imaginative and open-ended activities, rather than rule-bound, closed and cautious specialisms. They encourage anticipations of the future to pursue ambitious goals, make use of small steps and benefit from the most unexpected criticisms.

Proposals need not depend upon existing conditions, but can range widely among imaginative dispositions of existing and new resources. Bold and democratic objectives can be adopted, instead of burrowing into the analysis of existing constraints, as if these somehow represented the only form of possible reality. Public participation, too, will be much easier to design and more attractive to conduct once we have accepted that all competent thinkers have innate capacities to solve problems. Such transformational and responsive planning can reflect the dynamic but patterned nature of life, well expressed in Lavoisier's aphorism, quoted in the last chapter, that 'Nothing is lost; nothing is created: everything is transformed' (Graham, 1999; Lavoisier, 2010). The resulting objective-based planning is more realistic than the assiduous pursuit of the trend or the meticulous collation of statistics, based on the belief that out of them will emerge a useful idea, when in reality only useful ideas will be able to identify and breathe meaning into the most conscientious of observations and statistics.

COMMON GROUND BETWEEN SCIENTIFIC AND PLANNING METHODS

In summary, both science and planning are problem-solving activities, involving a cyclic process, which moves through:

- scanning the environment to sense aims, potentialities, problems and information needs;
- producing well-focused accounts of relevant information;
- developing hypothetical options;
- testing or evaluating options in the light of facts or values;
- refining hypotheses or options to form viable theories or feasible solutions;
- monitoring the performance of the theories or plans until anomalies or new problems arise to generate a further cycle of the theory or plan-building process.

Figure 6.2 relates planning methods to scientific ones. Both originate in a first phase when attention is directed to a situation or problem, resulting in interpretations, expectations and recognition of information needs. This gives rise to a second phase, collecting relevant information from direct or recorded observations. A third phase, combining the outcomes of the first two, is then able to produce hypotheses and options. In science, this may involve resolving the

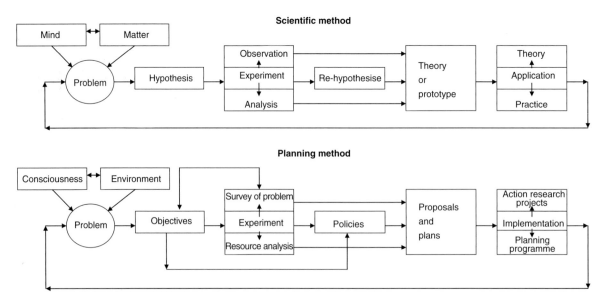

Figure 6.2 Models of scientific and planning method.

mismatch between expectations and evidence to stimulate an explanation of why observations are not as anticipated, such as the following notional syllogisms:

- The stars appear in different places each night; therefore either they are going round the world or the Earth is moving relative to them.
- Evidence of eclipses and relative positions suggests that the Earth and other planets move in different orbits round the Sun.
- Time is divided into day and night; therefore either the Sun is circling round the Earth each day or the Earth is rotating on its axis once a day.
- Evidence that the Earth orbits the Sun suggests that the phenomena of day and night must result from the rotation of the Earth on its own axis.

Such conclusions can then be tested in operation, by predicting and measuring future effects. In a similar way, more normative planning proposals can be produced and tested, such as:

- The five thousand tons of carbon dioxide being dumped in the city atmosphere every day by vehicular emissions on the journey to work are having devastating effects on health and climate; therefore we need to reduce either emissions per vehicle or vehicle distance travelled.
- If journeys to work in the city centre are to double, the proportion of them taken by single-occupancy private cars needs to be halved from 80% to 40%, if pollution rates are not to get even worse.
- This can be accomplished by reducing city centre car parking spaces by 60% and increasing provision of public and active transport to make this possible.

Figure 6.3 illustrates the logic by which critical rationalists explain how problem-solving contributes to human and social progress. People's initial awareness of problems results directly from consciousness of their environments, bringing their innate values and drives up against the constraints of the given world. Thus, both human and scientific problems are the products of innate drives to understand and control events. Where this conflicts with constraining reality, people's goals and objectives can be identified from the resulting problems.[ix] Although planning and science differ in that science seeks to establish universal laws, while planning is always returning to the particularity of place and people, they can be seen to share a strong commitment to creative problem-solving

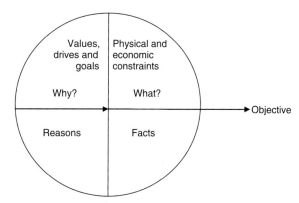

Figure 6.3 Generation of planning problems and objectives.

and objective-based explanation. However, planning also needs to have ready tools constantly available to shape events and resources to meet specific requirements. In this, it is more akin to the role of a craft, which is explored in the next section.

Planning as a craft

CRAFTSMANSHIP

It is clear from the first two sections that planning method derives creative solutions from art, and the use of measurement and tests from science. Nevertheless, planning is also a craft which must be regularly applied in cycles of repeated practice. In this way, it is similar to skills such as carpentry, weaving or computer programming. The characteristics and virtues of this kind of practical craftsmanship have been interestingly explored by Richard Sennett (2008), who argues that creativity is less the outcome of abstract mental pattern-making than the coordination of hand and eye in practical problem-solving. Sennett offers a different explanation to Popper of how the mainspring of problem-solving works in human progress. It develops, he argues, within the brain circuits connecting the activities of the hand and the eye. Later on, major shifts of associative logic[x] may result in developing new methods in quite different fields, which can then be refined by repeated practical application to become truly useful and reliable.[xi] Sennett argues that practitioners, whether they are musicians, carpenters, computer programmers or community planners, therefore need to master specific detailed skills and to practise long and purposively. To do this, they must be able to understand

(a)

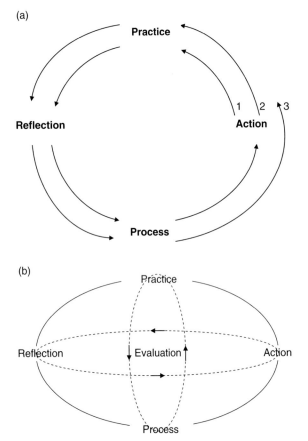

(b)

Figure 6.4   (a) Review in the action–reflection spiral;
(b) Evaluation in the action–reflection process.

and master all the component practices, each a kind of invention, which go to make up their crafts, such as chiselling mortise joints, fingering a violin string, elaborating a Linux program or designing an engaging and relevant method of community consultation. This sequence of improvement is illustrated in Figure 6.4.

This diagram is intended to show how people's instinctive responses to everyday needs for action naturally develop into accustomed practices, which, when reviewed in the light of stored experience and ideas, are refined to produce self-conscious processes. These can then revise and improve the next cycle of actions. Adjustments introduced by the reflective phase provide in this way the dynamic that converts this cycle into a spiral capable of keeping pace with the constant and inescapable changes of physical and human life.

THE FOUR PHASES OF PLANNING

This four-phase cycle involves a number of more specific stages, indicated in Figure 6.5. In the first phase, the state of awareness which gives rise to the intention to plan will also involve spontaneous *appraisal*. The second phase of *understanding* includes both the interpretation and projection of information about current situations and available resources, demanding some form of modelling (which is discussed in more detail in the next chapter). The *development and evaluation of options* of the third phase will involve both synthesis of information and reflection on results. In the fourth phase, refining these actions, practices and reflections into *proposals* for new ways of doing things should lead to both plans and programmes for their implementation and monitoring. This four-phase process, far from being intimidating, should reassure and empower practitioners, who can be confident that each of them can be applied at different levels of intensity, depending upon the scale and complexity of the planning situation. These can vary from the 'back of an envelope' record of existing knowledge before briefing a committee or a community group to a major two-year programme of search conferences and research investigations required for a community planning strategy for a major city or region.

In summary, planners, like any other practitioners, need to have a series of steps that they can apply, with minor amendments, to handle all the situations that may confront them. In this, they are like craftsmen, who, having acquired a working knowledge of each stage of their process, frequently find it possible to cut corners, to merge stages and to improve the quality of work by thinking ahead. In so doing, the best craftsmen (say a Chippendale, a William Morris or a Stradivarius) may breathe an almost perfect unity into their work, achieving a beautiful harmony between the materials, style and relations of the elements to reflect the original objectives.[xii] Similarly, skilful planners will aim to ensure that each stage of their process reflects their scheme's overall intentions. For example, an action research project (which may normally come later in the process) may be brought forward because a particular scheme can test and amplify ways to satisfy some particular objective, at the same time as involving significant stakeholders at an early enough stage to secure their engagement and support and to incorporate their knowledge and objectives. Equally, ultimate solutions that may occur intuitively at the outset of a planning scheme should not be puritanically excluded, but instead recorded for

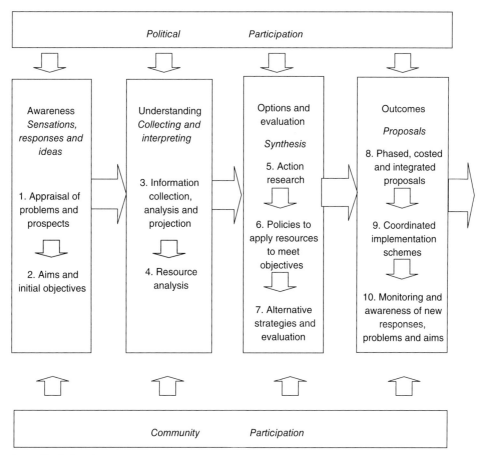

Political   Participation

Awareness
*Sensations,
responses and
ideas*

1. Appraisal of
problems and
prospects

2. Aims and
initial objectives

Understanding
*Collecting and
interpreting*

3. Information
collection,
analysis and
projection

4. Resource
analysis

Options and
evaluation

Synthesis

5. Action
research

6. Policies to
apply resources
to meet
objectives

7. Alternative
strategies and
evaluation

Outcomes

Proposals

8. Phased, costed
and integrated
proposals

9. Coordinated
implementation
schemes

10. Monitoring and
awareness of new
responses,
problems and aims

Community   Participation

Figure 6.5   Generalised planning process.

further development later on when options are being
generated.

TEN PLANNING STAGES

Within the general framework of these four phases, a
ten-stage process can be identified, as shown in Figure
6.6. Each stage constitutes an important step in the
overall journey from values through social, economic
and physical facts to community plans.

Whether plans are concerned with health, work, recreation, transport, housing or land use, these same
four major phases and their related stages can be
applied to provide a regular and direct path to reflect
the experiences and meet the needs of the people who
will use and bring life to their proposals. They are
designed to develop plans that are logical and responsive to the values of their users. The method should

also be open at each stage to external contribution and
scrutiny from other professionals, community
members and political leaders. By providing a common
set of activities and sequences, they can support cooperation and mutual adjustment between people undertaking and planning a very wide range of activities.

At present, coordination often founders on the different requirements, methods and timescales involved.
For instance, natural resource planners may be working
to achieve very long-term goals of global conservation,
often set by political commitments, while transport
planners may be driven by established programmes
developed to meet the requirements of trend projections of such pressing problems as traffic accidents and
local vehicle flows. Land use planners may be trying
to reconcile the conflicting aims of longstanding professional resolves to achieve urban intensification with
those of more immediate market pressures for land

Social process   Technical process   Political process

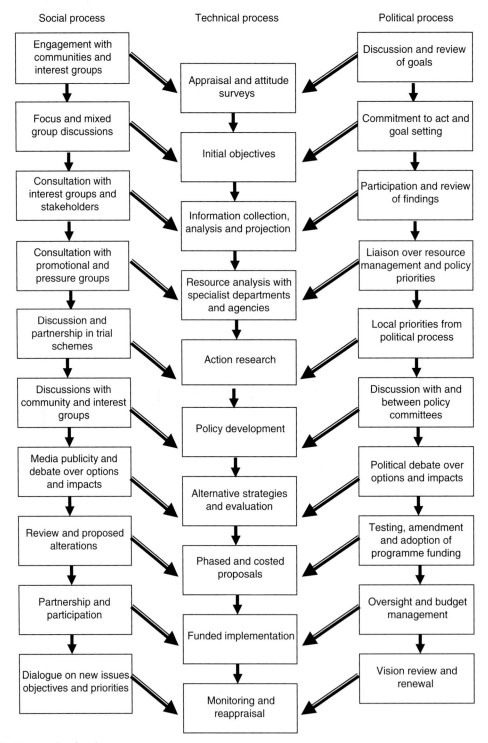

Figure 6.6   Community planning process.

Table 6.1 Comparison of phases of cabinet-making and community planning processes

Phase	Cabinet-making	Community planning
Appraisal	People's current use of products and views of their strengths and failings	Characteristics and problems of the area and its community, and views of the people involved
Initial Objectives	Client and market wants and designer's interests	Needs, problems and potentialities of the community and area and their current and future members and occupants
Information collection and analysis	What is needed from the product and the likely level of demand	The nature and extent of existing provisions and deficiencies, and their effects and causes
Resource analysis	Available materials and their capabilities, limitations and attractions	Resource availability, particularly land, finances, skills, powers and incentives
Action research	Making working models of different components to test their strengths and weaknesses	Small-scale implementation of key elements in partnership with local groups, firms or council departments
Policy Development: assembling and shaping of ideas and outcomes	Combining of techniques, funds, resources and materials to meet requirements	Policies to combine available resources to meet identified objectives, involving actions, agencies, funding, powers and performance indicators.
Alternative strategies and evaluation	Different available styles and materials and the relative advantages of different working models, making use	Alternative options, forms and physical strategies to fulfil policies and meet objectives and their costs and benefits in combining best features to achieve identified objectives
Costed and phased proposals	Designs for production, assembly of components and distribution of products	Integrated proposals, including vision, policies and performance indicators for each activity, with location maps and agreements required between cooperating partners
Implementation	Arrangements for materials, labour, finance and marketing, leading to commencement of production	Development of specific costed programmes for identified agencies and departments and an infrastructure plan and programme
Monitoring and review	Market review and research. Design adjustment to match market needs and preferences	Performance observation and testing by public attitude surveys, to review of objectives, adjust schemes and commence new cycle of planning

release and economic stimuli. These are all legitimate elements in a pluralist democracy. They can be openly expressed and transparently balanced within comprehensive sets of objectives and phased programmes of action. Progressive problem-solving can help. Mixed uses and phased implementation over regularly reviewed time horizons, for instance, can help to accord fair attention to each of a number of potentially conflicting priorities, and these can be integrated in comprehensive plans. In the words of the old proverb: 'You do not need to do everything at once. That is why time is spread out!' A common vocabulary and simple methods such as the sequence of awareness, understanding, options and outcomes demonstrated in Figure 6.3 can provide the necessary starting point for this process of mutual understanding. Such communities of method can enhance cooperation to harness the roles and energies of individuals, community groups and public authorities. The complex shaping of community life to meet the inevitable needs and pressures

of social and physical changes can benefit from this collaboration.

In order to clarify the roles and relations of each of these stages, Table 6.1 presents a simple description of the ten stages of this values-based approach to planning as a craft, illustrating its simple logic by equating each stage with that which a skilled cabinet-maker, similarly concerned to meet the demands of a large and diverse community market, would be drawn to adopt.

Before proceeding to discuss each of these stages of planning, it will be useful to establish agreement on the use of words and meaning of terms and this is provided in Box 6.1.

Stage 1: Appraisal of problems and prospects

Like people's innate capacity to create meaning through language, appraisal is exploratory and instinctive. This initial phase involves open-minded and

---

Box 6.1   Definitions of some key planning terms

Values
Concepts and states sought by individuals and groups, including both basic human drives essential to survival, such as *sustenance* and *health* and those which have evolved as a result of self-consciousness, such as *knowledge* and *social contact.*

Goals
Broad aims within society, which, being wider than specific and achievable end states, can provide necessary indications of desired directions, such as *lifelong learning* and *affordable housing.*

Objectives
Planning objectives:
Specific and achievable desired outcomes, e.g. *to provide adequate affordable rental accommodation* or *to provide adequate opportunities for student interaction.*
Operational objectives:
More precise statements, which translate planning objectives into a particular context, following more familiarity with the study area and the collection of more information, e.g. *to provide 300 units of rental accommodation in the social housing sector at rents of not more than 30% of the average income of the lowest quartile to meet projected needs in five years' time* or *to provide opportunities for informal interaction between arts, business and design students in residential, recreational and academic spaces before and after lectures and during daily activities.*

Policies
Statements of how operational objectives are to be achieved, demonstrating feasibility. They should include a justifying *rationale* answering the question, *Why?* referring to objectives. They should also answer the questions: *What should be done? How should it be done? Who should do it? With what powers and finances, and over what periods of time? And in what types of location?* Policies therefore require the collection and analysis of considerable amounts of information.

Proposals
Written and diagrammatic summaries of intended actions, including precise indications of where these will be located.

Plans
Comprehensive written, diagrammatic and mapped specifications of proposed activities and land uses, the changes necessary to bring them about and the agreements required between actors and agents.

Evaluation
Judgment about worth or meaning based on identified values. In planning, evaluation has two aspects:

1. The continuous weighing of observations and information to determine their worth or significance.

2. The systematic weighing of developed options or overall strategies in the light of their identified objectives to determine strengths, weaknesses and possible improvements.

---

open-hearted inquiry that includes senses, sympathies, chance contacts, experiences and previous practice. It can aptly be described as planning with our whole bodies and minds. Soaking the senses in the characteristics of place, patterns and problems can prompt creative responses which will help shape later proposals. Methods designed to capture a wide range of community members' and groups' perceptions and insights can contribute to an inclusive range of objectives for the next stage and assist later collaboration. Box 6.2 therefore emphasises its subjective nature. Contact with local people and stakeholders can prepare the ground for regular consultation that can avoid the devastating effects of developing a siege mentality, which can all too easily happen in situations where there are high stakes of money and impacts on people's lives.

Stage 2: Aims and initial objectives

The introductory appraisal of the first stage also plays an important role in exploring draft objectives. This may surprise some open-minded people, whose first feeling may be that such an important matter as plan-

Box 6.2   The appraisal

Aims

- To establish the scope, range, initial aims and approximate boundaries of the plan.
- To establish an initial sense of direction: 'What really matters here and now?'
- To establish contacts in the study area.
- To get a feel for the area, its people and their problems and hopes from both the inside and the outside.

Means

This stage involves personal evaluation based upon observation and reflection, which can be assisted in a number of ways:

- By briefing from members of residents and other local interest groups and stakeholders, including staff and students of the local school.
- Participating and observing in activities in local centres like shopping areas, parks, playing fields, school playgrounds and other community spaces.
- Exploring the study area in a random way with and without notebook and camera.
- Research from published local histories, fiction and poems; studies and policy statements; and notice boards and newspapers.
- Team discussions to promote exchange of ideas and perceptions.

Outputs

- Information and questions for a Consultation Kit.
- Contacts with groups and individuals.
- Personal understanding of some of the main local concerns.
- A report summarising the context, character, main activities, problems and potentialities of the area, which can be used to brief other team members and people becoming involved in the project.
- Provisional draft objectives.

Form

Words, sketches, photographs, maps, diagrams, tables and collages.

Style

Holistic, subjective, exploratory, imaginative, interpretive and qualitative rather than quantitative.

---

ning objectives should not be approached until careful research has been completed. There are two reasons why this is only partially true. First, in planning, as in life, nothing comes out of nothing, and one must be clear on general intentions at the very outset of an activity, in order to avoid becoming a mere commentator or pawn of present pressures. This early direction-setting, often involving personal reflection and group discussion of values, wants and needs, will not preclude later expansion, amendment and refinement. Rather, it may provide the basis on which such changes can be openly made, involving the kind of 'mixed scanning' discussed in Chapter 4, generating sequences of comparison between long-term goals and immediate needs, and between local problems and citywide

priorities. One example of the value of this mixed scanning in setting objectives is the the the need to reconcile insistent immediate pressures to accommodate high rates of urban population growth with long-lasting goals of equitable provision of affordable housing. Resultant policies will need to combine market dynamism with government controls.

A second advantage is the opportunity to gather and inscribe diverse community objectives at the very outset of the planning process, which may otherwise tend to be driven, by default, by the subconscious values, social assumptions or professionalised goals of the planning team. A third reason is that effective and informed investigation of facts itself requires research questions to focus inquiry. Logically, research cannot completely precede identification of objectives. The Aladdin's Cave of modern information sources ranges from the wealth of online national census information, through the rich array of information assembled by promotional and interest groups concerned with such systems as housing, environment, transport and employment, to the networks of human cooperation involved in Wikipedia. Only clear guidance from explicit initial objectives, provided by the compass of overall intentions, will allow the investigator to steer a purposive path through this potentially confusing landscape.

Of course, these objectives will not be interred, like buried treasure near where were discovered, but will be regularly checked and added to in the course of the journey. They will provide repeated reminders to consider 'what matters here and now'. Consultation must therefore play a large part in appraisal and objective setting, but it is important to emphasise that no phase should be regarded as 'the consultation stage'. As indicated in Box 6.2 and later in Figure 6.6, dialogue needs to be developed early and to become a theme of all stages.

Once broadly sketched, objectives need to be more systematically developed, analysed and applied. Starting early, they will continue to evolve throughout the process and will later provide the springboard for each succeeding stage. They perform a number of key roles:

- **Direction:** Objectives define what a scheme aims to achieve, and thus its intended ultimate effects, including answers to such key questions as 'Whose interests?' and 'What activities?'.
- **Consultation:** Objectives are an ideal basis for consultation: they can be used as identifiable and accountable inputs that can shape proposals. In this sense, they are a useful way of keeping planners honest.
- **Information requirements:** Clear objectives indicate the information that is required about activities and resources; without this focus, there is a tendency for facts to be collected mainly because they are available, causing plans to suffer from loads of irrelevant data resulting in 'analysis paralysis'.
- **Action research:** Objectives may suggest action research projects, which can increase understanding about feasibility, unintended consequences and implementation issues at the same time as generating public participation and political support.
- **Structure and content:** An integrated framework based on the range and links of objectives can be show the pattern and scope of the plan, so that its content and preparation can be organised, understood and improved.
- **Performance standards:** Objectives indicate what performance standards need to be developed, so that proposals can be measured relative to plan's intentions, rather than relying on whatever indicators happen to be statistically available.
- **Evaluation:** Objectives provide the best possible basis to judge alternative plans and compose best possible composite proposals.
- **Review:** They form the logical basis from which to monitor the performance of the plan, and to identify deficiencies that need correction.

It is clear that objectives permeate all phases of planning. The entire process could be viewed as their refinement, enrichment and synthesis through cycles of information collection, analysis, synthesis and evaluation, until they emerge as fully developed, integrated and action-orientated proposals. Objectives are thus the unifying themes of plans. An image that captures well this role is the inspiring clarion of the trumpeter, with objectives being the breath that gives life and energy to its call. They are modulated by the instrument's valves, mixed by the keys and reshaped by the experiences, ideas and musical knowledge of the performer to create a melody that transforms everyday breath into a clarion call capable of inspiring those who hear it to concerted action.

Stage 3: Information collection, analysis and projection

The possibilities suggested by the objectives will lack precision and hard edges. In order to produce effective solutions and policies it is necessary to collect information on aspects such as scale, frequency, interrelations and intensity. The analysis of this may involve seeking to infer causes by identifying the factors involved and seeing how their relationships have changed over time, as demonstrated in the worked example of housing demand projections which forms Appendix 1 of Chapter 7. Projection is a particularly interesting issue, both for what it cannot as well as what it can do. In the mid-1960s, projection was often equated with the whole planning process. The early system planners believed that the main purpose of planning methods was to identify the various activity systems, project their future states and then provide land to accommodate their growth (McLoughlin, 1968; Chadwick, 1972, 1987). There are a number of problems with this approach. The direction in which events are currently moving may be problematic or undesirable so that to follow the trend may not be helpful. Again, it is not possible to know for certain what is going to happen in the future, so accurate projection may be impossible. The act of projection actually involves a number of assumptions about unpredictable facts and values, and it is much better to acknowledge these rather than to pretend they don't exist. Finally, planning is the very attempt to control the future to accord with specified objectives rather than to accept the unmodified outcome of current social conditions.

Projection has, nonetheless, real value. On the positive side, it indicates the potential that present trends and existing arrangements have to fulfil identified objectives. On the negative side, it is a most powerful tool for indicating what might happen if no interventionary action taken. In this way, it may be a very useful indicator of necessary but currently hidden objectives. Impact assessments and 'doom watch' approaches are particularly useful forms of planning projection.

Stage 4: Resource analysis

The resources available to individuals are their time, their money, their land and their powers of motivation, influence and collaboration. Equally, the resources available to governments and communities are their skills, finances, physical resources of land, air and water – the so-called factors of production – and powers of enforcement and incentives. Each of these needs to be explored to find out the community's ability to fulfil its objectives.

- Skills will pose the question: 'Who?'.
- Finance demands: 'With what funds?'.
- Land and resources require: 'Where and how?'.
- Powers and incentives prompt: 'By what means?'.

Management, economics, land evaluation and legal and administrative studies will all be necessary. Analyses of land potential in particular have been developed into sophisticated systems of evaluation that have been appropriately linked to their underlying objectives (Forbes, 1969; Lichfield, 1976; Kaiser, Godschalk, & Chapin, 1995). Forbes' 'Potential Surface Analysis', Lichfield's 'Planning Balance Sheet' and the 'Land development impact measures' of Kaiser *et al.* provide clear systematic approaches to evaluating the land resources which play an important basic role in community planning.

Resource analysis is also frequently assisted by the deep and wide knowledge which practitioners have of their own activities and their remarkable willingness to share this with others. The rapidly expanding fields of information and communications technology that have developed since the 1990s can also produce valuable harvests from well-seeded inquiries. As a result, resource analysis can become a fertile source of new ideas for policy development and implementation. The sequence starting with early involvement of stakeholders and activists and continuing with collaborative objective setting and dialogue can result in energetic partnership with providers and policymakers in identifying the resources available to achieve objectives and improve performance in their own fields. The topic of systems of activity analysis forms a major part of the next chapter.

Stage 5: Action research

It is unwise (and unconvincing) to launch direct into policy development for massive spending on untried and essentially hypothetical proposals. There are legions of examples of such schemes devised and launched over great distances from remote and powerful centres in London, Moscow, Canberra and elsewhere, which failed to achieve their radical intentions and often created very damaging outcomes: Russia's Virgin Lands Campaign of the 1950s and 1960s (Cole, 1959; Ridley, 1996); Britain's Groundnut Scheme of the 1940s (Wood, 1950) and Australia's Ord River Development Scheme of the 1960s (Walker, 1992), Growth Centre proposals and the Australian Assistance Plan of the early 1970s (Stretton, 1989). As Robert Burns (1964) observes:

> The best laid schemes o' mice an' men
> Gang aft a-gley.

The alternative is to test them by carefully selected action research projects. Suitable ones can take the form of housing improvement schemes, area management proposals, pedestrianisation of streets, industrial training initiatives, social centre provisions and public transport improvements. For example, a newly elected local council might be interested in introducing positive, promotional and dispersed planning throughout its area. A local resident's action group in one particular neighbourhood might have already developed area improvement proposals jointly with, for instance, a team of university planning students, and might therefore be encouraged to participate in applying such an approach to their own area with small-scale council support. If it works, it can then be applied more widely in a streamlined version elsewhere, with considerable confidence. A number of advantages will have accrued. The participating departments and agencies will have gained experience of this kind of work. They will have learnt to work together. They will have confidence in forecasting costs, and thus in giving the council the estimates it needs to launch programmes. Public support can be marshalled on the basis of proven achievements to date. The local community will be energised by their high-profile role, and by the benefits that have flowed from the trial scheme. Finally, flaws and omissions in the original proposals can be identified and rectified at the small scale of a single locality or scheme before expensive and highly visible calamities occur. Out of such action research projects, accurately funded and integrated implementation programmes can be developed on a much larger scale.

Stage 6: Policies to apply resources to meet objectives

Developing policies is as creative a stage in planning as is making a design for the craftsman. (It is interesting that Ebenezer Howard always regarded his proposal for garden cities to replace industrial metropolises as an 'invention' rather than a theory or a proposal.) By this stage, all the materials have been obtained. We can picture the cabinet-maker or planning team seated at the kitchen or conference room table. They have an agreed list of achievable objectives; beside that is a slim pile of notes or succinct reports giving necessary details and statistics about the systems involved; on a third pile is information about the materials or resources available. The task is now one of synthesis. Material can drawn from each of the three piles and combined to produce mixes of ideas and information to shape alternative models of the intended design or plan. These can then be compared to see how well each achieves the plan's evolving objectives. Politicians and local people can also be involved in these discussions.

The objectives pile will provide the framework of what needs to be done. The information pile will describe what circumstances, opportunities and constraints will be involved. The resource analysis pile will tell them about the available physical, financial and human resources and incentives to get the design or plan into operation. In short, the resultant policies should indicate what should be done, how it can be accomplished, by whom, using what finances and powers, and over what period.

In order to ensure that policies are adequate, standards may often be necessary to stipulate what levels of performance should be achieved. These can be based on material drawn from the information and resource analysis reports. They may take the form of, for example, a requirement that there be no through traffic in residential streets, or that no dwelling be more than one kilometre from a local play space. Such performance standards and their indicators help to shape policies, and can provide an important test of how well they are subsequently achieved.

Stage 7: Alternative strategies and evaluation

The same policies can be expressed in very different strategies. Proposals may be based on different degrees of spatial intensity or concentration, or theories of settlement form; different levels of priority or investment; or different overall views of future social directions. Spatial strategies can employ different patterns such as those developed in *A Pattern Language* (Alexander, Ishikawa & Siverstein, 1977) and discussed in the first section of this chapter. Different strategies may be strongly correlated with spatial issues which will often turn upon balancing the economies of scale of facilities and services, on the one hand, with their degree of accessibility to those who will be using them, on the other. Linear, grid, circular, stellar and dispersed patterns, discussed in the final section of Chapter 10, will all offer varying costs and benefits to different groups.

In making choices between these alternatives, there are numerous useful evaluative systems to help. Cost-effectiveness, cost–benefit analysis, threshold analysis, planning balance sheets and ends–means analysis can all contribute to this process of judging and identifying elements, which can be recombined to shape a new optimal and preferred strategy (Lichfield, 1976; Kaiser, Godschalk & Chapin, 1995). As a result, the important considerations in developing alternative strategies are to ensure that they span a wide range of alternatives, so that many different approaches can be evaluated.

The purpose of evaluation is not to select the one best single strategy and discard all the others, but rather to see which elements of each are most suitable to different groups and then to recombine them into an optimum strategy bearing in mind the classic questions of 'Who pays?' and 'Who benefits?' Because each option should represent an alternative way of achieving the same objectives, they should all be directed towards the same policies and should be sufficiently compatible for a unified evaluation system to work well. Two basic questions must be considered:

How good are the proposals (in terms of achieving the objectives)?

What are the costs of implementation (in terms of money)?

It is best to treat these two considerations separately, so that the result of an evaluation will be in the form of a combination of ends–means analysis and cost-effectiveness, producing answers such as: 'This strategy provides these levels of benefits for those levels of cost.' Combining them into a single cost–benefit analysis based solely on monetary worth will involve the false assumption that it is possible to weigh factors such as the value of a human life (which depends upon imponderables such as love and unknowables such as psychological effects), time savings (whose value will vary between individuals and times) and community welfare and cohesion (which cannot be quantified) into one misleadingly precise calculation. Peter Hall memorably deconstructed such an approach in his discussion of the cost–benefit analysis conducted in the early 1970s to select a site for a third London airport in his book *Great Planning Disasters* (1980). Peter Self described it as 'nonsense on stilts'. Evaluation should aim to illuminate and not necessarily to quantify, because its aims are creative rather than judgmental.

Stage 8: Phased, costed and integrated proposals

Implementing and funding organisations may include both the policy and coordination committees of local or national government and the management boards of private and social enterprises and voluntary agencies. After one or more successful action research projects, the various planning bodies and departments involved should be in a position to recommend to their decision takers adoption of overall programmes that can incorporated in forthcoming annual operational plans and budgets. The scale of these proposals may be sufficiently large and important to justify the formation of special interdepartmental or inter-organisational project teams to achieve coordination, and this would certainly be the case in developments such as preparing and planning for hosting major international sporting events such as the Sydney, Beijing or London Olympics, building a new city, or implementing a large coastal reclamation scheme. Donald Schon explores the organisational and psychological advantages which can be derived from such an approach in his book *Beyond the Stable State* (1971).

In other cases, coordination must depend on more integrated systemic such as the annual cycle of a planning–programming–budgeting system, which indicates the contributions required from, and funding which will be provided to, each section of an implementing agency in the course of each of a number of years programmes. This formal allocative system needs to be assisted by the commonsense liaison of individuals in different departments and organisations at middle and junior officer levels. Thus, it is important that each participating agency has a clear and concise summary of the inputs to the total scheme of all others. Critical path diagrams will prove useful, and they can easily be distributed as diagrammatic attachments via email or in hard copy to the many desks of the numerous participants throughout all of the agencies and community groups involved in the plan. Electronic information and communication technology systems (like PB Works or Wiki networks) offer radical, and inherently enjoyable, communication systems to put people separated by significant physical and administrative distances into instant contact with each other. Community planners have much to gain from such developments in contemporary technology because they depend so significantly on good communications to identify and solve problem sequences. Rapid checking of interactions of specific initiatives through the wider systems of space and organisations can greatly improve review and efficiency.

Stage 9: Coordinated implementation schemes

Management theorists are increasingly concluding that successful corporate management is an attitude as much as a process (Drucker, 2002). At any level, from director to process operative, the personnel of different departments may choose to work together; to ignore each other's roles or to operate in parallel, despite personal antagonisms. Acknowledgement of the importance of good interpersonal relations has led to advocacy of team-building approaches to implement community programmes. Certainly, project team implementation, is an excellent framework for inculcating ideas of cooperation and team spirit, and ensuring that project personnel identify with the success of the community plan. The method normally involves individuals being seconded from each of the collaborating departments for the duration of the project, and being given identified responsibility for its successful implementation.

Where the timescale of the exercise is short enough or its priority high enough, this is likely to be an appropriate approach, but in other cases the necessary cooperation can be achieved by convening regular meetings of representatives of all the government and community agencies involved to learn about each other's work and decide how they can collaborate to achieve the best possible shared outcomes. In the overall context of cyclical community planning, where the interests of whole communities are involved and long-lasting relations between different agencies are essential, short-term approaches, involving limited information exchange, offer only partial solutions. Coordinated implementation will depend far more on combining the powerful new information and communications technologies with the time-honoured techniques of good personal communications and mutual acknowledgement, in open edged communication networks where all participants are encouraged to contribute ideas and concerns.

Stage 10: Monitoring and appraisal of new responses, problems and aims

Once the proposed innovations have been established and planning is nearing completion of a cycle, it is possible to start testing the plan's operation. Consultation with the consumers and local population, as well as the agencies involved, can help indicate successes, failures and unintended consequences. Performance indicators can be used to test the effectiveness of the plan's operation, providing a potent way of directing the evolution of the planning system into more effective channels. Effective, rapid and regular ways of monitoring will be needed to achieve annual review, to precede preparation of the authority's annual planning and programme budgeting system. New problems will suggest new objectives and the next cycle of the process can be started. Major reviews may take place every three to five years, if possible following local elections to establish ownership by the political representatives. Appraisal, review and reformulation of objectives can start again.

Political control and community participation

POLITICAL CONTROL

Community planning can usefully be envisaged as flowing in three parallel streams of social, political and technical processes, as shown in Figure 6.6. The diagram should be regarded as a cylinder bringing together community and political strands, rather than as a sheet separating them: exchange of ideas among the community members and their political representatives should be as continuous as that between the planners and service providers. The very decision to prepare plans for an area is a political one, and politicians will receive the most effective feedback in the form of continued support and votes, or their withdrawal, at weekly 'clinics' in their ward offices and at election times. Any action research projects identified

as suitable by local communities must be supported by politicians if they are to be funded and implemented. It is they who must adopt and stand by the policies prepared with the planners. They must therefore have a decisive voice in the selection of alternative strategies. Any general community planning scheme must receive their formal support, and be adopted by the council. Funding for proposals must be found out of the annual budget, which it is one of politicians' major responsibilities to oversee.

For all these reasons, planners must ensure that they maintain close, respectful and amicable working relations with politicians and members of boards of directors of social and private enterprise bodies for whom they are working. It is not only common sense to listen carefully to the views of people whose support is crucial to the success of one's work. Even more important, the ethics and political validity of community planning as a public activity mean that elected representatives must be in charge of the planning process. Planning not only opens up common opportunities but also proscribes the individual freedoms of people to take actions which may impinge harmfully on others, so that individual citizens and voters need a clear and current means of redress in the voting booth against perceived infringements of their rights.

Positive advantages will also accrue: well-briefed and motivated politicians will be far more likely to make well-informed and wise decisions than ones who have been intentionally kept in the dark, or disregarded as insufficiently knowledgeable to be treated as intellectual equals. Planners must remember that an academic degree is neither necessary nor sufficient to guarantee good decisions. Finally, politicians who take successful decisions in the public interest, may gain popularity and therefore become more aware of the benefits of planning, which they may come to see as effective and productive. Planning will thereby receive a powerful impetus along its upward spiral towards social improvement.

THE PLACE OF COMMUNITY PARTICIPATION

Dialogue with local communities, residents, progress associations and, indeed, developers should be constant, across the table, via local media and in local halls. Even where this rapport has yet to be established, there should be local consultation with residents and other interested parties over objectives at the outset of a planning scheme. Such relations will make the subsequent planning processes easier and more effective. The strong commitment to more collaborative planning in the 2010 Green Paper produced by the UK Conservative Party is a particularly interesting development (Conservatives, 2010). The policy, entitled *Open Source Planning*, stresses decentralisation and collaboration, advocating a 'rebalancing of power away from the centre and into the hands of local people' (Conservatives, 2010). Another of the Green Paper's commitments (2010) is to ensure 'that significant local projects have to be designed through a collaborative process that has involved the neighbourhood'.

This is interestingly similar to the requirement of the Oregon State Planning Goal Number One, Citizen Participation, for Citizen Involvement Committees with statutory rights of consultation, information, funding and policy involvement wherever local governments are proposing to prepare a planning scheme (Oregon Department of Land Conservation & Development, 2010). Other moves towards collaborative planning envisaged in the *Open Source Planning* paper (Conservatives, 2010) include the option for local people wanting to undertake householder developments to consult with their neighbours and attain their assent as an alternative to having to seek local government approval. Developers would also be encouraged to pay impact costs direct to those affected in order to avoid having to seek local government approval. There is clearly a strongly running tide in favour of both participation and community planning. The Green Paper, for instance, makes a commitment to 'make a truly local plan, built out of a process of collaborative democracy the centrepiece of the local planning system' (Conservatives, 2010).

The collaborative approach of community planning has political and ethical advantages. It can also be very useful technically, because local people usually know their own areas even better than the planners do. In many cases, energetic community involvement can produce critically important qualitative information such as where flooding is most acute, and when a particular non-conforming use first started operation or is likely to cease. Invariably, key issues and problem areas will be identified that require further survey and analysis. In some areas, local organisations will be keen to cooperate with planners in helping to compile a community profile through self-survey. Members collecting attitudinal information will develop skills that can be used again later in pursuit of community objectives.

Involving local people in the evaluation of policies and strategies is right ethically, on the basis that people's voices should be heard in their own causes. It is also politically helpful for planners to secure the whole-hearted support of local communities before proposals are finalised. Action research projects carried out with local residents and groups can help build trust, and collaboration can maximise political advantage for politicians whose support the plan will need. Part of the purpose of such schemes is to test, modify and develop support for revised programmes to be carried out later on a larger scale. Good publicity and enthusiastic community support are thus important.

Community participation can also assist implementation. Because people's perceptions of buildings and built environments are significantly influenced by the richness and sensory quality of their details and user characteristics, public involvement is an effective way to ensure detailed relevance and usability. This may take the form of deciding the location and materials of street furniture in a new pedestrian mall or older people's incidental seating area or in the location of bus stops in a new suburb regular meetings with local groups should improve not only the quality and acceptability of plans for their areas but also the community's view and sense of identification with the planning agency.

When monitoring plan performance, self-survey carried out by local groups in conjunction with council planners and local schools and universities can be an effective way of identifying successes, priorities and deficiencies. There are other ways. Workshops convened jointly by the council and local residents associations and interest groups can promote communication, trust and participation. Local authorities can carry out regular 'public attitude' surveys, either in conjunction with rates notices for local property taxes or by follow-up surveys in areas where schemes have been completed. In each of these situations, opportunities should also be taken to identify new objectives that can lend direction to the next cycle of the planning process. The ideal of communities promoting continuous discussion and understanding among their members is becoming daily more feasible and attractive. Rapid advances in information and communication technologies are increasingly able provide electronic systems to help coordinate activities and mutual understanding throughout entire communities.

Conclusions: values as the basis for communities of method

At each stage, planning can provide vital links between governments and the communities they represent, through processes that are sensitive to the needs and hopes of both local and wider communities. Ensuring that those who will the ends also will the means can include full and just compensation after open public scrutiny of options wherever urban redevelopment is proposed (Prest & Turvey, 1965). Political decisions about plans and budgets can then be informed by accurate knowledge of impacts and preferences as well as available resources. One of the advantages of a values-driven planning approach is the shared basis of human experience and needs that it provides as a meeting place for the contributions of its many different activities and practitioners. Instead of having to try to interpret a jarring cacophony of conflicting proposals and plans, the many different practitioners involved in different aspects of community planning should be able to create proposals that mirror, at different scales and in different activities, the needs and experiences of the many people who make up these communities.

Communities of method are built on respect for each others' values and roles. They can practise and benefit from collaboration between planners who share common values-based methods. Practitioners and consumers within the fields of health, education, economy, environment, communications, transport and many others can communicate with each other and with their own communities of concern in a continuous conversation that can promote the understanding, negotiation and adjustment necessary to deal holistically with other communities of policy and place. Adjusting focus from scale to scale, and activity to activity, we can view each situation both through the prism of our own values, wants and professional commitments and also through those of others. The next chapter applies this common understanding to a number of the actual activities which make up community life.

Endnotes

i In a similar way, Upper Palaeolithic figurines of stylised human forms of 20 000 to 25 000 years ago, particularly female ones, seem to be searching for the very essence of human fertility. Unlike the little models of animals which may have been made to assist hunting, they are not naturalistic but almost surreal. They have a wide distribution in Upper Palaeolithic sites over much of Europe and eastward as far as Western Siberia and Ukraine. Although they vary a good deal, Campbell observes that they have some significant things in common. Arms, legs and heads are extremely small in proportion to the torso, and in some cases are merely suggested. All the emphasis is on the bodies, with their female characteristics – breasts, belly and buttocks – greatly exaggerated in size. They look like tiny earth goddesses or fertility figures, and that is probably what they were. The early artists were doing

much more than mere recording – they were interpreting, celebrating and proclaiming their values and beliefs.

ii Although ideas casting their shadows ahead of events should assist evaluation of unintended consequences, the effect is often the opposite, committing leaders and investors to uncritical support of schemes such as proposals for a 'world's tallest building' or for new dams which will immerse whole landscapes and drown settlements and habitats, in order to meet the water and energy needs of great metropolises such as Cairo, Mumbai or Wuhan, irrespective of human and geographical consequences.

iii This ultimate reliance on creative insight and intuition unifies art, science and planning The Impressionist painters of the nineteenth century, for instance, created very beautiful new patterns of light and colour by moving their focus of interest from the objects themselves to the pattern of light which they refracted. Stimulated by new ideas about the nature of light and perception, painters such as Monet, Seurat and Pissarro explored how to capture and communicate the momentary perceptions which imprint themselves so vividly on our minds. For Monet, this concept of focusing on the light itself rather than the object which was refracting it unifies all his work, including the series of the face of Chartres Cathedral, the Gare du Nord railway station and the bridge over the water lily basin at Giverny. They celebrate the dazzling richness of the colours by which we are all constantly confronted and constitute among the best-loved paintings in Western culture. For Pissarro and the Pointillists, the resulting approach was different: by faithfully reproducing the tiny dots of colour which go to make up light, they sought to replicate the process by which our eye and brain re-create reality. Van Gogh, Gauguin and Toulouse-Lautrec were inspired by the opportunities presented by the new use of light to achieve powerful effects, but the focus of their interest shifted back onto the essence of the subject – whether it was a chair, a Tahitian girl or a Parisian *demi-mondaine* – and also their own emotions about these objects. Both Impressionists and Expressionists created art which celebrated life in radical reinterpretations of often everyday reality.

iv Renaissance art often expresses timeless and universal ideas of great originality. Michelangelo (1475–1564), infuses this poetic vision into all his work. The gigantic fresco with which he decorated the barrel vault of the Sistine Chapel and the 12-window lunettes and intervening panels in St Peter's cathedral in Rome extends over an area 132 feet long and 45 feet wide and took four years to complete (Chastel, 1972). Its conceptual scale is even more remarkable: the entire biblical story of God's creation of the sun, moon, earth and humanity, and the origin of sin and of its consequences. The charge of current that seems to flow from the outstretched finger of God to enliven the awakening Adam could be seen as symbolising in one gesture the extraordinary creative energies of the entire age. Then, in his last pietà, he 'made his final effort to span the unbridgeable gap between matter and spirit … to translate into stone the pure and perfect idea whose reflection flashes out from an amorphous mass' (Rizzati, 1968). This process of the emergence of ideas from matter can be vividly sensed in the *Rondanini Pietà*, where the figures of Mary and the lifeless Jesus, just taken down from the cross, emerge from the block of marble out of which they are carved, and melt one into the other in a stricken mass (Chastel, 1972).

v These qualities of urban elegance of European renaissance cities, starting in twelfth-century Perugia, Siena and Bologna, and spreading north to include sixteenth-century Paris, seventeenth-century London and eighteenth-century St Petersburg, reached an acme of design that has never since been surpassed. Even though crowding and poor health and safety practices occasionally gave rise to plagues and fires, these cities developed physical forms that were highly appropriate to their roles as centres of craft production, regional commerce and administration and to the foot, cart and carriage transport of their times. Bramante with the design of St Peter's Square in Rome, Alberti in Urbino, Vasari in Florence, Palladio in Vicenza and Venice, Le Vau in Versailles and Wren and Nash in London, Oxford and Bath designed urban spaces and created models of whole cities that celebrated a wide range of values, including godly, kingly, ducal and commercial power, defensive strength, order and elegance. The huge tourist industry that they continue to generate is a tribute to their quality.

vi New examples are constantly occurring, and include the village choir of a community riven by religious conflict, depicted in the 2007 Swedish film *All that is in Heaven*, the theme of the triumph of mutual aid and affection over self-interest, suspicion and exclusion of the 2008 British Broadcasting Commission's television series *Heart and Soul* and Australia's award-winning *Choir of Hard Knocks*, founded in 2006 to help homeless people in inner Melbourne overcome their frailties and marginalisation, which has formed the subject of two award-winning documentary television series by the Australian Broadcasting Corporation. There is much evidence that people naturally respond to the self-expression of song.

vii In both *Babel Tower* (1996) and *Possession* (1990), A. S. Byatt has written a series of parables in the form of stories within stories to explore the psychological and economic roots of totalitarianism and human choice. In her mid-career, Doris Lessing wrote a series of novels transcending the boundary between science fiction and imaginative parables to discuss gender, class and human relations, and later her *The Good Terrorist* returned to conventional storytelling (2007) to explore the nature causes and effects of good and evil societies. Margaret Attwood's *Oryx and Craik* (2004) and several of her other novels place this moral exploration in the immediate future. Nadine Gordimer and J. M. Coetzee locate their explorations of good and bad forms of community in the recent past or present. Coetzee resurrects the literary form of the sermon in his *Elizabeth Costello* (2004) in the guise of a series of lectures and letters arguing the importance of environmental concerns in community planning, and Gordimer's *Burger's Daughter* (1985) describes and transcends the injustices of 1970s South Africa to point the way to a better future; it is significant that she subsequently agreed to serve on Nelson Mandela's Constitutional Committee to develop a more equitable government system for the newly democratic country. Arundhati Roy, in her novel The God of Small Things (1998) traces the powerful links between community life and values and individuals' capacites for human development.

viii The most celebrated example of this upward spiral of conjecture and refutation is the radical modification of Newton's laws of physics, mechanics and optics by Einstein's theories of relativity. After two and a half centuries of success in explaining, predicting and exploiting the physical environment (embracing both the microcosm of the atom and the macrocosm of the universe), Newton's laws helped to produce sufficient new knowledge to necessitate their revision. Einstein's conjecture that their clockwork logic broke down in situations of high scale and volatility when energy, speed, and matter all became relative to each other was confirmed by new observations. For good or ill, it was an understanding of the relativity of energy and motion which gave humanity the ability to split the atom.

ix The development of the more positive approach associated with appreciative inquiry (Hammond & Royal, 1998; Ludema, Cooperrider & Barrett, 2006) and 'strengths based' social planning (Cuers & Hewston, 2007), however, has shifted attention back onto the more positive methods of identifying people's natural advantages. Successes using these approaches suggest that they can also provide useful paths to develop objectives for future actions and developments. It will be seen from Figure 6.3 that this is moving the focus of analysis further back from the experience of problems to the underlying values from which they may result. In effect, the same problem-solving cycles of action, reaction and environmental modification are involved, but there are real advantages in the more positive stance which appreciative inquiry encourages.

x The concept of 'bisociation' was coined by Arthur Koestler (1989) to describe the process of developing new ideas by shifting concepts from one context to another.

xi Sennett (2008) traces the development of the warp and woof of weaving through the mortise and tenon of ship building in the first millennium BC to standard use in cabinet-making and thence to town planning in the interlocking grid form of the Sicilian colony of Selinous and Hippocrates' ideas for ideal settlement patterns.

xii In this way they are similar to composers like Mozart and Beethoven in whose symphonies the three or four different movements may be unified by a number of themes that run through all of them.

References

Alexander, C. (1979a) *Notes on the Synthesis of Form*. Cambridge, MA, Harvard University Press, (first published 1964).

Alexander, C. (1979b) *A Timeless Way of Building*. New York, Oxford University Press.

Alexander, C. (2002–4) *The Nature of Order, Book One: The Phenomenon of Life; Book Two: The Process of Creating Life; Book Three: A Vision of a Living World; Book Four: The Luminous Ground*. Berkeley, CA, Center for Environmental Structure.

Alexander, C., Ishikawa, S., Siverstein, M. (1977) *A Pattern Language*. New York, Oxford University Press.

Alexander, C., Silverstein, M., Angel, S. *et al.* (1975) *The Oregon Experiment*. New York, Oxford University Press.

Alexander, C., Neis, H., Anninou, A., King I. (1987) *A New Theory of Urban Design*. New York, Oxford University Press.

Attwood, M. (2004) *Oryx & Craik*. Virago, London.

Burns, R. (1964) 'To a Mouse'. In: *Robert Burns*. London, Oxford University Press.

Byatt, A. (1990) *Possession*. London, Vintage.

Byatt, A. (1996) *Babel Tower*. London, Chatto & Windus.

Campbell, B. (1985) *Humankind Emerging*. Boston, Little Brown.

Chadwick, G. (1972) *A Systems View of Planning: Towards a theory of the urban and regional planning process*. Oxford, Pergamon Press.

Chadwick, G. (1987) *Models of Urban and Regional Systems in Developing Countries: Some theories and their application in physical planning*. Oxford, Pergamon.

Chastel, A. (1972) *Italian Art*. London, Faber & Faber.

Clark, K. (1956) *Landscape into Art*. London, Penguin.

Coetzee, J. (2004) *Elizabeth Costello*. Sydney, Random House.

Cole, J. (1959) *Geography of World Affairs*. Harmondsworth, Penguin.

Commoner, B. (1972) *The Closing Circle*. London, Jonathon Cape.

Conservatives (2010) *Open Source Planning Green Paper*, http://www.conservatives.com/~/media/Files/Green%20Papers/planning-green-paper.ashx, accessed 18 November 2010.

Cuers, S., Hewston, J. (2007) *The Strong Communities Handbook*. Brisbane, Community Practice Unit, Queensland University of Technology.

Desroches-Noblecourt, C. (1976) *Tutankhamun: Life and Death of a Pharaoh*. New York, The New York Graphic Society.

Drucker, P. (2002) *Management Challenges for the 21st Century*. Oxford, Elsevier.

Forbes, J. (1969) A map analysis of potentially developable land. *Regional Studies* 3(2): 179–95.

Goel, N. (2010) *Squatter Settlements: The urban vernacular*. Urban Transformation, Controversies, Contrasts and Challenges, 14th Conference of International Planning History Society, Istanbul, July, 2010, (PowerPoint presentation on companion website).

Gordimer, N. (1985) *Burger's Daughter*. Harmondsworth, Penguin.

Graham, D. (1999) Anaxagoras. In: R. Audi (ed.), *Cambridge Dictionary of Philosophy*. New York, Cambridge University Press.

Hall, P. (1980) *Great Planning Disasters*. London, Weidenfeld & Nicolson.

Hammond, S., Royal C. (1998) *Lessons from the Field*. Plano, TX, Practical Press.

Heywood, P. (1987) *Felda & Bustee: The management of population growth in town & country*. Unpublished paper available from author, Brisbane, Queensland University of Technology.

Hume, D. (1990) An enquiry concerning human understanding. In: S. Cahn (ed.), *Classics of Western Philosophy*. Indianapolis, Hackett.

Kaiser, E., Godschalk, D., Chapin, F. (1995) *Urban Land Use Planning*. Urana, IL, University of Illinois Press.

Koestler, A. (1989) *The Act of Creation*. London, Arkana.

Lavoisier, A. (2010) *Antoine Lavoisier*, http://www.directessays.com/viewpaper/41663.html, accessed 4 April 2010.

Lessing, D. (2007) *The Good Terrorist*. London, Harper, (first published 1985).

Lichfield, N. (1976) *Evaluation in Planning*. Oxford, Pergamon.

Ludema, J., Cooperrider, L., Barrett, F. (2006) Appreciative inquiry: The power of the unconditional positive question. In: P. Reason, H. Bradbury (eds), *Handbook of Action Research*. London, SAGE.

McLoughlin, B. (1968) *Urban and Regional Planning: A systems approach*. London, Faber & Faber.

Magee, B. (1973) *Popper*. London, Fontana/Collins.

Mannering, D. (1981) *The Art of Leonardo da Vinci*. London, Hamlyn.

Metro Portland (2003) *Metro 2040 Vision*. Portland, OR, Metropolitan Service District of Greater Portland.

Mill, J. S. (1983) *Utilitarianism: On liberty and considerations on representative government*. London, Dent, (first published 1861).

Mumford, L. (1961) *The City in History: Its origins, its transformations, and its prospects*. New York, Harcourt World & Brace.

Neale, M. (1998) *Emily Kame Kngwarreye: Paintings from Utopia*. Brisbane, Queensland Art Gallery.

Oregon Department of Land Conservation & Development (2010) *Statewide Planning Goals*, http://www.oregon.gov/LCD/goals.shtml, accessed 12 April 2010.

Passmore, J. (1980) *A Hundred Years of Philosophy*. Harmondsworth, Penguin.

Popper, K. (1959) *The Logic of Scientific Discovery*. London, Hutchinson, (first published 1935 in Vienna as *Logik der Forschung*).

Popper, K. (1972) *Conjectures and Refutations*. Oxford, Oxford University Press.

Popper, K. (1989) *Objective Knowledge: An evolutionary approach*. Oxford, Clarendon.

Popper, K., Eccles, J. (1984) *The Self and its Brain*. London, Routledge & Kegan Paul.

Prest, A., Turvey, R. (1965) Cost–benefit analysis: A survey. *The Economic Journal* **300**(LXXV).

Putnam, R. (1993) *Making Democracy Work: Civic traditions in modern Italy*. Princeton, Princeton University Press, (with Leonardi, R., Nanetti, R.).

Queensland Government Office of Urban Management (2005) *South East Queensland Regional Plan*. Brisbane, Author.

Ridley, M. (1996) *The Origins of Virtue*. London, Viking.

Rizzati, M. (1968) *The Life and Times of Michelangelo*, (trans. C. J. Richards). London, Hamlyn.

Roy, A. (1998) *The God of Small Things*. London, Flamingo.

Schon, D. (1971) *Beyond the Stable State: Public and private learning in a changing society*. London, Temple Smith.

Sennett, R. (2008) *The Craftsman*. London, Penguin.

Stretton, H. (1989) *Ideas for Australian Cities*. Melbourne, Transit.

Suzuki, D. (2009) *The Sacred Balance*. Sydney, Allen & Unwin.

Walker, K. (1992) The neglect of ecology: The case of the Ord River Scheme. In: Walker, K. (ed.), *Australia Environmental Policy*. Sydney, University of New South Wales Press.

Whitehouse, R. (1977) *The First Cities*. Oxford, Phaidon.

Wood, A. (1950) *The Groundnut Affair*. London, The Bodley Head.

Wordsworth, W. (1946) 'Composed Upon Westminster Bridge'. In: *Collected Poems*. London, Oxford University Press.

7 Activities and their Analysis

This chapter explores the roles of human activities in shaping community life and examines techniques that can assist their effective planning, by discussing four related issues:

- the links between activity systems and values;
- the uses of models of activities;
- the role of systems theory within the planning process;
- activity systems analysis in practice.

It concludes with a consideration of the roles of activity systems in community planning.

The links between activity systems and values

Chapters 5 and 6 demonstrated the important roles that values play in shaping and evaluating community plans. However, the temptations of speed and simplicity may offer strong inducements to plan activities without regard to human values, by simply observing existing conditions and power relations and arranging for the land, capital and labour that will roll these forward, amplified or unchanged, into the future. This was how countless trend planning schemes came to produce the tower blocks, urban freeways and out-of-town shopping centres that marked much urban development throughout the mid-twentieth century in Europe and North America (Heywood, 1974; Hall, 1980, 2002). Ignoring underlying human values in order to promote currently fashionable or profitable activities in this way may seem to make the business of community planning much simpler, but it may also produce tragic and wasteful mistakes and violate people's rights. Seeing activities as expressions of human values, by contrast, provides a clear understanding of their purposes and possibilities.

Activities occupy much of people's everyday lives. They are the middle ground between objectives and plans. Observing the ways in which they develop in the absence of formal planning systems can aid understanding of the underlying links between causes, influences and effects. An essential first step is to clarify how the impulses for these activities are motivated by ideas which can later be expressed in purposive actions. Models of this process can then be expanded to incorporate motivating values and goals. Later in this chapter, we shall also look at how this understanding is applied in systems theory.

As used by social and planning theorists such as Le Play (Fletcher, 1969), Geddes (Mairet, 1957), Lynch (1981) and Foley (1968) the term 'activity' implies functional organisation that can express values in material outcomes. Lynch writes perceptively of the:

> degree to which one can directly perceive the operation of the various … activities and social and natural processes that are occurring within the settlement. Can one actually see people at work, hear the waves strike the shore … see what a truck is carrying or where the sewage soaks away, watch the transfers of money or messages? Some of these processes are important, some trivial … They convey a 'sense of life' in any settlement and, with congruence, are the direct perceptual basis for deeper meanings … Functions presented immediately to our senses help us to understand the world. (Lynch, 1981)

Insightful commentators, such as Lynch (1981) and Foley (1968) (whose ideas are discussed later in this section) offer sophisticated understanding of these processes. They also recognise that other individuals, immersed in the flux of daily living, may develop their own, more spontaneous, awareness from personal

Community Planning, First Edition. Phil Heywood.
© 2011 Phil Heywood.
Published 2011 by Blackwell Publishing Ltd.

experience, often only becoming aware of an activity when encountering a problem or impediment to their natural needs. Initial perceptions and interpretations of transport, for instance, may start when children's daily journeys to school in a nearby suburb, make them subconsciously aware of the modes of foot, cycle, car, bus and train transport, and they embryonically start to construct in their minds the whole complex pattern of the organisation of urban movements. To begin with, we are not so much aware of the overall structure of external reality as that portion of it which appears to be responding to our immediate interests or impinging on fulfilment of our wants. Reflection may later help us identify the underlying and driving values to reconstruct the system in ways that can reshape activities and overcome the problems. These revised activities will link different actions in stable patterns of cause and effect and reflect intentions to produce desired outcomes. Activities are thus more composite than single actions or events. Being more patterned and durable, they are also more predictable and significant for planning.

This process by which activities and land uses are generated through social and economic evolution emerges as being the mirror image of the sequence by which we tend to recognise and become aware of them. This process is illustrated in Figure 7.1, which shows how interpretation can trace back observations to identify the underlying activities and the causal values and needs which gave rise to the whole process.

In effect, this process forms a design 'W' with the letter laid on its side. Perception is traced back from its starting point in awareness of land uses through recognition of activities to their origin in values. This in turn can be reconstructed as a link of causation which creates the land uses. Analysis can then trace this back to a fuller understanding of the generative values. These, expressed as goals, can subsequently provide the directing force for policies that can drive plans to solve the initial problems and optimise the physical conditions, the perception of which gave rise to the whole process. A useful analogy for this is provided by the flow of electric current which results when opposite polarisation of ions occurs simultaneously in both directions.

Once recognised, this process can be stood firmly on its feet to plan better activities and make tangible provisions that can solve problems and build healthy communities.

PROBLEMS AS WINDOWS ON VALUES

Later in this section, we shall examine the dangers of short circuiting this process and charging straight down the land use column, towards a favourite or preconceived solution without searching out the underlying causes. Alternative approaches and unintended consequences may both be overlooked. Such unreflecting or perfunctory responses to problems may respond directly to poor conditions by attempting to remove obvious obstructions, but they may also divert attention from underlying causes and result in long-term frustration of people's values. For example, routine solutions like post-World War Two 'slum clearance' schemes (Jacobs, 1961; Anderson, 1964) or demolition of low-cost dwellings in shanty towns in developing countries (Turner, 1976) may ignore necessary activities like affordable inner-city dwellings and disregard the deeper values and needs of residents and users, such as social justice, urban economy and personal autonomy. This temptation to adopt standardised solutions has often exerted damaging effects on local communities, economies and people's capacity to create and maintain social life (Heywood, 1974, 1987).

A typical example could be found in a situation where planning is being undertaken to solve the problems of rush hour traffic flowing through a residential area. Residents may be concerned about problems of danger, noise, road congestion and atmospheric pollution, giving rise to calls for street closure and removal of all through traffic. Investigation may establish that

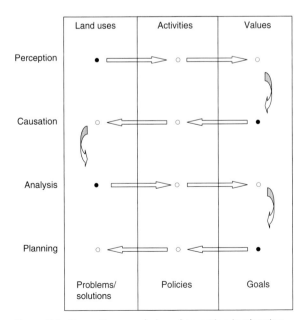

Figure 7.1   Perceptions, analysis and causation in planning.

the causes of these traffic flows lie in the activities of city and district centre employment, outer residential living areas and people's choice of means of journey-to-work. On reflection, this traffic may be seen to express underlying needs for work, shelter and movement, each with its own associated objectives, and many alternative ways of being tackled. Analysis may indicate that the problematic traffic conditions may be resolved by a combination of means, which will be far more effective than simply closing roads to through traffic and thereby diverting flows onto other residential streets. For instance, parking charges in the city centre may divert people onto public transport, including use of the railway system. Relocation of traffic-generating industries to a new planned industrial estate, perhaps on disused marshalling yards adjacent to a rail line, may reduce offensive heavy traffic. The designation of a heavy vehicle route system, accompanied by access licensing, should further improve conditions. The introduction of a 'slow-way', with linked traffic lights set to keep rush hour traffic flowing at a steady 20 to 30 kilometres per hour would reduce drivers' expectations and improve safety by reducing the speed of vehicles closer to that of pedestrians. The further we trace the activities which underlie land uses towards their causal values, in this way, the more we shall open up possibilities for solving problems in ways which truly reflect people's needs and avoid mere displacement of difficulties from one, most vocal or well-organised group, activity or location, to others.

THE FEATURES AND FAILINGS OF IMPULSIVE PLANNING

Impulsive planning, which merely seeks to reallocate land uses, irrespective of underlying activities or human values, has produced many failures. One of those which imprinted itself earliest and most force-fully upon my own mind occurred in the great port of Lagos, which was then the capital of Africa's most populous nation, Nigeria, and dates from the early years of the country's independence in 1963/4. It is described in Box 7.1, together with another case, involving a recurrence of a similarly over-optimistic belief in the power of purely physical controls, which occurred fifteen years later in the provincial capital of Akure, 250 kilometres to the north-east, and was ably documented by a then student of mine, Mr Owolabi Faseki (1981), who had worked in the provincial planning office.[i]

Nevertheless, personal insights and pet solutions can play a useful role in exploring issues and options, if they are regarded as bright ideas needing to be carefully evaluated for adequate focus or unintended con-sequences. For people with a highly intuitive cast of mind, they can be convenient entry points to a coherent planning process. Their proposals can become part of an analytical framework that relates them back to underlying activities and values. They can then be tested for worth, feasibility and unintended consequences, along with other possible solutions, instead of being uncritically adopted. The fact that they may have to be discarded because of adverse impacts, or failure to achieve the actual objectives of the scheme, will not then saddle society with crippling encumbrances like high-rise towers or decks of public housing or concrete spaghetti arrays of urban motorways in inner cities. As with Popper's celebration of the value of mistakes, which was discussed in the previous chapter, such errors can even suggest better solutions.

RELATIONS AMONG LAND USES, ACTIVITIES AND VALUES

Just as land uses and structures develop to accommodate activities such as residence, work, play, movement and governance, so these activities are themselves responses to the basic needs and wants constituting our values.[ii] Not only logic but also social justice may prompt us to look behind everyday activities to discern the values they serve, for two very important and cogent reasons:

1. There may be better and more effective ways of fulfilling these values than by maintaining existing activities, and good method should encourage, rather than preclude, the search for alternatives.
2. People do not act as they do solely because they want to; they may be coerced into that pattern of behaviour by existing power relationships and conditions. Their objectives and values may be frustrated, but be nonetheless available through the questioning methods of consultation.

In searching to understand the ways that land uses and activities are influenced by deep-seated values, the American planning theorist Donald Foley developed a useful diagrammatic framework of a metropolitan spatial structure (1968). Foley argues that, although they are at one level very physical artefacts of bricks, mortar, steel and bitumen, cities only exist to accommodate and promote activities such as production, exchange, play, administration, security and communal living, which have in turn been developed to satisfy the deeper human needs and values of prosperity, sustenance, creativity, choice, contact and so on.[iii] He sees planning as a process that develops understanding in order to transform existing

Box 7.1   Contravention in Lagos and Akure

1. The case of Lagos' Ebutte Mette
Lagos is the chief port and was the first national capital of the newly independent state of Nigeria. The city occupies a beautiful location astride the coastal lagoon that formed the original port and spreads out across a number of islands to the new deep water docks on the Bight of Benin. One of these islands, Ebutte Mette, is joined to the mainland by a bridge, and has always been a busy and crowded centre of market activity, with a lively mix of traditional trading, modern commerce, and heavy traffic flows. In the first flush of post colonial energy, the new government resolved to clean up this confusion by removing the market stalls and the stall holders' traditional mud brick and palm thatch dwellings. They planned to relocate the occupants to a garden suburb on the northern fringes of the city at Surulere. Despite protests, the structures were cleared and the land prepared for new government and commercial offices.

However, within weeks, amid the rubble of the old trading stalls of the market, the former residents re-appeared to build shanty structures where they could sleep and trade, because they could not afford to live in their new, expensive rental dwellings, where they had no local means of livelihood and were separated from the city centre by slow, erratic and expensive public transport. Equally the city centre workers missed their cheap and convenient source of consumer goods and traditional food. Very quickly the old patterns of roadside market stalls and informal housing re-asserted themselves through a mixture of necessity and the powerful drive of human values to find expression in sympathetic activities and land use.

2. Contravention in Akure
Over fifteen years later, a study by Owolabi Faseki (1981) investigated a similar failure of physicalist planning to control productive activities or replace established values. Faseki established that nearly one in five of all new developments in the bustling West Nigerian town of Akure, capital of Ondo Province, contravened the pattern book town planning scheme prepared by British trained town planners. Between 1973 and 1979, no fewer than 1536 contraventions were recorded, few of which subsequently complied or were removed. In 1979 alone, there were 291 recorded contraventions, of which 200 were ignored, 24 subsequently complied, and 67 were demolished. Faseki investigated the reasons for the very high rate of informal building and very low rates of subsequent enforcement. Public officials and general public respondents agreed that non-involvement of the public in planning and corruption of public officials were significant causes of contravention. Even more important was their recognition of cultural reasons including:

- the need to fragment compounds to create dwellings for a number of wives in the traditionally polygamous Yoruba society conflicted with European patterns of residential planning;
- people caught up in long running disputes over land ownership were unwilling to become involved in slow and legalistic planning processes, a problem which similarly bedevilled rehousing of the 60000–70000 families whose dwellings were destroyed by militia in the Timor-Leste Independence conflict of 2000 (Heywood, 2002).

While officials believed that the major causes of contravention were poor literacy, building and design skills, inadequate finances, widespread poverty, and undue political influences, the general public were more aware that employment and shelter needs forced people to use any available land they could to ply their trades and house their families. They had to build using any available materials, and to do so as quickly as opportunities arose.

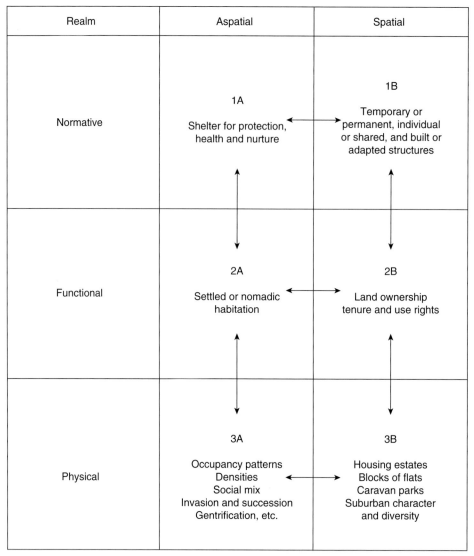

Realm	Aspatial	Spatial
Normative	1A Shelter for protection, health and nurture	1B Temporary or permanent, individual or shared, and built or adapted structures
Functional	2A Settled or nomadic habitation	2B Land ownership tenure and use rights
Physical	3A Occupancy patterns Densities Social mix Invasion and succession Gentrification, etc.	3B Housing estates Blocks of flats Caravan parks Suburban character and diversity

Figure 7.2 Relations between normative, functional and physical realms of shelter in metropolitan spatial structure. *Source:* Based on Foley, 1968.

conditions. Figure 7.2 lays out his schema, which is the basis for his argument that all events and spatial arrangements must take their origin from normative, aspatial concepts, and must ultimately result in physical outcomes occupying space. This process of transformation will involve a series of changes of domains, in many ways anticipating the ideas of Lefebvre (1991). Foley (1968) points out that there are various paths that an idea may take on its journey to physical actuality. (Some of these are explored in Figure 7.3., which has been developed for simple explanatory

purposes at a very low level of scale and complexity.) Figure 7.2, based on Foley's approach, can itself be used as a 'thinking machine' into which different values, activities or land uses can be inserted in order to determine whether better ways can be identified to fulfil human needs and wants.

The interpretation of this figure is largely self-explanatory. A simple example has been incorporated, which explores the significance of the basic human concerns of shelter: protection from the elements, maintenance of health and promotion of nurture.

	Human process			Planning and design process
	conceptual	**Spatial**		
Values	**1A** Sensory pleasure Food supply Cultivation	**1B** Blossom, stones, water, foliage, fruit, vegetables	**Objectives**	**1C** To achieve sensory pleasure, cultivation and food supply through provision of accessible trees, shrubs, flower, blossom, foliage and attractive stones and suitable controlled water.
Activities	**2A** Observing Touching Smelling Soil sustenance	**2B** Pre-breakfast walking Relaxation Informal eating Sunbathing Reflection Entertaining Digging and mulching	**Policies and proposals**	**2C** Detailed statement of activities and provisions selected to achieve objectives including actions, agencies, timing and funding (what, who, when and how)
Land Uses	**3A** Cultivation Rock arrangement Water storage Recirculation	**3B** Shrubs, flower and vegetable seedbeds, planted trees, rock assemblies, ponds and fountains	**Plans and designs**	**3C** Scale diagrams and drawings showing located elements detailed enough for implementation

Figure 7.3 A model of garden design.

Reading from cell 1A to cell 1B, the normative expression of this concept can be related across to alternative forms of temporary or permanent, individual or shared and built or adapted structures. Following an alternative route, staying within the aspatial dimension but moving into the functional domain, from cell 1A to 2A, shelter is expressed in activities such as settled or nomadic habitation. These in turn will have spatial dimensions expressed in cell 2B as land ownership, tenure and use rights (which could also be traced back within the spatial dimension to cell 1B with concepts of temporary or permanent, private or shared, and natural or adapted structures). The spatial activities of cell 2B can then give rise in cell 3B to the housing estates, blocks of flats, caravan parks and other forms of habitation that we encounter in our daily lives.

It is also clear that one may proceed through this diagrammatic field from the pure concept of shelter to the reality of residential accommodation by a number of other routes. Starting points may be variable. It is not necessary to always start from pure platonic ideals and proceed to the world of pragmatic physical outcomes. Any starting point will provide an effective entry to explore the set of relationships, which constitutes the real value of this 'thinking machine'. To make well-informed choices, we need to explore carefully the links between conceptual and spatial dimensions as well as the domains of values, activities and physical forms. Foley's framework is thus an encouragement to explore and translate rather than an instruction to follow a rigid sequence of method. This perspective has many practical benefits, including:

- focusing attention on the causes and relationships of existing land uses and activities;
- providing stimulus to recognise or invent more appropriate alternatives;
- developing capacity to trace impacts of changes through the whole system.

Figure 7.3 applies this model to the landscape design of a small garden in order to demonstrate that the approach is also relevant to issues with which most people are familiar in their everyday lives.

The diagram illustrates in a very simple way how values-based planning can create solutions to match the values that clients and users will want to satisfy in their garden. Early discussions can initiate the practical dialogue and consultation, which should continue throughout the design process. In this case, the main interests are identified as sensory pleasure, contemplation and plant and food cultivation. These take on the spatial forms of blossom, foliage, stones, water, fruit and root crops, with the precise list being amplified by direct discussion with the users. Activities identified to express these values include observing, touching, smelling, tasting and moving, taking on the physical forms of pre-breakfast walking, family relaxation and games, informal eating, sunbathing, personal reflection, entertaining and general gardening. These activities can generate specific land uses and structures that go to make up the elements of the garden's design. Together, the values and activities suggest such land uses as flower and vegetable beds, rock arrangements, water storage and recirculation, and pathway systems. These in turn require physical features: shrub, flower, seed and vegetable beds; pathways; planted trees; rock assemblies; ponds and fountains. Depending upon the values and preferred activities of the users, a garden pond and other water features may or may not be included. A family whose values strongly inclined them to playing ball with a pet dog would want a clear space for running, catching and performing.

In parallel with understanding how the physical garden can reflect the personal values of its users, self-conscious planning can start to explore the meaning of these values as well as the character of the site. Lists of initial aims can be developed, which will suggest what site characteristics need to be surveyed and analysed, and what materials and resources will need to be researched. Two kinds of mixing will be required to develop proposals. The first will draw together objectives and information to create general options for potential solutions. The second kind of mix will combine different activities, such as movement, cultivation and observation, to form physical designs of

attractive features and patterns, using the processes of synthesis of form developed by Christopher Alexander (1964) and outlined in the third section of Chapter 6, discussing planning as a craft in the subsection on policies and standards.[iv]

This logic, originally developed by Foley to explain and assist the planning of metropolitan spatial structure, emerges from this application to the finer grain of garden design as being equally effective at smaller scales. The ideas of Henri Lefebvre on the production of space (1991) provide reassurance that similar transformative logic can also be productive in different fields of concern. His argument that the production of space unifies perceptions, conceptions and lived experiences of spaces runs parallel to Foley's recognition of the normative, functional and physical aspects of space. Awareness is now spreading that social, economic, cultural and negotiative spaces may exist as effectively and be as influential as physical ones. This awareness is particularly important for community planning because of its holistic scope and intentions. For all these reasons, Foley's model of relationships between the conceptual and spatial worlds and the normative, functional and physical domains should prove no less relevant for health, housing and community and economic development than for overall land use and community planning.

The uses of models of activities

In order to obtain a better understanding of these possibilities, the process is now applied to the concerns of housing at the regional level, which have already been introduced in Figure 7.2. Few human values are more essential to personal fulfilment in contemporary society than shelter. A secure and safe home means that people can maintain health, learn and develop skills, obtain and retain work, and develop self-esteem. They can contribute to community life, which can in turn generate human development and sustain social institutions. Shelter is both a prime value in itself and a cradle for many of our other values. Our awareness of housing issues often commences with problems such as people sleeping rough, overcrowding, excessive densities, mismatch between household and dwelling sizes or poorly located and constructed new housing estates. Related to these physical land uses or structures are such conceptual factors as the existence of homelessness, inadequate or inappropriate housing stock and processes of housing demand and home-building. The activities which give rise to them may include boarding house accommodation and conversion, public and private housing investment, land use planning systems and, of course, processes of household formation. These in turn relate to such underlying values as adequate shelter, personal health, urban amenity, economic use of scarce resources and community life.

A parallel planning process can be developed to mirror this social process, starting from specific objectives, which express values in a particular context. As in the garden design, these objectives will indicate the activities that need to be analysed, and will provide the themes around which plans can be shaped. Analysis of activities will include resources, opportunities and constraints and will therefore provide the information

that is required to amplify objectives to develop policies and options. Finally, physical and located proposals can be developed to reflect the original values and aims, and the best possible use of available resources. The process is thus driven by values, shaped by functional information and expressed in specific proposals for physical provisions, as can be seen from Figure 7.4.

Figure 7.5 takes this process a stage further to show how conceptual norms of land ownership, family life and social mix express themselves in settlement processes, such as land supply, the housing market, gentrification and supporting infrastructure systems which in turn give rise to occupancy patterns, with their local area planning categories, housing actions plans and

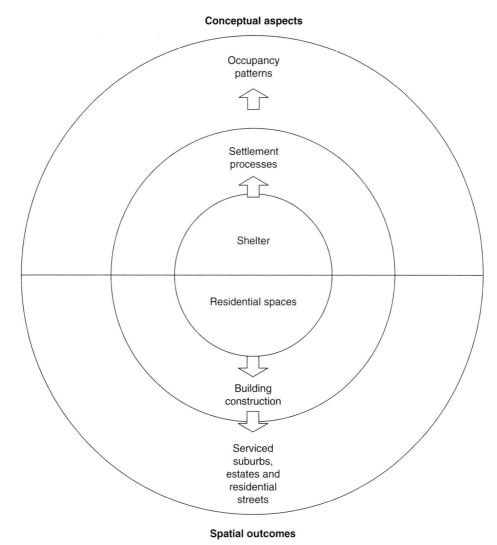

Conceptual aspects

Occupancy patterns

Settlement processes

Shelter

Residential spaces

Building construction

Serviced suburbs, estates and residential streets

Spatial outcomes

Figure 7.4 Values, activities and land uses in shelter.

	Values	Activities	Land uses and structures
Conceptual (aspatial)	**1A shelter** Land ownership Family life Personal providence Individual agency Social organisation Amenity; cultural heritage Aesthetics Security Health and convenience Social mix Health and comfort Self-expression and play Access	**2A settlement processes** Land supply, development and tenure Household formation House purchase, sale and rental Public participation Housing finance, investment and building Community planning processes Gentrification; dwelling adaptation and maintenance Community organisation and policing Water sanitation and power services Active and passive recreation Movement systems	**3A occupancy patterns** Residential planning strategies Total housing stock in different tenures Housing action plans and standards Community meeting places Private and public investment and mixed ventures Community networks, integrated local area plans, new urbanism and responsive environments Invasion and succession Family, single, emergency, cooperative, sheltered and mobile accommodation Service networks Open space systems

			Integrated movement networks
	⬇	⬇	⬇
Spatial	**1B residential spaces** Developable land Personal refuge Settlement form Spatial and density patterns Design choices and principles Conservation areas and heritage housing Housing mix Service channels Open space Movement networks	**2B building construction** Land title Land subdivision, purchase and leasing House building and purchase Residents' associations Building regulations Design and density controls Construction and conversion standards Housing conversion and demolition controls Play spaces Water sanitation and power networks Road, path and cycle systems	**3B serviced suburbs, estates and streets** New towns, town expansion schemes and transit-orientated developments Community spaces and buildings Housing estates, apartment blocks, mixed use developments, gated developments, infill housing, women's and youth refuges, boarding houses, retirement villages, sheltered housing Heritage housing Service trenches, pipes and cables Parks and gardens Roads and paths

Figure 7.5   Values, activities and land uses in the creation of shelter. *Source:* Based on Foley, 1968.

systems of housing tenure. At each stage these conceptual norms, activities and networks are paralleled by spatial systems such as residential densities, housing mix and design types, giving rise to built environments involving land titles, building regulations and processes of construction and conversion, which in turn create the physical reality of the living suburbs, new towns, housing estates, community spaces and physical services of roads, drains and water supplies which provide the arenas for our daily lives. By tracing out the relational links in this way, a far richer understanding of the wide-ranging and complex field of shelter can be obtained, allowing the interplay of normative elements such as values and objectives, functional ones including resources and technology and material ones such as structures and spaces to be fully appreciated and harnessed in innovative planning. A planning process has been developed which reflects David Hume's dictum, which introduced the previous chapter, that 'The mind is, and should only be, the slave of the passions' – we should study and reorder the world to fulfil our deepest values.

The role of systems theory within the planning process

This chapter has so far been exploring how an understanding of the logic of the processes which generate the daily activities of community life can help community planners to bring the often onerous and unjust organisation of realities into closer alignment with what people want and value. The remaining part of this chapter will explore ways in which these processes can be modelled and optimised. This tracing of quantifiable inputs, through identifiable processes to achieve desired outputs represents the third bar of analysis of the design 'W' illustrated in Figure 7.1. This process moves us from empirical data, through interpretation to the formulation of options.

The technological and social changes of the current century are presenting new ways to satisfy old values, including new fields of communication and research, whose definition is ultimately decided by the interests of those operating them, and the objectives they are pursuing.[v] In analysing these activities, great advantages can be derived from the use of basic systems theory which was developed in the mid-twentieth century to promote the twin objectives of describing complex sets of related phenomena (Emery, 1969) and optimising outputs from organisational systems (Ashby, 1969).

Systems theory dates from the fusion of the work of biologists seeking to understand the behaviour of organisms and of 'operations research' specialists aiming to optimise outputs for production processes. Basically, an analytical tool, it focuses on the relationships among inputs, processes and outputs and makes use of models to explain often complex relationships between elements in terms of correlations or formulae (Figure 7.6). For these purposes, systems can be regarded as sets of related material or immaterial elements, changes to one part of which will result in significant changes throughout other parts and elements. Systems thinkers recognised early that accurate description required the adoption of open systems theory in which each system is linked to the wider environment from which it receives inputs and into which its outputs flow. This led to interest in establishing a 'general systems theory', as a scientific doctrine, concerned with the principles which apply to systems in general. Though never fully achieved, this has remained a significant motivating interest and source of energy. A highly relevant aspect of this approach has been the recognition that each general category also contains a number of constituent subsystems which must in turn be identified and understood for control processes like planning to be fully effective.

Viewed through the lens of systems thinking, everything in the universe is related to everything else, so that we can identify a universal system with its own internal mechanisms of attraction, repulsion, space and time. Within that, scientists identify for the purposes of study the solar system, to explain day and night, and to provide the technology for measuring time and navigation. Geographers and geophysicists focus on the global system to explain vulcanicity and meteorology. Ecologists make use of the idea of the biosphere as a system, with very many levels of subsystem going down to and beyond the concept of photosynthesis. Each human being is himself and herself a system with many component systems – glandular, cardiac, nervous, respiratory and reproductive – each with its own stable pattern and predictable performance. Organisms themselves are vast, sequenced assemblages of matter, descending to the scale of atoms and molecules with component particles of electrons, neutrons and quarks. At each level, effective control and optimisation depends upon accurate understanding of the composition of the system and the relationships of its elements. Systems theory is thus a way of viewing linked phenomena to aid understanding and assist control (Chadwick, 1972, 1987; Emery & Trist, 1969). Systems theory becomes an empowering way of perceiving and managing the world of sensations and information.

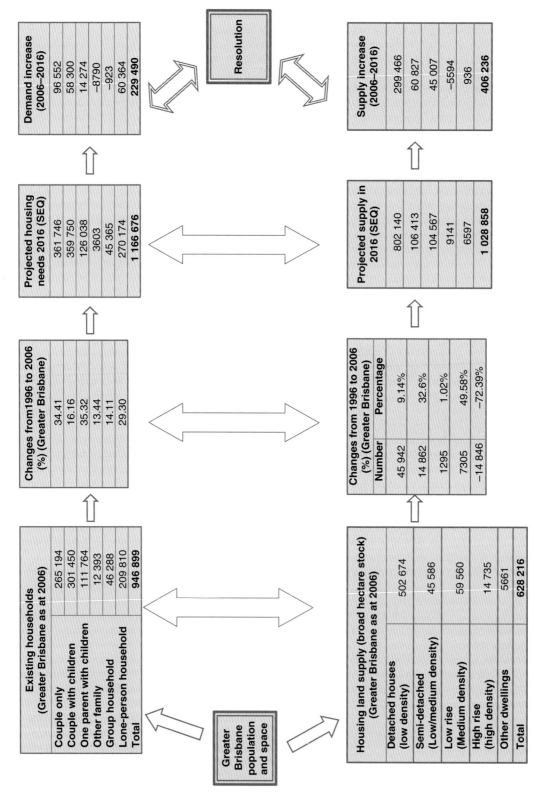

Figure 7.6 Projection of housing demand and housing land supply in Greater Brisbane, 1996–2016. *Source*: Adapted from research by Mark Conlan, presentation by Jessica Chatwin.

Activity systems analysis in practice

The first section of this chapter examined the place of activities in organised societies; the second section reviewed the relationships between values, activities and land uses, and applied its findings to propose a logical planning process using garden design and regional housing provisions as examples. The third section discussed in more detail the nature and uses of systems theory. This section now proceeds to apply the use of models in projecting trends and generating options. Four examples are used. Two, concerned with housing and employment are based in Greater Brisbane where the author works. Two more general ones, analysing transport systems and the human use of natural resources, are designed to relate to wider scales.

HOUSING IN GREATER BRISBANE

The model is based on two simple concepts:

- Households will require types of accommodation related to their size and composition.
- Dwellings will require different types of land relative to whether they are intended for:
  - detached family structures (separate family housing)
  - medium-density low rise ('townhouses')
  - medium-density medium rise attached dwellings ('apartment blocks') or
  - high-density, high rise ('high-rise flats').

Change in Greater Brisbane in different types of household between 1996 and 2006 is analysed in the categories of:

- lone-person households;
- couple families without children;
- couple families with children, one-parent families with children;
- other families;
- group households (largely student share households).

The official forecasts for these households have been calculated by the Queensland government's Population and Forecasting Unit (PIFU), based on population forecast interpreted in the light of current demographic patterns. The model makes use of these forecasts to project increased household demand for accommodation in the region up to the year 2016. This constitutes the housing demand, which is compared with the supply of housing land. Figures of available 'broad hectares' housing land from 2006 are compared with those from ten years earlier to determine if increased

provision has kept pace with the quite rapid growth of formation of households.

This land supply has been categorised by PIFU according to its suitability for detached, low-density family housing, townhouses, apartment blocks and high-rise flats. The model allocates the increase in households, to each of these categories in proportions based on existing patterns and behavioural assumptions, drawn from publications and informed review. This forms the basis for a resolution table shown in Figure 7.6, which allows us to view how existing provisions could be expected to fare in meeting the trend forecasts of housing demand.[vi]

In order to relate the household demand and housing land supply elements of the model, working assumptions have been made about the housing requirement and preference patterns of different households, which are incorporated in Figure 7.7.[vii]

Similar approaches could be used to allocate these projections of household change to different locations for land use planning, such as 'greenfield sites', 'centres', 'corridors' and 'inner area redevelopment' locations. A particular advantage of this approach is that it could be expanded to include preference patterns based on surveys of groups' own intentions and preferences, amplified by consultation with market suppliers and advocacy groups concerned with shelter.

As it stands, the model produces some interesting results:

- In 2006, the existing 'land bank' of 628 216 dwelling sites had not only succeeded in matching the demand of the previous ten years, but had also achieved a slight growth in available sites to meet the demands of the new decade.
- The projected increase in supply available by 2016 of 406 236 dwelling sites is over a third more than the total forecast housing demand of an extra 229 490 households needing accommodation.
- Three-quarters of the new provision is, however, in low-density separate houses, whereas less than half the forecast household growth will be in families with children.
- Nevertheless, the synthesis model shows that all categories of provision are adequate with the exception of the high-rise flats provision, which is not well addressed in a 'broad hectares study' looking essentially at, as yet, undeveloped peripheral land. A 'brownfield land' availability study therefore needs to be undertaken in suitable sectors of Greater Brisbane. These would include areas of such obsolescent uses as abandoned port sites and railway marshalling yards, areas of obsolete or inappropri-

Distribution	Separate houses (low density)		Attached (low/medium density)		Low rise (medium density)		High rise (high density)		Other dwellings	
	%	Number	%	Number	%	Number	%	Number	%	Number
Couple only	24	23 172	24	23 172	24	23 172	24	23 172	4	3862
Couple with children	70	40 810	30	17 490	—	—	—	—	—	—
One parent with children	45	6423	35	4996	15	2141	—	—	5	714
Other family	—	—	34	-2989	33	-2901	33	-2901	—	—
Group household	80	-738	20	-185	—	—	—	—	—	—
Lone-person household	—	—	35	21 127	20	12 073	40	24 146	5	3018
Total demand		70 945		66 785		37 386		47 318		7594
Total supply		299 466		60 827		45 007		-5594		936
Deficit/excess		+228 521		-5958		+7621		-41 724		-6658
Total excess						181 802				

Figure 7.7 Working assumptions on distribution of household demand categories between housing land supply types, based on forecast total changes, 2006–2016.
Source: Adapted from research by Mark Conlan; presentation by Jessica Chatwin.

ately located slum industries and areas within walking distance of major public transport nodes such as busways and railway stations. However, the total demand for such high-rise accommodation is not likely to exceed 50 000 units over the ten-year period spread throughout all the available brownfield sites in the city region, which includes five separately administered cities.

The model produces some reassuring results suggesting that the policy challenge facing Greater Brisbane in producing housing land for the next decade is one of selection and choice rather than radical change or drastic relaxation of regional policy directions. This is significant because housing industry lobbyists are arguing that there is a crisis looming in the provision of greenfield housing sites, which is simply not supported by an objective analysis of the situation.

Equally, crisis policies of massive inner-city redevelopment to provide sites for luxury high-rise flats do not appear to be justified. The Brisbane City Council has recently passed on to the State Government Department of Infrastructure and Planning for checking for matters of state interest a proposed South Brisbane Neighbourhood Plan and other inner area neighbourhood and local plans that would permit construction of 8-, 12- and 20-storey residential tower blocks in the suburbs of West End, Woolloongabba, Milton and Lutwyche (Brisbane City Council, 2010). That for South Brisbane (including the suburb of West End, which is currently the focus of the city's creative and cultural industry activities) would increase its current population of less than 5000 by more than five times to a potential total of over 27 000 (Brisbane City Council 2010), on the basis that there is an urgent need for this kind of increase to take pressure off the outer suburbs, which is a familiar scenario in cities undergoing rapid change and development. However, the model above indicates that the two different parts of the city region cater for a different kind of market, with the provision for family housing already being generously supplied in locations identified in the SEQ regional plan (Queensland Government, 2009). In the other four cities that make up the Greater Brisbane city region. Of the approximately 450 000 extra dwelling sites needed for the wider region in the period 2009–2031 only a third (158 000) are allocated to Brisbane City, the other 300 000 being proposed for the outer suburbs of the city region in the separate local government areas of Moreton Bay Region and Redland, Ipswich and Logan cities.

The model therefore shows that the kind of analysis of Robert Adams (2009), advocating the concentration of medium-rise residential development in corridors along major transport routes (discussed in more detail in the next chapter) also applies to Greater Brisbane. The kind of dwellings which will be most needed to meet growth in demand will be townhouses and medium density apartment blocks, not high rise flats which are more expensive to build, maintain, service and have very much higher carbon footprints. These townhouses and medium-rise apartments would best be located in the 'nodes and corridors' locations which are actually proposed in *City Shape*, the existing adopted strategy of the council (Brisbane City Council, 2006). However, current actions are instead concentrating on radical extension of the city centre into inner suburbs for high-rise accommodation, rather than distributing growth along public transport routes in the way proposed by Adams. In making possible this evaluation and critique, it becomes apparent that activity system projection has real advantages, not so much in producing new planning proposals, as in providing best the available basis for projection and analysis, against which different policy proposals can be usefully and realistically evaluated, and new options generated.

EMPLOYMENT PROJECTIONS IN GREATER BRISBANE

This model is based on two simple concepts:

1. Projected changes in population will produce related changes in the numbers of people in the working age groups and therefore the potential labour force. Since all of those seeking jobs in 15 years' time will be already born, projections of those requiring jobs can be confidently predicted for 15 years ahead, incorporating migration assumption and using well-established demographic survival rates.
2. General directions of changes in employment can be anticipated by reviewing current trends, as amended in the light of known investment, development and educational intentions. These will not be forecasts but projections of current employment situations and trends on the basis of stated assumptions; projected figures can thus be progressively reviewed in the light of emerging conditions.

Relating projected labour force numbers to the demand for workers should help to indicate if there are likely to be overall deficiencies or excesses in the availability of labour. It should also be possible to identify in which particular industries these are likely to occur, and the implications for education, investment and migration policies.

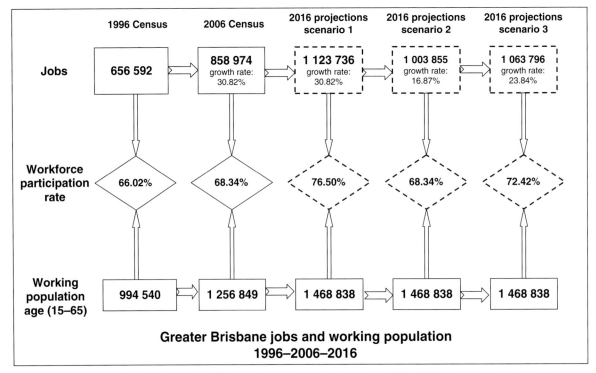

Greater Brisbane jobs and working population 1996–2006–2016

Figure 7.8 Projection of supply and demand for employment in Greater Brisbane, 1996–2006. *Source:* Research and presentation by Sherry She Juan.

The projection of Brisbane's employment situation, demonstrated in Figures 7.7 and 7.8, illustrates a typical rapid growth spiral in which environmental attractions are generating increases in both population and employment, which then further reinforce each other. In the decade up to 2006, jobs grew at the very rapid rate of 30% to reach a total of 859 000, outstripping the growth of population in the working age groups by 26.2% to produce a high and rising participation rate of 68.34%. Given continuation of current government policies and reviewing growth in the constituent industries, this straight-line projection of jobs growth (to reach approximately 1 124 000 by 2016) appears quite realistic. This is partly because the region is catching up on growth in knowledge-based industries elsewhere and partly because strong state government policies supporting port-based development of processing industry is likely to also maintain growth in the manufacturing sector, though at a lower rate than in other activities.

However, owing to falling birth rates in the 1990s and retirement of the 'baby boomer' generation, growth in people of working age is not predicted to keep pace with this demand for workers, especially in the health,

education, public administration and safety, retail and construction sectors, all of which significantly increased their proportion of total employment in the preceding decade by as much as 1.45% in health care and social assistance and 1.3% in retail. Overall anticipated growth in the numbers in the working age groups of 17% is little more than half that projected for the economy's demand for workers of over 30% to approximately 1 124 000. This would result in an unprecedentedly high participation rate of 76.5%, which is unlikely to be achieved, owing to the following reasons:

- Increased recognition of the need for more prolonged periods of paid leave to allow home care for newborn children.
- Increases in the 15–24 age groups in the proportions of people and the duration of studies in full-time education.
- Diminishing proportions of total population in the working age groups owing to retirement of the 'baby boomer' generation born in the period 1945–1955.

In recognition of the need to resolve this mismatch between supply and demand for workers, Scenario 2 has been developed, based on a continuation of the current participation rate of 68.34%. This would result in the labour force increasing by only 17% to just over one million, a shortfall of 120 000 against potential demand. Relating this outcome to individual industries, very high rises in productivity or shortfalls in provisions would have to result in the rapid growth activities of health services, public administration, retail and construction, in all of which current investment and policy trends are likely to create continued rapid job growth. Scenario 2 could thus result in harmful contraction in key human capital and social service areas of the economy, with damaging long-term results. Given contemporary high levels of personal mobility and the attractions of Brisbane as a place to live and work, it is also highly unlikely that this scenario will occur. Instead, the already high rates of migration into the region may be further increased and specifically targeted at the working age groups, to meet the projected labour shortage. There is, however, widespread opposition from environmental and community groups to this added impetus to the spiral of very high levels of inward migration and population pressure on resources.

In the light of these doubts over the plausibility and desirability of Scenarios 1 and 2, Scenario 3 has been developed, based on a participation rate of 72.42%, halfway between the current level of 68.34% and the straight-line projection figure of 76.55. Scenario 3 produces tight, but manageable, labour force increases in each of the major growth activities, at the same time as raising the possibilities of productivity increases managing the lesser labour force demands in other activities such as manufacturing, financial services and accommodation and food services.

It will be seen that Scenario 3, while producing viable outcomes, would still result in a regional shortfall of 60 000 workers compared with the potential numbers of jobs generated by the various industries, which could be met by a combination of policies for worker migration, increased productivity, industrial retraining, part-time vocational training and worker retention beyond retirement age in non-manual activities. The pattern of employment growth that would result from these three scenarios can be seen in more detail in the analytical tables in *Appendix* 2: *Employment Projections: Brisbane Statistical Division*.

This review also raises issues concerning the application of the state's current 'Smart State' policies to concentrate job creation schemes to attract the maximum number of jobs into the south-east region, which is routinely described as the powerhouse of the Queensland Economy. Early recognition that these

polices may need review came in her concluding address to the April 2010 Population Summit in Brisbane when the Premier, Anna Bligh, explicitly raised the possibility that population pressure in the south-east may best be met by encouraging growth elsewhere, in regional centres such as Townsville and other port cities (Queensland Government, 2010). These have good industrial and commercial infrastructure and could support some of the growth industries which are now being encouraged to develop in the 'Australian Trade Coast' along the lower estuary of the Brisbane River. It appears reasonable that some of the extra 265 000 jobs which are projected in Scenario 1 for Greater Brisbane over the period 2006–2016 would be better steered to developing regions with spare capacity along the north and central coasts. The model indicates that this could be done without endangering full employment in Greater Brisbane.

Other general issues that emerge are the desirability of pursuing the Commonwealth government's intention, announced in 2010, of reviewing the retirement age for females from 60 to 65 years to match the male level, and progressively raising the retirement age for non-manual workers from its present level of 65 towards 70 years to match increased longevity, vitality and health standards (Tanner, 2009). Consideration of a suite of employment policies is also prompted, including linking school and vocational training programmes to employment prospects in health, administration, construction, education and retail servicers. It will be seen that this kind of activity systems model can raise some most significant policy issues for community planners, at the same time as assisting in the development of options that can then be evaluated for balance of costs and benefits and possible unintended consequences. Such modelling, though not a planning outcome in itself, is a useful means to better-informed planning.

THE TRANSPORT SYSTEM

The transport system may be best understood through its roles in connecting different places and activities. The interpretative models below have been developed on this basis, which is expressed in the following two principles:[viii]

- Most journeys occur daily and start or finish in homes or workplaces.
- Total daily movements can be estimated from the numbers of people involved, the origin and destination of their journeys and the forms of transport they use.

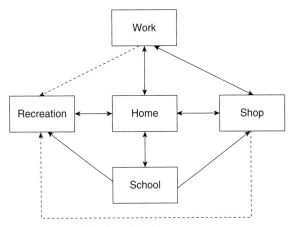

Figure 7.9 Simplified model of transport system.

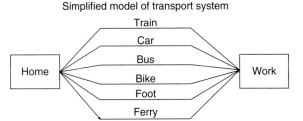

Figure 7.10 The journey to work subsystem.

These principles are demonstrated in Figure 7.9. Quantifiable descriptive and prescriptive models similar to those explored earlier for housing and employment can be extrapolated from this conceptual model by inserting numbers of people undertaking journeys in each of the elements of home, work, shop, learn and play. Figures for 'home' will be the total numbers of households in the study region; 'work' figures will the employed labour total from the census; and 'shop' figures can be based on estimates of total numbers of shopping trips made by each household (information which is usually available from transport planning colleagues who regularly conduct sample behavioural surveys). In the case of Brisbane it is estimated at approximately three visits a week or approximately 0.4 per day. Trips to learn are established by numbers of children and young adults in primary, secondary and tertiary education. Trips to recreation will require a little more research and interpretation, but can normally be obtained from sample surveys conducted by government departments of sport and recreation; sports management courses at local universities may also have developed information on recreational patterns that can be extrapolated to provide indications of regular recreational movements. As a general guide, every person over the age of five years tends to make approximately three recreational trips a week or 0.4 per day.

Not all trips go direct to one of these destinations from home. Work–work trips, for instance, are quite common, as are work–shop and work–recreation trips, particularly as part of return journeys from work to home. These variations amplify but do not distort the basic model, so that a total pattern of daily movements can be readily developed for most great and small cities and city regions. This is invaluable for understanding and developing overfall options from the movement system.

Such a model does not, however, provide route-specific information required for operational system planning. Within this overall transport system, individual subsystems linking different pairings of origins and destinations may be particularly significant and will help to identify which traffic flows can be allocated to particular routes. Because they offer opportunities to consider and interpret these key flows better, they also promote understanding of the motivations of travellers, and should suggest methods of altering current patterns of movement. Implications for investment and programme management can be considered, including encouraging people to change from one transport mode, such as the private motor car, to others, such as the bus, train, bike or ferry.

Such journeys between home and work (Figure 7.10) generally adopt one of these six main modes of travel, which are not difficult to quantify. Existing flows are normally well documented by departments of transport as part of their work of monitoring and accommodating traffic movements. In many countries, this information is also available from quinquennial censuses. A clear understanding can then be gained of the existing 'modal split' between different methods of making the journey to work. The effects of different distributions of total journeys between the various modes can be modelled and evaluated. This kind of modelling underlies the most successful transport policies of cities such as Toronto, London, Stockholm, Portland (Oregon), Bogotá and Curitiba in Brazil. Since the excessive use of the private motor vehicle for the journey to work is the largest single contributor to the carbon emissions which are increasing global warming, with its related problems of climatic volatility and rising sea levels, such descriptive, predictive planning models have a very important role to play in community planning, transcending both local and global levels. Well-constructed models of the journey-to-work subsystem can thus play an indispensable part in remedying this situation. It is not only that 'to understand all is to forgive all'; it is also the case that increased understanding is the surest path to good communication and wise management and control.

THE HUMAN USE OF NATURAL RESOURCES

Community planning must inescapably work within the framework of the finite world of physical resources. Recalling Lavoisier's dictum that 'Nothing is lost; nothing is created; everything is transformed', planners must be very concerned to ensure that the transformations for which they are responsible are beneficial or reversible. We have seen that Figure 5.4 in Chapter 5, is situated within this understanding. It is based on three propositions:

1. All human uses of natural resources result from the operations of mind, ideas and values on matter to create food supplies, raw materials and energy sources.
2. Natural ecological processes constantly transform matter between different states and reintegrate waste products back into sustainable sequences of change.
3. Human use may reach a scale and intensity where the production of bio-hostile matter accumulates in the form of production refuse and discarded items of consumption faster than they can be reintegrated into the natural environment by established ecological processes. Carbon pollution of the atmosphere is one such example.

The model identifies inputs to this cycle of energy, raw materials and food sources which are both natural and invented. Energy flows naturally from the sun, but humans have captured and concentrated it in the form of fossil fuels, fire and power generation to extend its use and effectiveness. Raw materials are freely available in the natural environment, but their potentialities have first to be recognised or invented. Food and water are freely available, but their current use depends upon people developing ways of amplifying and storing them to support a more bounteous existence and larger populations. Processes of human intention and understanding are thus required to transform the matter, which is offered for human use by natural ecological processes. However, these intentional processes have now reached a scale and intensity which has exceeded natural capacities for their reintegration. Outputs now include not only items for human use but also increasingly large volumes of discarded matter in the forms of production waste or time-expired items of consump-

tion. This cycle of inputs, processes and outputs has exceeded the capacity of natural ecological processes for self-regulation. Though intentionally very general, this model is, like that for transport, capable of being amplified by similar ones relating to the subsystems of land, water, air and living matter, as well as to specific outcomes such as carbon production and water pollution and land contamination by toxic chemicals.

Such models can be quantified and applied widely to determine outputs which may include current and predicted carbon footprints and accumulations of solid waste or polluted water. Applied to regular 'ecological audits', they can help to indicate levels of sustainability, as well as anticipated origins, locations and levels of projected waste production. Creatively interpreted, they may help to suggest options for programmes of consumption and waste reduction and reintegration, by means of recycling, reclamation and reformed production methods. Recycling links the phases of technological transformation and human use by reprocessing such waste and discarded materials as water, metal, paper, glass, sewerage, plastics and animal waste so that they will no longer accumulate in toxic concentrations which threaten natural ecological processes. In addition, they may reduce demands for new natural resources such as timber for paper pulp and sand and gravel for roads and other major construction work, including air- and seaports.

Proactive reclamation can bring back into productive use concentrations of toxic or destructive waste, including mining spoil, chemical discharges and derelict land (such as that which still pockmarks the landscapes of pioneer industrial regions of parts of northern Britain and the mining regions of central Appalachia in the United States). Reclamation programmes and grants and use of regulatory frameworks favouring new developments on brownfield sites can reduce the effective costs of using these kinds of resources to the levels where they become more profitable than extracting virgin resources. Other examples of such policies include recycling 'grey water' for appropriate reuse and developing old quarrying and sand and gravel extraction sites for recreational uses for watersports, BMX tracks and motorsport.

A third set of actions to reform production methods which is currently generating much international discussion and diplomacy relates to the proactive steering of productive processes towards more sustainable methods by carbon pricing (Avaaz.org, 2009; United Nations Framework Convention on Climate Change, 2009). This could take the form either of a carbon tax administered by national governments which has the very great advantages of simplicity and ease of enforcement, but might be harder to introduce in economically disadvantaged countries aiming to raise their people's material standards of living. The alternative approaches of emissions trading schemes (ETSs) would create large flows of funds to finance carbon reduction and forest preservation schemes in developing countries, but in the absence of international government and police powers ETSs are very insecure in their effectiveness.[ix] Combinations of such approaches offer the best possibilities of achieving sustainable futures. The model of the human use of natural resources not only alerts us to the imperatives of searching for paths towards environmentally sustainable policies in these ways but also suggests ways and locations where such options may be found.

Conclusions: the roles of activity systems in community planning

This chapter has focused on the ways that activities can be understood, interpreted and optimised to express values in order to achieve successful human outcomes and promote productive community life. Though they cannot provide the inspiration for a community's planning, present and potential activities do offer invaluable indications of the means by which those plans may be achieved. Techniques of activity systems analysis offer effective ways to understand, interpret and optimise these activities. The relationships between inputs, processes and outputs can be identified and adjusted. Inputs can be varied and new processes invented to produce beneficial outcomes, more closely aligned to community values and objectives. Because human value systems are themselves evolving, the dynamic role of intention is constantly being brought into play to optimize activity systems and meet new objectives. The ways in which this operates in the four important fields of human activity of shelter, work, education and health are explored in the next two chapters.

Appendix 1 Household demand and housing land supply statistics, Greater Brisbane 1996–2016

SEQ Residential Market Assessment: Housing Land Supply								
SEQ Existing housing stock analysis (PIFU)								
SEQ broadhectare stock and expected dwelling yield by local government area								
	Broadhectare stock (hectares)				Expected dwelling yield (dwellings)			
Local government area	Higher density[2]	Detached urban	Low density	Total stock	Higher density[2]	Detached urban	Low density	Total dwellings
Brisbane (C)	578	2253	10	**2841**	32645	24795	15	**57455**
Gold Coast (C)	681	2836	1159	**4676**	30086	18176	1183	**49445**
Ipswich (C)	3399	4129	1312	**8840**	88129	28241	1965	**118335**
Lockyer Valley (RC)	8	896	3176	**4080**	438	6250	3194	**9882**
Logan (C)	630	4211	2305	**7146**	12335	29875	3044	**45254**
Moreton Bay (RC)	600	2509	2904	**6013**	15329	22033	2334	**39696**
Redland (C)	94	593	100	**787**	3018	6239	150	**9407**
Scenic Rim (RC)	8	1386	307	**1701**	164	9213	595	**9972**
Somerset (RC)	10	162	28	**200**	287	1076	50	**1413**
Sunshine Coast (RC)	591	5144	971	**6706**	18053	43922	1111	**63086**
Toowoomba (SD)[1]	0	2050	2176	**4226**	10	8573	2412	**10995**
Existing SEQ Res. Stock:	**6599**	**26169**	**14448**	**47216**	**200494**	**198393**	**16053**	**414940**
Dwellings per hectare:	**30.38**	**7.58**	**1.11**	**8.79**				

[1]Toowoomba Statistical District includes the former Toowoomba City and surrounding residential areas of Cambooya, Crows Nest, Jondaryan and Rosalie
[2]Higher density urban includes attached housing and small lot subdivisions.
Source: 2009 DIP SEQ Broadhectare Executive Summary (page 6)

2006 SEQ Household Demand Analysis

Household Size Category*

ABS Statistical Region	1 Couple family with no children[1]	%	2 Couple family with children[1]	%	3 One-parent family with children[1]	%	4 Other Family[1]	%	5 Group Households[2]	%	6 Lone-person Households[2]	%	Total	%
305 Brisbane	169764	26.62%	211699	33.20%	75146	11.78%	9429	1.48%	31589	4.95%	140114	21.97%	637741	67.35%
307 Gold Coast	52907	29.47%	52178	29.06%	21721	12.10%	1935	1.08%	9956	5.54%	40856	22.75%	179553	18.96%
309 Sunshine Coast	34449	32.84%	29641	28.25%	12218	11.65%	789	0.75%	4092	3.90%	23719	22.61%	104908	11.08%
312 West Moreton	8074	32.69%	7932	32.12%	2679	10.85%	240	0.97%	651	2.64%	5121	20.74%	24697	2.61%
Totals:	**265194**	**28.01%**	**301450**	**31.84%**	**111764**	**11.80%**	**12393**	**1.31%**	**46288**	**4.89%**	**209810**	**22.16%**	**946899**	**100.00%**

'ABS and PIFU categories.
1Source: 2006 ABS Basic Community Profile B24 FAMILY COMPOSITION.
2Source: 2006 ABS Basic Community Profile B30 HOUSEHOLD COMPOSITION.

2001 SEQ Household Demand Analysis

Household Category '

ABS Statistical Region	1 Couple family with no children[1]	%	2 Couple family with children[1]	%	3 One-parent family with children[1]	%	4 Other Family[1]	%	5 Group Households[2]	%	6 Lone-person Households[2]	%	Total	%
305 Brisbane	149450	25.31%	198984	33.70%	70253	11.90%	9030	1.53%	29052	4.92%	133644	22.64%	590413	69.11%
310 Moreton	79451	30.11%	76087	28.84%	31318	11.87%	2664	1.01%	12906	4.89%	61443	23.29%	263869	30.89%
Totals:	**228901**	**26.79%**	**275071**	**32.20%**	**101571**	**11.89%**	**11694**	**1.37%**	**41958**	**4.91%**	**195087**	**22.84%**	**854282**	**100.00%**

'ABS and PIFU categories.
1Source: 2001 ABS Basic Community Profile B17 FAMILY TYPE.
2Source: 2001 ABS Basic Community Profile B32 HOUSEHOLD TYPE BY NUMBER OF PERSONS USUALLY RESIDENT(a).

1996 SEQ Household Demand Analysis

Household Category*

ABS Statistical Region	1 Couple family with no children[1]	%	2 Couple family with children[1]	%	3 One-parent family with children[1]	%	4 Other Family[1]	%	5 Group Households[2]	%	6 Lone-person Households[2]	%	Total	%
305 Brisbane	130061	24.56%	190426	35.96%	58862	11.11%	8643	1.63%	28161	5.32%	113469	21.42%	529622	70.32%
310 Moreton	67246	30.08%	69094	30.91%	23728	10.61%	2282	1.02%	12402	5.55%	48793	21.83%	223545	29.68%
Totals:	**197307**	26.20%	**259520**	34.46%	**82590**	10.97%	**10925**	1.45%	**40563**	5.39%	**162262**	21.54%	**753167**	100.00%

*ABS and PIFU categories.
[1]Source: 1996 ABS Basic Community Profile B24 FAMILY TYPE BY WEEKLY FAMILY INCOME.
[2]Source: 1996 ABS Basic Community Profile B26 HOUSEHOLD TYPE AND FAMILY TYPE BY NUMBER OF PERSONS (USUALLY RESIDENT(a)).

DATA ANALYSIS

1996 2001 and 2006 Residential Land and Site Supply Analysis

Dwelling Type	1996	%	2001	%	% change 96-01	2006	%	% change 01-06	% change 96-06	Av % annual change
Separate Houses Low Density	632878	74.65%	670697	75.38%	5.98%	718233	76.96%	7.09%	13.49%	1.35%
Semi-detached Low/medium density Medium Density	61462	7.25%	75616	8.50%	23.03%	87188	9.34%	15.30%	41.86%	4.19%
Low-rise (<4 floors) Medium Density	94687	11.17%	93753	10.54%	-0.99%	90179	9.66%	-3.81%	-4.76%	-0.48%
High-rise (>3 floors) High Density	23378	2.76%	28099	3.16%	20.19%	26955	2.89%	-4.07%	15.30%	1.53%
Other dwellings (Caravan) Other	35434	4.18%	21540	2.42%	-39.21%	10650	1.14%	-50.56%	-69.94%	-6.99%
Totals:	847839	100.00%	889705	100.00%	4.94%	933205	100.00%	4.89%	10.07%	1.01%
Persons/dwelling:	2.52		2.67			2.60				
Persons:	2133681		2372104			2425429				

SOUTH EAST QUEENSLAND HOUSEHOLD DEMAND TRENDS

Household Composition	1996 No.	%	2001 No.	%	2006 No.	%	2011 No.	%	2016 No.	%
Couple family with no children	197307	26.20%	228901	26.79%	265194	28.01%	310131	29.51%	361746	31.01%
Couple family with children	259520	34.46%	275071	32.20%	301450	31.84%	329354	31.34%	359750	30.84%
One-parent family with children	82590	10.97%	101571	11.89%	111764	11.80%	118803	11.30%	126038	10.80%
Other family	10925	1.45%	11694	1.37%	12393	1.31%	8501	0.81%	3603	0.31%
Group households	40563	5.39%	41958	4.91%	46288	4.89%	46124	4.39%	45365	3.89%
Lone-person households	162262	21.54%	195087	22.84%	209810	22.16%	238144	22.66%	270174	23.16%
Totals:	**753167**	**100.00%**	**854282**	**100.00%**	**946899**	**100.00%**	**1051058**	**100.00%**	**1166674**	**100.00%**

SOUTH EAST QUEENSLAND HOUSING SUPPLY TRENDS

Dwelling Type	1996 No.	%	2001 No.	%	2006 No.	%	2011 No.	%	2016 No.	%
Separate houses	632878	74.65%	670697	75.38%	718233	76.96%	759044	77.46%	802140	77.96%
Semi-detached	61462	7.25%	75616	8.50%	87188	9.34%	96447	9.84%	106413	10.34%
Low-rise (<4 floors)	94687	11.17%	93753	10.54%	90179	9.66%	94688	9.66%	104567	10.16%
High-rise (>3 floors)	23378	2.76%	28099	3.16%	26955	2.89%	23403	2.39%	9141	0.89%
Other dwellings (e.g. Caravan)	35434	4.18%	21540	2.42%	10650	1.14%	6283	0.64%	6597	0.64%
Totals:	**847839**	**100.00%**	**889705**	**100.00%**	**933205**	**100.00%**	**979865**	**100.00%**	**1028859**	**100.00%**

Appendix 2 Employment Projections: Brisbane Statistical Division

1. ABS CENSUS DATA, 1996–2006

	1996 Census		2001 Census		2006 Census	
	Persons		Persons		Persons	
Agriculture, forestry and fishing	6960	1.06%	7650	1.05%	5918	0.69%
Mining	2981	0.45%	3314	0.45%	4823	0.56%
Manufacturing	75390	11.48%	86738	11.86%	94156	10.96%
Electricity, gas, water and waste services	4887	0.74%	6931	0.95%	8640	1.01%
Construction	42568	6.48%	47118	6.44%	68702	8.00%
Wholesale trade	40701	6.20%	39035	5.34%	38874	4.53%
Retail trade	67844	10.33%	81939	11.21%	96319	11.21%
Accommodation and food services	39335	5.99%	45104	6.17%	50602	5.89%
Transport, postal and warehousing	35163	5.36%	40108	5.49%	47220	5.50%
Information media and telecommunications	16367	2.49%	16324	2.23%	14638	1.70%
Financial and insurance services	25277	3.85%	27302	3.73%	31654	3.69%
Rental, hiring and real estate services	12329	1.88%	14367	1.96%	17520	2.04%
Professional, scientific and technical services	47391	7.22%	52144	7.13%	63181	7.36%
Administrative and support services	19005	2.89%	25027	3.42%	28185	3.28%
Public administration and safety	44881	6.84%	47818	6.54%	61342	7.14%
Education and training	51095	7.78%	60642	8.29%	68299	7.95%
Health care and social assistance	65117	9.92%	74345	10.17%	93571	10.89%
Arts and recreation services	9207	1.40%	10020	1.37%	11064	1.29%
Other services	29964	4.56%	30131	4.12%	32330	3.76%
Inadequately described / Not stated	20130	3.07%	15154	2.07%	21936	2.55%
Total	**656592**	100.00%	**731211**	100.00%	**858974**	100.00%

Research and presentation: Sherry She Juan.
Source: T25 Industry of employment by sex for time series ABS.

2. PIFU POPULATION PROJECTIONS

	ERP	Medium series				
		Projected resident population				
Statistical Division (SD)	2006 no.	2011 no.	2016 no.	2021 no.	2026 no.	2031 no.
Brisbane (SD) 2006 ASGC	1819762	2004092	2204647	2392069	2564496	2726836

5 years to 30 June					25 years to 30 June	
					2031	
Statistical Division (SD)	2011 no.	2016 no.	2021 no.	2026 no.	2031 no.	no.	%
	no.		%			
Brisbane (SD) 2006 ASGC	36866	40111	37484	34485	32468	36283	1.6

Source: PIFU Future Population 2008 edition Medium Series.

Key Assumptions

1. POPULATION FORECAST BY AGE GROUPS:

Statistical Division (SD)	Population forecast by age groups							
	Age group (years)							
	Year	0–14	15–24	25–44	45–64	65 and over	TOTAL(a)	Median age
Brisbane (SD)	1996	312	240532	454471	299537	161157	1468617	32
	2001	335203	246092	487141	361054	176160	1605650	34
	2006	**364437**	**277599**	**546707**	**432543**	**198476**	**1819762**	**35**
	2011	391545	296646	586476	476568	252858	2004092	36
	2016	419939	316352	627995	524492	315870	2204647	37
	2021	443933	332416	662751	569333	383636	2392069	38
	2026	463383	344768	690551	610642	455152	2564496	39
	2031	**479372**	**354249**	**713026**	**649586**	**530603**	**2726836**	**40**

2. PROJECTED LABOUR FORCE

Year	1996	2001	2006	2011	2016	2021	2026	2031
Population	1468617	1605650	1819762	2004092	2204647	2392069	2564496	2726836
Potential working population (age 15–64)[1]	994540	1094287	1256849	1359689	1468838	1564500	1645961	1716861
Potential working population to total population ratio	67.72%	68.15%	69.07%	67.85%	66.62%	65.40%	64.18%	62.96%
Labour force	656592	731211	858974					
Labour force to potential working population ratio	66.02%	66.82%	68.34%					
Projected labour force to potential working population ratio[2]				66.26%	64.16%	62.07%	59.98%	57.88%
Projected labour force[3]				900927	942479	971086	987168	993724

Note:
[1]The potential working population aggregates the population from age groups 0–14,15–24, 25–44 and 45–64.
[2]The projected labour force to potential working population ratio follows the same trend of potential working population to total population ratio from 1996 to 2031.
[3]The projected labour force is calculated based on potential working population and the projected labour force to potential working population ratio.

3. PROJECTED LABOUR FORCE BY INDUSTRY TYPES

	1996 Census		2001 Census		2006 Census		2011		2016		2021	
	Persons	Share	Persons	Share	Persons	Share	Projected persons	Projected share	Projected persons	Projected share	Projected Persons	Projected Share
Agriculture, forestry and fishing	6960	1.06%	7650	1.05%	5918	0.69%	5051	0.56%	3536	0.38%	1841	0.19%
Mining	2981	0.45%	3314	0.45%	4823	0.56%	5379	0.60%	6133	0.65%	6841	0.70%
Manufacturing	75390	11.48%	86738	11.86%	94156	10.96%	98333	10.91%	100415	10.65%	100936	10.39%
Electricity, gas, water and waste services	4887	0.74%	6931	0.95%	8640	1.01%	10459	1.16%	12174	1.29%	13813	1.42%
Construction	42568	6.48%	47118	6.44%	68702	8.00%	76489	8.49%	87156	9.25%	97157	10.00%
Wholesale trade	40701	6.20%	39035	5.34%	38874	4.53%	33164	3.68%	26809	2.84%	19498	2.01%
Retail trade	67844	10.33%	81939	11.21%	96319	11.21%	106290	11.80%	115341	12.24%	123118	12.68%
Accommodation and food services	39335	5.99%	45104	6.17%	50602	5.89%	53307	5.92%	55295	5.87%	56489	5.82%
Transport, postal and warehousing	35163	5.36%	40108	5.49%	47220	5.50%	50342	5.59%	53332	5.66%	55640	5.73%
Information media and telecommunications	16367	2.49%	16324	2.23%	14638	1.70%	12203	1.35%	9050	0.96%	5496	0.57%
Financial and insurance services	25277	3.85%	27302	3.73%	31654	3.69%	32357	3.59%	33074	3.51%	33279	3.43%
Rental, hiring and real estate services	12329	1.88%	14367	1.96%	17520	2.04%	19124	2.12%	20769	2.20%	22185	2.28%
Professional, scientific and technical services	47391	7.22%	52144	7.13%	63181	7.36%	66420	7.37%	70133	7.44%	72930	7.51%
Administrative and support services	19005	2.89%	25027	3.42%	28185	3.28%	32309	3.59%	35622	3.78%	38581	3.97%
Public administration and safety	44881	6.84%	47818	6.54%	61342	7.14%	64368	7.14%	68778	7.30%	72351	7.45%
Education and training	51095	7.78%	60642	8.29%	68299	7.95%	73680	8.18%	77876	8.26%	81062	8.35%
Health care and social assistance	65117	9.92%	74345	10.17%	93571	10.89%	101823	11.30%	111118	11.79%	119229	12.28%
Arts and recreation services	9207	1.40%	10020	1.37%	11064	1.29%	11166	1.24%	11142	1.18%	10926	1.13%
Other services	29964	4.56%	30131	4.12%	32330	3.76%	30177	3.35%	27800	2.95%	24761	2.55%
Inadequately described/Not stated	20130	3.07%	15154	2.07%	21936	2.55%	18486	2.05%	16926	1.80%	14953	1.54%
Total	**656592**	100.00%	**731211**	100.00%	**858974**	100.00%	**900927**	100.00%	**942479**	100.00%	**971086**	100.00%

It is assumed that the growth of employment by industry type from 2011 to 2021 follows the historical trend from 1996 to 2006.
The estimated employment is calculated based on the projected industry shares.

Endnotes

i This is a case where checklist planning borrowed from another culture, using alien controls, failed to acknowledge local values and needs. Time-consuming and difficult as it would have been, the Ondo planners would have been better advised to go back to community values and needs and devise a planning system that served the purposes of shelter improvement, job provision and traditional urban and compound form and organisation. Table 7.1 below indicates the explanations provided by the public and officials for the failure of official planning system.

Table 7.1 Explanations for planning contraventions in Akure 1973–1979

Reason	Source	
	Public	Officials
Non-involvement of the public in planning	X	X
Corruption of officers of the authority	X	X
Fragmentation of residential compounds to accommodate traditional polygamy	X	X
Disputes over land ownership	X	X
Employment needs	X	
Cost of building materials in an inflationary economy	X	
Delays in planning application process	X	
Increasing cost of planning application process	X	
Fragmentation of the compounds to accommodate traditional polygamy	X	
Low literacy levels of the public		X
Inadequacy of artisans (carpenters, bricklayers)		X
Poverty of public unable to satisfy planning requirements		X
Incompetence and inefficiency of draftsmen		X
Undue political influence protecting defaulters		X

ii Work, for example, may be motivated by a number of values including prosperity and the provision of sustenance to maintain life for ourselves and our groups, as well as to express natural creativity, and to acquire wealth, power, status and self-esteem. Play expresses not only its own values but also others such as skills development and therefore prosperity. Similarly, movement may be made for reasons of choice, recreation, economy or autonomy.

iii Foley's approach is neutral on the question of the changeability of values. His argument does not depend on unchanging innate drives, but rather on acknowledging that the aims of plans and designs are to satisfy human wants, be they stale or evolving. Either way, proposals will ultimately have to take on physical forms, occupy space and be integrated within 'metropolitan spatial structures'.

iv In summary, synthesis will use cross-cutting policies which draw together information from many different activities to meet the intentions of clusters of objectives constituted to reflect their functional links. For instance, the objectives of garden access, maintenance, cultivation, construction and contemplation will all be linked in design policies that join different activity nodes by discrete paths that use natural materials and avoid the dangers of causing erosion. Objectives can be organised into a framework with most important bands at the top, and different activities, such as movement and cultivation, arranged along a horizontal axis. As a result, each policy bundle will consist of cluster of top-level, major and basic objectives, whose ranking will be determined by their importance to the garden's future users, as well as their contribution to the overall set of objectives. This process has been worked out in very effective practical detail by Christopher Alexander (1964) in his celebrated Indian Village case study.

v The dominant activities of dwelling, work and movement identified by Le Play and Geddes as the bases of human society in the nineteenth century (Mairet, 1957) have been amplified by twentieth-century extensions of choice and productivity to include health, administration, education and cultural activities, such as worship and art.

vi It is assumed that the market will, during the forecast period, continue to achieve a reasonable adjustment of housing occupancy to changing household size and characteristics, as family households move into 'couple only' and 'lone person' categories and households within those categories become 'couples with children'.

vii For instance the 96 552 forecast increase in the number of 'couple only' households requiring accommodation in the decade 2006–2016 has been distributed between the different types of housing land categories in proportions that reflect known patterns of needs and preference. Four per cent have been allocated to 'other dwellings' (largely caravan parks) to reflect realistic continuation of present needs during times of housing stress. Of the remainder, a quarter have been allocated to separate houses, to reflect current trends whereby a considerable portion of 'couple only' households choose to buy such dwellings as investments or in anticipation of starting a family. A further quarter has been allocated to attached (low/medium-density dwellings), often referred to as townhouses, which are the least expensive form of accommodation that often serve as starter homes. A further quarter have been allocated to low-rise, medium-density dwellings, which are the apartments that form an equally popular form of dwelling, often associated with good access to public transport. Finally, a further quarter has been allocated to high-rise, high-density dwellings, which reflects trends to increased residential development in inner metropolitan areas to which this kind of household is well suited, though the inherently above-average cost level restricts occupancy to the more affluent sections of the group.

Similar considerations have been made in deciding the allocations of the different types of households. For instance, 70% of couple households with children have been allocated to separate low-density dwellings to reflect existing patterns, preferences and needs of children for access to private open space, with the remainder being allocated to townhouses which are generally cheaper and have small associated outdoor spaces. One-parent families have been allocated more equally between separate dwellings (45%) and townhouses (35%) to reflect the reality of smaller incomes available to one-parent families with more restricted earning capacities. The largest proportion (40%) of the growing number of lone-person households have been allocated to high-rise accommodation on the basis of suitability and the quite adequate income available to the large number of retirees. Less affluent people will be seeking townhouse and apartment locations. These are reasonable allocations, but they are capable of refinement in the light of further analysis of existing patterns of occupancy.

viii There is a strong logical case for including transport and communications in a single 'access' system because the remarkable developments in the transmission of ideas and information of the last fifty years, to some extent reduces the needs to move goods and people, encouraging, for instance, increasing numbers of people to work from home. However, the two activities are in many other ways still quite separate and it is not yet, in practice, helpful to analyse their inputs, processes and outputs in the same system.

ix Those paying the funds from within developed economies would have little interest in ensuring that the carbon reduction schemes agreed for locations thousands of miles away were actually fully implemented. Equally, those receiving the funds would have strong economic interests in evading the carbon reduction processes, once funds had been received. Such outcomes are not inevitable but the creation of powerful international administrative agency would be necessary to avoid their occurrence. This then runs the further danger of lack of real support from governments within developed nations, who would see slices of potential gross national product transferred overseas. This analysis suggests that there is a strong case for national carbon tax regimes which contribute a portion of their income to international funds to promote carbon mitigation in developing economies.

References

Adams, R. (2009) *Transforming Australian Cities*. Melbourne, City of Melbourne.

Alexander, C. (1964) *Notes on the Synthesis of Form*. Cambridge, MA, Harvard University Press, (reprinted 1979).

Anderson, M. (1964) *The Federal Bulldozer: A critical analysis of urban renewal 1942–1962*. Cambridge, MA, MIT Press.

Ashby, W. (1969) Adaptation in the multistable system. In: F. Emery (ed.), *Systems Thinking*. Harmondsworth, Penguin.

Avaaz.org (2009) *The world wants a real deal*, https://secure.avaaz.org/jp/blog.php, accessed 21 April 2010.

Brisbane City Council (2006) *City Shape*. Brisbane, Author.

Brisbane City Council (2010) *South Brisbane Neighbourhood Plan*. Brisbane, Author.

Chadwick, G. (1972) *A Systems View of Planning: Towards a theory of the urban and regional planning process*. Oxford, Pergamon Press.

Chadwick, G. (1987) *Models of Urban and Regional Systems in Developing Countries: Some theories and their application in physical planning*. Oxford, Pergamon Press.

Emery, F. (ed.) (1969) *Systems Thinking*. Harmondsworth, Penguin.

Emery, F., Trist, E. (1969) Socio technical systems. In: F. Emery (ed.), *Systems Thinking*. Harmondsworth, Penguin.

Faseki, O. (1981) *The Problem of Contravention: Akure, Ondo State, Nigeria*. Research study submitted towards the award of the BA in Town & Country Planning, Gloucestershire College of Arts & Design.

Fletcher, R. (1969) Frederic Le Play. In: T. Raison (ed.), *Founding Fathers of Social Science*. Harmondsworth, Penguin.

Foley, D. (1968) Metropolitan spatial structure. In: M. Webber (ed.), *Explorations into Urban Structure*. Philadelphia, Pennsylvania University Press.

Hall, P. (1980) *Great Planning Disasters*. London, Weidenfeld & Nicolson.

Hall, P. (2002) *Cities of Tomorrow: An intellectual history of urban planning and design in the twentieth century*. Oxford, Blackwell Publishing Ltd.

Heywood, P. (1974) *Planning and Human Need*. Newton Abbott, David & Charles.

Heywood, P. (1987) *Felda & Bustee: The management of population growth in town & country*. Unpublished paper. Brisbane, Queensland University of Technology, (copies available from author).

Heywood, P. (ed.) (2002) *Planning for Independence*. Proceedings of the Timor Loro S'ae Planning Institute Annual Conference, Dili, Brisbane, Queensland Division, Planning Institute of Australia.

Jacobs, J. (1961) *The Death and Life of Great American Cities*. Harmondsworth, Penguin.

Lefebvre, H. (1991) *The Production of Space*. Oxford, Blackwell Publishing Ltd.

Lynch, K. (1981) *Good City Form*. Cambridge, MA, MIT Press.

Mairet, P. (1957) *Pioneer of Sociology: The life and letters of Patrick Geddes*. London, Lund Humphries.

Queensland Government (2009) *South East Queensland Regional Plan 2009–2031*. Brisbane, Department of Infrastructure and Planning, Planning Group.

Queensland Government (2010) *Population Summit Outcomes Communiqué*, http://growthsummit.premiers.qld.gov.au/resources.aspx#outcomes, accessed 21 April 2010.

Tanner, L. (2009) Speech to Association of Superannuation Funds of Australia Luncheon, Melbourne, Thursday 27 August 2009, http://www.financeminister.gov.au/speeches/2009/sp_20090827.html, accessed 21 April 2010.

Turner, J. (1976) *Housing by People: Towards autonomy in building environments*. London, Marion Boyars.

United Nations Framework Convention on Climate Change (2009) *The Copenhagen Climate Change Treaty Draft: Wealth transfer defined, now with new and improved 'dignity' penalty*, http://wattsupwiththat.com/2009/10/03/the-copenhagen-treaty-draft-wealth-transfer-defined-now-with-dignity-penalty/, accessed 21 April 2010.

8 People, Homes and Communities

This chapter explores the ways in which homes and communities can be planned to ensure that people's needs for shelter are met when, where and how they are required. The chapter is organised into the following four sections:

- demographic challenges in meeting global and local housing needs;
- technological responses and impacts;
- costs, means and access to provision and finance for housing;
- balancing demand and supply for shelter.

The chapter concludes with a consideration of the contributions of shelter to community life.

Demographic challenges in meeting global and local housing needs

By the end of the twentieth century, cities throughout the world were facing major challenges just to find adequate space and shelter for their rapidly growing populations. In developed countries, overcrowding and homelessness were rife. In many developing countries, in cities such as Lagos, Lima and Kolkata, millions were being forced into unhealthy and crowded dwellings in shanty towns and spontaneous settlements on flood prone land, along routeways and on city fringes. One cause of this pressure has been the doubling of global population from just over 2.5 billion in 1950 to over 6.8 billion in 2000. This growth was encouraged by remarkable improvements in public health, reduced infant mortality, increased life expectancy and advances in preventative epidemiology and was further amplified by tides of rural–urban migration (United Nations Department of Economic and Social Affairs, 2009). This movement towards the cities, assisted by radical new developments in transport and communications, resulted in the urban proportion of the total population increasing sharply from less than 30% in 1950 to almost 50% in 2000 (United Nations Department of Economic and Social Affairs, 2001).

Managing these flows was made more difficult by the high costs of housing land in the competitive markets of many of the host cities and by the planning regulations of an increasingly specialised and regulated world, which were restricting people's rights to make use of whatever materials were available to provide their own shelter (Turner, 1976). These factors continue to create complex and uncertain environments for humanity's 'struggle for shelter in an urbanising world', as much now as when Charles Abrams first coined the phrase many decades ago (Abrams, 1964).

THE CREATION OF NEW HOUSEHOLDS

Though very large, the challenges posed by population growth are not beyond effective management. There has actually been a marked but selective slowing of the very rapid rates of global population growth observed in the second half of the twentieth century, starting first in the most economically advanced countries of Western Europe, and then spreading to the newly developing ones of the global 'East', particularly among the 'young tiger' economies of Japan, South Korea, Singapore and Taiwan. This slowing of global population growth has resulted from increasing proportions of the population in all continents gaining access to modern methods of birth control (Davis, 1967; Salk & Salk, 1981; United Nations Department of Economic and Social Affairs, 2001). The current world population of 6.8 billion is expected to peak at around 9.15 billion by the middle of this century as the trend to self-limitation spreads to affect people in all continents, even those currently still experiencing high levels of population growth (United Nations Department of Economic and Social Affairs, 2009).

Community Planning, First Edition. Phil Heywood.
© 2011 Phil Heywood.
Published 2011 by Blackwell Publishing Ltd.

The current challenge for community planners is thus to manage a major and measurable surge in housing and infrastructure demand as opposed to trying to staunch a flow of ever-increasing demands for new dwellings and urban services. Demographic data and projections can thus support and inform current programmes to shape, intensify and judiciously enlarge existing cities and their regional settlement patterns, rather than justifying despair at the scale of the task.[i] Within this general strategy of accommodating 'peak population', a number of very significant demographic trends may be identified, including:

- mass urbanisation;
- household fission;
- increased mobility;
- population return and intensification in inner cities;
- ageing population profiles.

The changing pattern and distribution of the global population over the last half-century could well be described as 'macro nucleation and micro dispersal', with the overall increases concentrated in major cities being dispersed to the urban fringes in search of adequate space and cheap housing sites. These magnet cities, such as Los Angeles, Toronto and São Paulo in the Americas; Mumbai, Kolkata, Wuhan and Tokyo in Asia; Sydney, Brisbane and Perth in Australia; Istanbul, London and Milan in Europe; and Cairo and Lagos in Africa, have more than doubled their populations. Together with an approximate halving of average densities (Newman & Kenworthy, 1991), this has resulted in very rapid expansions in area, often more than quadrupling land consumption of large expanses of formerly productive farmland and posing great problems for urban transport and accessibility. In turn, this has fuelled increased use of motor vehicles to distribute goods and people, resulting in further problems of urban pollution, respiratory health and serious additions to global carbon emissions and climate change. It is not surprising that environmentalists, such as Paul Ehrlich (1978), have tended to attribute all of our environmental ills to population growth. This misinterpretation has had the unfortunate tendency of diverting attention away from more critical and durable planning responses involved in technological choices, improvements in social and economic organisation, increased levels of sharing and development of behavioural constraints. The evidence is that improvements in education, family-planning resources and personal autonomy result in people naturally adjusting family size towards replacement level. Top-down decision-making and unequal distribution of wealth, on the other hand, tend to result in poor levels of public health and life expectancy, which actually encourage high birth rates. This happened in India under the forcible population control experiments introduced by Indira Gandhi in the 1970s, and is still occurring in many parts of Africa afflicted by drought, floods, famine and AIDS, all leading to very high rates of infant mortality and consequent large family sizes.

Irrespective of reduced overall levels of global population growth, people will continue to be drawn towards the greater economic and social opportunities offered by major cities, encouraged by increased personal mobility and the spread of information and communication networks. It must also be expected that further numbers will be added to urban populations by the unpredictable but recurrent disasters of climate change and major famines. As a result, although total world population is only expected to increase by 20% between 2010 and 2030, the United Nations' forecasts predict that urban populations will grow by about 40% (United Nations Department of Economic and Social Affairs, 2001, Tables A2, A3, A4). Continued rapid growth can therefore be expected in demand for dwellings, often at around current levels of up to 2% a year. These inflows will be compounded by the ageing of the overall population and increased mobility of both existing and new households, with 50% or more of the population already moving house every five years in some developed nations.

Numbers in each household and dwelling, on the other hand, can be expected to trend downwards as falling birth rates and the general ageing of the population reduce family size, creating a need for smaller and more specialised designs than the standard detached family housing, which the market in developed countries has become used to producing. These increased densities of smaller dwellings will require more local public spaces and more sharing of circulation spaces in the form of mass transit and active transport options for journeys to work, school and play. More emphasis on footpaths, cycle ways and bus ways will provide opportunities to knit communities closer together than in many of today's cities, whose forms have often been badly affected by the social and physical dislocations of the scything motorways of the mid-twentieth century.

SUMMARY OF DEMOGRAPHIC CHALLENGES

Growing total demand for dwellings can be expected to peak by the middle of the century, and then remain stable. Demands will continue to be concentrated in the great cities and metropolitan regions consisting of one or more million people. By 2015, there will be over five hundred of these large-scale centres, accommodating more than 40% of the world's population of nearly eight billion people (United Nations Department of Economic and Social Affairs, 2009). Within these great cities, in the developed nations of the 'North' and 'East', increasing proportions of one- and two-person households will characterise the inner city, while family housing (averaging two parents and two children) will predominate in the middle and outer suburbs. However, in the developing nations of the 'South' in Africa, South America and South Asia, family sizes, though much reduced from their current average levels of six people, will still tend to be on average half as large again as those in the more developed nations of the 'North' and 'East'.

Technological responses and impacts

While new technologies of travel and production have transformed the size and scale of settlements, the design of domestic space has remained remarkably stable.[ii] At the larger scale of the residential area,

however, there have been far more significant changes. Formerly compact cities such as Greater London, Greater New York, Glasgow, Amsterdam, Milan and many others have spread along roads and railways into residential regions extending over many thousands of square kilometres.[iii] Transport technologies, not least the dispersing effects of electric power and electronic communications, clearly remain powerful factors in influencing the form, location and capacity of urban communities. A number of the most significant of these impacts and outcomes are identified in Table 8.1.

Roads, wheels, wagons and motor vehicles

The roads and wheeled vehicles which supported the development of the first settlements continue to exert powerful influences on the shape and growth of contemporary cities. By accommodating daily flows of workers from home to workplace, they make possible the regular distribution of food, raw materials and products, though with increasing difficulty as the scale

Table 8.1 Influences of invention, investment and infrastructure on the form and location of homes and settlements

Field of technology	Impact	Outcome or response
Road, wheel, wagon and motor vehicle	Dispersed dwellings, with road access to concentrated markets and workplaces	Clustered groups of mixed dwellings in increasingly widespread networks
Rail locomotion using steam and electric power	Focused and intensified settlements with pronounced central places of administration, work and exchange	Metropolitan growth with marked central place hierarchies and wide ranges of residential densities
Elevators and tall buildings	Make possible intensive central place high rise apartments developments of unlimited scale	'Radiant city' and 'city beautiful' development style of residential developments in New York, Chicago, Central London, Rotterdam and other post war provincial cities throughout the Western world
Tunnels	Mass movement of residents, workers and shoppers around intensively developed central cities	Underground Metro systems in London, New York, Singapore, Kolkata, Moscow and so on supporting high-density inner-city living
Power generation and transmission	Sequences of increasing dispersal of settlement from steam and gas to electricity power networks, including solar and bio-technical variants	Move from compact 'fenced' cities to spread city regions, with increasingly dispersed home and work locations
Water storage, recycling and reticulation	Stimulus to cities of garden suburbs and residential estates	Support for growth of regional hierarchies of metropolitan and urban networks
Telegraph, telephone, satellite and Internet communications	Parallel coexistence of traditional place-based communities of personal contact and growth of 'non-place urban realm' of global scale	Globalisation of settlement influences and a tendency to homogenise residential character
Construction technologies from mud and baked brick to reinforced concrete and prefabricated panels	A range of building materials and technologies including high-rise apartments, and rationalised traditional mass production of town houses and suburban estates	Development of intensive high-rise residential central cities and medium-rise, medium-density 'transit-orientated developments' along major route corridors, with low-rise estates in cities' outer suburbs

of urban growth elongates journeys and intensifies often conflicting volumes of traffic. The cheap fossil fuel and free disposal of waste matter, which fostered their rapid development, are likely to be reversed in the 'post peak oil' era we are now entering, in favour of smaller dwellings and denser, more clustered, and yet more populous cities. Active transport and mass transit initiatives will be required to encourage sharing of transport channels and reduction of carbon emissions.

RAIL LOCOMOTION

Railways are a good example of a technology invented to meet the social and economic needs of rapidly growing cities. They made possible the movement of large volumes of raw materials and workers from increasingly distant sources and locations to central places of manufacture, exchange and consumption that underpinned the Industrial Revolution. The inherited suburban structure of many contemporary cities, clustered around central places that are heavily influenced by public transport, may present a framework for sustainable city development in the coming era of scarce oil and more strictly controlled carbon emissions. Cities have largely created and relied upon railway systems, which provide effective frames for urban housing, because of their high volume capacity and unsurpassed ability to promote shared use of space and energy.

ELEVATORS AND TALL BUILDINGS

Technological inventions have intensified the development potential of central nodes by taking them upwards into air space, thus expanding the range of housing choices. By freeing tall buildings from the demands of the time and energy associated with climbing stairs, the invention of the mechanical elevator in New York in the mid-nineteenth century ushered in the growth of high-rise apartment blocks. Together with the use of reinforced concrete and pre-stressed panels, they assisted the birth of the towering city centres and rashes of post-war residential reconstruction of public housing in cities such as London, Birmingham, Rotterdam and Hamburg.[iv] High-rise building of this sort, advocated by Le Corbusier (1970), increased potential densities and decreased the balance between structures and natural environment, often resulting in unloved and unlovely 'concrete jungles' and slab blocks of the inner cities of places like London's Thamesmead, Sheffield's Park Hill and Hyde Park, St Louis' Pruitt Igoe and the disastrous

Moscow apartment blocks of the 1950s and 1960s (Newman, 1973; Bater, 1979). Nevertheless, when used with caution and careful resident and community consultation, multi-storey construction does offer one simple way to increase residential densities in inner cities.

TUNNELS AND UNDERGROUND DEVELOPMENT

Underground development has a more ancient history. Roman catacombs and subterranean dwellings and churches in Cappadocia, in what is now Turkey, date back over two thousand years.[v] However, the most significant influence on today's shelter lies in underground transport, which removes large volumes of traffic from the surface levels of cities into tunnels, often complete with shopping arcades, thus greatly improving the liveability and convenience of surface conditions in such great cities as London, Paris, New York, Moscow, Tokyo, Singapore, Kolkata and many others where they have resulted in removal of previously almost constant traffic jams and smog.[vi] Such underground rail systems also play a significant role in adapting growing metropolitan areas to absorb continued growth by concentrating and intensifying development along high-density, medium-height corridors animated by public transport both above and below ground (Adams, 2009).[vii] Used judiciously, tunnels can reduce the need for existing and proposed ground-level motorways, and make possible convenient and accessible car-free living in inner suburbs, which would otherwise be divided by urban freeways and polluted by exhaust emissions.

POWER GENERATION AND TRANSMISSION

Whereas steam power could only be transmitted over short distances, (and therefore concentrated employment and residence under pollution palls close to toxic and putrid discharges from chimney stacks, cooling ponds and spoil tips), electric power, with its capacity for very rapid, cheap and efficient transmission over long distances, has allowed settlements and workplaces to spread widely across growing urban regions like Greater London and the entire southern half of New York State. Homes could be located in garden cities and suburbs and endowed with the convenience of power-driven domestic appliances such as washing machines and electric irons and enlivened by the electronic communications of radio, telephone, television and, more recently, computers linked into the World Wide Web of information. All of this could be achieved without the need to be located near power sources.[viii]

Electric power is thus providing more choices in the scale and location of where we live, though with no guarantee of either good or bad results.[ix]

ELECTRONIC COMMUNICATIONS

The impact of modern electronic communications has rapidly expanded from the first invention of telegraphy and the magnetic telephone in the nineteenth century to become one of the major influences shaping contemporary society. This can be observed in the continually growing reach of the Internet and satellite communications universalising access to knowledge and information. These impacts are wide ranging and complex. Central command of information and media has been concentrated in the hands of investors, controllers and operators of the key nodes of the communications system. Nevertheless, the new communications are also simultaneously empowering more than a billion participants in the global network with equal access to knowledge, information and capacity to participate in generating and distributing their own ideas and knowledge in open access and open source networks. It is even possible that the medium is becoming the message. There is therefore no certainty whether the ultimate effect will be to empower or subordinate individuals and communities – or, indeed, whether there will *be* an ultimate outcome or instead continuing tugs of war between the incessant initiatives of commerce to achieve centrally controlled privatisation and community actions to achieve and expand open access. Meanwhile, global communities of interest like Oxfam, World Wildlife Fund, the Inter-Governmental Panel on Climate Change, Greenpeace and Avaaz are spreading their reach to empower and support more local communities.

WATER STORAGE AND RECYCLING

Technologies of bulk water capture, storage and reticulation can also widen choices to support the growth of independent family life. Trunk water mains and feeder systems from the times of the Roman aqueducts onwards have assisted the spread of well-serviced settlements across wide regions. In developing countries, the expansion of such systems has freed people from the necessity of taxing daily trips to fetch water from the local stream or neighbourhood pump or well.[x] These fall most heavily on women, already burdened with childrearing, housework and the cultivation of domestic gardens. However, massive dam-building projects can also flood valleys, displacing many tens of thousands of rural families as has occurred in China's Three Gorges Project and the Narmada Valley scheme in central India, designed to supply power and water to the booming economy of Mumbai (Roy, 1999). Recycling schemes too, which encourage the growth of stable and self-sustaining settlements and residential areas, may encounter cultural rejection from communities with strong taboos about consumption of anything linked to human waste (Lacey & Heywood, 2010). As an increasingly valuable and scarce resource, it is important to reflect carefully on the use of water and to ensure its open and inclusive governance within the regular cycle of plan making and provision, distribution and charging. Maximum provision, irrespective of unintended consequences, is not a merit in itself.

CONSTRUCTION TECHNOLOGIES

Construction technologies exert more immediate and direct impacts on the form and location of people's homes and living places. Early mud brick constructions of five thousand years ago produced the dense networks of low-rise communities and stepped ziggurats of Mesopotamia, North Africa and India. The availability of baked bricks and concrete made possible the rapid construction and extended service lines that have spread earlier intensive compact settlements outwards into extensive suburbs. However, this also posed unintended consequences of resource consumption and personal isolation. Composite pre-cast components and site-assembly methods have extended city centre development upwards in dense districts of high-rise apartments and office towers rising to heights of three and four hundred metres. The fact that these high-rise apartments are not always popular, as indicated earlier in this section, results from the difficulties that they pose for conventional family life. Container technologies and mobile homes seem to offer promising responses to meet growing needs caused by increasingly frequent emergencies and natural disasters, but their potential uses and likely impacts on future settlements and communities are not yet clear and need to be carefully evaluated. The lesson is that good design develops not from seizing each new technical opportunity to meet immediate market demands for increased supply but rather from careful evaluation of each new way of meeting existing and projected needs.

SUMMARY OF TECHNOLOGICAL IMPACTS

In summary, we can anticipate that human ingenuity will continue to create new technologies and inventions to meet needs for shelter resulting from social change and population growth. In the past, such capacities have flowed generously to produce new mass-volume infrastructure systems and communications networks. Designs can optimise new technologies by carefully adjusting them to fit with wider patterns of community life and organisation. Thoughtful planning can identify, monitor and interpret these changing needs and opportunities to predict and forestall harmful impacts.

Costs, means and access to provision and finance of housing

EVOLUTION OF INDIVIDUAL AND COMMUNITY ROLES

The political economy of housing can be seen as a chessboard whose squares offer different advantages to competing individual and community interests. Not surprisingly, the earliest traces of human shelter dating from 400 000 years ago at Terra Amata in southern France contain both family and community elements.[xi] The later valley civilisations of the Nile and Indus of five thousand years ago provide archaeological evidence of a more hierarchical society with a mixture of grand palaces, residential villas of the priestly and administrative classes, compact workers' dwellings rather similar to their Neolithic forbears and barrack-like regimented dwellings for workers involved in major building schemes for the ruling elite.[xii] This kind of evidence suggests that for many thousands of years shelter was provided both by families meeting their own needs and by ruling elites ensuring that their workforces were safely housed and securely enclosed. Housing was not primarily a commodity to be bartered but an essential support to the prevailing economic system, whether that system was based on collaborative subsistence farming and craftwork or centralised feudal theocracy.

The earliest signs of 'commodification' appear in the classical world.[xiii] The unprecedented growth of towns in Europe and North America which resulted from the Industrial Revolution of the nineteenth century – spreading to many parts of Asia, South America and Australia in the twentieth century – multiplied the scale of this longstanding way of meeting population growth and movement. Investment in dwelling construction was regarded as being 'as safe as houses', though the quality of the resulting accommodation was often very poor and living conditions could be severely overcrowded.[xiv] An increasing proportion of the housing stock was being captured within the mainstream of the capitalist economy through regular cash exchanges between necessitous buyers and willing sellers. Their dwellings rapidly became, for many of the labouring classes, a commodity which they could seldom hope to own themselves and made them heavily dependent upon the goodwill of landlords, who could increase their rents or evict them at will. Collaborative action on the part of workers tackled this situation by establishing mutual finance organisations called building societies to fund home ownership.[xv] As a result, more than half of the population of England and the United States came to own or be purchasing their own homes by the mid-twentieth century.

Nevertheless, around a third of housing in most advanced countries continues to be commodified as rental accommodation, built or acquired by investors for financial return. On the one hand, in prevalent mixed economies, this promotes freedom of movement and choice of workplace for mobile age and working groups. On the other, renters may face constant feelings of personal insecurity, economic exploitation and threats of arbitrary eviction, resulting in demands for public regulation of the housing market and direct public participation in the provision of affordable housing. Commodification of shelter thus emerges as a double-sided page. It can be considered capable, particularly in times of rapid growth and mobility like the present, of responding quickly to demographic movements and changes, but also needing careful management and active participation from the public, voluntary and cooperative sectors to prevent overcrowding and economic exploitation.

Prudential regulation by governments is also required to control speculative lending by bonus-driven financial operators to 'sub-prime' borrowers, whom the lenders do not know and who may possess very little creditworthiness. Lack of such regulation resulted in the cascading international financial crisis of 2008/09. Although lending by banks and permanent building societies is basically an investment activity, the resulting dwellings may pass between private ownership and rental tenure many times in the course of their life, so that much current owner-occupation provides an interesting mix of commodified and personalised provision of housing. To be fully effective, national and local housing policies require a mix of public, private and cooperative involvement to match the composite structure of the contemporary housing market.

HOUSING AFFORDABILITY

Housing affordability depends not only on achieving the necessary volume and speed of production but also on providing the appropriate variety of type, location and tenure of dwellings. Exclusive reliance on either the market or State monopoly has notably failed to achieve these outcomes. For example, State monopoly in Soviet Russia and Eastern Europe in the period 1945–1989 proved inflexible and unresponsive to people's needs, though quite effective at mass production of sheer numbers of dwellings (Bater, 1979).[xvi] Market systems have generally produced higher-quality dwellings but have been afflicted by recurrent crises of homelessness and affordability, where public involvement has been weak or remote, as has been the case in the United States and Australia. Spasms of expansion and contraction climaxed in the mortgage lending crisis of 2008/09, in the course of which millions of less affluent home purchasers were forced to walk away from their dwellings, leaving them to be resumed by banks, who were in turn unable to dispose of them in a collapsed market. Few would now argue that exclusive reliance on the free market can regulate, finance and produce a housing supply that is adequate, let alone affordable. By contrast, collaborative approaches are well suited to the mixed economy regimes which are increasingly common in all continents. Such approaches can effectively involve a variety of stakeholders, including governments, builders and consumers, and can weave together contributions from a number of different strands:

- social market housing polices to encourage commercial construction;
- government partnerships and social enterprises;
- direct provision of public and social housing.

SOCIAL MARKET HOUSING POLICIES

This approach, of governments encouraging market delivery to achieve social objectives, was first developed in the mid-twentieth century in Western Europe to support rapid post-war reconstruction.[xvii] It involves providing tax concessions to developers and builders who provide affordable and appropriate housing for sale or rent, has been widely advocated and is now being included in a number of the economic stimulus packages currently being applied to steer Western economies out of the 2008/09 Global Financial Crisis. For example, this approach is evident in Australia's Nation Building Economic Stimulus Plan for 2008–2012 (Australian Government, 2009).

AFFORDABLE RENT SCHEMES

Under these arrangements, the Australian Government is offering AUD$4 billion in tax incentives to develop-

ers to build affordable housing, with the intention of attracting enough money to achieve 50 000 new homes within a three-year period (2009–2012). The then Prime Minister Kevin Rudd offered to double the scheme to make available a further AUD$4 billion to build another 100 000 dwellings if it became a success. Under the scheme, owner-investors gained an annual rebate of AUD$8600 per home for developing and passing on to low- and moderate-income households at 20% less than market rates (Australian Department of Families, Housing, Community Services and Indigenous Affairs, 2009; Lenaghan, 2009). Benefits are paid annually over a ten-year period, as long as rental levels and conditions continue to meet the terms of the initial agreement. There is no restriction on who may participate in the National Rental Affordability Scheme (NRAS), but existing voluntary organisations, charitable bodies and mixed enterprises including state-subsidised 'housing companies' are particularly well situated to take advantage of the scheme because of their experience in managing affordable housing. Although initial responses from the Australian commercial sector have proved less enthusiastic than the 1950s response in Germany, the Australian government's initiative is receiving enthusiastic support from the not-for-profit sector (discussed later). Despite some initial caution, overall housebuilding rates are being maintained at more or less their pre-financial crisis levels and it is likely that government and commercial and superannuation funds management will negotiate agreements that meet the objectives of both sides.

PUBLIC–PRIVATE PARTNERSHIPS

Government agencies can also enter into direct partnership with commercial developers, as well as not-for-profit providers, to combine public powers of land designation and assembly with private sector skills in development, design and marketing, thus linking social benefits with commercial success. Such cooperation can also call upon and leverage earlier instances of successful cooperation. One particularly notable example is provided by the collaboration of the South Australian Urban Land Trust and a large private developer, Delfin Developments, over the period 1983–2003 to build the new community of Golden Grove in North Eastern Adelaide.[xviii] The new neighbourhoods rapidly developed into an attractive suburb and in 1998 Golden Grove was awarded the Prix d'Excellence as the world's Best Residential Development by the International Real Estate Federation (Delfin, 2003).

Similar approaches have been adopted in the schemes developed to prepare for London's Lea Valley

Olympic Games and the subsequent use of the sites. The regeneration strategy, launched by the London Development Agency and Thames Gateway Development Corporation, aims to create between 30 000 and 40 000 new homes and 50 000 new jobs, harnessing the Valley's unique natural environment. A mixed public–private body, Leaside Regeneration, is coordinating the overall development, conducting consultation and entering into partnerships with developers (Leaside Regeneration, 2009). Another very ambitious and carefully integrated scheme with a similar collaborative basis is being developed in Vancouver's South East False Creek area, on the site of the 2010 Winter Olympics village. Described in Box 8.1, the resulting developments are being shaped to meet social objectives, achieve economies of scale and accomplish sufficiently rapid rates of building to meet

pressing needs for new housing for a wide range of income groups. By contrast, 'go it alone' government approaches may lack responsiveness and deteriorate into sink estates, while exclusively private enterprise approaches prosper by pushing minimum prices up to levels which many of the neediest cannot afford.

PLANNING INFRASTRUCTURE PROGRAMMES AND SUBSIDIES

Affordable housing can also be promoted by governments planning and installing the infrastructure required to support new development, as an incentive to commercial developers to include affordable dwellings.[xix] One example of the capacity of infrastructure spending to achieve very effective results comes from the successful trebling of the population of Greater Toronto in the period 1953–1983, under the

---

Box 8.1 Vancouver's South East False Creek redevelopment: A public–private partnership for an affordable inner-city community

The deepwater inlet which separates Vancouver's bustling high-rise commercial core from the city's southern suburbs provided ideal locations for the docks, waterside industries and storage yards which crowded the waterline. As these declined, their sites became available for new uses and in the 1980s the western areas close to Granville Island were redeveloped for a mix of high-quality social and market housing of varying heights and densities, laced with excellent foot and cycle paths. The area rapidly became one of Vancouver's most welcoming places for both local residents and tourists. The waterfront areas to the south-east were developed as the Athletes Village for the 2010 Winter Olympic Games. The 44-hectare site, three-quarters in public ownership, has been developed as an integrated mixed use and mixed income residential area (Figure 8.1). The Olympic Village (Figure 8.2) occupies the central portion, accommodating 2800 athletes in buildings that were be converted after the Games finished in February 2010 to 1150 long-term residential units (City of Vancouver, 2009).

When complete, the development will have 6.5 million square feet of residential development, with family housing a priority. The housing stock will comprise approximately 6200 units, a third of them specifically designed and priced to be affordable, with an estimated total population ranging from 10 000 to 12 000 people, forming a vibrant new inner-city community. The overall development will contain a mix of uses, at a high density but not exceeding eight to ten storeys in height and designed to meet liveability and sustainability objectives with open space, parks, streets and pathways designed for pedestrians, cyclists and transit, connecting throughout and linking to nearby neighbourhoods. Two rail lines and bus ways run to the city centre and suburbs for access to employment, and goods and services are within walking distance. A wide range of parks and recreational spaces line the waterfront, including the seaside pedestrian/bicycle route. Parks and open spaces include the re-establishment of wildlife habitat and private and community gardens.

Integrated government planning and partnership with the private sector have made possible the inclusion of market and affordable housing within a comprehensive community with a community centre, boating facility, up to five childcare facilities, out-of-school care facilities, grocery store and community services, as well as an elementary school and interfaith spiritual centre. Five heritage buildings are being restored and ten hectares of park land, covering almost a quarter of the site, will include habitat, playgrounds and opportunities for urban agriculture. The closing ceremony of the Winter Olympics therefore marked the beginning, rather than the end, of the celebration.

Figure 8.1 South East False Creek redevelopment site. *Source:* Eagle Eye Flying Camera. Reproduced by permission of the City of Vancouver.

guidance of the region-wide Metro Council, whose role was to supply wholesale services of water, power and transport and to pass them on for retail distribution to the constituent local governments (Lemon, 1985; Sewell, 1993). Metro's and Toronto's city councils undertook a series of planning agreements with large development companies to provide tens of thousands of dwellings in agreed locations, to meet the very large population increases of migrants arriving from Europe and other parts of Canada to share in the success of the metropolitan economy (Sewell, 1993).[xx]

One of the most sophisticated and successful examples of how to manage housing provision by integrating planning with infrastructure supply comes from Oregon in the north-west of the United States, where the regional metropolitan government of Metro Portland was established as an elective council in 1978 with three constituent counties, 25 cities and two further unincorporated areas (Metro Portland, 2010). Metro has succeeded in shaping relatively high-density development within a number of transit-orientated

developments mostly located around stations of the publicly owned Metropolitan Area Express (MAX) light rail. Portland has thus also succeeded in increasing its urban density, preserving green space beyond its urban growth boundary and diminishing its annual total of vehicle miles travelled (VMT) by using planning powers conferred under the 1973 Oregon Land Use Act. This also forms the basis for Metro Portland's 2040 Growth Plan and Transportation Planning Rule (produced in 1994) that effectively restrict new development to transit-orientated developments around public transport nodes, particularly those served by the four lines of the 120 km MAX system (Adler & Dill, 2004). These successes, reinforced by the Regional Framework Plan (Metro Portland, 2005) have only been possible because the State of Oregon's statutory Planning Goals and Guidelines require compliance by state agencies once they have signed off on regional and local plans.[xxi] As a result, Metro Portland can be confident when negotiating with developers that the locations it is proposing will be practical in terms of

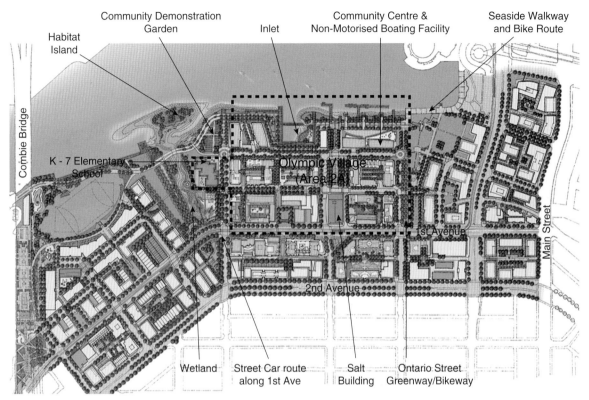

Figure 8.2 South East False Creek redevelopment plan. *Source*: Vancouver City Council. Reproduced by permission of the City of Vancouver.

transport, sewerage and other essential services, such as education and law enforcement. Such compliance requirements on government departments and agencies are invaluable levers to achieve coordinated provision of infrastructure and to build lively, well-serviced and socially integrated communities.

GOVERNMENT SUPPORT FOR SOCIAL ENTERPRISES

Government partnerships with not-for-profit housing associations were developed in many parts of Western Europe during the post-war reconstruction period. Initially, they were especially significant in France and Sweden but were later also widely adopted in the United Kingdom, where they were recognised by the 1964 establishment of the Housing Corporation, specifically to encourage the contributions of voluntary housing associations to affordable and accessible social housing By the time of its merger with other government housing agencies to form the Homes and Communities Agency in 2008, the Housing Corporation had grown to oversee and fund more than 2000 housing associations (all of whom are regulated

as 'registered social landlords'). The HCAs 'triennial investment programme for 2008/2011 of £9 billion is intended to fund over 153,000 homes, just over half for affordable rent and just under half for affordable sale, through 'Home Buy' initiatives that are intended to help people get a foot on the property ladder (Housing and Communities Agency, 2010a). This planned and funded construction rate of more than 50 000 dwellings a year constituted a sizable proportion of the country's total house building programme and was particularly significant in the current situation of very low confidence within the private house building sector. It also pointed to the important role of social market housing polices in managing difficult situations in times of volatile economics. Around half of all new homes built in England in 2009 were directly funded by the HCA (HCA, 2010b)

Australia's Nation Building Economic Stimulus Plan is also moving in the same direction, providing funding of AUD$5.238 billion over three and a half years from 2008/09 to 2011/12 for the construction of new social housing, which is doing much to encourage not-for-profit housing associations, housing companies and similar social enterprises dedicated to the provision of social housing in this country (Australian Department of Families, Housing, Community Services and Indigenous Affairs, 2009). It is providing a boost to both public housing and housing administered by the not-for-profit community sector and is designed to assist low-income Australians who are homeless or struggling in the private rental market.

THE POTENTIAL OF SOCIAL ENTERPRISES: DIRECT PUBLIC INVOLVEMENT IN HOUSING PROVISION

For over eighty years, the United Kingdom has maintained an ambitious policy of public housing, which had grown by the early 1970s to supply almost a third of the total national stock. This was achieved by balancing national funding through the Department of Housing and Local Government with local control provided by the housing departments of local governments themselves. Much sound and progressive accommodation was provided in this way but by the time the Thatcher government launched its crusade against public enterprises of all sorts in the 1980s, the country's many large public housing estates were beginning to attract the stigma often attached to client populations. The Thatcher government's policy of sale of council houses to their occupants or disposal of them to housing associations, supported and overseen by the Housing Corporation, did not attract very widespread criticism. Instead, housing activists diverted their energies into effective campaigning for more funding and targeted support for special housing projects by not-for-profit organisations, particularly the country's many housing associations.[xxii]

Social enterprises are particularly suited to provide housing because they have greater credibility and a more universally supported ethos than commercial bodies. They can also operate with more flexibility and on a more personal scale than government agencies. They are often associated with 'third way' politics aiming to avoid the brittle short-term profit maximisation of capitalism and the enforced conformity of communism. The Mondragon Corporation and the Grameen Bank are good examples of social enterprises. Housing versions of these enterprises tend not to grow to such a large scale because of their need to maintain good local communications and links. However, in aggregate, the United Kingdom's more than 2000 housing associations – all registered social landlords, responsible for more than 10% of the nation's entire housing stock – must be considered as a very significant part of the nation's life.

A relatively recently established Australian social enterprise dedicated to housing provision, which is in many ways based on those models, may serve to demonstrate the contributions which can be made quite rapidly to the provision of social housing. The Brisbane Housing Company (BHC) was officially established with the Queensland State Government and the Brisbane City Council as its major shareholders in 2003. It was registered as a charitable organisation for tax purposes, reflecting both its not-for-profit status and its commitment to providing affordable housing. Led by an energetic CEO, David Cant, with a background in inner-London housing associations, and a board of directors including representatives of government, business and the wider community, the BHC has benefited from access to the steady flow of government surplus land that is common in all mixed economy societies, occasioned by social and land use change and including old schools, public storage space, disused railways, works department and other residual land. By 2010, the BHC had completed approximately one thousand dwellings, many of them one-bedroom units in large and carefully designed apartment blocks, illustrated in Figures 8.3 and 8.4. These dwellings are offered for rent at levels not exceeding 75% of normal market levels, but some are now being offered for sale. The BHC also partners with private developers to build on parts of sites sold to them. Winning a number of awards, including the Planning Institute of Australia overall Award for Excellence in 2007 for a scheme conducted jointly with the Queensland State Government and the

Figure 8.3 Brisbane Housing Company conversion of former Richlands High School teaching block for 26 affordable rental dwellings, with small front garden spaces, nearing completion, 2009. *Source:* Reproduced by permission of the Brisbane Housing Company.

Figure 8.4 Brisbane Housing Company conversion of Richlands High School teaching block for 26 affordable rental dwellings, rear view with patio garden spaces, nearing completion, 2009. *Source:* Reproduced by permission of the Brisbane Housing Company.

Figure 8.5 Brisbane Housing Company, Fitzgibbon outer suburban greenfield site previously owned by Queensland Housing being developed for mixed rental and purchase medium-priced and affordable dwellings, using Commonwealth Fiscal stimulus funding. *Source:* Reproduced by permission of the Brisbane Housing Company.

Queensland University of Technology in the inner-city Kelvin Grove Urban Village, the BHC has established a reputation for attention to relationships with surrounding spaces and urban activities and for very high-quality design, illustrated in Plates 8.1, 8.2 and 8.3. With this is combined a major emphasis on policy implementation. Early construction of a large mixed use scheme at Fitzgibbon, a middle metropolitan suburb of northern Brisbane, is illustrated in Figure 8.5. This development is intended to relieve pressure in the housing market for more affordable and medium priced accommodation, at the same time as concentrating growing populations in transit orientated developments served by major commuter rail lines and the planned extension of the city's successful busway system.

Apartment blocks of one- and two-bedroom units to cater for the needs of young and elderly households are better located in inner areas, conveniently close to long-established community services, medical facilities and shops. Such apartment blocks are being built on land formerly owned by government departments and agencies in inner areas undergoing rapid redevelopment for mixed commercial and high-quality residential uses, as illustrated in Figure 8.6. Housing policy and investment is thus being made to serve community planning objectives of social mix, economic health, full employment and urban form and density, in support of values of social justice, economic prosperity and environmental sustainability.

While originally not intending to directly manage rental activities, the company has since established its own effective rental section which is now responsible

Figure 8.6 Brisbane Housing Company, Masters Street, Newstead inner-city apartment block under construction with city centre in background. *Source:* Reproduced by permission of the Brisbane Housing Company.

for over half of all the company's building projects. A recently established 'tenant participation section' is also encouraging the formation of 'tenant participation groups' in all of its buildings (Brisbane Housing Company, 2010).

The success of the BHC has led to its being used as a model by the state government to tackle wider housing problems in other regions such as the Gold Coast, the Sunshine Coast, Logan City and Mackay. Still others are being investigated in the Western Downs, Townsville and Roma regional council areas. An example of one particular site developed by the BHC is summarised in Box 8.2.

THE CONTINUING ROLE OF MULTIPURPOSE PUBLIC AUTHORITIES IN COMMUNITY DEVELOPMENT

Housing associations and government-sponsored housing companies represent a move away from tra-ditional public housing as supplied as a right by governments to the less affluent members of their electorates. Nevertheless, worldwide there is continuing success and relevance for one particular variant of public housing: that 'invented' by Ebenezer Howard in his proposal for garden cities to re-house the industrial workers penned in the overcrowded and polluted industrial towns of Britain at the turn of the twentieth century. Although Howard saw this not as public housing but rather as a community enterprise, with each of the residents being a shareholder in a garden city development association, the new towns which have been planned and built in all six settled continents have normally been developed as public housing bodies, designated and funded by central governments and managed by development corporations appointed by them (Hall, 1998, 2002). Such bodies continue to offer great advantages and potentialities for the provision of affordable housing. They can combine,

---

Box 8.2 Brisbane Housing Company, Columba Street redevelopment of Richlands High School site, Inala

The Richlands site, once occupied by a state school and later temporarily used as an employment incubator, was originally identified as a suitable place for affordable housing by a local community housing action group, Butterfly Housing, whose president, Tony Green, was a local resident. The eleven-hectare site also included an Aboriginal 'Yarning Place' and social centre in the old school library, as well as the proposed location for a new council swimming pool. The state government has a practice of making available its surplus lands for purposes supported by different departments, and Queensland Housing was persuaded to support the sale of four hectares of the site for a very reduced sum to the Brisbane Housing Company, which has developed it for a wide range of 2 two-bedroom terrace houses On one corner of the site, twenty-six low-rental two-bedroom dwellings have been converted from an old school block, shown in course of development in Figures 8.3 and 8.4, and made available at rents varying from $110 to $230 a week (levels not readily obtainable elsewhere in Brisbane). Each dwelling has its own ground level front door, patio, balcony and small garden and residents display considerable pride and pleasure in their secure and comfortable homes. Despite the high density of the development, they say that they find the place quiet, and enjoy good relations with their neighbours. Minor design problems with the organisation of the internal spaces, such as the bathrooms and cupboards, have been noted for design adjustment in future schemes. Elsewhere on the site, new dwellings have been built, also for rental in attached rows of two-storey town houses, and part of the site has been sold to a private developer who has also erected 21 similarly compact townhouses using Commonwealth 'Fiscal Stimulus' funding at a cost of AUD$4.9 million. They were completed in mid-2010, within a period of seven months from the agreement of funding to readiness for occupation.

The site is being shared with Mission Australia, which has established a major facility, some of whose clients are also residents of the new development. Newcomers are being put in touch with a wide range of other social, medical, financial and recreational support groups in the suburb. A street, Albert Holt Place, has been named after the local Aboriginal leader and author, who continues to play an important role in local community life and consultation. No less importantly, a meeting place has been maintained for Inala's thousand-strong Aboriginal community, many of whose children attended the former school in the 'Yarning Place' which now occupies the converted old school library.

for stipulated periods, coherent control over the physical, social and economic development of the new communities and in so doing can help to create integrated communities to respond to the needs of rounded citizens. They can also utilise the generally excellent credit rating that is enjoyed by many national governments to raise large development funds at low rates of interest and benefit from the financial increment resulting from increases in land value of their own making. They can charge tenants the rents they believe to be appropriate to their needs and the town's social health. As such, the model offered by the well-defined structure of the 'new town' development corporation remains a valuable option for communities facing the need for large-scale house building programmes to meet extensive population movements or increases. This approach does not have to be exclusively statist. For example, the new town development corporation board could well include public, private and community stakeholders in the spirit of contemporary collaborative planning.

Balancing demand and supply for shelter

Residential areas make up about half of the extent of most cities, so that the accuracy of projections of housing need and relevance of working assumptions regarding dwelling locations and densities is very significant. Methods of projection and planning based on balancing demand and supply have been widely adopted, and have a number of practical advantages, including:

- Regularly updated population and household forecasts are available for most major cities and provide transparent and easily understood bases for estimating housing need to support the necessary integration of land assembly, house building, health, education and transport policies.
- Analysis of demand also supports stakeholder involvement and public consultation about preferences and possibilities.
- Policies can be updated and amended as population forecasts and land estimates change.

The worked example accompanying Figure 7.6 in the preceding chapter should help to indicate the uses of this approach by analysing the balance of projected housing demand and housing land supply for the period 2006–2016 for Greater Brisbane. This provides the empirical basis for the following more general discussion of demand and supply factors.

DEMAND FACTORS

Housing demand is a function of future population and household size, both of which will be affected by factors such as ageing, net reproduction rates, migration balance and projected income levels. Locational preference will be influenced by family size, lifecycle phase, cultural norms and sense of social affiliation. Demand will be capable of refinement into different categories of dwelling size, tenure types and locational characteristics. Housing land supply will include greenfield sites on and beyond the city fringe and brownfield ones, which may take any of several different forms:

- areas for densification or redevelopment around designated activity centres linked to transit-orientated development;
- areas in metropolitan corridors of densification adjacent to existing major communication channels (Adams, 2009);
- areas in inner cities regarded as 'ripe for clearance and redevelopment' by property developers;
- lands becoming available through demographic change (such as school sites where populations of whole suburbs have aged) or land use change, resulting from the closure or movement of obsolete activities such as inner-city rail marshalling yards or port areas which have moved downstream to deeper water locations.

SUPPLY FACTORS

Barriers to land release, needing to be identified, include planning, financial and physical constraints. Periodic regulatory reform can ensure that unnecessary bureaucratic rigidities do not impede land release and processing of development applications. Shortages of investment funds can be resolved by government loan guarantees, participation in development schemes or requirements for superannuation schemes to invest a certain proportion of their funds in housing developments. Infrastructure planning and sequencing can coordinate land release, housing development and community building to match anticipated demands. This has been done in the series of infrastructure plans and programmes produced by the Queensland State Government in the period 2005–2009. These infrastructure plans have been developed to support the radical population increases of over one million people that are anticipated in the SEQ Regional Plan; the funding committed to new infrastructure development totals AUD$124 billion over a 22-year period (Queensland Government, 2009).

CURRENT POLICY OPTIONS

As the great cities of the mid-twentieth century reach maturity, redevelopment and densification become important. For instance, proposals to increase the population of Melbourne by approximately two million to five million people by 2029 propose to intensify new activities, particularly residential development in sites adjacent to existing major movement corridors of tram, train and intensive bus routes (Adams, 2009). In this case, new development would be limited to eight storeys, and the existing inner and middle suburbs behind them would be preserved as traditional housing and urban conservation 'green wedge' areas. These intensification corridors would occupy only 3% of the total metropolitan area and further development would be restricted beyond the recently declared 'urban growth boundary'. These investigations by the city of Melbourne and the Victorian state government recognise and use the very large capacity of medium-rise apartment blocks, from which European cities have benefited ever since the growth of the planned Baroque cities of the seventeenth and eighteenth centuries.

Coordinated infrastructure development can also help to shape future developments, as is happening in Portland, Oregon. Housing associations and housing companies can play important roles, as they have for several decades in Western and Northern Europe and are increasingly doing in Queensland, Australia. Funding is a major factor and schemes like the United Kingdom's £9 billion investment in its affordable housing programme for 2008–2011 (Homes and Communities Agency, 2010a) and Australia's National Rent Affordability Scheme (NRAS; Lending Guru, 2009) offer promising examples of the options that are available to governments aiming to improve the supply of affordable housing without returning to the often rigid and increasingly unpopular programmes of mass 'council housing' of the last century.[xxiii]

Options are needed for land, skills, funding and legal powers. Methods of land assembly include release of government-owned land, densification of existing low-density development in new transit-orientated developments and partnership with private developers to designate and develop new greenfield sites. Options to ensure that the necessary skills are available include links with the education sector, particularly vocational education and training (VET) programmes and support for Sweat Equity schemes, encouraging a return to traditional self-building methods. Funding options increasingly include taxation, incentive and market regulation mechanisms as well as partnership schemes with private and social enterprise providers. Finally, the power of positive planning should not be underrated. By presenting coherent pictures of intended futures and combining the actions of public, private and community stakeholders, community plans can create confidence and mutual understanding between the various key providers whose work is necessary to turn housing areas into active and healthy communities.

HOMES AND COMMUNITIES

These wider communities of association, interdependence and interest naturally provide the settings within which dwellings are embedded. For instance, it is difficult to sustain a satisfactory home life in isolation from other people or from activities supporting health, learning, sustenance, work or movement. The processes of integration, both intuitive and systematic, by which this kind of place-making can be achieved, are discussed in more detail in Chapter 10. Nevertheless, it will be useful to conclude this discussion of homes and communities by indicating how concerns for place-making and the structure of settlements should influence the ways we set about planning land and investment for housing. We need to take account of focus, function, access, scale and density, as well as merely matching allocations of space to projections of numbers.

A general model which relates different types and scales of housing to different types of locations can help practitioners in both housing and other systems to understand and integrate with each others' roles and work to promote equity and participation, as well as service efficiency. While never likely to provide universally applicable numerical indicators, such models can form useful bases to improve shared understanding, mutual adjustment and collaboration between agencies. Ideas about such central place hierarchies and networks of activity centres were first produced by scholars such as Johan von Thünen in the nineteenth century and Walter Christaller and August Lösch in the early twentieth century and evolved to play significant roles in twentieth-century regional planning practice (Glasson, 1974; Friedmann & Weaver, 1979). They continue to influence contemporary regional planning in the form of hierarchies and networks of activity centres, which are widely used in current regional planning to distribute government service functions and roles, including locations for government investment in public transport, health, education, cultural and entertainment facilities and focus points for community and social interaction

(South East England Regional Assembly, 2006; Queensland Department of Infrastructure & Planning, 2009a, b).[xxiv]

In considering these patterned systems, it becomes clear that the grain and positioning of settlements crystallise along a continuum: one end of which is permanently anchored in capacities for direct and recurrent contact between individuals, while the other end is constantly being redefined by the expanding capacity for individuals to receive and exchange more or less instantaneous messages and images over ever-greater distances, which have now reached the global scale. The range of communities thus already extends from the local neighbourhood to the 'global village'. In order to locate and link different kinds of housing need appropriately, some indication of the resulting spectrum and scope of settlements will be helpful. This is provided in Table 8.2.

This kind of table runs two kinds of risks:

1. The array of prescriptions may appear as an authoritarian template designed to simplify the lives of

Table 8.2 Community size and types of appropriate housing provision (developed countries)

Indicative thresholds of size	Frequency and intensity of contact	Predominant types of dwelling	Links	Governance
Neighbourhood or village (up to 1000 households and 100 hectares)	Capacity for daily and direct personal contact with neighbours	Mainly detached family dwellings	Corner store, pharmacy, kindergarten, child care centre, bus stop, ride share network, indoor/outdoor play space	Neighbourhood association, kindergarten committee
District or locality (from 3000 to 10000 households and from 300 to 1000 hectares)	Weekly and recurrent contact with people in shops, schools, buses and medical centres	Mix of detached family dwellings and some higher-density housing for young, ageing and specialised households	Secondary school, several primary schools, public transport hub (train station/bus stop/community transport and active transport networks for pedestrian and cyclists), local park/recreation area, local medical centre	Community Council with designated local government support and roles, secondary school council, parents and citizens associations
Town or suburb (from 10000 to 50000 households and from 1000 to 5000 hectares)	Focus for a number of different age, income, activity and interest groups	Wide array of housing types, styles, sizes, tenures, cost and densities with greater heights up to approx 20m or eight storeys around local transport hubs	District shopping and local government services, Multi Service Health Hub, public transport hub, active transport network focus, VET college	Ward councillors office and district federation of community councils
City or rural region (from 50000 to 200000 households and from 5000 to 20000 hectares (50–200km² within urban areas)	Interdependent specialists providing recurrent health, education, recreation and governance services	Mix of types and tenures, including owner-occupied family housing and public and private rental stock, including central high-rise (>50m) apartments	City/regional council administrative centre, central business district with public transport focus, regional health centre, public and active transport network hub, cultural centre/library/museum, regional university campus, city and regional parks	Local government council, local progress association, organised interest groups for housing, social service, environmental care etc.
Metropolitan or nodal region (1 million+ households and >1000km² area)	Specialist activities, balancing demands and supplies for services and resources	Full range of types and tenures including inner-city apartments, suburban villas and specialised student and retirement accommodation	State/provincial government offices and cultural centre, focus of national and international transport networks of land air and sea	Metropolitan regional governance

communities, which are, in reality, much more complex than any such simple table can reflect.

2. None of the categories will hold true across all situations. Some neighbourhoods in New York, Shanghai or Mumbai, for instance, may be more populous than whole districts or towns in Australia, New Zealand or Portugal.

Nevertheless, it is useful for community planners to have a general guide to different levels of social interaction and the kind of facilities that are required for each. The intention of the table is not, therefore, to compose or impose an ideal pattern or hierarchy of central places and functions, which could be rolled thoughtlessly out over whole cities and regions, but to raise questions and prompt answering options in the minds of those responsible for planning and providing such major community elements as schools, clinics, transport services, parks and economic development programmes. It has been included for these reasons and to illustrate the ways in which housing policy can take account of the many other activities which are required to contribute to the growth of successful communities, and to help those working in these allied fields to visualise how they might cooperate in building well-serviced communities able to accept responsibility for their own subsequent successful self-regeneration.

Conclusions: the contributions of shelter to community life

Safe, healthy and sociable homes provide the basis for many other aspects of successful living. Learning, for instance, is much easier for children who have access to space at home for study and regular rejuvenating rest. Social skills are best learnt in happy and welcoming home environments. Habits of work and personal organisation learnt at home can build future individual and community prosperity. Healthy communities develop and flourish where hygienic homes discourage the spread of disease and debilitation. Well-located and compact housing areas promote community accessibility because home is where most journeys start or finish. Personal independence is most secure where private space provides a refuge from which people can gain information and make daily choices about relations with the outside world. Equal opportunities to create or acquire safe and comfortable shelter promote social justice. Social sustainability, too, is enhanced by the stake in society which a secure home provides. Many of these housing outcomes are strongly influenced by decisions taken outside the home so that individual control and choice can only be achieved through active individual and community involvement in planning land uses, access systems and environmental standards.

Because shelter is the building block of communities and the basis of personal independence and family life, its provision inevitably calls together public, private and community concerns. The rights of the individual to affordable housing choice need constant reassertion in an age of mounting commercialisation. Community concerns are equally pressing, reflecting the powerful shaping effect which the quality and health of home life exerts upon each new generation. Collaboration between the public interest and private energies and initiative is particularly acutely involved in developing countries, where provision of shelter presents one of the greatest challenges facing twenty-first-century society, as people born in the peak period of population growth of the last few decades start to form their households and search for homes. In developed countries, the problem is scarcely less acute, focusing on the need, as the population ages, to meet the demands of growing numbers of smaller households, in ways that are personally and psychologically acceptable. Throughout the lives of people now born, shelter is likely to remain scarce. House prices are already resuming their upward trend and affordability will continue to be a major challenge.

Recent events connected with the Global Financial Crisis indicate that cooperation between governments, developers and builders is essential to ensure a safe and secure matching of supply to demand for future housing. However effective short-term profit maximisation may be in creating large numbers of dwellings attractive to potential buyers, it is now clear that considerable and continuing assistance of financial security and policy guidance is required from governments to achieve sustainable and beneficial long-term housing results. Further boom–bust cycles would not only cause great social stress and human suffering, they might well destabilise social organisation and promote social conflict. Community planning can help to identify and balance the nature and scale of needs against available resources and potential solutions. Simple models to match such demand and supply forecasts have therefore been included earlier in this chapter, and the roles of community organisations in actually helping to meet needs for affordable housing have also been described. However, practitioners in all three sectors of public, private and community housing also need to understand how the linked fields of education, health and work contribute to and benefit from well-housed communities, and this forms the topic of the next chapter.

Endnotes

i There are clear signs that 'peak population' is within sight. Worldwide declining male sperm counts and rising levels of female education and access to birth control information and technology, may within the lifetimes of people now entering the workforce or higher education be raising the need to manage or rectify selective and ultimately widespread population decline. We may well approach the situation which J. S. Mill described as 'the stationary state' (Mill, 1968) where attention can be refocused on improving the quality of life and communication instead of having to devote dominating attention to managing quantity.

ii For instance, the two-storey, shop-top dwellings of Akrotiri, on the southern shores of the Greek Island of Santorini, that were buried in the volcanic explosion of three and a half thousand years ago, display remarkably similar characteristics and spatial organisation to a modern townhouse in an English or Dutch new town, with similar human scale and cubic geometry combining to shape similar rooms that meet the requirements of family life. In the same way, the laterite mud dwellings of the Igbo, Yoruba and Hausa peoples of West Africa have surprisingly similar spatial organisation to the farm cottages of rural Kent or Gloucestershire in England.

iii Scholars have speculated over the reciprocal roles of the city and the road in generating this growth. Lampard (1964) notes that many interpret the great urban explosion of the second half of the nineteenth century as resulting directly from improved communications, which concentrated economic opportunities where there were the greatest cost advantages for collecting, producing and distributing goods.

iv Such techniques simultaneously increased the pace and scale of construction and removed the processes of feedback, mutual adjustment between form and context and cyclical elimination of error (discussed in Chapter 6) which had enabled earlier cities like Rome, Amsterdam and Paris to evolve with grace, harmony and aesthetic unity. The scale and impact of these tower blocks of flats were often achieved at the cost of humanity and responsiveness (Heywood, 1974). These developments were not cheap because construction costs mount for any structure above two storeys and are, as a rough guide, twice as expensive on level twelve as on ground level. High-rise technology as a means of meeting housing need provides an instructive lesson that 'is' does not imply 'ought', and that because something is possible does not make it desirable, indicating that technology is an incomparable servant but an unacceptably tyrannical master.

v Later and less salubrious industrial equivalents can be found in the basement slums of nineteenth-century Manchester and Liverpool where Mumford reports that one-sixth of the population lived in underground cellars and that 'even in the nineteen-thirties there were 20 000 basement dwellings in London, medically marked as unfit for human occupation' (Mumford, 1961). Subsequently, Paolo Soleri (1969) incorporated excavated settlements in his proposals for underground development in his concept of 'Arcology'.

vi Underground transport started in London in 1863 with the first construction of a network that has grown to include twelve lines with 288 stations (Watts, 2007; Transport for London, 2010) and is now administered by Transport for London, a branch of the directly elected Greater London Authority. This partly underground network has contributed powerfully to the success of the city's public transport network, supporting one of the world's largest metropolitan areas with over seven million people and more than 90% of its city centre journeys to work undertaken by public transport every day (Mayor of London, 2009, Chapter 3, Para. 89).

vii Other uses of the same technology, providing underground toll channels for private vehicle movements, through the inner suburbs of Australia's growing metropolitan areas of Melbourne, Sydney and Brisbane, will produce very different results, encouraging further penetration by private cars into central cities and inner suburbs (Brisbane City Council, 2009).

viii Lewis Mumford (1961) once famously speculated upon the transformation in urban development that would have resulted if the invention of electricity generation had preceded the introduction of the steam power which generated the 'cities of dreadful night' of the Industrial Revolution, depicted so well by Charles Dickens (*Hard Times*; 2003), Emile Zola (*Germinal*; 1968), Fyodor Dostoevsky (*Crime and Punishment*; 2003) and Upton Sinclair (*The Jungle*; 1973).

ix Left to themselves, the combined influences of technological determinism and market forces would be as unlikely to produce beneficial community life as an unprogrammed computer would be to write a good policy for community development. In the inspired words of Gordon Campbell, then Chair of the Greater Vancouver Regional District, addressing members of the Council of Councils in 1993: 'You can have anything you want. But you can't have everything and you can't have it right now: you must take choices!' Community planning is about the process of taking those informed and enlightened choices.

x There are enormous gains in health, convenience, time and energy from such installations of reticulated water supplies but the associated losses in recurrent community contact removes a powerful nucleating force, which needs to be recognised and compensated for by activities such as regular festivals and the creation of incidental meeting places to bring people together in casual and enjoyable contact to exchange information and emotional support. This issue provides a useful illustration of the importance of weighing the social implications of different technologies to optimise or mitigate impacts before innovations are introduced.

xi Richard Leakey (1981) describes the traces of the *Homo erectus* camp on the terraces overlooking the site of modern Nice as follows:

> a series of eleven large carefully constructed dwellings, each built on roughly the same spot as the previous year's, oval in shape and each measuring 12 metres by 6 metres … a hearth was built near the centre of each hut, and a scatter of stone flakes indicated the work of a tool maker.

These are clear indications of a communal grouping of family units clustered round their own hearths. Later Neolithic villages also comprised individual family dwellings closely clustered into compact settlements. Mumford (1961) describes this pattern as follows:

> A heap of mud huts, baked or of mud–and-reed construction, cramped in size, at first little better than a beaver's lodge … everywhere the [Neolithic] village is a small cluster of families, from half a dozen to three score perhaps, each with its own hearth, its own household, its own shrine, its own burial plot.

xii Desroches-Noblecourt (1976) describes the situation in Thebes of 3300 years ago as follows:

> The taste for luxurious comfort was the keynote in aristocratic dwellings: on the outskirts of the town they were set in large gardens, but in the central built up area where space was limited, some houses had as many as three stories … Palaces and hovels alike were built of unbaked brick, limestone was used only for thresholds, column bases or lintels … Around each estate was a high wall with a watchman's lodge.

xiii Plato's *Symposium* (2003) makes plain that leading citizens in ancient Athens owned their own houses, and there must have been a market in dwellings to meet the housing needs of slaves who had bought or otherwise gained their freedom to establish separate households. In ancient Rome, there are accounts of proto-capitalist entrepreneurs, building blocks of apartments rising to legislated height limits of 60 or 70 feet (probably seven and eight storeys) and renting them to the many traders and artisans who flocked to the city to share in the metropolitan prosperity. Hall (1998) quotes Lanciani as estimating that of the million population of Rome only 179 000 people lived in individual dwellings and the other 821 000 in tenements, apartment blocks known as *insulae*, accommodating a rich array of mixed uses with shops and workshops on the ground floor, and flats for rent on the floors above, with each floor having a lavatory and chutes for rubbish disposal, a form, as allH Hall observes, that can be found in Italian and larger French cities to this day (Hall, 1998).

A thousand years later, the early development of capitalism and the associated mobility of labour in the medieval market towns and cities of Western Europe repeated this pattern of speculative housebuilding and rental. Feudal kings and lords taxed the towns by the value of lands in different uses, including dwelling plots or tofts. In England the Domesday Book of 1086 records the value of the ground rent of each town parish and demesne. Throughout the country, abbots and lords of the manor subdivided their land and laid out villages and towns with building plots for sale or rent to accommodate the rapidly swelling urban populations. Shelter was becoming a commodity assessed by its capacity to produce cash value. Robert Beckinsale has explored this theme in his work on planned towns of the Cotswolds (1979), as has Margaret Allison (2003) in her work on the growth of a yeoman society that was favoured by a two-way flow between rental tenure and home ownership, with dwelling titles being acquired by occupants, in freehold or in 'fee simple'. Later, they could be rented to newly formed or recently arrived households or sold to other freeholders, providing an early link between land tenure, house-building and community planning. Similarly, in twelfth-century China, travellers such as Marco Polo and the traders of the Silk Road were able to find lodgings for quite prolonged stays, though it is uncertain whether these were provided by merchants or members of the ruling elite (Thubron, 2007). By Shakespeare's time, renting accommodation in London and provincial cities such as Stratford upon Avon was the accepted way for mobile workers like tailors and strolling players to secure a regular base in return for an agreed rent (Greenblatt, 2004). Building, in order to rent out, dwellings and rooms became a lucrative investment.

xiv This is well described by Friedrich Engels in *The Condition of the English Working Classes* (1971) and Elizabeth Gaskell in her influential novels *Mary Barton* and *North and South* (1985, 1998).

xv The celebrated initiative of Richard Ketley and ten other working men who combined to form the first recorded terminating building society, at the Golden Cross Inn in the rapidly growing metal working centre of Birmingham, consisted of an agreement to pool their annual savings to provide one dwelling each year for successive members, until all eleven had been housed. By the early decades of the nineteenth century, this approach had grown to include 'permanent building societies' and banks who advanced sums to house buyers for home purchase in return for guarantees of continued monthly repayments, which could be spread over periods of twenty years.

xvi It is nevertheless interesting that the West German social market housing policy, combining government incentives and private enterprise construction and management was equally successful in numerical terms, and far more so in achieving socially desirable dwellings (see Denton, Forsyth & Maclennan, 1968).

xvii This approach aimed to avoid the excesses of both National Socialist authoritarianism and capitalist profit maximisation. Making use of the economic theories of Professor Walter Eucken, West German Treasurer Ludwig Erhard provided very substantial tax benefits to construction and development firms that provided housing that met specified requirements of location, type, size, cost and tenure, in areas of housing stress. As indicators of housing adequacy were achieved, areas were removed from the schedule of further subsidisation. Within a period of ten years, West Germany succeeded in producing three million high-quality dwellings, starting from the basis of an infrastructure devastated by war (Denton, Forsyth & Maclennan, 1968). The difficulty of maintaining low housing prices in a sellers' market was met by limiting continuing tax concessions to organisations maintaining rents within stipulated levels.

xviii The development of this new suburb comprised nearly 10000 dwellings and a population of 30000. In 1983, the Trust approached Delfin to undertake a joint development on publicly owned land, with its value to be recouped in the form of new public housing units, which would be distributed throughout the new development and constitute 10–20% of the total new dwellings. Both parties also benefited from close cooperation between developers and government departments in the phased provision of schools, community facilities and public transport (Delfin, 2003). The social objectives of the South Australian Housing Trust (now Housing South Australia) were better met by securing attractively designed dwellings that were integrated into the physical fabric of the new community, than if they had attempted to construct an exclusive public housing estate themselves.

xix The alternative approach to levy 'betterment' charges on developers for infrastructure provision may not be so effective in bringing down house prices.

xx Looking back in 1993, John Sewell, the former Mayor of Toronto, doubted whether Metro had exacted sufficiently watertight or even-handed contributions from the private development companies such as Bramah Pty, but the 'planning agreements' approach certainly proved a more efficient and inclusive way to produce a wide range of large-scale development than that being adopted at the time in the sprawling, racially segregated subgroups being constructed south of the border in the United States who were making use of the very untargeted policy of the US Federal Housing Mortgage Authority. Later again, Sewell (2009) attacks the continuation of developer-driven urban sprawl in outer Toronto and proposes more proactive metropolitan governance and planning to contain it.

xxi In particular, Goal Number 2, Land Use Planning, requires that suitable implementation ordinances be adopted to put the comprehensive plans of cities and counties into effect. Goal Number 11, Public Facilities and Services, also mandates efficient planning of public services such as sewers, water, law enforcement and fire protection to ensure that public services are planned in accordance with a community's needs and capacities rather than being forced to respond to development as it occurs (Oregon Department of Land Conservation and Development, 2009).

xxii Registered social landlords (RSLs) are government-funded not-for-profit organisations that provide affordable housing. They include housing associations, trusts and cooperatives. They work with local authorities to provide homes for people meeting the 'affordable homes' criteria. As well as developing land and building homes, RSLs undertake a landlord function by maintaining properties and collecting rent.

xxiii NRAS is expected to supply up to 50000 affordable rental houses across Australia by 2012, with a further 50000 to be made available after 2012 at a cost of $623 million. If housing investors reduce rents by 20% of the normal market rent, the government will provide an incentive of $8000 per year ($6000 from the federal and $2000 from the state governments). This incentive, which in 2009 was $8672, is guaranteed for ten years, with increases in line with the Consumer Price Index. Eligible tenants are determined on an income basis with the service industries such as police, teachers and nurses prioritised as potential tenants. Because the incentives are tax-free, the incentives may have a real value of up to $13675 a year per dwelling (Lending Guru, 2009).

xxiv The spatial aspects of all of the suite of nine regional plans produced between 2004 and 2009 in Australia's north-eastern state of Queensland, for instance, are built around a physical framework based on designation of a network of activity centres, classified as 'principal', 'principal rural', 'major', 'major rural' and 'specialist', in metropolitan and urbanised regions, and 'major regional', 'major rural', 'district rural' and 'community centres', in the rural regions of the west. This network, in effect a hierarchy, has been specifically designed to aid in locating government investment and to help steer related private sector investment (Queensland Department of Infrastructure & Planning, 2009a, b).

References

Abrams, C. (1964) *Housing in the Modern World: Man's struggle for shelter in an urbanizing world.* London, Faber & Faber.

Adams, R. (2009) *Transforming Australian Cities.* Melbourne, City of Melbourne.

Adler, S., Dill, J. (2004) The evolution of transportation planning in the Portland region. In: C. P. Ozawa (ed.), *The Portland Edge.* Washington, Island Press.

Allison, M. (2003) *History of Appleton le Moors: A 12th-century planned village.* York, G. Smith.

Australian Department of Families, Housing, Community Services and Indigenous Affairs (2009) *National Rental Affordability Scheme,* http://www.fahcsia.gov.au/sa/housing/progserv/affordability/nras/Pages/default.aspx, accessed 23 December 2009.

Australian Government (2009) *Nation Building Economic Stimulus Plan,* http://www.economicstimulusplan.gov.au/housing/pages/default.aspx, accessed 23 December 2009.

Bater, J. (1979) *The Soviet City: Ideal and reality*. London, Arnold.

Beckinsale, R. (1979) *Planned Towns of the Cotswolds*. A lecture given to the Gloucestershire College of Art & Design Department of Town & Country Planning, based on articles written in the *Proceedings of the Cotswold Society of Naturalists*.

Brisbane City Council (2009) *Transport Projects*, http://bi.mipo.jsadigital.com.au/MIPO/Transport_projects/TransApex.aspx, accessed 25 December 2009.

Brisbane Housing Company (2010) *Innovation in Affordable Housing: Community cohesion*, http://www.brisbanehousingcompany.com.au/pages.php?p=tenantinfo_community, accessed 24 April 2010.

City of Vancouver (2009) *About South East False Creek and Community Village*, http://vancouver.ca/olympicvillage/about.htm, accessed 29 December 2009.

Davis, K. (1967) The urbanization of the human population. In: O. Flanagan (ed.), *Cities: A scientific American book*. Harmondsworth, Penguin.

Delfin (2003) *Golden Grove Named Australia's Best Development*, http://www.delfinlendlease.com.au/llweb/dll/main.nsf/all/news_20030321delfin, accessed 28 December 2009.

Denton, G., Forsyth, M., Maclennan, M. (1968) *Economic Planning and Policies in Britain, France and Germany*. London, George Allen & Unwin.

Desroches-Noblecourt, C. (1976) *Tutankhamen*. Boston, New York Graphic Society.

Dickens, C. (2003) *Hard Times*. London, Penguin.

Dostoevsky, F. (2003) *Crime and Punishment*. Harmondsworth, Penguin.

Ehrlich, P. (1978) *The Population Bomb*. New York, Ballantyne.

Engels, F. (1971) *The Condition of the Working Class in England*, (trans. W. O. Henderson, W. H. Challoner). Oxford, Blackwell Publishing Ltd.

Friedmann, J., Weaver, C. (1979) *Territory and Function*. London, Arnold.

Gaskell, E. (1985) *Mary Barton: A tale of Manchester life*. London, Penguin.

Gaskell, E. (1998) *North and South*. New York, Oxford University Press.

Glasson, J. (1974) *An Introduction to Regional Planning*. London, Hutchinson.

Greenblatt, S. (2004) *Will in the World: How Shakespeare became Shakespeare*. New York, Norton.

Hall, P. (1998) *Cities in Civilization: Culture, innovation and urban order*. London, Phoenix.

Hall, P. (2002) *Cities of Tomorrow: An intellectual history of urban planning and design in the twentieth century*. Oxford, Blackwell Publishing Ltd.

Heywood, P. (1974) *Planning and Human Need*. Newton Abbott, David & Charles.

Homes and Communities Agency (2010a) *Facts and Figures*, http://www.homesandcommunities.co.uk/factsandfigures, accessed 15 November 2010.

Homes and Communities Agency (2010b) *Top housing and regeneration facts*, http://www.homesandcommunities.co.uk/public/documents/housing-regeneration-facts.pdf, accessed 15 November 2010.

Lacey, J., Heywood, P. (2010) *Sustainable Urban and Regional Infrastructure Development, Technologies, Applications and Management*. Hershey, PA, IGI Information Science.

Lampard, E. (1964) The history of cities in the economically advanced areas. In: J. Friedmann, W. Alonso (eds), *Regional Development and Planning: A reader*. Cambridge, MA, MIT Press.

Leakey, R. (1981) *The Making of Mankind*. London, Abacus.

Leaside Regeneration (2009) *Leaside Regeneration: The sustainable regeneration company*, http://www.leasideregeneration.com/mission.php, accessed 23 December 2009.

Le Corbusier (1970) *Towards a New Architecture*, (trans. F. Etchells). New York, Praeger.

Lemon, J. (1985) *Toronto since 1918*. Toronto, Lorimer.

Lenaghan, N. (2009) Funds say numbers won't work, even with rebate. *Australian Financial Review* **19 November**.

Lending Guru (2009) *National Rent Affordability Scheme*, http://lendingtips.blogspot.com/2009/12/national-rental-affordabilty-scheme.html, accessed 10 April 2010.

Mayor of London (2009) *The Mayor's Transport Strategy*, http://mts.tfl.gov.uk/Read-the-strategy/Download-the-full-strategy, accessed 30 December 2009.

Metro Portland (2005) *Regional Framework Plan: 2005 Revision*, http://library.oregonmetro.gov/files/rfp_introduction.pdf, accessed 23 April 2010.

Metro Portland (2010) *Metro Portland, Mission, Charter and Code*, http://www.oregonmetro.gov/index.cfm/go/by.web/id=24270, accessed 23 April 2010.

Mill, J. S. (1968) Principles of political economy. In: *Selected Writings of John Stuart Mill*. New York, Mentor.

Mumford, L. (1961) *The City in History*. New York, Harcourt Brace.

Newman, O. (1973) *Defensible Space: Crime prevention through urban design*. New York, Macmillan.

Newman, P., Kenworthy, J. (1991) *Cities and Automobile Dependence: A sourcebook*. Aldershot, Gower.

Oregon Department of Land Conservation and Development (2009) *Statewide Planning Goals and Guidelines*, http://www.oregon.gov/LCD/goals.shtml, accessed 30 December 2009.

Plato (2003) *The Symposium*, (trans. C. Gill). London, Penguin Classics.

Queensland Department of Infrastructure & Planning (2009a) *South East Queensland Regional Plan 2009–2031*. Brisbane, Queensland Government.

Queensland Department of Infrastructure & Planning (2009b) *Draft North West Regional Plan*. Brisbane, Queensland Government.

Queensland Government (2009) *SEQ Infrastructure Plan and Program 2009–2031*, http://www.dip.qld.gov.au/regional-planning/south-east-queensland-infrastructure-plan-and-program-2.html, accessed 27 December 2009.

Roy, A. (1999) *The Cost of Living*. London, Flamingo.

Salk, J., Salk, J. (1981) *World Population and Human Values: A new reality*. New York, Harper & Row.

Sewell, J. (2009) *The Shape of the Suburbs: Understanding Toronto's sprawl*. Toronto, University of Toronto Press.

Sewell, J. (1993) *The Shape of the City: Toronto struggles with modern planning*. Toronto, University of Toronto Press.

Sinclair, U. (1973) *The Jungle*. London, Penguin.

Soleri, P. (1969) *Arcology: The city in the image of man*. Cambridge, MA, MIT Press.

South East England Regional Assembly (2006) *A Clear Vision for the South East*, http://www.see-in.co.uk/documentlibrary/2007/southeastplanaclearvisionforthesoutheast.html, accessed 10 November 2009; http://www.southeast-ra.gov.uk/sep_submitted.html#exec_sum, accessed 24 April 2010.

Thubron, C. (2007) *Shadow of the Silk Road*. London, Vintage.

Transport for London (2010) *Line facts*, http://www.tfl.gov.uk/tfl/corporate/modesoftransport/tube/linefacts, accessed 15 November 2010.

Turner, J. (1976) *Housing by People: Towards autonomy in building environments*. London, Marion Boyars.

United Nations Department of Economic and Social Affairs (2001) *World Urbanization Prospects: The 1999 revision*, http://www.un.org/esa/population/publications/wup1999/WUP99COVERPAGE.pdf, accessed 29 December 2009.

United Nations Department of Economic and Social Affairs (2009) *World Population Prospects: The 2008 revision*, http://esa.un.org/unpp/p2k0data.asp, accessed 29 December 2009.

Watts, P. (2007) *History of the London Underground*, http://en.wikipedia.org/wiki/London_Underground, accessed 24 December 2009

Zola, E. (1968) *Germinal*, (trans. H. Ellis). Gloucester, MA, P. Smith.

9 Facets of Community

Chapter 8 explored the crucial links between housing and community. This chapter proceeds to consider the roles of community planning in the three equally important activities of work, learning and health. Work is not only the source of people's capacity to survive and proper; it is the basis of personal independence and psychological self-esteem. Learning promotes the successful human evolution, allowing people to take control of their destiny in a world of constant but uncertain change, where survival depends upon the capacity to read, interpret and redirect environmental conditions. Health is also a prerequisite to survival, well-being and development. All three facets are of the greatest importance to communities and their planning. Accordingly, the chapter is organised into the following four sections:

- justifications for community intervention;
- planning and organisation of work;
- place of learning in community life;
- planning and delivery of health services.

The chapter concludes with a discussion of the many facets of communities.

Justifications for community intervention

Do the many links between the interests of the individual and those of the community in such activities as housing, work, learning and health justify collective responsibility in planning for each of these activities? On the one hand, it seems sensible that communities who wish for collective ends should be prepared to provide communal means. On the other hand, strongly argued objections have been raised against collective interventions into activities that could instead be managed by individuals in direct interpersonal negotiations (Hayek, 1944). Classical economists, for instance, have for many years argued that work can best be managed by the hidden hand of the laws of supply and demand, which can adjust market relations across whole regions and nations, by linking willing sellers and buyers. In education, there is a worldwide revival in the patronage of private schools. Development of online university courses and distance teaching is using the rapid development of information technology to mix public and private systems and simultaneously improve both access and profitability. In health, as well, contests between socialised and privatised medicine have never been fiercer as governments waver between the financial attractions of public reliance on private insurance schemes and concerns that such policies may produce unacceptable inequalities of life chances and expectation between classes. It is significant that this became as dominant a debate of Barack Obama's first presidential year as international terrorism or the management of the national and global economic recessions.

Mobility can also involve a wide range of private and public arrangements, from active personal movement, through communal provision of roads and wharves to public transport systems which may be operated by either public or private enterprises, in free-to-use or toll facilities. Play and recreation are also becoming more individual and commercialised through the spread of computer games. Social life, too, is evolving towards more private networks through such Internet organisations as Facebook and Twitter and other social networking sites, including dating agencies. In the field of political control, governments

Community Planning, First Edition. Phil Heywood.
© 2011 Phil Heywood.
Published 2011 by Blackwell Publishing Ltd.

have long had to face the challenge that 'that government is best which governs least'. Support for small government has led to proposals for the 'reinvention of government'. Osborne and Gaebler (1992), for instance, suggest more emphasis on 'steering not rowing'.[i] Without contesting the primacy of democratic control, such theorists advocate quite radical reductions in the spheres of public activities, in the interests of benefits that they believe would result in efficiency, incentives and economic progress.

THE CASE FOR COMMUNITY INVOLVEMENT

In response, the contrasting cases in favour of government involvement are grounded in six main arguments:

1. **Accountability:** In items of common consumption such as water supply, power distribution and public transport infrastructure, market failures of private monopolies can best be avoided by community regulation based on social objectives of equity and sustainability.
2. **Social and environmental impacts:** Control of damaging social costs and dangerous environmental impacts, which may include disease, pollution and carbon emissions, requires strong public powers and regulation, to prevent short-term private gains displacing long-term community interests.
3. **Flexible and wide-ranging capacities to respond to changed conditions:** The generation of sufficient options to support adaptation and survival in times of rapid external change like our own requires the nurturing of diversity rather than market elimination of deviations from a competitive norm, whether in gene pools or forms of social or economic organisation. (Kropotkin, 1939; Ridley, 1996).
4. **Collaboration:** The conflict management and consensus building involved in sustaining societies and their essential systems require public commitment to community services that can provide equal opportunities in education, health, social welfare and income security.[ii]
5. **Maintaining community 'voice' as an alternative to 'exit':** Building trust and cooperation will require collaborative management and operation of community services responsible to elective governance. In this way, it is possible to balance the social influences provided by voice with the social choices offered by exit (Cooke and Morgan, 1998; Putnam, 1993; Florida, 2005).
6. **Common goods:** Community or state partnerships may be required to prevent 'the tragedy of the commons' (Hardin, 2008) where private profit-seeking may rapidly extinguish a resource on which everyone relies, such as the common grazing land of the medieval European commons, the North African grain lands of the first millennium AD or the North Atlantic fisheries of the mid-twentieth century.

REGARDING THE SELF AND OTHERS

Differing levels of government involvement in the productive and service activities of communities offer significant but hotly disputed opportunity costs and consequences. Early attention was directed to these questions by John Stuart Mill (1983) in his classical work *On Liberty* of 1861. Mill applied 'self-regarding' and 'other-regarding' categories to distinguish between activities which should be left to the free choice of individuals and families and those where government intervention and control were needed to ensure efficiency or equity because of their impacts on others. This approach has strongly influenced subsequent practice in representative democracies, both directly and as part of their prevailing intellectual climate. Successive generations of politicians and administrators of a wide range of political affiliations and parties have used these criteria to decide whether national education, health systems and organisation of industries should be left to private initiative or be regulated or implemented by the public sector.[iii] Based on such analyses, there is now very widespread participation by national governments, and even international bodies, in all these systems.

An example which has already been referred to in Chapter 5, at the end of the section 'The values of liberty', refers to the United Kingdom's General Development Order, which originally contained 23 pages of exemptions and has survived in successive planning acts to continue to exempt from planning control domestic development, which, broadly speaking, does not impinge upon neighbours' senses of sight, sound or smell. No one wants to be prevented from making a small adjustment to their home or to be required to enter into a complex and formal application process before they can do so.[iv] Equally, no one wants to have massive and inappropriate new development imposed on their neighbourhood for someone else's benefit. In summary, community activities can be seen as the practices of a sociable species of exploratory individuals living in interactive communities. They require a combination of:

- individual initiative;
- community engagement, voice and review;
- social oversight and resourcing.

Combining these roles constructively will demand particular skills and methods of 'mixed scanning', community collaboration and communicative problem-solving (Etzioni, 1973). Mixed scanning can contribute the combination of scrutiny and understanding of wider social contexts with a clear focus on specific proposals with which people can identify and to which they can commit. Collaboration will make possible joint action between people responsible for different activities in community, commercial and government organisations. Communicative problem-solving can link many different actors and players in activities such as futures workshops, charettes and 'enquiry by design'.

The planning and organisation of work

Good decisions about the purposes and planning of work require careful consideration of its changing forms and people's personal experiences.

PURPOSES

Three related purposes of work can be identified:

- productivity to sustain individual, family and community life;
- creativity of individual self expression;
- the autonomy of personal agency arising from the first two, providing individuals with tradable capacities with which to justify their places and roles in the community (Jacobs, 1992).

Productivity

Economies of scale that maximise output and the division of labour that focuses energy and skills among trades and professions have fostered the extraordinary multiplication of material goods of the modern world, ranging from cell phones to tank-like SUV vehicles and from solar panels to orbiting communications satellites. An international division of labour has also emerged, dividing rich, poor and developing countries. Left to themselves, these processes produce the boom and bust cycles of the classic capitalist economies, whereas the emerging field of 'associational economics' (Cooke & Morgan, 1998) succeeds better in combining economies of scale with flexible forms of production and innovation. In the simplest terms, there is a growing acceptance of the need for primary cooperation in production to support secondary processes of competition within the global economy. This clearly has the greatest importance for community planning.

Creativity

Creativity can combine knowledge and imagination to transform ideas and matter into new uses. In so doing it stimulates the pleasure we feel in personal agency, fulfilling not only our own needs and visions but also meeting those of others. Both enrich life, as in Leonardo da Vinci's restless search for answers leading to the concepts of the flying machine, the parachute and the helicopter centuries before the technology became available to support his designs (Landrus, 2006). The computer programmer of contemporary times, working out how to shrink the size of book-length files to the scale where they can be attached to emails and despatched around the world, is also meeting personal and social needs (Sennett, 2008). This creativity is both an individual and a communal attribute, often involving a high degree of trust between related inventors and operators (Cooke & Morgan, 1998). Richard Florida (2005) draws attention to the need for interaction between individual practitioners and networks of associated knowledge industry workers within the loose networks of the new 'creative class' drawn to the fertile and welcoming environment of relatively unconstrained inner-city life in 'downtowns' of great cities like New York, London, San Francisco and Toronto. Planning for the creative aspects of work in contemporary societies should thus aim to combine the individual freedom and opportunities offered by tolerant and supportive communities with the introduction of activities to support and develop innovation. This aspect of creativity is strongly linked to the next criterion of autonomy.

Autonomy

A sense of personal agency is not only psychologically important to individuals. It can also provide a powerful protection against intrusions of power or privilege into people's private and productive lives, forming a basis for asserting individual rights. Jane Jacobs (1992) sees this capacity as a powerful 'system of survival' for individuals dealing with each other to weave networks of power that can withstand the control of self-appointed leaderships, whether they are Plato's 'guardians', Lenin's 'leading role of the party' or the financial operators of the big investment banks of the contemporary Western world. For these reasons, too, we need to ensure that communities and individuals have secure and self-sustaining economic bases.

THE EXPERIENCE OF WORK

Writers such as Emile Zola (1968), describing the heroic struggles of the lives of nineteenth-century coalminers, Leo Tolstoy (2002), capturing the elation of physical labour in the fields, and D. H. Lawrence (1994), celebrating the creative energy of craftspeople throughout the world, can provide telling insights into the human experience of work.[v] In a poem entitled 'Work', for instance, Lawrence (1994) wrote:

> There is no point in work
> Unless it absorbs you
> Like an absorbing game…
> When a man goes out into his work
> He is alive like a tree in spring.
> He is living, not merely working…

He goes on to describe how:

> When the Hindus weave thin wool into
> long, long lengths of stuff…
> They are like slender trees, putting forth
> leaves, a long white web of living leaf…
> As with cloth, so with houses, ships,
> shoes, wagons or cups or loaves
> Men might put them forth as a snail its
> shell as a bird that leans
> Its breast against its nest, to make it round

By contrast, the unthinking distinctions that we are accustomed to make between work and play and between our social and productive lives come not from conviction but from the historical dominance of workers' lives by investing, political and other elites. They are products of social organisation. Today's community planning can help to move work away from its associations with physical and wage bondage. Work opportunities can be planned that match people's natural creativity, interests and self-expression with the needs and aspirations of their communities. In so doing, we should also improve capacities for flexible responses to rapidly changing physical and social conditions. Creativity has survival value.

THE CHANGING NATURE AND LOCATIONS OF WORK

Five or six great waves of dominant activity, each associated with particular technologies, can be recognised in human history (Mumford, 1961):

- The first one of Palaeolithic food-gathering and hunting predominated for a million years up to about 10 000 years ago, and is still enshrined in such activities as big game hunting and whaling.
- The second one of Neolithic subsistence agriculture prevailed up to the Industrial Revolution of 250 years ago, and likewise continues as a very important source of food.
- Third was the epoch of mass manufacturing and exchange ushered in by the Industrial Revolution, which continues to produce millions of tons of consumer products every year.
- Fourth was the short-lived period in the first half of the twentieth centre when physical services for society and production dominated the employment structure, and continues to play an important role in contemporary society.
- Next came the knowledge, information and communications industries of today, with most workers employed in the development, exchange, processing and application of knowledge in activities like finance, insurance, research, education and information technology.
- Finally, one can postulate a sixth wave of integrated work where individuals and communities balance their time more equally between component, consumer and craft production, provision of human and physical services for their families and neighbours, food growing, devising and exchanging ideas across global networks and contributing to new collaborative enterprises. Such developments would also bring together the three main purposes of work discussed earlier, combining personal creativity, associational activities and individual independence. One example of such integrated and flexible work, termed 'associational economics', that is growing up in central Italy is described in Box 9.1.

Work locations have also responded to these successive waves of dominant activities. Hunter-gathers were immersed in the richly varied and multilayered natural environment of forest, range and river bank, always enlivening and sometimes dangerous. Subsistence agriculture contracted the workplace back to a few acres around the village and started the process of alienation of humanity from nature. Specialised craft production and commercial manufacture

Box 9.1 Community collaboration in central Italy

The central Italian regions are justly celebrated for their long traditions of social capital and collaborative social institutions (Putnam, 1993). Nevertheless, the end of the Second World War found the region of Emilia-Romagna with its old cities of Bologna, Reggio Emilia, Modena, Ravenna, Ferrara, Parma and Carpi impoverished and without any clear economic base. A tradition of small enterprises making straw hats around Modena provided an immediate post-war entry into the international clothing market, but this was rapidly overtaken by lower cost suppliers in Asia and Latin America. Nevertheless, the contacts established in the hat trade had familiarised the Modena producers with the changing dictates of the international fashion industry, encouraging small firms to diversify into production of T-shirts, sportswear, children's wear, men's dress shirts and women's upmarket knitwear (Cooke & Morgan, 1998). Regional producers, building on long-standing traditions of collaboration and exchange were able not only to interpret and anticipate but also to respond to the latest trends of the international fashion market by rapidly applying flexible skills to create new products.

These developments coincided with the 1971 introduction of regional government into the 20 Italian regions. The new regional government quickly established a regional development agency ERVET (*Ente Regionale per il Valorizatione del Territoria*) to encourage cooperation between the many small artisans of the region to compete in national and world export markets, involving the National Confederation of Artisans (CNA) as well as educational, technical and government bodies to encourage economic development by providing services of accountancy, vocational training, bulk purchasing, marketing, credit facilities, technical support and 'industrial incubators' to sponsor start-up processes. ERVET also established 'artisans clubs' to encourage people in supply chains to get to know each other and build mutual trust. A 'service centre' model was developed, with the one for the fashion industry in Carpi providing access to very sophisticated design software to encourage innovation and interactive links to offer direct contact with international consumers. The Information Centre, CITER, occupies two floors of a terraced house in a largely residential street, with a library of fashion, design catalogues and magazines, a lecture theatre and a workshop equipped with a CAD-CAM system linked to an automatic loom which can produce experimental designs on the spot. By 1991, the knitwear industry in the city and its neighbouring communes had grown to involve 2500 enterprises employing 18 000 people, giving a good indication of the small-scale units which have combined to create the area's associational economy. Similar arrangements have been established for ceramics, footwear and generic technology transfer in Bologna, earthmoving equipment in Ferrara, agricultural machinery in Reggio Emilia and mechanical engineering and subcontracting in Parma (Cooke & Morgan, 1998).

The results have been to promote the region to be one of the two most prosperous in the European Union, with a flexibility based on the continuing innovation which is essential to survival in the rapidly changing global market. The organisational pattern is one of many small enterprises, forming a collaborative economy involving cooperation between state, region, innovators and producers. The model relies heavily both on government support and services and cooperation between local producers. It is neither totally organic nor totally planned but rather a collaboration which allows continuous evolution to meet the demands of a constantly changing market. As a model, it is highly appropriate for community planning and development.

progressively drew people into yet tighter and less healthy habitats of mine-top and quarry-side settlements and industrial towns, with close 'horizontal' integration of related processes, transport terminals and workers' housing. Further specialisation and zoning regulations resulted in increasing 'vertical' integration of large free-standing production plants on the edges of major cities like those of Ford Motors in Detroit and its Dagenham plant in England, both approaching a hundred hectares in extent, Austin Motors at Longbridge, also in England, and Volkswagen at Wolfsburg in Germany. City regions were rapidly expanding and mechanising, and sociologists were identifying the rise of industrial anomie (Wirth, 1964). Production line workers were beginning to lead lives of deadening alienation.

This degree of gigantism and over-specialisation also proved economically rigid and unsustainable, and the highly segregated cities that resulted have begun to evolve back to favour the mixed uses familiar in, for instance, the central areas of London, New York, San Francisco, Pittsburgh and Kolkata. Reference has already been made to the ideas of Richard Florida on the roles of the creative class in building new economies based on the human capital of inner cities and of Philip Cooke and Kenneth Morgan in drawing attention to associational economies drawing on the pools of social capital of well-established regions such as northern Spain, western Germany and central Italy.[vi]

PLANNING AND PROVIDING JOBS

Planning aims to identify and interpret relevant facts to help fulfil widely debated and justified values (see Chapter 5). Employment planning is thus more than either a trend exercise in statistical analysis or an imaginative invention of an ideal world based on personal conviction. A number of sometimes competing values will have to be assessed,[vii] and facts to be collected and analysed to determine forecastable needs and available resources. Valid future scenarios, of the sort illustrated for Greater Brisbane in Figure 7.7, in Chapter 7, can be developed to balance social demand for goods and services with supplies of products, and these can then be reviewed and adjusted in the light of available skills and investment funds, as indicated in Table 9.1:

Table 9.1 Values and trends in projecting demand and supply for goods, services and jobs

	Demands	Supplies
Goods and services	Forecast levels of consumption Currently suppressed demands Emerging wants Trend forecasts	Projections of energy, raw materials and labour stocks Substitution estimates Satisfaction of quantified needs
Jobs	Projected populations of working age Personal preferences Social priorities for health, education and community services Social and political choices Time allocations between work and leisure Childcare arrangements	Investment policies and production needs Retirement and pensions policy Social needs and wants Skill stocks Technological change Social policy, regulation and funding

The building of practical and desirable futures will depend upon collaborative planning and communicative winnowing of options. Models of this sort have been pioneered for a number of years in forums such as Portland's Portland Future Focus and Portland Development Commission (Seltzer, 2004) and in numerous advisory boards in cities like Amsterdam and Cambridge in the United Kingdom; (Healey, 2007). Their greatest potential is to stimulate ideas for future policy options rather than providing precise quantified projections or proposals.

PROJECTIONS OF JOB NEED

Figure 9.1 suggests how community values can provide the dynamic to drive the work system. The ways that changing populations will be maintained and employed in producing goods, services and knowledge and the kinds of workplaces they occupy will in part be decided by predominant visions of the future of society.

This diagram is intended to provide a generalised understanding of the links and relationships involved in the complex work and employment systems. For purposes of quantified projection, a more linear model, such as that developed for the purpose in Chapter 7 is required. Figure 7.7 examines more precisely the options and possibilities confronting a particular community. Adopting a supply-and-demand approach to the questions of work in the growing city of Brisbane, capital of Queensland in Australia, the supply of recent, current and projected jobs is compared with the demands for work that the city has experienced in the recent past, at present and projected in the future to indicate the anticipated balance and the contributions that employment trends in different industries may make to that balance. Some interesting conclusions emerge. The changing age structure of Brisbane's population can be expected to reduce the rate of increase in the working population, and therefore the demand for jobs (from 26% in the last ten tears to 16% in the next). On the other hand, continued growth in employment in the knowledge and health industries and the construction and services sectors catering for the needs of the rapidly growing overall population is likely to maintain the rate of growth in jobs at almost double that level (around 30%), suggesting a real need to consider policy options to meet this shortfall. These will include:

- incentives to retain members of the mid-twentieth century 'baby boomer' generation in employment in the knowledge and service industries, where

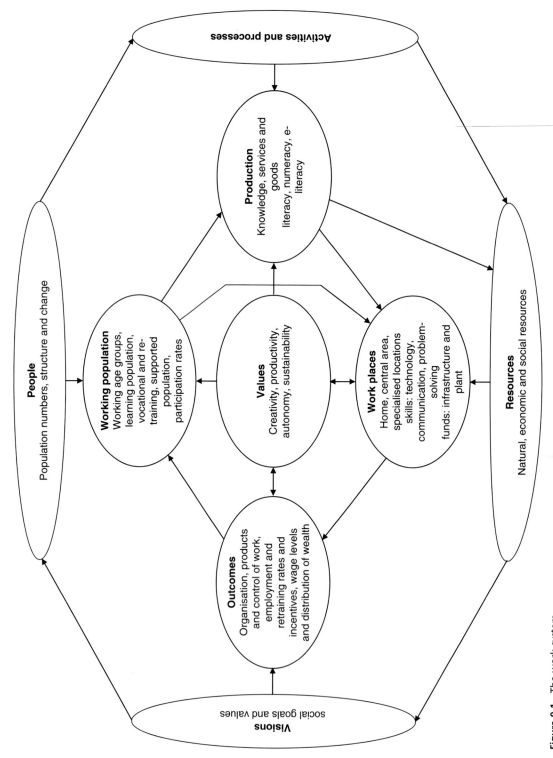

Figure 9.1   The work system.

their skills may be particularly suitable, after the official retirement age of 65 years;

- industrial retraining programmes to move people from potentially contracting industries like manufacturing and wholesale trades into expanding ones such as health care, education and professional scientific and technical services;
- extra incentives to encourage school leavers to undertake higher education to improve their skills, work productivity and flexibility of potential employment, before entering the workforce;
- the introduction of 'social housing' schemes that will encourage people with needed skills, such as teachers and health workers, to stay or settle in the city.

This figure incorporates a very simple approach to modelling job creation and need which can be applied in a wide range of contemporary situations, wherever, in fact, population and employment records are kept and demographic projections are made. Readers may find it interesting to insert statistics for their own communities to determine likely outcomes for job creation and worker supply. Such models will not, in themselves, produce instant answers but they can assist communities to identify the trends that are currently operating and some of the issues and options that need to be considered in the light of the values and priorities that emerge from continuing community discussion and dialogue.

WORK LOCATIONS

Changes, started in the 1980s that continue today, in technology, transport, communications and production processes have revolutionised industrial location. Gone are the days when a modelling expert could create a 'Model of Metropolis' (Lowry, 1964) using predictions of where manufacturing and national market service jobs would be, as the basis to allocate residential areas in terms of distance from those workplaces, and then where local services would be, relative to those living places. Some trends that will grow in significance to exert strong influences on future work locations have as yet barely surfaced. Others identified in Table 9.3, can be confidently predicted and their potentialities incorporated into creative community planning. It is, for instance, widely accepted that 'sunbelt and snowbelt' environments of high natural quality and pulling power will attract skilled people who will in turn create employment growth. Similarly, the changing proportions of jobs in different sectors have had powerful locational impacts. Manufacturing

employment in Western nations has declined from around 50% at the beginning of the twentieth century to around 10% at its end, resulting in a major shift in jobs from pioneer industrial regions like the Moselle, Tyne and Clyde valleys to more environmentally attractive locations such as the French Riviera, southern England and the Firth of Forth. The vocational pressures on operators in the 'knowledge industries' have far more to do with the lifestyle choices and access to information technology of Richard Florida's (2005) 'creative class' than with deepwater ports or raw materials, which no longer act as basic industries pulling towards them metropolitan growth. The main factors of influence and their predicted locational effects are summarised in Table 9.2. It will be seen that

Table 9.2 Influences and outcomes in employment locations

Influencing factor	Predicted locational effect
Growth and spread of knowledge industry	Increasing use of educational and health investment, particularly for new regional university campuses, research institutes and major hospitals to promote regional economic development
	Increased emphasis on industrial clusters and mixed uses in inner areas of cities and suburbs
Growing policy support for the development of regional economies through the establishment of horizontal links of association	Support for development of creative industry nodes in inner areas of great cities
	Evolution of large vertically integrated activities (like vehicle manufacture) into flexible swarms of component industries
Increased locational pull of high-quality environments	Increased attention to environmental quality of employment areas
Increasing costs of energy and transport	Increasing concentration on long-life and high-quality products rather than mass production of very cheap items
Increasing costs of raw materials	Expansion of recycling and conservation industries along major transport routes
Increasing move to home occupations	Increased proportion of people working from home
Increased levels of personal productivity	Reversal of recent trends and consequent reduction in the average size of new productive units
Diminished rates of growth in aggregate output and national and global economies	Re-sorting and redevelopment of existing industrial and employment sites

Table 9.3 Workplace provisions

Facility	Indicative thresholds of scale and size of location	Links	Size and Governance
Home, office or workshop of 1–10 people	Neighbourhood (up to 5000 people)	Local phone lines and Internet connections Circulation systems and foot and bike paths Corner shops	Family life Neighbourhood committees
Internet café Office supplies and services Producers clubs	District (10 000–15 000 people)	Public transport Interchange, active transport network focus District community service centre (local government services) District health clinic	Ward councillor Community council/ board
City centre administrative and commercial employment. Service Centre to promote local hard and software production Creative industry and info tech networks in inner areas	Town/suburb (40–100 000 people)	City business centre Vocational education and training (VET) Public transport focus	City council, economic promotion bureau and economic advisory board Chamber of commerce
Metropolitan employment node with 'back office' support facilities in the inner city	Urban region/city (250 000–500 000 people)	Regional university campus Cultural centre/library/museum Mass transit and active transport network hub Regional health centre Main offices of municipal/regional council Inner-city accommodation pool	Regional administrative, business, academic and interest group councils, involving government, industry, professions, advocates, academic and student representatives
Major metropolitan centre with national scale administrative and commercial services, including finance, research and development, packaging and marketing	Regional and national scale catchments 2–10 million people	National business and cultural centre National university campus state/provincial government Focus of national and international financial and transport networks of land, air and sea	National policy and research advisory committees National and regional councils, involving government, industry, professions, staff and student representatives

there is a pervasive shift from 'natural' locational factors such as raw materials and even such physical ones as rail lines and port facilities towards such factors as environmental quality, urban aesthetics and educational opportunity, which are much influenced by public decisions, choices and investment. As a result, these trends significantly increase the important role of community planning in ensuring future productivity and prosperity.

WORK PROVISIONS

While it is neither possible nor desirable to impose on communities a hierarchy of central places into which all employment, education, health and other services are expected to fit, there are tangible advantages in ensuring that appropriate provisions and facilities are available to residents and users of the different levels of settlement which go to make up contemporary communities. Table 9.3 is intended to act as a prompt to assist economic, physical, social and educational plan-

ning to take account of the need to integrate these workplaces in convenient and accessible centres.

CONCLUSION: THE LINKS OF WORK WITH OTHER ACTIVITIES

Rapid development of new fields of work may be one of the driving forces of contemporary change, but they are not independent prime movers, but are rather held within a net of relationships. As we have seen, the cultural environment and its attractions determine to a large extent where creative workers will congregate in concentrations that can produce the new activities which are increasingly dominating today's employment structure. Likewise the physical environment of coast, climate and resort characteristics exert major influences on the vocational decisions of managers and entrepreneurs. Education and knowledge industries can shape and transform regional economies as in the San Francisco Bay area, the Greater Boston metropolitan region and the Bangalore node of the information and communications industry in southern India.

Economic and labour force planners need not only to look sideways to understand their links with all these activities. They can also benefit from entering into direct discussions and dialogues, both official and informal, with their fellow practitioners. As well as standing to gain from this responsive approach, they also have great contributions of knowledge and understanding to make to the shaping of active, confident and self-reliant communities.

The place of learning in community life

INTRODUCTION: THE SIGNIFICANCE OF EDUCATION

Although no single thread of community life and development can be singled out as the most important, because they are all inextricably woven together within the different skeins of human personality, nevertheless, education provides a unique impetus to the processes of growth and development of individuals and communities. Human learning flows continuously fresh to enliven each new generation. Individuals gain consciousness, start to collect and process observations, gather understanding and develop new ideas to add to the accumulated knowledge of their forbears. Grounded in the unfolding senses of each young child, this learning is borne forward by the wave-like force of more than a million years of communicated knowledge.[viii] Even in the fields of self-knowledge and the sciences of mind and society, great advances are being made, opening the prospect of improved capacity to shape relationships with our families, our communities and ourselves.

GLOBAL TRENDS: EDUCATION RESHAPING THE WORLD

Learning exerts powerful impacts on people's attitudes. By channelling the way we express innate capacities in personal behaviour, individuals can help to shape and influence the evolution of community life. These effects are not confined to formal education or the new explorations of science and technology. Mass literacy is also spreading rapidly to encompass more than half the world's population of six billion people (United Nations Development Program, 2010). Adult literacy rates in China are already above 90%, providing over a billion people with the potential capacity to participate in the worldwide communication of the Internet and mobile phone networks (Dreze & Loh, 1995). Literacy in India is also rapidly expanding, and has now reached more than 60%. Well over half of the world's six billion people can now read and write, representing not only a new peak of human learning but also a promising foundation for its continued growth.

Inevitably, controversial issues of control are associated with this wave of change. While Internet and mobile phone networks have disseminated capacity to originate and distribute information and ideas to more than a billion people in all parts of the world, power to control and extract income from this access is being concentrated in the hands of small numbers of carefully positioned gatekeepers of media systems, including print, satellite and electronics entrepreneurs. While proprietors and providers of satellite and information and entertainment organisations are seeking to protect market monopolies, public interest bodies such as Wikipedia, Wikimedia, Wikileaks and Linux are creating self-regulating storehouses of free information (Sennett, 2008).

In issues of validity and meaning, too, dangerous conflicts are arising, between groups battling for control of the definition of truth, which are closely linked to the field of education. Traditional bodies of knowledge associated with established religions and sciences are coming into angry conflict with challenging new ways of thinking and seeing the world. One example is presented by fundamental Christian groups who question the right of science to teach evolutionary theory. Others oppose the distribution of birth control information or material.[ix] All of this reflects theories of the nexus between knowledge and power (Foucault, 1980), making the issue of learning particularly significant for community planning. The strong links between knowledge, power and policy emphasise the importance for educational practitioners and planners (who define and transmit knowledge) to develop and maintain a perceptive understanding of the evolving place and role of their work within the wider society and its relationships with such closely linked systems as economy, culture, access, play and community life.

METHODS AND ISSUES

Like other forms of community planning, educational planning can benefit from various forms of mixed scanning, of thinking in context by switching focus from immediate needs to more distant goals and back again.

- First, there is the mix of facts and values, both accurate descriptions of current conditions, such as existing populations and their needs, and normative views of what people think to be right, based on their social, political and professional values.

This ability to distinguish between 'is' and 'ought' without confusing the two, and to combine measurements of both quality and quantity, is itself a major attribute of education.

- Second, there is the need to relate past, present and future situations in order to understand trends without being dazzled by them.
- Finally, there is the need to give detailed attention to learning systems, places and organisations without losing sight of their wider social context, including other linked systems such as work, access, culture and social life.

Rising levels of literacy, e-literacy and numeracy also encourage habits of mixed scanning, bringing formerly distant and conjectural possibilities into immediate contact. The twenty-first century is an era of quantification, where universal numerical symbols acquaint growing numbers of children with the power of number to provide instant access to an open sky of information and rewards. This way of learning applies even more strongly to technical skills. In Bangladesh, for instance, the micro credit policies of the Grameen Bank have combined with social network and positive discrimination practices to create the situation where there are now more than 40 000 villages boasting a 'telephone lady', who can walk phone calls to almost every household in the village, familiarising the whole population with digital accessing systems (Yunus, 1998). The Grameen Bank, whose activities were discussed earlier in Chapter 1, has invested a small portion of its large body of members funds in creating Grameen Telecom to produce mobile phones, and has encouraged at least one member of each its 40 000 village branches to borrow funds to buy a phone, repaying the loan by acting as the village messenger, or 'Mercury', allowing people anywhere in the global communications network to contact local villagers who can have the phone walked to their homes to talk to relatives, friends or future business contacts, thus revolutionising the country's level of community linkage and access (Yunus, 1998).

Teaching at all levels from the primary school to the university and research institute can build on these naturally acquired skills of e-literacy and numeracy to develop competencies that become routine parts of people's daily lives, helping them to integrate and interpret the floods of new information which are characteristic of the contemporary world. Once developed, these skills can make invaluable contributions to productive, well-informed and tolerant societies. They can link people's natural drives to understand with preparation for the wider social roles of collaboration and

production. In these ways, the educational system can reflect individuals' learning experiences, in keeping with Noam Chomsky's insight that 'humanity is a species programmed to understand' (Lyons, 1991).

The third aspect of mixed scanning, defining relations with other systems, is demonstrated in Figure 9.2, illustrating the place of the learning system in a changing world. It will be seen that the context of the education system is provided not by static principles but by the certainty of change in each of the four of fields of population, physical environment, society and technology. The figure explores aspects of the internal structure and subsystems most relevant to planning, which are viewed in terms of people, processes, resources and outcomes. Both operational demands and external changes require links to other systems. Educational access, for instance, will influence, and be influenced by, where people live and the central place patterns of settlements. Equally, education to provide up-to-date skills and good interpersonal communications will influence work arrangements and capacities to create personal wealth and maintain social vitality. Other feedback loops can test whether technological changes are well designed to produce desirable work outcomes, help control environmental devastation and resource depletion and support public participation in the continual reshaping of shelter and settlements to reflect the needs and preferences of their occupants. In these and other tasks, learning and communications can be closely allied to prompt positive adjustments to inevitable external changes and thus to assist positive social evolution.

The generally high standards of demographic recording in the contemporary world provide information on current numerical requirements and future projected needs, in the way indicated in Figure 9.2. Basic census data on age by five-year-old cohorts, and population projections based on widely available statistical models, modified by migration assumptions, produce useful forecasts of future need for different levels of pre-school, primary, secondary and tertiary education. These can be related to different curricula options in terms of desired skill levels and employment patterns and requirements for educational facilities and teachers. These can, in turn, be related to positive social and physical links within the activity centres of the evolving settlement pattern, in the form adopted in Table 9.4.

EDUCATIONAL PROVISIONS

Because learning lies at the heart of human society, it helps to generate places which attract other functions,

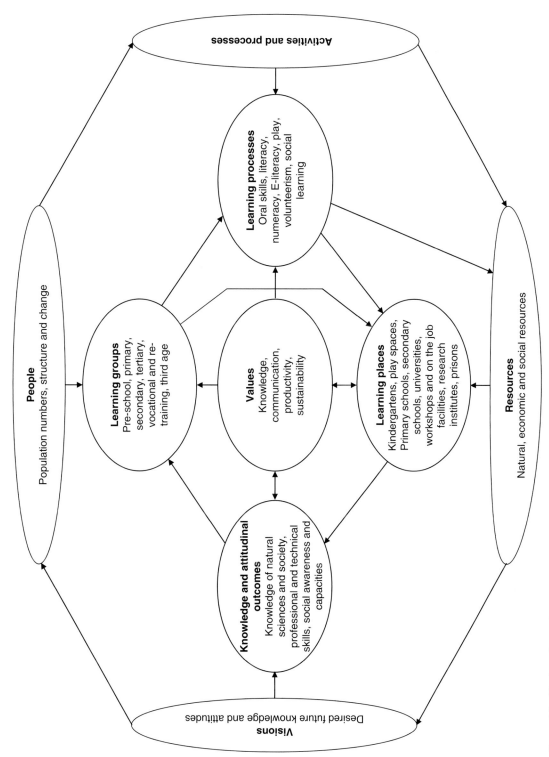

Figure 9.2   The learning system.

Table 9.4 A model of standard educational provisions in a developed country

Facility	Scale	Links	Size and governance
Pre-school childcare centre and kindergarten (2–5 years)	Neighbourhood (500–1000 people)	Indoor/outdoor play space Corner shops	20–30 places User committees Parents and teachers circle
Primary school (normally 5- to 11-year-olds)	Locality (4000–6000 people)	Public transport access (bus stop or community transport drop off) Active transport system (pedestrian/cyclist priority path systems) Local park/recreation area Local medical centre	400–800 pupils School board, parents and citizens committees Parent teacher association Government department of education
Secondary school (normally 12- to 17-year-olds)	District (10 000–15 000 people)	Public transport interchange, active transport network focus District community service centre (local government services) District health clinic	1000–1500 students School board, parents and citizens committees Parent teacher association Government department of education
Vocational education and training (VET) (normally 17- to 25-year-olds)	Town/suburb (40–100 000 people)	City business centre Public transport focus	1000–2000 full- and part-time technical and further education (TAFE) students Joint industry, staff and student liaison committee
Regional university campus (normally 18- to 28-year-olds)	Urban region/ city (250 000–500 000 people)	Cultural centre/library/ museum Mass transit and active transport network hub Regional health centre Municipal/regional council main offices Inner-city accommodation pool	10,000 – 20,000 full and part time, undergraduate and post graduate students. University academic council involving government, industry, professions, staff and student representatives
Major metropolitan/ national university campus National research institute	Regional and national scale catchments 2–10 million people	State/provincial government, business and cultural centre Focus of national and international transport networks of land, air and sea	40 000–100 000+ students University academic council, involving government, industry, professions, staff and student representatives

while also requiring close contact such as shelter, work and transport. Table 9.4 examines some of the more significant of these links within social and physical space and provides some very broadly indicative figures of the scale of facilities and hinterlands which may be involved. These will vary with the circumstances of particular societies, especially their population density, wealth, infrastructure levels and cultural traditions, so that few places will exactly replicate the figures presented here. Nevertheless, the intention of the table is to provide an example of one working pattern appropriate to current situations in an urbanised, economically advanced nation, which should be capable of adaptation to meet the different conditions and needs in less affluent developing societies. Questioning such standardised provisions should itself help to generate productive options such as making use of radio, TV and Internet instruction to

spread the catchment of metropolitan-scale tertiary education throughout networks of much more widely spread rural settlements. Rather different arrangements would be suitable for the most local scale in a developing country, including incorporating a village madrasah or community school into the neighbourhood scale of the system.

Education plays formative social, economic and community development roles at each of these levels, providing focal and meeting places from the neighbourhood kindergarten or pre-school centre, where recently arrived parents mix with long-standing residents, and children learn to socialise, to the university where lifelong friendships, romantic relationships and future professional and business alliances are formed. Economically, crucial skills are learnt at each level, the most formative ones of literacy and numeracy in the early years and the most advanced ones of applied knowledge and research in later vocational and university training. Often, links between these different levels of education and their wider communities can be more fully developed; collaborative planning can draw in extra resources at the same time as improving the relevance of teaching and learning programmes. Among the greatest benefits from collaborative planning is the community building which can include many activities, ranging from sharing facilities for such activities as sport, recreation, art classes and library provision, through community service programmes for disabled and older people and environmental care activities to participation in community visioning and governance programmes

The North American approach of placing responsibility for education policy in the hands of locally elected schools boards can help to integrate school life into that of the wider community, as well as providing a productive path for local people into political activity. Elsewhere, where education is a responsibility of central government, community involvement may be through parent teacher associations or parents and citizens committees. Though having fewer formal powers, they may take many individually small decisions on the conduct of school life and provision of new infrastructure for sports equipment or information technology which cumulatively come to shape the quality and style of school life. Educational planners may choose to ignore these organisations as irrelevant to the hard business of curriculum development and site acquisition, but they will benefit from integrating them as grassroots partners in the process of total quality management and consistent system improvement. Religious and charitable foundations will have their own systems of school administration, and may require guidelines to ensure parent, pupil and teacher participation as in the publicly provided system. A community which participates in directing and enlivening its own learning systems is taking command of new knowledge and engaging with some of its most talented members.

CONCLUSION: LINKS OF LEARNING WITH OTHER ACTIVITIES

Learning and education provide the driving forces for beneficial change in contemporary society. Not only do they produce the cognitive development to power new inventions that can create economic well-being and manage mounting changes and challenges in the social and physical environments, but they also expand human sympathies to forestall conflicts caused by misunderstanding, fear of the unknown and unthinking anger at the shock of the new. Their links to the population, economic, shelter and health maintenance systems of settlements and society rest on their unrivalled capacities to produce the ideas and social skills needed to support community life. Education itself receives essential contributions of access and information from the transport and communication systems, and therefore needs to have a say in their organisation, development and planning.

However, because education is such an important system with such large public budgets and the status of one of society's highest merit goods, there is often a tendency for its planning to be undertaken in a rather independent way. Demographers employed by education departments cooperate with educational architects and site planners to acquire the necessary sites well in advance of new suburban developments. Integration of educational facilities with community development of the sort identified in Table 9.4 is therefore only patchily achieved at present. There is thus great scope for better integration of educational impetus, energy and facilities within community planning.

The planning and delivery of health services

INTRODUCTION

Although personal wealth and providence can bestow on favoured individuals the privileges of good food, clean water and appropriate medical treatment, they cannot banish the spectre of epidemics of diseases which may endanger all members of the community. Public health programmes are needed to provide inclusive protection against these recurrent scourges, as they are in other measures to safeguard overall vitality, especially those affecting communal activities of work, social life and recreation. In planning such programmes, desired levels of population health and vitality can be related to proposed processes of health reporting, disease prevention, caring, treatment, self-medication, disaster response and scientific investment and research. Subsystems can be identified, including such key aspects as child delivery and care, cardiac treatment, physiotherapy, radiology, reproductive health and specialist attention to such different limbs and organs as knees, ankles, ear, nose and throat, dentition and the brain. The relations and links between these elements are indicated in Figure 9.3. Understanding external influences, especially the powerful impacts exerted on health by housing, income, education and communications, can be assisted by use of social statistics of changing

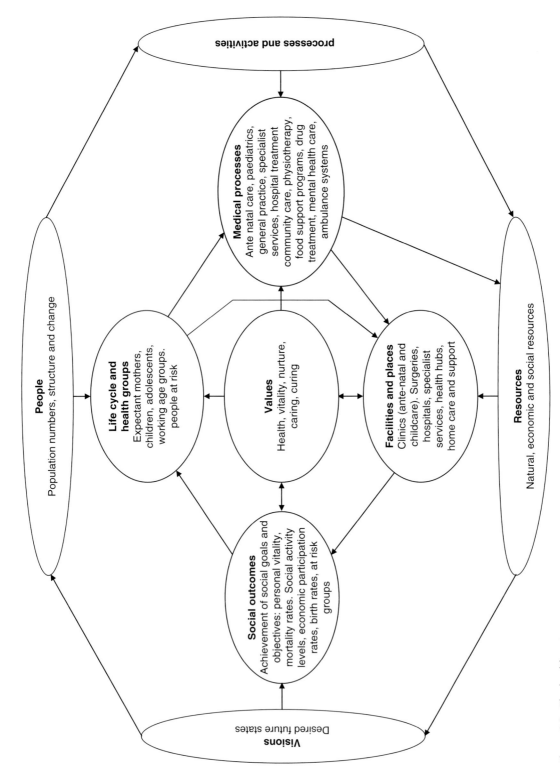

Figure 9.3 The health system.

population totals and components, which provide invaluable information, including fertility and mortality rates and vitality levels.

GLOBAL TRENDS

Health maintenance has been an important concern throughout human history. At times of major social change and disruption like the thirteenth and fourteenth centuries in Europe and Asia, epidemics and famines have threatened to reduce human populations to dangerously low levels. At others, such as the twentieth century, improved health and sanitation practices have contributed to dramatic population increases. Table 9.5 summarises a number of the most important and intrusive problems that affect health provision throughout the contemporary world, indicating that many of them have global causes, such as climate change and desiccation, but require locally planned and applied solutions such as water supply and recycling and introduction of new crops. However, the

most remarkable implication of the table is the high level of linkage with other systems: clean water depends on infrastructure, settlement planning and governance; food supply depends on governance, community development and agriculture; limitation of pollution depends on natural environment, work and governance; control of epidemics depends on national and international governance; climate change response depends on natural environment and governance; management of ageing populations depends on community development, social organisation and local governance; and equal access and justice depend, again, on governance. Health planners clearly need good awareness and links with the governance system at all levels from the local and regional to the national and international.

PRACTICAL METHODS AND TECHNIQUES

Health planning, like educational planning, requires mixed scanning between its universal scope as an

Table 9.5 Global health trends: challenges and responses

Current challenge	Potential responses
Clean water supply Desiccation, water shortage and pollution	Increased supply through recycling, desalination, new dams to increase storage capacity, reduced demand through demand management; pollution control through sanitation systems and effluent control
Adequate available food Increased famine and starvation	Negotiative and incentive-based processes to build civil peace; community development programmes involving cooperation between local and international non-government organisations; water-retention and irrigation schemes, improved agricultural practices; women's education and support programmes; voluntary spread of birth control practices
Pollution control Increasing pollution of air, water, land and sea causing breathing, skin, digestive, lymphatic, liver and other disorders	Emissions monitoring and control through regulation, taxation and trading; technological innovation and social initiatives to reduce waste generation and discharge
Management of epidemics Epidemics and pandemics	International cooperation through World Health Organization (WHO) and similar bodies such as Médecins Sans Frontières (and international organisations such as the European Union, the North American Free Trade Agreement and the Association of Southeast Asian Nations); coordinated programmes by regional and national community health networks
Climate change response Increasing prevalence of natural disasters of floods, storms and droughts	Improved forecasting and monitoring methods; emergency planning and relief programmes; coordinated long-term adjustment measures, including cooperation in evacuation and resettlement programmes
Ageing populations Increased life expectancy	Healthy lifestyles programmes to reduce lifestyle ailments such as obesity, diabetes and substance abuse and addiction; incentive and deterrent taxation; active transport; community health activities; care for the elderly; techno medicine (e.g. eye lens implants, organ donation and transplant and micro and nano surgery)
Equal access and rights Social inequities (unequal access to medical support; physical, sexual and economic exploitation; differential life expectancy and chances)	National health systems: Britain's NHS, Medicare systems in Canada and Australia Global guarantees for rights of low-cost production and distribution of generic drugs for mass diseases such as malaria, stomach ulcers, AIDS, tuberculosis cholera etc.

aspect of all human life (indicated in Tables 9.5 and 9.6) and the necessarily targeted applications of specific programmes and facilities. It is therefore logical to focus on the set of key questions and objectives identified early in the planning process in the way recommended in Chapter 6, rather than attempt comprehensive review of all available data. The analogy of a series of small magnets inserted into a field of iron filings can help to indicate this process of selecting data, with the magnets being the initial planning objectives while the iron filings are the items of information available from the rich array of demographic and scientific information available at all scales, from the local to the international. This invaluable secondary research material can also be amplified by primary research carried out in cooperation with local health providers and practitioners, universities, medical research institutes and government depart-

ments, in the form of statistics and trends of the reporting of symptoms and treatment of ailments. In conducting such research, health planners will benefit from certain simple guidelines:

- Focus information collection and analyses on issues relevant to the initial objectives identified for the health system and contribute this to the wider community planning process.
- Express all statistics in percentage terms to assist comparisons over time and between localities and scales.
- Include figures and percentages relating to a larger unit of reporting to that which is the main focus of the study, to illuminate the significance of local figures.
- Develop time series comparisons to identify trends and shape tentative projections.

Table 9.6   Health provisions

Facility	Scale	Links	Size and Governance
Pharmacy and non-prescription medications	Neighbourhood (500–1000 people)	Indoor/outdoor play space Corner shops Fitness circuits	Pharmacist plus 2–3 staff. Government pharmacy and Fair Trading regulations
Medical centre–primary health care (doctors, nurse practitioners, physiotherapist, ante- and post natal clinic, blood testing and x ray facilities)	Locality (4000–6000 people)	Public transport access (bus stop and community transport drop off) Local park recreation area/fitness circuit gym/fitness centre Primary school, community hall/church/mosque etc.	Medical staff and primary health care facilities Reviewed and regulated by regional health board or 'Medicare Local'
District health clinic Secondary level health care Day care centre Community outreach facilities Multipurpose service hub in rural areas	District (10 000–15 000 people)	Public transport interchange, active transport network focus District shopping centre Sheltered accommodation/retirement village Secondary school	1000 m² of grouped health facilities District health forum Planning, review and regulation by regional health board or 'Medicare Local'
Town/suburb public and private health insurance administrations, home support system, separate but related drug and alcohol treatment	Town/city suburb (40–100 000 people)	Vocational and educational training health courses for allied health Business centre Public transport focus District suburban community service centre (local government services)	1000m² of linked administrative offices Link to local government and regional health board or 'Medicare Local'
Regional/city hospital Tertiary health care multiservice agency with specialist surgical and treatment facilities and referral systems	Urban region /city (250 000–500 000 people)	Public and active transport network hub Regional university campus City/regional council main administrative centre	200- to 500-bed hospital of 4000–10 000m² floor space Regional health board or 'Medicare Local' (representatives of medical service users, practitioners and government departments)
Major metropolitan medical research institute	Regional and national scale catchments of 2–10 million people	National scale medical research institute and university State/provincial government, business and cultural centre Focus of national and international transport networks of land, air and sea	100+ health researchers; 40 000–100 000 students University and Institute Councils involving government, industry, professions, staff and student representatives

- Research and incorporate standards of accepted leading practice or widely acknowledged adequacy when discussing levels of service provision.

By adopting these simple approaches, health planners will both ensure the relevance of their work to key problems in health and increase mutual understanding, compatibility and collaboration with those planning other systems such as education, governance and settlements. By contributing to banks of well-targeted data and indicators, these methods should assist policy formulation and monitoring both in health planning and in the health-related aspects of the overall community plan.

LINKS TO OTHER SYSTEMS

There are strong linkages that need to be recognised between health and other community activities. Healthy children have more energy to learn, and well-educated societies, particularly those with high levels of female literacy, are better at both preventing and curing disease than those afflicted by superstition and ignorance. Environmental quality and resources exert continuous impacts, too, on community health, and healthy communities generate the kind of active awareness that is an important safeguard for environmental quality. Relations with work are close and influential, shaping the size and vigour of the workforce, and in turn influencing public health through workplace conditions, pollution and emission practices and environmental consequences of products and energy sources such as hydrocarbons, asbestos and radioactive waste. Other impacts include those exerted by culture, which affects health practices, and community development, which can transform people's sense of control over the factors affecting their families' health. Health considerations are also important in decisions about housing quality, form, density and location: the UN-sponsored Healthy Cities programme of the 1990s and 2000s highlighted the need for health standards and indicators to be a basic concern in town-planning decisions. Reciprocal influences of shelter and settlement on health planning include the impacts of the scale and grain of settlements on location of public health facilities and the possibilities for co-location of community facilities in neighbourhood and district hubs. In the same way, access is an important factor in health planning. Medical facilities both rely on good public transport and may be important contributors to the demand and supply aspects of community and public transport.

Health planners therefore need access to:

- demographic information and skills of analysis and projection;
- exchange of information on policy aims and instruments with education, housing, transport, industry, culture, environmental resources and governance systems and practitioners;
- awareness of issues of urban and regional planning and capacity and opportunities to participate in setting planning objectives at local, urban and regional scales;
- an informed interest in spatial and social aspects of option development;
- well-developed skills of public engagement and consultation;
- capacities to balance and integrate issues of professional expertise and public preference and concern in health planning.

HEALTH PROVISIONS

Health is regarded as a merit good in most societies, and figures prominently in their annual budgets. The location and scale of facilities have been much influenced by transport technology and scientific progress. The scale of hospitals in Western societies increased steadily throughout the nineteenth century, from small hospices caring for a few dozen patients to the large and highly specialised hospitals of the mid-twentieth century. Problems of diseconomies of scale, perceptions of patient anonymity and endemic infection such as *Staphylococcus aureus* (sometimes called 'golden staph'), legionnaire's disease and sepsis have led to a review of this policy of 'bigger is better', and careful thought is now being given to the most appropriate levels for the provision of different services, in an approach that has many similarities with the administrative principle of 'subsidiarity', by which each activity is allowed to subside to the lowest level at which it can be effectively performed.

Conclusion: the many facets of community

This chapter has outlined the significant advantages for each activity and for the wider community when activities such as work, learning and health are planned and provided within the context of overall community life, making use of values and objectives-based methods that can promote collaboration. Many other activities require similar approaches, including play and open space use, transport and access, and community life and culture, as well as the homes and communities which were the subject of the preceding chapter. All require community planning because of their powerful influences on each other and on the overall life of their communities. Education and health are matters of universal concern: education develops the skills on which the whole society will have to rely for its future prosperity. Health is common to everybody as a universal good because epidemics are no respecters of people. In activities such as public transport, economies of scale can result from community provision, while others, like water supply, communication networks, policing and defence, are natural monopolies unsuitable for private ownership.

Shared use of common locations has benefits which go beyond urbanisation and localisation economies. There are great benefits in co-location of facilities where hubs can offer people not only convenience and access but also the experience of intensity, contrast, and a sense of citizenship, but also the safety that comes from continual use throughout all hours of the day and deep into the night. The opportunity to shop, meet friends, pick up a prescription, visit a gallery or museum, go to a cinema and wait for one's child to come out of school all in one place requires careful collaboration and planning. This physical quality of shared spaces is a function more of well-planned mixed uses than of abstract design principles. Methods which build on this multifaceted approach to community planning to create vivid and engaging places at a variety of scales and in different parts of cities and districts are the subject of the next chapter.

Endnotes

i Individualistic values, proclaiming the supremacy of 'the selfish gene', are also being espoused with increasing confidence by evolutionary geneticists such as Richard Dawkins (1975, 2006) who challenge the very existence of such collective values as being inherently illogical and misleading. For a through philosophical review of this important matter, see Mary Midgley's *Beast and Man: The roots of human nature* (1979).

ii This may take one of two forms: extensive social provisions as in the 'monsoon cultures' of East Asia or State action to ensure equal life chances as in the 'longboat cultures' of Europe's Nordic nations. Either way, extensive state participation or intervention will be required in the provision of community services (Wilkinson & Pickett, 2009).

iii Mill argued that those activities which were primarily self-affecting, such as the profession of personal faith,

practice of sexual morality, disbursement of personal wealth and income and rights of public assembly, should be left to the choice of the individual and not subjected to attempts at regulation by governments. He also noted that these were precisely the activities for which the extensive legislation of the time in England sought to prescribe people's behaviour, imposing legal penalties and exclusions on dissidents and non-conformists. On the other hand, activities which impinged heavily on the rights and prospects of others in society, such as conditions of health and safety in workplaces, housing provisions, building standards and rent levels, educational opportunities and environmental impacts and conservation of physical and social heritage, should all be subject to strong and continuous public control and regulation (though he again observed that these were precisely the matters in which ordinary English working people were left unprotected by legislation or religious sanctions). As a result, cholera was rife, overcrowding of housing resulted in whole generations of working people in industrial and port cities, like Liverpool and Manchester, being forced to live in conditions with up to six people sharing a room in the basement dwellings and work in factories or mines that shortened life expectancy and damaged health. Mill's theories enunciated in *Utilitarianism* (1983) are widely recognised as laying the basis for the modern welfare state, with its commitment to mixed economies, progressive taxation, selective public investment and encouragement of private initiative, community activity and public regulation of social outcomes.

Mill also recognised that all actions, however self- or other-regarding they may be, must inevitably exert impacts on the individual and the community. He examined the interplay of this mixing of public and private issues in the field of education, which is fundamentally important to the success and evolution of society. On the one hand, the education of one's children, with direct implications for their moral development, faith and personality, is a field where parental control is justified. On the other hand, the future prosperity, safety and conviviality of society will be strongly influenced and shaped by the quality of the intellectual, technical and moral education which they receive. Society as a whole, therefore, has an interest in ensuring that this content meets prescribed minimum standards.

Mill's resolved this dilemma in a way which is still relevant today. Parents, teachers and religious groups should be free to plan, develop and manage schools to reflect their religious and social values, as long as they remain compatible with principles of universal tolerance and justice. The state, on the other hand, should provide free and compulsory education for all those not attending their own sectarian schools and should inspect all schools, regardless of their doctrinal allegiance, to ensure that they achieve acceptable standards of health, safety and educational content. This combination of the roles of private, community and societal actors has played a significant part in the remarkable educational advances of the last one and half centuries. Where national and sectarian or minority group interests have appeared to conflict, Fabian principles of voluntarism have been successfully introduced to resolve new difficulties. Divisions in the Australian Labor Party in the 1950s, for instance between Catholic supporters and those they suspected of being Marxist sympathisers, were effectively resolved by adoption of a policy of generous government subsidies for religious schools, provided that they met required levels of teaching curriculum and quality.

It is significant that such mixed economy prescriptions have outlasted the dramatic totalitarian political and economic experiments of the twentieth century (Popper, 1998). This position lends strong support to the contractarian idea of bills of rights, to guarantee basic human freedoms from interference by repressive elites or majorities. The Universal Declaration of Human Rights, for instance, states in Article 18:

> Everyone has the right to freedom of thought, conscience and religion; this right includes freedom to change religion and belief; and freedom, either alone or in a community, with others and in public or private, to manifest this religion or belief in teaching, practice, worship and observance.

Article 19 continues:

> Everyone has a right to freedom of opinion and expression; this right includes freedom to hold opinions without interference and to seek, receive and impart information and ideas through any media, regardless of frontiers.

iv This cautious and constructive approach of weighing consequences against values and principles has many helpful applications in the practice of community planning, encouraging participants or disputants to join in discussion and problem-solving. Although not intended or suitable for use as a formula, it does offer a method to allocate appropriate roles and a vocabulary for common planning methods between different parties.

v Growing up in an old mining area at the end of the nineteenth century, with a father who had worked underground from the age of ten and a genteel but embittered mother who had been a private school teacher and was frustrated by her role as a miner's wife, the writer D. H. Lawrence was well aware of the social consequences of the division of labour (Callow, 1997). As a child, he observed the men's weekly escapes into Friday night drunkenness and the ritualised and repressive labours of the school classroom. His many later journeys round the world, exploring culture, place and time suggested other, less alienated forms of labour, where work could express personality and provide a focus for community life and learning, instead of being a form of drudgery.

vi A further lesson of these naturally occurring processes is that community planning should be more concerned with facilitating than rule making, and that planners need to establish and maintain community dialogues that can identify and promote growth buds in the economy and community rather than attempting to subject proposed development to tests of conformity with standardised templates of segregation.

vii These will include, for instance, the competing influences of productivity and creativity, social justice and personal freedom, individual consumption and environmental sustainability, and economic competition and personal autonomy. Such debates can drive the public discussion on which community planning must depend for its validity and vitality.

viii If, as suggested in Chapter 3, we are now immersed in a period of very rapid physical and intellectual change, punctuating the mid-twentieth century plateau of equilibrium, it is no surprise that knowledge is multiplying in a crescendo of activity; understanding of the external world is being driven far beyond the limits of our own solar system and galaxy to distant extremities of space and time. At the same time, our understanding of matter is intensifying to identify ever-more-minuscule particles, giving us the power to initiate nuclear chain reactions that can both create vast supplies of energy and devastate the material and living worlds. Learning seems to be endowing us as a species with the double-edged capacity for constantly increasing power over our environment.

ix Disputes over equal rights to education between the sexes divide Islamic societies. Some Hindu groups react against equal educational opportunities for different castes. Elsewhere, Australia has recently experienced the so-called History Wars with former Prime Minister John Howard leading a campaign to ban a 'Black Armband' view of history which would acknowledge past injustices against the country's indigenous people, including mass murders, rapes and removal of children from their parents. Similar conflicts exist between those who proclaim and those who deny the truth of the Holocaust of six million Jews in the mid-twentieth century across Nazi-controlled Europe, despite the existence of massive photographic and documentary evidence of these events.

References

Callow, P. (1997) *Son and Lover: The young D. H. Lawrence.* London, Allison & Busby.

Cooke, P., Morgan, K. (1998) *The Associational Economy: Firms, regions and innovation.* Oxford, Oxford University Press.

Dawkins, R. (1975) *The Selfish Gene.* Oxford, Oxford University Press.

Dawkins, R. (2006) *The God Delusion.* London, Bantam.

Dreze, J., Loh, J. (1995) Literacy in India and China. *Economic and Political Weekly* **30**(45).

Etzioni, A. (1973) Mixed scanning: A third approach. In: A. Faludi (ed.), *A Reader in Planning Theory.* Oxford, Pergamon Press.

Florida, R. (2005) *Cities and the Creative Class*. New York, Routledge.

Foucault, M. (1980) Truth and power. In: P. Rabinow (ed.), *The Foucault Reader*. London, Penguin.

Hardin, G. (2008) The tragedy of the commons. In: R. Dawkins (ed.), *The Oxford Book of Modern Science Writing*. Oxford, Oxford University Press.

Hayek, F. (1944) *The Road to Serfdom*. London, Routledge & Kegan Paul.

Healey, P. (2007) *Urban Complexity and Spatial Strategies: Towards a relational planning for our times*. London, Routledge.

Jacobs, J. (1992) *Systems of Survival*. London, Hodder & Stoughton.

Kropotkin, P. (1939) *Mutual Aid*. London, Penguin.

Landrus, M. (2006) *The Treasures of Leonardo da Vinci*. London, Carlton.

Lawrence, D. (1994) *Collected Poems of D. H. Lawrence*. London, Penguin.

Lowry, I. (1964) *A Model of Metropolis*. Santa Barbara, CA, RAND Corporation.

Lyons, J. (1991) *Chomsky*. London, Fontana.

Midgley, M. (1979) *Beast and Man: The roots of human nature*. London, Methuen.

Mill, J. S. (1983) *Utilitarianism: On liberty and considerations on representative government*. London, Dent, (first published 1861).

Mumford, L. (1961) *The City in History*. New York, Harcourt, World Brace.

Osborne, D., Gaebler, T. (1992) *Reinventing Government: How the entrepreneurial spirit is transforming the public sector*. Reading, MA, Addison-Wesley.

Popper, K. (1998) *The Open Society and its Enemies: Volume 1: Plato*, 2nd edn. London, Routledge & Kegan Paul, (first published 1945).

Putnam, R. (1993) *Making Democracy Work: Civic traditions in modern Italy*. Princeton, Princeton University Press, (with Leonardi, R., Nanetti, R.).

Ridley, M. (1996) *The Origins of Virtue*. London, Penguin.

Seltzer, E. (2004) It's not an experiment: Regional planning in metro 1990 to the present. In: C. Ozawa (ed.), *The Portland Edge*. Washington, Island Press.

Sennett, R. (2008) *The Craftsman*. London, Allan Lane.

Tolstoy, L. (2002) *Anna Karenina*. New York, Penguin.

United Nations Development Program (2010) *Human Development Report, Table 13: Educational Achievements*, http://hdr.undp.org/en/, accessed 5 November 2010.

Wilkinson, R., Pickett, K. (2009) *The Spirit Level: Why more equal societies almost always do better*. London, Penguin.

Wirth, L. (1964) Urbanism as a way of life. In: L. Wirth (ed.), *Louis Wirth on Cities and Social Life: Selected papers*. Chicago, University of Chicago Press.

Yunus, M. (1998) *Socially Conscious Capitalism towards a Poverty Free World*. Public Lecture Transcript, Brisbane, Queensland University of Technology.

Zola, E. (1968) *Germinal*, (trans. H. Ellis). Gloucester, MA, P. Smith.

10 Places, Spaces and Community Design

This chapter draws together the activities of housing, work, learning and health, discussed in Chapters 8 and 9 with others, including play, access and assembly, to explore how they create the places which people actually experience. To these ends, it is organised into the following five sections:

- places and their properties;
- collective, communal and private spaces;
- the vocabulary and language of community design;
- place-making: designing to make life;
- models of settlement form.

The concluding section discusses the role of design in bringing places to life

Places and their properties

Places are what we make them. They become detailed maps of myriad sets of our aims, needs and skills, drawing together the attitudes and abilities of their occupants into perceptually solid forms. We love or resent places because they express so faithfully the values which shape our lives and the activities which occupy our days. The inescapable link between our characters and interests and the events in which we become involved means that we often come to *be* our own situations: the places, as well as the times, that we inhabit are shaped by our shared values and activities.

If we wish to improve the places where we live, we must therefore reshape the activities of the communities themselves. Creating a beautiful street picture, where there is no sanitation or regular waste disposal, will be neither possible nor productive, but an underground sewage system can transform the stagnant water bodies of a cholera-ridden slum into a vivid and vital public water play area. This happened, albeit in different ways, in both the bustees of inner Kolkata in the 1980s and the formerly dangerous and disused

docks of Salford Quays in the north-west of England in the 1990s. This story of place-making in Kolkata is told in Box 10.1 and illustrated in Plates 10.1 and 10.2.

The equally remarkable reclamation of Salford Quays to form a public water sports centre is no less important for the city of Greater Manchester, even though the scale of the achievement is, of course, less numerically significant given that the population of Greater Manchester at 2.5 million is only one-sixth that of Greater Kolkata's. For nearly a century, Salford Docks had provided a major port at the inland terminal of the Manchester Ship Canal. This was before the decline of the Lancashire textile industry and the contraction of much of the rest of the city's manufacturing sector caused its closure in 1982. Following a different path to that taken by the privatised and global policies of London's Docklands, the Salford City Council purchased the site and established a public corporation to redevelop the area for a mix of public and private purposes. The council was primarily interested in regenerating the inner area of the conurbation, and opening the notorious dock area again for public use after a hundred years of segregation and dislocation, which had made Salford a byword for urban blight.[i] In 1983, Salford City Council purchased the docks from the old Manchester Ship Canal Company and, two years later, established the Salford Quays Development company. Design and development studies continued apace with strong

Box 10.1 Place-making in inner Kolkata

Clustered around Kolkata's intensive inner city, a series of inner metropolitan residential areas stretch out at a distance of about two to four kilometres to accommodate more than three million people, or a fifth of the city's total population. These 'bustees' are defined as 'areas in excess of 700 square metres composed of huts for habitation'. They are built on often recently reclaimed land interspersed with water areas of normally five to ten hectares (accurately described as 'borrow pits'), from which the silt has been taken to raise the house sites above water level. The bustee dwellers are legal tenants having acquired their tenure at the end of a three-stage process commencing with the original landowners, who leased sizeable blocks to intermediaries and built large numbers of cheap houses in varying materials – mud bricks, wood, tin and thatch – which they then rented out to recently arrived families, often from the home state of the intermediary. As a result, these bustees tend to have a strongly clustered physical form, with a traditional cohesive village character and social structure, incorporating small shrines and holy trees.

When the Calcutta Metropolitan Development Authority (CMDA) was first formed in 1970 with World Bank backing, one of its intentions was to rehouse many of the bustee dwellers in modern accommodation. However, the selective clearance and rehousing policy had very limited success owing to a combination of expense, the impracticality of achieving sufficiently rapid land acquisition and development on the fringes, and economic dislocation of the relocated communities. In the twelve years between 1970 and 1982, a totally inadequate number of 44 707 dwellings were completed (Calcutta Metropolitan Development Authority, 1983, Table 50). Equally importantly, the policy suffered from social rejection. The bustee dwellers refused to occupy the new maisonettes, which were on the periphery of the city, had no economic base, did not reflect their social values or organisation and were very much more expensive to rent than their current accommodation. The engineers of the CMDA acknowledged that their original top-down physicalist solution had failed and they carried out surveys and discussions to discover a more relevant approach.

They discovered that the problems of the bustees were four-fold:

- First, they were subject to flooding, which made them frequently unpleasant and permanently unhealthy.
- Second, the rudimentary sanitation systems deposited human waste in the water areas, increasing health dangers and giving rise to endemic and epidemic cholera and malaria.
- Third, water supplies had to be drawn from the very sources which were contaminated by waste.
- Finally, many of the internal routes, which were simply composed of compacted silt, became impassable during the long monsoon season (Heywood, 1987).

These were factors outside the control of the local residents or their landlords. On the other hand, they felt positive about their own homes and were happy to take responsibility for them. It appeared that the original relocation policies of the CMDA had been tackling the wrong problems. Since the option of total replacement was neither feasible nor popular, the CMDA engineers decided instead to produce a series of specific solutions to tackle these problems in collaboration with local community groups. Local drainage and water supply schemes were designed to be laid on a manpower-intensive, area-by-area basis at depths of approximately two metres below newly paved paths. If the paths were wide enough to walk along, they were wide enough to swing a pick and to take a drain. This resulted in 500 kilometres of drains, mains and paved paths, as well as 51 000 communal latrines, at an average density of 1 per 25 people, providing local employment through both production and installation of pipes and sanitary ware.

Local communities felt a strong sense of communal responsibility for the maintenance and cleanliness of the communal latrines. Standpipes for the mains supply of clean water were also installed. In the period 1973–1986, nearly two million bustee residents had their living and health conditions significantly improved. Cholera was eradicated. The borrow pits emerged as popular and safe swimming, washing and amenity areas, and are no longer needed as sources of domestic water. Piped water has been installed on the basis of one standpipe for every 50–100 people. The paths have been paved with

Box 10.1   Place-making in inner Kolkata—cont'd

bricks and street lighting attached to the neighbouring dwellings. The cost of these internal improvements amounted to a total of 30 million rupees a year, the equivalent of approximately US$2 million. Ten times this (or approximately $US20 million a year) was spent on necessary improvements to urban infrastructure of sewage treatment plants and water supplies, amounting over the 13-year period to the considerable sum of nearly $US300 million. The results for the dynamic and productive inner-city economy of Kolkata suggest that this was money well spent, and there have been huge savings on the social costs of trying to construct new accommodation for the bustee dwellers, which would have proved simply impractical.

What have been the outcomes in terms of place-making? The high-density, inner-city residential areas have great vitality and preserve a strong atmosphere of sociable urban villages, with their density being relieved by the balancing effects of numerous water bodies, reflecting the changeable skies of Bengal (Plate 10.1). During festivals such as the annual Hindu Puja of September and October, which involves the celebration of water as an agent of renewal and cleansing, the large lagoons come alive with many families playing and washing in the shallows, alongside strings of gleaming white laundry. Young children dive and splash. Equally important, the preservation of these residual areas has supported their mixed economic activities. An extraordinary array of productive and culturally valuable mixed uses line the vehicular streets with shrines, different forms of transport, shops, eating houses, homes, workshops, classrooms, commercial and administrative offices and service industries (Plate 10.1), in a remarkable low technology anticipation of the kind of milieus which Richard Florida (2005) describes and advocates as the breeding ground for the creative classes in cities like San Francisco, Pittsburgh and Austin, Texas. It is important to remember that this form of place-making had its origins in community involvement and in re-prioritising public action away from the top-down policies of housing clearance towards supportive policies of mass scale service provision.

council and community participation. Queen Elizabeth opened the Lowry Creative Arts and Cultural Centre in 2000. Now the old docks are occupied by a lively water sports centre offering windsurfing, kayaking, powerboat training and dinghy sailing. During the 2001 heatwave, the water body was full of young people splashing around in the old docks, in a way very reminiscent of the use of the Kolkata Borrow Pits during the Puja Festival a dozen years earlier.

The Salford Quays project includes a large plaza and terraced areas leading to the canal with a lifting footbridge to Trafford Wharf. It is surrounded by the Imperial War Museum and the Lowry Centre, which is a high-technology business development providing serviced premises for the Digital World Society. This is a new think tank opened in 2003 to promote innovative projects in digital technologies with support from the English Arts Council and Millennium Commission, English Partnerships, Salford City Council, Trafford Park Development Corporation as well as the European Regional Development Fund, and the private sector.

The contrast between the mixed public/private, recreational-business style of the Salford Quays redevelopment and the place-making in London's old

docks, where the spectacular business developments of Docklands and Canary Wharf have been designed as a focus for the global economy, could not be more emphatic. Contrasting cultural traditions, political choices, geopolitical locations and cultural values have all combined to produce two very different examples of place-making. The similarities, on the other hand, between the place-making processes in inner Kolkata and Manchester are equally striking, and involve partnerships between governments, communities and semi-independent public agencies.

PLACE-MAKING AND ITS PRINCIPLES

However much good place-making may be driven by social, economic and technological causes, places remain very important to people as ends in themselves. In a study on social planning issues and methods conducted on behalf of the Local Government Association of Queensland (LGAQ) in the mid-1990s (Menzies, Rogan, Heywood & Smith, 1996), it was discovered through running a series of regional workshops that participants attached the highest importance to 'urban design'. The study team concluded that this was because of the direct and palpable impacts which immediate surroundings exert upon people's lives. Throughout their lives, most people display a strong attachment to the places and images of their childhood and to later locations where they experienced significant events or personal achievements. Because places provide the context for our first perceptions, which then shape the framework within which we construct understanding and meaning, radical changes to familiar places can be very threatening. A constant or common sense of place can, on the other hand, provide a positive starting point for a shared sense of community.

The messages we derive from places are initially ones which respond to our basic survival demands for food, water, security, sunlight and space. Places may thus be reassuring or threatening, promising or intimidating, attractive or repellent. In short, their perceived character results from how well they respond to our human needs and wants. These capacities underlie Jay Appleton's (1996) celebrated landscape interpretation theory of Prospect and Refuge, which classifies landscapes according to the extent to which they offer human users the stimulus of distant views or the promise of personal safety. When we look at the beauty of a natural landscape of distant mountains, winding valleys, sweeping estuaries and majestic curving shorelines, our appreciation reflects the awareness of the hundreds of millennia of adaptation and exploratory action by which humanity has come to shape that landscape by use of technologies invented to fell the forests, train the streams, plough the slopes and create the harbours. Beauty is, indeed, in the eyes of its beholders, and those eyes reflect human values. Likewise, our communities and settlements are expressions of our nature, evolving along paths whose future courses are not yet fully determined. In the oft quoted words of Winston Churchill, 'We make our cities and then our cities make us.'

Christopher Alexander (1964) points out that this cumulative causation cycle worked far better when there was time for the latest inventions of technology to be tested and bedded down within the wider social and urban context. It is no longer so practicable for settlements to evolve by 'elimination of misfit', as described in Chapter 6. Instead, we must develop self-conscious processes of design to replace the winnowing effects of time, systematically testing proposals for unintended consequences before they are adopted in practice and cause disastrous results, such as high-rise public housing and inner-city urban motorways. As Alexander's ideas have evolved over the last fifty years, his recommended methods

of spatial design have become increasingly linked to direct personal and community involvement (Alexander, 2002a, b, c, d). In the first volume of his *Nature of Order*, he argues that centralised comprehensive designs must always fail because they are too rigid to respond to the great natural diversity of life and its myriad evolving new combinations. Instead, he argues, designs at all scales should unfold from their existing internal elements interacting with the surrounding situations, which will very much include the values, goals, experiences and capacities of their intended users. This approach provides strong support for community control of the design process. He has been involved in a number of schemes in India, California, Japan, Mexico and England incorporating these methods, which often produce results of very great originality and beauty (Alexander, 2002b, c).

Although he believes that individuals and communities themselves can best choose the patterns for their own plans and environments, Alexander does not ignore the contribution of skilled and motivated designers, who are schooled and experienced to understand and apply the design language of the many universal patterns developed over the past five thousand years. The knowledge of these patterns can be applied in particular situations to meet local needs and desires in truly original ways. Such applications are best achieved when specialists work closely with communities and their voluntary representatives. In his influential and imaginative *A Pattern Language*, Alexander (Alexander, Ishikawa & Siverstein, 1977) aims to help people facing design challenges to identify the general shape of the universal patterns which are available to meet their needs and hopes. He and his collaborators identify, discuss and illustrate 253 of them, starting with 'independent regions' and concluding with 'things in your life', many representing the outcomes of *A Timeless Way of Building* (1979), which is the title of the companion volume. The four titles of the more recent series *Nature of Order* summarise the views that he has now come to hold: they are: *The Phenomenon of Life*, *The Process of Creating Life*, *A Vision of a Living World* and *The Luminous Ground*. He adopts the reasoned starting point that designed environments should aim to enhance and extend 'lifefulness', and he develops fifteen principles (Box 10.2), centring on the enhancement of life and the creation of wholeness, which are intuitively derived to achieve this end. These are demonstrated in layer upon layer of examples and aspects throughout the two thousand pages and more than one thousand illustrations composing the four volumes.[ii]

Box 10.2 Alexander's 15 properties of good design (*Source:* Alexander, C, *The Phenomenon of Life* (2002a))

1. Levels of scale.
2. Strong centres.
3. Boundaries.
4. Alternating repetition.
5. Positive space.
6. Good shape.
7. Local symmetries.
8. Deep interlock and ambiguity.
9. Contrast.
10. Gradients.
11. Roughness.
12. Echoes.
13. The void.
14. Simplicity and inner calm.
15. Not separateness.

1. **Levels of scale:** This principle promotes the relay of patterns and provisions from one scale of community or space to another to encourage coherent, equitable and accessible distribution of space and resources.

2. **Strong centres:** This principle projects the structural qualities of matter, as fields of interacting centres, each composed of its own sub-centres, onto the analysis and design of community life and spaces, thus emphasising their relational qualities.

3. **Boundaries:** This principle helps in determining the extent, scope and relations of different centres to their boundary zones in the organisation of community life and space.

4. **Alternating repetition:** This principle recognises the capacity of rhythm, pulse and repetition as equitable ways to manage scale and diversity.

5. **Positive space:** This principle encourages design that respects and values the qualities of existing spaces and the roles of communities in their evolution and development.

6. **Good shape:** This principle applies Alexander's belief that people have evolved to possess a natural appreciation of good shape, expressed in works of art and craft which can form a basis for collaborative design.

7. **Local symmetries:** Pattern, diversity and order are supported by this principle, which also promotes reciprocity and equity.

8. **Deep interlock and ambiguity:** This principle supports interconnectedness and open-endedness as attributes of successful places and communities.

9. **Contrast:** Diversity, dialectic and communication of healthy community life are promoted by this principle.

10. **Gradients:** This principle recognises and supports the transitions which favour variation and the coexistence of different activities and levels of intensity.

11. **Roughness:** This principle celebrates the open-endedness and variability of life, making spaces for growth buds of future development, which transcend current practice.

12. **Echoes:** This principle promotes the replication of past successes, the preservation of living heritage and repetition of unifying characteristics throughout communities.

13. **The void:** Settling at the centre of social and physical spaces, this principle creates space for reflection, problem-solving and innovation, and is akin to the architectural concept of 'loose fit'.

14. **Simplicity and inner calm:** This principle promotes the reflection and meditation required for personal fulfilment and balanced community life.

15. **Not separateness:** Living design should create inclusive spaces that will foster and link the many different activities required for fulfilling lives for fully rounded people and communities.

Later in this chapter, we shall explore the valuable ideas and methods offered by other design theorists, including Kevin Lynch, Randy Hester, the Responsive Environment theorists of Oxford Brookes University, including Bentley, Alcock and Murrain, and from the United States the New Urbanists, all of whom have much to offer in the field of community design. However, Alexander's combination of locally grounded objectives, universal methods and robust pattern language provides a uniquely open-minded and creative perspective for people engaged in community planning. It combines psychological, physical and aesthetic insights that can make community collaboration a process of discovery as well as one of mutual appreciation. A particular merit of his approach is its capacity to apply equally to each of the domains of public, private and community space and to draw them together to support integrated community life. Nevertheless, each of these elements tends to be produced by different sequences, involving different stakeholders and at different times. The following section explores the nature and design options that are involved in each of these domains.

Communal and collective spaces and places

Places are both the physical stages where we enact our daily lives and the gathering grounds for the structures which give form to our values and activities. Space is itself, therefore, a latent dimension waiting to be given purpose and character by our intentions and activities and will differ in meaning between the ages, experiences and intentions of its users. The categorisation being used here into communal and collective places, illustrated in Figure 10.1, reflects the focus of this book on community planning. It goes without saying that another book on physics, aesthetics or psychology would adopt different standpoints and

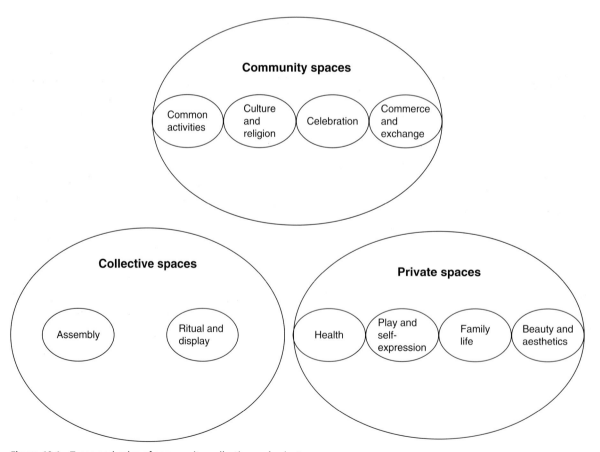

Figure 10.1   Types and roles of community, collective and private spaces.

Plate 2.1 People bathing at Brisbane's Southbank.
Source: photo by author.

Plate 5.1 An image of prosperity: David Hockney's *The Road across the Wolds*, 1997. *Source:* © David Hockney. Courtesy of Steve Oliver.

Plate 6.1 Emily Kngwarreye's *Earth's Creation*, painted at Utopia, Alice Springs in 1994. © Emily Kame Kngwarreye/Licensed by Viscopy, 2010.

Alex O'Reilly writes of Emily's *Earth's Creation*: 'This painting to me has a strong energy with elements of centres, traces of space and passages of movement . . . at a deep level, it implies that community and community planning have many different perspectives, ultimately with changing shapes that unite in art both collectives and individuals.'

Plate 6.2 David Hockney's *The Diver*, painted in California in 1978. © David Hockney/Tyler Graphics Ltd.

Plate 8.1 Brisbane Housing Company: Barbara and George, residents of Earnshaw Haven, single-storey, medium-density affordable rental dwellings, enjoying small back garden space. *Source:* Reproduced by permission of the Brisbane Housing Company.

Plate 8.2 Brisbane Housing Company, Hartopp Street: apartment block, high-density medium-rise affordable rental dwellings, communal landscaped interior garden space. *Source:* Reproduced by permission of the Brisbane Housing Company.

Plate 8.3 Brisbane Housing Company, Musk Avenue, Kelvin Grove: 12-storey, affordable rental apartment block, interior of one-bedroom apartment, with a view towards the city centre. *Source:* Reproduced by permission of the Brisbane Housing Company.

Plate 10.1 Kolkata water space at Puja Festival after installation of Metropolitan sewage system. *Source:* Photo by author.

Plate 10.2 Kolkata, inner-city street scene awash with clean water for Puja Festival *Source:* Photo by author.

Plate 10.3 Tolga village enhancement: new street signage and historic fig tree. *Source:* Reproduced by permission of John Mongard Landscape Architects to whom warm appreciation is expressed.

Box 10.3   Definitions of communal, collective and private spaces

- **Communal spaces** are places where people regularly meet for purposes of exchange, spectacle, recreation, discussion and access to essential common provisions such as water, food and transport.
- **Collective spaces** are places where large numbers of people may be gathered for the purpose of collective ceremony, cultural and ritual performance and acts of collective allegiance, tending towards periodic and high-intensity activities.
- **Private spaces** are places owned and occupied by individuals and families from which others may be excluded, and where personal values may be expressed in activities and forms of people's own choosing.

classifications. Each would have relevance for the other, but their interests and categories would be different. Community planning is concerned with communal spaces because they accommodate community life; and with collective spaces because they combine cultural symbolism with means of physical control where great numbers of people can be assembled. Private spaces are also important because of their role in shaping the physical and psychological health and family life of the individuals who compose communities, but they are not the focus of this book, and are not considered in equal detail. These interests give rise to the definitions listed in Box 10.3.

Figure 10.2   The Great Bath at Mohenjo-daro.
Source: International Council of Monuments and Sites.

COMMUNITY SPACES

The story of civilisation over the last five thousand years has been written most vividly and indelibly in its communal and collective spaces. Communal spaces have been characterised by the major community themes, evident from the earliest times, of cultural expression, celebration and commerce. They express shared needs and responsibilities, responding to and promoting sociability, and forming places where people can gather, pause, talk, meet, barter, reminisce and negotiate. In these ways, they promote personal relationships and public life. One of the earliest records of such a space is the Great Bath of Mohenjo-daro in the Indus Valley, dating back almost five thousand years. The city is particularly interesting in the way public and private spaces are related and linked to the necessities of life such as water supply and craft production. This civilisation owed its existence to elaborate irrigation schemes which controlled the waters of the Indus and its tributaries to support wheat farming and specialised city life, very much as the Egyptian civilisation was doing two thousand miles to the west in the Nile Valley. However, whereas Akhenaten's

pleasure gardens of Maru-Aten used the Nile waters to create a pharaonic playground (Desroches-Noblecourt, 1976), the 'Great Bath' (Figure 10.2), which was one of the centre pieces of Mohenjo-daro, and the earliest public water tank in the ancient world, was clearly intended for communal public use[iii] (International Council of Monuments and Sites, 1980). Close by on the stupa are other functional communal spaces, designated by the excavation teams as the Great Granary, the Great College and the Pillared Hall. This was a large and highly organised city with an estimated maximum population of around 35 000 people and an area of no less those 240 hectares. The civilisation is thought to have lasted for over a thousand years before its final disappearance around 3800 years ago.[iv]

Similar communal spaces characterise the classical world of the Eastern Mediterranean, Ancient Greek amphitheatres such as those in Delphi, Delos and Athens. These theatres were designed and used to stage rituals and plays exploring themes of major human concern including war, revenge, loyalty, incest, destiny and terror, as well as airing current controversies and political debates, and are discussed in more detail in the following section dealing with celebratory spaces. The amphitheatre, expressing the equality of the circle, with its equidistance of all points on the perimeter to the central focus, and its public performances, must have contributed strongly to the communal life and resilience of the constantly warring, waxing and waning Greek city states.

Squared forms, more characteristic of the highly regulated character of the Roman Empire, incorporate other aspects of organised community, including imposed order, ease of land allocation and rapid construction of services in new settlements. Perhaps coincidentally, grid development also results in the replication of numerous pathways, thus maximising movement and meeting at each of the many intersections where streets cross and people can meet to discuss the issues of the day, climaxing in the central forum or city square which often forms the commercial and social focus of the whole city. In the Middle Ages, after the collapse of the Roman Empire, these forums and squares became the sites for the great markets which provided one of the most important activities of the communal life of the emerging towns and city states. Religious life, too, echoed the clarity and organisation of the square in the form of the cloister, which emerged in the early years of Christianity to provide reflective and secure communal space where members of religious orders could gather to exercise their minds and bodies.

Time and again, abbeys and cathedrals reproduced these forms to combine the individual life of the spirit with that of the community. Lewis Mumford (1961) suggests that the communal space of the cloister is also reflected in the development of the university college quadrangles of Bologna, Oxford and Cambridge, and many later universities. It is also echoed in the central squares and marketplaces of the re-emerging medieval towns, like Perugia and Padua, as they matured to become the models for the great Renaissance cities with their central spaces such as the Piazza San Marco in Venice, and the Piazza dei Signori in Florence. In Siena, the city field (the *campo*) evolved to provide the city with the wonderful combination of circle and square which is so celebrated and well used today, vividly illustrating the importance of Alexander's principle of 'the void' as a space for people to gather and ideas to be exchanged. In urban design, the square (or *piazza*, *place* or *platz*) continue to be the symbol and space for sociability and exchange. They are the places

such as London's Trafalgar Square, New York's Times Square, or Milan's Piazza del Duomo, where the city celebrates its communal activities, be they cultural, festive or commercial, as discussed in the following sections.

CULTURAL SPACES

These reflect shared values. The dramatic and awe-inspiring monuments of Stonehenge (Figure 10.3), Avebury and the Alignments at Carnac in Brittany provide early instances of religious values from the Neolithic era of more than five thousand years ago, which are believed to celebrate the life-giving powers of the sun and its annual progression, driving the waxing and waning of the seasons, so crucial to agricultural civilisations.

Both the mystical and the managed aspects of religion are expressed in the long tradition of religious and sacred places. Bernard Campbell (1985) speculates that the extensive galleries of the Lascaux caves of the Acheulian culture of around 30 000 years ago may have been places where people assembled for religious and fertility rites and hunting rituals. The temples to the Sun God in Akhenaten were certainly dedicated to religious purposes (Desroches-Noblecourt, 1976), as were the great concourses of Aztec and Mayan culture in the Americas. The Renaissance cathedral squares in Europe became some of the most memorable and best-loved urban spaces of all with the wonderful eye-shaped ellipse of St Peter's Square in Rome, and in Venice the almost perfectly balanced interplay between the vast trapezoid and arcaded perimeter of the Piazza

Figure 10.3 Stonehenge. *Source:* Reproduced under the terms of Creative Commons licensing.

San Marco, and the façade of St Mark's Cathedral, accentuated by the slim symbol of the campanile, which forms a powerful but not overpowering feature. No less faithfully, the Varanasi waterfront with its merging of the elements of water and land, river and city, temples and people expresses and sustains the sense of mystery and merging of Hindu culture. A few hundred kilometres to the north-east, the spaces of Swayambhunath above Kathmandu bring together the elements of religion, learning, community, pilgrimage and assembly in the thousand-year-old Buddhist and Hindu hilltop temples, meeting places, monastery and library, creating a place where everybody feels at home (Figure 10.4). Further west, the spectacular combination of the Great Square in Mecca and the mystical dominance of the central Kaaba draws millions of pilgrims every year to celebrate the Prophet Mohammed's birthday, in a vivid demonstration of the significance that the spirit and form of place hold in people's lives.

New Zealand's marae represent a more localised example of the importance of cultural planning and spaces in contemporary societies. Marae are places where Maori culture is celebrated, where community and family occasions such as weddings and birthdays can be held, and where important ceremonies can be performed, not only welcoming visitors or saying farewell to the dead but also celebrating the continuing cultural values necessary to maintain personal pride and mutual support. Often the marae is the open space in front of the iwi, or tribal meeting house. Because it has both cultural and legal status, it cannot be bought or sold, and is protected by law[v] (Marae Community Operating System, 2010). This model could also be applied to preserve and create cultural space in many other societies and settlements.

Cultural spaces do not have to adopt massive scale to be effective. In Kevin Lynch's comparative study of people's urban imagery, the space in front of Jersey City's Medical Center occupied by a small landscape garden plot emerged as a more important identifying characteristic than the great bulk and skyline silhouette of the building that towered behind it (Lynch, 1960). In a similar way, the little statue of Eros in London's Piccadilly Circus has become a major symbol of London life. The urban farms discussed in Chapter 1, which are spreading throughout cities in all parts of the world, also perform important roles as cultural spaces that remind their workers and visitors of the importance of natural forces in human life.

'Celebratory space' has its own, rather different, qualities, more explicitly designed to influence the sensations which visitors take away from the space. The whole resplendent assemblage of temples and statues of Athens' Acropolis (Figure 10.5), celebrating the city's gods and the artistry and creativity of its people, continues to provide the city with a sense of focus in time and space. The more contemplative spirit of Moorish meditation, celebrating the arrival of desert Berbers in the well-watered plains of Andalusia, is expressed in the calm and beautifully proportioned spaces of Granada's Alhambra, where central pools reflect the building and gardens and fountains provide a constant reminder of the presence of the life-giving element of water (Figures 10.6 and 10.7). In a similar way, the perfect clarity of the Taj Mahal commemorates the love of the Mogul Shah Jahan for his queen, lost in childbirth, in forms that transcend political and religious affiliation. Modern spaces may also touch the spirit of those who observe and pass through them. The Berlin Holocaust Museum and the spaces which it defines constitute one such example, emphasising the restorative forces of the natural vegetation, which draw back into the life of the city the jagged edges of a structure that both crumples space and cuts into its fabric like a knife (Figure 10.8). New York's monument to the Twin Towers of the New York Trade Center,

Figure 10.4 Swayambhunath Temple and forecourt, Kathmandu. *Source:* Reproduced under the terms of Creative Commons licensing.

Figure 10.5 Acropolis of Athens. *Source:* Reproduced under the terms of Creative Commons licensing.

Figure 10.6 Timeless elements in community design: rhythm and alternating repetition in Granada's twelfth-century Alhambra Palace. *Source:* Image courtesy of Catherine Oakley.

Figure 10.7 Court of the Lions, Alhambra Palace. *Source:* Image courtesy of Catherine Oakley.

destroyed by the air attack in 2001, also relies on the shade and symbolism of natural materials and urban forestry to proclaim resilience. The works of Agnes Denes in her Environmental Art also take this form of symbolic expression of natural forces, for example a wheat field reclaiming the blank expanses of a cleared site surrounded by block-like tall buildings in New York City (Denes, 2003).

COMMERCIAL SPACE

The progressive spirit of contemporary commercialism is expressed in spaces which pulse with variety, con-trast and communication, whether they are the night-time galaxy of light to be found in New York's Times Square or Bangkok's night markets, or the swirling vitality of London's Leicester Square and Piccadilly Circus. The commercial roles of community spaces date back at least 2500 years to the *stoa* surrounding Athens' Agora, where traders erected their stalls. It

Figure 10.8 The Jewish Memorial Museum and associated spaces in Berlin. *Source:* Reproduced under the terms of Creative Commons licensing.

was continued in Europe's medieval market squares and the great markets and kasbahs that were threaded along the Silk Road connecting China and the Mediterranean for a thousand years until superseded by the sea routes of the seventeenth century. In Europe's medieval towns, the market square formed the focus of both the physical form and social life of the community, enlivened by weekly and even daily occurrences, as in the cases of Padua's Piazza della Fiore, Frutta and Erbe. Such spaces still display the irrepressible vitality of individualism and character which commercial life brings to public space everywhere. Whether they are Padua's market squares, Bangkok's floating markets or Kuala Lumpur's night markets, such activities transform the dead space of daytime car parks with food, clothing and craft items. Commercial enterprise, which can fashion public space out of wasteland by the sheer force of its energy, regularly creates street, riverfront and lakeside markets everywhere.

Open-air and covered markets combine the pleasures of spectacle and bargain hunting. The wide range of ages and styles of local people and visitors creates an inclusive feel, and local craft wares portray a sense of cultural appreciation. Food is on sale and displays are arranged with freshness and an eye for colour and form. The presence of crowds of visitors becomes a cultural experience in itself; the criss-cross network of pathways and stalls presents repeated choices and the variety and density of the scene creates a sense of abundance and opportunity. The custom of a visitor who may be unregarded at home or at work will be eagerly sought and an air of good humour and occasion pervades the scene. Such recurrent market

activities, occupying spaces also used for other purposes at other times, occur worldwide. San Francisco's Fisherman's Wharf is a particularly celebrated example, as is London's street market in Petticoat Lane. In the north Italian lakeside town of Luino, the entire town of 30 000 people is closed to traffic on Thursdays and the streets are filled with stalls stretching from the Embarcadero on Lake Maggiore to where the streets start to zigzag upwards towards the Alpine passes, offering everything that can be carried away on foot from jewellery to jackets and from trousseaux to truffles.

Such commercial activities can actually create community space from more restricted and privatised uses such as docks, land banks and redundant waterfront and road space. John Forester in *The Deliberative Practitioner* (1999) describes in detail the negotiative process by which a very significant part of the Oslo Waterfront that was being used or held in reserve for port purposes was opened to public access and enjoyment, thus transforming the city's waterfront. Open-air markets and communal spaces offer very significant opportunities for community planning, as evolution of activities and land uses brings obsolescent uses into review, creating opportunities to introduce new ones that may include public access and community spaces. For instance, the State of Oregon in the north-west of the United States has developed a comprehensive and creative set of planning goals, guidelines and rules which safeguard public access to coastal and riverside land and monitor their development, design and management, so that changes of land use always protect community uses on waterfront sites (Oregon Department of Land Conservation & Development, 2010). Immediately to the north, however, Washington State has very different traditions. Access to the magnificent waterfront of Puget Sound is largely privatised, from Everett in the north, through Seattle to the port of Tacoma in the south. Many planning situations lie between these two extremes, with such spaces becoming 'contested terrains'. Readers will find a typical example of this process of contestation over land undergoing a radical change in use, in Chapter 2, Box 2.4, tracing the development of Brisbane's Southbank Gardens. A more consensual process is illustrated in Chapter 8's Box 8.1, concerning the development of Vancouver's South East False Creek Olympic Village. Similar outcomes are being sought in London's Lea Valley in connection with the 2012 Olympic Games. As the pace of technological change accelerates, such opportunities occur increasingly frequently in cities throughout the world.

A special and significant case of reverse movement towards privatisation of communal space results from the twentieth-century introduction of privately owned and often gated shopping centres. Such centres are often patrolled by private security guards, authorised to exclude any unwanted visitors or groups suspected of being 'unruly elements', particularly young people drawn to the centres by their general atmosphere of material affluence, well-controlled microclimates and glamorous displays of consumer items (Heywood & Crane, 1997). Again, issues of access, community and security need to be balanced, and thoughtful community planning can do much to achieve the necessary physical permeability and social inclusion by introducing provisions for improved public access into approvals to build or modify shopping centres. Design modifications can also be negotiated, to integrate shopping centres into the regular street pattern of the surrounding community on whose custom their shops depend for their commercial success.

COLLECTIVE SPACES

Collective spaces occupy the other side of the urban coin, expressing the power of rulers and elites to create central places where their subjects can be assembled, inspired and controlled. The vast but oppressive Avenue of the Sphinxes at Karnak (Figure 10.9) is one such space, as is the even more psychologically overpowering space in front of Queen Hatshepsut's temple (Figure 10.10) at Luxor.

Figure 10.9 Temple, Ceremonial Way and Avenue of the Sphinxes: entrance to Karnak Temple. *Source:* Reproduced under the terms of Creative Commons licensing.

Figure 10.10   Temple of Hatshepsut, Processional Way and Forecourt. *Source:* Reproduced under the terms of Creative Commons licensing.

Similar celebrations of grandeur and power are often expressed in collective spaces displaying the power of centralised authorities to assemble and reinforce their control over urban and even national communities. Such spaces often have a memorable magnificence. One early example is the Great Court in Akhenaten. Prominent among numerous instances from the European Renaissance are Milan's Piazza del Duomo where the Sforzas combined the forces of Church and State close to both castella and cathedral, and Louis XIV's and Le Vau's great ceremonial avenue leading from the centre of the town to the Royal Palace of Versailles itself. Later, Baron Haussmann's monumental set pieces of the Place de la Concorde and the Champs-Elysées celebrated the power of Emperor Louis Napoleon and the central role of rule from Paris in French society. Kremlin Square in Moscow not only expressed the might of

tsars such as Ivan the Terrible but continued to provide the focus of Russian society where, for more than four decades, Communist regimes staged their annual massive May Day displays of military power. Tiananmen Square has played the same role in the Chinese State ever since the Ming Dynasty moved the national capital to Beijing six hundred years ago (Figure 10.11). In 1989, it became the site of one of the modern world's most explicit displays of centralised State power when the Chinese People's Army opened fire on demonstrators resulting in the deaths of many of its own citizens, variously estimated from several hundred to several thousand, mainly young students. These are spaces for rulers and elites to review their troops, display their power and exact expressions of loyalty and tribute from the masses. They are not intended for political discussion or cultural debate.

Figure 10.11 Tiananmen Square, Beijing. *Source:* Reproduced under the terms of Creative Commons licensing.

The language of design and the vocabulary of space and place

The language developed by physics to describe space relates observations of the behaviour of matter to its different elements and properties. Such descriptions, however, tell us little about how people understand and use spaces and places, or what arrangements evoke their pleasure or discomfort. For those purposes, a vocabulary based on perceptions and sensations is needed, which must ultimately be based on human values, including such basic concerns as those of liberty, choice, continuity and productivity discussed in Chapter 5. The initial section of this chapter indicated how positive design, reflecting health-giving and life-sustaining values, created places of surprising quality, interest and vitality in the improved bustees of

inner Kolkata, and the new cultural set pieces of the Lowry and Water Sports centres in the heart of the Manchester conurbation, which previously had been stagnant and decaying docks. The expression of values has resulted in activities which are transforming spent spaces into memorable new places. If such processes are to become widespread, they need a language that can express ideas and images in productive activities and solid shapes, and a grammar of design to link these labels to form living places.

Brunelleschi's invention of the principles of perspective in fifteenth-century Italy is often seen as the beginnings of the development of this language of design. It must have done much to shape the great European set pieces of Louis XIV's palace at Versailles, John Churchill's Blenheim Palace and its grounds laid out by Capability Brown at Woodstock in England and

Catherine the Great's Hermitage Palace in St Petersburg. Theories of perspective may have also influenced the magnificent composition of the Gardens of the Taj Mahal in Agra, embellishing public spaces with depth and organisation. Other principles had already emerged in Ancient Egyptian and Greek practice, such as contrast, variety, association and the characteristics of prospect and refuge, which have been discussed earlier. By the mid-nineteenth century, Humphrey Repton in the United Kingdom, L'Enfant in Washington and Olmsted in the great city parks of New York, Baltimore and Chicago were consciously incorporating these kinds of elements in their designs to create new public places. However, many of these places retain a rather formal character, constituting decorative and often grand containers, without responding immediately to their users' experiences or activities. It was left to Kevin Lynch (1960), in the democratic spirit of mid-twentieth-century America, to search for a language of places that could express people's actual use and enjoyment of space.

Lynch's starting point was that people's views of their environments are subjective mental maps, often amplified into three or four dimensions, including not only length and breadth but also height and history, which allow them to find their paths between activities and through spaces. These images are therefore more than mere aesthetic reactions. They are navigational maps, initially composed of series of disjointed fragments which are subsequently linked to form sequences within a unified network, inside which they can locate many significant destinations. Images form mental codes enabling us to understand, memorise, master and enjoy our environment. In order to understand this process, Lynch devised three original types of participatory survey. The first consisted of intensive office interviews with about one hundred local residents in each of Boston, Jersey City and Los Angeles, specially selected for their perceptiveness and articulacy, with the aim of discovering what elements of the city they found most memorable, what emotions they associated with different places and vistas, and which features they used as reference points in their journey through the city. The second set of surveys consisted of asking the same questions of random samples of people stopped in the street, producing very similar general results. For the third, a system of urban classification was developed, using features found to be significant in the first two sets of surveys, and intensive field discussions were conducted by trained staff to find out why interviewees had found certain features and districts more memorable and pleasant than others (Lynch, 1960). The conclusions were as interesting as the methods. City features were perceived as being of one of five major types:

- paths;
- nodes (focal points);
- landmarks;
- districts;
- edges.

Routes that passed through areas of distinctive character were preferred to more direct but less varied ones, with the most popular being those passing through activities of changing intensity, or progressing past notable landmarks. Landmarks were themselves remembered as much for contrast, prettiness, association or colour as for sheer bulk. Districts were associated with interesting activities and unusual types of topography such as Boston's Beacon Hill, with its steep slopes and well-maintained and beautiful buildings. Clearly defined edges helped structure the overall shape of the mental map of the city, particularly where they marked the boundaries between districts, such as along waterfronts, railway lines or industrial areas. Lynch also mentions the existence of seams, bordering areas which they link as much as separate, like creek corridors, waterside esplanades and old rail tracks turned into routes for active transport.

Lynch's vocabulary and analysis offers the basis for a common language which can promote productive cooperation between many different participants in community planning. It is also important to remember the participatory basis by which these ideas were developed. Time and again, students I have been supervising have benefited from his inspiration to go into communities to discover what their members value about their environments, what they see as needing improvement and how new development should combine with existing spaces and places to help shape and integrate and to unfold an evolving sense of place.

Lynch has reservations about Christopher Alexander's 'pattern language' (Alexander, Ishikawa & Siverstein, 1977). While praising its imagination, humanity and participatory emphasis, he criticises Alexander for the universal and timeless nature of his 253 patterns, fearing that they will become tablets of stone that may produce standardised places for very different societies and cultures (Lynch, 1981). However, Alexander is at pains to explain in his later work that his patterns are intended as universal models which can be consulted as the basis to prompt local and original solutions. Names such as 'pools of light' (number 252) and 'warm colours' (number 250) illustrate this point. They may not yet constitute a fully developed language of design, but they do combine the elements of Lynch's invaluable vocabulary into a grammar which can apply universal properties and thus help transform local spaces into living places.

Recognition of the importance of people's values and feelings has also helped to shape the work of Randy Hester (1985, 1989), who applies some of Lynch's participatory techniques to provide evidence for the importance of 'subconscious landscapes of the heart'. Work he did in the 1980s in the small Californian fishing town of San Mateo produced results which were at first sight surprising. When he asked local people on the streets, in gathering spaces and at meetings about the most valued environments in the town, their responses nominated several that had the appearance of being almost derelict, including an old decaying pier. It transpired that people valued the opportunity to meet and talk in a place of strong historical associations and environmental character, even if it was not very well maintained. Many readers will be able to think of examples in their own home towns or favourite visiting places which could be kept in their current informal state, protected and improved by designation and modest funding to maintain their communal quality and continue to provide well-loved meeting places. An example of one such space is in the inner Brisbane suburb of New Farm, where I was working in the 1990s with a local community development officer, Fiona Caniglia, to identify places of heritage and cultural significance to be incorporated in a local development plan. Using a technique of Hester's, during an afternoon working session with the neighbourhood action group, we had distributed three stick-on 'purple hearts' to each participant to place on sites of particular importance to them. One boarding house resident placed one of his three hearts on a derelict site on the edge of a little-used park located well above the main activity areas of the suburb.

'Are you sure that's where you meant to put that sticker, Joe'? I asked.

'Sure am,' he said. 'That's where the breakfast coffee cart comes every morning and I start my life again.'

The lessons for urban design are legion: the need for spare spaces, the question of who makes up the community, the methods of consultation we adopt and the partners we work with in planning for inclusive places. When we combine Hester's 'subconscious landscapes of the heart' with Lynch's vocabulary of urban elements and Alexander's universal patterns

and commitment to unfolding existing places to reflect the needs and values of their members, we begin to see emerging a community-based approach to urban design that involves local people shaping public places that can in turn build and sustain the life of local communities.[vi]

Place-making: designing to make life

Happily, examples of effective place-making abound in most societies because individuals and communities are good at shaping their environments to match their activities and values, in much the same ways as birds shape their nests, badgers their warrens and beavers their lodges. For instance, an intensive investigation by Christopher Alexander (2002b) of the evaluation of the Piazza San Marco over a thousand-year period in Venice identified ten linked stages, dating from its first establishment as a space behind the waterfront in the seventh century, through a series of adaptations and extensions as existing uses were strengthened and new ones were added:

1. Church and waterfront fortification on the site about 560, reflecting shared religious values and defence needs.
2. First Basilica Built in 832 – extending the existing functions and strengthening the space's centre.
3. Construction of the Campanile in 976 – amplifying and reinforcing the existing roles of religion and defence by adding a bell tower.
4. St Marks developed to its present cruciform shape in 1071 – extending and enriching the religious role.
5. Piazza extended into lagoon in 1100 intensifying the existing commercial uses where the square meets the lagoon.
6. Northern gateway built in 1250 – creating a defined link to the larger settlement.
7. The Ospicio Orseolo built at the eastern end of piazza in 1309 – expanding the existing religious and charitable functions.
8. Doges Palace built in 1450 – amplifying existing roles to include governance.
9. Old Procuria built in 1523 – further enriching governance roles.
10. New Procuria added in 1600, reinforcing governance and developing a new spatial (and functional) new centre to balance Basilica and Campanile).

This process, which Alexander identifies as 'unfolding', has succeeded in evolving a perfectly adapted space which blends and balances the three functions of religion, commerce and governance, and has even succeeded in managing remarkably well the new one of tourism. Alexander believes that at each stage the participants who needed to be involved (who would be called stakeholders today) were able to review options and make choices informed by their knowledge and personal experience and commitment. This was a case of design being firmly located in what Habermas would term the 'lifeworld', as distinct from the 'systemworld' of automated design systems such as computer-aided design (CAD). Linked to his fifteen properties of good design discussed earlier (which integrate ideas of interaction of centres and achievement of wholeness through recognition of the roles and rights of each element), this process of unfolding offers a significant guide to positive community design.

Other important contributions have been made by the schools of 'responsive environments' associated with Oxford Brookes University in England (Bentley *et al.*, 1985), and 'new urbanism' which has been driving much urban design and planning in the United States since the 1990s and is strongly linked to the 'smart growth' movement, which is attempting to increase urban densities, promote active transport and concentrate new development in 'transit-orientated communities' (Calthorpe, 1993; Calthorpe & Fulton, 2001).

PLACE-MAKING: A CASE STUDY IN THE ATHERTON TABLELAND OF NORTH QUEENSLAND

A third instance, particularly relevant for community planning, comes from the continuing social and physical renewal of three North Queensland country towns. This process was initiated in 1995 by John Mongard, a landscape architect and urban designer working with the local Shire Council and community groups. Mongard studied on an integrated landscape and planning course and combines the skills of both disciplines in his environmental design practice. For more than a decade he has been working in the beautiful but economically stressed tropical tableland area of Atherton in North Queensland (Figures 10.12 and 10.13).

The Atherton Tablelands is a beautiful cluster of rural villages surrounded by internationally significant rainforests. In 1995, Mongard was invited to develop some ideas for the main street of Atherton, the Shire's main settlement. This started a collaborative planning and place-making process that would span ten years and whose continued evolution has caused a major cultural and environmental reorientation of the four settlements of Atherton, Tolga, Tinaroo and Kairi.

Working from a vacant store on the main street, Mongard established a 'set-up shop' collaborative design process, involving residents, councillors, planners and garden staff in describing what made each place special and listing suitable ideas and strategies to enhance these qualities. The excitement that this generated provided the springboard for over twenty other small plans that would, over time, rebuild each town.

The place-making strategies for the original four small towns were embodied in community plans that created physical improvements to streets, parks and entry points and supported local trade and tourism. By promoting productive new and existing uses, the plans responded to needs for economic vitality. They were enacted piece by piece, usually one or two plans per year, supported by civic improvements in each village and informed by consultation processes that led to more detailed information and ideas. Thus, an overall strategy for the town of Atherton was whittled down into smaller plans (for example the railway lands plan, the main street plans, the key park plans) each designed and implemented through a collaborative process, in ways which recall Alexander's emphasis on the need for good designs to unfold rather than be imposed by a brittle short-term blueprint.

Mongard came to the Atherton Tablelands for visits of four to seven days every month or two over the next ten years, developing a strong relationship with the four villages and their people. The underlying motive was to give the local communities the processes, skills and confidence to evolve their towns in better and more environmentally sustainable ways. For example, when a new park at the lookout was to be planned, a rainforest verge needed re-vegetation, or when trees were proposed for the main street, the development team would meet with the council gardeners and a retired rainforest expert from the town. The local nursery would also become involved in the planning so the local and special trees would be grown years in advance of the civic improvements, with everyone knowing what would be needed. This allowed for resources to be both available and cost-effective. The plans mixed disciplines, scales and resources. For example, strategic planning happened in tandem with the making of civic furniture, or the design of a new visitor centre.

Small rural shires do not have the funds to rebuild themselves quickly or easily. Building new parks, for instance, may require employing more gardeners, and making cultural facilities may require more management staff. By firming up 'big visions' for the four villages, the community plans made possible grant applications for State and Federal co-funding to meet

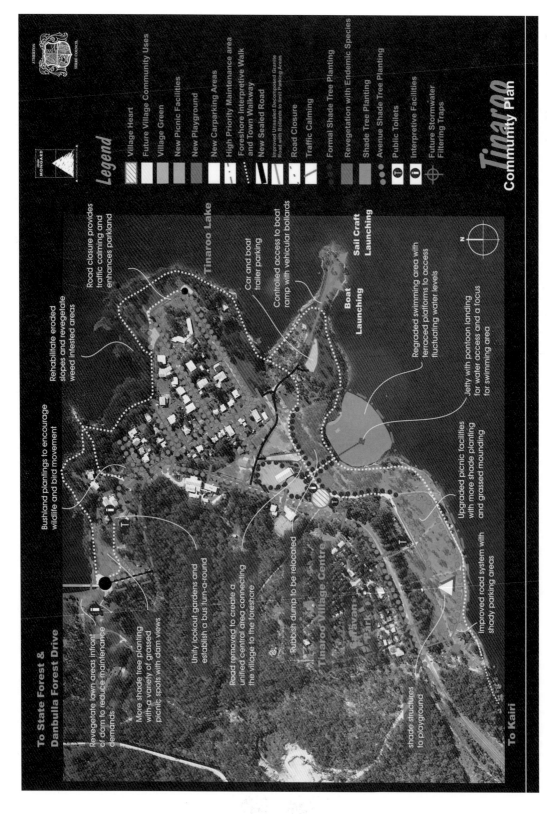

Figure 10.12 Tinaroo community plan, showing village centre, lakefront access and conservation and re-vegetation areas. *Source:* Reproduced by permission of John Mongard Landscape Architects to whom warm appreciation is expressed.

Figure 10.13 Community planning workshop with local residents. *Source:* Reproduced by permission of John Mongard Landscape Architects to whom warm appreciation is expressed.

these needs. As a result, Atherton rebuilt its whole main street, built a visitor centre, a destination park and town gateways. While these larger projects were developed, a range of small ones were enacted to provide immediate tangible outcomes. The first step was to create village entry signs which captured the aspirations of each place. Then a range of locally made furniture, bus shelters and picnic structures were designed and created in a Tablelands style using local hardwood, steelwork and farmyard boulders. Over time, all of the public toilets and amenities were also renovated with the improved look and finishes.

The Tablelands have rich volcanic soils supporting remnants of outstanding rainforest which have been isolated by progressive clearing for agriculture. One of the key strategies was to restore the forest by developing parklands and ovals next to creeks and rainforest, which were linked together by street and swale corridor plantings, creating wildlife stepping stones. As one village grew with new housing, water-sensitive urban design was created to clean and filter storm water before it reached the main lake. Finally, the statutory town plans were strongly shaped by the community plans, thus ensuring that the place-making was embodied in both private and public spaces.

Though small towns may lack the venues, density and diversity of big cities, they have their own cultural direction and arts, which the four villages' community plans helped to foster. Creative people, interesting or unique assets resources and materials were identified,

creating the basis for ongoing place-making projects. For example, when Atherton's Lookout Park was improved, six public art and craft projects were incorporated, allowing local woodworkers, schools and emerging artists to help fashion and focus Halloran's Hill's new interpretation centre. Later on, when the Entrance Park was built with garden staff, local Rotary members became inspired and went on to make art and craft to place in the park Thus, a cultural process emerged which gave the community the confidence to express and create its own artistic vision. The four local village community plans aim to help foster local culture and the arts. Creative local people and interesting or unique assets and resources have been brought together in place-making projects which feature such beautifully appropriate environmental art as the huge sculpture of a pumpkin or melon, hewn out of naturally occurring rocks within Atherton's Entrance Park (Figure 10.14). People in the village of Tolga wanted to improve its visual quality but retain its rural character and sense of integration with the surrounding tropical rain forest. Plate 10.3 shows how the ancient fig tree, a major feature of the village centre, was not only retained in the median strip but also enhanced with sympathetic planting of rain forest plants, ensuring that it continues to provide shade and frame the elegant new signage of the village shops. Old and new have been combined in a simple design that maintains character and expresses traditions in an authentic way while actually involving the local people in the work of enhancing their community.

Models of urban form

From time to time, communities will be called upon to face bigger decisions, often involving choices over investment in major infrastructure, with long-lasting impacts upon the opportunities and limitations which they and future generations will face. Roads and railways will have to be built, and choices between them made. Greenfield sites will have to be subdivided or brownfield land cleared and released for redevelopment. New public investment may be needed for existing or new centres. All of these choices will affect the form of the city and will, in turn, be affected by existing settlement forms and those being developed, either consciously or through inattention. The available alternatives can be grouped into four main categories, evident since the earliest days of settled societies, and related to the basic geometry of the circle, the square, the line and the sheet. Each has its

Rainforest revegetation
to volcanic crater
Picnic
terraces
Sculptural
playground
Interpretive
centre
Telstra
tower
Environmental
sculpture trail
Hallorans hill
lookout &
interpretive park

Interpretive signs at
hou wang temple

Sculptural landmarks
at the lookout

Atherton rotary park

Figure 10.14 Creating a culture of appreciation: Atherton community sculptures, plan and vistas. *Source:* Reproduced by permission of John Mongard Landscape Architects to whom warm appreciation is expressed.

own characteristics and implications for the communities which it accommodates:

- The circle generates radial concentric forms.
- The square creates grid forms.
- The line is expressed in corridor development.
- The sheet gives rise to galactic patterns.

RADIAL CONCENTRIC DEVELOPMENT

The compactness, sociability and ease of contact within circular settlements have ensured their popularity as community forms throughout the last ten thousand years. This shape has been adopted in the widest possible range of times and places: early hunting encampments, Neolithic villages of mainland Europe and Britain, Italian hilltop towns, agricultural villages throughout Africa, the bastide fortified settlements and market towns of Europe's Renaissance and the garden cities and most planned new towns of more recent times. They have offered economy in the use

of space and the consumption of resources, starting with the wickerwork branches protecting the semi-nomadic camp at Terra Amata (see Chapter 8) and still relevant in the central work locations in the contemporary metropolis. The circular form can be relied upon to concentrate the maximum area and activity within a given distance to a central point. For this reason, 'organic' settlements often grow into roughly circular shapes and schools of urban design frequently favour circular forms for their strong central image and easy access to central services. They also have the capacity to cluster different neighbourhoods, each gathered around its own focus in a hierarchy of centres, all contained within an 'urban growth boundary' or 'greenbelt'. Such arrangements support the co-location of essential urban facilities of medical centres, schools, local shops and recreation areas, creating economy and convenience. Advocates of the 'new urbanism' school of design also embrace the idea of basically circular 'transit-orientated communities' grouped around rapid transit stations to encourage higher densities, more use of active transport such as walking and cycling, and provision of a mix of housing styles and densities. In summary, circular settlements offer compactness, promote social contact, achieve optimal economies of service and distribution within a given radius or perimeter and are appropriate to bounded forms of urban containment and greenbelts.

Many great cities have evolved from different forms to develop into 'radial concentric' shapes, passing through stages of incremental peripheral growth, as they have grown outwards along radial routes, and in-filled behind them, to evolve into a star-shaped metropolis. Public transport, as in Tokyo, London, Stockholm, Toronto, Washington and Melbourne, can assist these stellar metropolises to continue to function to serve high population levels (for example in Greater Tokyo the population exceeds twenty million people). Stellar cities thus favour incremental growth within market economies, driving successive rings of invasion and succession, as the 'zone in transition' ripples outwards from the centre, redeveloping old areas for more lucrative uses (Burgess, 1972). Some degree of habitability may be maintained by the development of green wedges along floodplains or ridges of steeper terrain separating the swathes of development along major roads and rail lines. However, though it is one of the current world's dominant settlement forms, the stellar metropolis is inherently prone to problems of centralised congestion and conflict, as regional traffic flows arriving daily at the centre attempt to fit into relatively narrow channels, which can only be expanded by destroying the activities of the central area itself. Even public transport faces limitations of headway time between trains and lengths of railway platforms. At some stage, the elongating journeys to work and distances between activity centres ordain that activities start to decentralise and to evolve into a more multi-centred settlement form (Hall, 1977).

GRID CITIES

Grid cities, by contrast, can disperse flows and destinations about wide fields of organised space and provide a convenient basis for advance planning. Both the Indus and Nile Valley cities of four to five thousand years ago demonstrate this form, with Medinet Habu (Manley, 1996) and the systematic layout of the lower city of Mohenjo-daro (International Council of Monuments and Sites, 1980) offering good examples. Later, this form proved ideal for Greek and Roman *coloniae*, capable of being replicated wherever a new settlement was being established. Throughout western

and southern Europe, the squared shape of old Roman *castrae* can be identified in the modern city centre street pattern. Grid forms proved just as suitable for the colonial settlements of the new world in the Americas and Australasia. New York is perhaps the most celebrated example, but the pattern is replicated in Philadelphia, Baltimore, San Francisco, Kansas City, Melbourne, Brisbane, Adelaide, Christchurch and countless other cities. This is a settlement form which is ideal for planning and organising growth, as it maximises the movement and consumption of resources. However, it can also give rise to a sense of 'placelessness' and requires very sensitive adaptation to respond to natural features.

This form fell out of favour for planned new developments, after the development of 'garden city' concepts by Ebenezer Howard, Olmsted, Unwin and Stein brought organic analogies and natural settings into prominence. However, during the Western world's long mid-twentieth-century growth boom, conditions promoted both trend planning and a search for urban forms that could accommodate maximum use of the private car. The University of California planning theorist Melvin Webber (1964) speculated upon the 'non-place urban realm' and dismissed traditional views of urban design and place-making as anachronistic in an age of fast cars and even faster electronic communications. Called upon to act as a consultant for the design of Milton Keynes, last of the wave of English New Towns (located in the Midlands communications belt and bounded by the recently completed M1 motorway), Webber produced a low- to medium-density grid structure that spread for several hundreds of square miles over the Midlands plain with the explicit intention of promoting choice, ease of movement and 'modern' lifestyles. Milton Keynes New Town has fulfilled its allotted role of accommodating population, but its structure maximises resource consumption and does not favour either active or public transport or the development of social life. It is unlikely to be repeated as a public policy choice.

Nevertheless, advocates of both the responsive environment and new urbanism schools of urban design are attracted to the concepts of meeting places provided by central squares and the variety of route ways and permeability which can result from grid networks of surrounding streets. Their small-scale plans incorporate grid elements in the grain of their local designs. In particular, the reaction against cul-de-sacs and whimsical curves, which create spaces that cannot be easily overseen from neighbouring dwellings, encourages such use of grid forms at the most local scale of new communities. Later developments in settlement theory have merged the merits of order, logic and distribution of the activities of grid patterns with the incremental advantages claimed for linear development (discussed below) to propose a 'directional grid'. Such an approach is also well suited to meet the growth management and flexibility goals of current ideas of corridor development.

LINEAR SETTLEMENTS

These forms are also common throughout history. The street village and the waterfront fishing or trading settlement developed naturally as responses to commerce and topography and their modern versions continue to occur, generally now on the larger scale of the coastal conurbation, such as the urban region of the Puget Sound Regional Council which stretches from Everett through Seattle to Tacoma, or Greater Brisbane, the 'two hundred kilometre city' extending across two states from Noosa in Queensland to Tweed Heads in New South Wales, or the copper belt towns of Zimbabwe. In the mid-twentieth-century epoch of mass movement and the motor car, linear forms attracted much attention as ideal models for new development that would be able to accommodate the rapid growth of the times. Traffic engineering consultants added transport and regional planning to their advertised lists of activities and produced statistical models to promote maximal movement flows and continual growth. The international consultants Jamieson Mackay contributed a concept that combined the promotion of public and private transport in a 'three-strand linear structure': all new development would be located in chunky beads of new settlements strung along both sides of a central public transport spine, with motorways running along their outer edges providing through routes and bypasses for private transport.[vii]

Another aspect of linear settlement was developed by the Athens-based international planning consultant Constantinos Apostolou Doxiadis, for a universal linear system to link all new and proposed settlements in a global web termed 'ekumenoplis'. This formed the capstone in a new field of study called 'ekistics', described as the science of human settlements. A journal of the same name was founded in 1968 and continues to be published monthly, Doxiadis proposed, for instance, that settlement in England should crystallise into a coffin-shaped belt stretching from Liverpool and Manchester through Birmingham and Nottingham to London. This itself would form the Atlantic extremity of an even larger belt of continuous urbanisation linking western Europe with central Russia, and western and northern China to the sea-board cities of eastern China, Korea and Japan. These were seen as being connected by trans-Pacific trade routes with the rapidly expanding cities of the Pacific coast of North America, themselves linked by belts of continuous urbanisation to the East Coast metropolises, and via their trans-Atlantic routes back to Europe (Doxiadis, 1968).[viii]

Australian planners in the National Capital Development Corporation (NCDC), which is responsible for developing the new national capital city of Canberra, may have been influenced by this kind of prevailing conventional wisdom when they commissioned a firm of traffic engineers and transport planners from the United States to prepare a plan for the continued growth of the city. Canberra's design had originated in Walter Burley Griffin's winning entry submitted to a 1913 competition to design the city in which he proposed a compact, broadly circular city centred on a manmade lake. Faced with accommodating growth up to and beyond the quarter-million mark, the consultants produced a new transport-based plan which they termed 'The Y Plan'. This plan distributed growth in a series of new settlements such as Gungahlin and Belconnen and an expansion of the existing edge-of-town settlement of Queanbeyan to be joined by new motorways in a heavily modified version of the three-strand linear structure, but one which in the spirit of the times lacked a central public transport spine. Perhaps there was a mid-century assumption that public servants would all drive cars to work. The result is a structure that maximises daily movements, relies heavily on the private motor car and lacks ease of informal interaction at all levels above the local neighbourhood (where it is actually well organised and sociable). Subsequently, Canberra's planners have been encouraging increasing densities in the inner suburbs and the development of more of the intensive activities such as medium-density housing, street markets and open-air cultural festivals associated with the spirit of the circular city form of its original design.

Critics of linear structure have pointed to a number of basic fallacies and failings. First is the danger of privileging means of movement over the maintenance of the quality of the activities which they are intended to link. Urban freeways can destroy the inner-city communities which give life to cities. Second is the technical mistake of attempting to channel growth along a single line when people will inevitably seek access to central places throughout the breadth as well as the length of entire urban fields. Locations outside the proposed band, but laterally close to existing centres, which offer a wide range of activities, will inevitably attract residential development irrespective of the transport planners' intentions. Third, there are also criticisms of the very large resource demands of linear developments, maximising movements between different functions, consuming scarce energy and devouring whole belts of space for new roads, shopping areas, industrial estates and low-density car-based residential suburbs.

Responses to these criticisms by the transport and settlement planning theorists of the 1960s produced modifications of the original linear city proposals. For example, background studies conducted for the South Hampshire New City Study by Colin Buchanan and Partners (1968) investigated how to combine the capacities of grid settlement forms to distribute movement flows fairly equally throughout entire regions, with the flexibility and capacity of linear forms to accommodate continual growth without causing congestion in unique central areas. These resulted in a hybrid 'directional grid' giving equal respect to the needs of both public and private transport, and integrating central place concepts.

The settlement pattern was conceived as an elongated grid, focused around a hierarchy of central places adjacent to intersections of public and private transport routes. The major centres of Southampton and Portsmouth, for instance, were situated at the intersection of national rail lines with a proposed new regional motorway linking the two cities. Lower levels of centres were to be located where more local public and private transport routes intersected within the grid structure. This hierarchy of proposed centres was continued down to the local neighbourhood level: the meeting points of bike and walking routes with residential collector streets formed appropriate locations for the local primary school, recreational park and convenience shops. Ever since the publication of the South Hampshire study, directional grids have been routinely included amongst the options for new or restructured settlements (Puget Sound Regional Council, 2010; Walker, 2010). Their emphasis on public transport, central place access and continuous infrastructure lines, and their capacity to accommodate both mixed and segregated use areas, makes them effective structures for managing medium-term growth.

An interesting application of linear urban structure occurs in the 'corridor development' proposed by Melbourne City Council and the Department of Urban Planning of the State of Victoria (Adams, 2009). The study, *Transforming Australian Cities*, proposes to accommodate all of the two million population increase anticipated for the metropolitan area next forty years within narrow bands of high- and medium-density, medium-rise development. These would be located along major tram, train and bus routes and proposed new light rail additions. This proposal combines incremental growth along existing radial routes with linear settlement ideas, to allow large numbers of people to enjoy the intensive social, cultural and economic life of the city at the same time as being able to move conveniently about their daily activities. An interesting sidelight on this combination of settlement forms is provided by the recognition that the structure of Australian capital cities has been largely shaped by the original rail and tram lines running from the outer suburbs into the city centres, with suburban stations linked to their residential hinterlands by nets of footpaths and roads used as much by cyclists as motorists (Manning, 1984). Adams' (2009) proposals for intensification thus build on well established patterns of existing urban structure and grain.

In the longer-term however, problems may still arise from difficulties in managing the mounting pressure on central areas: the intensity of growth within the corridors and sideways growth that could change the intended structure into a high-rise and high-density sprawl. It may be significant that the most recent South East Queensland Regional Plan explicitly aims to divert much future growth away from the existing north–south coastal strip into a 'western corridor' towards and beyond the old mining and industrial centre of Ipswich (Queensland Government Department of Infrastructure & Planning, 2009). While this is proving very successful in its own terms, it is devastating the open spaces of the old Brisbane River valley with new motorways, water-recycling plants, shopping centres and residential estates, and ensuring continued pressure on the already congested centre of Brisbane, where the three northern, southern and western corridors converge. Similar problems may confront metropolitan Melbourne unless private vehicular traffic and toll roads are kept out of the central spines of growth corridors. They should instead be designed to serve as bypasses to these areas of intensive population concentration. Many city centre activities will also have to be decentralised to new 'knuckles' along the fingers of intensive urban development, which can then be linked by cross-city routes of effective rapid public transit, as in the inner and middle suburbs of Greater London and Toronto.

SHEET AND GALACTIC SETTLEMENT FORMS

In times of prolonged peace and in places of abundant supplies of water and fertile land, such as the plains of southern Germany and the prairies of North America, much early settlement occurred in isolated farmsteads spread quite evenly over wide areas. The rise of nation states with central systems that could impose peace and maintain service grids to distribute water and power to all parts of the countryside has created conditions where human settlement can similarly spread quite evenly over wide regions. Advocates of freedom and independence have often been attracted by the idea of dispersed settlement. Peter Kropotkin (1974) envisaged a flow out of the great cities to repopulate the countryside in networks of small farms and craft settlements. Frank Lloyd Wright, the apostle of American independence, encouraged in his Broad Acre City, a spread of independent family dwellings across the entire surface of North America, each ecologically well related to its surroundings and making its own contribution to the national productivity of goods and ideas (Fishman, 1982). Since he produced these ideas in 1933, and established his memorably beautiful model of independent living at Taliesin in Arizona, his ideas have become potentially more persuasive and relevant because of the dispersive capacities of new developments in electronic communications and the global reach of the Internet.

The significance of these trends was not lost on the Berkeley planning theorist Melvin Webber, who made them the basis of his influential essay 'The urban place and non-place urban realm' (1964), in which he argues that requirements of traditional settlement for direct spatial contact are being superseded by new communities of interest and association whose members are more likely to be distributed across whole regions and throughout the world than to be concentrated in one locality. This may have led Webber to his advocacy, discussed earlier, of grid settlements with their potentiality for dispersion. He certainly dismissed attempts to shape settlements to support traditional values of physical interaction and direct economic exchange. Later, he developed his ideas further to argue that planning should abandon 'narrow and negative constraints' and allow the natural forces of technological change to reshape society to a more dynamic and psychologically challenging exploration of new urban structures (Webber, 1968a, b). He termed this 'permissive planning'. My own critique of this approach is entitled 'Plangloss' (Heywood, 1969).

Kevin Lynch (1961, 1981) had anticipated the development of such ideas and later incorporated them into the broad framework of his explanations and evaluations of spatial form, without actually supporting their introduction. He examined what the forms would look like and how they would function. They would form sheets, he postulated, with regular small wrinkles occurring where local services such as petrol stations, schools or recreation centres were located at road intersections. Ecological concerns could also ensure that they did not extend into areas of vulnerable or precious natural environments such as floodplains, national parks, creek corridors or important natural habitats. They would require a comprehensive net of roads and infrastructure corridors and he proposed that these might best be arranged as a triangular pattern so as to add further directions of through movement (in short, to cut down the number of corners involved in travelling around a square grid). As a result, this form began to resemble Christaller's original hexagonal settlement pattern, prompting the idea that a new pattern of central place formation might naturally reoccur.

The question arises as to whether these are purely notional patterns or whether there are examples which we can study and whose performance we can evaluate. In many ways, the chosen lifestyle of the affluent has always tended towards such forms of rural retreat, whether it was the retirement villas of Roman aristocrats and writers in the hills of Umbria and Latium, the rural retreats of Mandarins in Han China or the chateaux established along the Loire Valley by the psychologically oppressed courtiers of Louis XIV. The suburban spread of the twentieth-century Western world marks a further stage in this flight from congested and polluted central places, which reached its climax in the rural residential patterns of 'exurban' development that have been spreading around North American and Australian cities for the last three decades (Nelson & Dueker, 1990) and whose international expression can be found in the purchase of Italian rural and lakeside properties by German business people and of French farmhouses by wealthy English retirees. Clearly, this settlement form still proves attractive to many who 'have it all'.[ix]

Residents of sheet settlements, often with above-average incomes and expectations, will require services and supplies whose distribution would (and does) demand large-scale diversion of energy and resources to meet their needs. Power, water, education, policing and roads all become problematic expenses, so that the settlement form is economically exorbitant. Socially, it is scarcely more sustainable, depending upon a combination of public services and above-average household wealth. Isolated dwellings can also be prone to random violence, with the associated rise of the gun culture which is common in many rural regions of the

United States. In Australia, threats of natural disasters such as floods and bushfires are a recurrent spectre and huge source of public expense. Culturally, this form of settlement can only reduce casual and informal contact, so that social and cultural capital seeps away and Jane Jacobs' 'systems of survival' (of people exchanging face-to-face knowledge and skills to build the trust on which both business and social life depend) becomes more and more difficult (Jacobs, 1992). For all of their good computer skills, Richard Florida's 'creative class' do not gather round virtual spaces in front of computer screens in their equipment-packed home offices, but they flock to the coffee bars, art gallery foyers and bookshops of the inner-city milieux, which can offer the intensity and surprise associations which trigger their contributions to economic growth (Florida, 2005). The non-place urban realm fails when it is asked to make the transition from virtual reality to the living world of human exchange, experience and physical demands. It fails on grounds of resource sustainability, personal sociability, mutual aid, economic productivity and visual interest and stimulus. When such ideas are elevated, as Wright and Webber advocate, into a major urban form, they prove simply unsustainable. Few planners would now advocate Webber's non-place urban realm. They would instead look for systems of infrastructure provision that can minimise the consumption of resources and the length of service lines and promote the sharing of space and culture.[x]

However, this model is not without its own valid social applications. The general concept of a more equal spread of activities and dwellings across available space can help equalise public access and thereby improve social justice. Reducing mass concentrations of people and production can also enable communities to step more lightly on their natural environments. Smaller clusters of population can also reduce nodes of congestion and improve the quality of people's contact with each other.

CONTRIBUTIONS OF EACH MODEL TO FUTURE SETTLEMENT FORMS

Each form has its own contribution to make. Compact circular settlements remain the basis of community life, promoting access, intensity and choice, but running the dangers of the self-destruction of success as their growth slowly turns them into centres of conflict and congestion. Grid forms can demonstrate five thousand years of successful organisation of space to manage development and exchange. They have also provided the classical squares for people to meet,

discuss, exchange and argue. They have become, in many ways, the symbols of civilisation from the Great Bath at Mohenjo-daro to the stoa-lined Agora of Athens, the Roman Forum, Oxbridge quadrangles and great Renaissance squares to the modern meeting places at the heart of all great cities, such as Times Square in New York and Trafalgar Square in London. However, grid cities can also maximise traffic flows and length of journeys, waste energy and resources and form urban regions that possess little sense of place or focus. Linear forms continue to evolve naturally in response to elongated spaces like coastal plains, lake shores and river valleys. They are well suited to flexible growth and the integration of land use, transport and infrastructure provision. However, they are even more prone than pure grid forms to maximise movements, and are inherently insensitive to the needs of communities to cluster around central places to obtain essential services. Sheet settlements respond to human values of personal independence and choice. They use to the full the capacity of modern technology for instant transmission of information and ideas across increasingly large areas of the world. However, they also create unsustainable demands for resources and deprive societies of the direct personal contact that is essential to the continuation of culture and to many of the chance contacts and experiences that make life worth living.

No settlement form therefore provides all the answers to the spatial needs of community life and none is devoid of contributions to imaginative plans. This is particularly welcome because we are currently immersed in the middle of a period of the most rapidly increasing pressure from demands for dwellings and places for work, health and learning in human history. The challenge of population growth is not unending. It is one whose conclusion we can already glimpse: world population should stabilise at less than ten billion people by the middle of this century (see Chapter 7). Nevertheless, we are confronted by the need to accommodate an overall population increase of about three billion people, or nearly 50% of our existing total, in a period of forty years. At the same time, we must strive to rectify gross deficiencies in existing provisions of shelter and standards of living, learning and health care. We must also manage major global population movements from poor to rich countries, from countryside to cities and from disaster-racked regions confronted by the periodic effects of global warming to the well-established world cities where they will arrive as refugees. We shall need as good an understanding of all the models of settlement form as we can assemble.

Rigid templates are as destructive in physical planning as they are in social, economic and educational planning. Thus, the following snapshot of how each of the elements of settlement form discussed above could be combined to meet the current needs of major metropolitan planning in Western nations is intended as a suggestive scenario rather than a nostrum or a universal prescription. With that qualification, it appears that the planned evolution of many great metropolises will benefit from steering future residential and employment growth into secondary centres, located throughout a well-defined urban region linked along corridors of intensive movement by high-quality public transport. Urban growth boundaries would mark the edge of the metropolis, and growth in the development corridors would be promoted by public investment and coordinated programmes of infrastructure. Intensive and often high-rise development would be encouraged on brownfield sites which become available through technological and land use changes, such as old docks and ports, storage sites (with remediation requirements to remove noxious chemicals where necessary), railway marshalling wards, industrial sites, relinquished or relocated military training areas and disused school grounds. Heights would be restricted to between six and eight storeys and densities of several hundreds dwellings per hectare would be encouraged. Behind these corridors, traditional detached family dwellings would be protected by limitations on height and density and the areas would be linked by universal systems of active transport to take cyclists and walkers to transport nodes located in the corridors.

The limited number of new greenfield communities which would be needed should be in places selected not for their ease of land assembly but for their appropriate locations in the regional transport, open space, conservation and economic systems. Their development should be based on the same principles of focused and shaped growth as those outlined above for existing major cities. Land would be acquired compulsorily at pre-designation market rates as determined to be fair by mixed public/private valuation authorities; development would be in the hands of new 'city development corporations' with memberships drawn from public, private, voluntary and academic sectors, consisting of eminent people with established professional expertise and a clear commitment to the public interest. Both the existing metropolitan araes and new cities would be planned to evolve as lively clustered neighbourhoods with compact local centres occupying the spaces between more intensively developed corridors. These medium-rise spines of mixed commercial, residential and cultural activities would be served by continuous flows of steady-paced public transport. Such cities would maintain their long-established neighbourhoods with mixes of grid and radial residential streets. Their visual imagery would nevertheless be strongly influenced by the corridors of intensified, higher-density development. They would radiate out to link major secondary centres, and themselves be linked laterally to each other by secondary belts of medium-rise shops and services.

The shape of such metropolitan cities would assume the form not of a flat sheet but rather of a big top tent, highest round the central pole where the grand ring accommodates the most intensive performances, while further out the poles support secondary high points where contributory acts are performed, while at the edges the height falls away to accommodate the many thousands of people whose contributions maintain the life of the whole enterprise.

Conclusion: bringing places to life

This chapter started by indicating that good design could not reclaim bad planning and that it is not possible to create beautiful spaces out of destructive or damaging activities. Over time, good planning, however, can become the mother to good design. In conclusion, it is useful to return to this theme of the relation between function, form and values. Four major human values were shown in Chapter 5 to be of particular importance for community life and organisation. (prosperity, liberty, justice and sustainability.) Table 10.1 demonstrates how these can be expressed in physical design principles (in this case, those of Christopher Alexander discussed earlier in this chapter). The intention of the table is not to provide a checklist of items that ought to be included in community planning but rather to illustrate how design principles may be applied to fulfil major human values and goals, in short to show how ideas and values can be combined to produce good physical environments. Different principles and values would produce different design proposals.

The beauty that people instinctively recognise in good design results from judgements about how well a scene reflects patterns of harmony and relationship, when compared with their stored sense of wholeness, as derived from previous experiences. It reflects how well the pieces of this scene fit together to make a unified pattern and how well shapes are adjusted to support their activities. Beauty therefore not only lies

Table 10.1   Design principles, community values and physical characteristics

Design principles	Values and Characteristics			
	Prosperity	Liberty	Justice	Sustainability
Levels of scale	Work opportunities and places integrated within local, urban, metropolitan and regional settlements. Encouragement for new economic activities to develop and thrive at each scale – from local workshops, through urban incubators to 'creative industry' clusters in the inner areas of great cities	Encouragement of mixed uses and activities within each level of settlement to provide wide ranges of opportunities and choices. Public and active transport links between scales and places to offer equal opportunities	Equal access to facilities and services at each scale for all income groups, indicating need for public and active, as well as private, transport between different centres	Adjustment of scale of development at each level within settlements to prevent concentration of resource and space consumption and energy demands that would accumulate as noxious waste and carbon emissions. This concern for levels of scale would lead to diffusion of activities down the urban hierarchy
Strong centres	Clustering of commerce, administration, education and entertainment in central places at all scales to achieve urbanisation and localisation economies	Communal spaces designed on the human scale to promote free association and assembly and ease of access by active transport of pedestrians and cyclists	Equal opportunities and access to central places and services by public, active and private transport for all social groups to central places	Balanced development with mixed uses and support for land use evolution and distribution of new activities between centres at different levels
Boundaries	Provision of well-serviced and accessible areas for noxious industry. Designation of bounded districts and protection from 'invasion and succession' of central commercial and industrial area expansion	Rights of existing residents and communities to retain the character of their dwellings and areas	Citizen participation in local planning, development assessment and design negotiation of their designated areas	Designation and reservation of natural habitat and regeneration areas at all scales from creek corridors to international marine parks and world heritage areas
Alternating repetition	Clustered settlement forms with fine grain, which can support the development of associational economies	Mixed land uses promoting freedom of people to do what they want where they want to rather than strict segregation of uses	Widely distributed and integrated community facilities of educational, medical, cultural and administrative services	Systems of conservation and ecological corridors and core areas
Positive space	Flexible planning that will allow evolution of new uses in existing structures and spaces	Community rights to design and maintain cultural and 'sacred' places for communal enjoyment	Protection rights for spaces and places of cultural significance	Conservation strips, urban farms and re-use of old buildings
Good shape	Local community consultation prior to new industrial and commercial development	Places where individuals and communities can shape their own activities and spaces (e.g. beaches and derelict land reclamation schemes) or contribute significantly to design, such as local parks areas	Collaborative community planning for local and neighbourhood plans and in development assessment and control	Use of aerial and satellite imagery to define extent of habitats and sequoias and conservation areas

Table 10.1 (*continued*)

Design principles	Values and Characteristics			
	Prosperity	Liberty	Justice	Sustainability
Local symmetries	Building new economic development on existing human and social capital. Promotion of spirit of place as with inner-city locations for new creative industries	Local design that recognises and enhances existing local character	Planning systems that protect local communities from out-of-scale change of uses and structures which may destroy local symmetries	Designation of conservation areas based on existing ecological associations and species
Deep interlock and ambiguity	Coexistence of different activities in close proximity. Opportunity for central places to change activities at different times of the day and night	Capacity for initiatives to change land uses (e.g. old power stations becoming art galleries and entertainment centres). Encouragement for innovation and variety	Equal rights of self-expression for all people and communities giving rise to contrasting activities and styles	Conservation planning for areas involving competing activities and impacts, such as estuarial wetlands and port facilities, metropolitan green wedges, coastal resorts and naval installations
Contrast	Integration of opposites: innovation and conservation; tranquillity and drama; intensity and calm	Rights to be different and to develop different forms and uses (e.g. spaces for city centre buskers and bike lanes on motorway corridors)	Mixed uses to reflect differing social needs and skills	Promotion of coexistence of opposites (e.g. urban growth boundaries, separating urban and rural development; coastal conservation zones next to port areas)
Gradients	Management of different activities and levels of intensity	Promotion of broad boundary zones and rights to have new proposals considered on their merits	Rights to have proposals considered on their merits in border areas of reservation zones	Buffer zones between conflicting use (e.g. intensive recreation for trail bike and motorsport activities between capital intensive industry and residential areas)
Roughness	Making space for growth buds of economic development, which may be different from existing land use categories, such as sale of food from petrol service stations or information technology workshops in shopping centres	Maximum freedom of action and development for individuals to do things differently consistent with sensory rights of others (e.g. coffee shops and convenience stores in suburban streets, and small workshops in residential areas)	Rights of people, communities and places to be themselves and not to conform to standardised patterns	Spaces for spontaneous regeneration of species
Echoes	Community planning that supports progressive unfolding of new activities and land uses, building on existing social capital and capacities to adapt to economic change, such as those of the associational economies of central Italy	Freedom to express oneself and one's cultural inheritance at speakers' corners, on spray art walls, skate parks and mountain wilderness areas	Extension of opportunities of elites throughout all parts of settlements, with web centres, public libraries, sculpture parks and child care centres in all local communities. Application of the principle of 'subsidiarity' to developed activities and their control to the smallest scale consistent with their efficient management	Conservation areas to conserve and restore habitats

Table 10.1   (*continued*)

Design principles	Values and Characteristics			
	Prosperity	Liberty	Justice	Sustainability
The void	Creation of focus and meeting points for exchange of ideas, goods and products – small squares, pocket parks, loose-fit spatial design generally	Designs that leave space for self-expression	Designation of common spaces and resources for protection	Preservation of spaces for natural life (e.g. wetlands, forest parks, habitat reserves)
Simplicity and inner calm	Non-intrusive central place and recreational design with inclusion of tranquil and reflective spaces	Creation of local, regional and national parks for active recreation and contemplation	Conservation of natural features of river valleys, creek corridors and wetlands for equal use and enjoyment of all	Open space systems that link local neighbourhoods, creek corridors, major valleys and countryside reserves to coastal wetlands and mountain wilderness areas
Not separateness	Mixed-use development that favours diversity and multiplicity of modern productive activities 'Associational economies' that link different specialist producers in chains of cooperation to meet changing market demands	Clustered communities that combine personal privacy with continual community contact in central places equally accessible to all Free personal movement able to percolate through localities Creation of many meeting places and opportunities for self-expression	Equal rights of participation, assembly, movement and celebration	Ecological audits and monitoring to ensure maintenance of mutual support between different species in the face of rapid climate change

in the eyes of beholders but also in their needs, wants and experiences. This grounding of good design in individuals' perceptions should affect decisions about the control, process and composition of development. The clear logical conclusion is that local residents and users should be effectively involved in design processes for their localities. This can start from the earliest stages, using the same participatory techniques that Kevin Lynch applied in developing his vocabulary describing how people see and value cities and districts.

A second conclusion about process is equally clear: neither architectural fashion nor engineering innovation has justifiable claims to shape community spaces or structures, though they may both be very valuable in generating interesting options. People's choices and decisions should therefore precede designs which give expression to them. For instance, design issues of grain, density, form and spatial arrangement of housing in new residential developments should be settled towards the end of a quite detailed process

that has reconciled and resolved objectives among participants and agencies. This logic demands that design be as much a bottom-up process of consultation and discussion as a top-down one of inspiration and leadership.

Communities can be helped to participate in design through discussions exploring the different physical forms available to fulfil their chosen plans. Given opportunity, people will often tend to choose different styles for different areas and activities, and urban design can reflect this diversity of scales, activities and lifestyles by a matching variety of forms that will add interest and legibility to everyday places. We need, for instance, local living areas that are deeply reassuring, harmonious and sociable and other, more central, intensive and widely shared spaces that can be confronting and inspiring. Different design principles and patterns can provide the raw materials for this stimulating variety. Taken as templates, abstract design patterns would consign control and potential destructive power to decision-makers far removed from the actual locations being developed. This could result in reducing cities and neighbourhoods to the deadening repetition of the cookie cutter or the ant heap. Used as models and palettes of portrayal, however, they can open the mind and spirit to the widest possible range of new combinations and innovations to match new situations. Rather than a separate and specialist activity, design should again become an enlivening part of everyday life. Political space for participation and empowerment and physical spaces for cultural expression and meeting can ensure the creation of well-loved and used places that can evolve in step with social and political change.

Endnotes

i   This reputation was epitomised in the theme of the song *Dirty Old Town*, which also celebrated the resilience and cultural courage of the local population. The song was written by Ewan McColl, who was born in Salford.

ii Alexander's argument proceeds from the basis that the best that intentional design can hope to achieve is to enhance or replicate the processes by which space, matter and life naturally come into being and continue to evolve, and which therefore form 'the nature of order'. As a mathematician by early training, he has a natural interest in science and structure and this has informed his inquiry into and understanding of the nature of order, which he interprets as consisting of repeated and self-sustaining relationships between greater and lesser centres. These relationships occur at many different levels: from galactic constellations, through solar and planetary systems, down to the structure of matter, composed of molecules, consisting in their turn of atoms formed of protons and neutrons in an ever-elaborating chain of repetition. The cellular structure of life follows a similar pattern down to the ordered genetic structure of the double helix of DNA. Alexander reaches the conclusion that the nature of life and order, which designers need to respect and promote, is the formation of new wholes through the recombination of smaller centres, creating a complex but coherent chain of being which ultimately unifies all matter in the universe.

The first of his principles, 'levels of scale', seeks to promote the idea of patterned repetition within evolving structures. In community planning terms, this will involve relaying patterns and processes from one scale of community to another, to encourage coherent, equitable and accessible distribution of space and resources. It also provides the frame within which the second principle, 'strong centres' is situated, reflecting the structural properties of matter and applying them to the analysis and design of community life and the coordination of services and activities in spatial concepts such as hubs. The third principle, 'boundaries', represents the combination of the first two. There are boundaries between different levels of scale and between different centres at the same level. Boundaries demarcate, for instance, both the greater extent of a major river basin and the lesser extent of its tributary valleys and define those valleys themselves. Alexander also draws attention to the fact that boundaries are not in reality the pencil-thin lines of conventional depiction but instead broad zones of transition offering the opportunity of choice and the possibility of change. 'Alternating repetition' recognises the capacity of rhythm, pulse and repetition to structure life and space in ways which can organise diversity into self-sustaining patterns and thereby manage situations of high variety. A million voters can form two contending parties; a million residents can be viewed as members of thirty different electorates each with both shared and competing interests.

'Positive space' once again reflects the natural disposition of matter into self-sustaining patterns of order and prompts us to respect the capacities of ourselves and others to recognise natural order and quality. Recognition of 'good shape' flows from Alexander's study of Middle Eastern carpets and their intricate designs and again expresses his confidence that people have an evolved capacity to recognise and value this quality, repeatedly expressed in works of art and craft that can form a sound basis for collaborative design. 'Local symmetries' inform and support this idea of good shape, through the elements of diversity, balance, pattern and order, as well as promoting reciprocity and equity. 'Deep interlock and ambiguity' take the idea of symmetry a stage further, incorporating interconnectedness and open-endedness as attributes of successful places and communities. 'Contrast' applies these characteristics to promote the diversity, dialectic and communication that lie at the heart of healthy community life. 'Gradients' recognise and support transition, favour variation and support the stable coexistence of differences. The acceptance of 'roughness' flows through many of these principles, protecting and celebrating open-endedness and variability of life, making space for growth buds of future development and transcending current practice. 'Echoes' (reflecting our own thought processes of experience and association) help to repeat past successes, avoid previous mistakes and preserve living heritage. Settling at the centre of social and physical spaces, 'the void' can create space for reflection, problem-solving and innovation. 'Simplicity and inner calm' reflect the psychological role of the void, promote the reflection and meditation required for personal fulfilment and balanced community life and create spaces for new life and centres. 'Not separateness' could also be described as 'wholeness' and reflects Alexander's aim to achieve designs that will foster and nurture new life.

His principles, starting from a scientific basis of the structure of matter with 'levels of scale' and concluding in 'not separateness' with an expression of holistic relationships, make use of cognitive, affective, sensory and psychological insights. In total, they constitute a rich and endlessly stimulating palette of materials to help develop integrated community design.

iii The Great Bath measures approximately 12 metres by 7 metres, with a maximum depth of 2.4 metres, two wide staircases leading down into the tank and small sockets at the edges of the stairs which are thought to have held wooden planks or treads, perhaps for ease of drawing water.

iv Nearby, the lower city is a complex site composed of private and public houses, wells, shops and commercial buildings along streets which are highly geometric in their layout, intersecting at right angles in an orderly system of planning also incorporating sanitation and drainage. Artefacts and remains suggest high levels of specialisation within the lower city, with different quarters concentrating on such products as armoury, leather goods, pottery, textiles and food production.

v Under the provisions of the Maori Reserved Land Act of 1955, the Resource Management Act of 1991 and the Te Ture Whenua Maori Act of 1993, marae are owned in perpetuity by the iwi and are controlled by designated traditional custodians.

vi The importance of public space in maintaining the political health of communities is strongly argued by the philosopher of communicative rationality Jurgen Habermas (1987). Public spaces are where the informal politics of personal discussion and the possibility of public demonstrations of support and dissent occur. Joe used the coffee cart site in New Farm to propound his quite radical views on the future of the suburb. Later, he discussed the competing rights of café owners and local people to ownership of the pavements.

vii A scheme to create a new city in central Lancashire (Chorley New Town), for instance, that proposed using the Liverpool–Preston rail line as the central public transport strand and the M6 Birmingham–Glasgow motorway as the eastern bypass reached quite an advanced stage of planning before being abandoned as too expensive and prone to problems of land subsidence and conflicting traffic flows. The development would have generated very large local traffic movements onto the M6, which was a national transport artery. It would also have created irresistible pressure for residential and related developments outside the bounding motorways in places close to planned centres. The logic of the proposal was to not only optimise but also maximise movement and relied on cheap fuel to move people around the city between home, work, shops, education and recreation. The 1973 fuel crisis spelt the final abandonment of the idea.

viii Such large-scale and beguiling ideas may deteriorate into mere pattern-making and may elevate pursuit of the trend into visionary prophesies. More seriously, they may be used to justify schemes that actually require more detailed local analysis of their economic impacts and unintended social and physical consequences. Nevertheless, they are still attracting influential adherents and supporters (Burdett & Sudjic, 2008).

ix It can also offer an escape, to rebuild their lives for others who are finding the achievement of basic necessities of shelter and sustenance beyond their reach in the competitive and congested cities of the mainstream (Delacouture, 2008).

x Logically an urban realm that has no spatial dimension has only virtual reality. Once it is applied to space, a number of hard questions emerge: 'Where will its portals be located?' 'Who will own them and have access to them?' 'Who will control the content of messages?' and 'How will the resulting cyber systems be mediated into spatial reality?' It is hard to escape the conclusion that Webber's 'non-place urban realm' does not exist in any dimension. His non-place realm is not urban; it is really a part of Karl Popper's 'World 3', as are other planning ideas. They cannot replace urban places, though they can and should influence them.

References

Adams, R. (2009) *Transforming Australian Cities for a more financially viable and sustainable future*. Melbourne, City of Melbourne and Victorian Departments of Transport and Planning & Community Development.

Alexander, C. (1964) *Notes on the Synthesis of Form*. Cambridge, MA, Harvard University Press.

Alexander, C., Ishikawa, S., Siverstein, M. (1977) *A Pattern Language*. New York, Oxford University Press.

Alexander, C. (1979) *A Timeless Way of Building*. New York, Oxford University Press.

Alexander, C. (2002a) *The Nature of Order: Book One: The Phenomenon of Life*. Berkeley, CA, Center for Environmental Structure.

Alexander, C. (2002b) *The Nature of Order: Book Two: The Process of Creating Life*. Berkeley, CA, Center for Environmental Structure.

Alexander, C. (2002c) *The Nature of Order: Book Three: A Vision of a Living World*. Berkeley, CA, Center for Environmental Structure.

Alexander, C. (2002d) *The Nature of Order: Book Four: The Luminous Ground*. Berkeley, CA, Center for Environmental Structure.

Appleton, J. (1996) *The Experience of Landscape*. Chichester, John Wiley & Sons.

Bentley, I., Alcock, A., Murrain, P. *et al.* (1985) *Responsive Environments: A manual for designers*. London, Architectural Press.

Burdett, R., Sudjic, D. (eds) (2008) *The Endless City*. London, Phaidon.

Burgess, E. (1972) The growth of the city. In M. Stewart (ed.), *The City: Problems of planning*. Harmondsworth, Penguin.

Calcutta Metropolitan Development Authority (1983) *Calcutta Metropolitan Statistics*. Calcutta, Author.

Calthorpe, P. (1993) *The Next American Metropolis: Ecology, community and the American dream*. New York, Princeton Architectural Press.

Calthorpe, P., Fulton, W. (2001) *The Regional City: Planning for the end of sprawl*. Washington, Island Press.

Campbell, B. (1985) *Humankind Emerging*. Boston, Little Brown.

Colin Buchanan and Partners (1968) *The South Hampshire Study*. London, HMSO.

Delacouture, J. (2008) *The Effects of Rural Residential Subdivisions on the Tara Shire 1970–2006*. Master's thesis, School of Urban Development, Queensland University of Technology.

Denes, A. (2003) *Agnes Denes Projects for Public Places*. Lewisburg, PA, Samek Art Gallery.

Desroches-Noblecourt, C. (1976) *Tutankhamun: Life and death of a pharaoh*. Boston, New York Graphic Society.

Doxiadis, C. (1968) *Ekistics: An introduction to the science of human settlements*. London, Hutchinson.

Fishman, R. (1982) *Urban Utopias of the Twentieth Century*. Cambridge, MA, MIT Press.

Florida, R. (2005) *Cities and the Creative Class*. New York, Routledge.

Forester, J. (1999) *The Deliberative Practitioner*. Cambridge, MA, MIT Press.

Habermas, J. (1987) *The Theory of Communicative Action*. Cambridge, Polity Press.

Hall, P. (1977) *The World Cities*. London, Weidenfeld & Nicolson.

Hester, R. (1985) Subconscious landscapes of the heart. *Places* **2**(3).

Hester, R. (1989) Social values in open space design. *Places* **6**(1).

Heywood, P. (1969) Plangloss: A critique of permissive planning. *Town Planning Review* **40**(3).

Heywood, P. (1987) *Felda & Bustee: The management of population growth in town & country*. Unpublished Paper available from author, Brisbane, Queensland University of Technology.

Heywood, P., Crane, P. (1997) *In or Out? Out and about: Report on young people in major centres*. Brisbane, Brisbane City Council, (with Egginton, A., Gleeson, J.).

International Council of Monuments and Sites (1980) *World Heritage Listing No 138: Mohenjo Daro*, http://whc.unesco.org/archive/advisory_body_evaluation/138.pdf, accessed 13 January 2010.

Jacobs, J. (1992) *Systems of Survival*. London, Hodder & Stoughton.

Kropotkin, P. (1974) *Fields, Farms and Workshops of Tomorrow*. London, Allen & Unwin, (first published 1899).

Lynch, K. (1960) *The Image of the City*. Cambridge, MA, MIT Press.

Lynch, K. (1961) The pattern of metropolis. *Daedalus* **Winter**: 77–98.

Lynch, K. (1981) *Good City Form*. Cambridge, MA, MIT Press.

Manley, B. (1996) *The Penguin Historical Atlas of Ancient Egypt*. London, Penguin.

Manning, I. (1984) *Beyond Walking Distance*. Canberra, Australian National University Press.

Marae Community Operating System (2010) *What is a Marae in New Zealand?* http://www.maraeonline.co.nz/, accessed 15 January 2010.

Menzies, C., Rogan, B., Heywood, P., Smith, N. (1996) *Social Planning Guidelines for Queensland Local Government*. Brisbane, Local Government Association of Queensland.

Mumford, L. (1961) *The City in History: Its origins, its transformations, and its prospects*. New York, Harcourt World & Brace.

Nelson, J., Dueker, K. (1990) The exurbanization of America and its planning policy implications. *Journal of Planning Education and Research* **9**(2).

Oregon Department of Land Conservation & Development (2010) *Statewide Planning Goals*, http://www.oregon.gov/LCD/goals.shtml, accessed 12 April 2010.

Puget Sound Regional Council (2010) *Vision 2040*, http://psrc.org/growth/vision2040, accessed 2 May 2010.

Queensland Government Department of Infrastructure & Planning (2009) *South East Queensland Regional Plan 2009–2031*. Brisbane, Author.

Walker, J. (2010) *Human Transit*, http://www.humantransit.org/2010/02/vancouver-the-almost-perfect-grid.html, accessed 2 May 2010.

Webber, M. (1964) The urban place and the non-place urban realm. In: M. Webber (ed.), *Explorations into Urban Structure*. Philadelphia, Pennsylvania University Press.

Webber, M. (1968a) Planning in an environment of change: Part 1: Beyond the Industrial Age. *Town Planning Review* **39**(2).

Webber, M. (1968b) Planning in an environment of change: Part 2: Permissive planning. *Town Planning Review* **39**(3).

11 Community Governance and Participation

Chapter 10 explored the ways in which many community activities, including housing, health, economy and transport, could be drawn together to promote vital places. This chapter now turns to a different kind of wholeness, that involved in integrating the management and control of conservation and change. In exploring the characteristics and methods of different scales and types of governance, the chapter is organised into the following six sections:

- governance, government and community participation;
- issues of freedom and order;
- the roles of negotiation and partnership;
- the development and evaluation of policies;
- roles and responsibilities in governance and participation;
- scales of community and their roles of governance and control.

The chapter concludes with a discussion of the contributions of participation and governance to community life.

Governance, government and community participation

The widespread view that 'governance' is simply a grand name for what governments do is far from true. Sustaining productive and fair community life has always involved far more than merely making laws demanding acceptance of common ground rules of behaviour. It extends to generating the participation necessary to achieve common aims. Governments cannot prosecute a war if people are unwilling to fight, as occurred with United States citizens in the Vietnam War. Nor can they achieve peace if many are unwilling to stop fighting, as happened for years following the United States' invasion of Iraq in 2003. Private organisations and voluntary associations may also play influential roles in the lives of pluralist societies. For example, in Britain the National Trust, Ramblers' Association and the Council for the Preservation of Rural England (CPRE) and in the United States the National Parks Conservation Association and the

Audubon Society are highly effective players in national environmental governance, and influence legislation. Religious and charitable bodies, trade unions and business organisations are also increasingly active in actually delivering public services, often attracting funding from governments (Etzioni, 2004). At the international scale, too, organisations like Greenpeace, the World Wildlife Fund, Oxfam, World Vision and Médecins San Frontières and many others all influence national and international policies. As a result, it would be a mistake to concentrate solely on the patterns and mechanisms of representation and election and to overlook the influences of the participation by community, market and interest groups. They well justify the equal attention they are given in this chapter.

There is much evidence that community participation helps to shape important political outcomes. The 2008 election of Barack Obama as president of the United States, for instance, owed much to the well coordinated activism of the multitude of his community supporters and their individually small financial contributions. His 2010 State of the Union speech was directed more to community members, whose participation in health promotion, job creation, the economy, education and taxes he was trying to mobilise rather than to supporters of any particular party (Obama,

Community Planning, First Edition. Phil Heywood.
© 2011 Phil Heywood.
Published 2011 by Blackwell Publishing Ltd.

2010). In a related way, the 2007 election of Kevin Rudd's Australian Labor Party owed much to a massive trade union campaign to oppose the 'Work Choices' legislation of the previous Liberal party government which had drastically restricted the legal rights and operations of organised labour. The lack of participation from civil society is also playing important roles in Iraq and Afghanistan, where elected governments are finding the winning of assent and maintenance of law and order almost impossible to achieve in the face of lukewarm participation from the majority and impassioned opposition from large disaffected minority groups.

At the urban level, cities struggle to find effective ways to maintain consensual government in multiethnic communities in all continents. In Copenhagen, in 2009, gang warfare flared between local right-wing youth gangs and ethnic minority groups in open street battles (Joumea, 2009) and later in the year there were street confrontations associated with the Climate Change Conference. In Mumbai, conflict simmers between Hindus and Muslims who are often blamed for such acts of terrorism as the 2008 hotel attacks which killed 179 people (Mahalo, 2009). In Urumqi in the Uighur province of Xinjiang, in western China, the June 2009 riots against exclusion of local people from equal participation with Chinese Han immigrants in the civil life of the region resulted in the deaths of nearly two hundred people and injuries to nearly two thousand (Li, 2009). Other examples occurring in the early years of the century will come readily to people's minds, including protest movements and civil unrest in Paris, the industrial towns of the United Kingdom and New York. The inescapable conclusion is that in considering issues of community governance, as much attention should be devoted to arrangements for participation by individuals and interest groups as to mechanisms to formulate and implement the official policies of government.

Issues of freedom and order

In balancing participation and governance, issues of freedom and order inevitably bring with them concerns of consent, negotiation and partnership. All government constrains freedom to some degree, and raises questions of the extent to which general rules can claim to be enlarging people's opportunities to live full and free lives. Order is one of the prime purposes of government, aiming to secure life and property in return for some sacrifice of complete freedom. Negotiation is the necessary process by which people who share resources, space and urban facilities can come to terms with each other to maintain the social fabric which they all share. Partnership is needed to ensure that the concerns of freedom, order and negotiation can be effectively achieved. In considering these issues, judgement should be guided by effects on people's capacities to live full lives. How, for instance, do proposals affect their ability to make full use of their natural endowments of speech, movement, understanding, belief, association and choice? Table 11.1 considers the ways in which values of freedom and order affect these capacities and their expression in community planning outcomes. Table 11.2 considers how attributes of policy development, evaluation and implementation interact with the concerns of partnership and negotiation.

FREE SPEECH

Free speech is one of the most treasured of human rights and is widely regarded as the guarantor of social justice and guardian of scientific truth (Popper, 1998). In its absence, communities rapidly deteriorate into assemblages of servile subjects like those of George Orwell's *Animal Farm* (1952). Nevertheless, civilised societies also need to provide protections against incitements to hatred, ridicule or contempt, which can be determined in processes of open trial. There is also a need for redress against the wilful publication of misinformation. As long ago as classical Athens, Plato (1976) warned of the ability of lucrative and self-serving plutocrats to shape public opinion to serve their own interests. Today, the much expanded power and reach of the mass media has further increased the dangers of this abuse. Redress against misinformation or wilful distortion needs to be secure and severe enough to discourage owners and editors of mass media from wilful propagation of untrue hearsay, intrusions into personal privacy and unsubstantiated allegations at critical moments of political campaigns preceding elections.

The most positive way to diminish the powers of media ownerships to control public information and opinion in their own interests is to guarantee publication of independent information and opinion. Significant issues affecting the current and future life of the community, particularly concerning proposed developments, can be explained, explored and debated. Throughout the world, there are many examples of such good practice at all scales from the open websites and newsletters of individuals and voluntary organisations to national broadcasting corporations such as the British Broadcasting Corporation (BBC),

Table 11.1 Community planning implications of freedom and order

Aspect	Freedom	Order	Community planning outcomes
Speech	Freedom of expression	Individual protection from incitements to hatred, ridicule and contempt	Guaranteed public rights to access, discuss and contest information
Movement	Rights to free movement across land, water and skies	Rights to secure enjoyment of safe movement in public places	Secure, accessible and safely regulated public and community spaces for meeting and exchanging
Information	Public and private access to public information	Prevention of criminal or demeaning performances, and redress for public misinformation	Open sourcing of information, with guaranteed rights of publication, debate and access to non-abusive matter
Belief and Observance	Equal and unfettered rights to religious and cultural beliefs and practices	Prevention of hate campaigns and actions	Promotion of the contributions to community life of legitimate interest, cultural and faith groups
Assembly	Rights of free assembly and demonstration	Protection of life, property and prevention of riot	Provision of open access to public spaces and places at all scales
Choice	Rights to unconstrained individual and community action and fair and free election to representative positions	Prevention of actions infringing personal and property rights and guarantees of respect for government decisions	Provisions of resources for both community participation and political programmes of elected governments
			Consistent devolution of roles to local groups and communities in line with principle of 'subsidiarity'

Table 11.2 Applications of negotiation and partnership in achieving community planning outcomes

Aspect	Negotiation	Partnership	Community planning outcomes
Development of policies and proposals	Early consultation with partnering communities. Continuous contact and continuity of dialogue. Human relationships within processes	Transparent allocation of roles. Appreciation of others' knowledge and expertise	Collaborative planning arrangements and processes. Community boards, neighbourhood associations and planning teams
Continuous evaluation and problem solving	Stakeholder engagement and negotiation. Spiral sequence of • Action→ • Practice→ • Reflection→ • Process→ • Revised action Charettes and enquiry by design	Role of engagement in planning and place making. Community involvement in social and environmental impact studies	Self-management and implementation by different types of communities. Development of consensual 'policy communities' and national planning doctrines
Community Initiatives	Mutual respect. Roles of communication and cooperation	Positive listening and dialogue. Recognition, encouragement and funding support	Shared roles and funding. Collaborative provision of shared support services

Canadian Broadcasting Corporation (CBC) and the Australian Broadcasting Corporation (ABC) and the United States Public Broadcasting Service (PBS). The adoption of universal blogging practices can also assist rights of comment, with free access to cyber space and open sourcing becoming important aspects of community planning. 'Wiki' type procedures can challenge and remove obscene and misleading material and can also stimulate dialogue and expand the scope of community evaluation of proposals. Wikipedia and Wikimedia themselves are powerful tools to support access to the best available knowledge-enhancing capacities for both community participation and democratic government.

FREEDOM OF MOVEMENT

Freedom of movement is scarcely less crucial to participation in the life of active and sociable communities.[i] Open pathways across the oceans and skies have always attracted those seeking self-expression and adventure (Saint-Exupéry, 1966; Roesdahl, 1998). Civil society has also been strengthened by maintaining and reclaiming traditional rights of way between settlements, and along river banks and coastal foreshores. Nevertheless, there are limitations to unrestricted free public access, which should not be extended to license individual or official trespass into private homes or personal spaces. Community planning therefore needs to distinguish between public and private space, with guaranteed free access to homes being limited to their rightful owners and users.

There is a third category of shared spaces, where use needs to be regulated, to ensure the essential movement of people and goods. Public rights of way on railway lines, roads, harbour entrances and air spaces are prime examples. Charging for the use of such corridors may well be justified both to meet the expenses of their maintenance and to control over-use and forestall congestion, resulting, for instance, from low levels of car occupancy during daily rush hour journeys to work in crowded city centres.

FREEDOM OF INFORMATION

Freedom of information involves open access and distribution via well-maintained public records, as well as the right to collect and distribute true information oneself. Both are required for consensual decision-making and inclusive community planning. However, this right to information should not extend to activities which may involve abuse of the rights of others, including pornography, gratuitous violence and techniques of terrorism. It is obvious that not everything that is personally profitable will always be publicly beneficial. Freedom of information in community planning should therefore be confined to guaranteed public access to material which is needed for fully informed public discussions and decisions.[ii] Information should be designed to avoid personal rancour, group labelling or gratuitous imputation of bad intentions. The ideal guarantee for these freedoms is some form of general bill of rights or set of planning principles such as the United States Declaration of Independence, or the Oregon Statewide Planning Goals, which are incorporated in the State's Land Use Act. Goal Number One, Citizen Involvement stipulates that 'a comprehensive plan shall adopt and publicise a program of citizen involvement that clearly identifies the procedures by which the general public will be involved … including continuity of citizen participation and of information that enables citizens to identify and comprehend the issues' (Oregon Department of Land Conservation & Development, 2010).

FREEDOM OF BELIEF AND OBSERVANCE

The past five hundred years have seen a revolution in societies' attitudes to faith in many parts of the world. Unquestioning commitment to the virtues of orthodoxy and piety are giving place to more widespread acceptance that belief is a matter of personal choice. However, shared beliefs and values remain powerful sources of motivation, energy and action, and as such we still need to consider how community planning will embrace matters of faith. Liberty demands unfettered rights of religious belief and observance, and cultural and ethnic rights and expression. Order requires that the activities stop short of permitting hate campaigns perpetrated by one group against another, or interference with their rights including particular styles of building, personal self-presentation or cultural practices. Equally important, creative community planning should encourage and support the roles of legitimate faith and cultural interest groups as partners in community organisation and programmes of community visioning and policy development.

FREEDOM OF ASSEMBLY AND ASSOCIATION

Freedom of assembly and association holds a particularly significant place in the evolution of democratic community life, as was indicated in the preceding chapter. Historically, command of the streets has been crucial to regime maintenance and change.[iii] The importance of public space as the arena of free political debate is emphasised by Jurgen Habermas, the philosophical champion of communicative action (1987). He emphasises its role of providing places where people can gather to discuss the issues of the day, listen to dissenting views and display their commitment to alternative public policies. It is significant that democratic societies from Periclean Athens to the United States of Bill Clinton and Barack Obama have succeeded in integrating the rights of free public assembly and demonstration while maintaining general support for the overall legitimacy of their regimes. It is a sign of stable regimes that they can tolerate free assembly in public places.

However, legitimate interests of order should also be considered in public spaces. Streets and squares should not be given over to such licensed thuggery as that of Hitler's Brownshirts during the *Kristallnacht* pogrom of 1938, attacking Jewish businesses and homes, or the 2005 riots on the beaches of Sydney's Cronulla, against people of Middle Eastern origin or appearance. Public places do need to be policed to preserve rights of free passage and assembly. The implications for community planning are that public spaces with unrestricted access are essential for the continuation of healthy community life at all levels – community gardens, neighbourhood parks, district centres, city squares and regional parks. Neither governments nor any particular community group can claim exclusive rights to their use and control. They belong to everybody and they should be equally available to all for any legal use.

FREEDOM OF CHOICE

Personal liberty implies not only the right to vote in free and fair elections to select representatives to take decisions on behalf of the whole community but also people's individual rights to take personal or communal action to achieve legitimate personal and group aims. This raises questions about how to establish the legitimacy of potential partners among interest groups, seeking to advance the concerns of their own members. Exclusion of collusive and criminal organisations intending to harm others for their own benefit requires careful attention and regular scrutiny. These are issues which collaborative community planning cannot avoid. Gary Miller (1981) in his telling and prophetic book on the abdication of representative government in Los Angeles County in the 1970s has shown how giving powers such as planning and property taxation to self-constituted, self-serving and privileged groups incorporating themselves as 'local governments' can lead to major break downs in social justice that prepare the ground for eventual civil disorder.[iv]

   There are, of course, effective and practical solutions to these dilemmas of authenticity. The model of the Office of Neighbourhood Involvement, evolved over three decades by the City of Portland in the state of Oregon, offers one particularly suitable example. Neighbourhood and community organisations are registered with the Office and receive financial, organisational, information supply and role sharing benefits. In return, they accept basic requirements for open and democratic selection of office holders and regular and recorded meetings (City of Portland, Office of Neighbourhood Involvement, 2010). Each association consists of groups of volunteers organised to act on issues affecting the liveability and quality of their neighbourhoods, including community engagement, crime prevention, disability and diversity support, graffiti abatement, information supply and referral, liquor licensing, mediation and other neighbourhood programmes and review of residential siting proposals. There are currently 104 Neighbourhood Associations, organised into seven not-for-profit district coalitions through which the city contracts to provide support to the member associations. Portland allocates an annual budget of around $1 million to support these programmes, which constitute a useful example of the application of the 'principle of subsidiarity'. This principle states that all governance functions should be devolved to 'subside' to the most local level at which they can be effectively performed, thereby increasing the opportunities for freedom of choice and increased levels of local participation. Freedom of choice is also expressed in the significant field of community action, which has formed a recurrent theme throughout this book.

The roles of negotiation and partnership

One of the most significant ways in which participatory governance differs from representative government is the greater opportunity that people are offered to negotiate outcomes for themselves and therefore to become partners in the shaping of events. Table 11.2 identifies some of the more important ways by which negotiation and partnership can help to develop, evaluate and implement policies and proposals. These are explored in more detail in the following paragraphs.

The development and evaluation of policies and proposals

Where communities are facing pressures of major change, early involvement of participants and stakeholders can help forestall rancorous conflicts and shape sustainable outcomes. Throughout New Zealand, for instance, 144 community boards now operate within local authorities in both urban and rural areas, providing local representation and advocacy at the grassroots level, and exercising powers delegated to them by local government. Any local government electoral division where one does not yet exist may vote to establish a community board which consists of 4–12 members, a majority of whom must be elected. They have a mandate to communicate with and encourage local community organisations and special interest groups and to contribute to decisions affecting their areas (Local Government New Zealand, 2009). Although a government-sponsored survey in 2008 indicated some limitations in the level of partnership offered by local government councils, two-thirds of community board members surveyed thought that the boards were able to do a good job of representing and promoting local interests (Richardson, 2008).

This participation does not always need to be official or programmatic. In *The Deliberative Practitioner*, John Forester (1999) discusses negotiations involving practitioners as diverse as harbourmasters, community development practitioners, rural health officials and educational administrators as well as city planners and architects. He explores how they engage through processes of imagination, sympathy and improvisation with people whose contributions are essential to mutually successful outcomes, in cultures as different as those of Norway, the United States, Mexico, Israel and Brazil. He shows how cumulative collaboration can lead from suspicion and opposition through discussion to the partnership which is necessary to achieve acceptable results for each of the participants, developing at the same time their ethical awareness and capacity for moral judgement.

Another well-known example is the involvement of neighbouring communities in the early negotiations that laid the groundwork for the 1993 extension of the Westpoint Sewage Treatment Plant on Puget Sound. By spending $32 million on improving existing neighbouring shoreline access and facilities, the Seattle city government gained the support of affected local communities (Municipality of Metro Seattle, 1993; Heywood, 1997). The scheme cost Metro Seattle far less than the alternative cost of establishing a new plant and cemented good relations with local communities. Such collaboration can often result from recognition of mutual benefit or escape from unproductive conflict. In the Norman Creek example discussed in Chapter 2 (Box 2.2), for instance, the city council's Departments of Engineering, Planning and Parks and Recreation and its Office of Economic Development only accepted key local groups as partners after all else had failed through four years of professional stonewalling. When they had to make good on the Lord Mayor's commitment to genuine community involvement under the shadow of forthcoming elections, negotiations benefited from the transparency which had been generated from the need to resolve earlier mutual suspicions. This proved valuable in maintaining momentum and forestalled the danger of co-option or collusion. Painstaking clarification of roles kept the process of plan preparation and adoption on track.[v] Other situations may involve professionally skilled and respected voluntary organisations tackling issues such as homelessness, aged care, drug treatment and cultural engagement, which are widely recognised as valid. In such cases, participation may be enhanced by more mutual trust, but transparency and clear role allocation remain essential safeguards against misunderstanding and unreal expectations.

A culture of collaborative community planning can develop from these processes. A wide range of professions, levels of government and sectors of the community may be drawn together to form 'policy communities', building on shared understandings to create mutual trust and achieve coordinated implementation (Healey, 2007). In the Netherlands, Faludi and van der Valk (1994) refer to the development of 'national planning doctrines' enshrining this kind of community consciousness to create practical partnerships having their own momentum. Well-known examples include the Netherlands' 'green heart' and the United Kingdom's 'greenbelt' policies. This 'Polder Model' of collaboration through recognition of shared interests (so named because of the traditions of Dutch communities of working together to protect reclaimed land threatened by floods and storms) is highly effective (Faludi & van der Valk, 1996). Healey (2007) also cites the economic primacy of central city interests in northern Italy in the 1990s shaping development in Milan.[vi] If expanded to ensure the inclusion of currently excluded participants such as unorganised communities, recent migrants, ethnic minorities, younger- and older-aged groups and people with disabilities, such approaches could add further positive dimensions to sustainable community planning.

Another collaborative approach is to involve existing local community organisations or establish new ones to act as steering committees for the preparation of community plans. As we have seen, this worked well and acted as a circuit breaker of deadlock in the case of Brisbane's Norman Creek corridor. Brisbane City's more recent experiments in this field, however, have attracted the criticism from community activists that they are based more on co-option than true community involvement. For instance, membership of neighbourhood and community planning teams, working with council officers in preparing neighbourhood and local plans, is decided by self-nomination and council selection; members are then required to sign a carefully worded commitment to confidentiality. Teams are disbanded once the plan is adopted. Neither condition favours wider and continuing community engagement or develops the kind of partnership which has been established in Portland or New Zealand. Nevertheless, Brisbane's 'community planning team' approach has potentialities to evolve into more inclusive roles and is generally well liked in the outer suburbs, where few radical changes are being proposed by the council. If developed to become better integrated and more participatory, accountable community planning teams could provide both outreach and involvement.[vii] In the long run, this process could contribute powerfully to mutual understanding and the collaboration on which progress and prosperity ultimately depend.

EVALUATION AND PROBLEM-SOLVING

If it is to respond effectively to the certainty of external change, planning must be a cyclical activity, involving regular review of schemes and monitoring of outcomes. This process should prompt continual evaluation and problem-solving, to drive the upward spiral of the cycle of:

Action > Practice > Reflection > Process > Revised action

described in Chapter 6. Such planning methods should stimulate reflection and provide a positive framework for the conduct of negotiations. Commonly used techniques such as 'charettes' and 'enquiry by design' promote collaborative evaluation and problem-solving across activities and sectors. Charettes involve short periods of intense collaboration among different stakeholders supported by an architect or graphic designer. They aim to produce sketch designs that can resolve conflicting preferences and combine ideas in unified schemes.[viii] The technique has limitations because negotiation is cut short by the restricted time available and is often confined to intuitive glimpses of potential solutions and future situations. 'Feel good' outcomes are thus favoured, which may not stand the test of the 'morning after' reviews of subsequent analysis. As a result, the outcome of charettes are often relegated to roles of sketching beguiling options and providing 'what if' examples, which are useful in themselves, but as snapshots rather than durable visions.

Enquiry by design expands the collaborative approach by involving more systematic preparation and integration with processes of governance. Time and resources are provided for exploration of unintended consequences, engaging a wide range of stakeholders and often extending over periods of three or four days. A staged investigation of one or more options for an area or for a scheme explores both what different stakeholders can contribute and what they may stand to gain or lose. The process is well suited to support collaboration, and to test feasibility and impacts. Members of Healey's 'policy communities' would be suitable participants, as long as the participation of other strongly affected parties, such as representatives of local communities and current and prospective users of the area, was also ensured. One of the advantages of this approach is the possibility that schemes will fail the tests provided by these enquiries. Such a capacity for falsifiability provides critical evidence of whether a process is valid (Popper, 1969).[ix]

Another aspect of the capacity of negotiative processes to favour participation and improve policies is highlighted by an interesting case in a major Australian city. This involved a proposal to build a 'green' bridge to provide a public and active transport link across a major river to a large university campus, with a combined student and workforce of 40000 people. The bridge was intended to link the campus directly to a public transport catchment of a million people (half of its total commuting hinterland) and reduce the need for those using public transport to have to traverse the city centre, removing many personal trips and bus journeys every day, many of them in peak hours, from the city centre, thus significantly reducing travel times. Nevertheless, the university's initial response was noncommittal, uneasy about city council intrusion into its prerogatives of campus planning and fearing that the penetration of the campus by buses would damage the campus environment and be the thin end of the wedge for subsequent opening of the bridge to private vehicles, thus flooding the academic environment with queues of private cars taking short cuts from one part of the city to another.

The project director, a transport planner with qualifications in land use and community planning, established an advisory committee and invited a number of senior university representatives to join. One by one, concerns were discussed and recognised as being important and valid, but all were shown to be capable of being resolved by feasible policies and practical concessions. Movement by buses into or through the campus could be prevented by creating a cul-de-sac turn around for buses at the university end of the green bridge. Subsequent escalation of the use of the bridge to include private vehicles could be prevented by structural limitations, and university control over campus planning of roads and car parks. All of this could be included in protocols signed by the university and city council.

During the course of negotiations, both parties became enthralled by the possibilities of improvements that could result. The university Manager of Sites and Services started to see the bridge as the good idea it was, as one by one university objections resulted in major design improvements and amplifications. Not surprisingly, the result has been an outstanding success and an astonishing improvement to the aesthetic and functional quality of the formerly somewhat suburban campus. The previous and rather dreary car access remains, though now it is less congested. The new entry point for pedestrians, bikes and buses across the green bridge affords stunning views of the forested river banks. It is quite different from the old one, strewn with an inheritance of multi-storey car parks and decades of assemblages of academic buildings that until the 1990s had never been given adequate thought to relate them to each other or to shape pleasing open spaces. The Green Bridge entrance now brings university staff, students and visitors into a welcoming planted space from which pathways lead off to riverside, educational buildings, campus shops and offices, playing fields and the swimming pool. These paths wind up though cool and elegant gardens and shrubberies to conveniently close destinations. Some traverse the shores of the university lake. Others skirt heavily planted rain forest gullies. People arrive at their destination calmed and in states of heightened harmony compared with those hurrying in from the hot and crowded car parks of the old road entrance. The sense of ownership by the university hierarchy is an important guarantee of their continued support. It is also a tribute to the negotiative planning skills of the project director and the then university Manager of Sites and Services capacity of collaborative planning to create sustainable environments.

COMMUNITY INITIATIVES

Negotiation is also involved in developing and shaping community initiatives, helping them to evolve from origins in rejection of unwanted proposals to create new contributions to community life and governance. As indicated in Chapter 2, there is often a sequence of

Opposing agendas > Conflict > Negotiation > Resolution

which can produce positive outcomes, as was the case with both the Norman Creek Waterway Park and Brisbane's Southbank Gardens, which have been discussed earlier. However, if the sequence is not allowed to unfold, owing to one or other party believing that it has access to a better BATNA (best alternative to a negotiated agreement) than can be obtained through collaboration, the situation may end in stalemate or the crude imposition of a destructive scheme which may leave one party deprived of living space, livelihood or treasured environmental resource and harbouring a permanent sense of grievance. Such tragic injustices do not have to occur. More collaborative outcomes can be achieved through legislatively mandated negotiation.[x]

For community planning initiatives to be successful, a dialogue has to be established and maintained both within the community and with power-holders in government and business. A particularly good example of this is provided by Kolkata's long-running Bustee improvement programme throughout the 1970s and 1980s. As has been described in the preceding chapter, this brought together local neighbourhood groups with the engineers of the Calcutta Metropolitan Development Authority (CMDA) to identify areas for upgrading and the location of standpipes and latrines. It benefited from using local labour, materials and products and the whole programme became a shared endeavour. Communities, which had vigorously opposed the CMDA's original proposals for clearance and relocation in slab blocks on the city fringes, became effective partners.

DIALOGUES AND PARTNERSHIP

The application of Lewin's three principles of contact, continuity and democratic decision-making tend to advance negotiation towards dialogue and partnership (Lewin, 1997). Once established, this can be strengthened and enhanced in numerous ways. Recognition can be provided through publicity and awards, such as those annually made by the HCA Academy in support of the Homes and Communities Agency's community engagement and development programmes (Homes and Communities Agency, 2010). Funding and support for implementation can also be highly effective ways to consolidate partnerships. Contributions to the running costs of neighbourhood associations, creek catchment coordinating committees and community engagement groups have helped to give vital institutional continuity to bodies whose energies would otherwise be rapidly dissipated in the taxing demands of simply maintaining their existence. Similarly, governments who provide funding to independent charitable organisations to run sensitive programmes such as supported accommodation for homeless and disaffected young people are both supporting and benefiting from collaborative action.

Australia's Landcare programme has developed since the 1980s to provide an interesting example of the success of this approach. Growing out of an initiative originally criticised as being merely therapeutic, it now includes hundreds of local groups of rural people prepared to develop and implement small- and medium-scale schemes of environmental reclamation, conservation and improvement (Landcare Australia, 2010). Landcare has applied in a non-theoretical way the three principles of contact, continuity and democratic process. It has now grown to include new 'Water Care' organisations, which may prove powerful local partners in the Commonwealth Government's proposed new national initiative to improve water conservation, starting with the troubled Murray Darling Basin, which constitutes more than a sixth of the continent's total area.

Community planning based on this kind of partnership can lead to fully collaborative planning with local groups and networks assuming responsibility for major portions of community life. These may include open space management of urban farms, creek catchments and local parks; economic activities of industrial incubators and mentoring programmes; transport innovations, such as carpooling schemes and bikeway monitoring and promotion; and community festivals that celebrate the diversity and self-expression of different cultures.

Roles and responsibilities in governance and participation

Of the four widely accepted roles of government – representation, agency, service and regulation (Gunlicks, 1981) – representation is probably the most characteristic of contemporary society. Selecting a representative through competitive election responds to that fascination with personality which is a continuing theme in local and national politics throughout the world. Elections reflect current preoccupations with choice. Political contests feed our insatiable appetite for battles between opposing interests and views. The public display of winners and losers responds to widely held assumptions about social evolution through survival of the fittest. Finally, the selection of representatives enshrines democratic commitment to the rights of electorates to give and remove mandates.

REPRESENTATION

The fact that representation and participation are strongly linked was recognised over 150 years ago by J. S. Mill, when he wrote:

There is no difficulty in showing that the ideally best form of government is that in which the sovereignty or supreme controlling power ... is vested in the entire aggregate of the community, every citizen not only having a voice in the exercise of that ultimate sovereignty, but being, at least occasionally, called upon to take an actual part in that government, by the personal discharge of some public function, local or general. (Mill, 1983)

This ideal has never been abandoned and is now strongly advocated in the 'third way' politics of community engagement and social enterprise which is reflected every day in the voluntary activities of countless local communities. Ken Livingstone's campaign for the newly established Mayoralty of London in 1999 relied on the voluntary participation of individuals and local groups who supported his leadership on such issues as the development of London as an inclusive and welcoming World City, maintaining public transport in public ownership and strengthening local government participation in the provision of affordable social housing. He had the support of no major political party. The mayors of both Curitiba and Bogotá similarly called upon the support and commitment of local groups in pursuing public transport policies that favoured the mass of the working population rather than the affluent, car-driving elite (Meadows, 1995). As we have seen earlier in the chapter, Barack Obama won the 2008 Presidential election partly because of his ability to mobilise the voluntary participation of numerous groups of local enthusiasts determined by their numbers and organisational commitment to outweigh the huge financial resources of the business-supported Republican Party.

The roles of leadership

Such links between representation and leadership go back more than two millennia to the three decades of Pericles' repeated re-election as the *strategos* in 4th century BC Athens, and his conviction that Athenians were confirmed in their courage in defending their city because of their role as free citizens in selecting the city's leaders, who were required to regularly resubmit themselves for election or replacement (Popper, 1998; Fox, 2008).[xi] Thus in parallel with the rightly praised participatory democracy of the Athens of that time, there was an equally strong commitment to representative democracy.[xii]

This association has a number of practical advantages for both systems. A sense of participation provides the necessary stimulus for electorates to exercise their voting rights. Decisive action, which is often crucial in times of rapid internal and external change and threats, is also favoured. The importance of representative leadership is no less at the finer grain of local community life, where strong leaders can confront electorates with the need to take choices and to find resources for their implementation. Leaders must go beyond themselves accepting the need to provide the means, when they have willed the ends, to actively encourage their electorates do likewise, accepting the realities of a world largely governed by cause and effect. This role was well expressed by Gordon Campbell, later the Premier of British Columbia, when as Chair of the Great Vancouver Regional Council in the welcoming speech (quoted in Chapter 4) to members of the Council of Councils in Vancouver: 'You can have anything you want,' he said. 'But you can't have everything and you can't have it right now: you must take choices!' Such local and regional leadership is a crucial part of community governance.

Selection of representatives

In modern mass democracies, composed of communities which may consist of many thousands or even millions of people, choosing representatives to take decisions on behalf of electorates too numerous to be directly involved becomes a logical necessity. Nevertheless, we should not lose sight of the many ways in which community participation still plays an important part in maintaining the health of representative democracy. Sacrifice of direct personal power can be balanced by gains from the 'open society', where discussion and challenge can create a continuous climate of social dialogue (Popper, 1998). Representation of both people and ideas can be contested, and both can be accepted or rejected, so that political debate acquires the character of 'conjecture and refutation', giving rise to societies whose guarantee of freedom is the capacity for electorates periodically to reject and remove representatives and ideas that they do not support.

Links with quantity

Representation also has very strong links with the issues of quantity and measurement which are such strong skeins in contemporary society. It thrives on the counting of numbers and turns the arithmetic of popularity into dominating issues of media discussion and public interest. The recurrent dramas of elections and the counting of votes have been extended to include the regular review of opinion polls and reports of focus groups, which provide another link between representation and participation, sensitising governments to the likely electoral consequences of adopting particular polices. It is clear to the least curious observer that governments and political parties are increasingly using private opinion polls to test the popularity of policies before they are adopted.

The operations of representative democracy

Over the last three centuries, representative democracy has developed a number of useful mechanisms which have come to be regarded as best practice. These include the division and separation of powers, the rules of accountability, the encouragement of volunteering and the integration of contemporary technology. The familiar separation of powers between legislative parliaments, executive governments and independent judiciaries has become a standard principle in modern democracy. Montesquieu's (1989) formulation of the doctrine, in his 1747 book *The Spirit of the Laws*, was based on his interpretation of the British system. He advocated the separation of powers so that each role could act as an effective check on the others and thereby forestall the development of absolutist centralised control. Elective legislatures would represent many interests, so that laws would be framed by bodies informed by a wide range of facts and values. Executive governments should not go beyond the powers of these laws, but would need to devise compliant programmes for the good conduct and progress of their societies. This would require a public service sector including a law enforcement arm and a number of continuing departments to provide and regulate approved services. Finally, an independent judiciary would ensure that no one, not government, business corporations nor private citizens, would be above the law.

This doctrine has been criticised by some twentieth-century leaders in Africa and Asia as being excessively conditioned by Western political traditions of adversarial individualism, which are held to be inappropriate in more cooperative consensual societies (influenced perhaps by the 'monsoon culture' of necessary collaboration to manage the dramatic effects of annual inundations by monsoons and the need to maintain complex irrigations systems). The argument is made that there is a tradition of natural leadership in such societies, where everyone cooperates for the undisputed good of the whole community, which is the polar opposite of the doctrine, discussed earlier, of 'conjecture and refutations' as the lever of progress in Western societies. Leaders such as Premier Lee Kuan Yew in Singapore, President Mahathir of Malaysia, and President Suharto in Indonesia, for instance, consistently argued along these lines. In sum, these ideas have not been well supported by the test of outcomes. President Suharto has been discredited and superseded by a regime giving more respect to the separation of powers, and President Mahathir's imprisonment of political opponents has been subsequently overturned. The most successful economies and societies in East Asia include countries such as Japan, South Korea and Taiwan, which aim to incorporate the separation of powers in their government. These limitations exercised by independent judiciaries and legislatures over the powers of government provide an important balance, in whatever continent or stage of development they may be. They erect safeguards to protect the rights of individuals against the development of monopoly powers by central governments.

Another threat to good governance is the tendency for actual power to be concentrated in the hands of unelected and often overburdened bureaucrats. This could be described as the doctrine of the 'altruistic bureaucrat' inherent in the case made out for representative government by Jeremy Bentham. He argued that public interest legislation enacted by governments would be implemented by public servants, motivated by the 'pleasure/pain principle' to do good work and confer maximum benefits upon the wider society (Mill, 1983). In practice, the growth of huge bureaucracies has often resulted in the development of great social, psychological and physical distances between public servants and the people whose welfare has been entrusted to them. Franz Kafka has satirised this in his novels *America* (1949), *The Castle* (1974) and *The Trial* (1994). Jurgen Habermas (1987) refers to the displacement of the direct experience of the 'lifeworld' by the deadening formality (and often irrelevance) of the 'systemworld'. These kinds of critiques have led to the rapid rise to popularity and adoption of the 'principle of subsidiarity' discussed earlier in this section, to reduce the distance between decision points and action points and to involve local people both in decisions about their communities' governance and in actually taking over as much as possible of the delivery of services themselves. A further and particularly significant aspect of this is the recognition of the importance of voluntary organisations in participating in governance, which has developed into the idea of 'third way' politics, adopting unreservedly neither total state nor market interests, but assisting communities to identify and meet their own needs collaboratively. The increasingly common term 'social enterprises' provides an accurate description of bodies as diverse as housing associations and workers' cooperatives, which are aiming to make social rather than financial profits, and to do so with the energy and pride in performance often claimed for commercial organisations.

ACCOUNTABILITY

Safeguards over the responsibility of governments take the form of measures of accountability. Commentators have pointed out the key roles that regular and guaranteed publicity play in entrenching such accountability (Rawls, 1971) and this has been enhanced by the dramatic spread of information technology and public access to information of recent decades, including such initiatives as 'Wikileaks'. In community planning, this will require dissemination of the aims, programmes and intended processes of planning activities, so that actual performance can be judged against clearly stated intentions and standards. Since their adoption in the mid-twentieth century, expectations of accountability can be derived from above, from such sources as the International Declaration of Human Rights and the European Convention on Human Rights (Hellenic Resources Network, 1995) and from the grass roots from specific statements of the guiding principles of local planning systems, such as the Oregon Goals and numerous health, education and workplace charters. The adoption of these safeguards and their incorporation in the public record provide further examples of citizen participation in healthy representative systems. Accountability can also involve legal controls, specifying rights of redress, restitution and removal. Geoffrey Robertson has pointed out that the ultimate security against bad government and tyranny is the prospect of retribution (1999, 2005). In future, leaders such as Slobodan Milosevic or Radovan Karadžić or the perpetrators of mass killings in Rwanda and Sudan will need to be looking over their shoulders at those who may bring them to judgment against internationally accepted standards of human rights. In the same way, local communities who know and understand the principles and processes which should guide policy development and plan adoption are in a stronger position to participate in their future health and prosperity. Accountability therefore extends beyond the negatives of redress to embrace and support the encouragement of participation.

Voluntary activism

This encouragement is at its strongest in the activities of volunteers, which is discussed in more detail later in the chapter, reviewing 'agency'. Volunteer individuals and groups play increasingly widely recognised roles, in the operation of representative governments, and are ideal partners to help develop and implement policies. Qualified by both knowledge and commitment, their participation has become an established social advantage, an economic necessity and a potential political safeguard against centralist conformity and the dead hand of standardisation.

Flexible and innovative methods

All systems of government stand to gain from thoughtful adaptation to social and technological change. Monarchies, for instance, quickly incorporated the invention of the printing press five centuries ago to expand the scope and scale of government, and support the creation of nation states. Similarly, the spread of mass literacy of the last two centuries provided better informed and more alert electorates, which supported the practice of representative democracy. Now, the information technology revolution of the 1990s offers prospects of quicker and more widely based participation in identifying public needs and preferences. Cell phones have become mini computers, and well-sorted information is readily available to anyone with access to a phone network. We have seen in Chapter 8, that this may result in a two-way tug of war between the central control of technology by global scale communication giants such as Microsoft, Google and News Ltd., and networks of locally based interest groups committed to causes like environmental conservation, social justice, open access and reduction of income disparities. Mediating between them are new structures like Wikipedia, the Wiki movement of open access and sourcing and Wikileaks, based on the idea that good ideas will drive out bad ones, making use of challenges both to information and to attempted deletions or replacements. The well-established processes of developing knowledge, by speculation, publication, review and reformulation, can be replicated in the powerful accelerator of the Internet, to the ultimate benefit of all participants.

Representative democracy cannot escape responding to these new opportunities. The 2008 election of Barack Obama to the United States presidency, discussed earlier in this chapter, was assisted by these new techniques of more active mass participation. Throughout the country, people with community development interests pooled their support for a candidate who shared their commitments to both community development and community law, using electronic fundraising networks to outweigh large corporate sponsorships. Other applications could improve sensitivity of policy development to public prefer-ences, making use of such techniques as rapid opinion polling, use of referenda to illuminate public concerns and priorities and virtual community conferences. Such approaches are strongly supported by the increasingly clear evidence that people of all levels of education and attitude find that information technology is enjoyable, which is not always true of conventional contemporary politics.

Current confidence in representative government

It is easy to overestimate public concern at the failings of venality, dishonesty, self-seeking and extravagance of current representative systems. Commercial media, at least as prone to those vices as politicians, often enlarge on these themes in self-righteous indignation, particularly when it is expedient to provide an alternative focus for public resentment to remove attention from the extraordinary failings of national and international capital and bankers, as was the case in the height of the global financial crisis of 2008/09. Nevertheless, the routine misappropriation of allowances by many members of the UK Parliament, amounting in many cases to over £200 000 for a single Member of Parliament, was not an encouraging development for English politics and the 'Mother of Parliaments' (Wapedia, 2009). People expected their leaders to set an example of financial probity. Democratic regimes do seem to be experiencing a pervasive problem of political behaviour that can be both illegal and unapologetically self-justifying.[xiii] The power of modern information and communication technology is increasingly revealing situations where politicians go beyond the normal range of human behaviour to demonstrate failings that the community does not want to accept in public figures. This can result in voter apathy, abstention, non-cooperation or even in more extreme cases, in acts of violent political dissent.

Communities committed to maintaining representative democracy (perhaps on the Churchillian basis that, however bad it is, all the alternatives are worse) may be wise to search for ways to improve the quality and performance of candidates for political office. There is a case that, just as people need to qualify to practise as doctors, so we should seek evidence of the suitability of candidates to stand for electoral office. One plausible criterion could be the performance of a period, possibly between two and five years, of voluntary community service, in such activities as access support, aged care, community education or engagement, cultural promotion, environmental maintenance, social welfare or sports and recreation promotion. This would have the double benefit of establishing the genuine interest of potential political leaders in community life and progress and providing the opportunity for them to demonstrate capacity, honesty and public spirit. It would also provide an effective training ground in public affairs. Another approach consists of the systematic increase in the participation of elected representatives in public dialogues. People may be very interested to learn the views on current controversies of their Member of Parliament or local councillor. As societies, we are still awaiting the delivery of the 'technology dividend' of time saved by the power of automation and information technology, which is instead resulting in further material acquisition and amplification of activities. It would be very beneficial if that increase in individual productivity were to be applied to make time to participate in dialogue and debate about the ends and means of shared community life, involving the active participation of local representatives.[xiv]

AGENCY

The balance between public and private action in Western societies has swung backwards and forwards over the last two centuries between extremes of State abstention and involvement. As mercantilism gave way to free market economics in the eighteenth and nineteenth centuries, Adam Smith's view that 'that government is best which governs least' led to minimal agency on the part of governments, which were largely restricted to defence, policing and promotion of trade between individuals and companies (Barber, 1967). However, the results of this policy of laissez-faire rapidly became unacceptable. Cholera was no respecter of persons. Slum housing bred bad health and enfeebled workers. Duplicated and unsafe railway lines competitively erected by private entrepreneurs dislocated shared settlements, destroying regional landscapes long treasured by their landowning classes. In England, utilitarian philosophers and public policy practitioners such as Edwin Chadwick and John Stuart Mill (1983) urged that governments should recognise the need for concerted action to achieve common goals of progress and productivity.[xv] In rapid succession, first in Britain, then in Germany and France, governments at national and local levels took on dominating roles in health, housing, education, public transport, public open space and cultural promotion.

Reaction against these energetic and expensive roles set in by the mid-twentieth century, with such prominent examples as Freidrich Von Hayek's apocalyptic denunciation of the *Road to Serfdom* (1944) and Josef

Schumpeter's more cautious advocacy of the role of evolutionary capitalism in generating productive innovation (Schumpeter, 1934). Milton Friedman (1962) argued that J. M. Keynes' concern with 'demand side' regulation would not maximise prosperity as much as 'supply side' policies that allowed the people's predilections for consumption and investment to encourage maximum economic growth. The long mid-twentieth-century plateau of prosperity further encouraged governments to withdraw from welfare programmes. As a result, public housing was sold, public transport privatised, community spaces commercialised within developer-owned shopping centres, and enterprise zones, such as London's Docklands, established where developers could more or less make their own rules (Hall, 2002). By 1992, Osborne and Gaebler were rationalising these developments by arguing for the reinvention of government, where public authorities would be in engaged in 'not rowing but steering'.

By the time the crest of this wave of self-confidence broke in the 2008 housing crisis in the United States and the consequent 2009 Global Financial Crisis, alternative approaches were already available and widely advocated. 'Third way' policies, referred to earlier, were seeking to draw in the energy of communities and voluntary groups (Giddens, 2001; Mawson, 2008). Theories of worker cooperation, associational economics and micro finance were already being developed into sets of proposals for alternative policies, available for collaborative community partnerships (Whyte & Whyte, 1989; Bornstein, 1997; Cooke & Morgan, 1998; Yunus, 1998; Mondragon Corporation Cooperative, 2008).

These 'third way' options are timely for governments, which are newly motivated to take action to stimulate economies and employment. Working with not-for-profit regional and national agencies and voluntary providers in housing, transport, communications, power and water, governments can reclaim public control of activities that are essential to national economic health but are unsuited to market control, either because they are natural monopolies or because low-cost provision is required in the public interest. At the same time, the initiative of state and local governments may be bound by decisions of citizen referenda limiting government expenditure. Such instances include Propositions 13 in California, and various Citizen's Initiatives in Oregon throughout the 1990s (Citrin & Martin, 2010; Thompson & Green, 2004). As a result, the option of partnering with voluntary and community organisations becomes increasingly attractive. It is significant that Australia's financial stimulus initiative of 2008/09 was more successful in finding partners for its new housing programmes among the not-for-profit organisations than in the resurgent merchant banking sector (Lenaghan, 2009).

SERVICE ACTIVITIES

The traditional roles of local government, often described as 'roads, rates and rubbish', linked local provision of transport and waste disposal to local funding. Parks and public gardens also tended to become council responsibilities because they required local design and maintenance. In the evolution of local governance, public health was not far behind, with the introduction of roles such as 'medical officer of health' to protect the community against unsanitary practices which might give rise to threats to public health, and to oversee the conditions in private and charitable hospitals and clinics. The introduction of national health systems in the mid-twentieth century raised issues of system-wide organisation and integration. Education is another function which is administered at different levels in different countries. In the United States, school boards with their 85 000 members (Dye, 1988), often form the most local level of representative governance, while elsewhere, as in England, primary and secondary education tends to be allocated to counties or similar upper- or middle-tier authorities (Jackson, 1969). Elsewhere again, as in France, systems are more centralised. Worldwide, national governments are laying down national curricula and raising issues for educational administrators of articulation between national standards and content, state or regional coordination and local delivery.

It is clear that none of these activities will benefit from being monopolised by one tier or sector of the community. Links are required, for instance, between public, private and voluntary methods in providing health services, emphasising the need for collaborative planning and system management. In most countries, direct relations with patients assist local healers and doctors to take responsibility for running their own practices within general guidelines of medical ethics, though often with funding support from central governments. Regulation of hospitals may be either regional or central. Management may be either by public service models, as in Australia, or on contemporary business performance and monetised bases, as in the United Kingdom.

The situation is similarly complex in education and transport. In education, public, market and charitable foundations all contribute and may all adopt different and unrelated methods of governance and accountability. Energetic market innovations in child care centres and tertiary education require careful consideration to governance and integration with other educational and social systems.[xvi] In transport, too, there is a need to relate national systems, policies and funding with regional coordination and local delivery. Generally speaking, the most successful transport systems are those where most thought has been given to coordinated governance, as in the case of the Toronto Transit Commission (2010), with its integration of bus, subway, street car and rapid transit transport. This is of great significance to community planning: on the one hand, fully effective planning and implementation can only occur where there is collaborative and integrated governance; on the other, the necessary collaborative planning can be a very useful step towards recognising the factors and processes needed to achieve responsive and coherent governance.

In summary, four aspects must be reviewed in the governance of community services: first is their role in contributing to community well-being and prosperity; second are the often competing advantages and disadvantages of provisions by public, private and voluntary sectors; third is the extent to which governance arrangements can coordinate systems internally and externally and fourth are the conditions required to achieve acceptable levels of problem-solving and accountability.

Contributions to social well-being

Many of the ingredients of human, social and cultural capital which are being increasingly recognised as crucial to the success of communities can be nurtured by community services of education, health, recreation and culture (Putnam, 1993, 2000, 2004; Hutchinson & Vidal, 2004). Putnam has shown, for instance, how traditions of civic responsibility and cultural transmission in Tuscany, Veneto and Emilia Romagna have contributed to the economic success and social stability of those regions, compared with the less active public life of the regions of the Mezzogiorno further south. In Australia, too, the greater economic prosperity and social stability in the second half of the twentieth century, as compared with that of Argentina, has also been ascribed to the country's higher levels of investment in public education, health and housing programmes (Pusey, 1991). Between them, health and education do much to shape the human resources which build successful communities.

Public, private and community provision

As the dust settles on the disputes between public, private and voluntary provision of community services, it is becoming increasingly clear that each has valuable roles to contribute, and that these need to be integrated in some form of coherent governance and accountability. Some basic principles will assist. It is the responsibility of national governments to ensure the equitable provisions of health, education and access, involving the planning, provision and delivery of public systems. Individual, commercial and voluntary initiatives can often make valuable contributions to meet these needs, and performance levels will be able to ensure that this does not result in failures of quality or loss of consistent standards. As has been seen earlier, in Chapter 8, the commitment and energy of voluntary groups can provide innovation and outreach. Educational innovations, for instance, frequently come from imaginative individuals such as Maria Montessori, Friedrich Froebel, Rudolf Steiner and A. S. Neill. Later, their insights can be integrated into wider systems. Health is now big business and the private sector is often eager to invest large sums in such activities as radiology, diagnostics and elective and cosmetic treatment, which may well contribute to later improvement of the public sector, but must be carefully regulated to avoid abuses.

Coordination of systems

Given the power of modern information technology, it is possible to create systems which integrate the different levels of delivery of these services, giving as much priority to 'bottom up' services like regular provision of general medical practice by private doctors as to 'top down' ones of national policies like immunisation, family planning, drug and alcohol abuse management and supply systems for prescription drugs. Since 1986, Australia has been practising a composite but coherent system linking public hospitals, largely run by the states, but funded federally, with voluntary (but subsidised) health insurance linked to both public and private hospitals. Meanwhile, the bulk of day-to-day health care is provided by local general practices, which are also subsidised. Recent proposals, discussed below and summarised and developed in Figure 11.1, would streamline the system by combining Commonwealth funding and quality control with local management by district health boards or 'Medicare locals'. Details of governance arrangements for these bodies have not yet been resolved, but Figure 11.1 integrates proposals made twenty years earlier in Canada by the Ontario provincial ministries of Health and Community

Services but never introduced owing to a change in government. Such a composite system may be well suited to the United States, which is currently struggling to introduce health care that can combine universal access and required minimum standards of service with acceptability to the health care professionals and industry. Similarly, in education, national curriculum, literacy and numeracy policies and examination standards can be related to local educational needs and potentialities.

Accountability

It is clear that a final question remains: how to achieve accountability for the integrated local delivery that will guarantee access, convenience and quality to individuals and communities? Debates have raged for decades about the relative advantages of different systems of accountability for services. District boards have been proposed to bring governance back closer to action points, but these have been criticised as not reflecting the expanding scale of settlements and social geography, and therefore being confined to reactive rather than proactive roles. Wider regional boards have been proposed to meet these criticisms, but they have often been not well liked by central administrators who see them as potentially challenging and dissident bodies, and criticised them as lacking grassroots legitimacy. In order to achieve fitness for function, it will be helpful to explore appropriate governance structures for preferred systems of organisation and delivery. Questions of representation and authority have to be resolved.

A general pattern of integrated delivery of health, education and work systems in clustered hubs has been outlined in Chapter 8. It is useful to explore the governance implications of this approach. The proposal, mentioned above and developed in the Canadian Province of Ontario in the 1990s, for multi-service agencies to provide a full and integrated range of health services for populations of about 200 000, provides an example of how this could be done within the three fields of community development, social services and health (Province of Ontario Ministries of Citizenship, Community & Social Service and Health, 1993).[xvii] The model, incorporated within Figure 11.1, is particularly well suited to match the functional mix involved in the 'hub' approach, drawing together into governance boards caregivers and service providers, representatives from government departments (who will be providing substantial quantities of funds) together with consumers and clients from hinterlands defined by accessibility catchments. Control of the

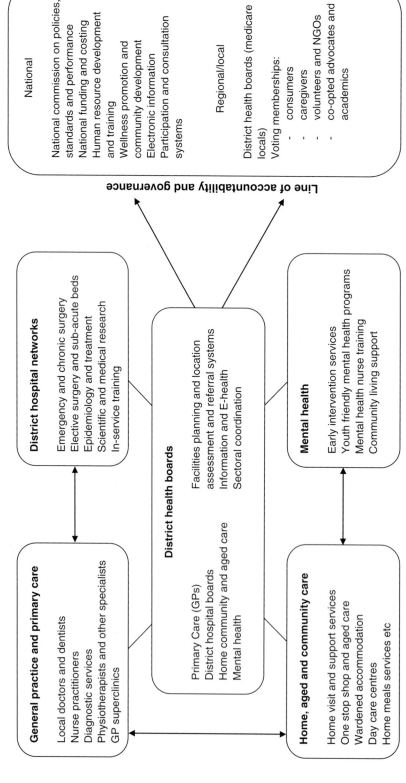

Figure 11.1 An integrated system of health governance and delivery. *Source: Province of Ontario, Ministries of Citizenship, Community & Social Services & Health (1993); Australian Government (2010).*

Medicare locals could thus be placed in the hands of a board representing both providers and consumers of services irrespective of whether they were in the public, private or voluntary sectors. The principle could be extended sideways to incorporate cooperative planning and management between systems. The hallmark of this approach to the governance of services is that it is democratic in fields where in the past inadequate attention has been given to this aspect of accountability. It is also collaborative in situations where very important gains can be achieved by linking the planning of space, support services, access and information exchange.

Regulation

Most aspects of government involve some form of regulation. For instance, in most contemporary societies, taxation regulates the contribution that each individual must make to the upkeep of community life. School attendance and standards aim to ensure that learning is universal and adequate for the transmission of knowledge and skills. Health standards are normally safeguarded by controls over house building and medical qualifications. Environmental quality is protected by waste disposal rules for households and businesses. Building regulation and inspections protect current and future generations from poor design and inadequate materials and workmanship. Development assessment and controls protect public interests, amenity and neighbourhood rights and test proposals for environmental and community impacts. Licensing of public premises safeguards neighbours' rights, and user safety. Traffic and transport rules ensure safe conditions on movement channels of road, rail, sea and air. All of these regulations should aim to balance maximum possible benefits for the wider community with minimum necessary intrusion to the rights of individuals. Lack of such regulations can result in loss of amenity, opportunity and even life.

It is clear that regulations should pay equal attention to the values of order, freedom, equity and prosperity. They define not only what people can't do but also what, by implication, they may do without permission. They imply equality before the law: all are equally liable to obey them, irrespective of wealth, birth or power. J. S. Mill (1983) argues cogently that the boundary of one person's liberty is that of his or her fellow's. The clear conclusion is that in other-affecting matters, we need regulations to provide a strong dividing line beyond which individuals may not trespass, whether it concerns payment of workers, impact on the envi-

ronment or treatment of their children. The qualities of individual and social rights gain precision and enforceability when they are expressed in terms of the quantities of numbers which must be reached or which may not be exceeded – whether noise levels, length of stay in a parking area, tensile strength of a beam or minimum lot size for construction of a dwelling. Nevertheless, the limiting case for regulations is supplied by the arguments of John Rawls (1971), that people should be wary of imposing excessive regulation on each other because they should expect the same rules to be applied to themselves in the largely unpredictable world of future events. In summary, order demands that regulations be enforced; equity that they apply equally to all; and liberty that they be regularly reviewed to ensure that they make minimum necessary inroads into people's personal choices. Good regulations can increase liberty by preventing some people from having too much at the cost of others who have too little, and can promote justice by ensuring that rules only restrict others in ways that we ourselves would be willing to accept restrictions.

Another aspect of regulation is the exemption which higher levels of government often claim from the jurisdiction of lesser ones (rather like a modern survival of the 'divine right of kings' to do as they like in their own jurisdictions). This approach can ride roughshod over community life and the good planning of local communities. For instance, a high proportion of the worst and most insensitive buildings in modern metropolises will be found, on enquiry, to have been erected by government departments exempted from normal processes of development control, by which contentious proposals are normally improved, thereby avoiding the processes of social and environmental impact assessment and testing of unintended consequences. Particularly dangerous evasions of prudential regulation occur when senior governments pass on such exemptions to commercial buyers for profit. Major airports previously owned by the national governments have recently been sold to private corporations, who may then enjoy the same legal exemptions from development control or liability to comply with regional, city or local plans as if they were being operated by elected governments in the accountable national interest. They are neither directly nor indirectly accountable to anyone but their own, often international, shareholders.[xviii] Good planning legislation, like that in Oregon, specifically removes such exemptions by making state government departments comply with regional, city and local plans once they have signed off on them (Oregon Department of Land Conservation & Development, 2010).

Nevertheless, ever-present dangers of over-regulation need to be scrupulously avoided. Such excesses were vividly demonstrated in the totalitarian regimes of the twentieth century, in Nazi concentration camps and Communist labour-force planning. Bater (1979) explains the *propiskaya* system of permits, which for thirty years regulated where soviet workers could and could not live and work, which Solzhenitsyn had earlier described in harrowing terms in his *Gulag Archipelago* (1974). Similar regulations operated at the same time in South Africa, compounded and overlain by brutal racism. Such excesses certainly can seem to give regulation a bad name. The best tests for valid regulations is that they can be shown to contribute to the sum total of human choice, and that limitations should only be imposed on individuals which they may wish to see imposed on others. For instance, fair consideration should be given to the arguments of supporters of enterprise zones that the removal of planning and development regulations in particular areas such as London's Docklands and tax liabilities in 'Freeports' in developing economies is justified because of the industrial growth and technology transfer that they hope will result. Such claims need to be considered on their merits, by means of rigorous and public social and environmental impact analyses, and weighing of unintended consequences against anticipated benefits.

No discussion of the effects of regulation on communities would be complete without reference to the far-reaching effects of the financial deregulation of the 1980s and 1990s – both worldwide and nationally. Rules of prudential behaviour, accountability and transparency now being developed in discussions among world leaders and finance ministers are clearly necessary to provide strong safeguards for local and national communities in an era of increasingly dominant global economics. Local and national communities need to be able to embark on energetic participation in global trade in the confidence that they can protect their community's ownership of the factors of production of land, labour and capital and prevent overseas operators from stripping their assets, colonising their workforces or buying out their resources of land and food production (Allen, 2010).

Both regulation and deregulation have therefore legitimate and important roles to play in governance. Regular review is required to dismantle such unacceptable intrusions as interference in individuals' rights of religious belief and freedom of speech and publication. Equally, governments and their advisers should constantly consider carefully the need to introduce new regulations to meet emerging problems of technological and social change such as polluting emissions and the need to establish and maintain transparent records for adults entrusted with the welfare of young people. Community and voluntary organisations can also play important roles in reviewing regulations. Environmental associations may assist in proposing appropriate standards in such matters as access and activity regulations in national parks or design and dimensions of bikeways and walking trails. Private enterprise organisations can also be involved as watchdogs to remind governments of the costs in time and money of excessive and inefficient regulation leading to proposals for appropriate reforms (such as introducing 'deemed approvals' for proposed development after adequate time for their consideration has elapsed). Public regulation is therefore a necessary watchdog to oversee human agency. Working together, they can provide energy and direction to create communities where no one individual or group will be able to lay exclusive claims to opportunities that should be equally open to all.

Scales of community and their roles of governance and control

It is clear that communities at many scales from local to global are based not only on shared physical spaces but also on shared interests, prospects and values. Figure 11.2 indicates the six different levels of governance which correspond to the different levels of community life identified in Table 3.1 at the beginning of Chapter 3 and discussed in Chapters 3 and 4: these levels are the local, urban, regional, national, supranational and global.

In each case, governance is a complex activity, consisting of the intertwining of the three strands of formal representation, organised interest groups and advocacy or promotional bodies, pursuing values to which their members are committed.

At the local level, community representation can take the form of organised Community Boards as in New Zealand and *panchayati*, in India (Mitra, 2001; Local Government, New Zealand, 2009). These may be integrated with local electoral units, or be more independent neighbourhood associations, owing their origins to a variety of reasons and subsequently growing to achieve recognised roles in representing the interests of the locality. The 104 neighbourhood associations of Portland, Oregon are a well-known example of this style, but there are countless others throughout the world in countries such as Canada, the Netherlands, the United Kingdom, the United States

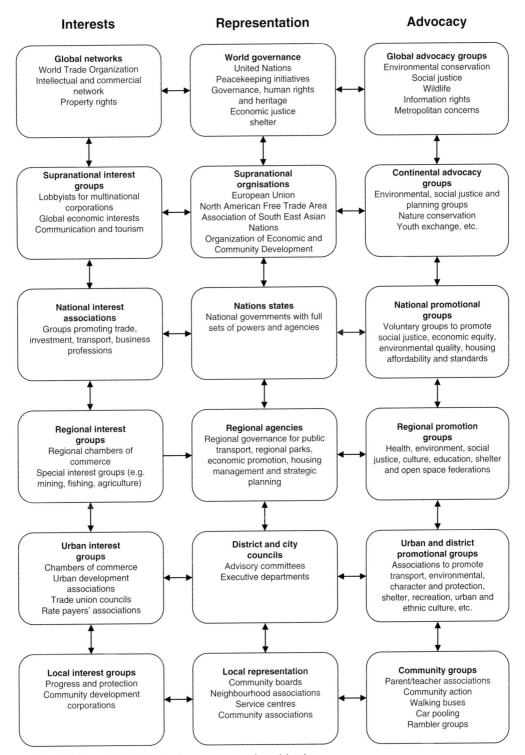

Interests

Representation

Advocacy

Global networks
World Trade Organization
Intellectual and commercial
network
Property rights

World governance
United Nations
Peacekeeping initiatives
Governance, human rights
and heritage
Economic justice
shelter

Global advocacy groups
Environmental conservation
Social justice
Wildlife
Information rights
Metropolitan concerns

**Supranational interest
groups**
Lobbyists for multinational
corporations
Global economic interests
Communication and tourism

**Supranational
orgnisations**
European Union
North American Free Trade Area
Association of South East Asian
Nations
Organization of Economic and
Community Development

**Continental advocacy
groups**
Environmental, social justice and
planning groups
Nature conservation
Youth exchange, etc.

**National interest
associations**
Groups promoting trade,
investment, transport, business
professions

Nations states
National governments with full
sets of powers and agencies

**National promotional
groups**
Voluntary groups to promote
social justice, economic equity,
environmental quality, housing
affordability and standards

**Regional interest
groups**
Regional chambers of
commerce
Special interest groups (e.g.
mining, fishing, agriculture)

Regional agencies
Regional governance for public
transport, regional parks,
economic promotion, housing
management and strategic
planning

**Regional promotion
groups**
Health, environment, social
justice, culture, education, shelter
and open space federations

**Urban interest
groups**
Chambers of commerce
Urban development
associations
Trade union councils
Rate payers' associations

**District and city
councils**
Advisory committees
Executive departments

**Urban and district
promotional groups**
Associations to promote
transport, environmental,
character and protection,
shelter, recreation, urban and
ethnic culture, etc.

Local interest groups
Progress and protection
Community development
corporations

Local representation
Community boards
Neighbourhood associations
Service centres
Community associations

Community groups
Parent/teacher associations
Community action
Walking buses
Car pooling
Rambler groups

Figure 11.2 The global context: six levels of governance and participation.

and Venezuela, in all six settled continents. They are well positioned to link upwards to city and district councils. They can represent and include local interest groups such as parents and teachers, progress and residents associations, as well as local promotional groups involving religious bodies, environmental action associations, creek conservation groups, heritage societies and mutual aid activities such as bulk food buying. Community planning at this local level can benefit greatly from recognising such local groups by involving them in such consultation and community action programmes as environmental maintenance, traffic monitoring, school support and response to development proposals.

At the urban level, city and district councils represent one of the longest and best-established forms of governance. Executive and planning departments undertake a wide range of roles, now including as well as the traditional 'roads, rates and rubbish' such crucial community functions as parks and open space, culture and festivals, public and active transport, social activation and planning. In some places, they play an important role in running and managing education; elsewhere they may provide social housing, and they are the most active of any level of community governance in promoting community development. Their links to the strongly entrenched urban interest groups of chambers of commerce, development associations and trades councils in many instances date back hundreds of years to medieval guilds. City councils may also develop links with promotional groups that may want to urge new policies and changes of emphasis or direction of urban management. There is increasing recognition that voluntary, charitable and religious groups may be invaluable partners for city councils looking to adopt 'third way' policies of devolution of responsibilities and subsidiarity of powers.

One version of regional government is based on direct election in regions and provinces with long historical traditions such as those of Spain, Italy and Germany providing longer-term and wider-ranging perspectives to steer and balance future development. In rapidly growing metropolitan regions, representative governance is normally based on indirect election, with members of constituent cities and districts working together to oversee such regional functions as strategic planning, environmental management, public transport, water and power supply and regional level health coordination. The continuing successes of Metro Portland and Metro Vancouver and the earlier ones of Metro Toronto in accommodating a tripling of the metropolitan population between 1953 and 1983 (Lemon, 1985; Heywood, 1997) are well known. By contrast, the administrative ingenuity of approaches such as the Greater London and Bangkok Authorities rest heavily on the election of a high-profile mayor responsible for developing a vision and strategies for the future of the metropolitan region. Both sorts of regional governments are well designed to liaise with regional interest groups concerned with business and economic promotion and advocacy bodies promoting concerns such as shelter, transport, environment, social justice, culture, health and education. The old belief that participation and consultation can only be conducted at the local level of face-to-face contact is discounted by the clear advantages which the regional level offers for consultation between representatives, interest groups and advocate organisations. Even in the days of Facebook and Twitter, there is much truth in the aphorism, ascribed to T. S. Eliot, that the only true cultures are regional ones, because localities are too small to contain a full cross-section of interests and nations are too large to allow face-to-face meetings, whereas regional associations allow people to meet and exchange ideas and interest in a number of different fields. Without diminishing the importance of the local and national levels, regional communities are a very effective tier for engagement and planning.

National parliaments remain the most effective representative bodies in the contemporary world because of their combination of law-making and law enforcement, cultural expression and cultural shaping and economic representation and control of benefits. Nations constitute large and diverse communities, where policies and programmes can be planned within the context of overall community benefits, and where unequalled powers provide the most significant control of outcomes for the regional, city and local communities. Diverse interests of investment, business and the professions all find powerful voices within this arena, but so do the promotional groups tirelessly concerned with environmental conservation, social justice, affordable housing and educational quality and justice. As we have seen in Chapters 3 and 4, various theorists of collaborative planning have demonstrated how regional and national level 'policy communities' of people who know and trust each other and understand each other's needs and ideals can be very powerful shapers of community planning at all scales (Faludi, 2005; Healey, 2006, 2007). Legislated transparency may be required to prevent this from deteriorating into collusive and exclusive self-serving, but at its best this kind of consensual cultural commitment can provide continuity and promote a climate of negotiation.

Supranational organisations like the European Union, the North American Free Trade Area and the

Association of South East Asian Nations are playing ever more significant roles in building new communities at continental and sub-continental scales. They are discovering common cultural traditions and reforming centuries' old traditions of dwelling on competition with their neighbours for roles and influence. The accumulated burden of past name-calling, demonisation and determination to exact retribution for old grievances has recently evolved towards a more rational examination of mutual dilemmas, shared development prospects and recognition of the economic advantages of mutual aid and exchange.

After many centuries frequently marked by internecine strife, mass persecution and even attempted extermination of minority groups, Europe is now leading the way in supranational community organisation, spanning political inclusion, cultural promotion and economic support for temporarily ailing national economies. The new continental level communities which are now emerging may well be slowed in their development by the obstacles created by different languages and sheer size but they do represent very real communities of interest, with capacities to forestall conflicts and to contain those which do occur. Their style and organisation is marked by a commitment to rational planning as a means to obtain mutual benefits.

The rapid growth of the idea and development of the reality of a global community has been strongly stimulated by recent developments. The explosion of communications technology, the spread of the global economy and the universal concern over the impacts of environmental change have fulfilled the forecasts of a global village. As we have seen earlier, commentators like George Monbiot (2003) argue powerfully that these changes demand the introduction of matching global governance. Monbiot does not believe that this can emerge from the United Nations, because of the structural control of the Security Council by the superpowers built into the organisation at the time of its establishment in the mid-twentieth century. Nevertheless, there is no doubting the organisation's great contributions to global governance, with its sponsorship and support for bodies such as the World Health Organization, the Food and Agriculture Organization, the United Nations Committee on Trade and Development, the United Nations Educational Scientific and Cultural Organization, Habitat and a dozen other such invaluable bodies that practise global governance in their own spheres. The global community is forging links of information and cultural exchange, as well as economic interdependence. Its membership is open to anyone who acquires the knowledge and skills to make use of modern communications technology.

Each of these six ascending scales of communities reflects the earlier definition at the beginning of Chapter 3 of 'groups of people who experience and acknowledge significant links, expectations and responsibilities towards each other'. Such mutual acceptance of shared destinies is the ultimate basis not just of community planning and governance but also of the community life which they exist to promote.

Conclusions: the contributions of participation and governance to community life

The very concept of community implies issues of governance. People who experience and acknowledge significant links and responsibilities towards each other have to decide how these links are to operate. In part, this can be accomplished through representative and democratic governance, in activities of agency, service and regulation and, of course, representation itself. In part, though, individual and group participation will be required to make representation responsive to people's actual intentions, and to give direct expression and effect to their values and preferences. These matters of choice in turn raise issues of freedom and order, rights of personal initiative to do what we think is right and the need to ensure that such freedom does not degenerate into activities of bullying or exploitation of others. Negotiation will be constantly required, both as a general approach to social relations and as a patterned process to reconcile opposing positions before disputes can turn toxic. At the most active end of the spectrum of governance, practices of partnership will offer the prospect of full personal involvement and control of community activities. This full array of involvement applies across the widening range of scales of community, from the urban and local to the global and supranational, and each one of us may find ourselves simultaneously active at several levels. Such multiple roles may produce strains between participation and governance that may sometimes become acute, but the same principles of communication, participation, negotiation and careful definition of roles and responsibilities should apply and assist in all situations and at all levels. As Mary Midgley (2003) observes:

> Morally, as well as physically, there is only one world, and we all have to live in it.

To do so well and comfortably, we must participate responsibly in its governance, and that participation implies a like role for others and a whole process of calculated community engagement.

Endnotes

i The freedom of serfs to leave the demesnes of their birth and move to work in the more productive and open towns contributed significantly to the evolution of Europe's regulated feudal communities into the civil societies of medieval cities (Fisher, 1956).

ii However, good order and personal protection should prevent publication of libels and slanders. Such criminal activities as recording and distributing performances of indecent acts, especially where these involve minors and disadvantaged individuals, can also claim no legitimate support from commitment to open government. Freedom of information is thus confined to public interest matters and must not be confused with license to distribute material which degrades or exploits others. Although the distinction is obvious, it needs to be re-stated to distinguish open governance from the fallacy that the unrestricted distribution of information working through the mechanisms of profit, loss and self-interest can safely be left to decide the future of communities.

iii The 1789 storming of the Bastille in Paris and the destruction of the Berlin Wall two hundred years later both spelt the end of exhausted regimes, and the mass shooting of the youthful protesters in Tiananmen Square in Beijing in the same year by the Chinese People's army announced the intention of the Communist Party not to relax its grip of centralised power.

iv Miller identifies, for instance a number of local governments which had been incorporated by special interest groups exclusively in their own interests. These included a number of cities with huge land values but very small populations, amounting in the case of the City of Commerce to less than one thousand. By incorporating as independent local governments under the 'Lakewood Plan' of 'Public Choice' in service provision, such very wealthy areas were able to freeload on the services of transport, education, policing, culture and health supplied by far poorer but more populous surrounding local governments where their employees often lived. By such means opulent communities and industrial areas were able to opt out of metropolitan service funding, while imposing exclusionary zoning on their localities.

v The city council officers requested a majority representation on the steering committee that was formed to guide the planning scheme and resolve the long period of stalemate. This was rejected by the local community activists because of their many years of experience of progress being stymied by official non-cooperation. A solution proposed by an academic member of the Lord Mayor's Citizen Advisory Committee was adopted, restricting membership of the steering committee to community representatives, with city council officers being co-opted as necessary, but acknowledging that the final adoption, amendment or rejection of the resulting scheme would be the prerogative of the duly elected city council. This careful and transparent role allocation was successful in steering the consultant's scheme which produced a widely praised solution with much in common with that produced five years earlier by QUT planning students and resolutely adhered to by the local community groups. This was rapidly adopted and implemented and gained the Planning Institute of Australia's Award for Excellence for the best strategic planning in Queensland in 1992. After five years' delay in adoption, it was actually implemented within a period of eighteen months and is now a well-loved feature of life in Inner Brisbane and the site of much conservation work by the Norman Creek Catchment Conservation Committee (N4C).

vi Although such doctrines offer a powerful basis for building consensus, this may sometimes seem to be a case of 'is' being used to imply 'ought', leading on to the justification of both processes and outcomes on the shaky basis that they each support the other – the classical functionalist fallacy that if something works, it works well. For instance, the interests of suburban, migrant and disadvantaged communities were often disregarded in the process of concentrating investment in Milan's city centre.

vii This is particularly valuable in cities like Brisbane where the most local level of representation involves wards with averages of fifty thousand people. In such circumstances, it is important to link locally grounded community planning with wider policies for district and city communities.

viii These design workshops are named after the French word for the wheelbarrow that was used to rush architecture students' final designs through the streets of Paris to the class's end-of-term display of work. They retain both the strengths of urgency and the weaknesses of often poorly resolved issues inherent in this approach.

ix An interesting example that occurred in Queensland's capital city of Brisbane involved a proposal by the state government to partner with a large developer to redevelop the North Bank of the Brisbane River, which is currently occupied by a convoluted string of freeway lanes and link roads separating the city centre from the river frontage. The government proposal was to link the riverside to the city centre over the concrete spaghetti of the braided freeways by elevated walkways that would allow development for office, hotel and residential towers and waterfront recreation and tourist activities. The open 'enquiry by design' held over a period of four days to examine the proposal became the focus for widespread professional and public unease. A number of serious objections emerged, including the hydrographic and climate change dangers of narrowing the Brisbane River by amounts variously estimated between 30 and 50 metres, the traffic generation implications of introducing tens of thousands of new workers and residents to the already congested traffic flows of the city centre and the insurance requirements and costs of constructing extensive pedestrian pathways over multiple lanes and link roads of a functioning freeway. The scheme was abandoned immediately after the enquiry. More imaginative and positive proposals have been considered for placing the existing freeway underground for a distance of 500 metres to allow the riverside to be redeveloped as an extension linking the city centre to the river frontage at ground level (Brisbane City Council, 2006).

  x If utilitarian considerations of the greatest happiness for the greatest number are taken to override the interests of significant minorities, this logically means that compensation in cash or alternative provisions are feasible and justified and can be paid out of the gains to the greater public interest (Prest & Turvey, 1965). This approach has the added advantage of acting as a truth test for an assertion that a sacrifice of minority rights is justified by benefits to the greater good. If the majority is obliged to pay just compensation, they should be led to weigh alternatives more carefully.

 xi A similar though less formal case of a leader regarding himself as responsible for the good government and welfare of his people is provided by the Indian King Asoka of the 3rd century BC (273–232 BC) who ordained peace throughout his kingdom and erected numerous still-surviving stellae enjoining tolerance, justice and social cohesion on all communities. While not democratically elected, Asoka represents an early example of the charismatic leadership on which representative systems also rely (Rawlinson, 1970).

 xii In modern times, representative government has continued to rely on such strong leadership as that of Abraham Lincoln in the divided USA of the American Civil war and Franklin Roosevelt, steering the country to recovery from the Great Depression of the nineteen thirties and through the challenging times of the Second World War. There are numerous other examples of the importance of strong leadership to representative democracy. Nelson Mandela in South Africa, Mahatma Gandhi and Pandit Nehru in India, and Charles de Gaulle in the turbulent situation of nineteen sixties France, divided between militant returned Algerian colonists and radical young left wing reformists, all sought to combine roles of representation and leadership.

xiii For example, a former Queensland cabinet minister, condemned to serve a long prison sentence for actively seeking out corrupt payments, perjury and interfering in the course of justice, has expressed no contrition, and made statements suggesting that he regards himself as an innocent victim of circumstances (The Australian, 2006). No Australian Commonwealth or state system has been free of major corruption scandals in the course of the last decade. Worldwide, few jurisdictions have.

xiv Other initiatives worth considering include the institution of youth councils of young activists selected by their peers and chambers of elders composed of people of acknowledged experience and achievement able to refer matters for the attention of legislatures and to comment on proposed legislation. Community boards on the lines of those in New Zealand, discussed earlier, could support activities within their communities, and perform such independent roles as commentary on planning applications, open space policy and organisation of community festivals and transport.

 xv Novels such as Charles Dickens' *Hard Times*, Elizabeth Gaskell's *North and South*, Emile Zola's *Germinal*, Upton Sinclair's *The Jungle* and A. J. Cronin's *The Stars Look Down* have provided vivid descriptions of what human misery can be produced by unregulated capitalism in cities driven solely by economic imperatives. The cautious reforming regulations of social democracy did much to reduce these problems and bequeathed improved situations to contemporary market democracies.

xvi *ABC Learning Centres* in Australia, for instance, experienced a meteoric growth based on the combination of government subsidies and parental payments, but collapsed through over-ambitious and rapid expansion, threatening many tens of thousands of families with sudden cessation of child care arrangements (Smart Company, 2008). Also in Australia, shady practices by Australian tertiary market organisations claiming to provide education for overseas students have been unmasked as providing largely worthless courses and qualifications (Wong, 2009).

xvii This proposal was worked out in administrative detail and was ready to be introduced. However, owing to a change of government, it was never implemented. The ministries responsible for health, social services and citizenship had combined to produce a strategy to integrate all 21 of their separate health, human services and community development programmes and deliver them jointly from regional 'multi-service agencies', whose design and organisation is reflected in Figure 11.1. Although funded by the provincial government, the 40–50 regional multi-service agencies would have been controlled by boards composed of representatives of their community, consumers and volunteers and accountable jointly to their voting memberships and the provincial government.

Uncertainty about the future direction of Commonwealth of Australia government policy following the change of leadership in June 2010 casts doubt on the implementation of the government's 2010 health proposals but they remain a promising model for integrating functions, levels of governance and social and physical aspects of service provision. This coordination and co-location of related services has much in common with the 'service hub' concept of human services planning identified by Dear, Wolch and Wilton (1994). In low-income parts of Venice and Santa Monica in Los Angeles County, a number of services, including cheap accommodation, food supply, day care, psychiatric and medical support and employment training, have been clustered close to safe outdoor meeting areas. Government and voluntary agencies have combined to upgrade a former 'skid row' area to a kind of low-income 'main street'. Dear and his colleagues argue:

> The challenge then is to find the optimal balance between decentralization and centralization … Decentralization … favours access and equity … Problems of remoteness [of necessarily centralized services] can be solved by developing an efficient referral system [with] rapid access to the higher tiers of care guaranteed.

The authors go on to identify population levels suited to local networks (10 000), ambulatory and residential care (100 000) and specialised day care (500 000+). These correlate very well with local, regional and metropolitan levels of integration. While it is neither necessary nor desirable for governments to provide all these services themselves, they are ideally situated to enable a variety of providers to co-locate and integrate their services (Brooke, 1989).

xviii This is the case with the recent sale by the Commonwealth Government of Brisbane Airport to a newly formed international body, the Brisbane Airport Corporation (BAC). The new corporation is developing a massive 'airport city' of offices, industry and a sprawling retail facility (termed the 'Direct Factory Outlet') six miles to the east of the existing city centre in a wetland area of extremely sensitive environment, that bears no relation to the *SEQ Regional Plan* or Brisbane's *City Plan* (Queensland Government Office of Urban Management, 2005; Brisbane Airport Corporation, 2009). Instead, it runs counter to many of their proposals for distributing regional traffic flows and establishing a hierarchy of centres. Endemic traffic congestion has now set in and is impeding movement on the regional system. The development will affect Brisbane City's spatial form for many decades in similar ways to that which resulted from the over-development of dockside industrial areas in London's East End and in Salford's 'Dirty old docks', before the introduction of planning. BAC's *Strategic Plan* is an eloquent testimony to the need for regulations to apply to all and to all equally.

References

Allen, K. (2010) Future of African farmland up for grabs. *Guardian Weekly*, 20 August 2010.

Australian Government (2010) *A National Health & Hospitals Network for Australia's Future*. Canberra, Australian Government.

Barber, W. (1967) *History of Economic Thought*. Harmondsworth, Penguin.

Bater, J. (1979) *The Soviet City: Ideal and reality*. London, Arnold.

Bornstein, D. (1997) *The Price of a Dream: The story of the Grameen Bank*. Dhaka, Grameen Press.

Brisbane Airport Corporation (2009) *Brisbane Airport Master Plan & Environment Strategy*, http://www.bne.com.au/files/pdf/Final%202009%20Master%20Plan/BAC%20ExecSummary_FINAL%20WEB.pdf, accessed 10 June 2010.

Brisbane City Council (2006) *Brisbane City Centre Master Plan*, http://www.brisbane.qld.gov.au/BCC:BASE::pc=PC_1860, accessed 1 June 2010.

Brooke, R. (1989) *Managing the Enabling Authority*. Harlow, Longman/Local Government Training Board.

Citrin, J., Martin, I. (eds) (2010) *After the Tax Revolt: California's proposition 13 turns thirty*. Berkeley, CA, University of California Press.

City of Portland, Office of Neighbourhood Involvement (2010) *Strategic Planning for Mission, Values, Goals*, http://www.portlandonline.com/oni/, accessed 30 January 2010.

Cooke, P., Morgan, K. (1998) *The Associational Economy: Firms, regions and innovation*. Oxford, Oxford University Press.

Dear, M., Wolch, J., Wilton, R. (1994) *The Service Hub Concept in Human Services Planning*. Oxford, Elsevier/ Pergamon.

Dye, T. (1988) *Politics in States and Communities*. Englewood Cliffs, NJ, Prentice Hall.

Etzioni, A. (2004) *The Common Good*. Cambridge, Polity Press.

Faludi, A. (2005) The Netherlands: A culture with a soft spot for planning. In: B. Sanyal (ed.), *Comparative Planning Cultures*. New York, Routledge.

Faludi, A., Valk, A. van der (1994) *Rule and Order: Dutch local planning doctrine in the twentieth century*. Dordrecht, Kluwer Academic Publishing.

Faludi, A., Valk, A. van der (1996) Planners come out for the Green Heart. *Journal of Economic and Social Geography* **97**(5).

Fisher, H. (1956) *History of Europe*. London, Arnold.

Forester, J. (1999) *The Deliberative Practitioner*. Chicago, MIT Press.

Fox, R. (2008) *The Classical World*. Harmondsworth, Penguin.

Friedmann, M. (1962) *Capitalism and Freedom*. Chicago, University of Chicago Press.

Giddens, A. (ed.) (2001) *The Global Third Way Debate*. Malden, MA, Polity Press.

Gunlicks, A. (1981) *Local Government Reform and Reorganization*. New York, Kennicutt.

Habermas, J. (1987) *The Theory of Communicative Action*. Cambridge, Polity Press.

Hall, P. (2002) *Cities of Tomorrow: An intellectual history of urban planning & design in the twentieth century*. Oxford, Blackwell Publishing Ltd.

Hayek, F. (1944) *Road to Serfdom*. London, Routledge & Kegan Paul.

Healey, P. (2006) *Collaborative Planning: Shaping places in fragmented societies*. New York, Palgrave Macmillan.

Healey, P. (2007) *Urban Complexity and Spatial Strategies: Towards a relational planning for our times*. London, RTPI/ Routledge.

Hellenic Resources Network (1995) *The European Convention on Human Rights,* http://www.hri.org/docs/ECHR50.html, accessed 6 August 2009.

Heywood, P. (1997) The Emerging Social Metropolis. In: *Progress in Planning.* Oxford, Pergamon/Elsevier.

Homes and Communities Agency (2010) *Homes & Communities Academy Awards Judging Panel,* http://skills.homesandcommunities.co.uk/awards/judges, accessed 7 November 2010.

Hutchison, J., Vidal, A. (2004) Symposium: Using social capital to help integrate planning theory, research and practice. *Journal of the American Planning Association* **70**(2): 142–92.

Jackson, W. (1969) *Local Government in England and Wales.* Harmondsworth, Penguin.

Joumea, A. (2009) *Copenhagen's 'Racial' Gang Wars,* http://english.aljazeera.net/focus/2009/03/200933194152661158.html, accessed 1 June 2010.

Kafka, F. (1949) *America: A story,* (trans. W. Muir, E. Muir). London, Secker & Warburg.

Kafka, F. (1974) *The Castle,* (trans. W. Muir, E. Muir). Harmondsworth, Penguin.

Kafka, F. (1994) *The Trial,* (trans. I. Parry). London, Penguin.

Landcare Australia (2010) *What is Landcare?* http://svc018.wic008tv.server-web.com/, accessed 1 June 2010.

Lemon, J. (1985) *Toronto since 1918.* Toronto, Lorimer.

Lenaghan, N. (2009) Funds say numbers won't work, even with rebate. *Australian Financial Review* 19 November.

Lewin, K. (1997) *Resolving Social Conflicts & Field Theory in Social Science.* Washington, American Psychological Association.

Li, Y. (2009) Notes on the Chinese government's handling of the Urumqi riot and the Chinese government reaction in *Xinjiang. China and Eurasia Forum Quarterly* **7**(4): 11–15.

Local Government New Zealand (2009) *Community Boards,* http://www.lgnz.co.nz/lg-sector/community-boards/index.html, accessed 30 May 2010.

Mahalo (2009) *Mumbai Terrorist Attacks,* http://www.mahalo.com/mumbai-terrorist-attacks, accessed 1 June 2010.

Mawson, A. (2008) *The Social Entrepreneur.* London, Penguin.

Meadows, D. (1995) City of First Priorities: Curitiba. *Brazil Whole Earth Review* Spring, http://findarticles.com/p/articles/mi_m1510/is_n85/ai_16816234/, accessed 1 June 2010.

Midgley, M. (2003) *Heart and Mind: The varieties of moral experience.* London, Routledge.

Mill, J. S. (1983) *Utilitarianism: On liberty and considerations on representative government.* London, Dent, (first published 1861).

Miller, G. (1981) *Cities by Contract.* Cambridge, MA, MIT Press.

Mitra, S. (2001) Making local government work: Local elites, panchayati raj and governance in India. In: A. Kohli (ed.), *The Success of India's Democracy.* Cambridge, Cambridge University Press.

Monbiot, G. (2003) *The Age of Consent: A manifesto for a new world.* London, Flamingo.

Mondragon Corporation Cooperative (2008) *Mondragon Corporacion Cooperativa, Spain,* http://www.iisd.org/50comm/commdb/desc/d13.htm, accessed 15 January 2008.

Montesquieu, C. (1989) *Spirit of the Laws: Cambridge texts in the history of political thought.* Cambridge, Cambridge University Press.

Municipality of Metro Seattle (1993) *Treatment Plants: WestPoint Treatment Plant East Division Reclamation Plant at Renton.* Metro Briefing Paper, 8/93, Seattle, Author.

Obama, B. (2010) *State of the Union Address,* http://stateoftheunionaddress.org/2010-barack-obama, accessed 1 June 2010.

Oregon Department of Land Conservation & Development (2010) *Statewide Planning Goals,* http://www.oregon.gov/LCD/goals.shtml, accessed 12 April 2010.

Orwell, G. (1952) *Animal Farm.* Harmondsworth, Penguin.

Osborne, D., Gaebler, T. (1992) *Reinventing Government: How the entrepreneurial spirit is transforming the public sector.* Reading, MA, Addison-Wesley.

Plato (1976) *The Republic,* (trans. A. D. Lindsay). Harmondsworth, Penguin.

Popper, K. (1969) *Conjectures and Refutations.* Oxford, Oxford University Press.

Popper, K. (1998) *The Open Society and Its Enemies: Vol. 1: Plato: Vol. 2: Marx and Hegel.* London, Routledge & Kegan Paul, (first published 1945).

Prest, A., Turvey, R. (1965) Cost–benefit analysis: A survey. *The Economic Journal* **75**(300): 683–735.

Province of Ontario, Ministries of Citizenship, Community & Social Services and Health (1993) *Partnerships in Long-term Care: A new way to plan, manage and deliver services and community support.* Toronto, Authors.

Pusey, M. (1991) *Economic Rationalism in Canberra: A nation-building state changes its mind.* Cambridge, Cambridge University Press.

Putnam, R. (1993) *Making Democracy Work: Civic traditions in modern Italy.* Princeton, Princeton University Press, (with Leonardi, R., Nanetti, R.).

Putnam, R (2000) *Bowling Alone: The collapse and revival of American community.* New York, Simon & Schuster.

Putnam, R. (ed.) (2004) Social capital. *Journal of the American Planning Association* **70**(2): 142–92.

Queensland Government Office of Urban Management (2005) *South East Queensland Regional Plan.* Brisbane, Author.

Rawlinson, H. (1970) Asoka. In: *Chambers Encyclopaedia: Volume 1.* London International Learning Systems.

Rawls, J. (1971) *A Theory of Justice.* Oxford, Oxford University Press.

Richardson, M. (2008) *Roles & Functions of Community Boards: Report to the Community Boards Executive Committee, June 2008,* http://www.lgnz.co.nz/library/files/store_020/Rolesandfunctionsofcommunityboards, accessed 1 June 2010.

Robertson, G. (1999) *Crimes against Humanity.* London, Hamlyn.

Robertson, G. (2005) *The Tyrannicide Brief.* London, Chatto & Windus.

Roesdahl, E. (1998) *The Vikings* (trans. S. M. Margeson, K. Williams). London, Penguin.

Saint-Exupéry, A. de (1966) *Wind, Sand and Stars*, (trans. L. Galantière), Ringwood, Victoria, Penguin.

Schumpeter, J. (1934) *The Theory of Economic Development*. Cambridge, MA, Harvard University Press.

Smart Company (2008) *Government to investigate ABC Learning Centres Collapse*, http://www.smartcompany.com.au/Free-Articles/The-Briefing/20081112-Government-to-investigate-ABC-Learning-Centres-collapse.html, accessed 7 June 2010.

Solzhenitsyn, A. (1974) *The Gulag Archipelago 1918–1956: An experiment in literary investigation: I–II*, (trans. T. P. Whitney). New York, Harper & Row.

The Australian (2006) *Secret $300k loan went to minister's kids*, http://www.news.com.au/national/secret-300k-loan-went-to-ministers-kids/story, accessed 1 June 2010.

Thompson, F., Green, M. (2004) Vox populi? Oregon tax and expenditure limitation initiatives. *Public Budgeting & Finance* **24**(4): 73–87.

Toronto Transit Commission (2010) *About the TTC*, http://www3.ttc.ca/About_the_TTC/index.jsp, accessed 7 June 2010.

Wapedia (2009) *United Kingdom Parliamentary Expenses Scandal*, http://wapedia.mobi/en/United_Kingdom_Parliamentary_expenses_scandal?t=4, accessed 1 June 2010.

Whyte, W. & K., 1989, *Making Mondragon: The Growth & Dynamics of a Workers Co-operative Complex*, Ithaca NY, ILR Press.

Wong, R. (2009) *Problems in Australia's Overseas Students Program*, http://asiapacific.anu.edu.au/newmandala/2009/07/13/problems-in-australias-overseas-student-program/, accessed 7 June 2010.

Yunus, M. (1998) *Socially Conscious Capitalism towards a Poverty Free World*. Public Lecture Transcript, Brisbane, Queensland University of Technology.

12 Conclusions: Community Planning Today and Tomorrow

Throughout this book, I have emphasised the importance of bringing together different ideas, activities, scales and people to match the very wide range of issues involved in the life, culture and successful evolution of communities. Creative synthesis has been a major theme. In the first part of this concluding chapter, I aim to draw out the connections between the topics of preceding chapters and explore their significance for the future development of community planning. In the second part, four unifying themes of inclusion, negotiation, adaptation to change and social inventiveness are explored. This combination of reflecting backwards and looking forwards results in the organisation of the chapter into two parts:

- The elements of community planning:
  - Challenges and options
  - Nature and levels
  - Values and methods
  - Activities and analysis
  - Place and governance.
- Themes, roles and future directions:
  - Inclusion
  - Negotiation
  - Adaptation
  - Invention.

The chapter concludes with a discussion of the future of community planning.

The elements of community planning

CHALLENGES AND OPTIONS

Rapid changes are affecting climate, economy, technology and politics. While they demand well-judged and energetic responses of community management and adaptation, they also reduce confidence in established methods of problem-solving and policymaking. The resulting growth of political and ethical uncertainty makes planning more difficult at the same time that it is becoming ever more necessary. Clear recognition of the importance of driving values is required if consensus is to be achieved on desired directions, and joint actions are to be adopted. Of the four predominant social goals of order, productivity, control and coop-

Community Planning, First Edition. Phil Heywood.
© 2011 Phil Heywood.
Published 2011 by Blackwell Publishing Ltd.

eration, no single one commands universal support or is entitled to exclusive consideration, but all can contribute some valid directions to help manage the tides of change affecting community life throughout the contemporary world. Order supports the search for established principles to rectify the disabling effects of uncertainty and indecision. Productivity promotes capacities to meet material needs. Control may help to tackle existing injustices, as with regulation of interest rates and noxious land uses. Cooperation is not only positive in itself but also provides the broadest path to collect and deliver the benefits sought from all other goals, including competition.

Underlying the necessary interaction among values, effective communication is essential to establish and develop understanding between individuals and groups. Needs must be discussed if mutual advantages are to be discovered. Such essential public and private goods as housing, transport, work, meeting places and conservation require concerted action which depends upon the communication of ideas. Though unevenly developed, there is evidence that collaborative community planning is already helping to solve problems resulting from the inertia of past injustices and current unprecedented rates of change. Examples of these successes are provided in the successful regeneration of places discussed in earlier chapters, such as Amsterdam's Bijlmermeer, Manchester's Longsight and the upgraded bustees of inner Kolkata; the successful economic cooperation of the Mondragon workers cooperatives in Spain's Basque Country; and the productive workers' networks of Modena and other cities in Italy's Emilia Romagna, the Veneto and Tuscany.

Communication and participation have wider social roles. The reach of communication, starting from its origins in personal experience and ideas, has been extended to the global scale by the universal span and instantaneous speed of information technologies. Dynamic new global communities of shared interests and influence have been created. In response, new planning methods can embrace more inclusive techniques of local community consultation and participation, even extending to include regular global review of new ideas and practices. Problems of unequal levels of knowledge, shortage of people's time, possibilities of conflicting objectives and limited resources to satisfy preferences are being tackled by methods of continuing community discussion. Such methods of dialogue, careful problem-framing, clear explanation of intentions and cyclical review can help community consultation avoid reliance on short-lived ad hoc programmes, which may degenerate into tokenistic projects of opinion management, and instead develop to provide the basis for effective participation and community empowerment.

Such participation lies at the heart of the community planning theories and methods explored in this book. A community without participation is like a colony of slaves or a barrack of robots. The democratic principle that the views of each person should count and count equally can only be fully achieved when people can and do directly influence decisions affecting the course of their own lives and the development of their communities. Competition for the use of scarce resources and differences in people's values and priorities mean that negotiation will also often be required to achieve this. If repetition of the tragedies and disasters of the twentieth century is to be avoided, it is imperative to resolve disputes before they fester to become cancerous resentments. Incorporating group dynamics and conflict resolution methods within routine planning processes can provide timely and constructive ways to identify and resolve such conflicts. Issues that may otherwise degenerate into the exercise of naked power can be aired and illuminated in public discussion. Examples of such topics include construction of religious buildings, redevelopment of long-established residential localities and locations of new transport facilities and industrial plants. Chapter 2 demonstrated how action and advocacy planning could employ old and new negotiative processes to resolve such questions of intensity and directions of acceptable change within communities.

There are other activities which can help to create and maintain healthy communities. Community action, development and organisation, discussed in Chapter 2, should all play important roles, and each constitutes an entire field of practice and study in its own right. Community action opens channels to local, regional and, increasingly, global communities, to help transform individual energies into communal activities. These may range in scale from the city farms outlined in Box 1.4, to the habitat conservation and global campaigns against blindness and disease conducted by such international charities as the Fred Hollows Foundation (2010) and Médecins Sans Frontières (2010). Community Development aims to discover and develop the capacities of individuals and communities to tackle their own problems and create better futures. Like community planning, its aims and methods include empowerment, devolution and subsidiarity.

Community organisation offers frameworks for innovations in governance and participation that can match the rapidly evolving politics, technologies and economies of contemporary societies. This is how the urban social movements of the second half of the twentieth century grew to help transform their wider political systems, often starting in quite local reactions to intolerable living conditions in urban communities in places such as Spain, South Africa and many of the countries of Eastern Europe (Castells, 1977, 1983). Now, new challenges of managing the increasingly scarce and contested resources of water, forests and fisheries demand new types of community governance (Lacey & Heywood, 2010). New ways to include marginalised individuals, groups and communities are also needed so that existing politics can be enlivened and helped to adapt and evolve. Such reforms can also help to develop new social and cultural capital. Despite successes in managing the potential disasters of the Global Financial Crisis of 2008/09, there are widespread signs of loss of confidence in democratic institutions. The infusion of new grassroots community organisations and their integration into the existing systems would be timely and valid. Community planning can provide a useful vehicle for such new forms of involvement and a recognised activity where the necessary roles and skills can be learnt and applied.

NATURE AND LEVELS

Throughout this book, I have aimed to demonstrate that broadly consistent methods of planning can be applied across the six different scales, or levels, of planning for local, urban, regional, national, supra-national and global communities. Whole cities and regions may face similar acute problems of internal tensions, population pressure density, poor communal organisation and inappropriate physical form that also confront local communities of daily contact. Such issues are often contested as much between different levels of community as within the communities themselves, emphasising the importance of related systems and compatible methods of problem-solving, policy development and planning. Common vocabularies and methods are needed to provide the necessary communication to help resolve such tensions.

In Chapter 6, I demonstrated how the clear translation of values into effective activities and desired proposals can produce new options to reconcile and resolve evident problems. Such problems will themselves have arisen from frustrated values. Proposals can then be negotiated, adjusted for compatibility and incorporated within collaborative community plans. At the local scale, issues of spatial justice may be particularly acute. Whole communities may be concerned that lack of access to facilities of health, learning, work and transport subordinate their needs to the interests of more favoured areas. Physical forms and memorable and culturally appropriate spaces are also very important to local communities. Participation and partnership are involved in all these concerns, and have been for more than two thousand years. Such arrangements date from the self-managing democracy of classical Athens, through the folk meetings and moots of the Anglo-Saxons in the eighth and ninth centuries and the guild systems of medieval market towns to the workers management exemplified in the modern Mondragon Cooperative with its 100 000-worker partners. Similarly, the venerable traditions of Indian gram shivas, or village councils, are being continued not only in the Gandhian movement for village democracy but also in the *panchayati* which now form the most local tier of Indian government (Mitra, 2001). Cultural recognition and promotion as well as formal

designation of such bodies can do much to improve and extend the roles of community governance to promote effective problem-solving. This local community development may express itself in many ways, including community festivals, support for urban farms and gardens, and partnership with neighbourhood associations in promoting valued aspects of local community life. Examples of such partnerships include the more than one hundred neighbourhood associations supported by the city government in Portland, Oregon; village councils in rural India and China; and the almost 20 000 community councils which have been taken into partnership by Venezuela's national government to promote direct action to solve local problems (Ellner, 2009).

More structured and systematic examples include the commitment to citizen participation enshrined in the planning goals attached to the State of Oregon's Land Use Act, mandating citizen involvement committees wherever development is proposed (Oregon Department of Land Conservation & Development, 2010); the community board provisions of the New Zealand Local Government Act (Local Government New Zealand, 2010); India's conferral of powers upon village councils, in its Local Government Act, as noted above (India Government, 1992); and Amsterdam's community councils, as discussed in Chapter 2 (Freiling, 2004). Together, these provide evidence of widespread recognition of the important role of community participation in activating and energising representative democracy.

The larger spheres of the city, region, nation and international and global communities provide their own opportunities to manage the turbulent changes which can already be predicted in the activities of shelter, work, access, health, education and recreation, which are necessary for healthy community life. City communities, in particular, have essential roles to play. Their long-established successes in promoting prosperity and productivity by bringing people together to exchange ideas, goods and care will be in even more demand, as the creative activities of the new knowledge industries seek out their nurturing environments (Florida, 2005). Emphasis on social inclusion, physical containment within urban growth boundaries, political devolution and administrative subsidiarity are already combining to support and reinforce the vitality of civic life. City regions such as Hong Kong, Mumbai, New York–Boston– Baltimore, São Paulo and Toronto, increasingly develop as almost independent actors in the global economy.

Regional scale communities reflect longstanding relationships between cities and their rural hinterlands, emphasising the balance between urban intensity and productivity on the one hand and the rural capacity for ecological recovery and conservation of natural resources on the other. Water, atmosphere, soil, agriculture, fisheries and forests may all be involved. Regulations to protect these often fragile systems of ecological recovery are best provided at this regional scale. Metropolitan regions, destined to accommodate nearly half the world's population by the middle of the century (United Nations – Habitat, 2010) may by then form the world's most dynamic and powerful communities, and it is crucial that their regional planning should include responsibility for maintaining the environmental health of their hinterlands. Bio-regions such as Cascadia in the north-west of the United States and western Canada, southern Ontario and the Thames and Rhine valleys are increasingly providing the outer boundaries for metropolitan regions, including Greater Seattle, Vancouver and Portland, Oregon; Toronto; Greater London; Strasbourg; and the Ruhr conurbation. Such regional communities of responsibility have essential roles to play in achieving the goals of sustainability discussed in Chapter 5.

At an even larger scale, national communities bring together unique powers with wide responsibilities, which show no signs of being diminished by the incursions of localism and globalism. Nations combine powers of control over national defence, law, economy and education with responsibilities for international relations, law enforcement, distribution of wealth and regeneration of culture. Their elites may themselves constitute policy communities, which become very significant players in shaping plans and activities. Where they are inclusive and open to entry by newcomers and upwardly mobile people, supported by democratic and humanistic traditions, they may provide effective paths to integrate new ideas, activities and people. Elsewhere, they may crystallise into exclusive and self-serving elites increasingly distanced from the rest of society. At their best, nations strongly reflect the definition of communities as groups of people who acknowledge shared interests and responsibilities. Their recognised roles in allocating resources and framing laws make them a crucial level of administration in the ladder of community governance.

Supranational and global communities of economy, interest and governance are radically expanding in number, membership, influence and self-confidence as a result of improved communications, global awareness and the flourishing technologies of transport and production. The growth of the global economy has created an urgent need for an effective level of community governance to match and manage its workings (Stiglitz, 2002, 2010). This has in part been met by the emergence of new supranational communities of economics and governance including the European Union, the North America Free Trade Association and the South East Asian Treaty Organization. Another type of organisation comes from the activities of such global non-government organisations as Oxfam, Médecins Sans Frontières, World Vision, the World Community Forum, the World Wildlife Fund, Greenpeace and many others, motivated by such values as human development, social justice and sustainability. Nevertheless, at the global scale there is a dangerous mismatch between the power of the global economy, well represented by the operations of the World Trade Organization, and the relatively weak and sometimes symbolic coordinating role of the United Nations, which has caused some commentators to call for a more radical advance towards a system of democratic and enforceable world government to serve the global community (Monbiot, 2003).

VALUES AND METHODS

One of the themes of this book is that community planning should be driven by human values and social goals. The four wide-ranging values of prosperity, justice, liberty and sustainability, explored in Chapter 5, were selected because of their capacity to reflect a broad spectrum of goals, including material abundance, personal freedom and choice, social cohesion and environmental conservation. The pursuit of such goals can help to ensure that communities thrive and develop. They can create and transmit productive skills and act as seedbeds for innovation. Human rights declarations and laws can ensure that the inviolable rights of personal choice and individual freedom are not infringed (Robertson, 2009). Communicative planning can promote the community involvement and open publication necessary to safeguard social justice. Conservation techniques, including re-use, recycling, rationing and reservation, can protect fragile resource bases. Social needs analyses and social infrastructure plans can support equal provision of social services and amenities in lively and accessible community hubs, helping to sustain consensual community life and support social justice.

The many ways that these values can assist each other have been explored in Chapters 5 and 6. Prosperity can support the personal independence and capacity for choice and providence which make possible free and sustainable living. In return, liberty should promote the creativity to sustain prosperity and equity, which are essential to social justice. Justice itself requires a prosperous life, which is the just expectation of all living creatures. Intergenerational equity will support conservation. Sustainability is also supported where people are prosperous enough to use resources with forethought; where social justice offers a stake in maintaining existing systems; and where personal liberty promotes the testing of ideas to develop a sound knowledge of repercussions and unintended consequences. Such values of justice, liberty and prosperity contribute to the understanding and will to conserve irreplaceable long-term resources of air, water and energy.

Values-based methods can also bring together practitioners and participants from different fields with often differing interests to share their concerns, acknowledge their responsibilities and discover new potentialities. In so doing, they can recognise that their actions impact on others in the same ways that those of others impact on them. Mutual understanding and adjustment will be assisted by the use of common methods and the development of shared objectives. Where objectives clash, processes of negotiation can help different parties recognise that combined plans need to incorporate the concerns of all. Such values-based planning methods can assist practitioners in a wide range of activities to communicate and cooperate with each other as they develop their own activity plans as related facets of overall community planning. Links between activities such as housing, transport, education and health can be reviewed and refreshed as planning proceeds through cycles of dialogue. In order to ground such methods in heart, mind and hand, it is necessary to draws upon the creative impulses of art, the investigative style of science and the regular routines of craft discussed in Chapter 6. The resulting four-phased method of awareness, investigation, proposition and implementation makes use of problem-solving at each stage to ensure that the comprehensive inclusion of interests, needs and objectives will lead on to effective outcomes. This will involve processes of progressive reconciliation, through elimination of misfit between different solutions and with their wider contexts. In these ways, it becomes possible to balance innovation of new development with conservation of existing valued features to meet continually evolving sets of consensual and monitored community objectives.

ACTIVITIES AND THEIR ANALYSIS

Within this cyclical process, plans for different activities can be adjusted to each other to help create integrated communities able to enjoy the benefits of shared spaces and healthy local economies. Activities can be studied and steered to meet identified needs and values. For this purpose, it will often be useful to produce estimates of aggregate needs for such items as jobs, land for housing, hospital beds and school places. Mixed scanning may be required, viewing the content of the individual activity system within the context of the wider community system. This kind of approach has two advantages. First, it enhances understanding and interpretation of the activity itself and its position within the larger system of community life. Second, it aids understanding of how to balance and adjust objectives between the different investment and development programmes of related activities, such as school building, housing subsidy and construction, and public transport, to take account of the place of each in the overall life of the community.

PLACES AND GOVERNANCE

Places where a lively mix of uses and activities bring together many people and events to exchange ideas, goods, services and companionship provide life throughout all hours of the day and deep into the night. Their quality is decided more by these activities than by abstract principles of design. Nevertheless, design, too, can enhance community values and culture, when it shapes the form of structures and spaces to reflect characteristics of psychology, perception and choice. Participation and governance provide other ways to draw together the many strands of community life. Both are equally important and operate at all community levels (global, supranational, national, regional, city and local). While continuing innovations in information and communications technology are daily increasing opportunities for more people to participate in one form of governance or another, at the same time these developments may threaten to exclude marginalised groups and individuals who lack proficiency or access to the new techniques. Such groups include the elderly, minority ethnic groups with limited knowledge of officially used languages and those whose educational and income levels exclude them from access to computer-based systems. Many of these problems can be resolved by methods such as translation systems, use of interpreters, provision of public access to Internet training and hardware, group consultation techniques and peer research methods. Community consultation and participation methods can thus be incorporated into decision systems and used to implement and link programmes of community-based implementation, often including the community development and community action discussed in Chapter 2.

Themes, roles and future directions

In looking towards sustainable futures, community planning needs to include and reconcile the widest possible range of participants. Change and adaptation must be accommodated. Processes must be able to invent new answers to resolve old and emerging problems. The four themes of social inclusion, negotiation, adaptive capacity and invention are clearly linked to each other. Inclusion will recognise and promote variety, and may well in turn demand negotiation and conflict resolution. Adaptation should be assisted by the necessary problem-solving. This will, in turn, involve invention, which is so important in times of rapid change and will draw stimulus from the systematic techniques of inclusion with which the cycle started. These four linked attributes form the themes for the following discussion of the future directions of community planning.

INCLUSION

Healthy societies need to embrace the widest possible range of ideas, activities and interests. Groups of people of differing incomes, ages, cultures and length of residence need to feel, and be, included if their societies are to be broadly based and sustainable. The originality of thought and ideas required to keep pace with a world of rapid and unpredictable change demands open and inclusive communication. Communicative techniques of developing objectives, evaluating options and reviewing outcomes will all benefit from different perspectives, and where these produce conflicts their resolution may itself generate new ideas. Such social inclusion is favoured by the objective-based methods described in Chapter 6 because they can garner aims and produce plans that reflect many concerns and command wide community support. By contrast, the exclusion of critical ideas may generate electoral opposition and hostility from those whose support is needed in democratic systems if the plans are to succeed. Inclusive techniques can also engage recent arrivals and immigrants and help to integrate the increasing proportion of newcomers within all communities This is important because overall, in most developed countries, about one-third of the population have moved to their present address in the past five years, often from elsewhere in the city, the nation or the world. In the current volatile physical and political climate, this proportion can only be expected to grow, as international migration increases in response to climate change, sea level rises and desiccation of marginal agricultural areas in Africa, Asia and Oceania.

The future of our societies and civilisation will be strongly affected by how well these newcomers are integrated into existing communities. Success could produce a similar flowering of new ideas, cultures and inventions to that achieved in seventeenth-century Holland, eighteenth- and nineteenth-century Britain and nineteen- and twentieth-century North America (Mumford, 1938, 1961). Failure could result in more of the conflict and blood-letting that followed the break-up of the old Yugoslavia and the failure of its constituent communities to resolve their differences and negotiate fair shares in shaping their governments and planning their own futures (Robertson, 2000). Similar problems have bedevilled all aspects of life in the last two decades in Afghanistan, Iraq and Kashmir. Rwanda is only now starting to create a society which looks to the future rather than to past differences. Because separation is often neither feasible nor desirable, thorough-going inclusion remains the most viable option, and the methods of community planning outlined in this book are intended to advance this through purposive and systematic engagement of all groups in full participation in community life and decisions, irrespective of when they arrived, where they came from or how prosperous, well-established or articulate they may be.

Ladders of participation can provide entry to the main thoroughfares of community life. If energetic action is taken within host communities to integrate newcomers into their life and culture, the paths trodden by successive waves of Jews, Armenians, Palestinians, Kurds, Vietnamese and Afghanis in European and Atlantic societies over the course of the last century could well be followed by many other groups over the next few decades. History suggests that immigrants can be relied upon to manage their own economic integration as they work hard to establish themselves and their families in their new homes. But if they or their children feel socially or politically excluded, some of the most energetic of the younger generation will inevitably become alienated or hostile in ways that no community should contemplate with complacency. Failure could spell the loss of the social consent and mutual trust on which societies ultimately depend. The rewards of successful integration, by contrast, are likely to include surges of cultural, creative and inventive energy.

Inclusion also extends to the dimension of time. Often a secure appreciation of how to manage the future requires a confident understanding of traditional values, derived from the past. Jewish and Armenian communities throughout the world provide good examples, but the same pattern emerges wherever an enquiring eye scans the contemporary world. Understanding and the conscious development of cultural traditions is a major advantage in coming to terms with changing futures. This is equally true among the indigenous communities of Australasia and the Americas, with the arts of painting and dance; membership of the English-speaking Commonwealth of Nations, with the common heritage of an unsurpassed literature; or the economically dynamic cultures of China and India with their long heritage of continuous written culture going back thousands of years to Confucius, Lao Tze, the Vedas, the Mahabharata and the Ramayana. All are building their futures on the social capital of longstanding traditions of communal culture.

Another particularly important aspect of inclusion, which relates to community governance and participation, is the relationship between participatory and representative democracy. Conventionally, these have often been seen as alternative or even opposing paths to accountable governance. Commentators as sophisticated as Karl Popper (1998) and Eric Reade (1987) often seem to be arguing this. Popper to some extent shared Plato's distrust of mass democracy as prone to deteriorate into populism and demagogic manipulation. Representative democracy, on the other hand, he praised as testable and accountable at regular elections and therefore valid. Eric Reade argued similarly that community objectives could only be validly derived from elected representatives who had put forward their agendas, and been selected on that basis by the electorate. Like Popper, he took comfort from the fact that if they failed to adhere to their own platforms, or their ideas were proved wrong, they could be ejected from office and replaced by others with better credentials. Such views certainly seem to have stood the test of tolerable outcomes better than the mass participation generalities of thinkers like Jean-Jacques Rousseau (1968), with their shadowy incapacity for either verification or falsification. His advocacy of 'the general will' was later adopted by the Jacobins during the French Revolution to justify executions of political opponents en masse.

Nevertheless, there are convincing illustrations of ways in which the two approaches can combine to create sustainable, just and inclusive politics in the cooperative doctrines of such Syndicalist thinkers as Peter Kropotkin (1939, 1974), José Arizmendi (Whyte & Whyte, 1988) and Mohamed Yunus (Bornstein, 1996). Participation by local representatives can maintain their connection with the grassroots and can nurture new generations of representative people. Subsidiarity and devolution of powers can pass responsibilities and funds down to the most local levels to include individual participation in activities as widely different as open space management, workers control, cultural development, community education and transport. Reciprocally, the support and scrutiny of representative democracy can help validate participation by individuals and groups through its regulating laws, by laws and distribution of public funds.

NEGOTIATION

Negotiation is therefore an essential element of successful community planning which is likely to become increasingly significant over the next few decades. Its well-developed theories depend on offering dissident or disadvantaged groups better alternatives than conflict or alienation through negotiated agreements (Susskind & Cruikshank, 1987). Negotiation thus often provides an invaluable opportunity to reconcile conflicting parties and viewpoints. Participation in community planning, with its clear processes of objective-setting, generation of alternatives, inclusive evaluation and cyclical review of problems, provides ideal means for this kind of conflict resolution. Because all members of communities have a stake in its outcomes, planning is an inherently public activity and offers a conveniently objective forum for public debate. In discussing what should happen in the future, dialogue can be promoted between groups who would normally find no reason to talk with each other.[i] This should have the further advantage of maintaining and enhancing social and cultural capital.

Many of these positive techniques of negotiation apply more widely beyond the boundaries of dispute resolution. Techniques such as 'appreciative inquiry' (Hammond & Royal, 1998; Cooperrider, 2008), which avoid the very idea of conflicting values, encourage participants to identify their own strengths and those of their colleagues to invent pathways to achieve new successes in positive negotiations. Community visioning, futures workshops and 'enquiry by design' all present ways in which latent resources of personality and place can be released, giving community planning the capacity to become a 'sum plus' activity.

Local planning offers one such example in the negotiation of the desired future character of precincts in community and neighbourhood plans. These can flow from discussions between people who may have come from different places, had different experiences and hold different values, but are nonetheless destined to share and care for common spaces and endow them with the vitality which makes for good community life. Issues which need to be aired and compared include density, height, access, vistas, open spaces, heritage values and spaces and buildings for education and health services. There also need to be seats at the tables where these matters are discussed for spokespeople of government agencies, city policy, environmental interests and commercial development as well as local residents. Without them, outcomes will be neither realistic nor well informed. When they are included, true problem-solving can occur, producing inventions that may draw the community forwards to new successes and achievements.

At a much larger, regional level, Dutch policies to combine retaining a 'green heart' within the heavily developed western part of the country, while maintaining appropriate residential densities and fair housing opportunities for everyone, succeeded because of the 'polder model' of consensus and local government participation in the supply of housing land. It provides an excellent example of how a negotiative stance can lead on to successful collaborative planning (Faludi & Van der Valk, 1994; Healey, 2006).[ii]

This kind of trading of interests is advocated by Jane Jacobs in *Systems of Survival* (1992), her important book on establishing communities of interest through negotiation. She contrasts the disastrous outcomes of attempts at centralised rule-making by self-proclaimed 'guardians' with the more open-ended and flexible capacity of negotiations which can produce contracts between participants who are trading their skills and capacities with others to achieve sustainable long-term relationships. These can be based on rational trust rather than imputed duties. Although such negotiative practices extend beyond the bounds of conventional community planning, they nonetheless constitute an essential skein within it.

ADAPTATION

Such collaborative approaches not only help existing communities adjust to evolving conditions. They can assist radical adaptation to the cascading changes of all sorts and scales of the contemporary world. In technical fields, many of the upcoming generation has acquired the necessary new skills of numeracy and learnt to master new developments in information technology with truly admirable adaptability. IPhones and BlackBerries have become instantaneous personal portals to global information and communications networks. Current generations have adapted to the arrival of the virtual world with widespread and spectacular success. However, our capacity to manage the changes that affect people's private lives have been far less successful. We are often uncomfortable with their emotional impacts and we may resent, for instance, having to accept those new neighbours to whom we are required to adjust. People frequently dislike the 'shock of the new', and find difficulty in accepting display of different styles of clothing, the public use of strange languages, the smell and appearance of different diets, the admission to equal access of educational and social opportunities of gender or ethnic groups previously regarded as culturally distinct, or equal sharing of power with castes or groups with whom they feel they have few common bonds.

Community planning, with its inherent and neutral acceptance that each person should count and count equally, offers an open path towards the necessary goals of inclusion and adjustment. At their best, therefore, socially inclusive community planning processes offer effective means both to help people to adapt to emotional and cultural change and to embrace and apply such material innovations as the rapid introduction of new technology. People whose own voices have been acknowledged in the public arena are more likely to understand the need to listen to the views of others, and those who have heard their own ideas voiced in public debate may become more apt to recognise that their own views may contain inconsistencies or contradictions, which need to be resolved.

INVENTION

As a problem-solving activity, community planning employs methods of progressive problem-solving through the elimination of misfit between possible solutions. This approach, associated with the ideas of Christopher Alexander (1964) and discussed in Chapter 6, welcomes the largest possible array of community objectives, including those held by different and even competing participants and stakeholders. Conflicts between objectives are resolved by inventing solutions that can solve old problems in new ways.[iii]

For instance, the invention of building societies in the late eighteenth century, described in Chapter 8, allowed workers in rapidly growing new industrial towns to build and own their own homes. Relying on social trust, groups of industrial workers agreed to pool their resources to build dwellings until all of them had acquired their own dwellings. Such institutions soon developed into the permanent building societies that were to transform British society: by the mid-twentieth century over half the country's dwellings were owner-occupied. By 1980, the proportion in Australia had reached two-thirds.[iv]

Other examples of influential social inventions are provided by the model industrial settlements of the nineteenth century of New Lanark, Saltaire, Bournville and Port Sunlight and elsewhere. Their example has entered the mainstream of community planning in the form of the hundreds of new towns which continue to be established in all six settled continents. No less significant have been the inventions of workers cooperatives enacted with spectacular success in Mondragon in the Basque region of northern Spain in the second half of the twentieth century (see Boxes 1.2 and 1.3 in Chapter 1). Because these inventions stem from practical problem-solving, their ideas are well adjusted to their times and situations. There is no better example of this good fit between a proposed solution and the context within which it will have to work than the micro credit arrangements of the Grameen Bank of Bangladesh (see Box 1.1). This invention was stimulated by the need to resolve the potentially conflicting goals of enhancing local community life and organisation and drastically reforming the economic system which kept local families impoverished and debt ridden, particularly those headed by women. Solving this problem produced the transformative invention of a quite intricate system of micro credit, where local community groups replaced the burden of producing economic collateral with the social collateral of trust between members of local groups and centres (Fugelsang & Chandler, 1993).

The questions arise of where such social inventions are to come from and how they can be encouraged. The spiral of community planning methods – values-based, inclusive, integrating different activities and solving problems – should provide a suitable array of ideas. The social entrepreneurship of the rapidly growing voluntary movements that already include housing associations, recycling cooperatives, community transport, cultural organisations and local employment transfer schemes can be expected to continue to produce new ideas. One particularly relevant example concerns the needs to embrace change and transcend traditional hostilities and toxic intercommunal competition within the central African state of Rwanda. Mass distribution of simple computers costing only around US$100 each to all schoolchildren is being partly funded by international charities (Beaumont, 2010). The programme is specifically designed to infuse optimism and an outward-looking focus into the new generation of a society infected by long-standing mutual suspicions between different tribes resulting in the appalling atrocities of 1993, in which more than a million people were slaughtered within a period of weeks by their neighbours. First indications are that the engagement of young people with the outside world and the future is achieving a dramatic change in attitudes and increase in levels of social optimism.[v]

Community planning relies heavily on the 'mixed scanning' discussed throughout this book. This ability involves scanning widely across different scales, relating patterns between different periods and linking immediate needs to long-term directions. The same way of thinking can also help to draw together strongly entrenched problems with previously unrecognised or apparently remote resources. Problem-solving skills can give rise to such new social inventions as business incubators, micro-credit organisations, housing associations, exercise and nature trails, urban farms and walking buses, to provide missing pieces in the jigsaw of community planning. Such initiatives maintain the flow of energy necessary to ensure that commitment to widely held values of liberty, justice, abundance and conservation are faithfully reflected in the collaborative planning of evolving communities.

The future of community planning

Looking to the future, there are positive prospects for all four activities of inclusion, negotiation, adaptation and invention, combining the skills of head, heart and practical action. The merit of inclusion should be promoted as numbers of previously isolated specialists recognise the reciprocal benefits that can be gained by linking their own roles and skills with those of others. Already, the practitioners of health, education, recreation and physical form are starting to cooperate for mutual benefit. Corrective service planners and environmental resource managers, for instance, also have much to contribute to, and gain from, integrated community planning. In each of these activities, input will be drawn from participants across government, voluntary agencies, the private sector and community activism. Sharing of skills, methods and community networks is among the many benefits that can result from this sort of cooperation. Developing friendships and trust relations across all these categories will help hold together the widening field of community planning.

Inclusion can be advanced by practical developments such as spreading information networks and online feedback opportunities, which should help consultation extend towards participation. People who respond to questionnaires can volunteer and be enlisted to become members of visioning and community planning and other engagement and activity groups. Transparent and prompt feedback is far easier via websites than through previous postal techniques, as is exchange of information between professionals. Because communication can be instant, these tools are often enjoyable and can engage people who would otherwise be too busy or preoccupied with daily events. The same information technology can also help in processing responses to combine many thousands of often conflicting individual preferences, into ranked and integrated representations of community preferences.

Nevertheless, fully valid and nuanced interpretations of these new mass techniques require the balancing of numbers with more searching insights and interpretations. Focus group methods developed by social and market researchers over the last three or four decades will continue to produce important insights into need and preference (Mackay, 2002). Empathy and emotional intelligence will also be needed, as well as the good habits of active listening. Well-judged community events will have a large role to play, including promotion of cultural fiestas and food-based festivities. These can both draw people together in enjoyable self-expression and exploration of new flavours of all sorts, and can be part of continuing programmes of community engagement and consultation. Such activities recognise that assimilation, however well intentioned, is not enough and that healthy communities need to incorporate, celebrate and harness the energies of difference.

The success of inclusion may well increase the need for good negotiation, as more minority and marginalised groups gain the confidence to demand a share in policymaking, seek seats at the decision-making tables and add their agendas to the range of concerns which have to be resolved. The place of negotiation will increasingly be brought forward from resolving conflicts between established adversarial positions to shaping discussions which may help to develop initial objectives or directions. Professionals who are very

skilled at their jobs and may have developed advanced skills of problem-solving in specific areas may also need to learn new capacities of facilitation, which often involves active listening rather than fluent expression. Good facilitators, for instance, may need to limit their own explanations, in order to evoke the fullest possible contributions from other members of groups. They will even need to accept silences while each participant reflects on his or her major concerns or interests and then states them in an organised sequence, so that everyone's voice and interests are heard, before giving way to more free-flowing discussion. Dedicated public officials have to learn to resist the temptation to engulf with exhaustive and elaborate justifications of existing policies the views of other participants with which they may not agree or which run counter to their current intentions. Such emotionally demanding skills require experience, practice and training, whether acquired in tertiary education or through in-service programmes.

However successful these formative community planning negotiations may become, conflicts will still occur and need to be resolved, as long as people retain their creative capacities for individuality and self-assertion. It is in everybody's interests to avoid 'knock down, drag out' fights that will only give rise to social division, resentment, alienation and abstention. Studies have shown that people will normally negotiate as long as that offers the possibility of a better outcome than a 'flight or fight' response (Susskind & Cruikshank, 1987). In other words, they have to have the prospect of a fair outcome that will be more durable than brittle reliance on money, power or threats of violence. The problem-solving and conflict-resolving methods of multiple-criteria policymaking, discussed in Chapters 2 and 6, incorporate such approaches within their planning processes. However, successful negotiation also depends upon genuine human fellow feeling and the desire to reconcile past misunderstandings and injustices. The capacity to practise emotional reciprocity – to recognise that if one experiences certain emotions and needs, it is probable that others will, too – plays a large part in successful negotiations. Such recognition will become increasingly important as communities at all scales evolve to incorporate growing numbers of people from different cultures and traditions. Negotiative processes will also need to shift the vocabulary of debates and visions from the dominantly economic terms in which people have grown used to thinking to ones reflecting the most important values of their own lives. The outcomes of successful negotiations can be truly transformational. Just as discussion between criminals and their victims can replace retribution with restitution, so community negotiations can divert latent anger and resentment into the discovery of new options and opportunities to enhance and reshape existing places and policies to meet new conditions.

The durability of community life over the past ten thousand years of settled society, and beyond to include the communal organisation of hunter-gatherers, has resulted from people's remarkable adaptability and the capacity of communities themselves to evolve. Basically stable values, such as shelter, nurture, productivity, communication and collaboration, have survived and succeeded in re-shaping existing activities and generating new ones to respond to radical changes in conditions of environment, climate and external competition. While ice ages have come and gone, fertile lands have become deserts, land bridges have appeared and disappeared, mega fauna have flourished and disappeared, each change has prompted the natural inventiveness to create adaptations that have in sum contributed to our survival and progress.

In the current phase of very rapid change, communities will have to continue to adjust to new challenges, including the impacts of new technologies, global warming, sea level rise, increased pressures to accommodate displaced coastal dwellers and new unprecedented of mass literacy and numeracy. In taking stock of such changing conditions, we need to acknowledge the needs of newcomers to link the cultures they have come from with the places they are coming to. In doing this, the aptness to innovation of the Western tradition and the remarkable resilience of the 'monsoon cultures' of the East will have important parts to play. However, to make full use of the wide range of ideas now becoming available, even more freely flowing exchange is required and the virtues of communicative action will be much needed.[vi]

One example of the need to balance carefully the impacts of technological change on existing settlement forms is provided by the effects of changing transport technology. Rapid growth in the scale and organisation of air transport in the past provides a vivid example. Urban impacts could result in consequences similar to those which transformed the inner areas of many coastal metropolises in the second half of the twentieth century following the movement of their port areas downstream.[vii] Airports and airport city extensions have already exerted dramatic impacts on the form and life of major metropolitan centres such as Amsterdam, London, Sydney, Tokyo and Hong Kong. Now, the predictable environmental and resource changes which seem likely to severely constrain their future custom, scale and profitability need to be taken into account. Careful thought is needed

when considering the future uses that these airports will be put to in the event of a rapid decline (and, indeed, eventual obsolescence) of current forms of air transport. Far-reaching adaptation plans may be needed. Alternative uses could include residential 'new-towns-in-town', new mixed-use suburbs, incubator sites for industrial promotion, city farm areas and locations for experiments in sustainable living. Recent records of spasms of over-expansion and contraction and of conflicting land uses and traffic flows suggest that it would be unwise to leave the redevelopment of these sites to the unconstrained operation of market forces.

The greatest cause for confidence in the future is offered by human capacities for invention[viii] and the same ingenuity is required in the social as in the scientific and technical spheres. There are some heartening examples: Ebenezer Howard's idea of the garden city; Mohamed Yunus's adaptation of capitalism to incorporate the traditional social support systems of rural village society in the specialised arrangements of the Grameen model of micro credit; the development of city farms to bring life and nature back into the inner areas of the most crowded metropolitan areas and the invention of 'wiki' techniques of collaborative knowledge development to make use of the universal access capacities of the Internet. The development and adoption of such life-giving inventions should be part and parcel of the processes of creative community planning. Other examples are available. The social entrepreneur's movement can help to fill the dangerously widening gap between governments and individuals (see Box 1.3 in Chapter 1). Another example which may well develop to span both economic and social spheres is the capacity for households to feed electricity back into power networks and therefore simultaneously to gain income and diminish the demands on more resource-consuming forms of power generation. Such economic and technical innovations to adapt changing situations to meet future needs and possibilities may frequently occur to alert participants in community planning processes. By linking community participation in defining needs to active policy development, community planning can help stimulate continuous adaptation and social invention. In a process involving so many cycles of inclusion and mutual adjustment, it is not surprising that communication also plays an essential role. Continuous community dialogue needs to be linked to exploratory actions. Such methods should lead to richer social communication, better opportunities for participation, more time and stimuli for problem-solving and a reduction in the consumption of scarce resources, as energy and materials are saved in physical and social innovations, encouraged by the spreading effects of miniaturisation. These decentralising processes will need careful and collaborative planning to ensure that they result in more amicable relationships between the many individuals and groups brought together by rapid change to create and re-create contemporary and future communities.

Endnotes

i The great achievements of the Truth and Reconciliation Commissions in South Africa and Timor-Leste are examples of this healing role of public speech.

ii Another example at the national and supranational level was afforded by the May 2010 summit meeting in Athens between the prime ministers of Greece, George Papandreou, and of Turkey, Recep Tayyip Erdogan, when they reviewed their bilateral and multilateral relations (Smith, 2010). Though not originally designed as a plan-making occasion, this provides a useful example of the potentialities of negotiation and problem-solving. By the end of the first day, both sides had agreed to consider cuts in their large military expenditures, mainly aimed at maintaining preparedness against each other. The switch in policies between neighbours who nearly went to war on three occasions in recent times came at a time of acute economic crisis for Athens and remarkable economic success for Ankara. There is a possibility that these negotiations could open the way to political and economic cooperation involving a succession of events that could improve the prospects for both countries and for the region. Increased trade with the more economically dynamic market of Turkey would help Greece to restructure and expand her own economy. This rapprochement with her old enemy could also help the country to rapidly reduce her 5% spending on defence – the highest of any country in the European Union – which could do much to relieve pressure on the country's financial credibility and credit worthiness and deter speculators who are gambling on the country's financial failure. Avoidance of this would in turn improve the prospects of a continued recovery for the wider European financial system.

Reciprocally, this evidence of good neighbour policies by Turkey and its newfound collaborative relations with Greece could reduce justifications for opposition to its admission to the European Union by France and Germany. If that occurs, then two of the world's most powerful supranational groups, the European and the Islamic worlds, could build a bridge that would be of lasting benefit to themselves, and the wider world. There is no guarantee that this outcome will be achieved, but it is a possibility which could thus avoid in this instance, the 'clash of civilisations' predicted by Samuel Huntington (1996).

iii The invention of walled cities by Sumerian rulers dating back five thousand years to Erech and similar Mesopotamian city states is one early example, maintaining interaction between specialists at the same time as keeping out marauding beasts and tribesman intent on plunder (Mumford, 1961). Later, the invention of democracy in Athens promoted the overall benefit of all by conferring responsibility for civic roles of justice, defence and urban maintenance upon local citizens. Everybody's needs became somebody's particular responsibility, breaking with a two-thousand-year tradition of the autocracy of the city states of Egypt and Mesopotamia. Later again, the Anglo-Saxons and Jutes invented the mechanism of the folk moot to help establish settled societies in their new homes in Britain and put down strong roots in the fertile soil of their new home.

Another social invention allowed the Igbo tribes of the Anambra, Cross and Lower Niger River basins to develop an effective system of development control. Meetings of the village elders allocated sites on the fringes of existing settlements for young couples forming their first households to build their new home (Innocent Nwoga, a district officer in the Eastern Region of Nigeria, 1964, personal communication). Later, as the encroachment on the agricultural lands surrounding the village became too severe, 'Umu' (son of) settlements were established to maintain traditional links within the clan and tribe that would allow new localities to be developed to provide necessary housing sites.

iv Societies, initially divided into rentier landlords and a subordinate underclass of powerless client workers, had transformed themselves into the property-owning democracies which have demonstrated considerable durability in withstanding the effects of world wars and international financial crises. In so doing, they have outlived the class rule systems which had been intended to replace capitalist exploitation by centralised apportionment of social wealth, which included mass-produced, state-owned rental housing (Bater, 1979; Dahrendorf, 2008). In this case, as so often, inventive problem-solving has proved more effective, as well as more humane, than centralised solutions. It is true that by the turn of the twenty-first century, the invention had been largely co-opted by free market financial institutions and large banks, which demutualised the building societies. Their objectives were then changed to maximising short-term profits rather than their original intention of promoting home ownership for those willing and able to commit to regular repayments. Following the resulting Global Financial Crisis of 2008/09, the re-establishment of the system of trust-based housing finance will require thought and thoroughness.

v In the field of teaching, a case in point is the opportunity to use information technology to increase interaction within teams of students working together in planning practice projects to improve exchange of information.

Programs such as Wiki Networks, PB Works and Blackboard allow team members to store information in virtual files, offering instant access to all members. Ideas can be developed, tested, adapted and then abandoned or incorporated in developing common work in progress. Team members can enjoy the comfort of their own homes, access to their bookshelves and electronic files, surf the Web for information and buzz their developing ideas around the team networks. The inherent power and playfulness of modern electronic communications can add a great deal to the long-established synergies of teamwork.

vi This movement between modes of thought occurred in the case of the Kolkata bustees improvement scheme (discussed in Chapter 10) where a preconceived approach to standardised clearance and rehousing failed in its own terms and was replaced by a more inclusive programme developed in discussion with the local residents themselves.

vii While impacts of 'peak oil', global warming, carbon taxing and international terrorism will increase the costs and constrain the scope of international air travel, there is likely to be a reduction in 'pull' factors resulting from diminished need for travel and transport associated with the increased use of teleconferencing and communication techniques such as 'Skype', and more equitable international division of labour between different regions around the world.

viii There are a number of prime examples of the extraordinary capacity of people to solve existing problems and create new solutions which transcend existing conditions and create new possibilities for individuals and communities. These include such inventions as Faraday's discovery of the electro-magnetic generation of electricity; Edison's use of filaments to disseminate electric light; Fred Hollows' low-cost laser-based mass removal of cataracts for whole communities of disadvantaged societies; the cumulative evolution of the microchip and other miniaturisation techniques; disseminate Ventner and Watson's genome sequencing; and the collaborative creation by many practitioners of the Internet.

References

Alexander, C. (1964) *Notes on the Synthesis of Form.* Cambridge, MA, Harvard University Press.

Bater, J. (1979) *The Soviet City: Ideal and reality.* London, Arnold.

Beaumont, P. (2010) *Rwanda's Laptop Revolution,* http://www.ubervu.com/conversations/www.guardian.co.uk/technology/2010/mar/28/rwanda-laptop-revolution, accessed 20 May 2010.

Bornstein, D. (1996) *The Price of a Dream: The story of the Grameen Bank.* Dhaka, Bangladesh, Grameen Press.

Castells, M. (1977) *The Urban Question.* London, Edward Arnold.

Castells, M. (1983) *The City and the Grassroots.* London, Edward Arnold.

Cooperrider (2008) *The Appreciative Inquiry Handbook,* [electronic resource]. San Francisco, Berrett-Koehler.

Dahrendorf, R. (2008) *The Modern Social Conflict: The politics of liberty.* New Brunswick, NJ, Transaction Publishers.

Ellner, S. (2009) *A new model with rough edges: Venezuela's community councils,* http://venezuelanalysis.com/analysis/4512, accessed 27 March 2010.

Faludi, A., Valk, A. van der (1994) *Rule and Order: Dutch local planning doctrine in the twentieth century.* Dordrecht, Kluwer Academic Publishing.

Florida, R. (2005) *Cities and the Creative Class.* New York, Routledge.

Fred Hollows Foundation (2010) *The Fred Hollows Foundation: Our programs,* http://www.hollows.org.au/our-programs/, accessed 26 May 2010.

Freiling, D. (2004) *Bijlmermeer: Compressed urbanism,* http://www.deltametropool.nl/v1/pages/english/Bijlmermeer,%20compressed%20urbanism.php, accessed 27 February 2010.

Fugelsang, A., Chandler, D. (1993) *Participation as Process: Process as growth.* Dhaka, Bangladesh, Grameen Trust.

Hammond, S., Royal, C. (1998) *Lessons from the Field.* Plano, TX, Practical Press.

Healey, P. (2006) *Collaborative Planning: Shaping places in fragmented societies.* New York, Palgrave Macmillan.

Huntington, S (1996) *The Clash of Civilizations and the Remaking of World Order.* New York, Simon & Schuster.

India Government (1992) *74ᵗʰ Amendment to the Constitution (Article 40),* http://india.gov.in/knowindia/local_govt.php, accessed 26 April 2010.

Jacobs, J. (1992) *Systems of Survival.* New York, Random House.

Kropotkin, P., 1939, *Mutual Aid,* Penguin, London first published 1899).

Kropotkin, P., 1974, *Fields, Farms & Workshops of Tomorrow,* London, Allen & Unwin, (first published 1899, Boston), Faber.

Lacey, J., Heywood, P. (2010) The ethics of regional water planning: Planning and management of water resources in a growth region. In: T. Yigitcanlar, (ed.), *Sustainable Urban and Regional Infrastructure: Technology, planning and management,* New York, IGI.

Local Government New Zealand (2010) *Community boards,* http://www.lgnz.co.nz/lg-sector/community-boards/index.html, accessed 28 May 2010.

Mackay, H., Maples, W., Reynolds, P. (2002) *Investigating the Information Society.* London, Routledge.

Médecins Sans Frontières (2010) *Delivering Obstetric Care.* Broadway, New South Wales, Author.

Mitra, S. (2001) Making local government work: Local elites, panchayati raj and governance in India. In: Atul Kohli (ed.), *The Success of India's Democracy.* Cambridge, Cambridge University Press.

Monbiot, G. (2003) *The Age of Consent: A manifesto for a new world.* London, Flamingo.

Mumford, L. (1938) *Culture of Cities.* London, Secker & Warburg.

Mumford, L. (1961) *The City in History*. New York, Harcourt Brace.

Oregon Department of Land Conservation & Development (2010) *Statewide planning goals*, http://www.oregon.gov/LCD/goals.shtml, accessed 12 April 2010.

Popper, K. (1998) *The Open Society and Its Enemies: Vol. 2: Marx and Hegel*, 2nd edn. London, Routledge & Kegan Paul, (first published 1945).

Reade, E. (1987) *British Town and Country Planning*. Milton Keynes, Open University.

Robertson, G. (2000) *Crimes against Humanity*. London, Penguin.

Robertson, G. (2009) *The Statute of Liberty*. Sydney, Vintage.

Rousseau, J.-J. (1968) *The Social Contract*, (trans. M. Cranston). London, Penguin.

Smith, H. (2010) Erdogan urges arms cut on Athens visit. *Guardian Weekly*, 25 May 2010.

Stiglitz, J. (2002) *Globalization and its Discontents*. London, Penguin.

Stiglitz, J. (2010) *Freefall: America, free markets, and the sinking of the world economy*. London, Penguin.

Susskind, L., Cruikshank, J. (1987) *Breaking the Impasse: Consensual approaches to resolving public disputes*. New York, HarperCollins.

United Nations – Habitat (2010) *State of the World's Cities 2010–2011*, http://www.unhabitat.org/pmss/listItem Details.aspx?publicationID=2917, accessed 2 April 2010.

Whyte, W., Whyte, K. (1988) *Making Mondragon: The growth and dynamics of a workers co-operative complex*. Ithaca, NY, ILR Press.

Index

Community Planning, First Edition. Phil Heywood.
© 2011 Phil Heywood.
Published 2011 by Blackwell Publishing Ltd.